POLITICS AND THE MEDIA

Richard Davis

Brigham Young University

POLITICS AND THE MEDIA

Prentice Hall, Englewood Cliffs, New Jersey 07632

Library of Congress Cataloging-in-Publication Data

Politics and the media / [edited by] Richard Davis.
    p. cm.
    ISBN 0-13-145897-3
     1. Mass media—Political aspects—United States. 2. United
States—Politics and government—1981-1989. 3. United States—
Politics and government—1989- I. Davis, Richard.
P95.85.U6P66 1994
302.23'0973–dc20
                                        93-17302
                                           CIP

Editorial/production supervision and interior design: **Joan E. Foley**
Acquisitions editor: **Charlyce Jones Owen**
Editorial assistant: **Nicole Signoretti**
Copy editor: **James Tully**
Cover designer: **DeLuca Design**
Production Coordinator: **Mary Ann Gloriande**

Additional credits appear on page 419
and constitute a continuation of the copyright page.

Printed in the United States of America
10 9 8 7 6 5 4 3 2 1

ISBN 0-13-145897-3

Prentice-Hall International (UK) Limited, *London*
Prentice-Hall of Australia Pty. Limited, *Sydney*
Prentice-Hall Canada Inc., *Toronto*
Prentice-Hall Hispanoamericana, S.A., *Mexico*
Prentice-Hall of India Private Limited, *New Delhi*
Prentice-Hall of Japan, Inc., *Tokyo*
Simon & Schuster Asia Pte. Ltd., *Singapore*
Editora Prentice-Hall do Brasil, Ltda., *Rio de Janeiro*

To **Dan and Delilah Gilfillan** and **Mack and Ferroll McCowin,**
for lives well lived

CONTENTS

9 The Future: Technology and Democracy 379

PREFACE

What is the news media's role in American politics today? This book answers that question by offering much of the very best work available on the subject of the place of the mass media in American politics. This compilation of readings ranges from political communications classics to very contemporary treatises and empirical studies. It includes works by scholars, journalists, politicians, and pundits. The student of political communications will not find in a single volume as complete an offering of selections on the subject as is found here.

The text is organized into nine chapters or sections reflecting the broad array of intersecting points in American politics where mass media role exists. The first chapter—the introduction—provides a broad overview of why the news media possess power in American politics and under what conditions that power exists.

Chapter two places current media role in a historical context. Classic readings on the history of journalism's political role alert the reader that the interaction of politics and press in the United States is hardly new. However, the nature of that interaction has changed over time, which has contributed to the current relationship examined in the subsequent sections of the text.

Chapter three analyzes the culture of the media by examining the types of influences that affect the news-gathering and news-reporting process. Political bias is only one influence included. Also discussed is the power of professional norms and the news organization's imperatives in the shaping of the news product.

The fourth chapter focuses on government regulation of the press. Changes in regulatory policy during the 1980s and the debate they have provoked are addressed.

Media effects on mass political attitudes and behavior, one of the best-researched subjects in the field of political communication, is the subject of chapter five. The readings range from classics in the field to current work with greater methodological sophistication and a focus on more subtle effects.

In chapter six, attention shifts to the media's role in political campaigns and elections. How does the press cover campaigns, how do candidates attempt to use media coverage for image making, and how has the media role affected the electoral process? Three of the readings address the media impact on the 1992 presidential election.

Chapter seven centers on the news media's relationship with political institutions and organizations. These include the presidency, Congress, the Supreme Court, the bureaucracy, and special-interest groups.

The public policy-making process and the role of the media are examined in chapter eight, which covers domestic, foreign, and national defense policy.

The final chapter, number 9, serves as a conclusion by looking to the future. By exploring current developments in communications technology affecting American politics, these works offer predictions about the future effects of technological change on media role. Finally, this section raises questions about how a democracy functions in a media-oriented age.

The author wishes to thank the following reviewers: Daniel C. Hallin, University of California—San Diego; Daniel Hellinger, Webster University; Timothy S. Prinz, University of Virginia.

Also, thanks is extended to the College of Family, Home, and Social Sciences and the Department of Political Science for research support. David B. Magleby, the department chair, was especially helpful in facilitating the completion of this book.

My special thanks go to my family for appreciating my need to spend long hours on books like this one.

chapter 1

POLITICS AND THE MEDIA

Presidents criticize, yet fear them. Presidential candidates solicit their favor, yet deride their influence. Other political officials crave their notice, but often attack them when they do not serve them. Interest groups are dependent on them for their goals. And many people are wary of them, but still spend part of each day with them.

Few players in American politics receive so much attention as those in the news media. This is true partially because journalists talk so publicly about their work. Moreover, the news media's influence has been the subject of discussion by political pundits, presidential candidates, policymakers, and even the mass public.

Much of the discussion is in the nature of criticism—criticism of the tone and extent of news media coverage of American political life. Yet, despite the criticism, there are no signs that the news media's role has diminished. In fact, evidence points to the contrary.

Polls indicate Americans are uneasy about the role of the news media today, but newspaper circulation is at an all-time high, and broadcast news—CNN, C-SPAN, morning news, evening news, and nighttime news—has never been more pervasive. We are still watching and reading the news despite what we think about the news media itself.

We do this because the news media perform a task today unmatched by any other institution. Few people have alternative sources of information on presidential candidates, White House activity, or state, national, or even international events. The news media and those who run it have become our primary window on the world outside our own communities. In the area of national politics, they usually are exclusive as an information source.

WHY THE NEWS MEDIA HAVE BECOME POWERFUL

The various news media have become powerful in American politics only because we have let them become so. If Americans do not like the role of the press, we must look not solely at the news organizations but also at ourselves as causes.

The causes of media power in American politics are intertwined and not easily sorted out. However, some of these causes stem from changes in our political system that have bolstered and extended the power of the news media.

THE DECLINE OF POLITICAL PARTIES

One cause of the news media's power has been the decline of the political party. Although American political parties have never exhibited the organizational cohesiveness of their European counterparts, they once played a much greater role in American politics than they do now. Parties have organized electoral campaigns, aggregated public support for public officeholders, and mobilized voters to participate in electoral politics.

The major political parties have lost control of the nomination process. The rise of primaries as the means for selecting party nominees has weakened the party organization and limited its power over its own candidates. Candidates for elected office are now self-starters who often thumb their noses at party leaders rather than work to earn their blessing. Once in office, they owe little allegiance to a party that did not assist them to gain the nomination and provided little help in the campaign or election.

Moreover, campaign finance has contributed to the parties' dilemma in electoral politics. Political parties have not been the primary beneficiaries of campaign reform; interest groups have. At the national level, parties are restricted in the amount of financial support they can provide their own candidates. Candidates naturally turn to interest groups for campaign funding, which enhances the interest groups' role in the campaign process.

As the parties have lost their power as a linking mechanism between elected officials and the citizenry, particularly as an organizing force in electoral campaigns, the news media have filled the vacuum. Reporters now play a greater role in organizing the electoral campaign, especially at the presidential level. They handicap the candidates and provide news coverage accordingly. They do not do so without relying on political pundits for expert advice. However, some may view themselves as politically adept enough to serve as their own experts.

THE NATIONALIZATION OF POLITICS

Historically, power in American politics has been decentralized. Central government long struggled to acquire power over activities traditionally delegated to the state and local governments.

In the 1990s, as a result of a steady 200-year trend accelerated in the 1930s and again in the 1960s and 1970s, much state and local power has gravitated to Washington.

The news media have contributed to and benefited from a centralizing trend in American politics. National news organizations have become the primary linking mechanisms between the citizenry and a more remote national government. Town and city hall are still accessible through interpersonal communication. Legislators in some states, particularly those with smaller legislative districts, are similarly close to their constituencies.

However, as power shifted to the national level, the necessity of mass communications has become more pronounced. Policymakers at the federal level—agency officials, members of Congress, the president—are remote from most Americans. Many Americans do not even know the name of their senator or representative in Congress; fewer still have met that individual. The greater the distance, the more mass communication becomes the mode of choice for personal interaction.

But unlike interpersonal communication, the mass media have been almost exclusively unidirectional. Transmission of information is the task of public officials and candidates, whereas individual citizens do little more than receive this information.

Some efforts have been made to correct the disparity. Organized groups do so through pseudo events—demonstrations, marches, and protests—that allow them to transmit information as well. Some groups acquire a quasi-legitimacy as news sources. Experiments in mass democracy, which will be discussed later, possess interactive capabilities that restore some measure of balance. Also, public-access broadcast channels offer what their name implies. (However, one wonders who is actually watching or listening.)

Thus, mass communication, unlike interpersonal communication, severely limits the two-way communication process inherent in the concept of democracy. But the nationalization of politics has guaranteed that, for the representative function at the national level, mass communication will become the primary linking mechanism.

THE DEMOCRATIZATION OF POLITICS

Another reason why the news media have become powerful is the movement toward greater mass democracy in American politics. Over the course of American history, democratic reforms designed to expand the role of the electorate—such as extension of suffrage, more direct election of public officials, and party primary elections—have succeeded.

We have discarded elements of the aristocratic democracy embodied in the Constitution. This is a conception of democracy where the electorate uses elections to choose between competing groups of elites. James Madison's conception of democracy, with its preference for representative government rather than direct democracy, probably comes closest to this theory.

But in American politics, we have become infatuated with the notion of mass democracy. We have evolved from a polity where elections determine policy direction to one where elections and constant reference to public opinion are the guides for elected officials.

Thus, it is this greater democratization of American politics that has added to the news media's influence and power. With public opinion constantly measured and reported, as well as alluded to even when not being measured, the imperative of knowing and responding to the public's views dominates American political life. As the only tool of communication capable of reaching the masses of Americans quickly and efficiently, the news media serve as linking mechanisms between elected officials and public opinion.

In fact, we go further than that. We expect the news media to organize and mobilize public opinion. This is true during electoral campaigns where the news media affect the process of winnowing candidates and organizing the agenda for the public discussion of issues by both candidates and voters.

This is also true in nonelectoral contexts. Public officials watch the news media for reaction to their pronouncements on specific issues. They attempt to use the news media to create interest in certain issues. Interest groups hope to use the news media to mobilize public opinion by attracting press attention to their key issues. In addition, the news media often have their own agenda.

None of these players always wins. Nor even often wins. But the basic assumption that the news media serve as critical linkages in the political process is no longer even challenged.

WHEN THE NEWS MEDIA ARE POWERFUL

Taken together, these causes have contributed to a position of enormous potential power for the news media. The word "potential" should be noted. The power of the news media in American politics rests on the existence of certain conditions in the political system. Two of these conditions are the media role in filling a power vacuum in the political system and the supply of and demand for information available to be disseminated.

FILLING A VACUUM

One of these conditions is the development of a political power vacuum created by political institutions and organizations that the news media then come to fill. In some cases, other institutions forfeit their roles. In others, functions shift owing to public expectations and the institution's or organization's needs.

Political parties are a classic example of the former. The deterioration of grass-roots organization, which included a valuable communications component, has enhanced the news media's function of presenting political information to the party faithful. Also, the lack of control over the nomination process by the party has empowered the news media by allowing them to fill a role as winnower of candidates.

The presidency has become heavily dependent on the mass media for pursuit of policy objectives. The decline of political parties has weakened the president's reliance on that base. But presidents also chose to unhitch themselves from their party because that independence offered freedom from domination by party leaders.

Presidents casting around for a means to communicate with the American public, to mobilize public opinion, and to go over the heads of a recalcitrant, sometimes lethargic Congress found the mass media a useful tool. Theodore Roosevelt called the presidency a "bully pulpit." Today the presidency has become an electronic pulpit with nationally televised "fireside chats," participation in call-in programs, small-group or one-on-one press interviews, and press conferences.

Public expectations of presidential action, especially in a nuclear age, have enhanced the president's dependence on some means of communication. A vacuum between presidential needs and public expectations on one hand and the means for mass communication on the other produces reliance on the media to fill that role.

The legislative function, including communication between an elected representative and constituents, at the federal government level (and in many states) has become a media-oriented process and another example of a power vacuum in American politics. Members of Congress rely less on town meetings than on press releases and press interviews to communicate with constituents. The former they hold occasionally, while the latter they do virtually every day.

Moreover, members of Congress increasingly are turning to media that grant them more control over their messages. These elected officials use their own cable television programs and newspaper columns to deliver messages to the folks back home. As with public-access channels, the question legitimately may be raised about whether anyone is actually watching the TV programs or reading the newspaper columns. But that concern speaks to the effectiveness of the communication in actually informing constitutents, not to its existence and use. Ironically, one contributing factor to the rise of these alternate forms of communication may be the limitation on use of alternative communication outlets such as congressional mass mailings, which used to be the primary form of mass communication with constituents.

SUPPLY AND DEMAND

Another reason for the potential power of the news media is the locus of control over information. When members of the media face a scarcity of sources for information they value, they are more prone to manipulation by others. For example, when the president holds information keenly sought after by the White House press corps, power shifts to the president and away from the press. The White House is in a position to determine how much of the precious information is parceled out to the press and in what forms.

It is under these circumstances that television reporters charge that the president has captured their cameras because the White House decides what images will be portrayed on the nightly news. And, more broadly, reporters complain that the top White House staff become quasi-news directors by establishing the themes for daily news emanating from the White House.

A real-world example of the president's power over information is news about presidential negotiations with foreign leaders at summit meetings. The White House usually holds a monopoly on information concerning such negotiations since no others—not Congress, not the bureaucracy, not interest groups—are as much aware of the proceedings. (The same may be true, although on a less frequent basis, for a government agency or a congressional committee. Congressional ethics committees, for example, have exclusive possession over information about ethics scandals involving their colleagues.)

One of the president's advantages in this interaction with the news media is the media's definition of news—whatever the president says or does is news. Thus, since the White House can effectively control media access to that information, the president often holds the balance of power in the tussle with the press.

However, when the supply of information outstrips demand, the tables are turned. When there is a plethora of sources for information the press desires, then those sources become pleaders at the gates of the media for inclusion in stories. Cabinet secretaries, members of Congress, and leaders of interest groups all vie for press attention. Even presidents sometimes are reduced to this level either when they do not possess information desired by the press or other events outstrip their activities in terms of newsworthiness.

An example of the former is the Iran-*contra* scandal when congressional committees and even Lt. Col. Oliver North himself possessed information the president apparently did not have (or did not remember). And an example of the latter is during the primary stage of a presidential campaign when the out-party's candidates acquire large doses of media attention in contrast to the incumbent president who is running unopposed for nomination.

Two factors contribute to the media's power in the supply–demand equation. One is the sieve-like nature of most of the federal government. This precludes the formation of permanent information monopolies.

Another is the extent of information-rich competing sources available to the press. This is partly due to the web of interaction between Congress and the bureaucracy and within Congress. Information is tightly held by the bureaucracy when possible, but information sharing is mandated by law and greases relationships. Moreover, it is used by bureaucrats to accomplish either policy or personal objectives. Within Congress, the fact that committee jurisdictions overlap also assures that information is passed around to more than a small group of players in a policy area.

As a result, for the press there are usually several possible authoritative sources for desired information on a certain topic. No one of the sources controls how much of the information will be revealed or in what form. The individual reporter possesses that power.

Moreover, the existence of specialist networks in policy areas means interest groups, think tanks, and academics are co-holders of information and potential sources for journalists. This variety of potential sources enhances the ability of the reporter to "pick and choose" what will become news and who will be part of the story.

The principle of supply and demand also enhances media power over mass political attitudes and behavior. The more exclusive the information is that the media possess and present, the more dependent are citizens on the news media's information and analysis of that information. However, when the individual has alternative sources of information—such as personal experience or interpersonal sources—the news presentation is less important.

For example, news about inflation and unemployment usually is tempered or accentuated by personal experience or interpersonal communication. People notice inflation when the price of ground beef rises. They know about unemployment when a local factory closes and layoffs hit their neighborhood. National news reports supplement the individual's personally acquired information.

But news about a Washington scandal or a foreign-policy development in Asia is usually the only information they will receive on that subject or event. News media become important as the sole source of information.

A key limitation on the power of the press as exclusive medium is the fact that most Americans are more concerned about issues that touch them personally—inflation, employment, education—than about issues and events far away and much removed from their daily lives. These are also issues where they have alternative sources and become less reliant on the news media as their information base.

But the more demand for news by the audience, the more powerful the news media become. During the Persian Gulf War, news of the war was constantly monitored by most Americans. The media's power to shape attitudes and beliefs was dramatically increased. (In that particular case, the Pentagon's leverage over war-related information aided the military's power over the news media message.)

When information the press desires is in great supply, reporters and commentators become the gatekeepers over the news and their power in the political process is enhanced. But when demand outstrips supply and control shifts to the possessors of sought-after information, the news media's power declines.

MEDIA POWER IN AMERICAN POLITICS

Media power is a creation not solely of news media organizations. It is also a product of systemwide developments altering the functions of the political system in a way conducive to increased media role. Over time, we have created a role for the news media unique to democratic systems. News media organizations did not push and shove to play a greater role in American politics. The system opened a door and invited the media in by making adjustments to accommodate the media. Although the system changes did not have that purpose in mind, the effect was practically the same as if it had.

chapter 2

HISTORICAL DEVELOPMENT OF THE POLITICAL ROLE OF THE PRESS

INTRODUCTION

The political power of the press did not emerge with the invention of television or the practice of investigative journalism. Reporters and politicians have interacted in American politics ever since the birth of American politics. As long as the press has been a vehicle for reaching potential voters (especially when other vehicles were absent), political leaders have realized the press's potential as a political tool.

The history of the role of the press in politics has been characterized by two parallel, but contrasting, trends: the successful claim of sovereignty by the press as a political actor, and a growing dependency on the press by the political system.

From the 1790s to the 1990s, through the acquisition of financial independence and professional status, the press has been transformed from a mouthpiece of political leaders and organizations to a highly autonomous participant in the political process with the capacity to influence that process. Today's press roles as an organizer of presidential campaigns, as a catalyst in the policy process, and as a force in public opinion are the products of that transformation.

The process was gradual and was stimulated by major developments along the way. Some developments were press-related—the rise of the penny press, the dominance of media conglomerates, professional trends such as adversarial journalism and advocacy journalism. Others inhered from alterations in the political system— the rise and fall of the political party organization, the democratization of elections, and the waning influence of partisan affiliation in voter choice.

The readings in this section highlight stages of the evolution of that relationship, and they provide snapshots of the historical development of the press's role.

First, we examine the early role of the press as a partisan organ rather than an independent force. The partisan press reflected the interests and opinions of the press's benefactors—political organizations and partisan leaders.

Next is a discussion of the emergence of the penny press. The demise of the partisan press was hastened by a new type of newspaper governed not by political ideology but by commercial profit. Factors contributing to the success of the penny press as replacement for the partisan press are explored.

Finally, the spotlight moves to the turn of the century when the muckrakers (a phrase coined by Theodore Roosevelt) scoured the political landscape for corruption and newspaper circulation. The Progressive Era saw rapid changes in the press's self-evaluation of its political role and the uses to which it would be put by the presidency.

1. PARTY AND PRESS

Culver H. Smith

Thomas Jefferson once remarked in a letter that "were it left to me to decide whether we should have a government without newspapers, or newspapers without a government, I should not hesitate a moment to prefer the latter."* But rather than having to choose, Jefferson and other politicians at the founding of the American republic helped create both government and the newspapers that covered it.

Convinced of the potential of the press in influencing public opinion, political leaders employed a variety of techniques to create a press tightly bound to the aims of the fledgling party organizations and factions. These financial incentives included government printing contracts, authority to publish government documents, patronage appointments, and outright loans and grants. Also, essays by political leaders, usually published pseudonymously, became staples of newspapers, which enhanced their credibility as organs of information.

As Culver H. Smith demonstrates in the following selection, newspapers and political leaders were highly intertwined in the first fifty years of the existence of the United States. Smith describes the system of reliance on the press by the two major political leaders of the 1790s—Alexander Hamilton and Thomas Jefferson. The linkage between political party and newspapers created by these two eminent Americans served as the model for the partisan press over the next half-century.†

Culver H. Smith, author of *The Press, Politics, and Patronage* (1977), was a professor of history at the University of Chattanooga. He died in 1980.

---

*Adrienne Koch and William Peden, eds., *The Life and Selected Writings of Thomas Jefferson* (New York: The Modern Library, 1944), pp. 411–12.
†From Culver H. Smith, *The Press, Politics, and Patronage* (Athens: University of Georgia Press, 1977), pp. 12–23.

George Washington was elected president of the United States without benefit of newspapers, one of the many facts that distinguished him from his successors. Very likely Washington would have needed or used newspapers had he been a candidate in the period of Jefferson or of Jackson, for by their time the situation that had enabled the first president to be elected twice without a dissenting electoral vote had changed. Political parties, which did not exist when Washington took office in 1789, emerged during his two administrations, and by the election of 1796 two parties, though rudimentary, could be identified by their opposing presidential candidates.

One of the by-products of parties was the political newspaper, for controversy over principles, issues, and men led to the use of the printing press as a means of presenting divergent views and winning adherents to them. The partisan pamphlet and newspaper were not American peculiarities; eighteenth-century England, where faction and party existed, provided the prototype for the American partisan press. However, in the United States the Constitution and the rapid extension of the franchise gave to the political newspaper a special value, if not, indeed, a peculiar character. Parties and the press were both ignored by the Constitution, yet parties developed in spite of this fact, while public concern forced an amendment to the Constitution that recognized the press, thus opening the way for a free use of newspapers by political parties when they appeared.

Even before Washington's first term was up newspapers were doing service for the leaders of political thought. They had, indeed, been utilized during the debates over the adoption of the Constitution; the now-famous arguments of Madison, Hamilton, and Jay for the Constitution, the *Federalist* essays, first appeared in contemporary newspapers. But such uses were those of normal publicity and education and did not represent attachment of newspapers to a party or a political leader. Washington himself in his eight years in office did not use any particular newspaper as his personal or official organ. But his leading cabinet members, Hamilton and Jefferson, were not long in adopting, if not creating, newspapers to represent their views. They soon found themselves in disagreement over fundamental principles of government and these principles became the basis for the Federalist and the Jefferson Republican parties. Soon there were newspapers that identified themselves with one side or the other. Certain papers, published in the capital, came to be regarded as the personal organs of Hamilton and Jefferson, giving authoritative expression to the questions at issue between them.

The first of this character was the *Gazette of the United States*, a semiweekly newspaper that appeared in New York almost as soon as the government was established there. John Fenno, its publisher and editor, had come from Boston where he had been connected with Benjamin Russell and his *Massachusetts Centinel*, a strong Federalist journal. Having lately suffered misadventures in trading, Fenno turned to New York to seek financial rehabilitation in printer's ink. He was introduced to Federalist Rufus King by Christopher Gore as a person of literary accomplishments whose talents as an editor were "unrivaled" in Massachusetts.[1] Apparently Fenno called on King to solicit an arrangement with the Federalists for publishing a newspaper in their interest. The question in the mind of the thirty-eight-year-old applicant was whether he could depend upon getting government printing. Satisfied on this point, he brought out his four-page paper April 15, 1789. Later, with the transfer of the capital to Philadelphia, Fenno moved his paper there because the proposals for printing it had stipulated that it should be "published at the seat of the federal government."[2]

John Fenno represented a new breed; he was not a professional printer but an editor. For a long time persons who issued newspapers had been identified as printers, for job printing was more common than newspaper publishing, the latter often being merely one product of a print shop. Yet issuing a newspaper did not necessarily make a printer an editor, and those who entered journalism as editors were exceptional. Fenno in regarding himself as an editor indicated that his function or purpose was dissemination of news and opinion.

The new paper did secure some much-wanted government patronage. Hamilton fed it printing orders from the Treasury Department, while it did some printing for the Senate. Jefferson assigned it the printing of the laws for a short time while the capital was still in New York. With this recognition, Fenno started displaying the masthead caption, "By Authority," proclaiming his paper's official status and its distinction.

Yet the *Gazette* required about two years to get fairly well established. At the end of its first seven months, trying to operate without advertising, it did not have enough subscribers to pay expenses, and the editor appealed to "the wealthy part of the community" for support.[3] He tried to extend the paper's circulation and influence by distributing it to other newspapers, expecting at least some of them to advertise it by inserting reprints. Two years later, in an appeal for advertising, Fenno declared that the *Gazette* was being sent to 120 postmasters and printers, as well as to a thousand subscribers, throughout the Union.[4]

Editorially Fenno was assisted by men who became prominent in the Federalist party, among them Rufus King, John Adams, and Alexander Hamilton. Their contributions were made in the form of letters to the editor signed by such pseudonyms as "Publicola," "Davila," "Camillus," "Metellus," "Amicus," "Pacificus," "Catullus," "An American," and "Plain Facts."[5]

With Hamilton as its patron, the *Gazette of the United States* became the medium through which his views were expressed, expounded, or defended. Fenno's statement of policy stressed the "union of the states," protection of "commerce," arrangement of the "national funds," and the establishment of "public credit," the quoted terms being printed in capital letters as if suggesting the features of the Hamiltonian program. Later, when the paper needed funds to keep going, Fenno turned to Hamilton, who undertook to honor Fenno's request for a loan of $2,000.[6] By then the paper was too valuable to Hamilton and the Federalists to let it die.

To Thomas Jefferson, however, now an opponent of Hamilton's policies, Fenno's *Gazette* in two years had become politically odious, "a paper of pure

Toryism, disseminating the doctrines of monarchy, aristocracy & the exclusion of the influence of the people."[7] Jefferson wanted a paper to counteract its influence. Although in the new capital at Philadelphia a pro-Jefferson paper, Benjamin Franklin Bache's *General Advertiser*, was at hand, it was not suited for wide distribution; it was a daily, therefore more expensive than a weekly, and its advertising had slight appeal outside the local area. Jefferson wanted a weekly or semiweekly suitable for national circulation, interesting in content, free of advertising, and serving as "a whig vehicle of intelligence." A new paper with a selected editor seemed necessary. More than a half-year of negotiations ensued before an editor and a new paper were secured.

The much-desired editor was Philip Freneau, a newspaperman who had served the New York *Daily Advertiser* and contributed to other publications. A graduate of the College of New Jersey in his home state, he was a classmate of Henry Lee, who suggested Freneau to [James] Madison, another classmate, who recommended him to Jefferson and did most of the urging, while Jefferson offered him inducements. Influenced by Madison, Jefferson, who was only slightly acquainted with Freneau, wrote him early in 1791 offering him the clerkship for foreign languages in the State Department at Philadelphia. This was a translator's job paying only $250 a year but requiring so little time "as not to interfere with any other calling."[8] Jefferson did not mention a newspaper in this letter, but he probably hoped that Freneau would appreciate the possibilities and take a hint. Freneau, however, declined the offer with the excuse that he was trying to establish a newspaper in New Jersey.[9] Madison now undertook to change Freneau's mind, and Jefferson fed Madison some suggestions he could use in persuasion. If Freneau would set up a paper in Philadelphia, Jefferson would let him use the foreign newspapers and other foreign "intelligence" received by his office and would assign him the paid printing ordered by the Department of State, including the printing of the laws, all of which would mean "considerable aid" to his income.[10] Madison kept up his negotiations with Freneau, who after several months yielded to the pressure and promises and moved to Philadelphia.

The *National Gazette*, Freneau's new paper, appeared October 31, 1791, as a four-page semiweekly, similar in format to the *Gazette of the United States*, at the price of three dollars per year. General Henry Lee, Madison, and Jefferson all helped get subscribers. Madison expected some circulation under the franks of friendly members of Congress.[11] With such influential sponsorship, prospects of success were good.

The thirty-nine-year-old editor of the *National Gazette* had been conditioned by toughening experience as a sea captain that left him with no love of England. He now had a reputation not only as a patriot but as a man of literary talent. Jefferson said his character "marked him as a good whig" and he himself took for granted that Freneau "would give free place to pieces written against the aristocratical and monarchical principles" of Fenno's *Gazette.*[12] This was another way of saying that Freneau could be counted on to play up Jefferson's principles. Madison, who had worked hardest to enlist him, declared that there was not to be found "in the whole catalogue of American Printers a single name that can approach towards a rivalship" of Freneau.[13]

With the establishment of Freneau's *National Gazette*, Philadelphia had two newspapers identified with government officials, Fenno's with the secretary of the treasury and Freneau's with the secretary of state. They were not the only newspapers in the capital, not even the only partisan papers, but the peculiar distinction that resulted from being known as the organ of a political leader made these two papers the journalistic leaders of the nation's political press. Neither had a large circulation, about fifteen hundred, but by copying from one another newspapers in other cities and states spread the message of the capital organs to a reading public many times the size of either paper's subscription list.

Freneau lost no time attacking Hamilton's cherished measures and Fenno's paper. Hamilton's first reaction was to reproach Madison for getting Freneau and his paper established, for Freneau was a "known anti-federalist," wrote Hamilton, so distressed that he equated Madison's opposition to his policies with subversion of the principles of good government and the "peace and happiness of the country."[14]

Between the two rival papers a sharp and bitter feud developed to which Hamilton lent his pen and service and which brought into the open the smoldering differences between Jefferson and Hamilton. President Washington had to intervene to keep the peace. Freneau's paper provoked the battle in the spring of 1792 by attacking Hamilton's funding scheme by which, it said, some fifty million dollars had been thrown into the hands of the wealthy, thus drawing them by motives of private financial interest to support the other various features of Hamilton's plan.[15] Continuation of attacks along this line over such signatures as "Brutus," "Centinel," and "Sydney" brought Fenno's paper to the defense, in which it suffered more than it gained. Finally Hamilton himself came to Fenno's aid. In July he contributed a letter anonymously signed "T.L." in which he stated that the editor of the *National Gazette* received a salary from the government. Was this salary paid him for making translations—the duty his job called for in the Department of State—or was it "for publications, the design of which is to vilify those to whom the voice of the people has committed the administration of our public affairs"? Was it "to oppose the measures of government, and by false insinuations, to disturb the public peace"?[16]

A few days later, Hamilton, signing himself "An American," struck at Jefferson, calling him the head of a party and Freneau merely his faithful and devoted servant. Furthermore, Jefferson had opposed some provisions of the Constitution when it was being drafted and had since been opposed to "almost all the important measures" of the government. The writer declared that "a newspaper instituted by a public officer, and the editor of it regularly pensioned with the public money in the disposal of that officer," was "an experiment somewhat new in the history of political manoevres in this country." In a later letter signed "Catullus," Hamilton again called Jefferson the "institutor and patron" of the *National Gazette*.[17]

Freneau replied by printing an affidavit, which he had made to the mayor of

Philadelphia, declaring that there had never been any negotiation between him and Jefferson for the establishment of the *National Gazette*; that his coming to Philadelphia was his own voluntary act; that he had not been urged, advised, or influenced by the secretary of state; that the *Gazette* had never been directed, controlled, or attempted to be influenced by the secretary or any of his friends; and that "not a line was ever directly or indirectly written, dictated or composed for it by that officer." The editor, he claimed, had been "free, unfettered and uninfluenced."[18]

Hamilton replied to Freneau with the second installment of "An American," almost three columns in length, dismissing the affidavit as the sort of thing one could expect from a pensioned tool. He then proceeded to state "the facts," which were designed to convince a person of "correct mind" that the connection "acknowledged to subsist between you and Mr. Jefferson . . . is indelicate and unfit, and consequently of a nature to justify suspicion."[19]

It is startling that Hamilton allowed himself to be drawn into a controversy with the newspaper editor and thus risk the dignity of his official position. But Hamilton was touchy, and the barbs of the *National Gazette* pricked his political skin. He did not profit from this wrangle; he especially lost grace by his insinuations about Freneau's honor. Not only did he have to acknowledge that he could not prove his charges, he was in a vulnerable position because he had been doing what he was criticizing Jefferson for doing, and Freneau did not let the opportunity pass to remind him that Fenno, whose paper was Hamilton's shadow, was being given all the printing of his department, the value of which was ten times the salary Freneau received from the State Department. Furthermore, scoffed Freneau, it is understood that "the immaculate Mr. John Fenno is printer to the Senate . . . , the emoluments of which are very considerable." Presumably $2,000 or $2,500 a year could not but have some sort of influence on the editor of the *Gazette of the United States*, "especially when his avaricious principles are brought into view."[20]

Jefferson kept himself out of the controversy, discreetly refusing to meet Hamilton directly through the newspapers. But he was represented by friends, including Madison, Monroe, Hugh Brackenridge, George Tucker, and Attorney General Edmund Randolph, whose writings, over pseudonyms, took up much of the available space in the *National Gazette*. James Monroe in collaboration with Madison contributed a series of six articles to Dunlap's *American Daily Advertiser* late in 1792 under the general title of "The Vindication of Mr. Jefferson." These articles gave a documented reply to Hamilton's charges that Jefferson had not supported or favored the Constitution and was misusing his office and Freneau's *Gazette* to oppose the government.[21]

Jefferson did reply to Washington's letter pleading for peace, describing his attitude and explaining his relation to the *National Gazette*. He related that Freneau applied for a position in his department while the government was still in New York, but that he could not offer him a clerkship until a vacancy occurred when the capital was removed to Philadelphia. Jefferson could not recollect whether it was before or after the application that he was told Freneau had in mind setting up a newspaper. "But whether then or afterwards, I considered it a circumstance of some value, as it might enable me to do, what I had long wished to have done, that is, to have the material parts of the Leyden Gazette brought under your eye, and that of the public, in order to possess yourself and them with a juster view of the affairs of Europe than could be obtained from any other public source."[22] On the establishment of the *National Gazette*, wrote Jefferson, he furnished Freneau with the *Leyden Gazette*, from which Freneau was at liberty to translate and publish news, but he did not give "any other direction or indication of my wish how his press should be conducted." Neither did he write or dictate anything for the paper to which his name was not attached.[23]

In this letter Jefferson also made two interesting admissions. He knew that Freneau was "a good whig" and he "took for granted" that Freneau would "give free place" to articles written against the monarchical principles expressed in the writings of "Publicola" and others in Fenno's paper. The second admission was that he had procured subscriptions for the *National Gazette* ("as I have with pleasure done for the labors of other men of genius"). Thus while saving himself from the ignominy that befell Hamilton, Jefferson nevertheless avowed his interest in having a partisan news organ. "No government ought to be without censors," he philosophized, and implied that this was sufficient justification for the *National Gazette*. He was not concerned with the merits of the paper, he said; Fenno and Freneau were rivals for the public favor; "the one courts them by flattery, the other by censure, and I believe it will be admitted that the one has been as servile as the other severe." For Hamilton, Jefferson unbosomed a blistering scorn: "Is not the dignity, and even decency of government committed, when one of its principal ministers enlists himself as an anonymous writer or paragraphist" for either of the papers, "spelling my name and character at full length to the public, while he conceals his own?" Jefferson's loathing had been provoked by "a man whose history, from the moment that history can stoop to notice him, is a tissue of machinations against the liberty of the country which had not only received and given him bread, but heaped honors on his head."[24]

Jefferson gained the advantage in the controversy without contributing articles himself, not only because he had able friends who wrote for him, but also because his editor was more effective than Hamilton's. The heavy-witted name-calling Fenno provoked Freneau to light, satiric verse about his "preaching, screeching, barking, whining" adversary. Fenno's columns, wrote Freneau, were filled with abuse, and, with great events breaking at home and abroad, he suggested that Fenno's readers would rather "be treated with news." Then a blast at Fenno's servile role in the government:

> One Printer for Congress (some think) is enough
> To flatter and lie, to palaver and puff,
> To preach up in favor of monarchs and titles,
> And garters and ribands to prey on our vitals.[25]

Freneau's verbal darts could hit his target with bull's-eye scores.

One conclusion is indisputable. Both Hamilton and Jefferson (as well as Madison) believed in the value of a partisan newspaper, and each in his own way established, encouraged, and maintained a journalistic organ. Each paper was in the nation's capital close at hand, instant in service. Both papers circulated throughout the Union—thanks partly to cheap postage—finding their way to the political leaders in the states and the printers of other newspapers, giving the form for partisan writing and thinking.

When Jefferson resigned his office at the end of 1793, Freneau had to give up his clerkship in the Department of State, resigning October 11. His paper came to an unplanned end on October 26, 1793. The *National Gazette,* which had claimed as many as 1,300 subscribers or more, had not paid expenses and would have ended sooner had not Childs and Swaine furnished the money to keep it going. In 1793 the divisions over the French Revolution and the strains caused by Citizen Genet's undiplomatic indiscretions may have had an adverse effect on circulation. Perhaps the yellow fever that struck Philadelphia that fall contributed to its financial difficulties; but the *Gazette of the United States,* after a three-month interruption because of the epidemic, was able to continue, and Fenno remained the Federalist party editor until his death in 1798. This paper had received enough printing jobs from Congress and the departments to help it survive.[26] Bache's Philadelphia *Aurora* became the leading Jeffersonian newspaper, but without benefit of government patronage.

The year 1798 became a pivot point in the fortunes of the Federalist party and in the relations of both parties to the press. The Federalists, irked by repeated criticisms of their policies by Republican newspapers, secured the enactment by Congress of the Alien and Sedition laws, the excuse being the threat of war with France and the necessity of protecting the country from subversive persons. The Jeffersonians charged that the acts were a political measure aimed at them, designed to limit the press and cripple the opposition. And when prosecutions were begun under the acts the charge seemed warranted, for the victims were mostly Republican editors, some of whom were aliens. Hamilton himself supported enforcement. Jefferson and Madison drew up resolutions of protest, claiming the acts violated the Constitution, and the legislatures of Virginia and Kentucky adopted them. The Sedition Act particularly was attacked because it provided a fine and imprisonment for anyone convicted of writing, uttering, or publishing "any false, scandalous and malicious writing or writings against the government of the United States, or either house of the Congress of the United States, or the President of the United States, with intent to defame . . . or to bring them, or either of them, into contempt or disrepute." The Virginia resolutions asserted that Congress was here exercising a power expressly forbidden by the First Amendment to the Constitution— "a power which more than any other ought to produce universal alarm, because it is levelled against the right of freely examining public characters and measures, and of free communication among the people thereon . . . the only effectual guardian of every other right."

The Federalist defenders argued that the Sedition Act, by providing that the truth could be pleaded as defense in libel cases and that the jury might decide both fact and law, offered more protection than the common law, which did not have these provisions; therefore, only the untruthful and malicious editors had anything to fear. Madison answered this argument with a closely reasoned exposition of all points involved. Giving the truth as evidence was not enough, he said, in cases where "opinions and inferences" are inseparable from the facts and where they may "often be more the objects of the prosecution than the facts themselves." To prohibit the "intent" to excite unfavorable sentiments against public officers was "equivalent to a prohibition of discussions having that tendency and effect." The use of penal laws against the "strictures of the press" would be a "protection of those who administer the Government" when they "may deserve to be exposed."[27] Opponents further argued that a federal law of libel was not needed; any person libeled had recourse to the state courts. Although only about fifteen indictments were made under the Sedition Act, these prosecutions provided the Republicans with sufficient evidence for their charge that the Federalists were against liberty of the press, and the press spread the alarm.

The Federalists were not against newspapers; they wanted to control them. They were not opposed to a free press, as they interpreted the term; they were over-sensitive about being criticized by it and were intolerant of exposure. Their reactions were inept and not conducive to winning friends. The parties divided on the question of whether libel laws should be federal, as well as state. Both parties had newspaper support through the election of 1800. Some papers even approved of the Alien and Sedition acts. Republican papers increased in number and they claimed the Federalists were undermining the Constitution with their repressive legislation and were bent on destroying freedom of dissent—a threat against the liberty of the citizen to be informed.

It appeared to the Republicans that the Federalists intended to use the Sedition Act to keep themselves in power. Madison pointed out the significance of the period of the act's duration. Between its passage in 1798 and March 3, 1801, when it was due to expire, there would be two elections for the entire House of Representatives, an election for a part of the Senate, and the election of a president.[28] Indeed, the timing of the prosecutions of the leading Republican newspapers had the earmarks of a preconceived plan to silence or intimidate the press during the elections. It was rather flattering to the newspapers that the party leaders should think the press could influence the outcome. In this period the Federalists in Congress beat back attempts to repeal the Sedition Act, and it expired according to its own provision on March 3, 1801. The next day Thomas Jefferson became president of the United States. There was, of course, more than one reason for his victory, but had newspapers been of less concern to the American people the issue of a free press would not have been a vote-getter for the Republicans in the election. The myopic Federalists with their Alien and Sedition acts had insured their own defeat. The Republicans had emerged from the struggle as champions of the press.

Jefferson as president released from jail those who were still serving sentences under the Sedition Act, and the federal government abandoned the field of legislation against its critics.[29]

The question of just how free the press should be had still not been definitely settled. During Jefferson's two terms in office he had occasions to calculate the value of an unlimited press. There were still more Federalist newspapers than Republican, including most of the city dailies. There were times when they tried his patience sorely, for he was as much abused by the newspapers as his predecessors had been, and at times he was provoked by their licentiousness. He deplored their calumnies and showed as much sensitivity to their vilification as had Hamilton. The man who as much as anyone had developed a press for party uses found his sporting spirit strained when the press of another party was used against him as president. Jefferson even reached the point of suggesting that "a few prosecutions of the most prominent offenders would have a wholesome effect in restoring the integrity of the presses."[30] But he did not depart from his basic philosophy. He did not go so far in his bitterness as to recommend that newspapers be denied the privilege of publication, nor did he propose that they be eliminated as an instrument in the functioning of the government. He merely insisted that printers be held responsible for libel under state laws, with truth as their protection. And he seems to have felt that truth was sufficient protection against "false and defamatory publications" for the holders of public office.[31]

In the post-Jefferson period the legal questions concerning freedom of the press, including the various kinds of libels and the authority to punish them, tended to become largely academic. Of greater importance was the force of public opinion. As the American people perceived more and more the usefulness of newspapers in the democratic process, such as providing needed information and evaluating public servants, they would not be without them, and they and public officials would tolerate unpalatable and even untruthful statements because under the competitive party system there would always be newspapers to challenge other newspapers in matters of public concern. The tendency was to give the press more and more latitude and allow the fun of verbal combat. Public legal actions involving liberty of the press became relatively rare, and in such cases the outcome was affected by that grass-roots body, the jury. Newspapers became remarkably free, regardless of legal interpretations of constitutions and statutes that might limit them. In fact, Professor Chafee has declared that in the nineteenth century newspapers were "the freest in modern times," both in the United States and in England.[32]

Neither Hamilton nor Jefferson was the elected head of the government when their gazettes were serving them. As leaders of opposing political philosophies they were heads of incipient political parties. Their newspapers, therefore, were essentially party organs, a situation that made it easy and natural for either of them to have an administration paper if he became president. Their experience pointed the way to a combination party and presidential news organ that appeared with Jefferson's presidency, setting a precedent for more than half a century. Had

Hamilton become president it is altogether likely that he too would have secured an administration organ, even if it were necessary to create it himself.[33]

After political parties became recognized and established, a few party newspapers achieved special distinction as presidential organs. They succeeded one another as did the presidents and were dependent upon presidential favor for their special status. They expected and got government printing, by which they were partially sustained. Of the papers already mentioned, the *Gazette of the United States* most nearly fits this character. Each president from Jefferson to Buchanan had such a paper, and all were in Washington.

NOTES

1. Gore to King, Boston, Jan. 18, 1789, *Life and Correspondence of Rufus King*, 1, 357. The term "Federalist" is used here in its later meaning as a party label, not in the current more general meaning such as that used during the ratification of the Constitution.

2. *Gazette of the United States*, Sept. 18, 1790.

3. *Gazette of the United States*, Nov. 25, Dec. 2, 12, 16, 19, 26, 28, 1789.

4. Ibid., Dec. 7, 1791. In May of 1791 Fenno claimed the number of copies distributed "is at present fourteen hundred." Postmasters in many cases could relay the contents of newspapers about as effectually as another newspaper.

5. The "Discourses on Davila" were a series of essays written by John Adams. Much like lectures on government, they tried to dampen the American ardor for the French Revolution, provoking so much criticism that Fenno asked Adams to discontinue them, which he did. Page Smith, *John Adams*, 2:797–802. Assistance of "several distinguished literary characters" was acknowledged by the *Gazette*, April 27, 1791.

6. Fenno to Hamilton, Nov. 9, 1793; Hamilton to Rufus King, Nov. 11, 1793, *Life and Correspondence of Rufus King*, 1:501–502; *Papers of Alexander Hamilton*, ed. Syrett, 15:393, 395, 418.

7. Jefferson to Thomas Mann Randolph, May 15, 1791, *Works of Jefferson*, ed. Ford, 6:263.

8. *Writings of Thomas Jefferson*, ed. Lipscomb and Bergh, 8:113.

9. Nathan Schachner, *Thomas Jefferson*, 1:442. Freneau had contributed to the *United States Magazine*, owned by his college mate Hugh Brackenridge, and been editor for three years of the *Freeman's Journal* of Philadelphia.

10. Jefferson to Madison, July 21, 1791, cited by Schachner, *Thomas Jefferson*, 1:442.

11. S.H. Gay, *James Madison* (1892), p. 172. Francis Childs and John Swaine, publishers of the New York *Daily Advertiser*, with a branch office in Philadelphia, assumed the expense and risk of the *National Gazette*, thus leaving Freneau free to concentrate on editorial work.

12. Jefferson to Washington, Sept. 9, 1792. *Writings of Thomas Jefferson*, ed. Lipscomb and Bergh, 8:404. Freneau was appointed clerk of foreign languages Aug. 16, 1791. Victor H. Palsitts, *Bibliography of the Separate and Collected Works of Philip Freneau* (1903), p. 8.

13. Madison to Jefferson, May 1, 1791, Writings of James Madison, ed. Hunt, 6:47n. Freneau's younger brother Peter, a printer, editor, businessman, and secretary of state of South Carolina, became Jefferson's political manager in that state. Richard B. Davis and Milledge B. Seigler, "Peter Freneau, Carolina Republican," *Journal of Southern History*, 13 (Aug. 1947): 395–405.

14. Hamilton to Edward Carrington, May 26, 1792, *Papers of Alexander Hamilton*, ed. Syrett, 11:426–44.

15. *National Gazette*, March 15, 1792.

16. *Gazette of the United States*, July 25, 1792. Reprinted by *National Gazette*, July 28, 1792. Freneau said it was "beneath a reply," although he did give a brief rebuttal. Hamilton's contributions are now available in his *Papers*, ed. Syrett, the "T.L." articles in 12:107, 123–25, 193–94; the first article from "An American," here cited, on pp. 157–64, the two later ones on 188–93, and 224 respectively.

17. *Gazette of the United States*, Aug. 4, Sept. 15, 1792. Madison denied that Freneau's paper was designed to "sap the Constitution." In a private letter to Attorney General Randolph, Madison affirmed that he had recommended Freneau for a government appointment (though not only in the Department of State) because of his "acquaintance of long standing," his respect for Freneau's talents, and knowledge of his "suffering in the course of the revolution." He had advised Freneau to establish his projected newspaper in Philadelphia rather than elsewhere because he thought Freneau's interest "would be advanced by it." But Madison added that he had also hoped as a consequence "a free paper for general circulation and edited by a man of genius and republican principles . . . would be some antidote to the doctrines & discourses circulated in favor of Monarchy and Aristocracy." He confided his belief that Hamilton's attack on Jefferson would "be of service" to both Jefferson and the public. Madison to Edmund Randolph, Sept. 13, 1792, *Writings of James Madison*, ed. Hunt, 6:117–18.

18. *Gazette of the United States*, Aug. 8, 1792.

19. Ibid., Aug. 11, 1792; *Works of Hamilton*, ed. Lodge, 7:236–42; *Papers of Hamilton*, ed. Syrett, 12:192.

20. *National Gazette*, Aug. 15, 1792. This was in the form of a letter to the editor, signed "G." Freneau also wrote anonymously a series of "Odes on Various Subjects" in which he used his poetic talent in lampoons. For example, an ode "To the National Gazette" belittled the paper's critics in verse that opened thus: "For nine months past, a host of busy foes / Have buzzed about your nose / White, black and grey, / By night and by day; Garbling, lying, / Singing, sighing:". "Ode IV," ibid., Aug. 4, 1792.

21. Philip Marsh, "The Vindication of Mr. Jefferson," *South Atlantic Quarterly*, 45 (1946): 61–67; Marsh, *Monroe's Defense of Jefferson and Freneau Against Hamilton*, pamphlet, 56 pp. (Oxford, Ohio, 1948); Claude Bowers, *Jefferson and Hamilton*, p. 169; Irving Brant, *James Madison*, 3:362.

22. For a brief time Jefferson got Fenno to publish translated extracts from the *Leyden Gazette*, partly to counteract the bias of English journals on which Fenno was drawing, an arrangement that ended by Aug. 1790, because Fenno gave up the effort to satisfy both Hamilton and Jefferson in his *Gazette of the United States*. An informed account of Jefferson's interest in the *Gazette de Leide* and connection with Fenno is given in an editorial note in *Papers of Thomas Jefferson*, ed. Boyd, 16:237–47.

23. Jefferson to Washington, Sept. 9, 1792, *Writings of Thomas Jefferson*, ed. Lipscomb and Bergh, 8:394–407.

24. Ibid. Hamilton held that it was all right for a paper to get government subsidies if it supported government measures, but not if it criticized them. If Jefferson wanted to use a newspaper in opposition he should resign his government office. Miller, Alexander Hamilton, p. 349.

25. *National Gazette*, July 28, 1792.

26. A considerable amount of literature on Freneau now exists, including his own writings that have been brought to light. Two major biographies are: Lewis Leary, *That Rascal Freneau: A Study in Literary Failure* (New Brunswick: Rutgers University Press, 1941), and Jacob

Axelrad, *Philip Freneau: Champion of Democracy* (Austin: University of Texas Press, 1967). Numerous periodical articles deal with aspects of Freneau's career, most notably those of Lewis Leary and Philip M. Marsh. Freneau's experience with the *National Gazette* is treated from various approaches in many different works, including Samuel E. Forman, *Political Activities of Philip Freneau* (Baltimore: Johns Hopkins University Press, 1902); Bowers, *Jefferson and Hamilton*; Noble E. Cunningham, *The Jeffersonian Republicans . . . 1789–1801*; and Donald H. Stewart, "Jeffersonian Journalism . . . 1789–11," Ph.D. diss., Columbia University, 1950. (Ann Arbor: University Microfilms, Publication No. 2132). See also Donald H. Stewart, *The Opposition Press of the Federalist Period* (Albany: State University of New York Press, 1969). My unplanned involvement in Freneau literature has yielded two conclusions: that Freneau merits fuller coverage than this chapter could afford him; that Madison and Jefferson showed remarkable perception in seeking his services.

27. Madison's report on the Virginia Resolutions, *Writings of James Madison*, ed. Hunt, 6:396–97.

28. Ibid., p. 395.

29. For full treatment of the debatable acts see John C. Miller, *Crisis in Freedom: The Alien and Sedition Acts*. For relevant documents on liberty of the press with background see the source book edited with an introduction by Leonard W. Levy, *Freedom of the Press from Zenger to Jefferson* (Indianapolis, 1966). In addition to the Virginia and Kentucky Resolutions, Madison's committee report on the resolutions in 1799–10 is basic material. A good brief, general interpretation is J. Morton Smith's "The Sedition Law, Free Speech, and the American Political Process," in *William and Mary Quarterly*, 3rd ser., 9 (Oct. 1925): 497–511. The able arguments of H.G. Otis for the constitutionality of the Sedition Act are noted in S.E. Morison, *Harrison Gray Otis*, pp. 119–20.

30. Jefferson to Governor McKean, Feb. 19, 1803, *Writings of Thomas Jefferson*, ed. Ford, 8:218.

31. Jefferson's second inaugural address. For a short, clear presentation of Jefferson's attitude, see Frank Luther Mott, *Jefferson and the Press*.

32. Zechariah Chafee, Jr., *Free Speech in the United States* (Harvard University Press, 1964), pp. 505–507. I am indebted to this author for buttressing with his legal approach a conclusion I had developed from another approach. Chaps. I and XIII have been especially helpful.

33. Even with the Federalist defeat, Hamilton made sure that a new Federalist paper was established in the *New York Evening Post*, with a prominent young Boston-born Federalist, William Coleman, as its editor. Hamilton aimed to match the best Republican journals. The paper did become a strong one. Allan Nevins, *The Evening Post*, chap. 1; *Correspondence of Rufus King*, 3:514.

2. THE RISE OF THE PENNY PRESS

Michael Schudson

The clientele of the partisan press consisted of the social elite of America in the early nineteenth century. This group made up the primary participants in American politics. Not only did they meet the suffrage requirements, which included property ownership, but they were the objects of deference by the mass public. They were expected to provide the political leadership for the country because they were uniquely qualified to lead.

However, with the onset of the age of the common man, social attitudes began to reflect a new equality. Electoral changes followed, which encouraged mass participation. In 1828, voter turnout was 50 percent higher than it had been just four years earlier.*

Democratization of American politics began to affect the press. No longer were the elite-oriented partisan newspapers appropriate for a mass audience. Moreover, the news content of the press changed as it appealed to a mass, rather than an elite, audience.

A fundamentally new press emerged. Initially termed the "penny press" because of its cost per copy, this new type of newspaper lacked partisan ties—in fact flaunted that fact—and existed primarily for commercial rather than political interests. Thus it relied on circulation and advertising rather than partisan affiliation and government subsidy. Because it sold for one-sixth the cost of the partisan press, it appealed to the working and middle classes and created a truly mass press for the first time in American history.

Michael Schudson describes how the penny press changed the concept of news. He also explains the birth of news gathering.†

Michael Schudson is professor of communication at the University of California–San Diego. He is the author of *Rethinking Popular Culture: Contemporary Perspectives in Cultural Studies* (1991), *Reading the News* (1986), and *Discovering the News* (1978), from which this excerpt is taken.

The penny press was novel, not only in economic organization and political stance, but in its content. The character of this originality is simply put: the penny press invented the modern concept of "news." For the first time the American newspaper made it a regular practice to print political news, not just foreign but domestic, and not just national but local; for the first time it printed reports from the police, from the courts, from the streets, and from private households. One might say that, for the first time, the newspaper reflected not just commerce or politics but social life. To be more precise, in the 1830s the newspapers began to reflect, not the affairs of an elite in a small trading society, but the activities of an increasingly varied, urban, and middle-class society of trade, transportation, and manufacturing.

The six-penny papers responded to the penny newcomers with charges of sensationalism. This accusation was substantiated by the way the penny papers treated the news (there were no sensational photographs, of course, no cartoons or drawings, no large headlines) than by the fact that the penny papers would print "news"—as we understand it—at all. It was common for penny papers, covering a murder trial, to take a verbatim transcript of the trial and spread it across most, or all, of the front page. What the six-penny press decried as immoral was that a murder trial should be reported at all. The typical news story was the verbatim report, whether it be of a presidential address, a murder trial, or the annual statement of the United States Treasury.

News became the mainstay of the daily paper. The penny papers did not depend on the usual trickle of stale news but sought out the news. They took pride in their activity, as the *New York Transcript* made clear in 1834:

*See Richard P. McCormick, *The Second American Party System* (New York: W.W. Norton & Co., Inc., 1966), pp. 390–91.

†From *Discovering the News* (New York: Basic Books, 1978), pp. 22–28.

There are eleven large and regularly established daily papers in this city; and with the exception of the *Courier and Enquirer*, and perhaps the *Times*, not one of them employs a news reporter or takes any other pains to obtain accurate and correct local information—on the other hand there are two small daily NEWS papers (ourselves and our contemporary), and those two employ four reporters, exclusively to obtain the earliest, fullest, and most correct intelligence on every local incident; and two of these latter arise at 3 in the morning, at which hour they attend the police courts, and are there employed, with short intermissions, till the close of the office at 8 in the evening, while others are obtaining correct information about the city.[1]

In 1835 the *Herald* joined the *Transcript* and its "contemporary" the *Sun* and, by the end of 1837, boasted two Washington correspondents, permanent correspondents in Jamaica and Key West; occasional correspondents in London, Philadelphia, and Boston; two Canadian correspondents during the MacKenzie Rebellion of 1837; and a correspondent roving New York State to report on the wheat crop. This was expensive, the *Herald* noted, but it was done to gratify the public.[2] A year later the *Herald* had hired six European correspondents as regular contributors.[3]

The institution of paid reporters was not only novel but, to some, shocking. Until the late 1820s, New York coverage of Washington politics relied mainly on members of Congress writing occasionally to their home papers. Some regular "letter writers" passed on dull reports and summarized speeches. James Gordon Bennett, writing in 1827 and 1828 for the *New York Enquirer*, initiated more lively reporting with his dispatches on "the court of John Q. Adams."[4] Adams never accommodated himself to the impudence of the new journalism. He wrote with disgust in his diary in 1842 that sons of President Tyler "divulged all his cabinet secrets to a man named Parmalee and John Howard Payne, hired reporters for Bennett's *Herald* newspaper in New York. . . ."[5] His use of "hired" to qualify "reporters" suggests how new, and perhaps disreputable, the institution of a reportorial staff was.

One way to see the dominance of the newspaper by news, which the penny press initiated, is to regard it as the decline of the editorial. This is much less than the whole story, but it was one of the ways in which contemporaries understood the change they were witnessing. In an article in *North American Review* in 1866, Horace Greeley's biographer James Parton sought to explain the phenomenal success and influence of James Gordon Bennett's *New York Herald*. Parton reviewed current opinion about the *Herald*. One view was that the *Herald* rose to prominence because it was a very bad newspaper, pandering to the bad taste of the public. A second view, and Parton's own view, was that the *Herald* succeeded because it was a very good newspaper—but that the newspaper had become something different from what the *Herald's* critics assumed it to be. Parton argued that people who thought the *Herald* a bad paper spoke mainly of its editorials which, he admitted, were execrable. Bennett was ornery, prejudiced, misanthropic, and opportunistic, and his editorials reflected his nature. But, Parton went on, the editorial is dying and only the news is the "point of rivalry" between papers. The success of a journal had come to depend "wholly and absolutely upon its success in getting, and its skill in exhibiting, the news. The word *newspaper* is the exact and complete description of the thing which the true journalist aims to produce."[6]

News was, indeed, the point of rivalry with the penny papers. We have so completely identified the concept of "news" with the newspaper itself that it may be difficult to understand how dramatic a change the penny press represented. Until the 1830s, a newspaper provided a service to political parties and men of commerce; with the penny press a newspaper sold a product to a general readership and sold the readership to advertisers. The product sold to readers was "news," and it was an original product in several respects. First, it claimed to represent, colorfully but without partisan coloring, events in the world. Thus the news product of one paper could be compared to that of another for accuracy, completeness, liveliness, and timeliness. The *Herald* in 1840 crowed over the accuracy and fullness of its report of a speech by Daniel Webster and ridiculed a Mr. Stansbury, reporting for a six-penny paper, who "knows nothing of stenography and wrote out some thirty or forty pages of small quarto foolscap, in long hand."[7] The *Herald* patted itself on the back, on one occasion, for having had the only reporter on the school-visiting trip of the City Council and School Fund commissioners and, on another, for having been the only paper in the city to print the United States Treasurer's report in full.[8] As for the timeliness of news, the *Herald* and the *Sun* rivaled each other in printing "extras" and praising themselves for it. The *Herald*, for instance, boasted on November 21, 1840, of its extra on the day before announcing the arrival of British forces in Canton: *"No other newspaper establishment in New York had the news at that time, nor could they get it, they are so inefficient and lazy."*[9]

During the first decades of the nineteenth century, newspapers had increasingly tried to be up-to-date, especially in reporting the arrival of ships and in printing the news they brought with them. The New York papers began to send out small boats to incoming ships to gather up news; in the late 1820s, several papers formed an association which bought a fast boat to meet the ships for all association members. But only with the penny press was the competition for news "beats" firmly established as the chief basis of the newspaper business. Thanks to James Gordon Bennett, even advertising became more timely. Until the 1840s advertisers paid a flat fee, often on an annual basis, to place the same notice in a paper day after day. In 1847 Bennett announced that, beginning January 1, 1848, all ads in the *Herald* would have to be resubmitted daily. This encouraged changing ad copy so that Bennett's managing editor, Frederic Hudson, exclaimed in his history of American journalism:

> the advertisements form the most interesting and practical city news. They are the hopes, the thoughts, the joys, the plans, the shames, the losses, the mishaps, the fortunes, the pleasures, the miseries, the politics, and the religion of the people. Each advertiser is therefore a reporter, a sort of penny-a-liner, he paying the penny. What a picture of the metropolis one day's advertisements in the *Herald* presents to mankind![10]

The penny papers' concept of news not only created news as a marketable product whose attributes—particularly timeliness—could be measured, it invented a genre which acknowledged, and so enhanced, the importance of everyday life. In literature until the eighteenth century, aristocratic conventions had dictated that the common aspects of everyday life could receive only comic treatment, if they were dealt with at all.[11] A similar convention appears to have prevailed in journalism—newspapers simply did not report on the lives of ordinary people. Although the War of 1812 ended the almost exclusive dominance of foreign news in the American press, local or hometown news, before the penny papers, remained a minor feature. The commercial press proved less reliable in reporting local prices of commodities or stocks than in reporting foreign news and shipping news.[12] The penny press, in contrast, focused on the nearby and the everyday, and for the first time hired reporters on a regular basis to cover local news. Reporters were assigned to the police, the courts, the commercial district, the churches, high society, and sports. The penny papers made the "human interest story" not only an important part of daily journalism but its most characteristic feature.

The penny papers saw news in ordinary events where no one had seen anything noteworthy before. This is nowhere better indicated than in those moments when even the most aggressive penny papers had a hard time claiming there had been any news. In an item headed "The News of the Week," the *Herald* of March 12, 1837, wrote:

The News of the Week

> Is not of very much importance. Yet the most insignificant events can be swelled to matters of great moment, if they are traced up eternity to their causes, or down eternity to their consequences. Not a single incident—not the slightest event that does not become a part of the time past or the time to come, and thus mix with the greatest everlasting both in time and in space. The news of a day—of a week—is supposed by the superficial blockheads who conduct newspapers and govern nations—or cheat the public—or sell quack medicine—or stir up politics—or shave in Wall Street, to be of trifling moment. And so it is to them. To the philosopher who dips deeply into things, it is different.[13]

The penny papers inaugurated this democratic attitude toward the happenings of the world: any event, no matter how apparently trivial, might qualify for print in a newspaper. . . .

NOTES

1. *New York Transcript,* June 23, 1834, quoted in Bleyer, *Main Currents,* p. 165. The "contemporary" referred to is the *New York Sun.*

2. *New York Herald,* December 8, 1837.

3. Pray, *Memoirs,* p. 251.

4. James Gordon Bennett, quoted in Frederic Hudson, *Journalism in the United States* (New York: Harper and Brothers, 1872), p. 286. Bennett's self-report of his innovation is corroborated in Ben: Perley Poore's recollections, which recall Bennett's "lively" letters which "abounded in personal allusions" about politicians and their families as an important new development in Washington correspondence. Ben: Perley Poore, *Perley's Reminiscences of Sixty*

Years in the National Metropolis, 2 vols. (Philadelphia: Hubbard Brothers, 1886), I:58.

5. John Quincy Adams, *The Diary of John Quincy Adams*, ed. Allan Nevins (New York: Frederick Ungar Publishing, 1969), p. 543.

6. James Parton, "The New York Herald," *North American Review* 102 (April 1866): 376.

7. *New York Herald*, September 30, 1840. Stansbury is Arthur J. Stansbury, an important figure in the early development of Washington correspondence, who wrote out his accounts of speeches with his own contractions of longhand. See L.A. Gobright, *Recollections of Men and Things at Washington During the Third of a Century* (Philadelphia: Claxton, Remson, and Haffelfinger, 1869), p. 401.

8. *New York Herald*, December 24, 1841.

9. *New York Herald*, November 21, 1840.

10. Hudson, *Journalism*, p. 470.

11. Erich Auerbach, *Mimesis* (Princeton: Princeton University Press, 1953), p. 31.

12. Frank Luther Mott, *American Journalism: A History 1690–1960* (New York: Macmillan, 1962), pp. 196–97.

13. *New York Herald*, March 12, 1837.

3. THE CIVICS AND ANTI-CIVICS OF MUCKRAKING

Thomas C. Leonard

The Progressive Era was a time of dramatic political upheaval and reform in American politics. The historian Richard Hofstedter concluded that "to an extraordinary degree the work of the Progressive movement rested upon its journalism."[*]

Throughout the 1800s, the penny press became financially profitable. The mass circulation wars and the embrace of yellow journalism by large segments of the press furthered the political role of the press by expanding its reach as a political medium. By the beginning of the Progressive Era, the press possessed the potential through its pervasiveness in American life and its autonomy from political parties to aid a national reform movement. Moreover, the trend in journalism was toward a description of social realism. Given that trend, a focus on the sins of the political system was a natural outgrowth.

But, according to Thomas C. Leonard, the work of muckraking transcended a certain reform movement.[†] Rather, it contributed to a societal consensus that politics was cheap and tawdry. Leonard contends the muckrakers aided in the development of a general distrust in, and distaste for, not merely political corruption but the political system itself. Leonard also describes some journalistic practices employed to reinforce the message that politics is dirty. Notice that some modern journalistic practices received their birth in that era.

Thomas C. Leonard is associate professor of journalism at the University of California–Berkeley. He is the author of *Above the Battle: War Making in America From Appomatox to Versailles* (1978) and *The Power of the Press: The Birth of American Political Reporting* (1986), from which this excerpt is taken.

[*]*The Age of Reform* (New York: Vintage, 1955), p. 186.
[†]From Thomas C. Leonard, *The Power of the Press* (New York: Oxford University Press, 1986), pp. 204–205, 207–210, 211, 213.

In the first years of the twentieth century David Graham Phillips took political reporting where few journalists had dared to go. His steps were the ones reporters dreamed of; his conclusions were bolder than successful journalists had been willing to make. Phillips was a celebrity and a scoffer. The gray routine of a reporter's life was not for him, nor the pulling of punches. Phillips snarled at the political process. He brought to the surface an antagonism toward government that was at the center of muckraking.

Phillips led a double life: the man of letters standing free of the demands of the newsroom and the reporter in harness who would chase any story. Phillips is easy to spot in the photographs of the press corps of this era, the peacock amidst the dark, wrinkled suits. His first editor in Cincinnati was so appalled by his fashionable tailoring that he would not speak to the young man for several days. In New York, conversations started over his white flannels and the large chrysanthemum he chose each morning for his lapel. Editors could not find an assignment too trivial, humiliating or dirty to discourage him. He scored on the stories other reporters found hopeless. Colleagues credited Phillips with finding a missing child and then wringing the last tear from the discovery. He got a full account of a British naval disaster into the New York *World* before the Admiralty knew the details.

Phillips's advancement followed the daydreams of a generation of colleagues in the newsroom. Reporters were paid the wages of clerks and often lived as if they were paid less. Phillips commanded the unprecedented sums that Pulitzer and Hearst bid for star talent in New York. Many reporters worked themselves sick as they supplemented writing for a newspaper with stories for other publishers. Phillips could take or leave newspaper work as he chose, and for a time he happily covered a beat during the day and wrote fiction through the night. (In the photo chosen by Phillips's admirers for the memorial biography, the journalist stands at his writing table for the night, wearing an embroidered robe, pencil poised.) He published seventeen novels, seven short stories, and one play before his death at age forty-three. Phillips was assassinated in Gramercy Park in 1911 by a deranged reader of his novels. Somehow this self-sufficient, nocturnal dandy thrust himself into the middle of the great public questions of the Progressive Era. It was Phillips's series on government for a Hearst magazine in 1906 that provoked President Theodore Roosevelt to brand it "muckraking" and to warn the American people where such reporting was taking them.

Any reader who even skims the nine installments of "The Treason of the Senate" soon notices two things: the pictures that tell Phillips's story and the reporter's insistence, over and over again, that the words of senators mean nothing. These may be the most important things about this reporting, for they upset the conventional way of telling political stories.

William Randolph Hearst had bought *Cosmopolitan* in 1905, and the Senate exposé was his first opportunity in a magazine to show his characteristic extravagance. Phillips was allowed to name his price. Talented researchers were hired. The series was relentlessly advertised. There was full-color art work on the first covers, and important cartoonists produced frontispieces. The most striking feature was the photographs Hearst obtained. The first installment of March 1906 began with New York's junior senator, Chauncey Depew, tilting his head back and laughing in the reader's face. This shot was followed by photos of the senator's three imposing residences and his drawing room in Washington. Depew was shown at play in his automobile and at work at the Republican convention. Three more senators were caught on the street with snap shots in the first six installments, and the story was frequently interrupted by architectural specimens. The fine modern edition of "The Treason of the Senate" reproduces only the cartoons from this run of illustration, and this is unfortunate. The photos said something about politics as startling as Phillips's words.

Cosmopolitan was the first magazine to find a place for photographs in the tested format of the exposé. Juxtaposing public servants with their lavish possessions had been a staple of illustrated journalism since the rise of *Harper's Weekly* a half century earlier. Without making an argument, without attempting to prove graft, the sumptuous setting of men in power was a visual indictment. Hearst used the new half-tone process to fit photographs into this scheme, and editors made sure readers got the point. The photo of Senator Depew in his auto had been published a year earlier by *Leslie's Weekly* captioned "A Statesman-Automobilist-Senator Depew, of New York, en route to the Capitol at Washington in his Horseless Carriage." The wide view of the avenue did make it seem the senator was going to work. *Cosmopolitan* cropped the photo to take the senator off the road and chose a caption to make it seem that he was idly sitting in his plaything—"one of the Senator's Favorite Recreations." Hearst's editors added the off-guard shot to this syntax of derision. Officeholders no longer control their public face. They can be "snapped," feet in the air or frozen to the sidewalk; they usually appear to be fleeing the camera or caught at playing a children's game of statue.[1]

The governed were not used to seeing the governors in this way outside a cartoon. *Cosmopolitan* had not published an unposed photo of an American politician before "The Treason of the Senate." The magazine had gone beyond the studio portrait before Hearst took control, showing reformers bent over a desk or gripping a telephone. Also, like the Hearst newspapers, candid shots of the rich at play were common, but *Cosmopolitan* had never printed a photograph designed to fit a political exposé. *McClure's* had been just as conservative with pictures. The boodlers and bosses of Lincoln Steffens's series appeared as they chose to appear before the camera. "Snap shots" in political stories were not unprecedented in 1906, but they had not stung. Wounding photographs linked to an attack with words formed a new arsenal for the press. A few months after the Phillips's series, for example, a photograph of the political establishment in California appeared in most of the progressive publications in that state as well as in national muckraking magazines. The camera had caught a Republican celebrating his nomination for the governorship in the company of the biggest money men in the state. The candidate's fingers gripped the shoulder of Boss Abraham Ruef of San Francisco. The photograph acquired a name, "The Shame of California." Veteran reformers, especially working for Hearst, made much bolder use of photographs towards the end of the first decade of the century. Muckraking had hit upon a new way to picture men in power, anticipating candid shots and even the "ambush" techniques of television.[2]

"The Treason of the Senate" overturned conventional reporting because it changed what the reader was to hear as well as see. Phillips had contempt for the debates of Congress, and he wanted the public to stop listening. He rarely quoted a senator and gave only the haziest account of what their positions were on the issues. Repeatedly he dismissed public debate as "sham battles" designed only to fool naive citizens. "Orators of the treason" pretended to disagree in order to disguise the conspiracies arranged in the committee rooms. To listen to these men was to be caught up in this deception, Phillips explained, for "all the speeches of these secret traitors to country and people . . . abounded in virtue, piety, and patriotism. . . ." An honest minority felt bound by senatorial courtesy and muffled criticism so the hypocrisy of the majority was never exposed. Phillips spoke of "the dust of senatorial debates" and described an atmosphere so close and fetid that a healthy citizen must keep away. He marveled that the senators who sat through the debates did not break into laughter.[3]

"The Treason of the Senate" began by pointing out the "stupidity" of the electorate and frequently offered a sneer at the gullible public. Taunts at the average citizen crept into muckraking after the first discoveries about government. The general public was scorned in *The Jungle* by Upton Sinclair, an exposé that was frightening Americans at the time Phillips's series appeared. After 1906 Americans were not allowed to forget how little they knew or to escape blame for their ignorance. The deceptions worked! This was the chorus of the investigative magazines, with Phillips and Sinclair the loudest voices. Sinclair took his story through several election campaigns, showing how bread and circuses produced any outcome the capitalists wanted. Voters were handled as efficiently as cattle in Packingtown. Phillips drew attention to the occult nature of politics, "the mysteries of the Senate—all its crafty, treacherous ways of smothering, of emasculating, of perverting legislation." A reader might reasonably conclude that the upper house consisted of nothing but buncombe speeches. "Slathering treason with cant," Phillips said, was the normal business of lawmakers. Behind the "black art of politics" stood "the Interests"—a term Phillips coined to describe the American plutocracy. He predicted that the lower and middle class would be crushed by this exercise of power in Washington. The humble citizen had only himself to blame. Phillips baited his readers, asking if the Senate's contempt was not justified.[4]

Phillips had built his reputation in fiction by mocking the political process, so his reports on the Senate could not have surprised his large number of faithful readers. The Americans in these novels, like Jurgis in Sinclair's *The Jungle*, lived through an anti-civics lesson. Machines decided elections. Bosses controlled their own party and, usually, the other one as well. Higher up "the Interests" bought the outcome plutocrats favored. Politics was a matter of "puppet peoples and puppet politicians" according to *The Cost* (1904). This was a tour of the "sewers of politics." "The Plum Tree, or, the Confessions of a Politician," made the cover of *Success Magazine* a month before the nation elected a president in 1904. The novel was a great success on the book lists the following year. In sending Phillips to the Senate in 1906 Hearst was asking little more than to make fact follow popular novels of the day. . . .[5]

It was politics itself that was attacked in a good deal of the literature of reform. In *Success Magazine* Charles E. Russell condemned "the fatal virus of 'practical politics,' the very name of which is always a sign of something rotten." Alfred Henry Lewis told readers of *Human Life* that "politics is the art of arousing the ignorance of mankind." There was contempt not only for the compromises a practical politician must make but also for the calculating mind that seeks partial good in the political process. . . .

What were readers supposed to make of this reporting? How could a political process worthy of such contempt be fixed so quickly? How could a government of traitors doing the bidding of the wealthy disappear?

****

The editors of muckraking magazines were obsessed by charges that they were too negative, and they responded with demonstrations that this was not so. As in Phillips's and Sinclair's work, exposés were almost always connected with a piece of legislation that would set things right. Open one of these magazines at random and read for a half hour: there is assurance (probably more than once) that an aroused public opinion will fulfill the promise of democracy. But this said, the President [Roosevelt] was a discerning critic of the literature of muckraking. The process of government was usually denigrated so effectively that participation in it—even as a voter—was made to seem futile. The imaginative literature and reporting repelled the citizen from political life. . . .

NOTES

1. *Leslie's Weekly*, C, 30 March 1905, 304. All of the photographs save one are reproduced in the reprint edition published in New York in 1953.

2. The only precedent I have found for the snap shots of senators appeared in a story favorable to the upper house: Walter Wellman, "Operating the United States Senate," *Success*, VII (Oct. 1904), 559–61. What the New York *Times* called "Promiscuous photographing" (snap shots of the Democratic presidential candidate) arose in the 1904 campaign, 16 July 1904, p. 2.

"The Shame of California—Photographed" appeared in *American Magazine*, LXV (Dec. 1907), 144 as part of Lincoln Steffens, "The Mote and the Beam." George E. Mowry, *The California Progressives* (Berkeley and Los Angeles, 1951), pp. 60, 174.

Charles E. Russell's series, "What Are You Going to Do About It?" *Cosmopolitan*, XLIX–L (July–Oct. & Dec. 1910) is a striking example of how composite photos brought a new element to the work of a veteran muckraker. In his earlier, celebrated work on the Beef Trust and the tenements owned by Trinity Church, documentary photographs had come without theatrical effects.

James Creelman, "The Romance and Tragedy of Wood Engraving," *Pearson's Magazine*, XVII (March 1907), 293, called the half-tone process a "revolution" in illustration and emphasized the economy. A master engraver fetched $150 to $200 for a picture that could now be made ready for the press for $6 to $30. The savings in time was just as dramatic. See also Neil Harris, "Iconography and Intellectual History: The Half-Tone Effect," in *New Directions in American Intellectual History*, ed., John Higham and Paul K. Conkin (Baltimore, 1979).

3. David Graham Phillips, *The Treason of the Senate*, George E. Mowry and Judson A. Grenier, eds. (Chicago, 1964) pp. 59, 85, 92, 99, 114–15, 121, 126, 146; "Orators of the treason" appeared in a conclusion at the end of the third installment in *Cosmopolitan*, the phrase is not reproduced in this edition. Phillips also dismissed speeches in the Senate writing in *Appleton's Magazine* (April 1906). David J. Rothman, *Politics and Power: The United States Senate, 1869–1901* (Cambridge, 1966), is the best single demonstration of how little of his subject Phillips understood.

"The Treason of the Senate" was longer, but not more extreme than other exposés of Congress in these magazines. Alfred Henry Lewis said that his political reporting was modeled after the rattlesnake's approach to intruders, and Lewis was frequently as good as his word. See, for example, "Confessions of a Newspaper Man," *Human Life*, II (Nov. 1905), 4; "Some Presidential Candidates," *ibid.*, VII (April 1908), 9–10, 32–33; "What Is 'Joe' Cannon?" *Cosmopolitan*, XLVIII (April 1910), 569–75. Samuel Merwin, "Taking the Hoe to Congress," *Success*, IV (Sept. 1906), 604–605, 647–48. Hearst's long-drawn-out release of the "Archbold Letters" was an assault on the integrity of the Senate, see *Hearst's Magazine, The World To-Day*, XXI (May 1912), 2201–16, and *ibid.* (June 1912) 2362–2776h.

4. Phillips, *The Treason of the Senate*, pp. 60, 69, 92, 99, 104, 194, 214. Upton Sinclair, *The Jungle* (New York, 1906), see especially pp. 110, 308. Virtually all of the fiction I use first appeared in muckraking publications. I cite the books as a convenience. There was much taunting of the reader in Russell, "At the Throat of the Republic," pp. 150, 260, 475. Alfred Henry Lewis spoke of "a numskull public" in "The Revolution at Washington," *Cosmopolitan*, XLIX (July 1910), 245.

5. John Graham (David Graham Phillips), *The Great God Success, A Novel* (New York, 1901), p. 173; Phillips, *The Cost*, p. 241; Phillips, *The Plum Tree*, pp. 220, 252. For dispiriting testimony about how politics worked see, for example, Eltweek Pomeroy, "An Outsider's Experiences with Inside Politics" and the editorial "Popular Government; 1904," *Independent*, LVI, 5 May 1904, 1006–10 and 1039–40; William Hemstreet, "The New Primary Law," *Arena*, XXVIII (Dec. 1902), 585–95.

SUGGESTED READINGS

Bailyn, Bernard, and John B. Hench, eds. *The Press and the American Revolution*. Worcester, Mass.: American Antiquarian Society, 1980.
A collection of readings by Robert M. Weir, Stephen Botein, James Russell Wiggins, and others on the role of the press in the pre-Revolutionary years as well as the Revolutionary War period.

Davidson, Philip. *Propaganda and the American Revolution 1763–1783*. Chapel Hill: University of North Carolina Press, 1941.
A classic history of the role of American newspapers in the development of a separatist climate prior to and during the Revolutionary War.

Juergens, George. *News From the White House*. Chicago: University of Chicago Press, 1981.
A history of the relationship between Progressive Era presidents and the press. Juergens describes the growing use of the press by presidents as a tool for policy-making.

Levy, Leonard. *Emergence of a FREE PRESS.* New York: Oxford University Press, 1985.
A revisionist history of the development of the concept of a free press. Levy argues that the Framers were not committed to a libertarian notion of the press.

Rubin, Richard L. *Press, Party, and Presidency.* New York: W.W. Norton & Co., Inc., 1981.
Rubin traces the evolution of the press from a mouthpiece of the political party to an intermediary between presidents and the public. His macro-analysis of media relationship with political institutions helped broaden political communication studies beyond mass behavioral effects.

Schiller, Dan. *Objectivity and the News.* Philadelphia: University of Pennsylvania Press, 1981.
Schiller documents the rise of the penny press and the changes in journalism that created the standard of objectivity. His book critiques objectivity as a journalistic standard and, in contrast to Michael Schudson, argues that the penny press became a government and capitalist tool.

Stewart, Donald H. *The Opposition Press of the Federalist Period.* Albany: State University of New York Press, 1969.
A detailed history of the Republican press during the 1790s, this book documents the emergence of the press in the success of the Jeffersonians over the Federalists.

Tulis, Jeffrey K. *The Rhetorical Presidency.* Princeton, N.J.: Princeton University Press, 1987.
Tulis describes the transformation of the role of the presidency into a public opinion leader, particularly by Theodore Roosevelt. The news media became a vital tool for presidential success.

chapter 3

MEDIA CULTURE

INTRODUCTION

When attempting to describe the forces that determine the news product, journalists often become vague. Some claim that the news is no more than a reflection of reality. They hold a mirror up to their audience and the image displayed is the reality that exists.* A president of CBS once remarked that "what the media do is to hold a mirror up to society and try to report it as faithfully as possible."†

Others are prone to treat the news process mystically. U.S. Supreme Court Justice Potter Stewart, now deceased, once remarked about obscenity that he could not define it but "I know it when I see it." The news process is regarded by some news professionals as similar to Justice Stewart's definition of pornography.‡ Reflecting this attitude of the news not originating from any definable process, Edward J. Epstein titled his study of news organizations, *News From Nowhere*.**

Although this may not be the intent, the result is a process known only to professionals and beyond the capacity of others to examine. Moreover, the adequacy of the product can be properly judged only by professionals.

*See, for example, Sig Mickelson, *The Electric Mirror* (New York: Dodd, Mead, 1972), and William Small, *To Kill a Messenger: Television News and the Real World* (New York: Hastings House, 1970).
†Quoted in Edward J. Epstein, *News From Nowhere* (New York: Random House, 1973), pp. 13–14.
‡See, for example, John Chancellor and Walter R. Mears, *The News Business* (New York: Harper & Row, 1983).
**Ibid.

These approaches have been rejected by social scientists. Empirical studies have demonstrated that the news does originate from somewhere. And it is impossible for the news product to be merely a reflection of the larger social reality. Too many events occur in a 24-hour period for events to be reported fully in the time and space constraints of today's news media. Many decisions are made in the news-gathering and news-reporting process to produce a daily issue of a newspaper or a 22-minute evening news program. That process guarantees that the news will reflect particular individual or group perspectives on reality.

Kurt and Gladys Engel Lang were the first social scientists to challenge directly this notion of news gathering. In their classic study of the 1951 General Douglas MacArthur parade in Chicago, they found a sharp distinction between the reality of observers along the parade route and the television portrayal of the event. Television coverage, through rapid cutting and the choice of visuals displayed, added greater drama to the event than existed in reality.[††] A similar study of the 1972 Democratic National Convention discovered a discrepancy between delegates' recall of the convention and the television coverage.[‡‡]

Studies of the newsroom editors who must sort through the plethora of stories from wire services, news syndicates, and their own local staff have identified elements used to cull those stories that will become the news. Conflict, timeliness, proximity, drama—these are the elements that editors and reporters seek in determining what is news.[*]

Social scientists approaching the news media from a variety of perspectives have identified social forces impacting the shaping of news. Two models of the news process have emerged in the study of news gathering.

The first, and more controversial model, holds that the news is a product of the political biases of news professionals—the reporters, editors, producers, and executives who gather, write, edit, and organize the news.

Under the second model, the professional values and norms of reporters, editors, and producers determine the nature of the news. News is determined largely by the professional's approach to what constitutes news.

The following sections describe each of these models, but allow you to decide which, in isolation or in combination with others, is the best fit in explaining the process of making news.

[††]See Kurt and Gladys Engel Lang, *Politics and Television* (Chicago: Quadrangle, 1968).

[‡‡]David L. Paletz and Martha Elson, "Television Coverage of Presidential Nominating Conventions: Now You See It, Now You Don't," *Political Science Quarterly* 91 (Spring 1976): 103–32.

[*]For the early gatekeeping studies, see David M. White, "The Gatekeeper," *Journalism Quarterly* 27 (Fall 1950): 383–90, and Walter Gieber, "Across the Desk: A Study of 16 Telegraph Editors," *Journalism Quarterly* 33 (Fall 1956): 423–32. For more recent work, see Mark D. Harmon, "Mr. Gates Goes Electronic: The What and Why Questions in Local TV News," *Journalism Quarterly* 66 (Winter 1989): 857–63; Eric A. Abbott and Lynn T. Brassfield, "Comparing Decisions on Releases by TV and Newspaper Gatekeepers," *Journalism Quarterly* 66 (Winter 1989): 853–56; and Dan Berkowitz, "Refining the Gatekeeping Metaphor for Local Television News," *Journal of Broadcasting and Electronic Media* 34 (Winter 1990): 55–88.

A. POLITICAL INFLUENCES

The most common explanation for the nature of news is political bias—that is, journalists organizing their work around their personal prejudices. The subject has provoked discussion of media effect ever since the beginning of the Republic.

As discussed in Chapter 2, the press does have a history of "carrying water" for politicians. Throughout the nineteenth century and early twentieth century, newspapers biased not only editorials but also their news stories.

The standard of objectivity has been of more recent origin and was a direct response to the past partisan affiliation of the press. The Fairness Doctrine, which required presentation of more than one side of an issue, was an attempt to limit the power of broadcasting to achieve partisan ends.

That objectivity has been rejected by many critics of the press. Despite journalists' protestations of adherence to evenhandedness, many critics and the mass public believe journalists hold biases and that those biases affect the way they approach their work.*

The direction of that bias, however, has not achieved consensus. Two broad but contradictory camps have emerged, largely based on the ideological predispositions of the critics.

Conservatives have charged the news media with a liberal bias. News stories, they contend, reflect their own liberal ideology and their interest in liberal causes.

Those on the political Left accuse the news media of harboring a right-wing bias. They argue the press fails to challenge the underpinnings of the political system and uses its gatekeeping power to exclude individuals and groups who offer radical political alternatives.

One cause of the discrepancy is the level of analysis. The former usually concentrates on the newsroom and those who are directly involved in gathering and reporting news, while the latter focuses primarily on the corporate boardroom at media organizations and its influence on the news operation. The Right targets the political and cultural liberalism of reporters and editors, while the Left emphasizes the salience of the economic conservatism of news executives and publishers.

Although much of the literature from the Left and Right is largely polemical, empirical studies of bias have been conducted. The first selection in this section is an empirical study examining the background and attitudes of journalists at the prestige news organizations in the United States. Next, a prominent internal critic of the press charges bias in its treatment of one particular issue—abortion. The remaining selections are representative samples of the two camps discussed above.

You decide which camp's argument carries greater weight.

---

*See, for example, "The People & the Press, Part 5, Attitudes Toward News Organizations," Times Mirror Corp., November 1979.

4. THE MEDIA ELITE

S. Robert Lichter, Stanley Rothman, and Linda S. Lichter

Who are the journalists who bring us the news every day? Drawing from a study that elicited a major controversy among intellectuals, Lichter, Rothman, and Lichter offer a portrait of an elite group—the media elite.* The elite they identify—journalists and editors at the leading media outlets in the nation, including the *New York Times, Washington Post, Wall Street Journal, Time, Newsweek*, the three major commercial networks, and public television—enjoy an upper-class social status unknown to their peers of earlier eras.

They describe a media elite that is politically liberal and cosmopolitan, but somewhat uncomfortable with the gap between themselves and middle-class Americans.

It must be noted that their conclusions cannot be generalized to all media profession-als. Other research suggests those journalists who are not in the "media elite" do not fit the group profile drawn in this article.†

However, the national media do possess an agenda-setting power in national politics and over nonelite media that justifies their isolation as a salient group in the study of politi-cal communication.

S. Robert Lichter and Linda S. Lichter direct the Center for Media and Public Affairs. Stanley Rothman is professor of government at Smith College. They have written exten-sively in the field of political communication. Most recently, they co-authored *Watching America* (1991).

> This business of us being a bunch of parlor pinks, limousine liberals and Harvard-educated pink-tea types who look down our noses at anybody who was born west of the Hudson River is a lot of baloney.—*James Deakin, White House Correspondent*

Are the media biased? . . . [T]he question is wrongly phrased. Between overt bias and pristine objectivity exist infinite shadings, subtle colorations, and elective affini-ties between personal outlook and news product. The trail that leads from journal-ists' perspectives to the news they report is often poorly marked. It winds through conscious attitudes, unquestioned assumptions, and inner motivations. This chap-ter examines the first factor in this complex progression, the actual backgrounds and outlooks of leading journalists.

WHO ARE THE MEDIA ELITE?

During 1979 and 1980, we directed hour-long interviews with 238 journalists at America's most influential media outlets: the *New York Times, Washington Post, Wall Street Journal, Time, Newsweek, U.S. News & World Report*, and the news organizations

---

*From *The Media Elite* (Bethesda, Md.: Adler & Adler, 1986), pp. 20–53. Some tables omitted. Reprinted with permission.

†See, for example, David H. Weaver and G. Cleveland Wilhoit, *The American Journalist* (Bloom-ington: Indiana University Press, 1986).

at CBS, NBC, ABC, and PBS.[1] Within each organization, individuals were selected randomly from the news staffs. From print media, we sampled reporters, columnists, department heads, bureau chiefs, editors, and executives. From television, we selected correspondents, anchors, producers, film editors, and news executives. The result is a systematic sample of the men and women who put together the news at America's most important media outlets—the media elite.[2]

To provide comparisons with a more traditional leadership group, we also surveyed 216 executives at six *Fortune*-listed corporations, ranging from a multinational oil company and a major bank to a public utility and a nationwide retail chain. They were chosen randomly from upper and middle management at each company.[3] The focus of our inquiry is the media elite. At appropriate points, however, we will compare their responses to those of the corporate executives.

ORIGINS AND DESTINATIONS

In some respects, the journalists we interviewed appear typical of leadership groups throughout society (see Table 1). The media elite is composed mainly of white males in their thirties and forties. Only one in twenty is nonwhite, and one in five is female. They are highly educated, well-paid professionals. Ninety-three percent have college degrees, and a majority attended graduate school as well. These figures reveal them to be one of the best-educated groups in America.

Geographically, they are drawn primarily from northern industrial states, especially from the northeast corridor. Forty percent come from three states: New York, New Jersey, and Pennsylvania. Another 10 percent hail from New England, and almost 20 percent were raised in the big industrial states just to the west—Illinois, Indiana, Michigan, and Ohio. Thus, 68 percent of the media elite come from these three clusters of states. By contrast only 3 percent are drawn from the entire Pacific Coast, including California, the nation's most populous state.

TABLE 1

Backgrounds of the Media Elite

White	95%
Male	79
From northeast or north-central states	68
From metropolitan area	42
Father graduated college	40
Father's occupation "professional"	40
College graduate	93
Postgraduate study	55
Individual income $30,000 +	78
Family income $50,000 +	46
Political liberal	54
Political conservative	17
Religion "none"	50

Journalism is a profession associated with rapid upward mobility. Yet we found few Horatio Alger stories in the newsroom. On the contrary, many among the media elite enjoyed socially privileged upbringings. Most were raised in upper-middle-class homes. Almost half their fathers were college graduates, and one in four held a graduate degree. Two in five are the children of professionals—doctors, lawyers, teachers, and so on. In fact, one in twelve is following in his or her father's footsteps as a second-generation journalist. Another 40 percent describe their fathers as businessmen. That leaves only one in five whose father was employed in a low-status job. Given these upper-status positions, it is not surprising that their families were relatively well off. Nearly half rate their family's income as above average while they were growing up, compared to one in four who view their early economic status as below average.

A distinctive characteristic of the media elite is its secular outlook. Exactly half eschew any religious affiliation. Another 14 percent are Jewish, and almost one in four (23 percent) was raised in a Jewish household. Only one in five identify as Protestant, and one in eight as Catholic. Very few are regular churchgoers. Only 8 percent go to church or synagogue weekly, and 86 percent seldom or never attend religious services.

In sum, substantial numbers of the media elite grew up at a distance from the social and cultural traditions of small-town middle America. Instead, they came from big cities in the northeast and north-central states. Their parents were mostly well off, highly educated members of the upper middle class, especially the educated professions. In short, they are a highly cosmopolitan group, with differentially eastern, urban, ethnic, upper-status, and secular roots.

As in any such group, there are many exceptions to these general tendencies. On the whole, though, they are rather homogeneous. For example, we could find few systematic differences among media outlets or job functions. Even television and print journalists differ mainly in their salaries. The proportions of men and women, whites and blacks, Jews and Gentiles, religious observers and abstainers are all roughly equal at the networks and the major print media. Moreover, the family backgrounds of print and broadcast journalists are similar in terms of national and ethnic heritage, financial status, parents' educational levels, and political preferences.

A NEW ELITE

What do journalists' backgrounds have to do with their work? In general, the way we were brought up and the way we live shape our view of the world. And journalists' perspectives on society have obvious relevance to their work. Indeed, this [study] is devoted to exploring systematically this basic point.

Of particular concern is the impact of leading journalists' rising social and economic status. At the time of our survey, one in three had personal incomes above $50,000, and nearly half (46 percent) said their family incomes exceeded that amount. As salaries continue to rise, these data understate their current income levels. By 1982, the *National Journal* found that well-established reporters at the *Washington Post* and the Washington bureaus of the *New York Times, Newsweek,* and *Time* earned from $55,000 to $60,000.[4] Reporters and editors at the *Washington Post* are now required to file financial disclosure statements detailing holdings in stocks, bonds, and real estate. According to a financial department editor, "it used to be rare that staffers had such investments, but now that annual salaries average in the mid-forties and two-worker families have incomes of $100,000 or more, they are more common."[5]

Moreover, there is sometimes a considerable difference between salaries and overall incomes. Columnists, investigative reporters, and television correspondents are all in demand on the lecture circuit, where they command four- and even five-figure fees. In a 1986 article entitled "The Buckrakers," *The New Republic* reported that television anchors command up to $25,000 for a speech, well-known columnists charge from $12,000 to $19,000, and *Time*'s Washington bureau chief recently raised his fee from $3,000 to $5,000.[6] Thus columnist Jody Powell recently castigated his colleagues for potential conflict of interest over speakers' fees:

> Washington correspondents, anchors, bureau chiefs, columnists and editors are frequent travellers in the lecture circuit too. We speak to groups that have a definite interest in how we make the subjective judgments that are an inherent part of our job. And most of us get paid a good bit more than senators and congressmen who are limited by law to $2,000 for a speech.[7]

This is not to suggest that these journalists do not earn or deserve such incomes. By way of comparison, newly minted law school graduates may earn over $50,000 annually in major New York firms and over $40,000 per year in Washington firms. As this comparison suggests, the figures merely demonstrate that leading journalists are now solidly ensconced in the upper middle class.

Print personnel are still at the bottom of the media income ladder. It is television that can make millionaires of journalists. Anchors at all three major networks now make over $1 million annually, and six-figure salaries are common among reporters and correspondents.[8] Even public television can pay enough to attract some network stars willing to trade top dollar for increased creative freedom. For example, correspondent Judy Woodruff joined PBS's "MacNeil/Lehrer News Hour" for $150,000 a year, half her former salary at NBC.[9] As James Deakin comments, "Over the years, newspapers and magazines have written breathlessly about the incomes of entrepreneurs and entertainers: John D. Rockefeller, Andrew Mellon, the Hunts of Texas, Clark Gable, John Wayne, Elizabeth Taylor. Now it is the anchorpersons and superstars of television news."[10]

The journalist as millionaire celebrity, star of the lecture circuit, filer of financial disclosure forms—it is enough to make Hildy Johnson turn over in his grave. It also makes many current journalists uneasy. David Broder, a highly regarded columnist and *Washington Post* reporter, recently wrote, "The fact is that reporters are by no means any kind of cross-section. We are over-educated, we are overpaid in terms of the median, and we have a higher socioeconomic stratification than the people for whom we are writing. . . . There is clearly a danger of elitism creeping in."[11]

Note that Broder's concern goes beyond income level to encompass journalists' new social and educational status as well. Ironically, not so long ago media critics complained instead of the profession's low-status insularity. As journalist turned media critic Ben Bagdikian writes:

> Before World War II newspapering was one of those occupations that afforded working-class families . . . middle class status or better. College educations were seldom required and were often a disadvantage . . . [this] produced a majority of journalists whose only perceptions of the outside world after they left junior or high school were what they saw and heard in the newsrooms. . . . It also provided a simplistic view of society and . . . the strong strain of anti-intellectualism that characterized American newsrooms for generations.[12]

Now the worry is that urbanity and cosmopolitanism bring their own distortions, or at least limitations, of perspective. Thus, the *Post*'s White House correspondent, Lou Cannon, complains, "As reporters climb up the income scale, their social values change. . . . The gulf is growing between reporters and working-class Americans."[13] Columnist Henry Fairlie gives this line of thought more bite:

> The most certain avenue to celebrity and considerable wealth [in Washington] is not now in the institution of government. . . . It is through the intricate networks of the media . . . the people of the media are today the wheelers and dealers. Point to any others so skillful at using the machinery of Washington, and so protected from any public challenge or scrutiny. . . . The media have removed themselves from all contact in their daily lives with the ordinary middle-class life and tastes of the community.[14]

For a modest example of the perspective that worries some journalists, consider a recent magazine article by syndicated columnists Jack Germond and Jules Witcover. The subject is how reporters survive the rigors of the campaign trail. But the underlying theme is the upper-status cosmopolitan's scorn for parochial middle America. The authors' advice: "If you're in some enclave of civilized conduct such as New York . . . have a few belts in the Oak Room at the Plaza . . . if you're in some backwater town like Columbia, South Carolina, your choice is to eat early . . . and then find a decent bar. . . ." They offer survival tips on various "uncivilized" cities. Cleveland: "If you're going to be in a plane crash in Cleveland, it's preferable that it happen going in." Indianapolis: "Pray you don't have to go here. . . ." Birmingham: "Never go there, certainly not overnight. . . ."[15] Such patronizing attitudes can be viewed as following in the great "boobseoisie"-baiting tradition of H.L. Mencken. But it's difficult to imagine many of today's high-flying columnists choosing to live out their lives in Baltimore, like the Sage of Menlo Park, far from the civilized surroundings of the Plaza's Oak Room.

Another alleged result of wealth and celebrity is a sense of self-importance that redefines the role of journalists as newsmakers themselves. For example, the naming of a network anchor is now front-page news in the major dailies. When Roger Mudd was demoted at NBC, the *Wall Street Journal* informed its readers that his "abrupt removal" was one of "two big stories in the national news this week," along with a presidential press conference. The *Washington Post*'s ombudsman responded tartly, "With highest regard for Mr. Mudd . . . it is respectfully suggested that people paid to convey the news have no business becoming front-page news themselves." He noted, however, a colleague's rationale for the contrary position: "They come into your living room. They set out the complexities of life, like the clergy used to do."[16]

More serious is the question of how journalists' enhanced status has affected their relations with the newsmakers they cover. Some critics maintain that journalists' elite status has undermined their independence or compromised their proper role as public tribune. In Fairlie's words, "The very profession that should be the acid, relentless critic of the affluence and cynicism of Washington is now the most ostentatiously affluent and cynical profession in the city."[17]

Others argue the opposite, that the formerly low status of journalists led them too often to revel in vicarious participation in the hails of power. Bagdikian criticizes old-school journalists for their "habit of close association with formal power which came to be seen as a natural reward of their occupation."[18] By contrast, today's leading journalists may be better paid and better educated than the politicians and bureaucrats they deal with. They may also be even more in demand socially. A publicist for Gray and Company, the influential Washington public relations firm, says matter-of-factly, "When we're putting together a guest list, including a journalist is just as important as including a diplomat or a Cabinet member."[19]

It would not be surprising if many of his colleagues agree with Jack Nelson of the *Los Angeles Times*, "I don't see any reason why we shouldn't consider ourselves on equal footing with those we cover."[20] The extent to which the tables have turned is illustrated by an encounter between Senator (and presidential candidate) Alan Cranston and CBS's Dan Rather during the 1984 New Hampshire primary. The two were having lunch when a CBS aide approached Cranston to say, "Senator, Mr. Rather will only have time for one more question."[21]

If society treats newscasters as more important than senators, it is unrealistic to expect the newscasters to reject society's opinion for long. Nor should we be surprised if journalists make use of their rising status to wrest control of politicians and other newsmakers. In keeping with their newfound status, leading journalists are increasingly likely to see themselves as professionals who translate the news rather than craftsmen who merely transmit it.[22]

Thus, the much-debated adversary relationship between media and government may be partly a function of reporters' changing lifestyles as well as their outlooks. They no longer need defer to the newsmakers they cover. As the late columnist Joseph Kraft wrote in 1981, "those of us in the media enjoyed an enormous surge of status and power in recent years. That surge coincided with the decline of various other groups, to the point where we could perceive ourselves as the only institutional force left on a well-nigh devastated plain . . . increasingly the media are an unrepresentative group—a group that is better educated, more highly paid, more sure of itself and more hostile to the system than the average."[23]

Kraft's analysis concludes that increases in the social, economic, and educational status of journalists are linked to liberal or anti-establishment attitudes. This is an issue our survey addresses in depth. So let us turn from the demography to the outlook of the media elite.

THE VIEW FROM THE NEWSROOM

POLITICS AND PERSPECTIVES

How do the leading journalists describe their own political leanings? A majority see themselves as liberals. Fifty-four percent place themselves to the left of center, compared to only 17 percent who choose the right side of the spectrum. (The remainder pick "middle of the road.") When they rate their fellow workers, an even greater difference emerges. Fifty-six percent say the people they work with are mostly on the Left, and only 8 percent place their co-workers on the Right—a margin of seven to one.

These subjective ratings are consistent with their voting records in presidential elections from 1964 through 1976. Of those who say they voted for major party candidates, the proportion of leading journalists who supported the Democratic candidate never drops below 80 percent.[24] In 1972, when more than 60 percent of all voters chose Nixon, over 80 percent among the media elite voted for McGovern. This does not appear to reflect any unique aversion to Nixon. Despite the well-publicized tensions between the press and his administration, leading journalists in 1976 preferred Carter over Ford by the same margin. In fact, in the Democratic landslide of 1964, journalists picked Johnson over Goldwater by a sixteen-to-one margin, or 94 to 6 percent.

More significant, though, is the long-term trend. Over the entire sixteen-year period, less than 20 percent of the media elite supported any Republican presidential candidate. Across four elections, the Democratic margin among elite journalists was 30 to 50 percent greater than among the entire electorate.

Also consistent with their self-descriptions are the media elite's views on a wide range of social and political issues (see Table 2). In the economic realm, over two-thirds agree that the government should reduce substantially the income gap between the rich and the poor. They are more evenly divided over the issue of guaranteed employment, with a slight majority opposing the entitlement issue. Most are anything but socialists. For example, they overwhelmingly reject the proposition that major corporations should be publicly owned. Only one in eight would agree to public ownership of corporations, and two-thirds declare themselves strongly opposed. Moreover, they overwhelmingly support the idea that people with greater ability should earn higher wages than those with less ability. Most also believe that free enterprise gives workers a fair shake, and that some deregulation of business would serve the national interest.

There is no contradiction between such praise for private enterprise and sup-

TABLE 2

Media Elite Attitudes and Voting Records

	AGREE
Economics	
Big corporations should be publicly owned	13%
People with more ability should earn more	86
Private enterprise is fair to workers	70
Less regulation of business is good for U.S.	63
Government should reduce income gap	68
Government should guarantee jobs	48
Political Alienation	
Structure of society causes alienation	49
Institutions need overhaul	28
All political systems are repressive	28
Social-Cultural	
Environmental problems are overstated	19
Strong affirmative action for blacks	80
Government should not regulate sex	97
Woman has right to decide on abortion	90
Homosexuality is wrong	25
Homosexuals shouldn't teach in public schools	15
Adultery is wrong	47
Foreign Policy	
U.S. exploits Third World, causes poverty	56
U.S. use of resources immoral	57
Goal of foreign policy is to protect U.S. businesses	50
CIA should sometimes undermine hostile governments	45
*Presidential Elections**	
1964	
Goldwater	6%
Johnson	94
1968	
Nixon	13
Humphrey	87
1972	
Nixon	19
McGovern	81
1976	
Ford	19
Carter	81

*Electoral percentages based on those who reported voting for major party candidates. Third party vote never exceeded 2 percent.

port for government action to aid the poor and jobless. These attitudes mirror the traditional perspective of American liberals who (unlike many European social democrats) accept an essentially capitalistic economic framework, even as they endorse the welfare state.

In contrast to their acceptance of the economic order, many leading journalists voice discontent with the social system. Almost half agree that "the very structure of our society causes people to feel alienated," and five out of six believe our legal system mainly favors the wealthy. Nonetheless, most would reject calls for a "complete restructuring" of our "basic institutions," and few agree that "all political systems are repressive." But they are united in rejecting social conservatism and traditional norms. Indeed, it is today's divisive "social issues" that bring their liberalism to the fore. Leading journalists emerge from the survey as strong supporters of environmental protection, affirmative action, women's rights, homosexual rights, and sexual freedom in general.

Fewer than one in five agrees that "our environmental problems are not as serious as people have been led to believe." Only 1 percent strongly agree that environmental problems are exaggerated, while a majority of 54 percent strongly disagree. They are nearly as united in supporting affirmative action for minorities. Despite both the heated controversy over this issue and their own predominantly white racial composition, four out of five media leaders endorse the use of strong affirmative action measures to ensure black representation in the workplace.

In their attitudes toward sex and sex roles, members of the media elite are virtually unanimous in opposing both governmental and traditional constraints. A large majority opposes government regulation of sexual activities, upholds a pro-choice position on abortion, and rejects the notion that homosexuality is wrong. In fact, a slight majority would not characterize adultery as wrong.

They overwhelmingly oppose traditional gender-based restrictions. Ninety percent agree that a woman has the right to decide for herself whether to have an abortion; 79 percent agree strongly with this pro-choice position. Only 18 percent believe that working wives whose husbands have jobs should be laid off first, and even fewer, 10 percent, agree that men are emotionally better suited for politics than women.

Only 4 percent agree that government should regulate sexual practices, and 84 percent strongly oppose state control over sexual activities. Seventy-five percent disagree that homosexuality is wrong, and an even larger proportion, 85 percent, uphold the right of homosexuals to teach in public schools. Finally, 54 percent do not regard adultery as wrong, and only 15 percent strongly agree that extramarital affairs are immoral. Thus, members of the media elite emerge as strong supporters of sexual freedom, and as natural opponents of groups like the Moral Majority.

We also inquired about international affairs, focusing on America's relations with Third World countries. The majority agrees that American economic exploitation has contributed to Third World poverty and that America's heavy use of natural resources is "immoral." Precisely half agree that the main goal of our foreign policy has been to protect American business interests.

Two issues dealing more directly with American foreign policy also elicit a nearly even division of opinion. A majority would prohibit the CIA from undermining hostile governments to protect U.S. interests. Just under half would ban foreign arms sales altogether or restrict them to democratic countries. About the same proportion would supply arms to any "friendly" country, regardless of the regime. Only

4 percent would be willing to sell arms to all comers. Thus, in several controversial areas of international relations, the media elite is deeply divided.

In sum, the media elite's perspective is predominantly cosmopolitan and liberal. Their outlook reflects the social (rather than economic) emphasis of what political scientist Everett Ladd calls the "new liberalism"[25] of upper-status groups. Leading journalists criticize traditional social norms and establishment groups; they are very liberal on social issues such as abortion, homosexual rights, affirmative action, and environmental protection. Many endorse an expanded welfare state, but they also emerge as strong supporters of the free enterprise system. Most describe themselves as liberals and most support Democratic presidential candidates.

Not surprisingly, these attitudes place them to the left of business executives, a traditional conservative elite, on virtually every issue the survey addresses.[26] On issues ranging from homosexuality and abortion to income redistribution, the gap between the two groups nears 40 percentage points. For example, 60 percent of the executives agree that homosexuality is wrong, 76 percent call adultery morally wrong, and only 29 percent favor government action to close the income gap between rich and poor. Even journalists' substantial support for free enterprise pales somewhat before businessmen's overwhelming endorsement. For example, 90 percent regard private enterprise as fair to workers, and 86 percent favor less government regulation of business. These figures exceed journalists' support levels by 20 and 25 percent, respectively.

It may seem obvious that corporate executives would be more conservative than leading journalists. The differences are documented here in order to establish that the businessmen are indeed an appropriate comparison group for the journalists. . . .

JOURNALISTS ON THE MEDIA

Some years back, columnist Joseph Kraft criticized his colleagues for holding such liberal perspectives. He argued that the major media had adopted an elitist and adversarial perspective on American society that made them combatants rather than observers of the political wars. Kraft wrote:

> We no longer represent a wide diversity of views. We have ceased to be neutral in reporting events. . . . The media have been taken in tow by the adversary culture. . . . We are skeptical about established authority. . . . We are sympathetic to the claims of those with grievances—whether black or brown or Indian or senior citizens. We tend to favor helping them, even though the benefits—integrated neighborhoods, school busing, affirmative action—tend to be paid for by middle America. As for middle America's complaints—about gun control, anti-abortion rulings, abolishing the death penalty, yielding Panama—we tend to write them off as disconnected single issues. Not only are we not representative, we are aligned on one side in the hottest class contention now dividing America.[27]

Such criticisms are not new, but rarely have they issued from such a prominent member of the journalistic profession. Our survey also asked journalists to evaluate some of these and other commonly voiced criticisms about themselves: Can journalists be unbiased when they are emotionally involved with an issue on which they are reporting? Do they have a liberal bias? Are they too attentive to minority groups and too critical of the establishment? Alternatively, are they too easily co-opted by the establishment? Should the media play a central role in promoting social reform?

A surprising number of leading journalists are willing to admit to problems of bias, at least in principle. At the same time, they strongly reject more specific criticisms of their practices and product. They are almost evenly divided over their role in promoting social reform; a slight majority agrees that the media should play a major role. At the same time, a majority agrees that the media have a liberal bias, and almost one-third believe that journalists cannot be impartial when they feel strongly about issues on which they report.

These findings suggest division within the media elite over their role in American society. In acting as the public's tribune against the powerful, journalists may seek to combine personal satisfaction with social service. But involvement in social issues may mean a loss of impartiality. This tension between professional objectivity and personal involvement in the newsroom will prove a leitmotif of this study.

However, specific criticisms about news coverage seem to produce a closing of ranks. Over four out of five reject the allegation that the media are too attentive to minorities, and an even greater proportion deny that they are too critical of United States institutions. Only 1 percent agrees strongly with either of these criticisms, while the proportions disagreeing strongly are 48 and 60 percent, respectively. Nor do many give credence to the notion that journalists are easily co-opted by government officials. Once again, fewer than one in four agrees, and about half disagree strongly. Overall, then, concerns about the media's political role seem more likely to be expressed in general terms than on specific issues.

THE BIG PICTURE

Thus far we have examined elite journalists' opinions on the great and small issues of the day. By charting their responses to numerous social issues, we try to understand their general perspectives on society and politics. The results, though, may be deceptive. They create the impression of a broad ideological portrait of the media elite without ever asking journalists to deal with the "big picture." Their attitudes toward issues like abortion, affirmative action, and arms sales provide benchmarks for understanding their outlook, since most people have opinions on such pressing and hotly debated questions. But they do not address some of the most basic underlying issues of political life: What directions should American society take? What groups exert the most influence over social goals and political processes? How much influence should be wielded by such forces as business, labor, minorities, and the media?

These issues are as old as political philosophy. But it is not only philosophers who grapple with questions like "who should rule?" and "what is the good society?" Most people have answers to these questions, even if they haven't consciously arrived at them. Their answers express basic values that underlie their transient opinions on current social issues.

The interviews we conducted tried to tap these fundamental predispositions of political thought. First, journalists were asked about the goals America should pursue during the next decade. From a list of eight choices, they selected the most important, second most important, and least important goal. The list, created by political scientist Ronald Inglehart, includes:

1. Maintaining a high rate of economic growth
2. Making sure that this country has strong defense forces
3. Seeing that the people have more say in how things get decided at work and in their communities
4. Trying to make our cities and countryside more beautiful
5. Maintaining a stable economy
6. Progressing toward a less impersonal, more humane society
7. The fight against crime
8. Progressing toward a society where ideas are more important than money.

Inglehart classifies these choices as "instrumental" and "acquisitive" values, on one hand, vs. "expressive" and "post-bourgeois" values, on the other.[28] In this list, the post-bourgeois choices are those dealing with participation, a humane society, a beautiful environment, and placing ideas above money. Unlike standard polling items, these choices are not presented periodically to cross-sections of the American public. So the sample of business leaders functions here as a comparison group. As archetypal representatives of a bourgeois society, they should be oriented toward more conservative "acquisitive" values.

Substantial segments (though still a minority) of the media elite endorse the post-bourgeois value orientation that Inglehart calls a "silent revolution" transforming the political culture of advanced industrial society. One in three journalists (33 percent) deems citizen participation, a humane society, or a society less oriented toward money as our most important goal—more important than either economic well-being or national defense. By contrast, only one in eight (12 percent) business leaders picks any of the "expressive" values as America's most pressing concern.

Even among the journalists, a majority (52 percent) favors economic stability as the most important value. However, almost half the media elite (49 percent) pick post-bourgeois values as their second choice, compared to 30 percent of the business elite. Forty percent of these leading journalists select a humane society as either their first or second priority, more than double the proportion among business leaders. Conversely, the businessmen list national defense more than twice as often as the newsmen. Finally, the journalists are almost twice as likely as the executives (by 39 to 21 percent) to choose acquisitive values as the *least* important for America to pursue. Overall, the media elite show a substantially greater preference for post-bourgeois goals than the business elite.

For many leading journalists, liberal views on contemporary political issues apparently reflect a commitment to social change in pursuit of the good society, as they visualize it. Such a commitment would align them with emerging forces of social liberalism who are pitted against more established leadership groups. Therefore, the survey also examined the media elite's evaluation of its competitors for social influence.

Beyond inquiring about the direction our society should take, we asked a more pointed question: Who should direct it? Specifically, journalists were asked to rate seven leadership groups in terms of the influence each wields over American life. Then they were asked to rate the same groups according to the amount of influence they *should* have. They assigned each group a rating from "1," meaning very little influence, to "7," representing a great deal of influence.

The seven groups represent a cross-section of major competitors for social power in contemporary America. They include black leaders, feminists, consumer groups, intellectuals, labor unions, business leaders, and the news media. Media leaders see four of the groups as relatively disadvantaged in the competition for social power. They rate feminists as weakest, just behind black leaders, intellectuals, and consumer groups. All four are clustered tightly together in their ratings, well below the "big three" of labor, business, and the media. The unions rank third, leaving the media close on the heels of business leaders, whom they perceive as the most powerful social group.

When the journalists were asked about their preferences, this picture changed drastically. They would strip both business and labor of their current influence, while raising the status of all the other groups. In the media elite's preferred social hierarchy, business leaders fall from first to fifth position, and unions drop to the very bottom of the ladder. Feminists move up only slightly, but blacks, intellectuals, and consumer groups would all have more influence than either business or labor. Emerging at the top of the heap, as the group most favored to influence American society, is the media.

There is a certain irony in the media elite's choice of itself as preeminent in the race for influence. The press is traditionally ambivalent about its power, and journalists often either deny or decry the notion of a powerful media elite. In a 1976 study of elites conducted by the *Washington Post* and Harvard University, the media leaders were the only group to claim they want less influence than they already have.[29] In fact, one could say the same of the subjects in our survey, but it would be a deceptive interpretation. In absolute terms, leading journalists would assign themselves a lower influence rating than they now have. Yet they would assign even lower ratings to other groups, thereby leapfrogging themselves from second position to the top spot.

The business leaders, by the way, return the compliment. They perceive the media as far and away the most powerful influence on American society, with labor a distant second and business only third, followed by the four emergent groups. Not surprisingly, they would also prefer to sit atop the influence hierarchy, while burying the media well back in the pack in fifth position (precisely where the media elite would place business). Indeed, the antipathy these two elites seem to feel toward each other is noteworthy. Business leaders regard the media as the most influential group listed and would reduce the influence of journalists more than any other group. Media leaders perceive business leaders as the most influential group and would likewise strip away most of their influence. One might speculate that these elites view one another with such mistrust precisely because each attributes great influence to the other. In the ongoing struggle over social influence, each appears wary of the other as its strongest competitor.

The media elite is also homogeneous in its politics. We found only slight ideological differences across media outlets or job functions. To illustrate this, we compared self-described liberals and conservatives across various subgroups. The Left-Right split is quite similar among print and television journalists. Fifty-three percent of those in the print media call themselves liberal, compared to 19 percent of those who choose the conservative label; among broadcast journalists, liberals predominate by 56 to 14 percent. Within the press, moreover, reporters and editors hold nearly identical political self-images. The liberal-to-conservative margin is 52 to 16 percent among reporters, 51 to 20 percent among editors. The gap narrows somewhat at the top of the newsroom hierarchy. Among senior print editors and executives, the margin closes to 41 vs. 24 percent; among senior television producers and executives, however, it remains more than two to one (44 vs. 16 percent).

Thus, ideological diversity among leading journalists seems confined to a relatively narrow band of the political spectrum. By contrast, no more than 22 percent of the general public have ever placed themselves to the left of center in Gallup polls conducted over the past decade. Nor has this group ever equalled the proportion of those who place themselves on the political right. At the time our survey was conducted, conservatives outnumbered liberals by 31 to 17 percent nationwide.[30]

OLD ATTITUDES, NEW FREEDOMS

SURVEYING THE SURVEYS

There is considerable evidence from other sources to corroborate our portrait of liberal leading journalists. No other studies have focused on precisely those journalists we term the media elite. But a group that overlaps ours in membership and influence, the Washington press corps, has been surveyed repeatedly. In 1976, a *Washington Post*-Harvard University survey of accredited Washington reporters found that 59 percent called themselves liberal and 18 percent conservative.[31] This is strikingly close to the 54 to 17 margin we found among the media elite four years later. Moreover, these self-descriptions were reflected in Washington reporters' voting preference in the 1972 election. Of those who voted, 70 percent chose McGovern and only 25 percent picked Nixon.

The *Post*-Harvard study also found, as we did, that management is less liberal than working reporters but not nearly as conservative as the general public. Their companion survey of newspaper managing editors and TV and radio news directors around the country revealed a liberal-conservative split of 40 to 17 percent. Thus, there were fewer self-styled liberals, more moderates, but no more conservatives in management than among the Washington reporters. This group was also less Democratic in its voting preferences, but a slight majority still supported McGovern over Nixon (51 to 45 percent).

In 1978, the Washington press corps was again surveyed by Stephen Hess of the Brookings Institution. He found fewer reporters willing to call themselves liberal (42 percent) but virtually no rise in the proportion of conservatives (19 percent).[32] Thus, the liberal vs. conservative ratio remained greater than two to one, though less than the three to one margins found elsewhere. (The difference may be accounted for either by a slightly different wording of the questions or by the low response rate, under 25 percent.) Hess also found, as we did, that a slight majority of journalists themselves found a political bias in their ranks. Of those who considered the Washington news corps biased, 96 percent felt it was liberal. By contrast, only one percent complained of conservative bias.

Another well-known study, conducted in 1971, reported self-descriptions of journalists at "prominent" news organizations, including the networks, newsmagazines, and major newspapers. Among executives, 73 percent placed themselves on the Left and 10 percent on the Right. Among staffers, the comparable figures were 53 and 17 percent, respectively.[33]

A more recent study of the politics of journalists was conducted in 1982 by scholars at the State University of California at Los Angeles. This survey of journalists at America's fifty largest newspapers found 50 percent self-described liberals and 21 percent conservatives.[34] The voting breakdown of this group during the 1972 election was McGovern 77 percent, Nixon 21 percent. This study also reports results for the 1980 election. The newspeople interviewed gave a slight majority to Carter (51 percent), with the remainder split almost evenly between Reagan (25 percent) and Anderson (24 percent). At about the same time, a group of scholars at Indiana University interviewed a random sample of 1,001 journalists around the country. Among those in "prominent" news organizations, 32 percent claimed a Left orientation and 12 percent a Right orientation.[35]

The most recent, most thorough, and perhaps most remarkable survey of journalists was conducted in 1985 by the *Los Angeles Times*.[36] Almost 3,000 newspaper reporters and editors, randomly selected at over 600 papers around the country, were polled on over 100 questions, including some of the same ones we asked. Equally important, the same questions were asked of a national random sample of about 3,300 adults. This makes possible direct comparisons between press and public attitudes.

The results document a wide disparity between the attitudes of journalists and the general public, with the former consistently to the left of the latter. On the average, for all questions, the *Times* reports a gap of 25 percent between the attitudes of journalists and their audience. . . .

On several issues we asked about, this massive survey replicates our findings while also demonstrating a gulf between news producers and news readers. Thus, 82 percent of journalists are pro-choice on abortion, vs. 51 percent of the public; 81 percent support affirmative action for minorities, vs. 57 percent of the national sample; and 89 percent uphold homosexual rights in hiring, vs. 56 percent of the public. Only 26 percent of the journalists voted for Reagan in 1984, a figure that resembles our findings from previous elections, as well as the Cal State 1980 results.

Economic issues constitute a partial exception to the overall pattern. Here the poll finds that journalists are "slightly, but not markedly more liberal" than the public.[37] They are much more likely to favor government regulation of business, by 49 to 22 percent. But they are slightly less likely (by 50 to 55 percent) to favor government action to reduce the income gap between the rich and poor. The leading journalists we surveyed are more liberal on this issue, with 68 percent agreeing that government should close the gap. Still, journalists around the country seem to echo the media elite's strong support for private enterprise and low opinion of business and labor alike. The pollsters conclude, "It appears that on questions that affect their interest, as opposed to purely ideological matters, journalists behave like other high-status elites."[38]

To return to the ideological self-description we have used as a benchmark, 55 percent of these journalists call themselves liberal and 17 percent conservative, a difference of one percent from our own finding. On the other hand, 24 percent of the general public term themselves liberal, a figure 31 percent lower than among journalists. In fact, the pollsters report that newspaper journalists are also "markedly more liberal than others of similar educational and professional standing."[39] Thirty-seven percent of other college-educated professionals say that they are liberal, an 18 percent drop from the press percentage. And 57 percent of other professional people give Reagan a positive rating, compared to 30 percent of the journalists.

Finally, the pollsters took on the Herculean task of questioning every news and editorial staff member of the *New York Times, Washington Post,* and *Los Angeles Times.* Despite a low response rate at the *Post,* they completed about 500 interviews at these major newspapers. They found that, "The combined staffs of the two *Times*es and the *Post* would seem, if anything, slightly more liberal than journalists on other papers."[40]

These results from numerous independent surveys are uniformly consistent with our own. Although the number of self-described liberals varies somewhat, the conservative population among major media journalists ranges only from 10 to 21 percent across the various surveys. Thus the liberal to conservative ratio always exceeds two to one. Similarly, the proportion of Nixon voters in 1972 ranges from 19 to 25 percent (except among news managers), about 35–40 percentage points below the level of Nixon's support among the electorate that year.

The *Los Angeles Times* findings on journalists' issue stands are also in line with our findings, despite the more elite status of our subjects. Indeed, the final portrait etched by the *Times* pollsters bears strong resemblance to the media elite: "They are emphatically liberal on social issues and foreign affairs, distrustful of establishment institutions (government, business, labor) and protective of their own economic interests."[41]

THE NEW PROFESSIONALS

Liberal and Democratic sympathies among journalists are not new. What may have changed more over the years is the relevance of journalists' social attitudes to their news product. When Leo Rosten conducted the first systematic survey of the Washington press corps in 1936, he found reporters to be mostly Democrats but very much under the thumb of their superiors. At a time when most newspapers were controlled by Republican publishers, 64 percent of the reporters favored Roosevelt in the coming election, and 6 percent favored Socialist or Communist candidates. Rosten compared these results to a contemporary Gallup poll showing that only 50 percent of the public favored Roosevelt, while 2 percent chose left-wing third parties.[42] At the same time, over 60 percent of reporters agreed with the statement, "My orders are to be objective, but I know how my paper wants stories played." Even more telling, a majority admitted having their stories "played down, cut, or killed for policy reasons."[43]

By 1960, this situation had changed dramatically. In 1961, journalism professor William Rivers again surveyed the Washington press corps. He found that Democrats still outnumbered Republicans among newspaper and broadcast correspondents, by margins exceeding three to one.[44] However, only 7 percent recounted ideological tampering with their work. In fact, Rivers concludes, "of all the changes in the Washington press corps during the past twenty-five years, none is more significant than a new sense of freedom from the prejudices of the home office."[45] He cites one longtime correspondent who recalled the difference from the old days: "The publishers didn't just disagree with the New Deal. They hated it. And the reporters, who liked it, had to write as though they hated it, too."[46]

Seventeen years after Rivers' study, Hess concludes from his own survey that "writing to fit the editorial positions of publishers [has] simply disappeared as an issue of contention. . . . The near absence of disagreements over political slant is a by-product of higher professional standards as well as the passing of the press 'lords' . . . who view their publications as outlets for their own views."[47] Hess notes further that today's Washington reporters initiate most of their own stories, which usually receive little or no editing. Journalism has come a long way from the days when Henry Luce could defend *Time*'s partisan coverage of the 1952 election with the comment, "it was *Time*'s duty to explain why the country needs Ike. Any other form of journalism would have been unfair and uninvolved."[48]

Our study corroborates the notion of a new era for reporters. We asked subjects how much influence they generally have over the content of news stories with which they are involved. They marked a scale ranging from "very little" to "a great deal" of influence. By far the lowest or least influential scores were recorded by executives of both print and broadcast outlets. So it is not only the press watchers who argue that the influence of reporters has increased relative to that of their bosses. This perception is shared by the journalists themselves.

The new authority structures influence media content only insofar as they permit different values to shape the news product. There is little doubt, however, that this has happened. In 1974, Ben Bagdikian summarized this dramatic shift of journalistic standards:

> There has been a rapid change within news institutions in the last decade. The received conventions that decade after decade automatically conditioned each novice journalist to comply with traditional values are being rejected and reformed. Standards of "legitimacy" are being questioned. The primacy of direction from above is being challenged from below. A different kind of novice professional has entered the field.[49]

THE ONCE AND FUTURE MEDIA ELITE

How did journalists come to their liberal views? Are they liberal and cosmopolitan in outlook because their profession makes them so, or do the media attract people with ready-made liberal leanings? Many journalists argue that their professional milieu is a natural source of liberalism. As an Atlanta *Constitution* columnist recently wrote, "Experience impacts attitudes, and journalists have more of the kinds of experiences that would challenge cozy conservative assumptions than most folks do. . . . It is far easier to harrumph in a country-club bar about welfare than it is . . . in a tenement listening to a welfare mother who can't pay her winter heating bill."[50]

This so-called nature vs. nurture question could be answered with certainty only by going back in time to determine what today's top journalists thought and felt at the beginnings of their careers. Despite the impossibility of securing such information, there are other ways of gaining insight into this question. First, we sought to determine whether liberalism related to age among leading journalists. If their experience in the profession is a liberalizing factor, one would expect older journalists to be more liberal than younger ones, who lack experience.

Yet just the opposite occurs within the media elite. We divided journalists into the old guard (over fifty years old), the mid-career group (between thirty-five and fifty), and the post-Watergate generation (under thirty-five). Among the old guard, 43 percent place themselves left of center, not quite double the 23 percent who pick the right side of the spectrum, with the rest choosing the middle of the road. In the mid-career group, the proportion of liberals rises to 52 percent and that of conservatives drops to 16 percent, about a three to one ratio. Among the rising generation who joined the profession in the wake of Watergate, 70 percent are liberals and only 13 percent conservatives, a ratio exceeding five to one. So younger journalists, by their own descriptions, are substantially more liberal than older ones.

Another approach is to look not to today's journalists but tomorrow's. If students at an elite journalism school are already liberal, it would support the position that liberal journalists are born into their profession, not made by it. If, on the contrary, those about to enter the profession are more conservative than working jour-

nalists, it would support those who see the work itself as the primary agent of journalists' liberalism. Interviewing today's journalism school students also provides a
glimpse at the future of the profession. By comparing today's media elite with a
select group of young people poised to enter the field, one may gain some sense of
what to expect from tomorrow's leading journalists.

THE NEXT GENERATION

Among journalism schools, one graduate program stands out as particularly prestigious. The cream of the crop among aspiring journalists attend Columbia
University's Graduate School of Journalism. Columbia offers not only excellent academic credentials, but also valuable contacts with the major New York–based media
outlets.

We surveyed a random sample of the school's 1982 degree candidates, excluding foreign students. . . . Twenty-eight students were interviewed, representing one-
sixth of the entire class.[51] They answered the same questions asked of the media
elite, as well as a few new ones. The results provide a striking portrait of some of
tomorrow's potential leading journalists.

The student group is less dominated by white males than today's leading journalists. Nearly half are female, more than twice the proportion of women among the
media elite. One in five of the students comes from minority groups, four times the
percentage of those already at the top.

In most other respects, though, the students are even more homogeneous
than their elders. They are drawn even more heavily from the northeast. They are
also almost twice as likely to come from metropolitan areas. Fewer than one in five
were raised in small-town or rural America.

Seventy percent of the journalism students have college-educated fathers, up
from 40 percent of the media elite. A majority rate their family's income as above
average, and only one out of nine say they were raised in homes with below-average
incomes. Thus, while the media elite are products of a comfortable background, the
students hail from an even more select and privileged stratum of society. Like
today's leading journalists, most of the students are not religiously observant. Nearly
half claim no religious affiliation, and only one in twelve say they attend religious
services regularly.

On the eve of their entry into the profession, what do these young people
believe about politics and society? First, an overwhelming majority place themselves
to the left of center. Eighty-five percent describe themselves as political liberals,
while only 11 percent consider themselves conservatives. So the journalism students
see themselves as substantially more liberal than today's media elite, and over three
times as liberal as the general public. Moreover, their self-assessment translates into
political behavior. In 1980, only 4 percent voted for Ronald Reagan, compared to 59
percent who backed Jimmy Carter and 29 percent who cast their ballots for John
Anderson.

The students' presidential choices and self-descriptions are consistent with their views on a wide range of social and political issues. They are more critical than today's media elite toward business and private enterprise, more alienated from the political system, and about as liberal as their future colleagues on social and cultural issues. On economic issues the students are stronger supporters of an expanded welfare state and much more severe critics of the capitalist system. A large majority views the government as responsible for both guaranteeing jobs (63 percent) and reducing income disparities (82 percent). Only one in three students believes that private enterprise is fair to workers, compared to over two-thirds of their elders. While almost two of three elite journalists believe that less regulation of business would be good for the country, nearly the same percentage of Columbia journalism school students rejects this idea. Finally, the students are over three times more likely than the current journalists to advocate public ownership of corporations. Almost two in five subscribe to this notion.

The students' dissatisfaction with the economic order is accompanied by pronounced political alienation. While just under half the media elite view the structure of our society as causing alienation, over seven out of ten students endorse this criticism. Similarly, half the students believe that our social institutions need to be overhauled completely. Although the students far surpass the media elite in their unhappiness with the economic and political order, the two groups are united in their rejection of traditional morality and their support for social liberalism. They are almost equally strong supporters of environmental protection, affirmative action, women's rights, homosexual rights, and sexual freedom in general. The students are more unified than their elders, however, in criticizing American policies abroad. For example, three out of four believe the U.S. exploits Third World nations. . . .

In sum, these elite journalism school students are at least as critical of traditional social and cultural mores as today's leading journalists. They express greater hostility toward business, heightened political alienation, and a more critical view of America's role in world affairs. In light of these attitudes, it is not surprising that they choose post-bourgeois goals for our society in greater numbers than their elders. A majority of the students, compared to only one-third of the media elite, selected the post-bourgeois choices in the survey over instrumental ones. In particular, they are more likely to favor the goals of community participation and an idea-oriented society. Of those students who focus on acquisitive goals, most are concerned with economic growth. Finally, the students rank national defense below all other goals. None considers it most important, and over two out of five consider national defense the least important of all goals listed.

To gain a sense of how their views might affect their perceptions of the current political scene, we solicited the students' opinions of several prominent national and international newsmakers. They could indicate strong or mild approval or disapproval, or feelings of neutrality toward each. The results show that their perspectives on leading newsmakers accord with their broader social outlooks. The most positive ratings all go to prominent liberal figures. The most popular is consumer advocate Ralph Nader, followed by feminist Gloria Steinem, Senator Edward Kennedy, Atlanta Mayor Andrew Young, and economist John Kenneth Galbraith.

The students' strongest disapproval is reserved for conservative groups and individuals. Seventy-eight percent disapprove of Ronald Reagan, a negative rating exceeded only by their rating of the Moral Majority. By margins greater than three to one, the students also reject two Reagan allies, then United Nations Ambassador Jeane Kirkpatrick and British Prime Minister Margaret Thatcher. In fact, they rate Cuban Premier Fidel Castro almost as highly as Thatcher, and considerably more positively than Ronald Reagan. Two out of three strongly disapprove of Reagan, compared to only one in four who feel as negatively about Castro. Nicaragua's Sandinistas, a bete noire of the Reagan administration, are viewed more positively than any of the conservative figures listed. Forty-one percent approve of the Sandinistas and only 26 percent disapprove.

Finally, we wanted to know where tomorrow's news gatherers get their perspectives on the news. So the students were asked to rate the reliability of a dozen organs of fact and opinion, including liberal and conservative journals, as well as avowedly nonpartisan outlets. They rate the *New York Times* and the *Washington Post* as highly reliable, along with public television. But they also rate a journal of the intellectual Left, the *New York Review of Books*, as highly reliable. *Time, Newsweek,* and *U.S. News* all weigh in as moderately reliable. Yet they rate the *New Republic* and the *Nation*, longtime representatives of liberal and left opinion, respectively, as no less trustworthy than *Time*, a major newsweekly. They reserve their lowest ratings for two more conservative journals of opinion, *Commentary* and *National Review,* along with TV network news.

More liberal and cosmopolitan than today's leading journalists, more alienated from both our economic and political institutions, sympathetic to liberal newsmakers and hostile toward conservatives, Columbia "J-School" students may be on the cutting edge of a new wave in American journalism. However, we cannot be certain of how their political or professional values may evolve as they become integrated into their chosen profession. Theirs may be the "progressivism" and skepticism of youth, yet to be tempered by the experiences or responsibilities of age. Of course, this would mean that integration into the news business is a conservatizing experience. We began by considering the opposite hypothesis, which presents journalism as a liberalizing force. So this possibility would challenge the notion that today's media elite became more liberal over time.[52]

For the most part, though, one could not expect so liberal a group as these students to turn very far to the right. Thus, Senator Daniel P. Moynihan's prediction some years back may yet come to pass:

> The political consequence of the rising social status of journalism is that the press grows more and more influenced by attitudes genuinely hostile to American society and American government. This trend seems bound to continue into the future . . . the young people now leaving the Harvard *Crimson* and the Columbia *Spectator* for journalistic jobs in Washington will resort to the [Lincoln] Steffens [muckraking] style at ever escalating levels of moral implication.[53]

CONCLUSION: AN AMBIVALENT ELITE

Many leading journalists are uncomfortable with both their newly proclaimed elite status and any liberal "do-gooder" self-image. Thus *Washington Post* editor Richard Harwood defends his colleagues against Moynihan's charges of elitism with the hypothesis that they are part of the working class: "An alternative hypothesis . . . might be that newspapermen are Democrats and liberals because they see themselves as part of [the] working class. . . . They are not, after all, 'professionals' in any classical or reasonable sense of the word. They pursue a 'trade' or a 'craft' for which there are no entrance requirements. Most of them are members of . . . a 'working class' union. . . ."[54]

This argument against media elitism might not be appreciated in other contexts. One need only refer to the *New York Times*'s outrage over a state court decision refusing "professional" status to journalists. In opposing the judicial opinion that "a journalist is not, legally speaking, a professional," the *Times* printed a stinging editorial that concluded, "There is no byline on the court's opinion, suggesting that it didn't deem it worthy of more than boilerplate. The modesty is appropriate."[55]

In fact, the rapid rise to elite status has produced a deep ambivalence in many leading journalists. Few people in any profession are so embarrassed by newfound prominence that they give back their paychecks and renounce their influence. On the other hand, the loss of identification with the hoi polloi is a genuine problem for those who pride themselves on representing the little guy against the powerful, and standing up for individuality and idiosyncracy against the gray flannel suit crowd.

In his account of life on the press bus during the 1972 election campaign, Timothy Crouse quotes Dan Rather as giving voice to the old and cherished image of the journalist as outsider: "The average journalist, including myself, is a whiskey-breathed, nicotine-stained, stubble-bearded guy. . . ."[56] Crouse suggests that this represents a triumph of self-image over reality: "Rather was wearing a beautifully tailored blue suit and he gave off the healthy glow of a man who has just emerged from a hotel barber shop. I had never seen him smoke and I doubt whether, on a typical day, his strongest exhalation could budge the needle on a breath analyzer."

Torn between an emotional commitment to an older professional image and the obvious advantages of a newer one, today's leading journalists would not be the first to try to have it both ways. A similar kind of denial often operates when journalists have to choose between the self-images of Menckenesque cynic and committed social reformer. Our survey found that a majority of leading journalists do see social reform as a major role of the media. On some level, many probably identify with David Halberstam's recollection of his youthful motives in becoming a journalist: "I believed deeply that . . . journalism had a crucial role as the societal conscience of last resort."[57]

Yet this image conflicts with another powerful persona—the journalist as the cynical outsider, the man in the trenchcoat, Bogart in the first reel. As James Deakin recounts,

Most journalists do not like to talk about [their] public-service motive. They are hard-boiled, realistic, worldly. It does not fit their self-image. In some strange way, they think it makes them vulnerable. Reporters tend to regard their idealism as sex was formerly regarded. It is embarrassing. The subject comes up only rarely. When it does, someone usually introduces a distraction. Another drink is suggested.[58]

Despite disclaimers and inner conflicts, the basic sociological profile of journalists at national news outlets is clear. They are a largely homogeneous group that is cosmopolitan in background and liberal in outlook. And they are an elite in terms of economic status, public perception, and social influence. . . .

NOTES

1. The interviews were conducted for us during 1979 and 1980 by Response Analysis, a survey research firm in Princeton, N.J. The public broadcasting sample included public affairs staffers at PBS and three major producing stations (WNET, WETA, WGBH), along with independent producers whose work has appeared on PBS outlets. We originally reported the number of cases as 240. However, we later ascertained that two respondents who completed the interview had declined to answer virtually every question. Therefore, they were dropped from the analysis.

2. Seventy-six percent of those contacted completed the interview. This response rate was high enough to ensure that our findings provide reliable insights into the composition and perspective of this group.

Many journalists are uneasy about the term *elite*, although they might be more at ease with appellations like *successful* or *leading* journalists. We use this term in descriptive fashion to refer to the members of the most important media organizations in America. By this definition, a reporter at the *New York Times* qualifies, while the editors and publishers of the *Miami Herald* or the *Boston Globe* do not, although they undoubtedly could be included under another definition. We have already discussed the rationale for our approach, which flows from theoretical concerns about the changing role of the national media in American society.

3. The business sample included top- and middle-level executives from three *Fortune 500* industrial firms, and one firm each drawn from *Fortune* lists of the fifty leading American retail outlets, banks, and public utilities. In each case, we developed a randomly based sample of top- and middle-management personnel from official company lists. The response rate among this group was 95 percent. We can identify the media outlets sampled because personnel were interviewed as individuals. We approached the business firms as organizations, however, and a requirement for their cooperation in each case was a promise of anonymity. Our statements about the nature of our samples and response rates can be verified by Response Analysis, the independent survey research organization that conducted the interviews for us.

4. Dom Bonafede, "The Washington Press—Competing for Power with the Federal Government," *National Journal*, April 17, 1982.

5. *Washington Post*, April 4, 1984.

6. Jacob Weissberg, "The Buckrakers," *New Republic*, January 27, 1986, 16–18.

7. Jody Powell, *Washington Post*, May 31, 1983.

8. James Deakin, *Straight Stuff* (New York: William Morrow and Co., 1984), 340–41.

9. *Washington Post*, May 7, 1984.

10. Deakin, *Straight Stuff*, 340–41.

11. Cited in Deakin, *Straight Stuff,* 345.

12. Ben Bagdikian, "Professional Personnel and Organizational Structures in the Mass Media," in W.P. Davison and F.T.C. Yu, eds., *Mass Communications Research* (New York: Praeger, 1974), 135.

13. Cited in Deakin, *Straight Stuff,* 345.

14. Henry Fairlie, "How Journalists Get Rich," *Washingtonian,* August 1983, 81–86.

15. Jack Germond and Jules Witcover, "Never Eat the Rubber Chicken," *Washingtonian,* January 1983, 58, 62, 63.

16. *Washington Post,* August 3, 1983.

17. Fairlie, "How Journalists Get Rich," 86.

18. Bagdikian, "Professional Personnel," 81.

19. Charlotte Hays and Jonathan Rowe, "Reporters: The New Washington Elite," *Washington Monthly,* July-August 1985, 21.

20. Ibid., 22.

21. *Washington Post,* February 28, 1984.

22. This distinction was originally applied to network and wire service journalists in Michael Robinson and Margaret Sheehan, *Over the Wire and On TV* (New York: Russell Sage Foundation, 1983).

23. Joseph Kraft, "The Imperial Media," *Commentary,* May 1981, 39, 42.

24. No more than 2 percent ever voted for third-party candidates.

25. Everett Ladd, Jr., "The New Lines Are Drawn," *Public Opinion,* July/August 1978, 48–53.

26. Stanley Rothman and S. Robert Lichter, "Personality, Ideology and Worldview: A Study of Two Elites," *British Journal of Political Science* 15 (Fall 1984), 1–21.

27. Kraft, "The Imperial Media," 42.

28. Ronald Inglehart, *The Silent Revolution* (Princeton, N.J.: Princeton University Press, 1977).

29. Barry Sussman, "Media Leaders Want Less Influence," *Washington Post,* September 29, 1976.

30. The Gallup poll results are reproduced in *Public Opinion,* April-May 1985, 35.

31. *Washington Post,* September 29, 1976.

32. Stephen Hess, *The Washington Reporters* (Washington, D.C.: Brookings Institution, 1981).

33. J.W.C. Johnstone, E.J. Slawski, and W.W. Bowman, *The Newspeople* (Urbana, Ill.: University of Illinois Press, 1976).

34. Fred J. Evans, "The Conflict Surveyed," *Business Forum* 9 (Spring 1984), 18.

35. G. Cleveland Wilhoit, David Weaver, and Richard Gray, *The American Journalist* (Bloomington, Ind.: Indiana University Press, 1985).

36. *Los Angeles Times,* August 12, 1985.

37. William Schneider and I.A. Lewis, "Views on the News," *Public Opinion,* August/September 1985, 7.

38. Ibid., 8.

39. Ibid., 7.

40. *Los Angeles Times,* August 12, 1985.

41. Schneider and Lewis, "Views on the News," 8.

42. Leo Rosten, *The Washington Correspondents* (New York: Harcourt, Brace, 1937), 191.

43. Ibid., 352.

44. William Rivers, "The Correspondents after 25 Years," *Columbia Journalism Review* 1 (Spring 1962), 5.

45. Ibid.

46. Ibid.

47. Hess, *The Washington Reporters*, 5.

48. Quoted in Robinson and Sheehan, *Over the Wire and On TV*, 277.

49. Ben Bagdikian, "Professional Personnel," 134.

50. Tom Teepen, "Press' Liberalism Is Force-Fed," *Atlanta Constitution*, May 22, 1985.

51. The response rate was 60 percent. . . .

52. To help ascertain whether the students' liberalism was attributable to their youth, we compared them to a random sample of forty students at New York University's Graduate School of Business. This provides a comparison analogous to that of media and business elites, while eliminating the influence of generational effects. The two student groups are also roughly matched for background characteristics: both share differentially northeastern urban, upper-status, and Jewish backgrounds. Despite these similarities, the journalism students prove the more liberal. On most issues the differences are roughly as great between the two student groups as those we found between their adult counterparts. Thus, the attitudes of aspiring journalists and businessmen already diverge sharply. This supports the hypothesis that journalists tend to acquire their liberal outlooks more at home than on the job.

53. Daniel P. Moynihan, "The Presidency and the Press," *Commentary*, March 1971, 43.

54. Richard Harwood, *Washington Post*, April 12, 1971.

55. *New York Times*, June 8, 1984.

56. Timothy Crouse, *The Boys on the Bus* (New York: Ballantine Books, 1974), 244.

57. David Halberstam, "Starting Out to Be a Famous Reporter," *Esquire*, November 1981, 74.

58. Deakin, *Straight Stuff*, 328.

5. COVERING THE ABORTION DEBATE

David Shaw

The issue of abortion has polarized the American public, but how has the subject been covered by American journalists? David Shaw argues that, in the year after the *Webster vs. Reproductive Health Services* decision in 1989, media coverage was frequently unfair to opponents of abortion.

The following selection is an exposé of journalistic bias by an insider.* It is uncommon among the bias literature because Shaw possesses no ideological agenda. Rather, Shaw's objective is to warn many journalists that, however unintentionally they have become advocates of one side, not independent observers of the abortion debate.

In his discussion of abortion coverage, Shaw demonstrates the origins of bias and the methods for transmitting it into newswork. He links journalists' abortion views to their cul-

*From "Covering the Abortion Debate," *ASNE Bulletin*, December 1990, pp. 10–19. This material is excerpted from the first story in a four-part series on media coverage of abortion written by Shaw and originally published in the *Los Angeles Times*, December 11–14, 1990.

tural and social background. He points out that journalists take sides by adopting the language of one side of the debate, allowing one side to define the terms by which it will be called—that is, pro-choice rather than pro-abortion—while the other side is defined in terms not of its choosing—anti-abortion rather than pro-life.

Shaw is a staff writer for the *Los Angeles Times* assigned to media criticism. He is the author of *Media Watch* (1984).

When reporter Susan Okie wrote on page one of the *Washington Post* last year that advances in the treatment of premature babies could undermine support for the abortion-rights movement, she quickly heard from someone in the movement.

"Her message was clear," Okie recalled recently. "I felt that they were . . . [saying] 'You're hurting the cause' . . . that I was . . . being herded back into line."

Okie says she was "shocked" by the "disquieting" assumption implicit in the complaint—that reporters, especially women reporters, are expected to write only stories that support abortion rights.

But it's not surprising that some abortion-rights activists would see journalists as their natural allies. Most major newspapers support abortion rights on their editorial pages, and two major media studies have shown that 80 percent to 90 percent of U.S. journalists personally favor abortion rights.

Moreover, some reporters participated in a big abortion rights march in Washington last year, and the American Newspaper Guild, the union that represents news and editorial employees at many major newspapers, has officially endorsed "freedom of choice in abortion decisions."

On an issue as emotional as abortion, some combatants on each side expect reporters to allow their personal beliefs to take precedence over their professional obligation to be fair and impartial.

Although reporters (and editors) insist they don't let that happen, abortion opponents are equally insistent that media bias manifests itself, in print and on the air, almost daily.

A comprehensive [Los Angeles] *Times* study of major newspaper, television and newsmagazine coverage over the last 18 months, including more than 100 interviews with journalists and activists on both sides of the abortion debate, confirms that this bias often exists.

Responsible journalists do try to be fair, and many charges of bias in abortion coverage are not valid. But careful examination of stories published and broadcast reveals scores of examples, large and small, that can only be characterized as unfair to the opponents of abortion, either in content, tone, choice of language or prominence of play:

The news media consistently use language and images that frame the entire abortion debate in terms that implicitly favor abortion-rights advocates.

Abortion-rights advocates are often quoted more frequently and characterized more favorably than are abortion opponents.

Events and issues favorable to abortion opponents are sometimes ignored or given minimal attention by the media.

Many news organizations have given more prominent play to stories on rallies and electoral and legislative victories by abortion-rights advocates than to stories on rallies and electoral and legislative victories by abortion-rights opponents.

Columns of commentary favoring abortion rights outnumber those opposing abortion by a margin of more than 2 to 1 on the op-ed pages of most of the nation's major daily newspapers.

Newspaper editorial writers and columnists alike, long sensitive to violations of First Amendment rights and other civil liberties in cases involving minority and anti-war protests, have largely ignored these questions when Operation Rescue and other abortion opponents have raised them.

Throughout the media, print and broadcast alike, coverage of abortion tends to be presented—perhaps subconsciously—from the abortion-rights perspective. When the U.S. Supreme Court ruled in the *Webster* case in July 1989 that states could have more latitude in regulating abortion, for example, ABC News—among others—termed the decision "a major setback for abortion rights." Couldn't it also have been called "a major victory for abortion opponents"? Yes. But most reporters don't identify with abortion opponents.

It's not that there's a conscious bias on abortion. Rather, "the culture in the newsrooms just assumes that abortion is right," contends John Buckley, longtime media spokesman for various conservative politicians and now a corporate consultant.

Abortion, Buckley says, is the first issue since the Vietnam War in which some journalists' instinctive "allegiance to their own social class and generational worldview is stronger than their professional allegiance to objectivity."

Surveys consistently show that abortion is essentially a class issue in the United States; the more money and education a person has and the less religious a person is, the more likely the person is to favor abortion rights. Since most big-city journalists tend to be better paid, better educated and less religious than the general public, it's not surprising that they also tend to favor abortion rights by a large margin; in fact, a 1985 *Los Angeles Times* poll of journalists on newspapers of all sizes showed 82 percent in favor of abortion rights.

Despite a growing evenhandedness in recent months, the personal preference of so many in the media for the abortion-rights position clearly "affects coverage very fundamentally, "in the view of Ethan Bronner, legal-affairs reporter for the *Boston Globe*, who covers the U.S. Supreme Court and spent much of last year writing about abortion.

"I think that when abortion opponents complain about a bias in newsrooms against their cause, they're absolutely right," Bronner says.

But James Naughton, deputy managing editor of the *Philadelphia Inquirer*, says abortion opponents feel so passionately about the issue that they would criticize the media no matter what was published or broadcast.

"They're seeing a conspiracy that doesn't exist," Naughton says. "They complain . . . even when we've gone fairly deliberately out of our way to . . . be exquisitely fair . . . to avoid giving them any reason to accuse us of . . . being unfair."

Both Bronner and Naughton make valid points. Still, it's clear from examining coverage of abortion that the very language used to frame the abortion debate in much of the media implicitly favors the abortion-rights side of the argument. As in any debate, "the language is everything," says Douglas Gould, former vice president for communications at Planned Parenthood of America; in the abortion debate, the media's language consistently embraces the rights of the woman (the primary focus of abortion-rights advocates), not the fetus (the primary focus of abortion opponents): When the networks broadcast an abortion story, the backdrop has often been the large word "abortion"—with the first "O" in the word stylized into the biological symbol for female. The networks could just as easily stylize the "O" to represent a womb, with a drawing of a fetus inside. But they don't.

When *Time* magazine published a cover story on abortion last year, the cover was a drawing of a woman; when *Newsweek* published a cover story on abortion two months later, its cover featured a photo of a pregnant woman. Neither cover depicted a fetus. (Of course, newsmagazines choose their covers in part to maximize possible newsstand sales. Women buy magazines; fetuses don't.)

When the *Washington Post* wrote about proposed anti-abortion legislation in Louisiana last month, it spoke of the state House of Representatives making a decision on "a woman's reproductive rights." As Douglas Johnson, legislative director for the National Right to Life Committee, pointed out, "In discussing abortion as a matter of 'a woman's reproductive rights,' the *Post* adopts both the paradigm and the polemic of the abortion-rights lobby."

When the *Los Angeles Times* covered the same story, it referred to the proposed legislation as "the nation's harshest." That's the view of abortion-rights advocates; it's "harsh" toward women's rights. But abortion opponents would describe the legislation as "protective"—"protective" of the fetus.

Wouldn't the word "strict" be more value-neutral, since the legislation would be "strict" both in its protection of the fetus and in its restriction of the woman?

Although the terminology used in abortion coverage is the primary responsibility of the reporters who actually put the words together, editors have the final say about what appears in a newspaper, so their views may often be even more important.

Ethan Bronner says that when he wrote a story for the *Boston Globe* last year on late-term abortions, a copy editor questioned his description of a surgical procedure "destroying" the fetus by "crushing forming skulls and bones."

Bronner says the editor told him, "As far as I'm concerned, until that thing is born, it is really no different from a kidney; it is part of the woman's body." To talk about "destroying" it or about "forming bones," the editor said, "is really to distort the issue."

Bronner felt the language he used was essential to the points he was trying to make, so he appealed to a higher editor; his view largely prevailed in the resultant compromise.

Like Bronner, advocates on both sides of the abortion debate recognize the power of language to define the debate and help determine its outcome.

John Willke, president of the National Right to Life Committee, devotes a chapter in his book *Abortion: Questions & Answers* to the terminology he thinks his followers should use to best advance their cause.

But Willke and other abortion opponents have been much less successful than abortion-rights advocates at insinuating their chosen terminology into the daily media lexicon, especially since the U.S. Supreme Court's *Webster* decision.

With that decision, the long-dormant abortion-rights movement was energized anew. Membership and fund-raising skyrocketed. Political activism blossomed. Courtship of the media began in earnest.

Representatives of the major organizations supporting abortion rights—the National Organization for Women, the National Abortion Rights Action League, Planned Parenthood of America and the American Civil Liberties Union, among others—formed a media strategies group, determined to overcome their opponents' pre-*Webster* head start in shaping the public dialogue. Radio and television commercials, full-page newspaper and magazine advertisements and press releases by mail, telephone and fax soon began flooding the media.

The campaign found a generally receptive audience. As Loretta Ucelli, director of communications for the National Abortion Rights Action League (NARAL), puts it, "There was a dramatic shift in the coverage of this whole issue post-*Webster*."

The energizing of the abortion-rights movement had "a lot to do with it," Ucelli says. "We've been able to communicate our message and at least see it coming through in what we would deem to be the fair and appropriate form." Eleanor Smeal, president of the Fund for a Feminist Majority, is somewhat less sanguine. She thinks the media "overstate the strength" of the anti-abortion movement and often accept its arguments uncritically, and she is particularly distressed by "the failure of the media to put abortion in a broader, international perspective . . . to go beyond who won and lost and who hired what public-relations firm and who spent what money."

But criticisms of the media by abortion-rights activists have been relatively mild since *Webster*, especially when compared with criticisms by abortion opponents.

Is that because abortion opponents are more passionate and committed than abortion-rights advocates? Or is it because they're less reasonable? Or more hostile to the press?

Or has there just been much less for abortion-rights advocates to complain about?

"Semantics . . . are the weapons with which this civil war is being fought," Ellen Goodman wrote in her syndicated column recently, and nowhere have the semantic weapons of the abortion-rights advocates been more effective than in the seemingly simple but extremely volatile issue of the labels the news media apply to each side.

Abortion-rights advocates made a shrewd tactical decision last year to try to shift the terms of the debate "from the question of whose rights will prevail, the woman's or the fetus's, to who will decide, women or the government," in the words of Frances Kissling, executive director of Catholics for a Free Choice.

Kate Michelman, executive director of the National Abortion Rights Action League, concedes that the battle cry "women have a right to control their bodies" didn't gain the movement "a lot of sympathy."

"It was not enough of a moral response," she says. "It didn't have the same . . . impact that 'murder' and 'when life begins' had."

A new slogan, "Who decides?," emerged from focus groups when abortion-rights advocates discovered the essential contradictions that public opinion surveys have consistently shown: Most Americans think some restrictions should be placed on abortion. Most Americans think abortion is immoral. Many even consider it murder—48 percent, according to a 1989 *New York Times*/CBS News Poll. But most Americans also think the choice of whether to have an abortion should be made by the individual woman.

Thus, abortion-rights advocates would like to be known as "pro-choice." But because abortion opponents think the real issue in the abortion debate is the life of the fetus, they would like to be known as "pro-life."

Traditionally, the media have called individuals and organizations by their chosen designation, whether it was "Negroes" wanting to be called "blacks," homosexuals wanting to be called "gays," or Cassius Clay wanting to be called Muhammad Ali.

So why not use both "pro-life" and "pro-choice"? That would be a balanced use of clear, simple terms that everyone recognizes and understands.

For a long time, most in the media bought at least half the argument. They used "pro-choice."

But not "pro-life."

The Associated Press, the largest news agency in the Free World, still follows that policy. So do many other news organizations, large and small, print and broadcast.

"In January, we issued a policy directive on how we'd label groups in the paper," says Ed Petykiewicz, editor of the *Ann Arbor* (Mich.) *News*. "We use 'pro-choice advocates' and 'anti-abortion advocates.' The staff was instructed to avoid the use of 'pro-life.' "

Why?

"We decided the issue was one of choice, not when life began," Petykiewicz says. "That's an issue yet to be decided. Accepting 'pro-life' is accepting their side of the argument."

But isn't using "pro-choice" accepting the other side of the argument, letting abortion advocates decide what the issue is, what the agenda is?

Many in the media have come to think so.

"To use the preferred terminology of one side and not the other . . . seems manifestly . . . unfair," says Cynthia Gorney, who writes about abortion for the *Washington Post.*

"Pro-life" is widely perceived as an emotionally loaded term that stacks the deck by implicitly suggesting the other side is "anti-life"—or "pro-death." So most in the media have long used the terms "opponents of abortion" or "anti-abortion" instead.

But "pro-choice" is also an emotionally loaded term that stacks the deck, as was demonstrated anew in a poll conducted last December by the *Boston Globe* and Boston television station WBZ. In that poll, 53 percent of the people surveyed said they would favor a constitutional amendment that would "guarantee a woman's right to have an abortion."

When the word "choice" was inserted in an identical question ("Would you favor or oppose a constitutional amendment which would guarantee a woman's right to make a choice to have an abortion?"), the number saying they would favor such an amendment jumped to 63 percent.

"Choice," like "life," is a powerful, positive word, and the use of "pro-choice" is especially unfair, critics charge, when the other side is referred to as "anti-abortion."

Karen Tumulty, a *Los Angeles Times* reporter who covered abortion for most of 1989, filed a memo with her editors last fall making precisely that point.

"In making one side 'pro' and the other 'anti,' we inevitably cast one in a positive light and the other in a negative," Tumulty said.

On March 22, eight years after the *Times* decided that "pro-life" was an unacceptable term, managing editor George Cotliar issued a memo to the staff, declaring that " 'pro-choice' . . . will no longer be acceptable."

In the interest of bringing "greater precision and fairness to our coverage of an emotionally charged debate," Cotliar said, the *Times* would henceforth use such terms as "abortion-rights advocates" and "supporters of legal abortion"—as it already used "opponents of abortion" and "anti-abortion"—formulations that most reasonable people on both sides agree are fair.

This policy is similar to those previously enacted at the *New York Times, Washington Post, Boston Globe, Philadelphia Inquirer, Omaha World-Herald* and *Milwaukee Journal,* among others. The *Journal*'s policy change last summer came amid a revealing newsroom contretemps.

Like most newspapers, the *Journal* had long used "pro-choice," without any complaint from the staff that is was unfair. But when Sig Gissler, editor of the *Journal,* wrote in a column that the paper would also begin using "pro-life," more than 80 reporters and editors petitioned him in protest before the column was even published.

Gissler spoke with several reporters and received memos from others. He considered their objections and revised his column—and the paper's policy. Both "pro-life" and "pro-choice" were now out. Mostly. Henceforth, the paper would "mainly use descriptive phrases such as 'anti-abortion groups' and 'abortion-rights advocates,' " he wrote.

Discussion about what labels the media use for the two sides in the abortion debate has become so heated in some quarters that at least three mainstream news organizations—the *Los Angeles Times, Washington Post* and Cable News Network—have done stories on it. But these labels are only one example of the implicit bias in the media's abortion terminology.

Abortion opponents are often described as "conservatives"; abortion-rights supporters are rarely labeled as "liberals."

Abortion opponents are sometimes identified as Catholics (or fundamentalist Christians), even when their religion is not demonstrably relevant to a given story; abortion-rights advocates are rarely identified by religion.

Abortion opponents are often described as "militant" or "strident"; such characterizations are seldom used to describe abortion-rights advocates, many of whom can also be militant or strident—or both.

In a story on the 16th anniversary of the U.S. Supreme Court's *Roe vs. Wade* decision, which legalized abortion, the *Courier-Journal* in Louisville, Ky., described an anti-abortion rally at which clergymen "ranted" against the decision; in the same story, abortion-rights advocates were said to have "hailed" the importance of the decision.

Moreover: The Associated Press, *Washington Post, Boston Globe* and *Time* magazine, among others, have referred to those who oppose abortion "even in cases of rape and incest" (circumstances under which most people approve of abortion). But the media almost never refer to those who favor abortion rights "even in the final weeks of pregnancy" (circumstances under which most people oppose abortion).

United Press International reported last year on a poll that showed a minority of all Americans take absolutist positions on abortion. The story said "only" 18 percent believed abortion should always be illegal. But there was no "only" before 27 percent who said abortion should always be legal.

Newsweek said last summer that under new abortion regulations, "Many women will be forced to seek out-of-state abortions—incurring travel expense and losing time and income in the process." But abortion opponents argue that no one is "forced" to have an abortion and that *Newsweek*'s statement is tantamount to saying that if guns were outlawed, "Many murderers would be 'forced' to use knives."

Some news organizations routinely say that polls show that "most" Americans favor abortions. But what the polls really show is that Americans are enormously ambivalent about abortion, their answers depending on precisely how the question is phrased. Indeed, as Charlotte Taft, director of a women's health clinic in Dallas, said last year, "Americans favor abortion only in the case of rape, incest and their own personal circumstance."

Abortion opponents say the media's mischaracterization of everything from scientific developments to Supreme Court decisions further undermines their cause.

Mary Ann Glendon, a Harvard law professor and abortion opponent who has written a book on abortion, says, for example, that the media's repeated mischaracterizations of the U.S. Supreme Court's 1973 *Roe vs. Wade* decision have helped undermine efforts to have the effects of *Roe* reversed.

When the Supreme Court issued *Roe*, initial news accounts emphasized the part of the ruling that said a woman would be allowed to have an abortion without restriction during the first three months of pregnancy, when more than 90 percent of the country's 1.6 million annual abortions are done, according to the Alan Guttmacher Institute, a special affiliate of Planned Parenthood that does research on abortion and family planning.

Even now, 17 years later, some in the media write about *Roe* in terms that suggest it legalized abortion only during the first trimester; the *New York Times, Los Angeles Times, Milwaukee Journal* and *Louisville Courier-Journal,* among others, have all mischaracterized *Roe* that way within the last year (although they have also characterized the decision correctly at times).

But the Supreme Court actually said a woman could have an abortion even in the last three months of pregnancy if that were necessary for "the preservation of . . . [her] life or health." Although only one one-hundredth of 1 percent of all abortions (about 100 a year) are done after 24 weeks of pregnancy, one-half of 1 percent (about 8,000) are done after 21 weeks and almost 9 percent (142,000, or almost 400 a day) are done after 12 weeks, according to the Guttmacher Institute.

Although that's still a very small percentage of the total number of abortions done, abortion opponents think support for legal abortion would be diminished if people knew *Roe* made that many abortions possible. And they don't think it's pure coincidence that such mischaracterizations in the media almost invariably seem to favor advocates of abortion rights.

Even some abortion-rights advocates (and some journalists) agree.

"My sense is that the pro-choice side is generally covered in a favorable way," says Frances Kissling of Catholics for a Free Choice.

Lisa Myers, who covers abortion for NBC, says some complaints of media bias by anti-abortion groups are "excessive," but "I do believe that some of the stories I have read or seen have almost seemed like cheerleading for the pro-choice side."

News media executives resent these charges.

"We're keenly conscious of how touchy this issue is," says Tom Bettag, executive producer of "The CBS Evening News." "I think we make a real effort to be even-handed. . . ."

Many journalists say they've taken special care to be impartial in their abortion reporting precisely because they realize that abortion opponents think the media is biased against them.

"I had my guard up all the time. I realized how easy it was to write a story in a way that would be perceived as partisan," says Eileen McNamara, who spent most of 1989 writing about abortion for the *Boston Globe.*

Reasonable critics of the media generally concede that most journalists try to be evenhanded. Most reporters—and most editors and television anchors and news directors—are conscientious professionals who struggle diligently (and usually successfully) to prevent their personal views from unfairly influencing their coverage.

Some may "bend over so far backwards to avoid letting their personal views color what they write" that they risk being unfair to the side they personally favor, says Soma Golden, national editor of the *New York Times*.

A few editors have created abortion "beats" at their newspapers, assigning one reporter to write about the subject full-time, specifically so that they can get to know the issues and individuals involved and provide coverage that is broad, informed and fair.

Nancy Myers, director of communications for the National Right to Life Committee, says she doesn't expect reporters to be totally objective about abortion because "anyone who spends any amount of time on abortion and professes to be undecided or impartial is either stupid or intellectually dishonest."

What Myers does want—and what she and others in her movement say they too seldom see—are reporters who are fair, who "recognize the validity of both sides of the debate and . . . convey the many facts and arguments to readers."

Editors insist that is exactly what their reporters do. "We've made an awfully big effort to be balanced, and I just don't see a pro-choice bias," says Jack Fuller, editor of the *Chicago Tribune*.

Fuller says he's not "blinded by a pro-choice bias" himself, since he personally favors some restriction on abortion. But he says he doubts that abortion opponents would be satisfied with fairness.

They don't want fairness, Fuller says. "They want support."

Abortion opponents deny this. But they are clearly worried that what they see as media "support" for the other side could ultimately have an enormous impact on both individual belief and the political process.

Indeed, a persuasive case can be made that abortion opponents received more favorable coverage than did abortion advocates, at least on television, from 1973, when the Supreme Court legalized abortion in *Roe vs. Wade*, until early 1989, shortly before the Court was scheduled to hear the *Webster* case, which the government was using in an attempt to overturn *Roe vs. Wade*.

Because abortion was legal and under no imminent threat during those years, the abortion-rights movement was essentially dormant. But opponents of abortion aggressively sought political and legal redress of their grievances, and the media covered their efforts, especially in election campaigns.

Network news in particular "paid it more attention and, in so doing, took a decided tilt to their side," *TV Guide* concluded after an examination of evening news programs from January 1983 to 1985.

"Everything [during that period] was biased on our side," one outspoken opponent of abortion conceded at the time.

That was before the *Webster* decision.

Times have clearly changed since then.

6. THE COMING BATTLE FOR THE MEDIA

William Rusher

Studies like those by Lichter, Rothman, and Lichter have supplied some critics of the media with support for the conclusion that since journalists share a political liberal perspective, the news product is dominated by a liberal bias.

The charge of a liberal slant in the news has been made by several media critics. Edith Efron was one of the first to detect bias in a quantitative study of press coverage of the 1968 presidential campaign.* Efron's methods were criticized and the general premise of a liberal news tilt has been challenged.†

Media watchdog groups such as AIM (Accuracy in Media) and the Media Research Center have formed to scrutinize media content—news and entertainment—to identify liberal bias. During the mid 1980s, a group of conservatives led by Senator Jesse Helms of North Carolina moved from argument to action by attempting a takeover of CBS through purchases of CBS stock.

One of those who claim there is a liberal bias in the news media is William Rusher. Drawing on the data of Efron and others, Rusher portrays a news product heavily influenced by journalists' biases.‡ William Rusher is former publisher of *National Review*. He is the author of *The Rise of the Right* (1984) and *The Coming Battle for the Media* (1988), from which this excerpt is taken.

Proving statistically that the media's demonstrated liberalism influences their handling of the news is no simple matter. The media clearly aren't going to do us the favor of admitting it, and the formidable human capacity for self-delusion makes it likely that many members of the media don't even realize it, at least not fully. A good many of them undoubtedly think their selection and treatment of stories is governed solely by their acute "news sense," where any objective observer would detect bias. And even when a member of the media knows full well that his handling of news stories is influenced by his biases, he is naturally prone to minimize that influence and make excuses for the residue.

Adding to the difficulty is the fact that evidence of bias, liberal or otherwise, is almost inevitably somewhat subjective. One man's "bias" is another man's "robust journalism," etc. Obvious as the bias may be to many thoughtful people, how can one nail it down?

****

In the *Wall Street Journal* for March 6, 1984, Holmes M. Brown, president of the Institute for Applied Economics, reported the results of a survey conducted by the IAE during the last six months of 1983. Once again the targets of the study were "the nightly news programs of the three major television networks."

---

*Edith Efron, *The News Twisters* (Los Angeles: Nash, 1971).

†R.L. Stevenson et al, "Untwisting the News Twisters," *Journalism Quarterly* (Summer 1973), 211–19. See also C. Richard Hofstetter, *Bias in the News* (Columbus: Ohio State University Press, 1976); and Michael J. Robinson and Margaret Sheehan, *Over the Wire and On TV* (New York: Russell Sage Foundation, 1983).

‡From *The Coming Battle for the Media* (New York: William Morrow, 1988), pp. 67, 74–84.

The particular significance of the last half of 1983 lay in the fact that the economic news was good during those six months: The country was unmistakably emerging from the recession that had darkened 1982 and the early months of 1983, and Ronald Reagan was, quite naturally, the political beneficiary of the change. Yet here is how Brown summed up the findings of the survey:

> During the entire period of the study, there were four to 15 economic statistics stories a month. Nearly 95% of these statistical reports were positive—however, of the 104 economic stories of an in-depth or interpretive nature that were aired during this period on the three network evening news shows, 89—or 86%—were primarily negative.
>
> The economic news was good in the second half of 1983. The coverage on network television was still in recession.

The technique, as Brown explained it, was simple:

> The transposition was done by concentrating on the pockets of recession within the overall recovery, thereby implying that behind the good news of falling inflation and rising employment there were black clouds of economic misery.

And he proceeded to cite examples of such distortion, drawn from all three networks:

> In November, unemployment dropped sharply to 8.4% from 8.7% a month earlier, the lowest level in two years. In just two months, the total of unemployed Americans dropped well over a million.
>
> ABC used the Dec. 2 unemployment announcement to focus on those left behind by the recovery. Although the November unemployment figures in 45 of the 50 states were down, ABC did a story that began, "Now those unemployment figures again; it's here in the Midwest that unemployment is most severe." They located two upper-middle-class men who had been unemployed for 1½ years and focused on their experiences with a story that lasted more than four minutes. A story that began with a 0.3 percentage-point drop in unemployment ended in complete despair and talk of suicide.
>
> Another major positive statistic during the time of the study was the increase in the gross national product. In the third quarter, it grew at a robust 7.7% inflation-adjusted annual pace, surprising even the most optimistic economists.
>
> NBC reporter Irving R. Levine, on Oct. 22, when the GNP boost was announced, delivered one of the most negative stories of the survey. The report focused on "pockets of poverty where recovery is still just a dream," undercutting President Reagan's economic policies and their relationship to the recovery. Mr. Reagan was shown saying "virtually every sector of the economy . . . is expanding, creating new hope in a more secure future." Mr. Levine focused on the limited areas where things were getting worse, stating that "beyond small programs to retrain workers, the administration is closing its eyes to regions bogged down in recession and sees no need to alter its economic policy. . . ."
>
> Inflation continued to abate during the year. The producer price index grew by only 0.6% in 1983, the smallest increase in 20 years.
>
> In July, the inflation rate for the first half of 1983 was announced at only 2.9%, a sharp decline from 3.9% a year before. CBS followed this news with a story featuring economist Pierre Rinfret, who said: "We kept the country in recession for three years, we've created unemployment as high as 13 million people, we idled most of the factories in this country, and put most of industry flat on its back. If you can't beat inflation with that, you can't do anything."

Such examples, however, though impressive, are not as important as the statistical totals. To repeat: Nearly 95 percent of the reported changes in United States economic statistics during those six months were positive (i.e., favorable); yet out of the 104 stories about them aired on the three networks' evening news programs, 86 percent were primarily negative.

. . . What is the explanation? Here we have people who have supported every Democratic presidential candidate since 1964 by margins of 80 percent or better, and who identify *themselves* as politically liberal by massive margins in poll after poll. Is it any wonder that they denied or minimized the economic upsurge in the latter half of 1983 to the best of their formidable ability? Bear in mind the very large component of wishful thinking that it is almost impossible to separate from economic analyses. These liberal journalists were not consciously deceiving their audiences. If they could have brought themselves to admit any bias whatever, they would undoubtedly have said they were simply warding off unjustified public optimism based on a few deceptive statistics, in the sure knowledge that "Reaganomics" would soon revert to form.

A somewhat narrower but still highly significant study was conducted by the Media Institute, of Washington, D.C., during March, April, and May 1985. The institute decided to focus on coverage, by the nightly newscasts of the three television networks, of two key areas in the great budget debate of that year: the Social Security cost-of-living allowance (or COLA), and defense spending. How were these issues treated?

Patrick Maines, president of the Media Institute, described the methodology of the survey as follows:

> Using a research technique known as content analysis, researchers analyzed all stories mentioning proposed COLA and defense cuts. The database comprised 56 stories.
>
> Researchers analyzed the coverage to determine its comprehensiveness and balance. A story was considered adequately comprehensive if it reported the provisions of the proposal at hand, mentioned at least one effect the proposal might have, and explained any specialized terms. Balance was determined by measuring the amount of coverage given opposing viewpoints.

Note that the Media Institute concerned itself with *comprehensiveness* as well as with the subject of our chief concern, *balance*. As it turned out, the networks received poor marks in both categories. To quote the Media Institute's report:

> Several key findings emerged regarding network coverage of Social Security COLAs and defense spending: Over half of all network stories were not adequately comprehensive: 56.4 percent of Social Security and 65.2 percent of defense stories failed to meet even minimal criteria.
>
> Network coverage was overwhelmingly opposed to freezing the Social Security COLA: 66.9 percent of issues coverage opposed a COLA freeze, 23.9 percent favored a freeze, and 9.2 percent was neutral. Network coverage was overwhelmingly opposed to increases in defense spending: 65.5 percent of the issues coverage opposed increased spending, 31.1 percent favored increases, and 3.4 percent was neutral.
>
> In summary, the networks offered comprehensive coverage of the COLA and defense-spending debates less than half of the time. In addition, coverage was clearly

imbalanced: It opposed freezing COLAs and it opposed increased defense spending, in both cases by margins of two to one.

The results of another statistical analysis of media bias on a specific issue were announced in the spring of 1986 by the (nonprofit) Center for Media and Public Affairs, in Washington. The authors were Robert Lichter and Robert Rycroft of George Washington University, Stanley Rothman of Smith College, and Linda Lichter of the Center. . . .

The authors reported that there is "a gap between what the experts think about nuclear power and what the media report." They first selected at random, from *Who's Who*, the names of 679 energy scientists and engineers, and polled these individuals on their attitudes toward nuclear safety issues. Then they analyzed news coverage of those same issues, for the entire period from 1970 to 1983, on the three commercial TV networks, in the three major newsmagazines, and in the *New York Times*.

On the basis of media reports, it comes as a surprise to learn that five-sixths of these energy experts rated the safety risks that presently exist in United States nuclear power reactors as "acceptable." Moreover, three out of four favored "rapid nuclear development" and would themselves be perfectly willing to live near a nuclear reactor. Finally, two out of three were "very confident" that they already knew how to solve nuclear safety problems.

Far different is the story we have been getting from our media. According to the aforementioned study, antinuclear stories have outnumbered pronuclear stories two to one in both television and newsmagazines. And a full 60 percent of all media judgments on specific nuclear safety issues have been negative.

The media achieved this impressive slant by picking very carefully the authorities they chose to cite. "Experts" critical of nuclear power outnumbered its supporters by more than two to one in newsmagazines and by a positively awesome five to one on the television networks.

The ancient journalistic precept that "good news is no news" may conceivably have something to do with these figures. The media would obviously adore a total meltdown, purely for its theatrical value, but alas there has never been one. (Even the ham-handed Russians, in botching Chernobyl, apparently avoided that.) But the media must be aware that, after forty years, there has yet to be in this country so much as a single radiation-related death at a commercial nuclear power plant. It is little short of appalling to reflect that American public policy on nuclear power issues must be shaped on the basis of "news" reportage so starved for sensationalism that this simple truth is not merely skewed but hustled completely out of sight in favor of alarmist reportage.

As a matter of fact, the study described above found that, of all the media investigated, only *U.S. News & World Report*'s coverage was, even by a narrow margin, pro-nuclear. As for ABC, NBC, CBS, *Time*, and *Newsweek*, their news coverage "was tilted in the anti-nuclear direction by wide margins."

Curiously enough, the environmental lobby spent the 1960s bashing utilities that burned the so-called fossil fuels (i.e., coal and oil) for polluting the atmosphere, and touting nuclear power in their legal briefs as an alternative that was both clean and safe. Then in the 1970s the "activists" suavely reversed themselves and went after nuclear power. Our liberal media, always ready for a lynching bee at the expense of American business, needed no encouragement to fall in line, and the war on nuclear power has been under way ever since. The chief casualty, as the above study demonstrates, has been the truth.

Finally, technology is beginning to make possible certain statistical analyses of media bias that would have been simply impracticable a few years ago. For example, Senator Jesse Helms is widely and rightly known as an outspoken conservative—as dependably and loudly conservative as Senator Ted Kennedy is dependably and loudly liberal. In 1984, Helms's ACU (American Conservative Union) rating (a conservative rating of votes on key issues) was 100; Kennedy's was 0. Helms's COPE (Committee on Political Education) rating (reflecting Big Labor's estimate of his performance) was 8; Kennedy's was 94. To make sure that its readers were warned of Senator Helms's rightward tilt and would be able to discount for it, the *New York Times*, during the years 1984 and 1985, preceded his name *in 21 percent of all news stories* (i.e., excluding opinion pieces and editorials) with some such cautionary phrase as "right-wing," "far-right," "archconservative," or "ultraconservative." On the other hand, however, the *Times* affixed a comparable qualifying phrase to Senator Kennedy's name (signaling his rigorously liberal slant) in only 2.3 percent of similar cases.

These striking figures are available thanks to the wonders of computer science. That ingenious conservative monitor of the liberal media, *Newswatch*, hit on the idea of asking Nexis, a computerized print-media data retrieval system, to come up with every story in the *Times* during 1984 and 1985 that mentioned either Senator Helms or Senator Kennedy. Setting aside opinion pieces and editorials, *Newswatch* then simply counted every labeling phrase that the *Times* gratuitously applied to either man.

And the *Times*, *Newswatch* discovered, was not by any means the only or even the worst offender in this matter. The *Washington Post* found it necessary to tag Senator Helms 22 percent of the time, but Senator Kennedy only 4.1 percent. In the case of newsmagazines, the makeup was applied with an even heavier hand: Helms was labeled 44 percent of the time in *Newsweek* and 47 percent in *Time;* Kennedy received comparable treatment only 5.6 percent and 3.5 percent of the time, respectively. Would anyone seriously contend that there is anything fair, or objective, or balanced about that performance?

Having pretty well given up on the issue of the personal liberalism of the media elite, the media's defenders have been understandably reluctant to abandon as well their fallback contention that this does not affect their treatment of the news. But as the studies we have just discussed rolled off the presses, they have consoled themselves with certain evidence suggesting that the media are, nevertheless, well regarded or even trusted by many or most Americans. This is technically irrelevant to the question of whether bias actually exists; but, assuming it does, it is understandably comforting to the media to reflect that a large segment of the public is unaware of this, or (better yet) thinks well of the media in spite of it.

. . . *Los Angeles Times* staff writer David Shaw made the point in the very first sentence of his report on the Times Mirror survey:

> American newspaper reporters and editors are substantially more liberal than the general public on a wide range of social and political issues, but readers seem largely convinced that the press does not permit this liberalism to unfairly influence its news coverage, a nationwide *Los Angeles Times* poll conducted over the last five months shows.

Gallup's own summary of the survey put it this way: "If credibility is defined as believability, then credibility is, in fact, one of the media's strongest suits."

Under a three-column headline, PEOPLE DO UNDERSTAND THE MEDIA (sub-head: AND THEY DON'T HATE THE PRESS AS MUCH AS WAS FEARED), James R. Dickenson, a political reporter for the *Washington Post*, discussed the glad tidings in a column, or think piece, in that newspaper on February 9, 1986:

> We in the press have been sensitized for years now to the fact that many conservatives believe that there is a liberal bias in the media. We understand that while few really think that many of us actually are subversives, they do harbor deep suspicions that—at the least—we have more than our share of irresponsible opportunists who are a burden to democracy and weaken the national security. . . .
>
> Whatever the reason, we tend to worry about the First Amendment and maybe feel just a little bit sorry for ourselves. A new and provocative study of public attitudes toward the media by the Times Mirror Co. suggests, however, that our biggest mistake may be our misunderstanding of what the American people think of us. . . .
>
> For all the criticism and lack of talk about us, people like us to a remarkable degree.
>
> About 70 percent are generally favorably disposed toward the media. Only about 15 percent find little or nothing good about us. Ten percent of these feel alienated from every major institution and the other five are our informed, vociferous, predominantly conservative and Republican critics who question our morality, patriotism, competence, honesty and independence.
>
> But most people like us because, for all the criticism, they think we're competent and believable—and they like the news. They like being informed.

In point of fact, the actual figures in the Times Mirror study are highly ambiguous on the subject of the public's opinion of the media. While most of the major media were given high ratings for "believability" (85 to 87 percent), and individual TV anchormen did even better (with ABC's Peter Jennings leading the pack with a rating of 90), only 55 percent of those surveyed were willing to agree that the press "generally [gets] its facts straight"; 34 percent, or over a third, disagreed. Just how do individuals or institutions whose *accuracy* is that suspect manage to score so impressively when it comes to "believability"?

A sharp criticism of the methodology of the Times Mirror poll was leveled by Accuracy in Media, a conservative organization that monitors the media, specializing in exposing liberal and leftist biases. An *AIM Report* in March 1986 took strong issue with the way in which Gallup (which conducted the poll for Times Mirror) evaluated the responses:

One question was designed to find out how the respondents rated various journalists, news programs and publications in terms of credibility. Here is how the question was put to the respondents:

"I am going to read another list. This time please rate how much you think you can believe each organization I name on a scale of 4 to 1. On this 4-point scale, 4 means you can believe all or most of what they say, and 1 means you can believe almost nothing of what they say. How would you rate the believability of _____ on this scale of 4 to 1?"

The respondents were asked first to rate a number of news organizations—TV network news departments, local TV news, Cable News Network, radio news, nationally influential newspapers, local newspapers, the Associated Press, and several magazines. They were also asked to use this same 4 to 1 scale to rate a number of prominent journalists, mainly those who appear on television.

When the results were tabulated it was found that on the average, 33 percent of the respondents rated the major news sources at 4, and 36 percent rated the major TV journalists at 4. In other words, about a third of those questioned said that they believed all or most of what these news dispensers told them. This was fairly close to the findings of a poll published in April 1985 by the American Society of Newspaper Editors [ASNE], which found newspaper credibility was rated high by 32 percent and television credibility rated high by 30 percent of those polled. This poll was widely viewed as revealing a serious credibility problem for the media.

The Gallup survey commissioned by the Times Mirror Co. magically caused this problem to vanish by a very simple trick. Nearly half of the respondents in its poll had rated the media organizations and the TV personalities at 3. Unfortunately, no one had told the respondents what 3 meant. Since 4 had been defined as meaning that you could believe all or *most* of what the journalists said, 3 had to mean that you could believe much of what they said, but not *most.*

Gallup's neat trick was to pin the label of "believable" on category 3 in writing up the findings of the survey. Category 4, labeled "highly believable," was then lumped together with 3 to produce highly gratifying believability ratings for all major sources of news and leading news personalities. The ASNE had concluded that "three-fourths of all adults have some problem with the credibility of the media."

An information source that can't be trusted most of the time certainly does not deserve to be labeled "believable." The failure to define 3 for the respondents when the question was asked was a serious error. Arbitrarily labeling 3 as "believable" is deceitful and misleading. The media were so eager to proclaim the death of the credibility crisis that they failed to tell their readers and viewers about this deception in reporting the results of the Gallup survey.

Since the published findings don't disclose how many respondents said they rated the media at 1, meaning they believed almost nothing of what they say, all we know from the Gallup survey is how many respondents believe all or most of what the media say and how many do not. This would have been a more accurate way of presenting the findings. Viewed this way, here is what Gallup found.

It may also be wondered just how Gallup's study for the Times Mirror squares with the many polls taken, by Gallup itself and others across the years, which suggest that the American people have, in fact, a much lower opinion of the media. In 1982, for example, the National Opinion Research Center at the University of Chicago asked 1,506 people to rate eleven major American institutions in terms of the con-

Can You Believe All or Most of What They Say?

		PERCENTAGES	
Electronic		*Yes*	*No*
MacNeil-Lehrer (PBS)		43	57
Cable News Network		38	62
Local TV News		36	64
ABC News		34	66
CBS News		34	66
NBC News		32	68
Radio News		30	70
All Things Considered (NPR)		25	75
Print		*Yes*	*No*
Wall Street Journal		45	55
Reader's Digest		40	60
Time		35	65
Newsweek		31	69
Local Daily Newspaper		29	71
Associated Press		28	72
Nationally Influential Papers		25	75
USA Today		25	75

Personalities	*Yes*	*No*		*Yes*	*No*
Walter Cronkite	57	43	Geraldo Rivera	31	69
Dan Rather	44	56	Sam Donaldson	30	70
Ted Koppel	41	59	Barbara Walters	30	70
Peter Jennings	40	60	Bill Moyers	28	72
John Chancellor	39	61	Diane Sawyer	28	72
David Brinkley	38	62	George Will	26	74
Tom Brokaw	37	63	Phil Donahue	23	77
Mike Wallace	35	65	Jack Anderson	17	83

fidence they had in them, and the press came in eighth—behind medicine, science, education, organized religion, the military, the Supreme Court, and major companies. Television ranked even lower: tenth—below the federal executive branch and just above Congress.

A much more recent poll by Gallup, also commissioned by the Times Mirror Company and conducted in late December 1986 and early January 1987 (i.e., after the outbreak of the Iran/*contra* controversy), modified somewhat the conclusions of the first. According to the report in the *New York Times* for January 16:

> The telephone poll of 1,502 adults . . . found that believability of news organizations had declined from June 1985 levels. Respondents were asked to rank believability on a scale in which 4 indicated total or near total belief and 1 indicated total or near total disbelief.
>
> Sixty-six percent of those polled gave network television a positive believability rating, meaning a 4 or a 3 on that scale, as against 83 percent in the 1985 poll. The believability rating of local newspapers was 63 percent, as against 80 percent in 1985. . . .
>
> The personal credibility of the three television network anchors had also de-

clined, the poll showed. Dan Rather, the CBS anchor, dropped to a believability rating of 69 percent from 81 percent in 1985. NBC's Tom Brokaw had a rating of 66 percent, as against 69 percent in 1985, and Peter Jennings' rating on ABC was also 66 percent, against 74 percent in 1985.

But these still essentially high figures were sharply challenged by others reported in the November/December 1986 issue of *Public Opinion* by Michael Robinson, academic director of the Times Mirror's "People and the Press" surveys. According to Robinson, a new survey had studied media believability as rated by three different age categories of the American national population: "Seniors" (age 50 and over), "the Woodstein generation" (from 30 to 49—the reference, of course, being to the presumed impact of the Woodward-Bernstein Watergate disclosures on this age group), and "the Post-Woodstein generation" (18 to 29 years old). The average rating of media believability was highest in the Post-Woodstein generation: 32 percent. For the Woodstein generation, media believability averaged a mere 27 percent. For Seniors, it was 28 percent. Scarcely, then, what one would call a rousing vote of confidence.

In the last analysis, however, the opinions of the public concerning such matters as the "fairness . . . believability" and "accuracy" of the media are hardly very useful as evidence of the actual facts. We have Abraham Lincoln's word for it, after all, that you can fool all of the people some of the time and some of the people all of the time. Fortunately, as he went on to say, you can't fool all of the people all of the time. And in recent years, as described above, depth surveys of the personal opinions of American journalists and careful quantitative analyses of their work-product have established beyond serious dispute what common sense has told objective observers for decades: that the members of the media elite are, in personal terms, vastly more liberal, politically, than the American people as a whole; *and* that they very frequently permit their personal views to bias and distort the "news" they produce. . . .

7. WHO CONTROLS THE NEWS?

Michael Parenti

At the other end of the political spectrum also come charges of media bias—a bias toward social and political conservatism. According to these critics, the media's corporate structure and ties to established political and economic institutions produce a tilt toward preserving the status quo. Journalists don't challenge capitalism because media organizations are capitalist and protective of capitalist interests. Their own upper socioeconomic class status, as demonstrated by Lichter, Rothman, and Lichter, militates against adoption of a reformist ideology.

Michael Parenti is one of the best-known leftist critics of the press. In the selection below, Parenti argues that the news is determined by the owners of media enterprises, the advertisers who provide the funding for continued operation, the editors who toe the line set by the first two, and reporters who impose self-censorship in order to please superiors.*

Michael Parenti is the author of *Power and the Powerless* (1978), *Make-Believe Media: The Politics of Entertainment* (1992), and *Inventing Reality* (1993), from which this excerpt is taken.

Does ownership of the media translate into control over information? Or are journalists free to write what they want? Reporters themselves offer contradictory testimony on this question. Some say they are independent agents while others complain of control and censorship.

CALLING THE TUNE: OWNERS

The people who own the media conglomerates along with their directors and chief executive officers are drawn overwhelmingly from the ranks of the rich. Not surprisingly, nearly all of them are politico-economic conservatives.[1] One media critic notes that among the top officers of the three major networks "there is not a person who I would judge is a liberal." The network bosses are "in general closer to the right of the political center than to the left."[2]

Do these rich conservatives preside over their empires without a concern for the ideological slant of the news stories and political commentary produced by their media organizations? If so, it would seem odd. An article in *Forbes*, a business magazine, noted that the Hearst Corporation enjoyed "considerable clout over network programming" because it owned the largest collection of non-network-owned ABC-TV affiliates. *Forbes* recognized that with ownership comes "clout" and saw nothing unusual about that.[3]

Rupert Murdoch was once asked: "You're considered to be politically conservative. To what extent do you influence the editorial posture of your newspapers?" He responded: "Considerably. The buck stops on my desk. My editors have input, but I make final decisions." Murdoch added that he thought of himself not as a mere conservative but a "radical conservative."[4]

Otis Chandler, publisher of the *Los Angeles Times*, readily admitted there existed an ideological selection process: "I'm the chief executive. I set policy and I'm not going to surround myself with people who disagree with me. In general areas of conservatism vs. liberalism, I surround myself with people who generally see the way I do." Chandler thinks of himself and his editors as "centrists."[5]

The top news executives are subject to the judgments of the ruling corporate directors and owners who exercise financial power over the organization and, if they so choose, final judgment over the news itself and over who is hired or fired at lower levels. When the Du Ponts owned the largest newspapers in Delaware they blatantly suppressed news reports and editorials that did not suit their ideological

*From Michael Parenti, *Inventing Reality*, 2nd ed., (New York: St. Martin's Press, 1993), pp. 33–42.

proclivities.[6] When Walter Annenberg owned the *Philadelphia Inquirer,* he regularly prohibited his editors from running stories that mentioned the names of persons he disliked, including individuals normally reported in the news. He also used the paper to attack a gubernatorial candidate who advocated policies that might infringe upon his own railroad interests in Pennsylvania—without ever informing readers that he had such interests.[7]

C. Peter Jorgensen, publisher of Century Newspapers Inc., advised all editors of his three Boston-area weeklies that he did

> not intend to pay for paper and ink, or staff time and effort, to print news or opinion pieces which in any way might be construed to lend support, comfort, assistance, or aid to political candidates who are opposed by Republican candidates in the November election. You are specifically instructed to submit any and all political stories which mention any candidate in any race and any photographs, letters, editorials, cutlines, or any other kind of written material whatsoever relative to the election or elected officials and their record, to the publisher prior to publication. . . . If this is unclear in any way, resolve every question in your mind with a decision NOT to print.[8]

No state censor could have been more thorough.

Owners often make a show of not interfering, but "the suggestions of powerful superiors are, in fact, thinly veiled orders, requiring circumlocutions in which commands are phrased as requests."[9] Sometimes suggestions made by owners can be brushed aside by editors, but not too often. And if the owner insists, then the editor obeys. Herbert Gans writes: "Older journalists at *Time* told me that Henry Luce used to flood them with story suggestions, many of which were ignored; but those he deemed most important and urgent were not."[10]

If an editor proves recalcitrant, the owner's velvet glove comes off. In the early 1950s Joseph Pulitzer [Jr.], publisher of the *St. Louis Post-Dispatch,* decided his liberal editors were being too critical of the anticommunist witch-hunting escapades of Senator Joseph McCarthy. Eventually Pulitzer's requests that his editors "lay off the McCarthy hearings" were replaced by a direct and silencing command: "I must ask that the words 'McCarthy' or 'McCarthyism' or any oblique reference to either shall not appear on the editorial page without my specific approval. . . ."[11]

Les Brown's observations about the ideological underpinnings of local TV stations hold for local radio and newspapers as well:

> Many of the stations are owned by persons of hard right-wing bias who are pillars of the local power structure and who believe their public service obligations to be met by promoting love for the flag. They would have networks concentrate on spreading patriotism and . . . would keep the air waves free from the voices of dissent.[12]

CALLING THE TUNE: ADVERTISERS

Owners themselves must have a care not to offend other large financial interests, especially those of big corporate advertisers. Todd Gitlin reports:

The knowledge of who pays the bills can't be dispelled, even though it doesn't always rise to consciousness. Network executives internalize the desires of advertisers. CBS's Herman Keld . . . didn't qualify his answer when I asked him whether ad agencies—and affiliates—are taken into account in programming decisions. "I would say they are always taken into account. Always taken into account. . . ."[13]

The notion that the media are manipulated by big moneyed interests is dismissed by some as a "conspiracy theory." But there is nothing conspiratorial about it. Because they pay the bills, advertisers regard their influence over media content as something of a "right." And media executives seem to agree. As erstwhile CBS president Frank Stanton said: "Since we are advertiser-supported we must take into account the general objective and desires of advertisers as a whole."[14]

Consider how, during the early 1970s, the *New York Times* covered the issues of auto safety and auto pollution. *Times* publisher Arthur Ochs Sulzberger openly admitted that he urged his editors to favor the automotive industry's position so as not to "affect the advertising." The industry was one of the *Times*'s biggest accounts at that time.[15]

Advertisers are not hesitant to exert pressure. Mobil Oil urged PBS to suppress a film that would offend its oil partner, Saudi Arabia.[16] Tobacco companies withdrew their ads from *Mother Jones* after the magazine ran articles citing cigarettes as a major cause of lung cancer and heart disease.[17] A study of five major women's magazines (which frequently reported on women's health and also regularly ran cigarette ads) found that they offered not a single article, review, or commentary on any aspect of the dangers of smoking.[18] When NBC ran a documentary on the terrible conditions endured by migrant workers, citing the abuses perpetrated by Coca-Cola Food Company, Coca-Cola sharply denounced the show, and the network was unable to find a single corporate sponsor for the program.[19] NBC was less courageous when its "Today" show managed to report a boycott without once mentioning GE even though the corporation was a major target of the boycott. As already noted, GE owns NBC.[20]

Locally owned media are also vulnerable to the pressures of advertisers and other business interests. While working for a paper in an Ohio mill town many years ago, Art Shields was cautioned by his editor to report nothing that might offend the town's merchants and brewers: "We can't live without their good will. Be especially careful when you write about the brewery. It's our best advertiser." Shields was further warned to check with the management of the big steel plant before reporting about it: "The steel mill runs this town," said the editor.[21]

A reporter for the *Willamette Week* in Portland, Oregon, was told by her editor that "business is where the power is and we have to rub their backs." She noted that "numerous articles containing mildly critical information on business" were rewritten because the editor wanted only "positive" pieces.[22] A study of how absentee mine owners dominated an impoverished Appalachian valley found that the media in the area never questioned the power of the coal company nor the baneful effects that the company's policies had on the local citizenry.[23] After reviewing many county weeklies published in the United States, one writer concluded that very few "ever print anything that might cause discomfort to anyone with any economic power."[24]

Advertisers will cancel ads when they feel the reporting reflects unfavorably on their own product or industry. But they just as frequently withdraw financial support because they dislike the "liberal biases" they think are creeping into the news.[25] Thus when the *New Haven Advocate* ran an article containing some positive things about revolutionary Grenada, a large department store responded by canceling its advertising account with the paper.[26] Years ago the owners of *Esquire* started *Ken*, "a magazine of liberal idealism" that attracted a good deal of reader interest. But big corporations unfriendly to the liberal views in its articles refused to advertise in the new publication and even threatened to withdraw their ads from *Esquire*. So the *Esquire* owners killed *Ken* even though it had met its circulation plans.[27]

Business viewpoints are abundantly represented with TV shows like "Nightly Business Report," "Wall Street Week," and "Adam Smith's Money World"—all of which have corporate backing. This country's most far-reaching wire service, Associated Press (AP), is also its most conservative.[28] AP is owned by big companies like Merrill Lynch. Corporate support also explains the plethora of conservative commentators such as Robert Novak, William Buckley, and John McLaughlin on political talk shows and the absence of progressive ones. The backing of rich sponsors explains the transformation of McLaughlin "from a fringe right-wing columnist in the late 1970s to one of the most prominent faces on public affairs TV."[29] In contrast, progressive commentators such as Jonathan Kwitny and Jesse Jackson— deprived of major advertisers—do not last long on public television, let alone on commercial outlets. Likewise, without big advertising support, progressive publications like the *Nation* and the *Guardian* are always facing insolvency, never able to launch the kind of massive mainstream promotional campaigns that might win the attention of larger publics.

Business interests rail against the "anti-business bias" in the news. It is a way of keeping the press in line. But actually very little of the "investigative reporting" of the last two decades has targeted big business. No wonder when corporate leaders were asked to evaluate the treatment accorded them by the media, only 6 percent said it was "poor," while 66 percent said "good" or "excellent."[30]

Almost all the discussion regarding freedom of the press focuses on government attempts to influence or limit the information flow. But most of the censorship occurs in the private sector, carried out by owners and advertisers who determine which facts and ideas will reach the public.

ON THE LINE: EDITORS

Actual responsibility for daily (or weekly) news production rests with the newspaper editors and radio and television program producers. Without having to answer to reporters, they can cut, rewrite, or kill any story they choose, subject only to final review by their executive superiors.[31] The top media executives meet regularly with editors and producers in order to keep tabs on story selection. They can recommend or veto a story whenever they like, even overriding their editors. However, since they have other duties and, within their corporation, are supposed to adhere to a division of labor, most often they refrain from imposing their power on a daily basis.[32] As one editor put it: "It is not what [the executive boss] will do or will veto, but what we expect that he will do or veto; that's his influence."[33] Daily censorship is made unnecessary by anticipatory self-censorship.

Many editors insist they are nobody's puppet. Infused with notions of professional integrity and personal autonomy, they will vehemently deny they are objects of corporate control. Indeed, editors are accorded a certain degree of independence—if they demonstrate their ability to produce what their superiors want: copy that generally does not challenge the interests of those of wealth and power. Editors perform without daily interference from their superiors because such interference is not necessary. An editor who has to be reined in every day by the publisher will not last long as editor. But we must not mistake this kind of conditional autonomy for actual autonomy. There is no reason to believe that compliant editors could oppose their publishers even if they wanted to.

Since many news editors and broadcast producers share the world view of their superiors, they seldom experience any ideological dissonance. They are free because they are in perfect agreement with their bosses and therefore give no cause for being called to account.

When an editor resists doing what the publisher wants, then the latter—like the boss of any business organization—is not above ramming his or her dictates down the editor's throat. If they want to keep their jobs, editors learn to swallow. On those relatively rare occasions when it is more than they can swallow, they will resign. The publisher of some local Michigan newspapers wrote a memo provoking his editor to quit. It read in part: "It will be our policy to aggressively support, promote, and report business organizations within our circulation area and/or those business organizations who support us with their advertising."[34] Sometimes editors are not given the choice of resigning and are unceremoniously fired for resisting the owner's directives or for allowing uncomfortable information or dissident opinions to creep into their pages.[35]

It is a rare event when a journalistic defender of capitalism stops pretending that he or she is an independent agent and explicitly admits that a class power relationship exists in the media. In 1983 and again in 1987, James Kilpatrick, a conservative columnist for the *Washington Post* and himself a former editor, wrote columns supporting the power of high school and college authorities to censor and suppress student newspapers. To give students "absolute freedom of the press is to let the animals run the zoo," he asserted. Furthermore:

> In a real, grown-up world an editor is subject to a publisher, and if the publisher says "Kill the piece," that's it, sweetheart, the piece is killed. The right of a free press attaches to the guy who owns one. Students do not own a school paper. They have invested not one dime in its production.[36]

Here Kilpatrick admits, indeed, proclaims that, contrary to the established mythology, freedom of the press is not a reporter's political right but is a prerogative of ownership and wealth. Owners thereby have license to exercise prior censorship over editors. Kilpatrick is right in saying that's how things work in the real world. It is just not often that mainstream commentators announce such truths about the real world. (However, if he seriously believes that those who pay should have the final say, then Kilpatrick should keep in mind that most student-run college newspapers are supported by student activities funds. It is the college administrators who "have invested not one dime" but who still claim the right of censorship.)

Editors are more frequently the conduits of, rather than resisters to, the owner's censorship. Former managing editor of the *New York Times* Turner Catledge notes how he used to pass his publisher's numerous criticisms to reporters and editors as if they were his own so that his staff would not feel "the publisher was constantly looking over their shoulders. In truth, however, he was."[37]

SELF-CENSORSHIP: REPORTERS

Like editors, reporters are granted autonomy by demonstrating that they will not use it beyond acceptable limits. They are independent agents in a conditional way, free to report what they like as long as their superiors like what they report. Journalistic competence is measured in part by one's ability to cover things from an ideologically acceptable perspective, defined as "balanced" and "objective." Like social scientists and other investigators, journalists rarely doubt their own objectivity even as they faithfully echo the established orthodoxy. Since they do not cross any forbidden lines, they are not reined in. Thus they are likely to be unaware they are on an ideological leash. This is why some reporters insist they are free agents. Only when they stray off the beaten path is the pressure from above likely to be felt. And they almost never do.

If every reporter had to be policed continually by superiors when producing the news, the system could not maintain its democratic appearance and probably could not function very smoothly. As it turns out, editors and owners do not have to exercise ubiquitous supervision; intermittent control will do. As already mentioned, the *anticipation* that superiors might disapprove of this or that story is usually enough to discourage a reporter from writing it, or an editor from assigning it. Many of the limitations placed on reporting come not from direct censorship but from self-censorship, from journalists who design their stories so as to anticipate complaints from superiors. This anticipatory avoidance makes direct intervention from above a less frequent necessity and leaves the journalist with a greater feeling of autonomy than might be justified by the actual power relationship.

After an extended study of major media, one sociologist concluded that self-censorship becomes a matter of habit, "in which case journalists may not be aware they are responding to pressure."[38] Gans mentions one reporter who considered arguing with an editor for deleting an uncomplimentary fact about the CIA but since "too much disagreement with superiors types people as 'cranks,' she decided to save her scarce political capital for an issue about which she felt more strongly."[39]

Many people who learn to hold their fire eventually end up never doing battle. After a while anticipatory avoidance becomes a kind of second nature. Former FCC chairperson Nicholas Johnson describes the process of self-censorship:

> A reporter . . . first comes up with an investigative story idea, writes it up and submits it to the editor and is told the story is not going to run. He wonders why, but the next time he is cautious enough to check with the editor first. He is told by the editor that it would be better not to write that story. The third time he thinks of an investigative story idea but doesn't bother the editor with it because he knows it's silly. The fourth time he doesn't even think of the idea anymore.[40]

One might add a fifth time when the reporter bristles with indignation at the suggestion that he is on an ideological leash and is not part of a free and democratic press.

Many reporters insist they owe their souls to no one. This despite the fact that they frequently wonder aloud to each other how the boss is taking things. They talk of good stories spiked or rewritten by politically motivated editors. They know of potentially combustible events that go unreported and of editors who decide to favor officialdom's version of events while ignoring abundant information to the contrary. They can recall instructions from above on how not to antagonize big advertisers and other powerful interests. They can name journalists who have been let go or banished to some obscure section of the paper. They know of political dissidents who have been invited to appear on opinion shows or write guest columns only to be suddenly disinvited when word of the event reached higher news echelons. Still most of them treat these incidents as aberrant departures from a basically democratic system of news production.

Journalists will treat their self-censorship as a matter of being "realistic" or "pragmatic" or "playing by the rules." In their ability to live in a constant, if not always conscious, state of anticipatory response while maintaining an appearance of independence, newspeople are not much different from professionals in other hierarchical organizations.

Journalists are subjected to on-the-job ideological conditioning conducted informally through hints and casual inferences that masquerade as "professional" advice. Thus, they might be admonished not to get too "emotionally involved" and not to lose their "objectivity," when they are producing copy that is disturbing to persons of wealth and power. While deputy editor of the *Washington Post* editorial page, Meg Greenfield advised a colleague on how to keep a safe distance from a particularly controversial subject as follows: "I don't know much. I'm like you. I've never been a 'cause' person."[41] Eventually Greenfield was promoted to editorial page editor.

Veteran newspeople "have remarkably finely tuned antennae for finding out the limits" to which they can go, remarked one former reporter.[42] Some even admit there are invisible restraints. ABC correspondent Sam Donaldson says:

There is a line when you're questioning public officials, particularly in public, beyond which you don't go. I can't define that line and I have never purposely gone over it, although once in a while I come close.[43]

NOTES

1. Ben Bagdikian, *The Media Monopoly*, 3rd ed. (Boston: Beacon Press, 1990), p. 6.

2. Les Brown, *Television, The Business behind the Box* (New York: Harcourt Brace Jovanovich, 1971), pp. 219–220.

3. William Barrett, "Citizen Rich," *Forbes*, December 14, 1987, p. 142.

4. Interview in *Cosmopolitan*, July 1986, quoted in *Extra!* July 1987.

5. Diana Tillinghast, "Inside the *Los Angeles Times*," unpublished monograph, 1980, quoted in David Paletz and Robert Entman, *Media Power Politics* (New York: Free Press, 1981), p. 15.

6. Ben Bagdikian, *The Effete Conspiracy* (New York: Harper & Row, 1974), p. 76.

7. Bagdikian, *The Media Monopoly*, p. 42.

8. Jorgensen memorandum published in *Columbia Journalism Review*, January/February 1985, p. 18.

9. Herbert Gans, *Deciding What's News* (New York: Vintage, 1979), p. 101.

10. Ibid., p. 342n.

11. Edwin Bayley, *Joe McCarthy and the Press* (New York: Pantheon, 1981), pp. 139–141.

12. Brown, *Television, The Business behind the Box*, p. 214.

13. Todd Gitlin, "When the Right Talks, TV Listens," *Nation*, October 15, 1983, p. 335.

14. Quoted in Eric Barnouw, *The Sponsor* (New York: Oxford University Press, 1978), p. 57.

15. Norman Bauman, "Newspapers: More or Less Put Together by the Advertisers?" unpublished monograph, 1977, p. 24.

16. Bagdikian, *The Media Monopoly*, p. 60.

17. Martin Lee and Norman Solomon, *Unreliable Sources* (New York: Lyle Stuart, 1990), p. 5.

18. Lauren Kessler, "Women's Magazines Coverage of Smoking Related to Health Hazards," *Journalism Quarterly*, 66, Summer 1989, pp. 316–322. The publications were *Cosmopolitan, Mademoiselle, McCall's, Woman's Day*, and the older version of *Ms.* Kessler also looked at *Good Housekeeping*, which did not carry cigarette ads but which ran nothing on the link between smoking and cancer.

19. Brown, *Television, The Business behind the Box*, p. 196.

20. "Boycotted News," *Extra!* May/June 1991, January/February 1991.

21. Art Shields, *My Shaping Years* (New York: International Publishers, 1982), p. 124.

22. Author's interview with Laurie Wimmer, November 9, 1982.

23. John Gaventa, *Power and Powerlessness* (Urbana: University of Illinois Press, 1981).

24. Calvin Trillin, "U.S. Journal: Kentucky," *New Yorker*, December 27, 1969, p. 33.

25. Gans, *Deciding What's News*, p. 254.

26. Author's interview, February 4, 1986, with George De Stefano, the former *New Haven Advocate* staff writer who wrote the article in question.

27. Bagdikian, *The Media Monopoly*, pp. 161–162.

28. Lee and Solomon, *Unreliable Sources*, p. 23.

29. Ibid., p. 89.

30. Bagdikian, *The Media Monopoly*, p. 57.

31. Gans, *Deciding What's News*, p. 94.

32. Ibid.

33. Ibid.

34. It was the publisher of News-Herald Newspapers Inc.; see *Workers World*, April 9, 1982.

35. For instances of editors resigning or being fired see Bagdikian, *The Media Monopoly*, p. 84; and Lee and Solomon, *Unreliable Sources*, pp. 196–197.

36. James Kilpatrick's column, *Washington Post*, February 14, 1987; also his column of February 18, 1983.

37. Turner Catledge, *My Life and Times*, quoted in Todd Gitlin, *The Whole World Is Watching* (Berkeley: University of California Press, 1980), p. 39.

38. Gans, *Deciding What's News*, p. 251.

39. Ibid., p. 196.

40. Quoted in Lee and Solomon, *Unreliable Sources*, p. 98.

41. Greenfield quoted in Roger Wilkins, *A Man's Life* (New York: Simon & Schuster, 1982), p. 329.

42. The author's conversation with a former AP correspondent, March 1, 1985, Washington, D.C.

43. Quoted in Howard Rosenberg's column, *Los Angeles Times*, June 16, 1986.

B. PROFESSIONAL INFLUENCES

The career path for budding journalists in the first half of the twentieth century began as errand boy in the newsroom and progressed to cub reporter, obituaries, and then to full-fledged journalist. Reporters learned about the news business, and especially how to write news stories, while actually on the job.

Today, however, almost all journalists hold college degrees, and a majority are the products of journalism schools.* Reporters learn first about the news business in the classroom, not the newsroom. As a result, journalists are more likely to share common values about news inculcated in standard texts and curriculums in schools of journalism or mass communications.

Professionalization of journalism has also been furthered by the establishment of societies and journals that foster group identity, by acknowledged professional standards, and by codes of ethics. Sigma Delta Chi, a national journalism society, supports greater professionalism in journalism. Journals such as the *Columbia Journalism Review, Washington Journalism Review,* and *Quill* enhance group identity and critique the profession.

Journalists are trained in what constitutes news. News elements have been identified. These include conflict, drama, known personalities, proximity, and time-

*David H. Weaver and G. Cleveland Wilhoit, *The American Journalist* (Bloomington: Indiana University Press, 1986), p. 43.

liness. Television news also requires compelling visuals to accompany stories with other elements. Not every story possesses all of these elements, but a story with none of them will rarely become news. Timeliness alone also is not sufficient, although it is usually a necessary condition for inclusion as news.[†]

Adherence to a definition of news as stories containing these elements results in a news portrayal that distorts political reality. V.O. Key once noted that "conflict, to judge from the headlines, is the entirety of politics."

The influences of the profession become another explanation of the nature of the news. The primary emphasis then is on the perspective of the professional. The perspective of the individual reporter—his or her definition of news, routines of news work, and perception of role—has become a significant element in the study of media culture.

8. THE INDEPENDENT REPORTER

James Boylan

Over the past century, power over editorial content in the news business has devolved from the publisher to the reporter. In their heyday, publishers such as Joseph Pulitzer and William Randolph Hearst exercised a powerful influence over the editorial direction of the newspapers they owned. Editors gained more authority (personified by high-profile editors such as Ben Bradlee of the *Washington Post*) as professionalization in the newsroom occurred and the media organization became part of a publicly owned conglomerate rather than a personal fiefdom.

By the 1960s, however, power had moved again—this time toward the individual reporter. Buoyed by increasing professionalism in the journalistic corps, reporters acquired greater control over their own product. Editors, most drawn from the ranks of reporters, shared with reporters the perspective that the reporter ought to take the initiative and that, almost as a work of art, the story should not be significantly altered without the reporter's knowledge.

James Boylan documents this revolution in journalism.[*] By narrating changes occurring over the past three decades, Boylan weaves a narrative demonstrating how journalists freed themselves from the constraints of their own organization.

Boylan is a former editor of the *Columbia Journalism Review*. He is co-author of *Mass Media: Systems and Effects* (1982) and author of *Our Troubled Press: Ten Years of the Columbia Journalism Review* (1971).

The late 1960s and early 1970s were an era of anti-organizational discontents. What Gay Talese wrote of *The New York Times* was representative of many newsrooms—that

[†]For example, see James Buckalew, "News Elements and Selection by Television News Editors," *Journal of Broadcasting* 14 (Winter 1969–1970): 47–54.

[*]From "Declarations of Independence," *Columbia Journalism Review* (November/December 1986): 37–39, 43. All footnotes have been deleted.

there was "frustration in writing for a place so large, so solvent and sure—a fact factory where the workers realize the too-apparent truth: they are replaceable." News staffers had little voice in determining the nature of their work; they were seldom asked for their ideas or listened to when they volunteered them. In particular, many reporters, witnessing the turbulence beyond the newsroom, found that their organizations were responding too slowly or not at all to the social and political crises of the Vietnam years; the magazines and the underground press seemed to get closer to the heart of things. Often, disaffection was expressed simply by leaving. Such departures usually did not alarm news organizations, which had always run on high turnover and an oversupply of labor. But even the *Times* must have found it disconcerting when it lost a parade of talent, including most of its crew of civil-rights reporters as well as [David] Halberstam.

Among those who stayed in the mainstream press there rose a new dissident movement, quite unlike anything seen before in the news business. Certainly there had been union organizing in newsrooms, but as [sociologist Warren] Breed had remarked, staff members had never ganged up on policy. Early activism took the form of violating the organizational taboo against politics: small numbers of journalists signed ads, wore buttons or armbands opposing the war, and even marched. But the focus soon began to shift to a general reappraisal of the individual journalist's place within the organization and a critique of the organization itself—of the standards of noninvolvement it imposed, of its supposed role in upholding established power, of the legitimacy of its least-examined premise, objectivity. Ron Dorfman, a Chicago reporter, commented: "Our 'objective' reporting is like the 'objective' scholarship of social scientists who study the powerless on behalf of the powerful, but never the powerful on behalf of the powerless." The movement contended that journalists literally had a right to autonomy—the right to determine the nature of their work without, as [Walter] Lippmann implied, commercial, political, or even patriotic hindrance.

The underground ferment burst out abruptly in Chicago in the wake of the street theater of the Democratic convention of August 1968, that maelstrom of police and demonstrators into which journalists were dragged willy-nilly and, many of them, professionally radicalized. Afterward, a core of thirty-five met at Riccardo's restaurant to plan their next move. What they decided on was, of all things, a journalism review. Why "journalism review"? The term had been around for nearly a decade, applied first to an annual publication issued by the University of Montana. The *Columbia Journalism Review*, issued by my old journalism school, which I served first as managing editor and then as editor, had been published since 1961. Thus the name had a certain recognizability, but it was clear that the Chicago group did not have in mind the Columbia model, which was viewed, not without justice, as being somewhat managerial in tone.

The Chicago founders wanted to create something completely different—a vehicle in which working journalists could criticize management and its policies. This was indeed a fresh departure, a million light-years from the assumptions of the

1950s about the proper role of the employee-journalist and particularly the younger journalist. But it worked. From its first issue in October 1968, the *Chicago Journalism Review* was a lively, wide-ranging forum of critical discussion of the Chicago and national press, presented in a clean newsletter format often adorned by Bill Mauldin drawings.

The *Chicago Journalism Review* inspired a string of local reviews, which were run on volunteer help and were similarly impecunious and fragile. Philadelphia, St. Louis, Providence, Hartford-Springfield, Dallas, Houston, Baltimore, the Twin Cities, San Francisco, and southern California all eventually had such reviews.

Chicago outlasted all but one or two. (Washington finally got its own long after most of the others were dead.) Like any volunteer effort, they tended to stumble as initial enthusiasm declined, but often managements took steps to hasten the end. The Philadelphia *Evening Bulletin* forbade its staff to have anything to do with the local review. A trial issue of an Atlanta review, published in the *Columbia Journalism Review*, cost one participant his job on the *Journal-Constitution*. A mimeographed *AP Review* lasted but two issues, the second of which revealed that the AP had suppressed Peter Arnett's references to looting by American soldiers during the 1970 Cambodia incursion.

Although the Chicago effort was the pioneer, the journalism review that took charge of the young dissident movement was *More*, founded in New York in 1971 by Richard Pollack and others. Not only did the publication tap a stable of vigorous young writers, such as Halberstam and J. Anthony Lukas, but it displayed a certain chic missing in other reviews—for example, in its corporate name, Rosebud Associates (cf. *Citizen Kane*).

More arrived at a propitious moment, when the original dissidence had flowered into what was called, in 1960s style, the "reporter-power" movement. Pollack's editorials helped to formulate a national program, and the A.J. Liebling Counter-Conventions, scheduled by *More* opposite the ANPA's [American Newspaper Publishers Association] spring fertility dance and named for the critic who had dissected those gatherings from time to time, became rallies for the new cultures of journalism.

The call to the first counter-convention, in 1972, stated the premises of reporter power succinctly: "The journalist is one of the nation's most foolishly wasted resources. In city rooms and television newsrooms across the country, thousands of men and women capable of giving their communities the kind of enlightened, tough-minded reporting they deserve are daily demeaned by the feckless institutions for which they work. And thousands more leave or refuse to enter the profession every year because of a system that rewards stenography and discourages enterprise. . . ." After the successful 1972 event in New York, attended by 3,000, a committee met to formulate a platform. It was as general as say, the American Society of Newspaper Editors' unenforced "Canons of Journalism," yet it represented a fresh departure, an alteration of previous understandings, claiming that "journalists must be as free from censorship and arbitrary interference by management as management is free from censorship and interference by government." It is possible that by the time this declaration was issued the newsroom movement had already crested. Although *More* dismissed The Newspaper Guild as hopeless, in fact the reformers often found that the collective-bargaining process, available only through the Guild, was the sole avenue to contractually protected reporter power. The Guild was not unsympathetic; it supported "a more direct voice in the product" and greater protection for the integrity of the individual's work and by-line. But it shunned the most foreign-seeming and radical-sounding of reporter-power proposals, borrowed from such newspapers as *Le Monde* of France—a veto over change in ownership and the election of editors. Somehow, not much reporter power ended up in contracts. In Chicago, where the most intensive effort was made, the proposals were gradually pushed off the bargaining table by both sides. The one place where the effort endured was in Minneapolis, where the "underground church" at the *Minneapolis Tribune* developed, with management encouragement, a staff consultative body of some influence.

The newsroom-democracy movement produced its list of martyrs, mostly reporters who violated the taboo against fouling one's own nest. Three reporters were dismissed for attending and writing for outside publications about the counter-convention. Donald Drake of the *Philadelphia Inquirer* was demoted for writing an article in the *Philadelphia Journalism Review* entitled "I Was a Whore for the Press"; *PJR's* editors eventually counted up seven such casualties among eight founders. Four of five *Houston Chronicle* reporters on the masthead of the first issue of the *Houston Journalism Review* were gone within weeks, via firing or forced resignation. David Deitch of the *Boston Globe*, who had campaigned for worker (not merely reporter) control was fired for writing an article in *The Real Paper*, a weekly that allegedly competed with the *Globe*.

In each of these cases, the commonsensical view was that the employer had had extreme provocation and that the employee had been disloyal. At the same time, management seemed in each case to be seeking to disregard the message that these journalists were conveying at such great risk to their careers. That rationale was well stated in the evanescent *AP Review*. "We seek change not because we are dissidents or militants—although some of us may be—but because we are journalists." The general management response to such assertions was that the contagion of wanting change had to be stamped out by strenuous measures before it could spread. . . .

****

ORDER RESTORED

It is impossible to tell when a whiff of Pulitzer Prize began to waft through the *Washington Post* in connection with Janet Cooke's story about an eight-year-old black heroin addict—no later, certainly, than the time it was published on September 28, 1980, under the headline JIMMY'S WORLD. In the account later offered by the *Post* ombudsman, it is clear that in the process that permitted the fabrication, Cooke, a neophyte reporter, was less important than her powerful organizational sponsors. The attacks by Washington officials on the story and the *Post*'s indignant defense of its right to conceal its sources seemed only to enhance the story's prize value. It was soon shipped off to the Pulitzer factory, where its quasi-realism, luminous detail, and implied sense of moral concern struck the jury and the advisory board as representing the very best in journalism (and, of course, it arrived under the best of aegises, that of the heroes of Watergate). On April 13, 1981, it received a Pulitzer. Within two days, anomalies appeared, first in Janet Cooke's résumé, then in the story itself, and the *Post* was compelled to return the prize.

Almost at once it became clear that the significance of the matter within the journalism community extended far beyond the circumstances that it involved the Pulitzer Prizes and the *Washington Post*, although these certainly gave it initial prominence. The incident mobilized the whole journalistic counter-reformation, for it crystallized among those whom the critic David Eason has dubbed the "conventionalists" everything that had gone awry in journalism over the previous two decades. Eason wrote: "The predominant thrust of this commentary—so predominant that few alternative conceptualizations were published—was that journalism had lost its way in the 1960s and 70s and that it needed to turn away from these new practices and reconnect with the better traditions of its history." In short, these commentators were ready to evoke an imagined past of tough-minded (and dead) city editors as a replacement for the uncomfortable present—somebody along the lines, say, of Walter Burns of *The Front Page*.

Editors even tried to put this romantic notion into practice. There was for a time a hot pursuit of news-fakers, and *The New York Times*, the New York *Daily News*, and the AP each had its petty embarrassment. A poll conducted a year later for the ASNE revealed that editors on nearly 30 percent of the responding newspapers claimed to have tightened controls on reporters—mostly over use of anonymous sources—as a result of the episode. Tellingly, four out of five respondents still said they considered it important for their newspaper to compete for prizes.

Yet it has long been clear that unwritten newsroom policies are more important than the written, and the unwritten rules that were in effect by 1982 mocked the notion that journalism could turn the clock back to an imaginary time. Stephen Hess, in *The Washington Reporters* (1981), observed that real-life editors, "not caring very much, not knowing very much, being too busy, deferring to experts, wanting to retain morale," exerted little control over the output of reporters.

At first glance, such an analysis might have made it sound as if reporter power had triumphed in the long run, that reporters at last had the autonomy envisioned in the 1970s. Yet any working reporter knew instinctively that it was not true. Certainly, as Hess observed, most stories were developed on reporter initiative and were left largely intact on the way to publication, but there were still rules guiding the work. A reporter still knew that a news story demanded a certain approach and political placement. Any major violation would, of course, result in nonpublication and eventually, perhaps, in nonemployment.

How could reporters be free and confined at the same time? One student of the problem, John Soloski of the University of Iowa, has concluded that the standards of professionalism, which were the symbols of rebellion in the 1950s, have been transmuted into a system of control: "The value of news professionalism for the news organization is that it establishes norms of conduct making it unnecessary for the news organization to arbitrarily establish elaborate rules and regulations for news staffers." What had once been the reporters' weapon against the parochialism of the organization had become the organization's weapon against their autonomy.

This was indeed a balance point in the equilibrium that returned to newsrooms after the disruptions of the 1970s. Hess saw it as a specific bargain: although reporters have less supervisory authority than employees of comparable rank in other fields, they have the quasi-professional prerogative of not having specific managerial judgments imposed on their work. He hardly needed to add that they also have careers in a sense not known to previous journalistic generations—salaries extending at the major institutions toward the upper reaches of five figures (and well beyond in television), as well as the comforts of professional prestige and social status. "This is a trade-off," Hess wrote, "that seems to satisfy both management and labor."

9. THE AMERICAN JOURNALIST IN THE 1990s:
A PRELIMINARY REPORT OF KEY FINDINGS
FROM A 1992 NATIONAL SURVEY OF U.S. JOURNALISTS

David H. Weaver and G. Cleveland Wilhoit

The rise of the salience of the reporter in the process of making news has made relevant the following questions: How do journalists see their role? Do they view their role as one of challenging the president or serving as a neutral carrier of information about current events? Do they have self-imposed expectations of interpreting the news for the audience?

The following selection is drawn from the authors' landmark study of journalists conducted in 1992. David Weaver and G. Cleveland Wilhoit sampled over a thousand journalists to determine, among other things, their conceptions of the role of the press. Their study replicated an earlier one the authors conducted in 1982–1983 and a 1971 survey by John Johnstone and colleagues published in *The News People* (1976). In the following selection, Weaver and Wilhoit contrast their findings with those of the earlier studies to illuminate an evolution of journalistic role conceptions.

The introduction offers an overview of the research design. They then present their findings of journalists' conception of their role and their success in fulfilling that self-assigned role. They conclude that journalists do not see themselves as political agenda-setters or as adversaries of government.*

David H. Weaver is Roy W. Howard Research Professor at Indiana University. G. Cleveland Wilhoit also teaches mass communication at Indiana University. They also co-

*From an unpublished report titled "The American Journalist in the 1990s: A Preliminary Report of Key Findings from a 1992 National Survey of U.S. Journalists," November 1992.

authored *The American Journalist* (1986) and *News Media Coverage of U.S. Senators in Four Congresses* (1980).

The professionalism of American journalism continues to be debated in these times of great change in the world.[1] In the past decade, as never before, the news and the journalists who produce it increasingly have become center-stage in American life. The "professional spirit" of journalists detected in Frank Luther Mott's classic history of American journalism, and in the ideas of Pulitzer and the founders of the first schools of journalism, has not been forgotten, but has never been fully developed, as documented in the 1971 national study of 1,328 U.S. journalists by Johnstone and colleagues,[2] and by our 1982–83 follow-up study of 1,001. . . .[3]

Nearly a decade has passed since the data were collected for our study of U.S. journalists in 1982–83, which was funded by the Gannett Foundation and which resulted in The American Journalist—a book that has been widely cited and used by those in journalism and in journalism education.

During this time, great changes have occurred in journalism and in the larger society. Even more dramatic changes have occurred since the 1971 benchmark study. These changes include the wholesale adoption of new technologies that have changed not only the speed of transmission of news, but also its nature.

But what of American journalists? Have they, too, changed dramatically in the past decade? As the following preliminary findings will suggest, the answer is both "yes" and "no," but mostly "no. . . ."

METHODS

Because this study was intended to be a follow-up to the 1971 and the 1982–83 national telephone surveys of U.S. journalists, we followed closely the definitions of a journalist and the sampling methods used by these earlier studies to be able to compare our 1992 results directly with those of 1971 and 1982. We also used many of the same questions asked in these previous studies, but we added some questions to reflect the changes in journalism and the larger society in the past decade.

Unlike the previous two studies, however, we deliberately oversampled journalists from the four main minority groups—Asian Americans, Black Americans, Hispanic Americans, and Native Americans—to ensure adequate numbers for comparison with each other and with White journalists. We kept these oversamples of minority journalists separate from the main probability sample when making comparisons with the earlier studies.

The findings that we report here come from 45-minute telephone interviews with 1,410 U.S. journalists working for a wide variety of daily and weekly newspapers, radio and television stations, and news services and magazines throughout the United States. These interviews were conducted by telephone from June 12 to September 12, 1992, by trained interviewers at the Center for Survey Research at Indiana University's Bloomington campus.

Journalists in the main probability sample of 1,156 were chosen randomly from news organizations that were also selected at random from listings in various directories.[4] The response rate for this sample was 81 percent, and the maximum sampling error at the 95% level of confidence is plus or minus 3 percentage points. It is, of course, higher for the individual media groups.

Journalists Interviewed in 1992 Main Probability Sample

MEDIUM	NUMBER
Daily Newspapers	636
Weekly Newspapers	162
News Magazines	61
News Services	58
Television	138
Radio	101
TOTAL	1,156

The oversample of 254 minority journalists was chosen randomly from the membership lists of the four main minority journalism groups—the Asian American Journalists Association (AAJA), the National Association of Black Journalists (NABJ), the National Association of Hispanic Journalists (NAHJ), and the Native American Journalists Association (NAJA). The response rate for this oversample was 61 percent, and the maximum possible sampling error is just above 6 percentage points, but higher for the individual minority groups.

The general picture . . . suggests most journalists do rate their organization as good or very good on informing the public. Those who are most positive are journalists for wire services, who cite high quality of editors and staff, and speed of news coverage. The least favorable ratings on informing the public are from television journalists, who mention small size of staff and limited resources (Table A).

A majority of journalists now say the editorial policies of their organization (68%) are very important in how they rate their job, an increase of 10 percentage points over the decade. Journalists in the print media are more likely to say editorial policies are important than are their colleagues in the broadcast media. . . .

The chance to help people remains a very important aspect of news work for a majority (61%), but altruism is somewhat more apt to be cited by journalists in broadcasting and on weekly newspapers than in other media, and especially by minority journalists. Job security (61%) and the extent of their autonomy (52%) also are very important in how journalists rate their jobs. As in the past, though, fringe benefits and pay are much less likely than other factors to be cited as very important to rating a job in journalism.

Our earlier study suggested that the number of journalists who planned to leave the field had increased, and that disgruntlement tended to be most visible among the more experienced and altruistic persons. The trend continues in the

1990s, as 21% of the sample—almost double that of 1981–82—say they plan to leave the field during the next five years mainly because of limited pay and the need for a change or a new challenge. Asian journalists are least likely (11%) to say they plan to leave journalism, and Native Americans are most likely to say this (29%).

The journalists in our sample were asked a battery of 11 questions about the importance of various aspects of the possible roles of the news media. Specifically, each journalist responded to questions such as this: "How important is it for the news media to get information to the public quickly?"

For the most part, the perceptions of journalistic role are broadly similar to those a decade ago. Journalists tend to see their responsibilities as pluralistic, with wide majorities agreeing that there is at least some importance for roles as disparate as surveillance and entertainment. The focus of the analysis, then, is on assessing which roles are seen as most important.

Two journalistic responsibilities are seen as extremely important by a majority: Getting information to the public quickly (69%) and investigating government claims (67%). There is no significant difference by race or gender on these journalistic roles, except that Native Americans are much less concerned about getting information to the public quickly (Tables B, C).

Compared to a decade ago, journalists are somewhat more likely to rank their role in providing information quickly as extremely important. Television and wire service journalists are much more likely to rank the information function higher than are persons in other media. Investigating the claims of government, which dropped in salience in the early 1980s, is unchanged in relative importance and is

Table A

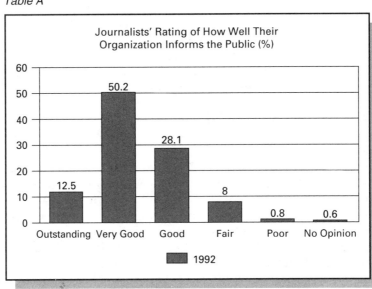

Table B

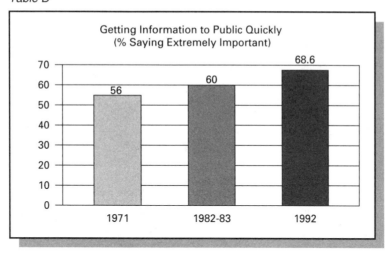

ranked about the same by staff on all media except radio. Journalists working for radio stations are much less likely to see this as a responsibility.

The analytical function of news media—providing analysis of complex problems—also remains about the same, at 48 percent saying it is extremely important. Journalists for the news magazines and daily newspapers are much more likely than news workers in other media to see analysis of complex problems as highly salient. Asian and Black journalists are also more likely to rate this role as extremely important (see Table D).

Amidst the post-Watergate climate of our earlier study, the question of journalists' perceptions of the importance of an aggressive stance toward government was of particular interest. We found the adversarial role was considered less salient in the minds of journalists in 1982–83 than many critics expected. Similar results are found in the 1992 survey.

Only a small minority of journalists see the adversary role—directed at either government or business—as extremely important. Print journalists, in general, are more likely to be adversarial than are their broadcast colleagues. Asians and Blacks are also more likely than other groups to rate the adversary role as extremely important (Tables E, F).

In the most recent study, a new question attempts to assess journalistic initiative in setting the political agenda, a topic that has received much attention over the last decade. Few journalists see their role in these terms, with only 4 percent ranking it extremely important and 41 percent rejecting it entirely. But three of the four minority groups (Blacks, Hispanics, and Native Americans) are more likely to say this is an extremely important role. Even among these groups, however, only about 10 percent see setting the political agenda as extremely important.

Table C

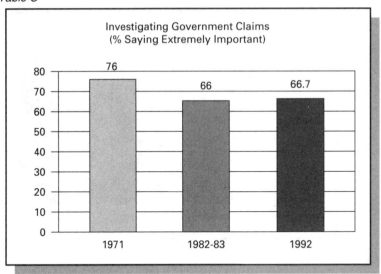

Another issue of currency is the extent to which journalists should attempt to give ordinary people a chance to express their views on public affairs. A little less than half of the sample say this is an extremely important role. Those working on daily and weekly newspapers are most likely to rate this as extremely important.

As some prominent journalists join the critics in claiming that mainstream journalists are sometimes guilty of yielding too easily to the marketing values on the business side, our findings on the perceptions of the importance of entertainment

Table D

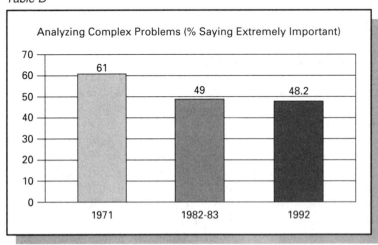

Table E

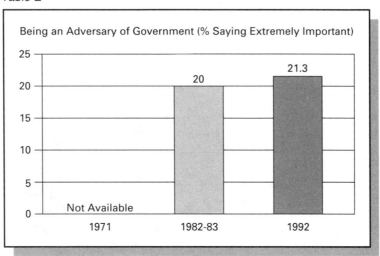

Being an Adversary of Government (% Saying Extremely Important)

are interesting. Fewer journalists now than a decade ago—especially among those in broadcasting—are willing to admit that entertainment is important to news organizations (Table G).

The effect of cable services and other new media in fragmenting the mass audience into specialized markets may explain one of the major shifts in journalists' perception of their work. When asked about the importance of trying to reach the widest possible audience, only a small percentage—significantly fewer than 10 years

Table F

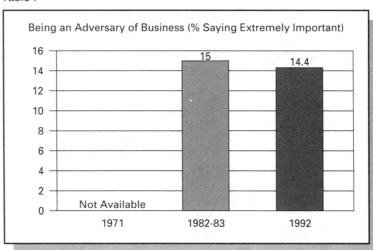

Being an Adversary of Business (% Saying Extremely Important)

Table G

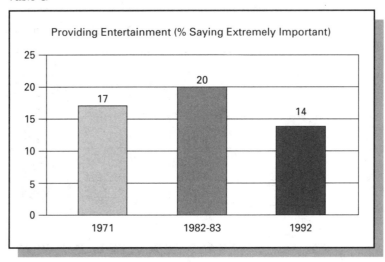

Providing Entertainment (% Saying Extremely Important)

ago—now agree that the pursuit is extremely important. Black journalists, however, are the most likely to say this. . . .

CONCLUSIONS

This massive data set of extensive interviews with more than 1,400 journalists has much more open-ended narrative from the respondents than our previous study. Much of that rich material is yet to be analyzed, and there remains considerable statistical analysis on all the questions. Our results, then, must be viewed as a preview from which conclusions are to be read with caution.

Some broad-stroke, tentative conclusions follow. . . .

Overall differences in ideas about journalistic roles and reporting practices, while not great overall, seem to be related more strongly to working for a particular medium than was the case a decade ago. And, in the 1992 results, gender and racial differences appear to account for many fewer differences than do the types of news media for which journalists work.

Changes in media audiences appear to be reflected in a perception among journalists that reaching the largest number of people in the audience is not as important as it was a decade ago. Speed in getting the news to the public—likely a reaction of new technology's capacity for immediacy—has become more salient. Investigating government claims remains a high value. On the other hand, there is a tendency to downplay entertainment as an important aspect of the news.

While recognizing the importance of the adversary role, journalists do not see it as their highest responsibility. In fact, there is evidence that journalists display considerable caution about playing an activist role in their news work. The idea of setting the policy agenda of the nation and their communities is not one they see as very salient to their job as journalists. . . .

More detailed analysis of these findings, and the reasons for them, will appear in our forthcoming book, *The American Journalist in the 1990s.*

NOTES

1. The authors' study was funded by The Freedom Forum, a nonpartisan, international organization dedicated to free press, free speech, and free spirit for all people, headquartered in Arlington, Virginia. The authors appreciate the autonomy and support given them for this study, especially that of Jerry Sass, Senior Vice President; and Brian Buchanan, Director of Journalism Professional Development. The assistance of Indiana graduate students Lars Willnat, Douglas Walker, and Scott Lewis is also much appreciated, as is the cooperation of the 1,410 U.S. journalists who took the time to answer the authors' many questions. The authors also thank John Kennedy and his staff at the Center for Survey Research, Indiana University-Bloomington, for extremely thorough and professional telephone interviewing.

2. John W.C. Johnstone, Edward J. Slawski, and William W. Bowman, *The News People: A Sociological Portrait of American Journalists and Their Work* (Urbana, IL: University of Illinois Press, 1976).

3. David H. Weaver and G. Cleveland Wilhoit, *The American Journalist: A Portrait of U.S. News People and Their Work* (Bloomington, IN: Indiana University Press, 1986; Second Edition, 1991).

4. These directories include the 1991 *Editor & Publisher International Year Book, The Broadcasting Yearbook 1991,* the 1991 *Gale Directory of Publications and Broadcast Media,* and the Summer 1991 *News Media Yellow Book of Washington and New York.* We used systematic random sampling to compile lists of 181 daily newspapers (stratified by circulation), 128 weekly newspapers, 17 news magazines, 28 wire service bureaus, 121 radio stations, and 99 television stations, for a total of 574 separate news organizations. Unlike the earlier studies, we did include photojournalists and network television journalists.

SUGGESTED READINGS

Altheide, David. L. *Creating Reality.* Beverly Hills, Calif.: Sage Publications, Inc., 1976.
Altheide argues that the perspective of the journalists transforms the event into news. By providing a context for the event, journalists shape its interpretation.

Bennett, W. Lance. *News: The Politics of Illusion,* 2nd ed. New York: Longman, 1988.
Bennett's study of news management found that decisions of allocation of organizational resources were made by a small group of managers.

Broder, David. *Behind the Front Page.* New York: Simon & Schuster, 1987.
A skilled political analyst, Broder directs his attention to the role of norms and ethics in journalism in news coverage of campaigns, institutions, and issues. A valuable critique of journalistic practices by a respected insider.

Efron, Edith. *The News Twisters.* Los Angeles: Nash, 1971.
A content analysis of news coverage of the 1968 campaign, which concludes the news media were biased against the candidacy of Richard Nixon. A classic in the literature on a liberal bias within the news media.

Epstein, Edward Jay. *News From Nowhere*. New York: Random House, 1973.
A classic study of the effect of organizational imperatives on news gathering, Epstein's book is a "must read" for students of political communication.

Fishman, Mark. *Manufacturing the News*. Austin: University of Texas Press, 1980.
Fishman's study of reporters on a police beat revealed that a product of organizational imperatives for news organizations is the ability for public officials to manipulate press coverage.

Gans, Herbert J. *Deciding What's News*. New York: Pantheon, 1979.
A classic in political communications, Gans's study examines the role of organizational imperatives, especially economic, in the news-gathering process.

Gitlin, Todd. *The Whole World Is Watching: Mass Media in the Making and Unmaking of the New Left*. Berkeley: University of California Press, 1980.
Gitlin describes a pattern of distortion in news coverage of the New Left. A classic on media coverage of new political movements.

Isaacs, Norman. *Untended Gates: The Mismanaged Press*. New York: Columbia University Press, 1986.
A practitioner critiques his own profession and argues that the ethics and standards of news practices must be reformed for the news media to regain public confidence.

Lee, Martin A., and Norman Solomon. *Unreliable Sources*. New York: Lyle Stuart, 1991.
A leftist critique of the press as too dependent on government and corporate sources.

McDonald, J. Fred. *Television and the Red Menace: The Video Road to Vietnam*. New York: Praeger, 1985.
A history of the mass media's support of anti-communism from McCarthyism through the Vietnam War. McDonald argues that both news and entertainment media glorified anti-communism and contributed to U.S. involvement in Vietnam.

Tuchman, Gaye. *Making News*. New York: Free Press, 1978.
One of the major studies of the sociology of the news, *Making News* describes how news organizations' imperatives affect how news professionals draw on their own professional values to frame news stories. Special emphasis is given to a case study of the evolution of news coverage of the women's movement in the 1960s and 1970s.

Tunstall, Jeremy. *Journalists At Work*. Beverly Hills, Calif.: Sage Productions, Inc., 1971.
One of the first sociological studies of journalistic norms and imperatives and their effects on the news-gathering process.

GOVERNMENT REGULATION OF THE PRESS

INTRODUCTION

Thomas Jefferson once remarked that "were it left to me to decide whether we should have a government without newspapers, or newspapers without a government, I should not hesitate a moment to prefer the latter."* Yet, later in his life Jefferson also declared that some of the Federalist papers criticizing his administration should be targeted for government action. "I have therefore long thought that a few prosecutions of the most eminent offenders would have a wholesome effect in restoring the integrity of the presses."†

Herein lies the dilemma for government regulatory policy toward the press. Rhetorically, press freedom is accorded great political weight in our democratic system. The First Amendment prohibits Congressional abridgement of freedom of the press, and the Supreme Court has restrained state and local press restrictions as well. Politicians rarely suggest First Amendment rights should be curbed. The press itself frequently speaks of the "chilling effect" on the role of the press of encroachment on press freedom.

However, the United States has rejected a libertarian view of the press. Prior restraint on publication, although rare, occurred during the Persian Gulf War when

---

*Adrienne Koch and William Peden, *The Life and Selected Writings of Thomas Jefferson* (New York: The Modern Library, 1944), pp. 411–12.

†Quoted in Leonard Levy, *Emergence of a Free Press* (New York: Oxford University Press, 1985), p. 341.

news copy by reporters in the field was subject to a security review before transmission back to home offices. Postpublication responsibility is common. Libel, national security, and obscenity proscriptions subject the press to possible postpublication governmental sanction or civil liability. The broadcast media are especially targeted by government regulation owing to its usage of the public airwaves. While print media utilize privately owned resources, the broadcast media have been entrusted with a public trusteeship stemming from a government-licensed monopoly over a certain bandwidth of the publicly owned airwaves. Broadcast regulations have included the Fairness Doctrine (no longer enforced), which mandated that broadcasters air more than one side of a controversy; the Equal Time Provision, which requires broadcast stations to provide equal access—either free or paid—to political candidates for office; and news and public affairs broadcasting requirements.

Broadcasters have contended that they have been unfairly singled out by government policy and that such regulations have a "chilling effect" on their ability to discuss controversial issues. In the area of programming content, they argue that they should be treated much like the print media.

The broadcasting industry was successful during the 1980s in convincing the federal government to deregulate broadcasting. Throughout the 1980s, the Federal Communications Commission (FCC), dominated by conservative Republicans, loosened government restrictions on programming decisions. One critical battleground was the Fairness Doctrine.

The Fairness Doctrine was initiated by Congress in 1959. It was intended to facilitate wideranging discussions of public issues. If a broadcaster broached a controversial issue, the broadcaster was required to offer reasonable opportunities for both sides in a controversy.

Proponents of the Fairness Doctrine argued that it was essential because the limited number of frequencies within the broadcast spectrum allocated for each geographical area would inhibit debate if broadcasters used their monopoly to advocate positions on controversial issues.

The U.S. Supreme Court upheld the Fairness Doctrine as constitutional in 1969.[‡] However, broadcasters objected to their special regulatory status, since print media were not so regulated. They argued they should enjoy First Amendment rights equal to the print media, which were not subject to the Fairness Doctrine. By the 1980s, they also contended that with the proliferation of cable channels there was no longer a scarcity of broadcast frequencies that may have justified the regulation initially.

In 1987, the FCC, dominated by Reagan administration appointees, ruled that the Fairness Doctrine was unconstitutional and should not be enforced. The FCC decision prompted a majority in Congress to attempt to codify the doctrine through statute, which the FCC would be bound to enforce. However, President Ronald Reagan vetoed the measure, and Fairness Doctrine proponents in the Congress failed to muster enough votes to override.

[‡] *Red Lion Broadcasting vs. FCC*, 395 U.S. 367 (1969)

The arguments pro and con on the value of the Fairness Doctrine are outlined in the first two selections that follow. These selections consist of statements made during the 1987 debate over codification of the doctrine. Since 1987, Fairness Doctrine advocates have been unable to enact legislation supportive of re-establishing the regulation.

But the issues of whether the Fairness Doctrine should be instituted and the degree to which government should regulate broadcasting are still current. The third and fourth selections in this section set forth that debate. They document changes in U.S. broadcasting regulatory policy in the 1980s and outline the future of regulatory policy. At that point, we go beyond the debate over specific regulation to the broader discussion of what the role of government regulation should be in the future in a democratic society.

10. VETO MESSAGE

Ronald Reagan

When vetoing legislation, presidents usually append a message to the house of Congress originating the bill, explaining their reasoning and implicitly urging Congress not to override the veto.

President Ronald Reagan's veto message succinctly states the arguments of opponents to the Fairness Doctrine.* Reagan reiterates many of the arguments of the broadcast industry: the dangers of government intervention in programming content, the current plethora of broadcast options, and the inhibiting role of the doctrine on broadcasters.

Ronald Reagan served as president of the United States from 1981 to 1989. Previous to his two terms as governor of California, Reagan was a film actor and a sports broadcaster.

MESSAGE TO THE SENATE RETURNING
WITHOUT APPROVAL THE FAIRNESS IN BROADCASTING BILL,
JUNE 19, 1987

To the Senate of the United States:

I am returning herewith without my approval S. 742, the "Fairness in Broadcasting Act of 1987," which would codify the so-called "fairness doctrine." This doctrine, which has evolved through the decisional process of the Federal Communications Commission (FCC), requires Federal officials to supervise the editorial practices of broadcasters in an effort to ensure that they provide coverage of controversial issues and a reasonable opportunity for the airing of contrasting viewpoints on those issues. This type of content-based regulation by the Federal Government is, in my

*"Message to the Senate Returning Without Approval the Fairness in Broadcasting Bill," June 19, 1987, *Public Papers of the Presidents of the United States: Ronald Reagan 1987, Book 1* (Washington, D.C.: U.S. Government Printing Office, 1989), pp. 690–91.

judgment, antagonistic to the freedom of expression guaranteed by the First Amendment.

In any other medium besides broadcasting, such Federal policing of the editorial judgment of journalists would be unthinkable. The framers of the First Amendment, confident that public debate would be freer and healthier without the kind of interference represented by the "fairness doctrine," chose to forbid such regulations in the clearest terms: "Congress shall make no law . . . abridging the freedom of speech, or of the press." More recently, the United States Supreme Court, in striking down a right-of-access statute that applied to newspapers, spoke of the statute's intrusion into the function of the editorial process and concluded that "[it] has yet to be demonstrated how governmental regulation of this crucial process can be exercised consistent with First Amendment guarantees of a free press as they have evolved to this time." *Miami Herald Publishing Co. v. Tornillo*, 418 U.S. 241, 258 (1974).

I recognize that 18 years ago the Supreme Court indicated that the fairness doctrine as then applied to a far less technologically advanced broadcast industry did not contravene the First Amendment. *Red Lion Broadcasting Co. v. FCC* 395 U.S. 367 (1969). The *Red Lion* decision was based on the theory that usable broadcast frequencies were then so inherently scarce that government regulation of broadcasters was inevitable and the FCC's "fairness doctrine" seemed to be a reasonable means of promoting diverse and vigorous debate of controversial issues.

The Supreme Court indicated in *Red Lion* a willingness to reconsider the appropriateness of the fairness doctrine if it reduced rather than enhanced broadcast coverage. In a later case, the Court acknowledged the changes in the technological and economic environment in which broadcasters operate. It may now be fairly concluded that the growth in the number of available media outlets does indeed outweigh whatever justifications may have seemed to exist at the period during which the doctrine was developed. The FCC itself has concluded that the doctrine is an unnecessary and detrimental regulatory mechanism. After a massive study of the effects of its own rule, the FCC found in 1985 that the recent explosion in the number of new information sources such as cable television has clearly made the "fairness doctrine" unnecessary. Furthermore, the FCC found that the doctrine in fact *inhibits* broadcasters from presenting controversial issues of public importance, and thus defeats its own purpose.

Quite apart from these technological advances, we must not ignore the obvious intent of the First Amendment, which is to promote vigorous public debate and a diversity of viewpoints in the public forum *as a whole*, not in any particular medium, let alone in any particular journalistic outlet. History has shown that the dangers of an overly timid or biased press cannot be averted through bureaucratic regulation, but only through the freedom and competition that the First Amendment sought to guarantee.

S. 742 simply cannot be reconciled with the freedom of speech and the press secured by our Constitution. It is, in my judgment, unconstitutional. Well-intentioned as S. 742 may be, it would be inconsistent with the First Amendment and with the American tradition of independent journalism. Accordingly, I am compelled to disapprove this measure.

RONALD REAGAN

The White House,
June 19, 1987.

Note: *The message was released by the Office of the Press Secretary on June 20.*

11. FAIRNESS DOCTRINE ENSURES THAT VIEWERS RECEIVE ALL SIDES OF CONTROVERSIAL ISSUES

John Dingell

Rep. John Dingell, Democrat from Michigan, offers the opposing argument. According to Dingell, the Fairness Doctrine is still an essential regulation for controlling broadcasters.*

Dingell presents the argument that scarcity still exists because more people want to broadcast than can do so. As long as that condition prevails, the Fairness Doctrine is a necessary limitation on broadcasters.

Another argument Dingell does not make but could is the public-trustee nature of the license provided broadcasters. The airwaves used for transmission are the public's. The government, in the name of the public, offers a monopoly over a broadcast frequency. However, with the monopoly comes a public trust. One aspect of that public trust is to stimulate, not stifle, public debate by presenting differing perspectives on controversial issues. And by requiring that responsibility to belong to each broadcaster individually, not to the broadcast industry as a whole, it personalizes the obligation of public trust. Although many broadcasters may hold this sense of responsibility out of an ethical obligation, the Fairness Doctrine assures that even those who lack that ethic will still act in the public's interest.

The issue of whether the Fairness Doctrine should be reinstituted speaks to the larger issue of the proper measure of government regulation over the broadcast media.

Rep. Dingell was elected to the U.S. House of Representatives in 1955. He serves as chairman of the House Energy and Commerce Committee.

FAIRNESS DOCTRINE ENSURES THAT VIEWERS RECEIVE ALL SIDES OF CONTROVERSIAL ISSUES

The Fairness Doctrine requires broadcasters to provide balanced coverage of controversial issues. It was given definitive statement by the Federal Communications Commission in 1949, pursuant to the requirement in the Communications Act of 1934 that broadcasters act in the public interest.

The 1959 Amendments to the Communications Act gave statutory approval to this requirement—referring to the "obligation imposed upon broadcasters under

*From *Television/Radio Age*, March 30, 1987, p. 153.

this Act to afford reasonable opportunity for the discussion of conflicting views on issues of public importance."

In its 1969 *Red Lion* decision, the Supreme Court held that as long as there were more people who wanted to broadcast than there was spectrum available, the Fairness Doctrine was a constitutional means of affirming the paramount right of viewers to receive differing viewpoints on essential public issues.

In a 1985 report the current FCC revised history by concluding that the Fairness Doctrine had a "chilling effect" on the First Amendment rights of broadcasters. The commission was poised to eliminate the doctrine but was constrained by congressional opposition and the apparent codification of the doctrine in the 1959 Amendments.

The FCC took a different tack by seeking to undermine the doctrine in court.

In its September, 1986, TRAC decision, the D.C. Court of Appeals concluded that the doctrine was not a binding statutory obligation. The FCC has viewed this decision as license to repeal the doctrine administratively, and in several recent actions, the commission has demonstrated its intention to do just that. The argument that the doctrine chills the First Amendment rights of broadcasters is not persuasive. Broadcasting differs fundamentally from other media such as newspapers. The limited electromagnetic spectrum creates a technical scarcity that requires government licensing.

SCARCITY STILL EXISTS

Some argue that scarcity no longer exists in broadcasting. They say that the number of broadcast stations has increased, that the number of newspapers has declined, and that alternative video distribution outlets have begun to grow.

All true. But none of these developments heralds the end of broadcast scarcity. One need only look at the escalating price of broadcast properties and the number of comparative renewal cases pending at the FCC to know that scarcity still exists in broadcasting. There continue to be more people who want to broadcast than there is available spectrum.

Broadcasters suggest that the Fairness Doctrine has actually made them avoid controversial topics. If only there were no obligation to be balanced, they say, we would be more daring.

To anyone who believes that I have a great looking bridge to sell. In fact, the Fairness Doctrine merely gives legal recognition to the ethical obligations of journalists to be balanced. Its whole purpose is to frustrate any intent to provide exclusively one side of controversial issues.

The Fairness Doctrine does not quell controversial speech—but it has been used as an excuse for broadcasters to shy away from hot topics. Broadcasters may indeed be allergic to controversy—but if so, this is because they think controversy offends advertisers, not because of the fairness doctrine.

The economics of the broadcast industry suggest that repeal of the Fairness Doctrine could diminish competition in the electronic marketplace of ideas. Without the fairness doctrine discussion of public affairs could be reduced to a bland, uniform pablum as broadcasters react to economic pressures from commercial advertisers—whether real or perceived.

Viewers benefit from the Fairness Doctrine because it enables them to receive opposing sides of controversial issues. The public benefit would be even greater if the Fairness Doctrine were more vigorously enforced. . . .

12. COMMUNICATIONS DEREGULATION

Jeremy Tunstall

In the 1980s, broadcast regulation in the United States underwent a major revolution. The Federal Communications Commission, controlled by anti-regulation conservatives, deregulated the broadcast industry. Not only was the Fairness Doctrine eliminated, but other restrictions on ownership and programming content, advertising, and franchise renewal were curtailed.

This anti-regulatory attitude has receded somewhat in the 1990s. However, the question of the proper role of the government in the broadcast industry is still highly germane.

In the following selection, Jeremy Tunstall describes the regulatory changes that occurred in the 1980s.* He also examines their effects on the broadcasting industry, particularly radio. As Tunstall points out, the new communications technology and the alterations it brings to the economics of broadcasting will make the issue not merely a philosophical question about government role. Rather, government regulation affects the economics of the broadcasting industry. The deregulation policies of the Reagan administration are still being sorted out. Their effects on the redistribution of income within the industry and the political role of broadcasting are yet to be determined.

Jeremy Tunstall is the author of *Liberating Communications: Policy-Making in France and Britain* (1990), *Journalists At Work* (1971), and *Communications Deregulation: The Unleashing of America's Communications Industry* (1986), from which the following is excerpted.

Significant deregulation of radio took place in 1980, and, after much Washington infighting, the FCC gave television deregulation a major impetus in 1984. The obvious difference was the much larger number of radio stations. A typical market—half the people live in larger, half in smaller population areas—then has 700,000 or 800,000 *households*, about 2 million people living within the radius of the main TV signals. In this size of city—Phoenix, Portland (Oregon), San Diego or Cincinnati— there are at least 20 local radio stations, but usually only 5 TV stations. The TV choice in such a representative city is usually three network affiliates, one commercial independent and one public station. Thus the competitive argument for extending deregulation to television had to rest partly on the spread of cable.

The advance in *technology* also buoyed up deregulation. Perhaps most significant was the use of satellites, which made national distribution of radio networks

*From *Communications Deregulation: The Unleashing of America's Communications Industry* (Oxford: Basil Blackwell, 1986), pp. 145–47, 149–54.

and packages much cheaper and thus much more varied; satellite distribution was also adopted by television. Electronic portable cameras, a huge switch to tape (instead of film) and the electronic newsroom were other changes. Under active policy discussion or early implementation were AM stereo radio, stereo sound for TV and HDTV.

The *advertising* fortunes of broadcasting greatly contributed to industry confidence. Advertising itself grew strongly, and broadcasting continued its traditional slow advance in taking a slightly larger slice of the whole advertising pie. In this strong commercial context, *network TV advertising* did especially well, growing a full 50 percent in the three years 1981–4.

The deregulation of both radio and television had gone most of the distance advocated by the deregulatory consensus in general and wanted by the broadcast industry in particular. Significant deregulation occurred on at least six fronts. These numerous tactical changes added up to an overall change that strengthened the status quo of station incumbents, while cutting back many of the constraints on those incumbents:

(1) *Advertising* rules, which had in any case been voluntary, were removed, leaving no constraints on either the number of minutes per hour or the spillover of paid advertising into programming.

(2) *Content* rules, operated by the FCC, had specified a minimum of 5 percent information, 5 percent local and a total of at least 10 percent nonentertainment programming. The multiplicity not only of stations but also of 'news' and 'talk' programming was quoted as justification for abolishing these content rules. In addition, stations were largely relieved of the traditional task of logging what they had broadcast.

(3) *Ownership rules* of several kinds were relaxed. The number of stations allowed to a single owner increased, in particular from 5 to 12 very high frequency (VHF) television stations. 'Attribution' rules were relaxed so that an individual could own up to 5 percent of a media company before being defined as an 'owner'. This provision alone stimulated stock market activity, because it allowed a major investor simultaneously to pursue several possible takeover targets. The period for which a station must be owned before it could be resold was reduced. And cross-ownership rules, which from 1970 to 1982 forbid broadcast ownership in cable, were relaxed.

(4) *Franchise renewal* procedures were heavily modified in favor of incumbents. Not only were the duration of incumbency extended and the programming requirements reduced, but so were the opportunities for threatening a costly franchise battle, which in turn could be used to extract public service or minority employment concessions.

(5) *More stations* were licensed, especially more independent commercial TV stations, but also hundreds more radio stations. This was potentially an unattractive increase in competition for incumbents, but was made palatable, even welcome, when placed alongside the extended group ownership provisions.

(6) *Equal opportunity* provisions for ethnic minorities and women were in gen-

eral cut back. Ethnic minorities still owned less than 2 percent of the broadcasting station industry. One major irritation to broadcasters—'ascertainment' of minority community provision, depending on elaborate interviewing and documentation—was removed. . . .

The deregulation of radio occurred in several stages. In 1980–1, just before the arrival of the Reagan appointees, the FCC proposed the formal abolition of most content restraints on radio. An early Reagan budget measure in 1981 extended radio licenses to seven years, which, together with the other relaxations, meant a 99 percent chance of license renewal. With voluntary constraints on amounts of advertising being also declared illegal constraints on trade, the main remaining regulations referred to what had always been the one and only key issue—the ownership of radio stations. Thus the FCC'S 1984 extension of the 7/7/7 rule to a 12/12/12 rule allowing one company to have 12 FM and 12 AM stations was the most important of all radio deregulation measures. ABC, for example, already owned radio stations in New York, Los Angeles, Chicago, Washington, Houston, San Francisco and Detroit, and it was now free to buy stations in the remaining 5 of the top 12 markets.

By 1980 the radio industry had much experience of adjusting to other media; it was now having to adjust to cable, much of whose cheaper programming (music videos, nationwide phone-ins) was really radio with pictures. According to FCC statistics, in 1980 over 2,000 radio stations were losing money. One key to radio station operation was keeping costs to a minimum. According to an NAB [National Association of Broadcasters] study released in 1984, the typical radio station had revenues of $540,000 and employed 14 full-time staff, mainly in general administration and in selling local advertising. At most, only 5 or 6 staff voices would ever be heard on the air, despite 24-hour operation. Even in bigger markets, the large amount of competition meant that a few stations tended to dominate in audience and revenue numbers; they did this by having the strongest transmission signals, by employing local celebrity 'personalities' or journalists, and by expensive promotion. But even leading stations in many markets used largely or entirely prerecorded material.

Nevertheless, despite the spartan economics of most stations, U.S. radio is in several respects the world's most pervasive mass medium. Americans 'listen' to radio for some three and a half hours each day, nearly as much as they 'view' television. Over half of what they hear is music, and radio's (and TV's) stars are *the* superstars of the moment. At least 20 percent of all radio is advertising, totalling almost $6 billion in 1984.

Radio is also much the most pervasive dispenser of news. The all-news stations are confined to a few major markets, and are sustained by a high audience proportion of senior executive males, who interest advertisers. But in the typical market, the average FM station runs 85 minutes of news per 24 hours, or 3½ minutes per hour. Ninety percent of stations admit to using news wire services as a primary source. And radio news, not TV or newspapers, is the most frequently and universally received form of news for the U.S. population. Typical adults who watch network news three times a week and read a daily paper four or five days a week listen to radio news three or four times a day. Few studies exist of this phenomenon, which is perhaps 700 million times a day broad, but less than 5 minutes deep. Radio news may well be the most headline-oriented and most violent of all major forms of news; these quick fixes of news several times a day dwarf in their huge numbers all other communications—apart from those other several-times-a-day quick fixes, the nation's daily telephone calls.

The steadily increasing number of radio stations, the deregulation of radio and television, plus the appearance of additional video media have made yet more competitive the already fierce competition for radio advertising. In 1984 radio still received some 7 percent of all advertising expenditure, the same figure as throughout the 1970s.[1]

Radio's attempts to survive the additional competition inevitably turned to new ways of providing attractive music and other programming. And this meant more *networking*, especially since satellite transmission enables the national broadcast networks to operate more cheaply and to meet FM standards of sound quality. ABC blossomed into no less than 7 separately targeted additional radio networks (with FCC deregulatory permission); a new league table of radio networks emerged, with multiple-networking efforts from ABC, CBS and NBC, taking 10 or so of the top dozen places. ABC was in 1984 claiming 1,744 radio station affiliates and NBC and CBS have both been following in ABC's footsteps.

But a small local station, which is not a network affiliate, now has several different sorts of *syndication packages* available from a fastgrowing new breed of suppliers. Westwood One and Drake-Chenault in Los Angeles and Clayton-Webster in St. Louis are leaders among at least fifty companies which syndicate radio programming nationally; these companies are not confined to greater Los Angeles and New York, but are liberally spread around Dallas, Boston, St. Louis, Chicago, Detroit and other top-twenty markets. The services they supply include the following:

1. entire 24-hour music services in the major music formats, with gaps left for local station commercials;
2. daily blocks of material targeted for particular times of day or night;
3. weekly specials, featuring interviews with current hit musicians, sports, religion and other features;
4. very short inserts, usually between 1½ and 3½ minutes, of humor, politics, business/finance news, leisure, hobby, travel or automotive talk, many of which are provided by newspapers, business magazines or hobby publications;
5. celebrity interview programming, syndicated by major stations.

Reliable information about the sales and use of these syndication packages is not available (or, if it is, has a suspect promotional ring), but many local stations undoubtedly use this material some, most or nearly all the time. Much of the material is bartered for free inserted advertising spots; other services are supplied for a few hundred dollars a month to smaller market stations. For $1,000 a month a station manager may be able to fill up a couple of hours a day, making it possible to program a 24-hour station for very modest sums. A syndicator with several such services selling to several hundred stations can still collect two or three million dollars a year.

Deregulated radio is thus even more prevalent, more nationwide, more fragmented and more unknown in its basic details than was the case before deregulation and before satellites (in fact most radio syndication is still done on tape).

Radio provides ever greater quantities of FM popular music; black voices are getting a much better hearing in 'adult contemporary' and more generally; radio is especially good at reaching young people, who are light users of both newspapers and television. Radio can be brilliantly local, especially regarding weather or emergencies. It is also extraordinarily flexible in pursuit of novel formats for delivering audiences to advertisers.

But this hyperflexibility is also a major weakness. Formats change with dizzying speed; most people have little idea of the full range available; many young people now stick to FM and never try AM; nearly everyone sticks to their two or three favorite channels; and the supposedly most intimate medium is dominated by hype, promotion, cynicism and plain old advertising for many minutes per hour.

Paradoxically, the most specifically targeted and specialized medium is also the medium that jumbles everything up together, so that the listener has difficulty telling apart the music, news, views and advertising. Much is not what it seems to be; the 'local' programming may come from 2,000 miles away; both music and talk tend to be free publicity for music groups, authors or other self-promoters; the views tend to be rabid; and phone-ins often offer voyeuristic excursions into unstable minds. The news itself is suspect: What presents itself as news may also be a plug for a business magazine or a particular company. Even the fast 'genuine' news, at which radio can be so brilliant, is too often not only undiluted mayhem and murder, but plain old self-promotion by your friendly, local police PR person.

Deregulated radio certainly exhibits plenty of both virtues and vices. . . .

NOTE

1. Christopher H. Sterling, *Electronic Media* (New York: Praeger, 1984), p. 85.

13. MASS COMMUNICATIONS POLICY: WHERE WE ARE AND WHERE WE ARE GOING

Henry Geller

Although Jeremy Tunstall has offered us a picture on the recent regulatory debates, in the next piece the theme is prescriptive rather than descriptive. Henry Geller outlines telecommunications policy recommendations spanning the spectrum of issues before the Federal Communications Commission.* The primary objective of reform is the promotion of demo-

*From Judith Lichtenberg, ed., *Democracy and the Mass Media* (Cambridge: Cambridge University Press, 1990), pp. 290–310.

cratic values through telecommunications policy. Geller argues the current regulatory structure fails in achieving that objective. He suggests alterations such as modification of Section 315—the provision which requires equal opportunity to airtime by political candidates, greater definition for the Fairness Doctrine (not its elimination) in keeping with the public-trustee function of broadcasting, and promotion of more public access to the airwaves. But Geller proposes other policy changes, some of which he considers highly pragmatic while others are, in his words, "blue sky." Either way, Geller's proposals should be analyzed and debated.

(This essay was originally published in 1990 and the legislation in Congress to give statutory status to the Fairness Doctrine that Geller refers to has not become law as of this writing.)

Henry Geller is director of the Washington Center for Public Policy Research at Duke University. He is a former general counsel to the Federal Communications Commission.

This essay discusses the current state of government policy concerning mass communications, with particular reference to news and public affairs: Does the policy promote democratic values or work against them, and, if the latter, what would constitute a different, better policy?

There are two initial caveats. First, it will be necessary to oversimplify in light of the enormous scope of the topic. And second, I shall oversimplify with respect to the definition of the key goal here: promotion of democratic values. I recognize that there can be heated argument concerning the term "democratic values." I intend to finesse this important area by focusing on a "motherhood" approach. We can all agree that, in the words of Learned Hand and Hugo Black, the United States has committed itself to a marketplace of ideas to robust, wide-open debate; that, although others may regard this as folly, we have staked our all on this approach. A democracy—in our case, a republic depending on representative government—critically depends on an informed electorate and, therefore, on a free and unfettered press bringing to it all worthwhile ideas and views.

A further corollary of this First Amendment goal of robust, wide-open debate is that the American people should receive information from as diverse and antagonistic sources as possible (the so-called *Associated Press* principle set out in *Associated Press v. United States*).[1] And obviously it is desirable that the citizens themselves have access to the media to bring to the fore their notions of issues or views. So the key questions that I shall be asking concerning government policy are, Does it promote or inhibit robust, wide-open debate? Does it promote or inhibit the press in discharging its important role of contributing to an informed electorate? Does the policy do all it can to promote access by the citizenry?

As a final initial matter, I also note the obvious: that First Amendment values, however vital to us, are not absolutes (Justices Black and Douglas to the contrary). Frequently they must be balanced against other, equally important values in a democracy, and a compromise struck.

I shall discuss the three main regulatory models that are important here and address the policy issues in the electronic arena and finally in the print arena.

THE THREE REGULATORY MODELS

It is not possible to pigeonhole each new mass medium under a particular regulatory regime. Hybrid technologies like cable TV appear to cut across several models (television, print, common carrier). Nevertheless, I think it is helpful to keep in mind those three main models—broadcasting, print, and common carrier—because often "law is determined by a choice between competing analogies."[2]

In *broadcasting*, there is government licensing to avoid engineering chaos and scarcity (defined as more people wanting to broadcast than there are channels available). The government bestows the scarce licenses on a short-term renewable basis in exchange for a commitment by the private licensee to serve the public interest. This public-trustee concept necessarily carries with it government supervision of overall programming, including an equal opportunities provision for candidates and, until recently, a fairness doctrine for the coverage of controversial issues of public importance.[3]

In print, licensing is unthinkable under the First Amendment, and so also there can be no overall government supervision of the operation—no public-trustee concept, with its equal time and fairness aspects.[4] And this is so even if there is economic scarcity—a monopoly resulting from the marketplace.[5] Government intrusion is strictly limited to narrow areas like obscenity or libel, although the latter is proving particularly troublesome, as we shall see in a subsequent section.

Finally, in the *common carrier* area, there is an indifferent holding out of service to the public at large; the information supplied by the customer will be transmitted for a price on a nondiscriminatory, first-come, first-served basis to the points specified by the customer.[6] From a First Amendment point of view, this separation of content and conduit has well served the nation in the print field (i.e., the use of the U.S. Postal Service by thousands of publications). It obviously would be the optimal model in the electronic publishing field—namely, a common carrier reaching into every home and delivering electronic intelligence. Indeed, a model exists for narrowband distribution of electronic material—the ubiquitous telephone line (93 percent penetration in the United States). No comparable model exists today for broadband wire distribution. Although this will undoubtedly change in the next century with fiber in every home (perhaps with the so-called broadband integrated service digital network [ISDN]), policy for the next decade must be made without this highly desirable technological breakthrough.

Based on experience with these three models, I would derive the following principles:

1. If the regulation—whether it be structural (access or common carrier) or behavioral (Fairness Doctrine)—interferes with editorial autonomy (e.g., by requiring the operator to give up control of some of its "publication" or to present some additional speech), there must be the "hook" of government bestowing a scarce license or privilege of operation. Thus, the government has no such "hook" with videocassettes or disks and thus no ability to impose access or fairness requirements

on these media. On the other hand, the government can properly insist, when franchising a telephone operation, that it be conducted essentially on a common carrier basis.

2. The reason for the regulation is generally the diversification principle—the notion that the diversity of sources of information is paramount. The First Amendment "rests on the assumption that the widest possible dissemination of information from diverse and antagonistic sources is essential to the welfare of the public, that a free press is a condition of a free society."[7]

3. As a constitutional matter, the approach taken to achieve the diversification principle must be the least intrusive interfering least with daily editorial operation.[8] As a policy matter, wherever feasible, the scheme to promote diversification should opt for structural (content-neutral) approaches rather than behavioral ones where the content of what is transmitted becomes the critical focus.

4. Regulation to promote diversification or robust debate in some other fashion should be clearly called for in the circumstances. Regulation serving no clear or solid diversity purpose is simply unwarranted government intrusion, even if it is structural in nature.

With the foregoing as background, I turn now to government policy as it affects *broadcast* journalism.

GOVERNMENT POLICY AFFECTING BROADCAST JOURNALISM

THE EQUAL OPPORTUNITY PROVISIONS OF SECTION 315

Broadcasting, especially television, is *the* most powerful mass medium. A majority of people rely primarily on television for news.[9] And candidates for important offices also place tremendous reliance on this medium. There are thus two ways in which broadcasting contributes to the informed electorate—a goal stressed at the outset of this discussion: broadcast journalism and the electronic soapbox. The first involves the broadcasters' own coverage of the political news—in newscasts, documentaries, interviews, special events such as staging a debate or covering a convention, and so forth. The second is the presentation of issues by the candidates themselves directly rather than through the editorial selectivity of the broadcast journalist. The equal opportunity provision of Section 315 works against the full use of broadcasting in both respects.

Because the broadcaster is a public trustee, Congress decreed in the Communications Act that if the broadcaster allows one candidate for office to use its facilities, it must afford equal opportunities to all other qualified candidates for that office. The difficulty arises because of the fringe party candidates—Socialist, Socialist Labor, Vegetarian, Prohibition, and so forth (e.g., in the 1960 presidential election, there were fourteen candidates on the ballot in the several states). If then the broadcaster presented a clip of one of the major party candidates in the evening news, it would have to afford precisely equal time to these other candidates. Because a 1959 FCC ruling so required, Congress amended Section 315 to exempt appearances of candidates on four newstype programs: (1) bona fide newscasts, (2) bona fide news interview shows, (3) bona fide news documentaries (if the appearance of the candidate is incidental to presentation of the subjects covered), and (4) on-the-spot coverage of bona fide news events (e.g., the political conventions).

The exemptions have certainly helped; indeed, recent FCC constructions of the fourth exemption have made possible coverage of the presidential debates and press conferences. A recent Court ruling has opened the possibility of one or all three networks presenting the two major party presidential candidates in a series of back-to-back speeches on the great issues (e.g., one session on the economy; another on social issues; another on foreign policy; still another on defense).[10] But if the broadcast activity does not fit within an exemption, it can be blocked by the Section 315 requirement that equal hours of prime time be afforded the fringe party candidates, and many worthwhile programs do not fit. For example, the following types of broadcast journalism are blocked: in-depth interviews with the major candidates, documentaries delving into their positions and backgrounds with extensive use of interviews or clips (thus not falling within the present exemption with its emphasis on *incidental* appearance), or the appearance of a candidate on an *advocates*-type program. The list could be extended greatly because it is not possible to forecast all the formats to which broadcast journalism might turn.

It is important to bear in mind that in these circumstances the Section 315 requirement accomplishes nothing: The program is not presented, so the fringe party candidates receive no time, and the public is simply deprived of many informational programs about candidates in whom it is really interested.

There are a number of good and readily apparent solutions to this problem. Congress could amend the law to make the equal opportunities requirement applicable only to paid broadcasts by candidates. This would maintain substantial protection against abuse and at the same time completely free broadcasters to make a maximum contribution to political discussion. As to the claim that they might abuse this freedom, the short answer is that we trust the broadcasters to act appropriately in the newscast area where they must make innumerable editorial judgments every day, so why shouldn't we trust them in the area of special events, where there is much more of a spotlight?

Or Section 315 could be amended to limit to major party candidates the applicability of the equal time provision in partisan general election campaigns. The term "major party" would be defined liberally to include all significant candidates (e.g., the candidate's party garnered 2 percent of the vote in the state in the last election or, if a new party, had petitions signed by 1 percent of the number of voters in the last election).[11] But so defined, it would eliminate the fringe party candidates who now block the presentation of so much worthwhile informational programming.

There are other approaches: Additional exemptions to 315(a) could be added to cover any bona fide journalistic effort that is under the licensee's control and not designed to advance a particular candidacy.[12] Or the equal opportunities provision could be made inapplicable to the presidential and vice-presidential races. After all, there is a spotlight on these races, and the 1960 suspension worked well in the general election: More than thirty-nine hours of free time were afforded the candidates (as contrasted with only about four hours four years later, when there was no suspension), with no abuses.

I have been making some obvious and quite pragmatic suggestions to improve the present situation markedly. There are other approaches that are more "blue sky" but would result in an *ideal* situation. There is, for example, the Voters Time proposal, put forth by the Twentieth Century Fund's Commission on Campaign Costs in the Electronic Era, which called for Congress to create a new form of nationwide television and radio campaign broadcasts for presidential candidates.[13] These programs would be presented in prime time simultaneously over every broadcast and cable TV facility in the United States during the thirty-five days before the election. Six 30-minute broadcasts would be allotted to candidates of major parties which had placed first or second in two of the three preceding elections. Candidates of parties on the ballot in three-quarters of the states accounting for a majority of electoral votes, which had won one-eighth of the votes in the preceding election, would receive two 30-minute program slots. And the candidate of a party meeting the three-quarters rule but not having obtained sufficient votes previously would be allowed one broadcast.

Other sweeping reforms could be examined in this field—for example, the British political broadcast election process of allocating set blocks of free television time to the parties to be used as they wish. I will not dwell on these far-ranging proposals because they have little chance of serious consideration, let alone enactment. The present major parties do not want them, and the electronic industries would strongly oppose them. Indeed, the bottom line here is that we cannot even take the easy and clearly called-for modest reforms I have listed above, so as to allow our most powerful medium, broadcasting, to make its full contribution to robust debate and an informed electorate.

THE FAIRNESS DOCTRINE

The Fairness Doctrine, as described in the 1959 Amendments to the Communications Act—see Section 315(a)—requires broadcasters to afford reasonable opportunity for the discussion of conflicting views on issues of public importance. As the Supreme Court has stated in the seminal 1969 *Red Lion* case, this imposes a twofold duty: (1) to devote a reasonable amount of time to the coverage of controversial issues of public importance; and (2) to do so fairly. The first duty has never been effectively implemented by the FCC and will be discussed later in this essay. I treat here the second duty, about which so much has been written.[14]

First, however, I must note the present controversy and uncertainty concerning the doctrine's validity. The court of appeals has held that the Fairness Doctrine is not statutorily mandated.[15] The FCC, relying heavily upon the 1985 report,[16] declared in a 1987 report that "the Fairness Doctrine chills speech and is not narrowly tailored to achieve a substantial government interest," and that therefore "the Fairness Doctrine contravenes the First Amendment and thereby disserves the public interest."[17] The FCC also eliminated the first duty as no longer needed.[18]

Upon appeal, the court affirmed the FCC upon statutory—that is, nonconstitutional—grounds.[19] The petitioners have filed a petition for certiorari in the Supreme Court. Congress is considering legislation to require the doctrine and will probably pass such legislation in this Congress (the 101st). What is not certain is whether President Bush will sign the legislation or, like President Reagan, veto it; and if the latter, whether this Congress will override the veto. If the legislation were to become law, there would undoubtedly be a new suit brought by a broadcaster like Meredith Corp. to test its constitutionality.[20]

In these circumstances, I put aside the litigation and legislative activities and will simply give my own views of how I believe this important issue should be treated.

First, the charge that there is no longer any scarcity justifying a Fairness Doctrine ignores the basis for the unique broadcast regulatory approach. In the 1920s, there was no effective licensing of radio stations. Many more people wanted to broadcast than there were frequencies available. Engineering chaos resulted: Without government licensing, no one could be heard.

But the government did not pass out the licenses by auctioning them to the highest bidder as in the case of other scarce, valuable privileges like offshore oil or mineral drilling rights. The licenses are bestowed free as a public trust. To promote diversification, the government could have given each frequency or channel to several licensees, dividing the broadcast day or week. That would be constitutional but poor policy. So the government chooses one licensee and enjoins everyone else from using the frequency. But it insists that this short-term licensee—which acknowledges it has no property right in the frequency—act as a fiduciary for all those kept off by the government. The broadcaster thus volunteers for this public trust accountable to the government both initially and at renewal of the short-term license.[21]

Thus, the key issue of scarcity was not a relative one (e.g., the number of broadcast outlets as against newspapers). At the time of the 1969 *Red Lion* decision, there were 45 radio stations in New York City, all under the Fairness Doctrine, and only three daily newspapers. Nationwide, there were about 7,000 radio stations and only 1,700 daily newspapers. Rather, the scarcity turned on the need to license, *and that more people want to obtain such licenses than there are channels available.* That is still true today: There are no frequencies available in the top fifty markets where close to 70 percent of the population resides, and if a frequency opened in, say, Washington, there would be a dozen applicants for it.

That brings me to the second key issue—whether the Fairness Doctrine has chilling effects. In *Red Lion* the Court held that there was no showing of chilling effects on robust debate and that even if there were such effects, the commission could take action to compel coverage of issues.[22] From the point of view of our study, resolution of this issue of chilling effects is the critical one. Does the Fairness Doctrine simply add more speech and thus contribute to robust debate and an informed electorate, or does governmental intrusion to ensure fairness add such costs and possible penalties that it results in less coverage of issues or a skewing of the coverage to "safe" topics?

The studies of the FCC on this issue are in conflict. In 1974 the commission, under a Republican chairman (Richard E. Wiley), concluded that there was "no credible evidence of a chilling effect."[23] In 1985, under Republican chairman Mark Fowler, the commission reached the opposite conclusion.[24] The FCC relied heavily upon the showing of broadcast commentators like the National Association of Broadcasters (NAB) (which cited forty-five examples of chilling effects in its comments). These examples were extensively criticized by proponents of the doctrine.[25] Proponents argue that the doctrine works well on an informal negotiating basis,[26] and does not interfere unduly with editorial operations, because the licensee is afforded so much discretion under the doctrine, with commission interference only in the few cases where the broadcaster's action can be said to be arbitrary.[27] As noted, the court affirmed the FCC's holding as not arbitrary, while itself observing "some perplexity" at the commission's insistence that "the doctrine's overall net effect was to reduce the coverage of controversial issues."[28] It pointed out the great difficulty of evaluating the "quality" of coverage.[29]

In my view, resolution of this issue results in a mixed verdict. The networks and large broadcasters are not chilled; they are "big boys" with adequate resources to defend themselves against any fairness complaint. They follow practices of fairness going far beyond the governmental requirements. Thus the doctrine does not call for balance in every program—yet in all network documentaries, there is a strong effort to achieve balance in *that* program, so that the same audience hears both sides. I would thus tend to agree that the Fairness Doctrine has not caused the large broadcaster to treat issues in any manner other than it would have done based on reasons of good journalistic practice.[30]

On the other hand, the smaller station might be adversely affected by the existence of the Fairness Doctrine. Such stations already tend to avoid controversy because it is not attractive to advertisers. The expense involved with the doctrine can reinforce this tendency, although it is thus not the major or controlling factor in why such stations avoid controversy (and why implementation of the first duty under the doctrine is so necessary).

Consider just one routine case, *Complaint of Sherwyn H. Hecht.*[31] The case was picked up in a Rand study of all fairness rulings in a six-month period.[32] The routine case seems at first blush to support the commission. The complaint was resolved in favor of the licensee. But the resolution took two and a half years, and the station's license was held up during the resolution process; it involved 480 man-hours of the station personnel's time and a legal bill of $20,000 (with station profits probably in the $50,000 range). This raises the question, What effect—perhaps even unconscious—does this have on the manager or news director the next time he is considering an editorial campaign on some contested local issue? What may be crucially important here is not the number of fairness rulings like *Hecht*, even if favorable.

Further, the government has a most difficult time in its effort to determine fairness or unfairness. Thus, the commission's practice of ad hoc fairness rulings has led it ever deeper into the journalistic process and has raised several serious problems:

1. *Defining issue or personal attack:* What is a controversial issue of public importance or a personal attack can be extremely difficult to judge; indeed, it is only after a commission ruling and court review that the matter can be definitively settled.[33]

2. *Defining balance or reasonable opportunity:* The doctrine requires that *reasonable* opportunity be afforded the contrasting viewpoints on an issue. Lurking in the doctrine's administration is a very difficult question—namely, at what ratio of overall time (e.g., 2 to 1, 3 to 1, etc.) would the FCC say that the opportunity for presenting opposing viewpoints has not been reasonable? Even more difficult, how does frequency (e.g., imbalance of 5 or 8 or 12 to 1) or choice of time (e.g., prime or nonprime time) affect this evaluation? I refer here to one example, the *Public Media Center* case.[34] It establishes conclusively that there is no way for the FCC to determine rationally fairness in the complex situations of amount, frequency, and different time periods (e.g., side A got 4 to 1 in amount, but 1 to 8 in frequency, and its times were two-thirds prime whereas side B was all prime—and so on). A broadcaster can know whether it has been fair or not only when the FCC by fiat so declares.

3. *The "stopwatch" problem:* In order to determine whether there has been reasonable balance, the FCC literally has used a stopwatch to time the presentations made on both sides of an issue.[35] Even more difficult can be the problem of judging whether a particular program segment is for, against, or neutral in regard to a particular issue. In the gray areas that are bound to arise in this respect, it is not appropriate for a government agency to make such sensitive programming judgments.

4. *The "stop-time" problem:* An associated problem arises from the fact that during and after the period in which the FCC makes a decision on a fairness complaint, a broadcaster often continues its coverage of an issue for a number of reasons, such as new developments. The commission then finds that the circumstances on which it made its decision have changed significantly.[36]

There are solutions to these problems, but the commission has refused to adopt them. In my view, it is not legally feasible for the commission to eliminate the doctrine. As long as the licensee remains a public trustee, the doctrine is called for. A public trustee cannot act as the station in Jackson, Mississippi, did in the late 1950s and the 1960s: WLBT-TV was run by a racist who presented only the segregationist point of view; such a station is not acting consistently with the role of public fiduciary.[37] But that is what the commission should focus on: complying with the public-trustee obligation rather than trying to ensure fairness on every issue. The latter leads the commission to interfere deeply with daily broadcast journalism.

Thus, I suggest that the commission consider fairness matters only at renewal (or anytime it decides to revoke a license) and only under a *New York Times v. Sullivan* standard[38]—namely, whether there is a malicious pattern of unfairness inconsistent with the notion of a public fiduciary. If there is malice (i.e., operation deliberately violative of the doctrine or a pattern showing reckless disregard of the doctrine), the licensee lacks the requisite qualifications. It is the character of the licensee—whether it is a responsible public fiduciary—that is critical here, and not whether the licensee has achieved fairness on some particular issue. Good-faith mistakes should be tolerated, in order to allow breathing space for robust, wide open debate. Thus, while appropriate complaints would be referred to licensees as received, they would not be considered at renewal (or revocation) absent a pattern of malice. And the FCC has the power to adopt this approach: It did not consider fairness complaints except at renewal until 1962, when it adopted the present ad hoc procedure over the protest of Congress.[39] Significantly, when the Fairness Doctrine was codified into law in 1959, it was applied at renewal on an overall basis.

The commission should also eliminate its personal attack and political editorializing rules. The FCC now does not apply the personal attack rule to most news-type situations (i.e., newscasts, interviews, on-the-spot coverage of news events). If those large-scale exemptions have proved satisfactory (as they have), why keep the rule for documentaries, and so forth? General fairness affords more flexibility to the licensee and suffices.

Similarly, the political editorializing rule makes no sense and is chilling. If the licensee has hours of programming on both sides of a ballot issue and then adds its editorial voice, it need do nothing; general fairness has been served. But in the same situation, if its editorial endorses a candidate, it must notify all the rivals and afford them opportunity to respond. Why, if fairness has been achieved in the station's programming?

Finally, the FCC should consider promoting voluntary access schemes instead of dumping cold water on them.[40] Indeed, Congress should consider requiring such access schemes (e.g., setting aside one hour per week for spot announcements and lengthier programming, like the "op-ed" approach that has worked so well for newspapers).[41] Access has the following advantages over fairness:

1. With access, a broader range of controversial issues will receive airtime. The licensee will be presenting issues on which it believes the public should be informed. But now there will be a valuable supplement: Persons granted access will be free to introduce significant issues that the licensee ignores.

2. The access scheme will render the great majority of fairness complaints nugatory. Only in the most egregious cases would the FCC have to resort to action. A substantial portion of complaints that reach the FCC come from disgruntled viewers with no other recourse. An access scheme thus provides an effective alternative to government intervention.

3. Access allows prompt response to controversial issues. Under the FCC's present complaint-oriented approach, it takes months and often years to resolve a fairness dispute.[42] By that time the issue may be moot or of much reduced importance.

4. Views aired during access time will come from partisan spokesmen, a factor

both the Supreme Court and the FCC have considered important, but which the commission has never enforced.[43]

EFFICACY OF PUBLIC TRUSTEE SCHEME WITH RESPECT TO INFORMATIONAL PROGRAMMING

The Communications Act requires the broadcaster to devote a reasonable amount of time to informational programmings that broadcasting will make its contribution to an informed electorate.[44] Although the FCC has stressed the importance of this duty since 1949,[45] it has failed miserably in its implementation of the policy. Thus, it has authorized operation with 0/0 percent in news and public affairs, and less than 1 percent informational service.[46] In a half century of regulation, it has never denied a license for failure to deliver sufficient news or public affairs programming.

The FCC today is still emphasizing the critical importance of issue-oriented programming (defined broadly in the dictionary sense).[47] Indeed, that is its entire focus for public service programming. Yet its implementation remains just as woefully inadequate.

The commission has eliminated the first prong of the fairness doctrine—the duty to devote a reasonable amount of time to controversial issues of public importance.[48] It has done so on most dubious grounds—that with the elimination of the second prong (the duty to be fair), the broadcaster will now present sufficient amounts of such controversial issue programming.[49] But what if the broadcaster simply wants to present entertainment fare like MTV or home shopping material? The plain truth is that the FCC now has no policy at renewal that would require a station to present controversial-issue programming.

There remains the duty to present community issue-oriented programming.[50] This programming category is much broader than controversial-issue material and really includes all nonentertainment fare.[51] But on this broad category the commission itself now receives no programming information. It renews stations with only a postcard before it, stating that all required information has been placed in the public file.[52] It is thus placing complete reliance on the public to bring to its attention any case of inadequate public service operation (i.e., insufficient issue-oriented programming). But the public is busy with its own matters; there is no basis, in theory or experience, for the agency to shift this statutory burden to the public.[53]

Incredibly, the FCC at the same time deprived the public of the information it needed to perform this "watchdog" function. For the commission eliminated its requirement of logs and instead simply required the licensee to list quarterly at least five example issues, with some illustrative programs under each.[54] Such a list shows only a minuscule amount of the station's issue-oriented programming[55]; to determine the overall amount, the public would be put to the extraordinary burden of monitoring the many stations in the area. Under court order, the FCC reluctantly made available sufficient programming material so that an interested person could petition to deny.[56] The final irony is that the licensee does keep records of its public service programming, as it can never tell when it will face a renewal challenge, ordinary or comparative.[57] The records are just not public, as the FCC is really hostile to public participation, despite the statutory command.

The commission itself has no notion of how its deregulatory policies are working; it gets no programming data and conducts no special studies. There has been one such study, conducted by the Radio and Television News Directors Association in 1984. It found that "radio stations across the country are reducing the amount of air time devoted to public affairs and news programming, as a result of Federal deregulation and the broadcast industry's changing economics"; in television, "some cutbacks are also being made, but to a much lesser extent." The research found that public affairs programming—the in-depth treatment of issues—has suffered a "substantial reduction in airtime" since the FCC's deregulatory act of 1981.[58]

There are, I believe, two main solutions to this regulatory botch. The first and most obvious one is to eliminate the comparative renewal, which is supposed to spur substantial as against minimal service,[59] and in its place simply establish percentage guidelines for substantial service for the two critical programming areas—local and informational (including children's informational). The percentage should reflect a reasonable notion of substantial service (i.e., around the median for stations appropriately grouped by their nature—large or small market; VHF or UHF; network affiliate or independent; and for the hours 6:00 a.m. to midnight and prime time). All stations would be required to meet the guidelines or establish good cause for not doing so, with a report to Congress of any waivers.

Sound policy, I believe, strongly calls for the rule rather than the ad hoc approach. The latter disserves the public interest for two reasons. First, it does not inform the broadcaster or the public of what the licensee's responsibilities are in this most important programming area. Terms such as "reasonable" or "substantial" amounts of informational programming are mushy. As former Chairman Dean Burch testified concerning such terms, "These are, in the vernacular, 'marshmallow' phrases—they mean almost nothing in and of themselves or, conversely, almost anything that one wants them to mean."[60] Vagueness, with its consequent "unbridled administrative discretion,"[61] creates a further danger that the renewal evaluation might chill the exercise of licensee First Amendment rights. As the court stated in *Greater Boston Television v. FCC*, "a question would arise whether administrative discretion to deny renewal expectancies, which must exist under any standard, must not be reasonably confined by ground rules and standards."[62]

This point is crucial. It is not a matter of the FCC's avoiding appraisal of the renewal applicant's programming under one approach as compared with another. Under the statutory scheme, the critical issue is the incumbent's record, and programming is the essence of that record. The question is whether in this sensitive area the First Amendment is served by examination of an incumbent's programming without any objective standards that the licensee has had the opportunity to meet.

Second, the ad hoc approach is ineffective. Because terms such as "reasonable" or "substantial" amount of time do not really inform the licensee of its respon-

sibilities, and because the commercial nature of the licensee militates against performance in this area, particularly in public affairs, many stations tend to perform
poorly. If the renewal applicant then faces a challenge to its operation on this score,
the agency also tends to protect the applicant against the challenge. For broadcasters are operating in the dark because of FCC failure, and the agency is thus a partner to the station's dilemma at renewal. If the FCC moves against the broadcaster
in the "subjective" circumstances, there is both unfairness and the serious First
Amendment problems noted in *Greater Boston*. In short, there is a wide gap between
the promise of the FCC's high-sounding proclamations and its performance in
implementing them on an ad hoc basis.

There is a second and much more sweeping reform. As noted, there has been
no effective FCC enforcement of these obvious public service requirements for the
last half century; the FCC has never denied a license for failure to provide sufficient
local, informational, or children's programming. The comparative renewal process
is just as great a charade. The incumbent always wins, no matter what its past record,
and the Court has roundly condemned the commission for failure to discharge its
statutory obligation.[63]

Further, the present content regulation strains the First Amendment, as
shown by several incidents (e.g., drug lyrics; topless radio; fairness complaints like
the *Hecht* one previously discussed).[64]

After more than half a century of failure, it is time to try a different approach.
Content or behavioral regulation cannot fill the real gaps in the marketplace, and
any attempt to do so would run afoul of the First Amendment.

Common sense establishes that there *are* gaps. The more than nine thousand
commercial radio stations do an excellent job in supplying a variety of formats, usually interspersed with brief news and other talk materials. People welcome these services—they stand the test of the marketplace.

But a public trustee should deliver significant amounts of worthwhile programming for children, who listen so much to radio. Commercial radio fails here.
Nor will one hear serious drama—Faulkner or Shakespeare or new playwrights—on
commercial radio. Commercial radio will not broadcast lengthy public affairs shows;
it will not provide a "newsmagazine" or gavel-to-gavel coverage of great national
issues like the Panama Treaty debate.

What I am describing is public radio, which now faces a serious financial crisis
in this country. And that brings me to my substitute scheme. Why not eliminate the
public-trustee concept (i.e., renewal and the Fairness Doctrine) and in its place exact
a modest spectrum fee—say, 1 percent of gross revenues, fixed for a 35-year term in
a contract? The broadcaster volunteered to be a public trustee, and it is now being
relieved of that responsibility. But the question then arises, Why is the broadcaster on
that frequency, with all others enjoined by the government? Why not selection by lot
or auction? Clearly this would be too disruptive in light of the long-established system, but it is not too disruptive to demand a reasonably modest fee for the govern-
ment-granted and protected privilege of "grazing" on the spectrum range.

The moneys obtained would go to the general treasury and could be appropriated by Congress periodically to accomplish more directly and effectively goals not fulfilled in the marketplace—for example, educational, cultural, dramatic, minority, and in-depth informational programming. This could be done through the Corporation for Public Broadcasting (CPB) for public radio or through funding minority ownership and would be reviewed periodically in the appropriation process.

Congress would thus have ended ineffectual content regulation, with its economic and First Amendment costs, and would now have a rational structure. It would no longer be saying to commercial broadcasters, "You are a business impressed with the public interest and must present educational and informational programming." The commercial broadcaster would be free to act as it does today, and the modest sums taken from it for exclusive "grazing" rights would support the public broadcaster, who is motivated to present educational, cultural, in-depth informational service. In this connection, Congress should also act to insulate the public broadcast system better from political interference (as was the case during the Nixon administration); nominees for CPB should come from a list of five names selected by prestigious special commissions, rather the present method of presidential choice on a purely political basis.

I see little downside to this spectrum fee approach. It is true that a station could then act as WXUR-AM did in Media, Pennsylvania[65]; but the public in the Philadelphia area, with its large number of radio outlets, will survive such partisanship. It is also true that with the end of the Fairness Doctrine, one side could outspend the other on, say, a ballot issue. But that is true today where the discrepancy can be quite large—5 to 1 in overall time—before fairness comes into play; significantly, we do not equalize war chests in the political area. In any event, I do not believe that we should hold on to this present scheme, with all its flaws, for this one purpose, when much can be gained by shifting to the alternative approach I have urged.

I would also favor this approach in television, but I recognize that Congress may be reluctant to move so rapidly in light of the much smaller number of TV outlets. Therefore, I would await the experience with radio deregulation and, if it is successful, use the same approach in television about five years later. In the meantime, the regulation of television should be made more effective along the lines I have described.

I would maintain the multiple-ownership rules. When the government bestows a scarce privilege in the mass media area, it makes sense to promote the *Associated Press* principle to diversify as much as possible the sources of information coming to the people. The most important aspect of diversification is in the local area. Certainly no one entity should own two TV stations in the same market or a local daily newspaper and a local TV station. Because people get their news primarily from TV and secondarily from newspapers, these two powerful media should be in different hands. Note that this does not prevent newspapers from owning TV stations. The *Washington Post* can readily own the TV station on Channel 4 in Detroit rather than Channel 9 in Washington.

The second most important area is regional concentration: One entity should not control the editorial policy of five or more stations in, say, the New York State area, as there are statewide political and ballot issues. The commission erred, therefore, in its refusal to adopt any effective regulation in this area.[66]

NOTES

1. *Associated Press v. United States*, 326 U.S. 1, 20 (1945).

2. H. Kalven, "Broadcasting, Public Policy and the First Amendment," *Journal of Law and Economics* 10 (1967):15, 30.

3. See Section 315(a), 47 U.S.C. 315(a); *Red Lion Broadcasting v. FCC*, 395 U.S. 367 (1969).

4. *See Miami Herald v. Tornillo*, 418 U.S. 241 (1974).

5. See *HBO v. FCC*, 567 E2d 9, 45-48 (D.C. Cir. 1977), *cert. denied*, 434 U.S. 829 (1977).

6. *National Association of Regulatory Utilities Commissioner v. FCC*, 533 E2d 601, 608 (D.C. Cir. 1976).

7. *U.S. v. Associated Press*, at 20.

8. See, e.g., *Hynes v. Mayor of Oradell*, 425 U.S. 610 (1976); *Gooding v. Wilson*, 405 U.S. 518 (1972); *Keyishian v. Board of Regents*, 385 U.S. 589 (1967); *Griswold v. Connecticut*, 381 U.S. 479 (1965).

9. See Roper Organization, *Public Attitudes Toward Television and Other Media in a Time of Change* (1985), pp. 10–11: 65 percent of the population rely primarily on TV for news, up from 51 percent in 1959.

10. See *King Broadcasting v. FCC*, Case No. 88-1367, D.C. Cir., decided November 1, 1988.

11. See First Report and Order, 48 FCC 2d 1, at par. 35 (1972).

12. Ibid., at par. 36.

13. See Hearings Before the Senate Communications Subcommittee, on S. 2876, 91st Cong., 1st sess., at 34–44.

14. See, e.g., Steven J. Simmons, *The Fairness Doctrine and the Media* (Berkeley: University of California Press, 1978); Ford Rowan, *Broadcast Fairness* (New York: Longman, 1984).

15. *See Telecommunications Research and Action Center v. FCC*, 801 F.2d 501 *reh'g en banc denied* (D.C. Cir. 1986) (TRAC), *cert. denied*, 107 S.Ct. 3196(1987).

16. *Inquiry into Alternatives to the General Fairness Obligations of Broadcast Licensees*, 102 FCC 2d 143 (1985).

17. *Syracuse Peace Council*, 2 FCC Rcd. at 5043, 5057 (1987), *recon. denied*, 3 FCC2d 2035(1988).

18. 2 FCC Rcd. at 5048–52; 3 FCC Rcd. at 2039-42.

19. *Syracuse Peace Council v. FCC*, Case No. 87-1516, D.C. Cir., decided February l0, 1989, pet. for rehearing pending.

20. *Meredith Corp. v. FCC*, 809 F2d 863 (D.C. Cir. 1987).

21. *See Red Lion.*

22. At 367. But see *Miami Herald v. Tornillo*, where the Court invalidated a print fairness approach on the grounds that it would be chilling, with no more evidence before it than in *Red Lion*. In my view, there is no real way to square *Tornillo* with *Red Lion*. See H. Geller and

D. Lampert, "Cable Content Regulation and the First Amendment," *Catholic Law Review* 32 (1983): 603, 617–18. Indeed, the proposition that there should be the least intrusive government action is contradicted by the Court's affirmation of the fairness approach in *Red Lion*, because contrary to the Court's observation in *CBS v. DNC*, 412 U.S. 94(1973), fairness, particularly as implemented by the FCC on a case-by-case basis, represents a deep intrusion into daily editorial decision making, whereas there are less intrusive content-neutral approaches to achieve diversification of sources of information. See Henry Geller, *The Fairness Doctrine*, The Rand Corp., R-1412-FF (December 1973); but see *NCCB v. FCC*, 567 F2d 1095, 1115–16 (D.C. Cir. 1977), *cert. denied*, 436 U.S. 926 (1977). I believe that the explanation rests on Holmes's aphorism "the life of the life is not logic; it is experience"; the broadcast system had become entrenched with the public trustee-fairness approach for a half century, and the Court would not disrupt this long "experience."

23. *Fairness Report*, 48 FCC 2d, at 8.

24. See *Inquiry into Alternatives*.

25. See comments of Media Access Project, Docket No. 84-262, at 27–37.

26. See Rowan, *Broadcast Fairness*, pp. 71–88.

27. *See Fairness Report, supra; Strauss Communications v. FCC*, 530 F.2d 1001, 1101 (D.C. Cir. 1976); C. Ferris and J. Kirkland, "Fairness: The Broadcaster's Hippocratic Oath," *Catholic Law Review* 34 (1985): 605, 614.

28. *Syracuse Peace Council v. FCC*, at 24.

29. Ibid.

30. Group W comments to the FCC in Docket No. 84-282, at 6.

31. 40 FCC 2d 1150 (1973).

32. H. Geller, *The Fairness Doctrine*.

33. See *NBC (Pensions)*, 44 FCC 2d 1027 (1974), *NBC v. FCC*, 516, F.2d 1101(D.C.Cir. 1971), vacated, *cert. denied*, 424 U.S. 910 (1976); Simmons, "The Problems of 'Issue' in the Administration of the Fairness Doctrine," *California Law Review* 65 (1977):546; Steven Simmons, "The FCC's Personal Attack and Political Editorial Rules Reconsidered," *University of Pennsylvania Law Review 125* (1977):990.

On personal attack, compare *Strauss Communications, Inc.*, 51 FCC 2d 385 (1975) (calling congressman a coward personal attack) with *Philadelphia Federation of Teachers*, 31 Pike and Fischer, Rad. Reg. 2d 26 (1974) (calling public teacher association guilty of "blackmail" and "blood money" not personal attack); *WMCE*, 26 FCC 2d 354 (1970) (charging persons with "deliberate lie" or being "paranoid" personal attacks); *WMCP Broadcasting*, 41 FCC 2d 201 (1973) (not a personal attack to charge public officials with "hiding" county funds, "hoodwinking" another agency about them, using them for "taxi service"); *University of Houston*, 11 FCC 2d 790 (1968) (stating that group engages in "physical abuse and violence" and "local terror campaigns" personal attack); 1. *J. Allen Carr, 30* FCC 2d 894 (1971) (calling university a "breeding ground" for "terrorists" and "guerrillas" not a personal attack).

34. *In Public Media Center*, 59 FCC 2d 9 (1976), the commission in effect tried to establish that if the two sides have had roughly the same amount of time, the frequency and audience factors are not to be considered. See, e.g., decision as to *KATY* (at 499–500) (503–4, 519); KJOY (505–6, 519); KPAY (505–6, 526); and *KVON* (509–23)—where the commission found "reasonable opportunity" relying solely on roughly the same amount of time, despite great disparities as to frequency—34 to 1, 25 to 1, 14 to 1, and 16 to 1. But see *Clarence F. Massart*, 10 FCC 2d 968 (1967); *George E. Cooley*, 10 FCC 2d 968, 970 (1967), where the commission found unfairness in two political editorializing cases because of an imbalance in frequency even though overall time was roughly the same. And see *KSRO*, 507–8, 522, where there was a 4-to-1 disparity in total time, so the commission looked to "frequency and audience" and, finding an 8-to-1 frequency ratio, found unfairness—but see *NBC*, 16 FCC 2d 956 (1969), holding a 5-to-1 total time and 8-to-1 frequency ratio to be reasonable. My point is

obvious: The area is confused and contradictory. Upon appeal, the court so found and remanded the matter to the commission to clarify its policies. *See Public Media Center v. FCC,* 581 F.2d 1322 (D.C. Cir. 1978). The commission simply ordered the other stations to give time but never clarified its policies, because it is impossible to do so.

35. *Complaint of the Wilderness Society against NBC (ESSO),* 31 FCC, 2d 729, 735–9 (1971). In that case the staff set forth the following "stopwatch" analysis of the material broadcast on the issue (pp. 738–9):

DATE OF BROADCAST	PRO	ANTI
June 7, 1970	4:40	5:35
September 10, 1970	:20	1:00
January 13, 1971	:06	:15
February 14, 1971	—	:10
February 16, 1971	:49	1:05
February 24, 1971	:15	1:30
February 28, 1971	1:32	—
June 4, 1971	1:58	—
July 11, 1971	:27	2:15
August 6, 1971	:45	1:10
August 26, 1971	—	:15
September 15, 1971	—	8:00
Total	10:52	21:15

See also *Sunbeam TV,* 27 FCC 2d 350, 351 (1971).

36. See, e.g., *Complaint of Wilderness Society against NBC,* at 733, 735.

37. See *Lamar Life Broadcasting,* 38 FCC 1143 (1965), reversed and remanded, *Office of Communication of the United Church of Christ v. FCC,* 359 E 2d 994 (D.C. Cir. 1966).

38. *New York Times v. Sullivan,* 376 U.S. 254 (1964).

39. *See Letter to Chairman Oren Harris,* 40 FCC 582 (1962).

40. *Fairness Doctrine,* 74 FCC 2d 163 (1979).

41. See Rowan, *Broadcast Fairness,* p. 165.

42. See Geller, *The Fairness Doctrine,* p. 37.

43. *CBS v. DNC,* 412 U.S. 94, 131 (1973).

44. See Section 315(a); *Red Lion Broadcasting v. FCC,* at 384; *UCC v FCC,* 707 F 2d 1413, 1.428, n–46 (D.C. Cir. 1983).

45. *Editorializing Report,* 13 FCC 1246 (1949).

46. See, e.g., *Herman Hall,* 11 FCC 2d 344 (1.968); *Simon Geller,* 90 FCC 2d 250, 265 (1982), *rev'd,* 737 F.2d 74 (D.C. Cir. 1984).

47. *See Radio Deregulation,* 84 FCC 2d 968 (1981), aff'd in part, rev'd in part, *Office of Communication of the United Church of Christ (UCC) v. FCC,* 707 F.2d 1413 (D.C. Cir. 1983); *Radio Deregulation,* 96 FCC 2d 930 (1984), remanded, *UCC v. FCC,* Case No. 84–1239, D.C. Cir., December 20, 1985 (holding that the FCC must make available to the public a significant accounting of the broadcaster's public service efforts); *TV Deregulation,* 98 FCC 2d 1076 (1984), 104 FCC 2d 358 (1986), rev'd in part on other grounds, *ACT v. FCC,* 821 F.2d 741 (D.C. Cir. 1987).

48. See *Syracuse Peace Council.*

49. The court of appeals affirmed this precatory holding as reasonable, with Chief Justice Wald issuing a strong dissent. See *Syracuse Peace Council v. FCC.*

50. See *UCC v. FCC,* 707 E 2d 1413 (D.C. Cir. 1983).

51. Ibid.

52. *See Postcard Renewal*, 87 FCC 2d 1127 (1981), aff'd *Black Citizens for a Fair Media*, 719 F.2d 407 (D.C. Cir. 1983), *Cert. denied, 104* S.Ct. 3545 (1984).

53. Ibid. at 434 (dissenting opinion of Judge Wright).

54. See note 45.

55. *UCC v. FCC*, at 1441 n. 95.

56. *UCC v. FCC*, 779 E 2d 702 (D.C. Cir. 1985).

57. *See Broadcasting Magazine*, September 26, 1985, pp. 39–40.

58. *See New York Times*, September 17, 1984 ("radio stations reduce airtime given to news").

59. *Central Florida Enterprises v. FCC*, 598 E2d 37 (1978).

60. Hearings on Broadcast License Renewal Before the Subcommittee on Communications and Power of the House Committee on Interstate & Foreign Commerce, 93d Cong., 1st sess., Ser.93–96, pt. 2 at 1120 (1973).

61. Ibid. at 1119.

62. *Greater Boston Television v. FCC*, 444 F.2d 841, 854 (D.C. Cir. 1970), *cert. denied*, 402 U.S. 1007 (1971).

63. *Central Florida Enterprises v. FCC.*

64. *Yale Broadcasting v. FCC*, 478 F.2d 594, 603 (D.C. Cir. 1973), *cert. denied*, 414 U. S. 914 (1973); *Illinois Citizens Committee for Broadcasting v. FCC*, 515 F.2d 397, 407, 427 (Statement of Ch. J. Bazelon) (D.C. Cir. 1975).

65. *Brandywine–Main Line Radio v. FCC*, 473 E2d 16 (D.C. Cir. 1972), *cert. denied*, 412 U.S. 922 (1973).

66. *In the Matter of Regional Concentration Rules*, 49 Fed. Reg. 19, 670 (May 9, 1984).

SUGGESTED READINGS

Friendly, Fred W. *The Good Guys, the Bad Guys, and the First Amendment.* New York: Random House, 1976.
A classic work on the legal history and application of the Fairness Doctrine by a former CBS News president.

Rowan, Ford. *Fairness Doctrine.* New York: Longman, 1984.
A critique of the Fairness Doctrine from a former news reporter.

Schmidt, Benno. *Freedom of the Press vs. Public Access.* New York: Praeger, 1976.
The best analysis of the constitutionality of public-access requirements placed on the press.

Smolla, Rodney A. *Suing the Press.* New York: Oxford University Press, 1986.
Smolla presents several case studies of libel suits involving well-known personalities. A proponent of fewer libel suits, Smolla analyzes recommendations for libel reform.

chapter **5**

MASS POLITICAL BEHAVIOR

INTRODUCTION

The question that has most intrigued students of political communication is the effect of media messages on people's political attitudes and behavior. The question is hardly insignificant in a democracy where individuals choose their political leaders. And in a democratic system where public opinion carries weight in the making of public policy, the answer becomes more critical.

If media messages shape political attitudes and behavior, then elections and public policy are being made under the influence of a force outside the sphere of constitutional checks and balances or the representative process and governed largely by commercial and journalistic imperatives. Media critics can charge that a small coterie of media executives or editors and reporters shapes voters' impressions of issues, candidates, and government and indirectly manipulates the political process.

Even in a more benign sense, media influence can distort the political process by focusing voters' attention on sensationalism and trivia that boosts newspaper circulation and audience ratings but does little to further public understanding of the policy choices placed before them.

The question, then, is highly relevant. Also, the question is hardly new. The persuasive ability of the media has been widely assumed since the founding of the

Republic. Thomas Jefferson called the news media a "powerful engine."* At the turn of this century, the press was blamed for instigating the Spanish-American War and causing the assassination of a president. A Hearst-owned newspaper editorial in 1898 proclaimed the power of the press when it stated: "Under republican government, newspapers form and express public opinion. They suggest and control legislation. They declare wars. . . . The newspapers control the nation because they represent the people."†

Up until the 1940s, the media's influence on individual attitudes was considered analogous to a hypodermic needle. Individuals had little defense or ability to filter the effects of the media. Adolf Hitler's radio appeals were cited as examples of the massive power of the media over people's minds.

But when the first empirical studies of media effects were conducted in the 1940s by a team of sociologists at Columbia University, little media impact was found. Researchers concluded that other factors such as social group identification and political party affiliation played much stronger roles in the formation of political attitudes.

These conclusions gave rise to the minimal-effects theory of political communication (i.e., media have little impact on public attitudes and behavior). The primary effect was reinforcement of attitudes already held. But the minimal-effects theory began to be challenged by empirical studies conducted in the 1970s and 1980s. Bolstered by more sophisticated methodologies, these studies began to find media effects in such areas as voters' perceptions of candidates and issues, levels of trust in political leaders, and feelings of alienation toward the political process.

Today, the questions have moved far beyond media effect on vote choice to a host of related issues: How do people make sense of the media messages they attend to? Does press coverage of issues determine an individual's sense of what issues are most important? Do individuals gauge majority opinion on issues by media portrayals? Is a person's analysis of candidate performance in presidential debates affected by press analysis of candidate performance? Does press coverage of campaigns affect voters' knowledge of and feelings toward candidates?

The result is a burgeoning field no longer restrained by the minimal-effects theory. We now know much more about the power of the news media over individual attitudes.

Although the minimal-effects theory has been rejected, the hypodermic needle theory has not filled the vacuum. Rather, a partial-effects paradigm has emerged. Media effects are not necessarily generalized. Media messages affect certain people under certain circumstances in different ways. Much depends on what individuals bring to the encounter and what they want to get out of it, as well as on the nature of the media message.

Such a theory is a far cry from the hypodermic needle approach because it

---

*Adrienne Koch and William Peden, *The Life and Selected Writings of Thomas Jefferson* (New York: The Modern Library, 1944), p. 542.

†Quoted in Gerald F. Linderman, *The Mirror of War: American Society and the Spanish-American War* (Ann Arbor: University of Michigan Press, 1974), pp. 165–66.

includes an "active" rather than a "passive" audience for news. Individuals are using, not being used by, media.

Not surprisingly, much research has focused on understanding the nature of the audience. Why do people choose to be in the news audience? What are the gratifications they receive from news?

The following chapters explain the minimal-effects theory that long dominated the field; they examine the role of the news media in political learning, the news media agenda-setting role, the influence on political participation, and the effect of media messages on vote choices.

A. MINIMAL-EFFECTS THEORY

14. THE PEOPLE'S CHOICE

Paul F. Lazarsfeld, Bernard Berelson, and Hazel Gaudet

The minimal-effects theory grew out of the studies of Paul Lazarsfeld and his associates at Columbia University. In the 1940s, they studied voters' responses to electoral campaigns to determine what factors shape the electoral choice. A major conclusion of their studies was the inadequacy of the news media as an explanation for voter attitudes and behaviors.

Lazarsfeld and colleagues found the media had only a small impact on the electoral outcome. They posited that media influence is filtered through a two-step communication process. Opinion leaders are tuned to media messages and they influence others. However, the filter of opinion leaders distorts the media message.

The primary impact of the media was reinforcement of previously held views. Few voters were subject to conversion by media messages, and those most susceptible to conversion were least interested in and exposed to media messages.

The "hypodermic needle" effect was put to rest. Media messages did not possess the overwhelming power over people's minds as widely perceived.

The classic work from which the following excerpt is taken is worth reading because of its seminal quality.* Even though subsequent research has discredited some of the findings of Lazarsfeld's team, and new technology—particularly television—has changed the role of the media, *The People's Choice* still stands as a landmark work, and many of its conclusions about the salience of sociological forces are relevant today.

Paul F. Lazarsfeld, Bernard Berelson, and Hazel Gaudet were sociologists at Columbia University at the time of publication of *The People's Choice* (1948). Professors Lazarsfeld and Berelson, along with William McPhee, also co-authored *Voting* (1954).

Paradoxically enough, campaign propaganda exerted one major effect by producing no overt effect on vote behavior at all—if by the latter "effect" we naively mean a *change* in vote. Half the people knew in May [1940], before the campaign got

*From *The People's Choice* (New York: Columbia University Press, 1948), pp. 87–93, 150–57. Charts and footnotes have been deleted.

underway, how they would vote in November, and actually voted that way. But does that mean that campaign propaganda had no effect upon them? Not at all. For them, political communications served the important purpose of reinforcing prior decisions instead of initiating new ideas. It kept the partisans "in line" by reassuring them in their vote decision; it reduced defections from the ranks. It had the effect of reinforcing the original vote decision.

The importance of reinforcement can be appreciated by conjecturing what might have happened if the political content of the major media of communications had been monopolized, or nearly monopolized, by one of the parties. European experience with totalitarian control of communications suggests that under some conditions the opposition may be whittled down until only the firmly convinced diehards remain. In many parts of this country, there are probably relatively few people who would tenaciously maintain their political views in the face of a continuous flow of hostile arguments. Most people want—and need—to be told that they are right and to know that other people agree with them. Thus, the parties could forego their propagandizing only at considerable risk, and never on a unilateral basis. So far as numbers of voters are concerned, campaign propaganda results not so much in gaining new adherents as in preventing the loss of voters already favorably inclined.

Whenever parties stand in substantial competition—as they do throughout most of the country and as they did in Erie County in 1940—party loyalties are constantly open to the danger of corrosion. Party propaganda—from his own party— provides an arsenal of political arguments which serve to allay the partisan's doubts and to refute the opposition arguments which he encounters in his exposure to media and friends—in short, to secure and stabilize and solidify his vote intention and finally to translate it into an actual vote. A continuing flow of partisan arguments enables him to reinterpret otherwise unsettling events and counter-arguments so that they do not leave him in an uncomfortable state of mental indecision or inconsistency. For example, Republicans who might be disturbed by [Wendell] Willkie's relationship to utility interests were equipped with the notion that his experience in business would make him a better administrator of the national government than Roosevelt. Similarly, Democrats uneasy about the third term as a break with American tradition were able to justify it by reference to the President's indispensable experience in foreign affairs at such a time of world crisis. (In fact, this latter argument *was* the answer to the disturbing third-term argument for many loyal Democrats.)

The provision of new arguments and the reiteration of old arguments in behalf of his candidate reassure the partisan and strengthen his vote decision. Should he be tempted to vacillate, should he come to question the rightness of his decision, the reinforcing arguments are there to curb such tendencies toward defection. The partisan is assured that he is right; he is told why he is right; and he is reminded that other people agree with him, always a gratification and especially so during times of doubt. In short, political propaganda in the media of communication, by providing them with good partisan arguments, at the same time provides orientation, reassurance, integration for the already partisan. Such satisfactions tend to keep people "in line" by reinforcing their initial decision. To a large extent, stability of political opinion is a function of exposure to reinforcing communications.

PARTISANSHIP, PARTISAN EXPOSURE, REINFORCED PARTISANSHIP

The availability of partisan propaganda in Erie County in 1940 was somewhat out of balance. There was much more Republican material available, but it was still reasonably easy to read or listen to the Democratic side. If the exposure of the partisans paralleled the partisan distribution of available communications, they would always be running up against the case of the opposition, especially the Democrats. Thus reinforcement would take a step forward and then a step back, and its effect would be halting and lame at best.

But, of course, actual exposure does not parallel availability. Availability plus predispositions determines exposure—and predispositions lead people to select communications which are congenial, which support their previous position. More Republicans than Democrats listened to Willkie and more Democrats than Republicans listened to Roosevelt. The universe of campaign communications—political speeches, newspaper stories, newscasts, editorials, columns, magazine articles—was open to virtually everyone. But exposure was consistently partisan, and such partisan exposure resulted in reinforcement.

By and large about two-thirds of the constant partisans—the people who were either Republican or Democratic from May right through to Election Day—managed to see and hear more of their own side's propaganda than the opposition's. About one-fifth of them happened to expose more frequently to the other side, and the rest were neutral in their exposure. But—and this is important—the more strongly partisan the person, the more likely he is to insulate himself from contrary points of view. The constants with great interest and with most concern in the election of their own candidate were *more* partisan in exposure than the constants with less interest and less concern. Such partisan exposure can only serve to reinforce the partisan's previous attitudes. In short, the most partisan people protect themselves from the disturbing experience presented by opposition arguments by paying little attention to them. Instead, they turn to that propaganda which reaffirms the validity and wisdom of their original decision—which is then reinforced.

One of the assumptions of a two-party democratic system is that considerable inter-communication goes on between the supporters of the opposing sides. This evidence indicates that such inter-communication may go on in public—in the media of communication—without reaching very far into the ranks of the strongly partisan, on either side. In recent years, there has been a good deal of talk by men of good will about the desirability and necessity of guaranteeing the free exchange of ideas in the market-place of public opinion. Such talk has centered upon the problem of keeping free the channels of expression and communication. Now we find that the consumers of ideas, if they have made a decision on the issue, themselves erect high tariff walls against alien notions.

REINFORCEMENT DESCRIBED BY THE REINFORCED

Partisans need reasons for being partisan, and the formal media supply them and thus reinforce their partisanship. At one point during the interviews, the respondents who maintained a constant voting preference were asked why they favored the candidate of their choice. Their answers sometimes showed the effect of reinforcement.

Faint beginnings of doubt about the wisdom were counteracted by appropriate propaganda, and corrosion is thus halted. For example, a young married woman, a Democrat with low income, reported: "In FDR's Wednesday night speech, he stated the facts of his administration. He mentioned several facts of which I had been unaware—for example, that there have been fewer bank failures in his administration than in previous ones. I cannot recall any others at present, but *I had no idea FDR had accomplished so much.*" The final phrase clearly expresses this partisan's relief and gratification in the apparent validity of her decision.

Similar reinforcement—the other side of the coin—is evident in the case of a young salesman on a low SES [socio-economic status]level who was for Willkie in 1940 just as he had been for [Alf] Landon in 1936. His actual economic position conflicted with his appraisal of himself as belonging to small business. He granted that "Roosevelt's policies were good but we don't need them now," and then continued: "I have been reading various articles about Roosevelt lately and he didn't do as much as I thought. . . . Read in *Nation's Business* about the NLRB. The basic idea was all right but they didn't push it far enough. *It just sounds like he has done a lot but he really didn't.*" This man's wife disagreed with him on politics. Under all these cross-pressures, perhaps insecure in his Republican vote intention, he turned to business publications to reassure himself, to convince himself that he was right, and to get good ideas for purposes of argument. Without such reinforcement, this man might have swung away from the Republicans.

But some respondents had more than the faint beginnings of doubt; they had enough doubts actually to leave their original choice for indecision or even the other party, after which they returned to their first decision. Such people are the waiverers. . . . The influence exerted upon them by the media of communication to return to their original decision is no less a reinforcement effect than that exerted upon someone who doubted but never actually left his party. It is just that they needed *more* reinforcement. . . .

An . . . illustration of the effect of reinforcement upon a waverer involves the vice-president of a bank, with strong Republican predispositions. In May he was Republican, but by June—after Germany's conquest of Western Europe—he was not sure: "My decision will depend upon who will keep us out of war. That is paramount in my mind." But all his attitudes and values, and probably associates, were so firmly Republican that his indecision was short-lived. By August he was back doing business at the same old stand: "For one thing, FDR's running for a third term made me very disgusted . . . *any man (Willkie) who has made such a success of himself in such a big business* as Commonwealth and Southern will do a lot for this country in a business way. I've read articles about him in the *Cleveland Plain Dealer* and also the *Chicago Tribune.* I have also read a book, *The Smoke Screen,* which woke me up to just how badly FDR is spending the taxpayers' money."

It is in comments of this kind that we find indications of the reinforcement functions of partisan arguments. They reinforce by validating, orienting, and strengthening the original decisions, by minimizing tendencies toward an internal conflict of opinions, by buttressing some opinions at the expense of others, and by countering possible or actual corrosion of partisan attitudes. . . .

THE NATURE OF PERSONAL INFLUENCE

In comparison with the formal media of communication, personal relationships are potentially more influential for two reasons: their coverage is greater and they have certain psychological advantages over the formal media.

PERSONAL CONTACTS REACH THE UNDECIDED

Whenever the respondents were asked to report on their recent exposure to campaign communications of all kinds, political discussions were mentioned more frequently than exposure to radio or print. On any average day, at least 10% more people participated in discussions about the election—either actively or passively—than listened to a major speech or read about campaign items in a newspaper. And this coverage bonus came from just those people who had not yet made a final decision as to how they would vote. Political conversations, then, were more likely to reach those people who were still open to influence.

For example, people who made up their minds later in the campaign were more likely to mention personal influences in explaining how they formed their final vote decision. Similarly, we found that the less interested people relied more on conversations and less on the formal media as sources of information. Three-fourths of the respondents who at one time had not expected to vote but were then finally "dragged in" mentioned personal influence. After the election, the voters were given a checklist of resources from which they got most of the information or impressions that caused them to form their judgment on how to vote. Those who had made some change during the campaign mentioned friends or members of their family relatively more frequently than did the respondents who kept a constant vote intention all through the campaign.

THE TWO-STEP FLOW OF COMMUNICATIONS

A special role in the network of personal relationships is played by the "opinion leaders." [I]deas often flow *from* radio and print *to* the opinion leaders and *from* them to the less active sections of the population.

Occasionally, the more articulate people even pass on an article or point out the importance of a radio speech. Repeatedly, changers referred to reading or listening done under some personal influence. Take the case of a retired school teacher who decided for the Republicans: "The country is ripe for a change. . . .

Willkie is a religious man. *A friend read and highly recommended* Dr. Poling's article in the October issue of the *Christian Herald* called 'The Religion of Wendell Willkie.' "

. . . The person-to-person influence reaches the ones who are more susceptible to change, and serves as a bridge over which formal media of communications extend their influence. But in addition, personal relationships have certain psychological advantages which make them especially effective. . . . We turn now to a discussion of five such characteristics.

NON-PURPOSIVENESS OF PERSONAL CONTACTS

The weight of personal contacts upon opinion lies, paradoxically, in their greater casualness and non-purposiveness in political matters. If we read or tune in a speech, we usually do so purposefully, and in doing so we have a definite mental set which tinges our receptiveness. Such purposive behavior is part of the broad area of our political experiences, to which we bring our convictions with a desire to test them and strengthen them by what is said. This mental set is armor against influence. The extent to which people, and particularly those with strong partisan views, listen to speakers and read articles with which they agree in advance is evidence on this point.

On the other hand, people we meet for reasons other than political discussion are more likely to catch us unprepared, so to speak, if they make politics the topic. One can avoid newspaper stories and radio speeches simply by making a slight effort, but as the campaign mounts and discussion intensifies, it is hard to avoid some talk of politics. Personal influence is more pervasive and less self-selective than the formal media. In short, politics gets through, especially to the indifferent, much more easily through personal contacts than in any other way, simply because it comes up unexpectedly as a sideline or marginal topic in a casual conversation. For example, there was the restaurant waitress who decided that Willkie would make a poor president after first thinking he would be good. Said she: "I had done a little newspaper reading against Willkie, but the real reason I changed my mind was from *hearsay*. So many people don't like Willkie. Many customers in the restaurant said Willkie would be no good." Notice that she was in a position to overhear bits of conversation that were not intended for her. There are many such instances. Talk that is "forbidden fruit" is particularly effective because one need not be suspicious as to the persuasive intentions of the speakers; as a result, one's defenses are down. Furthermore, one may feel that he is getting the viewpoint of "people generally," that he is learning how "different people" think about the election.

Such passive participation in conversation is paralleled in the case of the formal media by accidental exposure, e.g., when a political speech is heard because it follows a favorite program. In both conversation and the formal media, such chance communication is particularly effective. And the testimony to such influence is much more frequent in the case of personal contacts. The respondents mentioned it time and again: "I've heard fellows talk at the plant. . . . I hear men talk at the shop. . . . My husband heard that talked about at work. . . ."

FLEXIBILITY WHEN COUNTERING RESISTANCE

But suppose we do meet people who want to influence us and suppose they arouse our resistance. Then personal contact still has one great advantage compared with other media: the face-to-face contact can counter and dislodge such resistance, for it is much more flexible. The clever campaign worker, professional or amateur, can make use of a large number of cues to achieve his end. He can choose the occasion at which to speak to the other fellow. He can adapt his story to what he presumes to be the other's interests and his ability to understand. If he notices the other is bored, he can change the subject. If he sees that he has aroused resistance, he can retreat, giving the other the satisfaction of a victory, and come back to his point later. If in the course of the discussion he discovers some pet convictions, he can try to tie up his argument with them. He can spot the moments when the other is yielding, and so time his best punches.

Neither radio nor the printed page can do anything of the kind. They must aim their propaganda shots at the whole target instead of just at the center, which represents any particular individual. In propaganda as much as in other things, one man's meat is another man's poison. This may lead to boomerang effects, when arguments aimed at "average" audiences with "average" reactions fail with Mr. X. The formal media produced several boomerangs upon people who resented what they read or heard and moved in the opposite direction from that intended. But among 58 respondents who mentioned personal contacts as concretely influential, there was only one boomerang. The flexibility of the face-to-face situation undoubtedly accounted for their absence.

REWARDS OF COMPLIANCE

When someone yields to a personal influence in making a vote decision, the reward is immediate and personal. This is not the case in yielding to an argument via print or radio. If a pamphlet argues that voting for the opposite party would be un-American or will jeopardize the future, its warning may sound too remote or improbable. But if a neighbor says the same things, he can "punish" one immediately for being unimpressed or unyielding: he can look angry or sad, he can leave the room and make his fellow feel isolated. The pamphlet can only intimate or describe future deprivations; the living person can create them at once.

Of course all this makes personal contacts a powerful influence only for people who do not like to be out of line. There are certainly some people who gain pleasure from being nonconformists, but under normal circumstances they are probably very much in the minority. Whenever propaganda by another person is experienced as an expression of the prevailing group tendencies, it has greater chances of being successful than the formal media because of social rewards. For example, here is a woman who was for Roosevelt until the middle of the campaign: "I have always been a Democrat and I think Roosevelt has been all right. But my family are all for Willkie. They think he would make the best president and they have been putting the pressure on me." She finally voted for Willkie. . . .

TRUST IN AN INTIMATE SOURCE

More people put reliance upon their personal contacts to help them pick out the arguments which are relevant for their own good in political affairs than they do in the more remote and impersonal newspaper and radio. The doubtful voter may feel that the evaluations he reads or hears in a broadcast are plausible, for the expert writer can probably spell out the consequences of voting more clearly than the average citizen. But the voter still wonders whether these are the issues which are really going to affect *his own* future welfare. Perhaps these sources see the problem from a viewpoint entirely different from his own. But he can trust the judgment and evaluation of the respected people among his associates. Most of them are people with the same status and interests as himself. Their attitudes are more relevant for him than the judgments of an unknown editorial writer. In a formal communication the content can be at its best; but in a face-to-face contact the transference is most readily achieved. For example, here is the case of a young laborer who professed little or no interest in the campaign and who did not even expect to vote until late October: "I've been discussing the election with *the fellows at the shop* and I believe I'll vote, but I haven't decided yet who for." His constant exposure to the views of his fellow-workers not only brought him to the ballot booth but also brought out his final Democratic vote in line with his colleagues. . . .

Trust in another person's point of view may be due to his prestige as well as to the plausibility of what he has to say or its relevancy to one's interests. It is obvious that in all influences prestige plays a considerable role. The degree of conformity is greater the higher the prestige of the person in our group who seeks to influence us. The plausibility of the consequences he presents will seem greater if he is important. (Of course, the formal media are also important in this respect.) The heightening of trust through the prestige of certain personal contacts was clear in the case of the driver of a bread truck who changed to Willkie because the prominent president of a business firm had done him the honor of persuading him in that direction. . . .

PERSUASION WITHOUT CONVICTION

Finally, personal contacts can get a voter to the polls without affecting at all his comprehension of the issues of the election—something the formal media can rarely do. The newspaper or magazine or radio must first be effective in changing attitudes related to the action. There were several clear cases of votes cast not on the issues or even the personalities of the candidates. In fact, they were not really cast for the candidates at all. They were cast, so to speak, for the voter's friends.

"I was taken to the polls by a worker who insisted that I go."

"The lady where I work wanted me to vote. She took me to the polls and *they all voted Republican so I did too."*

In short, personal influence, with all its overtones of personal affection and loyalty, can bring to the polls votes that would otherwise not be cast or would be cast for the opposing party just as readily if some other friend had insisted. They differ from the formal media by persuading uninterested people to vote in a certain way without giving them a substantive reason for their vote. Fully 25% of those who mentioned a personal contact in connection with change of mind failed to give a real issue of the campaign as a reason for the change, but only 5% of those who mentioned the formal media omitted such a reason. When personal influence is paramount in this way, the voter is voting mainly for the personal friend, not the candidate.

B. POLITICAL LEARNING

15. PROCESSING THE NEWS: HOW PEOPLE TAME THE INFORMATION TIDE

Doris A. Graber

In a media-rich democratic society, the problem for most individuals is coping with the deluge of political information to which they are exposed. The problem is especially acute for those who feel a personal need to remain informed about politics. One of the holes in research on the linkage between media messages and an individual's cognitions and attitudes is an understanding of the process by which political information is learned through the media. Doris Graber has attempted to fill that hole through her research on information processing.

Following the approach of Robert Lane in his study of political ideology,* Graber interviewed twenty participants in an in-depth survey of the process of sorting political information. The twenty hours of open-ended personal interviews for each panelist and daily diaries elicited information on people's information-processing procedures.†

Graber concluded that individuals possess a news selection process that helps them sort out valuable from forgettable information. Even information that is remembered usually focuses on broad outlines and omits specific details.

In the selection below, Graber reiterates her primary findings, but she also suggests the implications of her work for the democratic process. She contends that Americans do not

*Robert Lane, *Political Ideology: Why the Common Man Believes What He Does* (New York: Free Press, 1962).

†From Doris Graber, *Processing the News: How People Tame the Information Tide* (New York: Longman, 1988), pp. 249–54. Reprinted with permission.

need more specific political information in order to participate meaningfully in American politics.

Doris A. Graber is a professor of political science at the University of Illinois–Chicago. She has published extensively in the field of political communication. In addition to *Processing the News*, she has authored *Mass Media and American Politics* (1992), *Media Power in Politics* (1990), and *Crime News and the Public* (1980).

The first major conclusion drawn from this study of information processing is that people tame the information tide quite well. They have workable, if intellectually vulnerable, ways of paring down the flood of news to manageable proportions. When they finish reading their newspapers, two out of every three stories have been excluded. Perusal of the remaining stories is simplified by taking advantage of the inverted pyramid style of news reporting. In this style, the most important information appears in the initial paragraph, allowing the reader to skip the remainder without fear of losing the story's focal point. Nearly half of the stories that people notice are handled through such partial reading. Only 18 percent of the stories in an average newspaper are read in full.

Similar winnowing goes on for televised and radio news. On an average, out of 15 to 18 stories in a television newscast, no more than one is retained sufficiently well to be recalled in any fashion shortly afterward. The total loss of information, however, is not as great as these numbers suggest. Many of the stories are ignored because the audience realizes that they are a repetition of previously reported information. Television and radio newscasts throughout a given day are especially repetitious. If one considers only genuinely new information, the proportion of actual "news" recalled is somewhat higher.

Although the initial news selection process is haphazard, in addition to being stringent, people manage to keep on top of the most important stories. When one focuses only on stories that political elites deem significant, the balance between skipping and paying attention is reversed. People exposed to high-quality news sources recollect to some degree two out of every three prominent stories that are likely to affect the course of politics substantially. The credit for this greater attentiveness to important stories is shared by newspeople. They use a series of prominence cues (for example, story placement, headline size, story length, pictorial treatment, and frequent repetitions) to attract attention to news that political leaders and media gatekeepers deem significant.

In addition to paring down the flow of information by ignoring large numbers of stories, people use a processing strategy that further reduces the amount of information that needs to be stored. This strategy is schematic thinking. It allows individuals to extract only those limited amounts of information from news stories that they consider important for incorporation into their schemata. The schema process also facilitates integration of new information into existing knowledge. Since news sources usually present the news in isolated snippets, without sufficient background, schemata allow the receivers to embed the news in a meaningful context. During relatedness searches, the information extracted from a news story may be integrated into a single schema, or it may be segmented and the segments embedded in several schemata. Alternatively, the whole story may become a part of several schemata. In this way, a single story may be used to broaden substantially an individual's store of knowledge. The schema process also facilitates discarding information by providing criteria for determining that new information is redundant or does not conform to previous knowledge that still appears to be sound.

Although the schema process does well in reducing the danger of information overload, it does not lead to the retention of a large amount of factual data about specific events. Understanding the nature of a problem, rather than rote learning of the reported facts, is the goal. This explains why most people are unable to provide full particulars for news that they have processed. Despite rigorous winnowing, people nonetheless learn some details because many news stories are reported repeatedly with essentially the same information. For instance, most people can provide stories about street crime, unemployment, pollution, and corruption among officeholders. Even when people cannot recall specifics from a particular story, they can make judgments about it. For instance, they know, on the basis of comparisons with familiar information stored in memory, when "nothing new" has been reported. Whenever information needs to be recalled, schemata can provide ready-made nonspecific answers. Schemata can even provide previously stored story details for other stories for which these details have been skipped.

Over time, an individual's fund of generalizations and specific knowledge grows, despite substantial amounts of forgetting. This is not surprising. Several daily lessons about current events, carried on year after year with frequent repetition of the same lesson, are bound to leave their mark, even when learning is purely passive. Since most of these lessons are used to flesh out preformed beliefs, a good deal of systematic error is likely to occur whenever these beliefs are wrong. That is the price people must pay for easing information-processing burdens through the use of schemata.

From the standpoint of average Americans, haphazard news processing is quite satisfactory. Interest in news is comparatively low. Therefore it does not justify great expenditure in time and effort when other things have a higher priority for the individual. But despite lukewarm interest in the news, average Americans want to keep informed because they have been socialized to consider this a civic responsibility. Many of them also want daily reassurance that they are not missing news items that might be personally significant. This combination of normative and personal pressures impels people to give at least cursory attention to news on a regular basis.

Most Americans have also learned to regard news as a form of entertainment. So they try to satisfy two goals simultaneously whenever possible. They scan the news for pieces of information that are important, diverting, and possibly both. The decision to select news or to reject it, therefore, is strongly influenced by an appraisal of the significance and the appeal of a particular piece of news. This fact makes it incumbent upon the media to cover essential stories in ways that capture and hold the public's interest.

IMPLICATIONS FOR AMERICAN DEMOCRACY

The broader political implications of the kind of news-processing behavior that we have depicted need to be considered. . . . The first of these is the capacity of average Americans to acquire enough political information to fulfil the obligations of democratic citizenship. . . .

THE CAPACITY FOR POLITICAL LEARNING

The American mass media supply a vast amount of current political information to average Americans throughout the days, months, and years. This news is mixed in with an even larger amount of nonpolitical information. All in all, no single person, even spending all waking hours in news consumption, could begin to pay attention to all of it, let alone absorb it successfully.

Our panelists demonstrated that people from all walks of life, endowed with varying capabilities, can manage to extract substantial amounts of political knowledge from this flood of information. All panelists had mastered the art of paying selective attention to news and engaging in the various forms of relatedness searches. All had acquired schemata into which they were able to fit incoming political information. All were able to work with an adequate array of schema dimensions, and all frequently used multiple themes in their various schemata. All had adopted culturally sanctioned values as the schematic framework into which schemata covering more specific matters were then embedded.

The differences among the panelists in the use of their processing skills were surprisingly minor. Largely, they were matters of degree in the use of various skills, such as segmenting and checking, and differences in coping with highly complex information drawn from settings remote from the individual's life. The high-interest groups generally processed more political information in greater detail and remembered it better than the low-interest groups. But basic choice and processing criteria were similar. Difficulties in access to news led to more selective processing and to combining attention to news with other activities. With some exceptions, interest and motivation to absorb specific information predicted learning better than education or expertise. Some processing differences were linked to needs created by life-style. Insofar as life-style coincides with demographic categories, such as age, sex, and ethnicity, life-style differences take on the appearance of demographic differences.

On balance, the verdict is clear. Average Americans are capable of extracting enough meaningful political information from the flood of news to which they are exposed to perform the modest number of citizenship functions that American society expects of them. They keep informed to a limited extent about the majority of significant publicized events. They also learn enough about major political candidates to cast a moderately thoughtful vote and make some judgments about post-election performance. Our findings show that "no opinion" replies often involved individuals who did have opinions but were afraid to express them until coaxed to do so. Fear of sounding stupid or uncertainty about the merits of particular opinions and the adequacy of their information explained their initial reluctance to reply.

Ideally, one may wish that expectations about the knowledge that citizens need were higher and that the social pressures to keep well informed were greater. One may wonder whether changes in news production and news processing might enhance the quality of citizenship. But answers to such questions are speculative and controversial and generally ignore the fact that people lead complex lives that permit only a peripheral involvement in politics.

Critics of current patterns often question whether people can fulfil citizenship needs adequately when they lack specific knowledge and when they base election choices largely on assessments of the candidates' personal qualities. Shouldn't well-informed people depend more on information about issues for voting decisions? Doesn't effective citizenship require that one remembers the name of one's representative or knows the length of a senatorial term? Isn't it essential for Americans in the 1980s to be able to locate Afghanistan on a map? I believe that the answer is no. One can judge the political qualifications of candidates without knowing their precise positions on issues. One does not have to know the name of one's representative or the length of a senatorial term to understand the role Congress plays in the political process. And one need not be able to locate Afghanistan on a map. . . .

Despite lip service to the judgmental criteria advocated by political elites, most people select their political judgment criteria in their own ways. Judged from the perspective of personal efficiency, these criteria appear to work well. Take the example of selecting political leaders largely on the basis of personality. This process makes eminently good sense,

> given the capacities and inclinations of the average voter. Information about personal qualities is the only information which the average layman, remote from the political scene, can appraise intelligently. . . . People may properly feel that a president who is "a good man, capable and experienced" can tackle any kind of problem. At the time of the election it may be uncertain in which areas a candidate's severest test will come. Therefore it may be best to concentrate on general leadership qualities and characteristics of integrity and trustworthiness, rather than dwelling on competence in a variety of areas.[1]

The intellectual abilities of average citizens have also been called into question because social scientists have been unable to find the kind of belief systems for which they were looking. We have indicated that people do have belief systems, although they are not the grand edifices of the researchers' dreams. Broad value principles are the closest thing to an overarching belief structure. Beyond these, people do make causal and other connections among their schemata. The fact that processing involves relatedness searches also shows that there is continual awareness of similarities and connections.

The multiplicity of approaches used in schema construction leads to substantial flexibility and diversity in organizing information. This makes patterns of beliefs far less predictable than the patterns expected as the result of previous belief system research, which envisioned liberalism and conservatism as the cores around which belief structures were built. A multiplicity of organizing principles is intuitively sound. One should not expect to squeeze or stretch the multifaceted problems of the political world into a single Procrustean bed. Taking flexible positions is sensible whenever choices are not clear-cut and present themselves in widely divergent contexts. Rather than worrying about the public's rationality, one may well wonder about "the unwillingness of many political leaders and commentators to accept the public's 'post-ideological' maturity, and their insistence that the public should either endorse the left's traditional affirmation of the state or the right's rejection of it."[2]

NOTES

1. Doris A. Graber, "Press Coverage and Voter Reaction in the 1968 Presidential Election," *Political Science Quarterly* 89(1974):96–97.

2. Everett Carll Ladd, "Politics in the 80's: An Electorate at Odds with Itself," *Public Opinion* 5(1983):3.

C. AGENDA-SETTING

16. NEWS THAT MATTERS

Shanto Iyengar and Donald R. Kinder

How do people become aware of issues not directly affecting their lives? How do they decide which issues are important ones our society should resolve? And how is the decision made about which important issues should be resolved first? This process is called *agenda-setting*.

The power of the news media in this process has been the subject of several studies.* Although scholars have found the news media do play a role in agenda-setting, the nature of that effect is conditioned by the type of issue and the news audience. Issues where the audience relies primarily on the media for comprehension are more likely to be placed on the public's agenda by the press. And individuals who are more likely to be influenced by the agenda-setting power of the press are those who are not typically in the audience for news. These include people who are less educated and politically less active or interested.[†]

*See, for example, Maxwell E. McCombs and Donald L. Shaw, "The Agenda-Setting Function of the Mass Media," *Public Opinion Quarterly* 36 (1972):176–87; Donald L. Shaw and Maxwell E. McCombs, *The Emergence of American Political Issues* (St. Paul: Minn.: West Publishing, 1977); and Donald L. Weaver et al., *Media Agenda-Setting in a Presidential Election* (New York: Praeger, 1981).

†Shanto Iyengar and Donald R. Kinder, *News That Matters* (Chicago: University of Chicago Press, 1987), pp. 47–62.

Agenda-setting has political consequences. The selection that follows is based on research demonstrating some of the political effects of the media's agenda-setting power. The authors, Shanto Iyengar and Donald R. Kinder, decisively reject the minimal-effects theory, as the title of their selection implies.[‡] They argue that television news shapes voters' attitudes by setting the agenda for the public. But they go beyond the previous agenda-setting research by contending that TV news actually affects voters' judgments of politics. Television news primes voters by influencing the standards by which people judge policies and individuals. Through the process of framing stories, television news impacts voters' assessments.

When television news makes linkages to other individuals or events, public assessment of that individual or event is affected. For example, when TV news attributes the state of the economy to the president's policies, people's assessment of the president's performance will be affected.

The research presented by Iyengar and Kinder has dramatic implications for the study of media role in American politics. If media messages affect people's assessment of political leaders and policies, then the potential influence on the direction of politics is enormous. Driven by an assessment cultivated by media messages, people may turn for or against a political leader or policy. A president's ability to govern could be undermined by media linkages. A proposed military intervention framed in the context of Vietnam will evoke different images from one compared to the Persian Gulf or Grenada. Television news, by offering a litany of policy failures or by setting expectations of resolution of irresolvable problems, will doom a presidency.

The power to determine the standards by which the electorate will judge performance is enormous. If the media hold this power it constitutes the ability to manipulate American politics.

Shanto Iyengar is professor of political science and communication studies at the University of California, Los Angeles. He is also author of *Is Anyone Responsible? How Television Frames Political Issues* (1991). Donald R. Kinder is professor of political science and psychology at the University of Michigan. He is the author of articles in journals such as the *American Political Science Review*, the *American Journal of Political Science*, and *Public Opinion Quarterly*.

. . . [T]elevision news does indeed influence the priorities the American public assigns to national problems. But the power of the networks does not end with viewers' political agendas. . . . [W]e take up the more subtle and more consequential possibility of what we will call priming. *By calling attention to some matters while ignoring others, television news influences the standards by which governments, presidents, policies, and candidates for public office are judged.*

Priming refers to changes in the standards that people use to make political evaluations. In assessing the performance of a government, a president, a policy, or a candidate, citizens can apply any number of standards. . . . According to the priming hypothesis, should television news become preoccupied with, say, the prospects of nuclear annihilation, then citizens would judge the president primarily by his success, as they see it, in reducing the risk of war. Should television news shift its attention to the economy, citizens would follow suit, now evaluating the president according to success, as they see it, in maintaining prosperity—at least according to the priming hypothesis.

. . . We develop a theory of priming, argue for its psychological plausibility,

[‡]From *News That Matters* (Chicago: University of Chicago Press, 1987), pp. 63–65, 106–11. Footnotes have been omitted.

and then test it against a series of television experiments focusing on presidential performance.

A THEORY OF PRIMING

For theoretical guidance we have drawn upon ideas developed within the information processing perspective in psychology. Our general point of departure is Simon's observation that "human thinking powers are very modest when compared with the complexities of the environments in which human beings live. Faced with complexity and uncertainty, lacking the wits to optimize, they must be content to satisfy—to find 'good enough' solutions to their problems and 'good enough' courses of action" (1979, 3). Like Simon, we find it useful to begin with the modest assumptions about human cognitive capacity typically made in psychological theory and corroborated in psychological research.

A major conclusion of such research is that people do not pay attention to everything. To do so would breed paralysis. Attention is highly selective; people notice only particular features of special consequence. Because of this fundamental limitation, the impressions we form of others tend to be organized around a few central themes (Asch 1946). With respect to the impressions we form of presidents, such themes might include the political party he represents, the policies he favors or opposes, his performance in office—the achievements and failures he has appeared to bring about, the kind of person he seems to be, particularly with respect to his apparent competence and integrity, the racial, religious, class and ethnic groups he stands for and against, and the general values he appears to embrace. These themes represent the central standards against which presidents are measured.

A second conclusion of research on judgment is that rather than undertaking exhaustive analysis, people ordinarily prefer heuristics—intuitive shortcuts and simple rules of thumb. One such heuristic is reliance upon information that is most *accessible*. When asked to evaluate a particular president, Americans do not consider everything they know. Nor do they even consider everything they know relevant to the central themes listed above. Instead, they draw upon a sample of what they know, and a sample of convenience at that. Some considerations prove decisive; others are ignored altogether. The relative importance of each depends in part on its momentary accessibility. Fischhoff, Slovic, and Lichtenstein put the general point well: "People solve problems, including the determination of their own values, with what comes to mind. The more detailed, exacting, and creative their inferential process, the more likely they are to think of all they know about the problem. The briefer that process becomes, the more they will be controlled by the relative accessibility of various considerations" (1980, 127). Under ordinary circumstances, judgments about the president are offered rather casually. Because the judgment process is seldom "detailed, exacting, and creative," judgments of the president depend less on the entire repertoire of people's knowledge and more on which aspects of their knowledge happen to come to mind.

The importance of accessibility as a heuristic device in everyday judgment is supported by considerable experimental evidence. Consider these examples: (1) Americans are more likely to say that they pay a fair share of federal income tax if they have just been asked a battery of questions probing their support for popular programs like aid to education and environmental protection than if they have not (Turner and Krauss 1978). Presumably, questions about particular and popular uses of tax monies primed people to take such uses into account when they decided whether their own tax burden was fair; (2) Americans report themselves to be substantially less interested in politics if they are first reminded of their limited political knowledge by being taken through a series of difficult questions regarding the activities of their representative in Washington, than if they are asked about their interest before this series of questions (Bishop, Oldendick, and Tuchfarber 1982); (3) More generally, Kahneman and Tversky have demonstrated that sizable shifts in choice can be produced by "seemingly inconsequential changes in the formulation of choice problems" (Tversky and Kahneman 1981, 453; also see Kahneman and Tversky 1979). Framing the problem in one way rather than in a logically equivalent alternative way can radically alter which options are chosen and which foregone.

The upshot of all this research is not that judgment in general or political judgment in particular is capricious. Indeed, Kahneman and Tversky offer their own prospect theory as a systematic alternative to the conventional theory of rational choice they attack. The point is rather that a person's judgment depends in part on what comes to mind—on considerations that are, for whatever reason and however briefly, accessible.

To a considerable degree, what information is accessible for presidential evaluations and what is not is a matter of circumstance. When political circumstances change, what comes to the citizen's mind most readily will also change. The circumstantial basis for judgments of presidential performance no doubt has many sources, but among the most important may be television news. We suggest that the standards citizens use to judge a president may be substantially determined by which stories newscasts choose to cover and, consequently, which considerations are made generally accessible. The more attention television news pays to a particular problem—the more frequently a problem area is primed—the more viewers should incorporate what they know about that problem into their overall judgment of the president. . . .

VOTING IN PRESIDENTIAL ELECTIONS

We turn . . . to the part priming might play in presidential elections. From the voters' perspective, contests for the presidency are nothing if not complex. They are partly a clash between the major parties, partly an ideological struggle over the poli-

cies government should pursue, partly a judgment on the administration's performance over the past four years and a comparative appraisal of what sorts of people the
candidates seem to be, partly a reflection of the particular feelings that the candidates evoke, and much more. Because so many elements may plausibly enter into
the voter's choice, the prospects for priming seem great.

THE CASE OF 1980

The 1980 presidential campaign may be a particularly telling case in point. Recall
that as election day neared, the race for the presidency seemed too close to call. By
most accounts Ronald Reagan was ahead, but his lead over President Carter was
tiny, and the unusually large number of undecided voters made the contest difficult
to predict. In election-eve surveys with large samples of probable voters, the
CBS–*New York Times* Poll found Reagan ahead by a single percentage point; the
ABC–Harris Poll reported Reagan's lead to be five percentage points; the Gallup
Poll had Reagan ahead by three points. A few days later, Reagan won decisively,
receiving 51 percent of the vote to Carter's 41 percent. Why did the polls perform
so poorly?

One possibility is that the polls were basically correct, but that large numbers
of voters shifted toward Reagan between the time the interviewing was completed
and election day. Most conspicuous in the campaign's final days was the chain of
events that appeared to promise the resolution of the Iranian hostage crisis. These
developments, and the ultimate collapse of the negotiations, were given enormous
and detailed attention by the press. On the night before the election, the three network news programs each devoted much of their broadcasts to a recapitulation of
the Iranian crisis, the taking of the American embassy in Teheran, the months of
stalled negotiations, the failure of the rescue mission, and especially the multiplying
complexities involved in meeting the Iranians' demands. Perhaps such coverage
dealt a devastating and fatal blow to the president's reelection chances, inducing
many voters to conceive of the decision they confronted as a referendum on the
Carter presidency's performance on foreign affairs.

This claim is certainly congenial to our theoretical perspective. It is simply a
particular—though particularly consequential—version of priming. . . . Our . . .
experiment was designed to reconstruct the priming effects, if any, associated with
the intensive coverage of the Iranian crisis in the closing days of the 1980 presidential contest.

AN EXPERIMENTAL RECONSTRUCTION
OF THE 1980 CAMPAIGN

Experiment 7 was conducted in June of 1982. Participants were recruited from the
New Haven community in the usual fashion and randomly assigned to one of three
treatment conditions. Participants in the neutral or control treatment were shown a

collection of nine recent network news stories compiled from the Vanderbilt University Television News Archive. Participants assigned to the hostage treatment saw the identical set, with two exceptions. Instead of a story on the endangered status of the California Condor, they watched a story from the final days of the 1980 campaign that described Iranian demands for the release of the hostages, concluding with Iran's threat that if such demands were not met, the hostages would be tried as spies. Then in place of a story devoted to the trans-Siberian railroad, hostage treatment participants watched a clip that featured Ayatollah Khomeini addressing militant students in Teheran while the correspondent described Iran as waiting to hear from Washington regarding its demands.

The major purpose of experiment 7 was to assess whether viewers primed with hostage crisis news stories relied upon foreign affairs in evaluating President Carter's overall performance more heavily than did those in the neutral treatment. An additional purpose was to see whether priming can be produced by good news as well as by bad. Participants randomly assigned to a third treatment saw the same broadcasts, but this time with two stories inserted that recapitulated Jimmy Carter's greatest triumph in foreign affairs—the signing of the Camp David Peace Accords. This treatment will enable us to ascertain whether stories that focus on achievements can trigger priming, just as stories that focus on failures can.

We tested for priming in experiment 7 by comparing the impact of viewers' ratings of Carter's performance in foreign affairs on their assessment of his overall performance as president across the three experimental conditions. We actually examined priming in four separate tests, each involving a distinct component of Carter's foreign affairs performance. Participants were asked to evaluate: (1) President Carter's management of the hostage crisis (most thought he had bungled it); (2) his performance at the Camp David Middle East negotiations (most gave him high marks); (3) the power and moral authority exercised around the world by the United States under the Carter administration (most viewers thought that U.S. influence had declined); and, finally, (4) President Carter's effectiveness in dealing with world problems (most believed Carter only modestly effective). If the priming hypothesis is correct, each of these aspects of Carter's foreign affairs performance should exert a greater impact on general assessments of the Carter presidency when television news dwells upon foreign affairs.

The results from the first two tests, those that involve specific aspects of President Carter's performance in foreign affairs, are displayed in Table 1. They demonstrate that priming can indeed be triggered by achievements as well as by problems. Stories about Carter's success at Camp David raised the significance of foreign affairs performance just as did stories that recapitulated the sorry history of the hostage crisis.

The results also suggest that priming requires a close correspondence between the judgment to be primed and the news story that triggers the priming. The importance accorded to Carter's management of the hostage crisis in evaluations of his overall performance was magnified by exposure to news about the crisis, but not by exposure to news about Camp David. In complementary fashion, the impact of

TABLE 1

Priming Presidential Evaluations: The Impact of Hostage Crisis and Camp David Performance on Evaluations of President Carter's Overall Performance as a Function of TV News Coverage: Experiment 7 (ordinary least squares estimates)

	TV COVERAGE OF CAMP DAVID	NO TV COVERAGE (BASELINE)	TV COVERAGE OF HOSTAGE CRISIS
Camp David performance	.43	.08	.30
Hostage crisis performance	.37	.31	.53*

$*p < .20$ (for difference between primed and baseline impact).

viewers' evaluations of Carter's management of the Camp David treaty on their evaluations of his overall performance was materially enhanced by exposure to Camp David broadcasts, less by hostage crisis stories.

Table 2 moves the tests of priming to a more general plane. One recurring theme in the 1980 presidential campaign was the alleged decline of American influence in world affairs, a theme that the Reagan campaign stressed repeatedly and which the hostage crisis seemed to typify. Row 1 [of Table 2] indicates whether news about the hostage crisis (or about Camp David) strengthened the extent to which viewers measured the Carter presidency against this standard. The answer is a resounding no: row 1 reveals not a trace of priming. Notice that the theme of declining American influence in world affairs was important. Viewers who believed that the position of the U.S. overseas had eroded during Carter's tenure evaluated Mr. Carter much less favorably on average than did viewers who believed the United States was as respected abroad during the Carter Administration as ever. But this substantial relationship was not augmented by television coverage of foreigners.

The results presented across the second row of Table 2 suggest that this failure is due not to the sheer generality of the theme of declining American influence overseas, but to its content. Row 2 indicates considerable priming at work on judgments of President Carter's effectiveness in dealing with foreign countries, the second general theme. And once again, priming is induced both by presidential achievements as well as by presidential problems. In each instance, moreover, the

TABLE 2

Priming Presidential Evaluations: The Impact of Sense of U.S. Decline and Carter's Effectiveness with Foreign Countries on Evaluations of President Carter's Overall Performance as a Function of TV News Coverage: Experiment 7 (ordinary least squares estimates)

	TV COVERAGE OF CAMP DAVID	NO TV COVERAGE (BASELINE)	TV COVERAGE OF HOSTAGE CRISIS
U.S. decline	.63	.65	.60*
Carter's effectiveness with foreign countries	.57	.63	.69**

$*p < .20$ (for difference between primed and baseline impact).
$**p < .05$.

effect is substantial. Exposure to news about Camp David or about the hostage crisis produced a doubling of the impact of ratings of Carter's effectiveness in dealing with foreign nations on evaluations of his overall performance as president.

A sense of how sizable these priming effects are can be had from the following exercise. Suppose two prospective voters, Smith and Jones, are identical in all ways except that Smith judges President Carter to have been generally effective in dealing with foreign countries (a score of two on our five-point scale) while Jones judges the president to have been generally ineffective (a score of four). If Smith and Jones were assigned together to the control condition in our experiment, this one difference would translate into a modest difference in their overall evaluation of President Carter's performance: Smith would have a slightly positive overall evaluation of Mr. Carter while Jones would be slightly negative. If, instead, Smith and Jones viewed television news stories about the hostage crisis, the difference of one point in their ratings of Carter's effectiveness in foreign relations would be much more consequential. Having been primed with stories about the Iranian crisis, Smith would now evaluate President Carter rather positively while Jones's evaluation would be sharply negative. Such a difference begins to suggest the part priming might play in presidential election outcomes in general and in the 1980 presidential contest in particular.

SUMMARY AND CONCLUSION

Our . . . election experiment . . . shows that priming operates on the choices voters make. The priorities that are uppermost in voters' minds as they go to the polls to select a president . . . appear to be powerfully shaped by the last-minute preoccupations of television news.

One reason for the strength of these effects may be that our news manipulations focused on events, outcomes, or considerations for which the candidates were unquestionably responsible. . . . [P]riming is enhanced when news coverage interprets events in such a way as to imply an intimate connection between the events and the target of judgment. . . . [O]ur experimental analogue of the final days of the 1980 presidential campaign emphasized either the Camp David Accords or the hostage crisis, both of which were widely interpreted as President Carter's personal triumph and tragedy, respectively. From this point of view, the magnitude of the results may seem understandable, if no less unsettling.

The election-day experiment contained two further lessons that bear repeating here. In the first place, priming can apparently be set off by achievements as well as by failures. Flattering stories about the Camp David Accords were just as effective in triggering priming in viewers' evaluations of President Carter as were grim stories about the hostage crisis. We do not mean to suggest, based on a single comparison, that achievements and failures will always be equally and symmetrically effective. Rather we regard this one result merely as a demonstration that priming can be triggered by both bad news and good news.

A second lesson is that priming may require a close fit between the domain of judgment that is the intended target of priming and the news stories that constitute the prime itself. This is suggested by two results. First, the importance granted President Carter's handling of the hostage crisis in the president's overall evaluation was enhanced by exposure to hostage crisis stories, but not by exposure to Camp David stories. Similarly, the impact of viewers' evaluations of Carter's success at Camp David on their evaluations of his overall performance was enhanced substantially by exposure to Camp David broadcasts, less by hostage crisis stories. Second, coverage of either the Camp David Peace Accords or the negotiations regarding the release of the hostages that took place during the 1980 campaign's last days induced viewers to weigh President Carter's effectiveness in dealing with foreign countries more heavily in their overall judgment of his performance as president, but not to weigh any more heavily the theme of American decline in world affairs. The first—Carter's international effectiveness—is directly and strongly implicated by the triumph of Camp David and the collapse of the Iranian negotiations. The second—the United States' declining power and prestige—is also implied, but less directly and less strongly. In the latter instance, more inferential work is required on the viewer's part, work that evidently few viewers were prepared to undertake. These results suggest that in some respects the public is admirably discriminating. Priming appears to depend heavily on how closely the pictures and stories that appear in the news correspond to the choices and judgments viewers are called upon to make.

By the verdict of this chapter, television news exerts a powerful influence on the electoral process. Should this influence be welcomed or deplored? Does television news contribute to democracy or undermine it? Without promising definitive answers, we take up such questions in the next and final chapter. Our purpose there is to draw out the implications of our findings for the practice and promise of democratic politics in the age of television.

BIBLIOGRAPHY

Asch, S.E. 1946. Forming Impressions of Personality. *Journal of Abnormal and Social Psychology* 41:258–90.

Bishop, G.F., R.W. Oldendick, and A.J. Tuchfarber. 1982. Political Information Processing: Question Order and Context Effects. *Political Behavior* 4:177–200.

Fischhoff, B., P. Slovic, and S. Lichtenstein. 1980. Knowing What You Want: Measuring Labile Values. In *Cognitive Processes in Choice and Decision Behavior*, ed. by T. Wallsten. Hillsdale, N.J.: Erlbaum.

Kahneman, D., and A. Tversky. 1979. Prospect Theory: An Analysis of Decision Under Risk. *Econometrica* 47:263–91.

Simon, H.A. 1979. *Models of Thought*. New Haven: Yale University Press.

Turner, C.F., and Krauss, E. 1978. Fallible Indicators of the Objective State of the Nation. *American Psychologist* 33:456–70.

Tversky, A., and D. Kahneman. 1981. The Framing of Decisions and the Psychology of Choice. *Science* 211:453–58.

D. POLITICAL PARTICIPATION

17. THE SPIRAL OF SILENCE

Elisabeth Noelle-Neumann

Are people more or less inclined to participate in politics because of the news media? The question has piqued the interest of some scholars, especially since the late 1960s when voter turnout at the polling places experienced a dramatic decline and feelings of voter apathy and frustration rose.* With the simultaneous expansion of television news as a source for political information, some scholars have linked the voter's sense of political inefficacy with media messages.†

The classic work on media effect on political participation was written by Elisabeth Noelle-Neumann. This German public-opinion researcher proposes a theory that integrates public opinion and media messages to predict political behavior. She posits that individuals assess their environment to determine whether their opinions are socially acceptable. If they perceive them to be so, they are willing to engage in public debate. If not, they remain silent.

She argues that this behavior provokes a "spiral of silence" where those who hold one side of an issue become increasingly silent and the other side appears to gain greater acceptance due to the lack of competition. The media play a critical role by affecting the perception that individuals have of the climate of public opinion in the world around them.

Noelle-Neumann's theory sparked a lively debate among communication scholars and political scientists. Her conclusions have been challenged as ignoring the importance of minority solidarity even in the face of majority opinion as well as public sympathy with the underdog often felt by Americans. The theory also has been criticized as treating media messages as monolithic.‡

But Noelle-Neumann's theory has implications for the role of the media in stimulating public debate. If individuals respond as Noelle-Neumann hypothesizes, then media messages that portray a consensus on some public policy topic will militate against public debate over the issue. If a consensus forms on candidate viability, electoral choices could be diminished as voters perceive that a certain candidacy is a hopeless cause. Third-party candidates claim such a consensus against their viability is fostered by the media and hampers their ability to

---

*For a discussion of these trends, see Angus Campbell, *The Sense of Well-Being in America: Recent Patterns and Trends* (New York: McGraw Hill, 1981), and Seymour Martin Lipset, *The Confidence Gap* (New York: Free Press, 1983).

†See, for example, Michael J. Robinson, "Public Affairs Television and the Growth of Public Malaise: The Case of the Selling of the Pentagon," *American Political Science Review* 70 (June 1976):409-32; Arthur H. Miller, Edie N. Goldenberg, and Lutz Erbring, "Type-Set Politics: Impact of Newspapers on Public Confidence," *American Political Science Review* 73 (March 1979):67–84; and Garret J. O'Keefe and Harold Mendelsohn, "Nonvoting and the Role of the Media," in Charles Winick, ed., *Mass Media and Deviance* (Beverly Hills, Calif.: Sage Publications, Inc., 1978).

‡For a critique of Noelle-Neumann's theory, see Keith R. Sanders, Lynda Lee Kaid, and Dan Nimmo, eds., *Political Communication Yearbook 1984* (Carbondale: Southern Illinois University Press, 1985).

acquire legitimacy. During the 1992 presidential campaign, independent candidate Ross Perot may have predicted such treatment and decided to forego it by quitting a serious race to win the presidency and instead waging a moral campaign.

Journalists as a group could be subject to the spiral of silence phenomenon as they respond to elite journalists' news priorities and assessments of politics and what they perceive as public opinion. For example, journalistic defenses of political figures such as Vice-President Dan Quayle or Senator Jesse Helms of North Carolina are rare, although a few journalists consider themselves political conservatives.

Noelle-Neumann's theory is one of the few holistic theories of media role in politics.** It deserves our attention and examination. (The two parties she speaks of—Christian Democrats and Social Democrats—are the major political parties in Germany.)

Elisabeth Noelle-Neumann is professor of communication research at the University of Mainz. She also has been a working journalist and past president of the World Association for Public Opinion Research.

. . . The hypothesis came to me out of the student unrest at the end of the sixties and the beginning of the seventies; I probably owe it to one particular student. I met her one day in the hall outside the lecture room and noticed that she was wearing a Christian Democratic button on her jacket.

"I didn't know you were a Christian Democratic supporter," I said to her. "I'm not," she said. "I just put the button on to see what it's like."

I met her again at noon. She was not wearing the button, and I asked about the change. "It was too awful," she said. "I took it off."

In the context of the commotion that characterized those first years of the new Ostpolitik, this was understandable. Followers of the Social Democrats and of the Christian Democrats might be equal in numbers, but they were far from equal in energy, enthusiasm, or in willingness to express and display their convictions. Only Social Democratic buttons and emblems appeared publicly, so it was no wonder that the relative strengths of the two parties were incorrectly assessed. A peculiar dynamic developed at this point. Those who were convinced the new Ostpolitik was right thought their beliefs eventually would be adopted by everyone. So these people expressed themselves openly, and self-confidently defended their views. Those who rejected the Ostpolitik felt themselves left out; they withdrew, and fell silent.

This very restraint made the view that was receiving vocal support appear to be stronger than it really was and the other view weaker. Observations made in one context spread to another and encouraged people either to proclaim their views or to swallow them and keep quiet until, in a spiraling process, the one view dominated the public scene and the other disappeared from public awareness as its adherents became mute. This is the process that can be called a "spiral of silence."

. . . The fear of isolation seems to be the force that sets the spiral of silence in motion. To run with the pack is a relatively happy state of affairs; but if you can't, because you won't share publicly in what seems to be a universally acclaimed con-

**From *The Spiral of Silence: Public Opinion—Our Social Skin* (Chicago: University of Chicago Press, 1984), pp. 4–5, 6–7, 154–64. Reprinted by permission. Footnotes and some tables have been omitted.

viction, you can at least remain silent, as a second choice, so that others can put up with you. . . .

****

"I have experienced the spiral of silence in my club." "I've seen it at work in my volleyball team." "That's just the way things are in my business." In this way people often confirm the concept of a spiral of silence. This is as it should be, for there are varied opportunities to observe this all too human conforming behavior. Experiences such as we all have in small groups are parts of the process. When public opinion is forming, identical or similar experiences across various groups lead observant individuals to suppose that "everyone" will think the same way. Something unique happens, however, as soon as the spiral of silence starts to develop in public; it is this blending with publicity that gives the process its irresistible force. The element of public attention is brought into the process most effectively through the mass media. In fact, mass media objectify publicity—shapeless, faceless, unreachable, immovable public attention.

FEELING POWERLESS FACING THE MASS MEDIA

Communication may be classified as one-sided or two-sided (a conversation, for example, is two-sided); as indirect or direct (a conversation is direct); as public or private (a conversation is generally private). The mass media are one-sided, indirect, public forms of communication, thus contrasting threefold with the most natural form of human communication, the conversation. This is why individuals faced with the mass media feel so helpless. In every survey where people are asked, who in today's society has too much power, the mass media are ranked right there at the top. This powerlessness is expressed in two ways. The first occurs when a person tries to gain public attention (in Luhmann's sense) and the media, in their selection processes, choose not to give that person attention. The same thing occurs if there are unsuccessful efforts to gain public attention for an idea, a piece of information, or a perspective. This may result in a desperate outbreak in the presence of the guardians who have denied access to public attention—someone throws a bottle of ink at a Rubens in an art museum in Munich; a bottle of acid is thrown at a Rembrandt in an Amsterdam museum; someone hijacks an airplane in order to borrow public attention for some message or cause.

The second aspect of powerlessness comes into play when the media are used as a pillory; when they draw faceless public attention to an individual who is surrendered to them as a scapegoat to be "exhibited." He cannot defend himself; he cannot deflect the slings and arrows. The means of rebuttal are grotesque in their comparative weakness, in their awkwardness compared to the polished objectivity of the media. Those who freely consent to appear on a television talk show or to give a television interview without belonging to the inner circle of media gatekeepers are putting their heads into the jaws of a tiger.

A NEW START FOR RESEARCH ON MEDIA EFFECTS

Public attention can be experienced from two viewpoints, from that of the individual who is exposed to it or who is ignored by it—which we have just described—and from the perspective of the collective event, when hundreds of thousands, when millions of people observe their environment and either speak or keep quiet, thereby creating public opinion. Observation of the environment has two sources; public opinion is nourished from two springs: the individual undertakes direct observation in his or her environment, and receives information about the environment through the mass media. Today, television with its color and sound creates extensive confusion between one's own observation and mediated observation. "Good evening," the weatherman said at the start of his television weather report. "Good evening," answered the guests in a hotel in which I was spending my vacation.

People have long been questioning the effects of the mass media, expecting a very simple, direct relationship between cause and effect. They have assumed that the statements in any one medium cause changes in opinion, or—also to be considered as an effect—reinforce opinion in the audience. The relationship between mass media and audiences is somehow likened to a private conversation between two persons, one saying something and the other being strengthened or converted. The reality of media effects is much more complex, and differs considerably from the individual conversation model. Walter Lippmann taught us this when he showed how the media imprint stereotypes through innumerable repetitions, and how these become building blocks in that "in-between world" which intervenes between people and the objective external world to serve as their pseudo-reality. This is the implication of Luhmann's agenda-setting function, the selection of what the public must attend to, of indicating what is urgent, which questions everyone must be concerned with. All of this is decided by the media.

Moreover, the media influence the individual's perception of what can be said or done without danger of isolation. And finally we encounter something that could be called the articulation function of the mass media. This brings us back, then, to the starting point of our analysis of the spiral of silence, the train test as a paradigm situation for a small group in which public opinion is created through talk and reluctance to talk. For the moment, however, we will remain with the topic of how persons experience the climate of opinion through the mass media.

PUBLIC NOTICE LEGITIMATES

Everyone who read reprints of the purported "memorial address" that was put out by a group of students on the occasion of the death of Buback, a federal prosecutor murdered by terrorists in 1977, knew that more was involved in the reprint than mere documentation. The text, brought out under the pseudonym "Mescaleros," was reissued, ostensibly, to let the widest possible circles have the opportunity to read the original and thereby form their own judgment of it. The active publicity attending its republication increased the text's impact. Despite mildly disapproving editorial comments that barely concealed an underlying approbation, the publicity created the impression that one might secretly be pleased to hear that a federal prosecutor had been murdered, and might publicly express oneself to that effect without running the risk of isolation. Something like this occurs whenever a tabooed behavior receives public notice—for whatever reasons—without being painted as evil, something to shun or pillory. It is quite easy to sense whether we are dealing with publicity that stigmatizes or condones the behavior. To publicize behavior that violates norms without strongly disapproving of it makes it more fit for polite society, more acceptable. Everyone can see that engaging in this behavior no longer makes one isolated. Those who break social norms are often eager to receive the merest hint of sympathetic publicity; and their eagerness is well founded, for the rule, the norm, is thereby weakened. . . .

PUBLIC OPINION HAS TWO SOURCES— ONE, THE MASS MEDIA

Early in 1976, half a year before the German federal election, the full resources of survey research instrumentation and observation were for the first time set up to trace the development of a climate of opinion and the resulting formation of voting intentions according to the spiral of silence theory. The principal method was the repeated interviewing of a representative sample of voters, technically called a panel study. In addition, normal representative surveys were used to keep track of developments. Two surveys among journalists were carried out, and the political broadcasts of the two national television networks were recorded on videotape. . . .

We had developed pertinent questions starting with the [German] federal election of 1965. These involved the voting intentions of the respondents, their beliefs concerning who was going to win the election, their willingness to demonstrate publicly their political preferences, their overall interest in politics, and their level of media use (newspapers and magazines read and television watched), with special attention to political broadcasts.

BEFORE THE 1976 ELECTION, A SUDDEN CHANGE IN THE CLIMATE OF OPINION

In July [1976], during the height of the vacation season, a set of completed questionnaires arrived at the Allensbach Institute. They constituted the second wave of questioning of a panel of around 1,000 voters, representative of the total West German population. I was staying in Tessin, Switzerland, at the time, enjoying the cloudless summer days, and I vividly remember the contrast between the broad green leaves in the vineyards and the granite table with the computer output spread upon it. It was a few months before the election and not the right time to forget about work altogether. One thing was emerging clearly from the printouts. The most important measurement, the question concerning people's perceptions of the climate of opinion, showed a dramatic deterioration for the Christian Democrats. The question was: "Of course no one can know for sure, but what do you think: Who is going to win the coming federal election? Who will receive the most votes: the Christian Democratic Union or the Social Democratic Party/Free Democratic Party?" In March of 1976, panel respondents gave a 20 percent advantage to the Christian Democratic Union, expecting that they would triumph at the polls, but now the sentiment had changed and the estimates for the Christian Democratic Union and the Social Democratic Party/Free Democratic Party were only 7 percent apart. A little while later the Social Democratic Party/Free Democratic Party overtook the Christian Democratic Union.

My first guess was that the supporters of the Christian Democrats had behaved about as they had done in 1972, remaining publicly silent and not indicating, even before the election campaign began, what their convictions were. I knew that the campaign leadership of all the parties, including that of the Christian Democratic Union, had tried to make clear to their supporters how important it was to affirm their position publicly; but, as we know, people are cautious and afraid. I telephoned Allensbach and asked for the results of the questions about willingness to stand up for a party publicly. The finding was puzzling; it did not fit the theory. Compared to the results for March, the supporters of the Social Democratic Party tended to be lazier than those of the Christian Democratic Union. In answer to the question of what they were willing to do for their party, and given a list of possible activities including the answer "none of these," between March and July, supporters of the Social Democratic Party saying they would do nothing increased from 34 to 43 percent, while supporters of the Christian Democratic Union stayed almost constant (38 percent in March and 39 percent in July said they would do nothing). The Christian Democratic supporters' declining willingness to stand up for their party could not explain the change in the climate of opinion.

WITH THE EYE OF TELEVISION

I then thought of the two sources we have for obtaining information about the distribution of opinions in our environment: firsthand observation of reality and observation of reality through the eyes of the media. So I ordered a tabulation from Allensbach recording the data according to who had read much or little in the press, and watched much or little television. When the results were spread out on the table, they looked as simple as a primer. Only those who had more frequently observed the environment through the eyes of television had perceived a change in the climate; those who had observed their environment without television's eyes had noticed no change in climate at all (Table 1). . . .

REPORTERS DID NOT MANIPULATE; THEY PRESENTED WHAT THEY SAW

In order at least to approach the solution to this riddle, we analyzed the surveys of journalists and the videotapes of political broadcasts during that election year. If one starts with Walter Lippmann's thesis, it was not at all surprising that television

TABLE 1

Concerning the Second Source of Public Opinion, Impressions from the Eye of Television, Regular TV Viewers Perceived a Worsening of the Climate of Opinion for the Christian Democrats, but Persons Who Saw Little TV Between Spring and Summer Noticed No Worsening of the Climate for the Christian Democrats.

Question: "Of course, no one can know for sure, but what do you think: Who is going to win the coming federal election? Who will receive the most votes—the Christian Democratic Union or the Social Democratic Party/Free Democratic Party?"

	FREQUENT VIEWERS POLITICAL TV BROADCASTS		PERSONS WHO SELDOM OR NEVER VIEW POLITICAL TV BROADCASTS	
	Mar. 1976 (%)	July 1976 (%)	Mar. 1976 (%)	July 1976 (%)
Total				
Christian Democratic Union	47	34	36	38
Social Democratic Party/				
Free Democratic Party	32	42	24	25
Impossible to tell	21	24	40	37
	100	100	100	100
N =			175	118
Politically Interested Persons				
Christian Democratic Union	49	35	26	44
Social Democratic Party/				
Free Democratic Party	32	41	26	17
Impossible to tell	29	29	38	37
	100	100	100	100
N =			144	23
Politically Disinterested Persons				
Christian Democratic Union	39	26	39	37
Social Democratic Party/				
Free Democratic Party	32	45	23	26
Impossible to tell	29	29	38	37
	100	100	100	100
N =			31	95

Source: Allensbach Archives, surveys 2178, 2185.

viewers saw the Christian Democratic Union's chances disappearing. The journalists themselves saw no chance for the Christian Democrats to win the 1976 federal election. In reality, the two political camps were of almost identical strength, and the Christian Democratic Union would have won on election day, 3 October 1976, if 350,000 persons from among about 38 million voters (0.9 percent) had switched their votes from the Social Democratic Party or the Free Democratic Party to the Christian Democratic Union. An objective assessment of the situation before the election should have led journalists to answer the question, "Who do you think will win the election?" with "It's completely up in the air." Instead, more than 70 percent answered that they thought the Social Democratic/Free Democratic coalition would win, while only 10 percent expected a Christian Democratic victory. Journalists saw the world quite differently than the electorate, and, if Lippmann is right,

TABLE 2

Journalists See the Political Situation Differently than the Electorate. Is Their Manner of Seeing Things Transmitted to the Television Viewers?

Question: "Of course, no one can know for sure, but what do you think: Who is going to win the coming federal election? Who will receive the most votes: the Christian Democratic Union or the Social Democratic Party/Free Democratic Party?"

		JULY 1976 NATIONAL SAMPLE 18 YEARS OF AGE AND OLDER	ALLENSBACH'S SURVEY OF JOURNALISTS
Predictions:			
Christian Democratic Union		40	10
Social Democratic Party/			
Free Democratic Party		33	76
Impossible to tell		27	14
		100	100
	N =	1265	1235
		NATIONAL SAMPLE AUGUST 1976 (%)	JOURNALISTS IN JULY 1976 (%)
Voting intentions:			
Christian Democratic Party		49	21
Social Democratic Party		42	55
Free Democratic Party		8	24
Other parties		1	x
		100	100
	N =	1590	87

Source: Allensbach Archives. Upper half of the table: surveys 2185,2187. A survey of journalists run parallel to this one by the Institut für Publizistik at the University of Mainz resulted in 73 percent expecting a Social Democratic Party/Free Democratic win, 15 percent a Christian Democratic win, 12 percent "impossible to say." N = 81. Lower part of the table: surveys 3032,2187. It presents the answers of persons who gave a specific party preference. x = less than 0.5%.

they could only show the world as they saw it. In other words, the audience had two views of reality, two impressions of the climate of opinion—an impression from their own, firsthand observations, and an impression from the eyes of television. A fascinating phenomenon arose: a "dual climate of opinion" (Table 2).

Why did the population and the journalists see the political situation so differently? After all, the electorate still believed (in the summer of 1976) that a Christian Democratic victory was a little more likely than a Social Democratic/Free Democratic one.

One reason was that the population and the journalists diverged substantially in their political convictions and party preferences. And, of course, as Lippmann makes clear, convictions guided their views. Supporters of the Social Democratic Party and the Free Democratic Party (Liberals) saw many more indications of a victory for their own parties, whereas supporters of the Christian Democratic Union thought their party more likely to win. This is true in general, and it was true for the population and for the journalists in 1976. Since the national sample was split about evenly between the Social Democratic Party/Free Democratic Party on the one hand and the Christian Democratic Union on the other, whereas the journalists were split about three to one in favor of the Social Democratic Party/Free Democratic Party, it was only natural that they perceived the reality differently.

E. VOTE CHOICES

As discussed at the beginning of this section, the question that has animated media studies more than any other has been news media impact on the vote choice. Do media messages result in changes in voter's candidate preferences? If so, how does that change occur?

The early research by the Columbia University researchers sought to answer this question. They found little media impact on the vote decision. Their conclusion of minimal media effect dampened subsequent research for two decades.

But the search for direct media impact was redirected toward less ambitious questions. These include: How are candidates portrayed in media messages? Does that portrayal affect voters' attitudes about the candidates? Do those attitudes then determine behavior in the voting booth?

The following two selections reflect this refocused research agenda, concentrating on voters' perceptions of candidates. Both selections conclude that media messages do affect voters' perceptions of candidates and raise the issue of the extent of media message impact on vote choices and the outcome of the election.

18. NEWS VERDICTS, DEBATES, AND PRESIDENTIAL CAMPAIGNS

James B. Lemert, William R. Elliott, James M. Bernstein, William L. Rosenberg, and Karl J. Nestvold

In 1992, the presidential debates became major media events. Following the debates, journalists and commentators weighed in with assessments of the candidates' performance. Eventually, a consensus developed about which candidate had won.

This process has become routine since modern presidential debates were instituted as campaign rituals. The question has been whether such journalistic analyses affect voters' conclusions about debate performance.

James Lemert, William R. Elliott, James M. Bernstein, William L. Rosenberg, and Karl J. Nestvold conducted a study of the 1988 presidential candidate debates and vice-presidential candidate debate that was designed to answer that question.* They conducted 2,000 inter-

*From *News Verdicts, Debates and Presidential Campaigns* (New York: Praeger, 1991), pp. 253–57. Reprinted with permission.

views and content-analyzed news coverage following the debates that year. They interviewed people immediately following the debates and before a media consensus on performance had formed; they interviewed respondents again later in the wake of news verdicts.

They concluded that news verdicts of a candidate's debate performance did affect voters' perceptions of candidate performance. Debate watchers who saw the subsequent media analysis were more likely to follow the journalistic consensus on who won than those who did not. However, the verdict effect on voters is short-term because other campaign communications intervene.

James B. Lemert is professor of journalism at the University of Oregon and author of *Criticizing the Media: Empirical Approaches* (1989) and *Does Mass Communication Change Public Opinion?* (1981). William R. Elliott is associate professor of journalism at Southern Illinois University at Carbondale and has written articles for *Journalism Quarterly, Communication Research,* and the *Journal of Broadcasting and Electronic Media.* James M. Bernstein is assistant professor of journalism at Indiana University. William L. Rosenberg is director of the Drexel University Survey Research Center and has authored articles in *Journalism Quarterly* and *Communication Research.* Karl J. Nestvold is professor and associate dean at the School of Journalism at the University of Oregon.

. . . [O]ur findings fairly consistently suggest that an important verdict effect results from post-debate news specials. How long the effect lasts seems to vary with the particular debate, as does whether the news analysis effect is limited to the beneficiary or also includes the victim of the media verdict about who "won" and who "lost."

Debate Performance. For the two presidential debates, the candidate evaluated most favorably during post-debate news commentary also showed in survey respondents' perceptions as the better performer in the debate. Content analysis showed that of the post-debate news verdicts about Michael Dukakis after the first debate, 70% were positive, compared with only 42% for George Bush. Those figures were almost exactly reversed after the second debate: Bush 76% positive comments, Dukakis only 36%.

Turning now to the surveys, people seeing both the September debate and a post-debate news special gave higher debater-rating scores for Dukakis than those watching the debate only or not watching at all. No parallel influence showed for debater ratings of Bush. As for the second Bush–Dukakis debate, the same "winner-only" pattern existed for Bush (defined as the "winner" this time) but not for Dukakis. On average, debate and post-debate analysis viewers rated Bush as a debater higher than those watching the debate only or not watching at all. Once again, no parallel pattern showed up for the "loser" of this particular debate—in this case, Dukakis.

These results were also supported in our analysis of the responses to the open-ended questions about Bush and Dukakis as debaters. Respondents interviewed immediately after the September debate who had watched both debate and post-debate analysis were more likely to use favorable words in describing Dukakis than those who had watched the debate only. After the October 13 debate, the same pattern of positive descriptions by exposure to post-debate analysis followed for Bush.

What about the Quayle–Bentsen debate? Lloyd Bentsen received 76% favorable verdicts in post-debate news specials, while Dan Quayle received only 36%

favorable verdicts about his debate performance. Exposure to post-debate analysis once again strongly predicted favorable ratings of Bentsen's debating skills. Those who saw both the debate and analysis gave Bentsen an adjusted average rating of 7.63 on a 0-to-10 point scale, compared with only 7.11 for those who had just watched the debate. Strictly in terms of his ratings as a debater, the post-debate analysis effect for the loser (i.e., Quayle, as defined by the media) was not as strong ($p < .10$) as for the winner ($p < .02$). Nevertheless, Quayle's ratings as a debater were lower (a mean of 4.51) when people saw both debate and post-debate news special than when they watched only the debate (4.94). Furthermore, people who watched both the debate and analysis were significantly more likely to say that Bentsen won by a lot than those who watched only the debate. So we have a verdict effect for the loser as well as for the media-declared winner in the case of the vice-presidential debate.

We also found evidence for a verdict effect on Quayle in terms of open-ended responses collected between the vice-presidential and second presidential debates. Despite the fact that both his questioners and Quayle himself referred to questions of his competence repeatedly during the debate, it was not until one night later that more than 20% of respondents negatively described Quayle's competence in the debate. This percentage—roughly twice as high as that just after the debate—once it was reached, on October 6, remained remarkably stable through October 12, the end of that time series. Similarly, the idea that Quayle himself might be a campaign issue increased from just 6.6% on debate night to 23.8% the next night. These and the other open-ended responses imply that Quayle's performance looked worse 24 hours after the debate than it did immediately afterward, and this effect held for both Republicans and Democrats.

Over time, Quayle's ratings as a debater remained about the same on debate night (5.14) and the next night (5.20), but kept falling lower and lower on the next three nights we measured (October 9, 11, and 12). Meanwhile, in the case of the two Bush–Dukakis debates, changes around debate night were of relatively short duration (roughly two days). The longer life of the changes for Quayle may reflect the fact that we heard relatively little that was new from or about him, but much that was repeated, in the period after the debate. So if one of the effects of the post-debate coverage was to convert Quayle from debater into campaign issue, and if the reaction of the Bush campaign was to "hide" Quayle, it might not be such a surprise that whatever happened to Quayle's reputation as a debater continued to happen during this time period.

In any case, over the three debates, our evidence strongly suggests that post-debate analysis influences viewers in very predictable ways. The candidate judged most favorably in the media verdicts benefits in the survey responses. In something of a contrast, the least-favored candidate does not necessarily suffer because of exposure to post-debate analysis, although in the case of Dan Quayle, who became a campaign issue to many of our respondents, post-debate analysis as well as media coverage hurt his evaluations as a debater and greatly damaged the chances that people would think he won his debate with Bentsen.

Taken across the three general election debates, then, we report strong evidence of a verdict effect upon debate performance perceptions. This evidence still holds *after* controlling for partisan predispositions and demographic variables.

Image. We used a composite scale to measure the images of the two presidential candidates, and viewer responses on this composite scale were analyzed for the September and October presidential debates. Once again, exposure to post-debate analysis acted the same way on presidential candidate image as it did on debater ratings. The candidate receiving the most favorable post-debate news verdicts immediately after the debate (Dukakis on September 25 and Bush on October 13) also experienced an improvement in his general image as a potential president. For the September debate, viewers watching both the debate and a post-debate analysis rated Dukakis higher (26.33) than debate-only viewers (25.54) or non-viewers (23.03). After the final debate, George Bush had higher image evaluations for debate plus analysis viewers (27.03), followed by debate-only viewers (25.63) and those who watched neither (24.66). No such image measurements were available to us for the two vice-presidential debaters, but it seems clear that debate performance perceptions are used by viewers in evaluating the presidential candidates' overall images as potential presidents. No wonder campaigns worry so much about debate performance verdicts!

For the September 25 debate, simple exposure to the debate itself seemed to influence the image of both presidential candidates. The influence of the debate itself seemed short—one or two days. Once again, many other campaign communications would seem to temper how long the debate itself would influence candidates' general image, unimpeded by other relevant influences.

Voting Preferences. For the candidates, the most important possible impact of the debates obviously concerns whether or not debating adds or subtracts to their vote totals. We have some evidence, at least from the first presidential debate and the vice-presidential one, that it does. The September debate—especially in combination with post-debate analysis—appeared to increase the self-described probability that our respondents were going to vote for Michael Dukakis. In addition, when we moved to a Bush vs. Dukakis forced-choice question, the highest Dukakis percentage (65.7%) was given by people who saw both the September 25 debate and analysis, the next highest by debate viewers only (52.7%), and lowest (48.7%) by non-viewers.

Somewhat to our surprise, the Quayle-Bentsen debate seemed to produce a strong carryover to presidential voting choice. Preferences for Dukakis stood at 58% on October 4, 48% on debate night (October 5), and (consistent with a post-debate analysis effect) increased to 65% on October 6. After that, this 65% preference figure changed hardly at all each night through the night before the final October 13 debate. In the aftermath of the final debate, however, voting preferences seemed to have been established, and no debate (or analysis) effect was visible in our survey data.

Summary. Exposure to post-debate analysis emerges as the strongest debate-related influence on performance impressions, a composite presidential candidate image measure, and voting intentions. For the presidential debates, the post-debate verdict effect seemed more potent for the candidate favored by the verdict, but for the vice-presidential debate the impact seemed to be upon both Quayle, very much the loser in media verdicts, and Bentsen, very much the winner in those verdicts. In general, the verdict effect did not last as long for the presidential debates as it did for the vice-presidential one. In the case of the presidential candidates, many other subsequent campaign events might have shifted attention away from each debate.

Ironically, the effort by the Bush campaign to hide Quayle from scrutiny might have helped extend the length of time that the Quayle verdict effect lasted. Had this debate been the final debate, or had either of the presidential candidates performed at a Quayle-like level, who knows what the outcome might have been?

19. THE MASS MEDIA ELECTION

Thomas E. Patterson

Will Rogers's famous line "All I know is what I read in the newspapers" applies, with the addition of television, to voters during presidential campaigns. Awareness of candidates and issues and perceptions about those candidates depend, at least partly, on media presentation of the candidates.

Presidential candidates are not treated equally in the presentation of campaign news. This is especially true during the early stages of primary campaigns when some candidates bask in media attention while others struggle for it.

In the following piece, which is excerpted from a landmark study of media coverage of a presidential campaign and the effects on voters' cognitions and evaluations of candidates and issues, Thomas E. Patterson demonstrates the linkage between news presentation and the voters' awareness of and cognitions about presidential candidates. Voters become aware of those candidates who receive significant news coverage. Thus, news coverage alerts voters to the alternatives and affects their ultimate vote choice.*

Thomas E. Patterson is professor of political science at the Maxwell School of Citizenship and Public Affairs, Syracuse University, and has written widely in the field of political communication. He is the author of *The Unseeing Eye: The Myth of Television Power in National Elections* (1976), *The Mass Media Election: How Americans Choose Their President* (1980), and *The American Democracy* (1990).

Today's presidential campaign encourages self-starters, candidates who enter the race not so much in response to public demand for their presence, but more because of a personal desire to be the next president. Self-starting candidates whose backgrounds include state or national office and periodical appearances in the

*From *The Mass Media Election* (New York: Praeger, 1980), chapter 10. Reprinted with permission.

national news usually are taken seriously by fellow politicians and the press. But if they have been just ordinary figures in the news in the years leading up to the election, they enter the primaries as politicians unknown to large numbers of voters.

An example from the 1976 campaign is Fred Harris. He first won national news attention in 1964 when he upset footballer Bud Wilkinson in Oklahoma's race for the Senate. Touted as a comer within the Democratic party, Harris continued to appear in national news—co-chairing Hubert Humphrey's 1968 presidential campaign, receiving the Democratic national chairman appointment, and making a belated bid for the 1972 presidential nomination. When he sought the presidency for the second time in 1976, he hit the campaign trail a full year before the first primary in New Hampshire, crisscrossing the nation in a motor home, stopping wherever he could attract a crowd or the press. Like most Democratic presidential aspirants that year, Harris seldom made front-page news, but he was nevertheless among the candidates regularly mentioned in news reports on the upcoming election.

Even so, the public remained largely unaware of Fred Harris. Only 47 percent of the respondents questioned just before the New Hampshire primary recognized even his name. More importantly, only 12 percent felt they knew something about him.* Eleven months of vigorous campaigning and nearly 12 years of occasional national exposure had produced for Harris very little public recognition.

Several of the other candidates' attempts to penetrate the public's awareness were just as quixotic. A majority of the people knew the names of Morris Udall, Birch Bayh, Jimmy Carter, and Frank Church, but only 20 percent indicated knowledge of any one of these candidates beyond his name. When asked about Sargent Shriver, most of the 44 percent who felt they knew him were unable to cite anything more than his Kennedy connection or his 1972 nomination for vice-president. A full 37 percent of the Erie [Pennsylvania] respondents did not even recognize by name the most publicized of the nation's governors, Jerry Brown. Even Henry Jackson, one of the more visible Democratic candidates prior to the campaign, was not very well known. After his long tenure in the Senate, years of speculation about his presidential ambitions, and his prominence in congressional hearings over détente, national defense, and oil prices, 37 percent of the people said they had never heard of him, and another 36 percent said they knew him only by name.

A comparison of these candidates with three familiar public figures provides a clear indication of just how unknown they were. No less than 99 percent of the respondents knew Gerald Ford, Ronald Reagan, and George Wallace by name; and most felt they knew each candidate better. Over 90 percent felt they knew something about Ford, the nation's president since August 1974. Reagan, whose film and television career and two terms as California's governor had made him a national

---

*Recognition of a candidate's name is the standard measure of public recognition of that candidate. As will be demonstrated later in the chapter, however, simple name recognition is relatively unimportant to vote casting. What matters is whether people feel they know something about a candidate; only when their familiarity with him reaches this stage are they likely to consider him when making their vote decision.

figure, was known to 85 percent. In his fourth presidential race, Wallace was familiar to 76 percent of the respondents.

CHANGES IN CANDIDATE AWARENESS
DURING PRIMARIES

When the presidential primaries begin, the focus of political news swings toward and stays on the candidates. They are no longer merely the occasional subjects of news reports, for hardly a day passes without mention somewhere in the news of every active campaigner. Of course, the amounts of coverage that the various candidates receive may be quite unequal. Among self-starting Democrats running in 1976, Carter clearly dominated the headlines and news space; Jackson, Brown, and Udall got moderate coverage; Church had some exposure; Harris, Bayh, and Shriver received very sparse coverage. . . . How did unequally weighted coverage affect these candidates' recognition levels? What happened, in other words, to the public's awareness of each one? Only Carter, who received most of the coverage, became dramatically more visible to the voters (see Table 1). The proportion of citizens who felt they knew something about him rose from 20 percent in February to 81 percent by June, a jump of over 60 percentage points during the primaries. Their recognition of his Democratic opponents, however, increased only modestly. Recognition levels rose by about 14 percent for Udall, Brown, and Jackson, and by only 9 percent for Church. They remained fairly constant for Harris, and even declined for Bayh and Shriver.

The amount of coverage a candidate received was strongly related to the public recognition he gained—the correlation exceeded +.90.[1] Importantly, though, the relationship was not strictly linear. Small amounts of coverage resulted in stable or even declining recognition, a moderate amount contributed modestly to the public's awareness of the candidate receiving it, and intense coverage led to a dramatic increase in the public's familiarity with a candidate. In other words, within the relationship were thresholds at which the impact of news coverage on public awareness changed significantly. Below a certain level of news coverage, the effect was muted; above that level the effect was magnified.

At the base of this threshold effect lies the voter's approach to political news. The names, facts, and events in the news are simply too numerous for anyone to comprehend or remember. Voters trying to gain awareness of all public personalities and problems, big and small, would simply bury themselves in a mound of data for which they have neither the time nor the interest. The only practical way for most citizens to proceed is simply to follow the news, paying attention only to its obtruding features, and thus being certain of acquiring only that information placed at the top of the news again and again. The news signals what and who are important and gets across the message with repetition and placement.

When a presidential candidate is fortunate enough to find himself constantly in the headlines, the effect can be as sudden as it is dramatic. Carter had become a well-known figure by April. He was known to four of every five adults only two

TABLE 1

Awareness of the Candidates at Different Times during the Primaries (percent)

| | PERCENT SAYING THEY KNEW SOMETHING ABOUT HIM IN: | | | |
| | Feb. | April | Change from June | Feb. to June |
Candidate				
Birch Bayh	21	27	–	–4
Jerry Brown (Erie)	–	25	43	+18
Jerry Brown (L.A.)	–	87	91	+4
Jimmy Carter	20	77	81	+61
Frank Church	20	21	29	+9
Gerald Ford	93	93	94	+1
Fred Harris	12	12	16	+4
Henry Jackson	27	42	34	+7
Ronald Reagan	85	89	88	+3
Sargent Shriver	44	36	–	–8
Morris Udall	23	37	37	+14
George Wallace	76	74	74	–2

Note. Respondents were read a list of candidate names and asked to indicate which of the following categories best described their recognition of each candidate:
  1. I've never heard his name before.
  2. I've heard his name, but I really don't know anything about him.
  3. 1 know something about him.
The proportions in the table are those giving the third response which, as later analysis will show, is the recognition level that is critical to vote choice. Except in their recognition of Brown, Erie and Los Angeles respondents have been grouped for this table. Los Angeles respondents, however, had somewhat higher recognition levels of the candidates throughout the period. No entry in the table indicates that respondents were not asked about the respective candidate in that interview. This method of measuring candidate recognition was validated with open-ended questions. Unless a respondent was in the third category, there was a 90 percent probability that the respondent would not be able to say anything about a candidate when asked an open-ended question about him.

months into a campaign he had entered as a virtual stranger. Other factors were involved in public recognition of Carter during the early primaries. He did, after all, best his rivals in seven of the first nine Democratic primaries, making him the favorite to win nomination. Surely, even if he had received only slightly more coverage than his closest rivals, he would have gained wider recognition.

Yet if the Brown candidacy is indicative, the amount of coverage a candidate receives matters greatly to his recognition. Brown was a late starter in the race; all of the primaries he entered were held during the final stage. In each state where he was on the ballot, Brown beat Carter but shared the headlines with winners of other contests, for all of his wins came on Tuesdays when two or more primaries were held. He received only about a fourth of the news space awarded the Democratic candidates during the late primaries, about as much coverage as Jackson had received earlier, when the calendar consisted of a single primary each Tuesday. The amount of recognition Brown gained as a result of his victories was very close to what Jackson had gained during the initial two months. Despite a primary performance that rivaled Carter's early showing, Brown's recognition level did not even double.

So complete was Carter's domination of the news in the early primaries that he became familiar even to a large portion of the citizens who were outside the regular news audience. The more closely people follow the news, the more likely they are to feel they know the candidates. But regular news exposure does not result in familiarity with each candidate, and infrequent news exposure may result in awareness of some candidates. As the following figures show, the proportion of nonregular news users who felt they knew Carter in April 1976 exceeded the proportion of regular news followers who thought they knew the two men who were his principal opponents at the time (figures are percents):

	NOT REGULAR READER OR VIEWER	REGULAR READER OR VIEWER
Carter	64	85
Jackson	24	55
Udall	23	48

Most people, regardless of how closely they follow the news, will become familiar with an intensely reported candidate, while only a few outside of a moderate amount of news regulars will learn to recognize a candidate who receives infrequent coverage.

NEWS EXPOSURE AND CANDIDATE AWARENESS

It is widely believed that recognition of any candidate is more likely to result from television viewing than from newspaper reading. Familiarity is thought to be gained more easily and more rapidly from watching and listening to a candidate than from reading about him. In the words of Robert Agranoff, television "can thrust unknown candidates into prominence."[2] Yet the evidence points to the newspaper as the most effective means of building public awareness. For each of the 1976 presidential candidates, recognition was higher at the end of the primaries among people who followed the newspaper regularly than among those who watched the evening news regularly.

Further, increases in recognition levels from one interview to the next were more closely associated with newspaper reading than with television viewing. . . . People who read a daily newspaper frequently became more familiar than infrequent readers with every candidate; only about 60 percent of the candidates became more familiar to frequent television viewers than to infrequent viewers. This is not to say that television viewing was without impact. For 36 percent of the candidates among Erie respondents and 18 percent among Los Angeles respondents, there was a significant relationship between heavier viewing and increased awareness. But heavier newspaper reading had a much more substantial impact on people's awareness—73 percent of the Erie relationships and 91 percent of the Los Angeles ones were significant.

The newspaper is in this dominant position for the simple but easily overlooked reason that voters' awareness results largely from the frequency and depth of their exposure. Seeing a candidate on television may help viewers to recognize him when he appears again, certainly a step toward a sense of familiarity, but meaningful recognition results from repeated exposure to a candidate and the reception of information about him. It is when the candidate becomes more than just a face or name that voters come to think they know who the candidate is. With greater news space, the newspaper is more able than the evening newscasts to communicate large amounts of information about the candidates.

Of course, most of this news material goes unheeded; if readers saw and remembered even half of it, every candidate would be readily recognized by most citizens. The odds are, however, that the more information a news source makes available about the candidates the more likely it is that its users will come to recognize the candidates. This can be seen even in the greater impact of newspaper exposure on candidate recognition in Los Angeles than in Erie. Most newspaper readers in Los Angeles subscribed to the *Times,* a paper whose candidate coverage is as extensive as that in any of the nation's dailies. By chance alone, readers of the *Times* would encounter more news of the candidates than would readers of the less comprehensive Erie dailies.[3]

The Erie dailies, in turn, provide several times the amount of national news presented in the evening newscasts. The words spoken on a newscast will fit with room to spare on the front page of the *Erie Times* or *News.* In Erie, newspaper exposure was more highly related to increased recognition than was television exposure. The network newscasts, however, made a greater difference to recognition in Erie than in Los Angeles, indicating that when the depth of newspaper coverage is not considerable, television news makes a more substantial contribution to public awareness of the candidates. Indeed, the nature of the media environment appears to affect overall awareness levels. In media-rich Los Angeles, about 5 percent more voters, on average, felt they knew each candidate than was the case in Erie, where the available media are limited.

People's newspaper habits are particularly important to their recognition of less-publicized candidates. When a candidate dominates the news, the extent of his familiarity to television viewers and to newspaper readers differs only marginally. At the end of the 1976 primaries, Carter's recognition was only a tenth higher among newspaper-only regulars than among television-only regulars. But for candidates who were not heavily covered by the press during the primaries, recognition was a fourth higher among people depending on the newspaper. Again, this seems to result from differences in the media's news space. Although the proportions of coverage given all candidates may be roughly the same for both television and the newspaper, the absolute volume of coverage given the lightly covered candidates is considerably greater in the newspaper. This is particularly true of a newspaper like the *Los Angeles Times*; in 1976, voters exposed to this newspaper were better informed about the less-publicized candidates than were readers of other newspapers.

The importance of the information people receive from the news to their awareness of the candidates is further revealed by differences in the media's impact on voters of high, moderate, and low interest. . . . Low interest voters benefitted the least from newspaper exposure; those who looked at the news pages more frequently became only slightly more familiar with the candidates than those who largely ignored the newspaper. The reason is that most low interest readers seldom put much effort into their reading of the political sections of the newspaper. They infrequently read more than the lead paragraphs of political news stories, and usually move on after a glance at the headlines, thus bypassing nearly all of the information that the newspaper provides. Indeed, low interest voters derive about as much benefit from exposure to television.

Among moderate and high interest voters, however, the newspaper's impact was significantly greater than television's. For citizens in these categories of interest, those who followed the newspaper frequently became substantially more aware of the candidates than those who paid infrequent attention to the newspaper. On the other hand, the frequency of television viewing was relatively unimportant to the candidate recognition of moderate and high interest voters. Whether they watched the evening newscasts frequently or rarely, they were nearly as likely to gain awareness. Those who were not heavy viewers had alternative and just as effective ways of learning about the candidates. The newspaper, however, contains enough information to have an independent effect. High and moderate interest voters include nearly all of the citizens who take the time to read the newspaper somewhat carefully. Those who read the newspaper frequently therefore gain significantly higher awareness of the candidates than their high and moderate interest counterparts who read the newspaper only occasionally.**

AWARENESS AND VOTE CHOICE

Austin Ranney and others have shown that primary election voters are more interested in politics than other citizens.[4] As could be expected, they also are more familiar with the candidates. It is not the case, however, that primary voters think they knew each of the candidates on their ballots. Democratic voters in Pennsylvania, for example, faced the choice of voting for Carter, Jackson, or Udall.[5] Of those respondents who voted, almost 90 percent felt they knew Carter, but only slightly more than 50 percent were familiar with Jackson or Udall.

These differences in candidate recognition were important to the voting decisions that Erie's primary voters made, for few people selected a candidate known to them only by name (see Table 2). Nearly all picked a candidate they knew something about, which provided Carter with a decided edge on Jackson and Udall:

About 25 percent of the voters knew only one of the three candidates. This candidate usually was Carter. He received 90 percent of the votes cast by the group.

** The relationship between recognition levels and party affiliation also was examined. It might be thought that a party's candidate would be more familiar to voters within that party. However, there was little difference across party lines; Republicans were actually slightly more likely to be familiar with the candidates of both parties, presumably the result of their slightly greater attention to politics.

TABLE 2

Relationship of Candidate Awareness to Vote Choice during the Primaries (percent)

CANDIDATES WHOM THEY FELT THEY KNEW	CANDIDATE FOR WHOM THEY VOTED		
Pennsylvania Primary			
Erie voters	Carter	Jackson	Udall
Only Carter	20	2	0
Only Jackson	0	1	0
Only Udall	4	0	0
Only Carter and Jackson	12	8	0
Only Carter and Udall	4	0	4
Carter, Jackson, and Udall	20	11	8
None of the candidates	4	2	0
Percent of total vote	64	24	12

California Primary				
Los Angeles voters	Brown	Carter	Church	Udall
Only Brown	3	1	0	0
Only Carter	0	1	0	0
Only Brown and Carter	18	8	0	2
Only Brown and Church	1	0	0	0
Only Brown, Carter, and Church	5	4	2	0
Only Brown, Carter, and Udall	8	3	0	2
Brown, Carter, Church, and Udall	23	9	4	5
None of the candidates	1	0	0	0
Percent of total vote	59	26	6	9

Note. Table omits categories that include no respondents. For example, there was not a single respondent in California who knew Udall and Church, but not Carter or Brown.

About 30 percent knew two candidates, usually Carter and Jackson or Udall. Carter received 60 percent of the votes of this group.

There were 45 percent who knew all three candidates. Carter received half of the votes cast by this group. Carter received about 12 percent more votes than he would have received if each candidate had been equally familiar to the voters. In many presidential primaries, this advantage would have exceeded the margin of victory.

California's primary presented a different situation, since two of its candidates, Carter and Brown, were highly familiar to the voters. Both were known to 95 percent of the respondents who voted. Church and Udall were the unfamiliar candidates on the ballots, known to only half of those who voted. As in Pennsylvania, almost all of the voting respondents cast their ballots for a candidate they knew. Church and Udall received virtually no consideration from the voters who knew them only as names, gathering from them only 10 percent of their votes; 90 percent of the votes they received came from the half who knew them.

Voter support obviously is not based on familiarity alone. Voters may regard one known candidate more highly than another, or they may not care for a candidate they know, a position that Wallace held for many voters in 1976. But a candidate has little chance of gaining support from those to whom he is not familiar, for the voters' awareness defines the range of alternatives they consider. In the right circumstances, this can result in votes that are won and lost almost by default. When a candidate is known and not widely disliked, as was Carter, and when each of his opponents suffers from a lack of recognition, as did Jackson and Udall in Pennsylvania, his advantage is enormous.

Thus the way in which the press distributes its coverage among the candidates can make a difference: its reporting helps to define voters' alternatives. The press's coverage does not necessarily determine how people will react to their known alternatives—a candidate who gains their recognition must still gain their confidence. Nevertheless, without party labels to guide their choice and often with limited information about what each potential nominee represents, some voters are primed for uncritical acceptance of a candidate. Few voters, moreover, will change their news habits to try to discover which of the presidential hopefuls is best for them. There may be another candidate out there who offers more of what they want in their party's nominee, but they are unlikely to plunge into the news looking for him. Most people simply take the news as it comes, skimming the top and even doing that in a casual way. Indeed, it is precisely the voters with fewer known alternatives who are less critical in their choices and less likely to gain awareness of additional alternatives. Under the appropriate conditions, such voters have a high probability of choosing the candidate emphasized by the press.

NOTES

1. Based on rank-order correlations in which the news sources respondents used were taken into account.

2. Robert Agranoff, *The New Style in Election Campaigns* (Boston: Holbrook Press, 1972), p. 258.

3. A separate analysis of newspaper readers confirmed that exposure to the *L.A. Times* had the highest relationship to increased candidate awareness.

4. Austin Ranney, "Turnout and Representation in American Presidential Elections," *American Political Science Review*, March 1972, pp. 21–37.

5. Wallace and Harris were also on the ballot in Pennsylvania, but they were essentially out of the race by this time and are not included in the analysis.

SUGGESTED READINGS

Blumler, Jay G., and Denis McQuail. *Television in Politics.* Chicago: University of Chicago Press, 1969.
Based on a British study that found media effects on voter alienation, this book was one of the first challenges to the minimal-effects theory.

Keeter, Scott, and Cliff Zukin. *Uninformed Choice: The Failure of the New Presidential Nominating System.* New York: Praeger, 1983.

Keeter and Zukin contend that voters learned little about the candidates' positions on issues from media coverage of the 1980 presidential primaries. This leads to a lack of informed choice in vote decisions.

Key, V.O. *Public Opinion and American Democracy.* New York: Knopf, 1965.
V.O. Key's contribution to the field of media studies is contained in two chapters on the media. Key's speculations on media effects were prescient in light of later research.

Klapper, Joseph T. *The Effects of Mass Communication.* New York: Free Press, 1960.
A classic in political communications owing to its comprehensive discussion of the minimal-effects theory.

Kraus, Sidney, and Dennis K. Davis. *The Effects of Mass Communication on Political Behavior.* University Park: Pennsylvania State University Press, 1976.
A synthesis of the studies of attitudinal change caused by media effects from the advent of the minimal-effects theory through to initial challenges in the late 1960s and early 1970s.

Iyengar, Shanto. *Is Anyone Responsible?* Chicago: University of Chicago Press, 1991.
Iyengar links news stories with the public's perception of accountability for social problems and responsibility for finding resolutions to them. Iyengar finds that the framing of TV news stories militates against the assignment of accountability to public officials.

Protess, David, and Maxwell E. McCombs. *Agenda-Setting: Readings on Media, Public Opinion, and Policymaking.* Hillsdale, N.J.: Lawrence Erlbaum Associates, Inc., 1992.
An edited volume including many of the major works on agenda-setting during the 1970s and 1980s.

Robinson, John P. et al. *The Main Source: Learning From Television News.* Beverly Hills, Calif.: Sage Publications, Inc., 1986.
In this study of audience comprehension of news, Robinson and colleagues dispute the survey results suggesting television is the main source of news. This comparison of broadcast and print media serves as an indictment of a TV news presentation that does little to enhance audience comprehension of the news.

Sanders, Keith R., Lynda Lee Kaid, and Dan Nimmo. *Political Communication Yearbook 1984.* Carbondale: Southern Illinois University Press, 1985.
Three of the works in this edited volume critique the spiral-of-silence theory. A response by Noelle-Neumann also is included.

Shaw, Donald L., and Maxwell E. McCombs. *The Emergence of American Political Issues.* St. Paul, Minn.: West Publishing, 1977.
The first monograph-length exposition of the agenda-setting theory. Shaw and McCombs demonstrated agenda-setting effects and initiated an ongoing debate about the nature and extent of such effects.

Weaver, Donald et al. *Media Agenda-Setting in a Presidential Election.* New York: Praeger, 1981.
The first application of the agenda-setting theories to the context of a presidential campaign.

Patterson, Thomas E., and Robert D. McClure. *The Unseeing Eye: The Myth of Television Power in American National Elections.* New York: Putnam's, 1976.
Patterson and McClure found viewers learned more about a candidate's positions on issues from political advertising than from television news. A landmark study in the field of political communications.

chapter 6

CAMPAIGNS AND ELECTIONS

INTRODUCTION

The 1992 presidential election confirmed a fact of life in presidential campaigns: The media are salient players in the conduct of the campaign and affect the electoral process. This is so because no other entity possesses the ability to reach voters the way the media can. Presidential candidates understand that power and solicit media coverage to communicate with voters. With the demise of grassroots party organizations, candidates who rely on political party organizations for communications throughout the campaign reach fewer individuals than a single broadcast news program or TV commercial.

Moreover, the mass media have become the voters' window on the campaign. Voters use media messages to acquire information about individual candidates and campaigns, as was discussed earlier.

With both candidates and voters assigning the mass media roles in the electoral process, it is no wonder that media coverage produces effects on the nature of the electoral process. The extent of those effects has animated political communication scholars since the landmark Columbia University studies mentioned earlier. Studies of media role in presidential campaigns have increased in volume since those studies, and presidential campaigns usually produce a plethora of books and articles discussing the subject.

Increasingly, however, media role in campaigns has moved beyond the sphere of scholarly interest to become a campaign issue. The question of bias in media coverage of campaigns is not new. In 1964, the Republican National Convention was marked by anti-media statements by speakers accompanied by a vitrolic reaction from delegates directed at the media booths high above the convention floor.

But in 1992, media role became a frequent point of discussion. Presidential candidates, including Bill Clinton, Ross Perot, and George Bush, openly chastised the press for coverage they disliked. A popular bumpersticker among Republicans read "Annoy the Media: Re-elect Bush."

The media also have become so pervasive in the conduct of campaigns that candidates with media-related backgrounds are viewed as having an advantage. Previous presidential candidates Ronald Reagan, Pat Robertson, and Paul Simon had pursued television or print journalism careers. Two candidates for national office in 1992—former columnist and commentator Pat Buchanan and former newspaper reporter Al Gore—had media backgrounds.

Moreover, media coverage has become a topic for media coverage. News stories in 1992 analyzed how the news media reported on the campaign. Some stories even presented the press's public agonizing over whether the scrutiny of candidates' private lives was a legitimate function. Such stories resort to reporters interviewing reporters about reporting.

The media, then, have become major players in the drama of a presidential campaign. They are a "common carrier" of information about candidate activity. But they do more. They scrutinize the candidates, they participate in setting the agenda, they affect the nature of campaigning, and they are even the subject of their own stories.

In this section we will discuss media coverage of presidential elections, with special emphasis on the 1992 presidential campaign. We will examine the roles the media played in this campaign to understand the roles they have played in the past and will perform in the future. We will see how candidates attempt to use mass media for communication of messages. We will also ask some questions about media effects.

This section, then, is divided into three parts. In the first part, we analyze one sample of news media coverage of the 1992 presidential campaign.

Next, we examine candidates' attempts to use the media for creating images in voters' minds. Both free and paid media strategies are explored.

Finally, the media's role in the electoral process has affected participants in the process. The effects on two of those participants—the voters and the candidates—are the subject of the last part.

A. NEWS COVERAGE OF PRESIDENTIAL CAMPAIGNS

The press played traditional roles in the 1992 presidential campaign. Once again it served as a winnower in the nomination process. The press now plays the role that political party leaders once played, which was to assess presidential candidates and decide which would be accorded the status of viability. The press winnows through its roles as mentioner, categorizer, agenda-setter, expectation-setter, and critic.

Over time the press has become a *mentioner* in presidential campaigns, primarily during the nomination stage. Candidates not mentioned in news coverage remain anonymous to voters. The press also *categorizes* candidates by placing labels on them to differentiate one from the other—the "prairie populist" candidate (Tom Harkin), the "war hero" candidate (Bob Kerrey), the preacher candidate (Pat Robertson). As an *agenda-setter*, the press helps shape the issues and events that will be perceived as important factors in the campaign. The press is an *expectation-setter* when it establishes expected standards of electoral performance of candidates and then assesses them accordingly. Finally, the press is a *critic* of the candidates, placing special scrutiny on the front-runners in the process. The selection that follows demonstrates the mentioner role at work as news organizations reject a presidential candidate who seeks to be taken seriously.

20. THE PRESS REJECTS A CANDIDATE

Joshua Meyrowitz

Voters following the Democratic presidential nomination race in 1992 probably knew a great deal about Bill Clinton, Paul Tsongas, and Jerry Brown. They also likely had heard something about Tom Harkin, Bob Kerrey, and Douglas Wilder. But hardly anybody was aware of a seventh candidate who took his candidacy very seriously even if the press did not.

Larry Agran, former mayor of Irvine, California, struggled to gain name recognition and viability as a candidate. Although Agran had more government experience than Ross Perot or Jesse Jackson and more executive experience than Tsongas or Harkin, he was dismissed by news organizations as a non-candidate.

The following selection relates Agran's efforts to win press notice and why such attention was not forthcoming. Agran's case is a classic example of the powerful influence of the news media's mentioner role in determining who will be considered serious presidential contenders.*

Joshua Meyrowitz is professor of communication at the University of New Hampshire. He is the author of *No Sense of Place: The Impact of Electronic Media on Social Behavior* (1985).

When a close aide to Czech Communist leader Klement Gottwald was charged with treason and hanged in 1952, the state propaganda apparatus quickly airbrushed the traitor out of all state photographs. Such a crude act is almost unimaginable in a democratic society, but airbrushing of a more sophisticated kind is not entirely unknown.

Take the case of Democratic presidential candidate Larry Agran. The national press almost never reported on his campaign. When his name did appear, he was

---

*An earlier version of this essay appeared in the *Columbia Journalism Review* (March/April 1992). Copyright Joshua Meyrowitz 1992. Reprinted with permission.

described as a "dark horse," a "fringe candidate," or "an obscure contender." Agran was barred from most of the televised debates on the basis of criteria that seemed to shift as he tried to meet them. When he *was* allowed to participate in forums with the "major candidates," he was often left out of news reports of the events or asked by press photographers to move aside. With Catch-22 logic, Agran had been told by news media executives that he had not earned the right to media exposure because, among other things, he had not received enough media exposure.

To be fair to those making such news judgments, much of Agran's dark-horse status derived from his unconventional credentials as a presidential contender. Although he is a Harvard Law School graduate and published author who has devoted twenty years to public service, he has never held statewide or national office. He has served for twelve years as an elected official in Irvine, California, America's largest master-planned city. Most national journalists I spoke with dismissed him on the ground that he has held only local office, just as they once would have dismissed anyone who was only a Congressman or was only a *former* Senator or Governor. As journalist Roger Mudd put it at the start of a rare TV interview with Agran: "It does stretch credulity to think that a Jewish ex-mayor can make it."

But Agran's supporters pointed out that, as Irvine's first directly-elected mayor, Agran received national acclaim for the numerous progressive programs he initiated, including: elderly housing, childcare, mass transportation, the nation's first curbside recycling program, preservation of undeveloped land, and hazardous waste regulations. They noted that, as Executive Director of the Center for Innovative Diplomacy, he played a unique role as a "global mayor," who pursued issues of international trade, arms reduction, and human rights, and earned his city a United Nations award for his pioneering legislation to eliminate ozone-depleting compounds—all from an unlikely base in deeply conservative Orange County. They described him as the most articulate presidential contender with the boldest and most specific blueprint for shifting cold war military spending to post-cold war domestic needs. And they argued that, regardless of anything else, since Agran's campaign had achieved access to forty primary and caucus ballots, the public deserved to be told something about him so as to be able to make an informed choice in the voting booth.

It is no surprise that Agran's supporters saw more in Agran than did most national journalists. What is surprising, however, is the extent to which Agran's campaign received encouragement from the coverage of the local New Hampshire press reporting on the first-in-the-nation primary, as well as from at least two nationally-known columnists, Colman McCarthy and Sydney Schamberg. In New Hampshire, there were dozens of newspaper articles, editorials, columns, and letters to the editor, which described Agran's exclusion and/or supported his right to be heard in the national debates. Beyond New Hampshire, McCarthy and Schamberg both wrote columns challenging Agran's designation as a "minor candidate" and endorsing his right to be heard and seen through debates and national news coverage.

Agran's anomalous status as a candidate made his campaign a good lens through which to see aspects of campaign coverage that normally remain invisible.

To his dismay, Agran found that for him one of the rules of the campaign was: "To get press coverage, you must be disruptive." When he was barred by the chairman of the state Democratic party from a televised Health Care Forum with presidential candidates in Nashua, New Hampshire, for example, he stood up in the audience and demanded by what criteria he was being excluded. Responding to a signal from a state party official, security police began to remove Agran from the hall, but the crowd's shouts of "Freedom of speech!" and "Let us vote!" embarrassed the men at the dais into inviting him to join them. The confrontation was Agran's first widely reported "campaign event"—but little mention was made of his innovative proposals for health care reform.

To prevent this sort of public call for inclusion from occurring again, the next state Democratic party debate was moved to a high-security TV studio with no audience. Agran stood outside the studio, among a crowd of four hundred people who braved zero-degree temperatures to protest the exclusion of their candidates from the debates. (Most of the protesters were supporters of Lenora Fulani of the New Alliance Party, who ran as a Democrat in New Hampshire, but several other "fringe" candidates were also represented.) As reported in the local press, the protest offered many dramatic moments, with the "major" candidates forced to pass "picket lines for democracy" as protesters shouted "Scab! Scab! Scab!" Yet perhaps because there was no violence, the protest went unreported in the *New York Times* and the *Washington Post*, and in all but Agran's home-county edition of the *Los Angeles Times*.

When local press coverage and protests had no impact on his national media profile, Agran's campaign staff became convinced that his status as a "fringe" candidate could be erased if he tied or passed one or more of the "major" candidates in the polls. They were wrong.

When Agran made his first measurable showing in a University of New Hampshire/WUMR-TV poll taken from January 6 to 11, the AP story on the poll grouped Agran's result into a total score for "minor candidates," without mentioning his name. When a January 22 poll, conducted by the American Research Group [ARG], showed Agran tied with former California Governor Jerry Brown and Iowa Senator Tom Harkin, the AP bluntly reported this finding two-thirds of the way through a story. When a follow-up ARG poll showed Agran doubling his support and moving ahead of Brown, the AP incorrectly referred to it as Agran's "first measurable showing." When the next ARG poll continued to show Agran ahead of Brown, ABC's *World News Sunday*—perhaps to avoid the complexity of explaining the identity of a candidate they had not been covering—reported on the poll by skipping all mention of Agran and moving directly from Harkin to Brown. Other news organizations solved the problem by reporting only on the top three names. ARG pollster Dick Bennett says that had Agran's surprise strength in the polls been played up by news organizations it might well have been a further rise in the polls. Instead, "the press completely ignored the story, and he began to sink."

Agran's unusual appearance with four of the so-called "major candidates" at the U.S. Conference of Mayors led to the first significant mention of his campaign in the *New York Times*. In a January 24 article, "Mayors Appear Unmoved by the Major Candidates," Richard L. Berke began by observing that "After hearing pitches from the Democratic Presidential contenders on how they would revive America's cities, dozens of mayors meeting here today seemed to agree on one thing: the single candidate who truly understands urban needs is Larry Agran." Yet the AP release on the event, as well as the TV reports I saw on the forum, did not even mention that Agran was there.

Similarly, when Agran participated with the "major" candidates in the Global Warming Leadership Forum in February, the audience "was very enthusiastic about Larry Agran and less enthusiastic about Bill Clinton and Bob Kerrey," according to the conference organizer Carole Florman. But the major news organizations covering the event—ABC News, CBS News (through a local affiliate), and the AP—omitted all mention of Agran from their reports.

By the end of March 1992, Douglas Wilder, Tom Harkin, Bob Kerrey, and Paul Tsongas had all suspended their campaigns, but the narrowed Democratic field did not generate any increased attention to Agran. After being ignored by the press for so long, there seemed to be nothing Agran could do to register with the national media. Even when Agran garnered more voter signatures to be placed on the New York ballot than Jerry Brown, only Brown was allowed to participate in New York City debates with Bill Clinton. At the start of one debate at Lehman College in the Bronx on the topic of urban problems—Agran's specialty—the hapless candidate stood up and said "I respectfully ask to be included in this forum." Agran was quickly tackled to the floor by plainclothes police, dragged down a flight of stairs head first, handcuffed, thrown into a police paddy wagon until the debate was over, and then kept in custody at a Bronx jail for four hours on charges of disorderly conduct, trespassing, and resisting arrest. Agran's campaign manager, who had been sitting quietly next to Agran, was also arrested. The TV cameras did not even turn away from the debate stage to focus on any of this drama.

Agran's arrest received some coverage in New York, including a brief mention in the *New York Times*. And Agran's home state paper, the *Los Angeles Times*, condemned the arrest in an editorial. But beyond that, there was largely silence. (The *New York Post* sort of covered it, reporting: "Two men were arrested inside the Lehman College auditorium when they started heckling the candidates, according to police.")

One criterion for coverage that journalists cited when I spoke to them early in the campaign was federal matching funds. Agran, they told me, was unlikely to qualify. But when Agran, without any significant press coverage, did eventually qualify for federal matching funds in mid-May, there was virtually no press mention of this, and no change in the attention level he received.

Agran did not win his party's nomination. But he did receive a few delegate votes at the convention. They were listed on the TV screens as votes for "Other. . . ."

****

Most of the national journalists I spoke with during the campaign expressed little surprise over the press treatment Agran received, and they offered similar explanations for it. Tom Rosenstiel, for example, who is based in Washington and writes on media and politics for the *Los Angeles Times,* suggested that there are several reasons. For one thing, political reporters tend to cover those candidates that their sources tell them are the "major candidates." Reporters ask them, What are you hearing? Who is lining up endorsements? Who is doing fundraisers for whom? This year, especially, Rosenstiel says, "the last thing the Democratic leaders want is to have attention paid to someone like Larry Agran, which would reinforce the impression that they are putting forward a 'field of unknowns.' "

Secondly, says Rosenstiel, it is difficult and confusing and expensive for the media to have to contend with a lot of candidates. "Journalists don't sit around in newsrooms asking, 'Whom else should we cover?' The big question is 'Whom can we *stop* covering?' " An election, said Rosenstiel, "is not a matter of who is the smartest, the most articulate, or who has the best ideas. . . . What it really comes down to is who can win the most votes." Ultimately, Rosenstiel notes, "if we think someone is not likely to win, then we don't think of them as someone to devote much time to."

But Jeff Cohen, Executive Director of FAIR, a New York based media watch-dog group, argues that "It's not up to the media to determine whom we get to hear and whom we don't. That's not reporting, it's censorship." He told me during the primary that "the media have made Agran a reverse Zelig. He's clearly at the right places at the right time, and they excise him from the picture."

Washington Post columnist, Colman McCarthy, who pressed for Agran's inclusion in televised debates, agreed with Cohen. He expressed disgust with the "incestuous" relationships between the media and party elites. "A major abuse in the media is not that we slant the news, but that we can arbitrarily choose the news. The Agran blackout exemplifies that this is a journalistic crime easily gotten away with. Who is going to report it? Not the criminals, for sure."

B. IMAGE MAKING

With the exception of a relatively few people, voters do not come to know candidates separate from the cognitions gained from the mass media. Therefore, the image of the candidate carried by the voter is media-created. This is especially true for candidates running for president for the first time.

However, this doesn't mean the candidate's portrayal is influenced only by the media. Campaigners understand this role of the media in the electoral process and act throughout the campaign to shape that media-conveyed image.

The two forms of media used for image-making purposes are free and paid media. Free media consists of news coverage of the candidate's activity including speeches, campaign appearances, debates, and campaign organization efforts. Paid media is political advertising.

Candidates employ both free and paid media to create images because each possesses certain advantages. Free media has the advantage of cost and credibility.

Although efforts to obtain free news coverage are not "free," owing to the campaign apparatus—press secretaries, event arrangements, etc.—involved, this coverage is far less costly than paid media. Free media is also more credible with voters since the candidate is not seen as controlling the message.

Paid media does provide that control because of the lack of an editorial filter provided by the press. The candidate can design the packaged advertisement to conform to the desired image.

In the following excerpts we see campaign image-making efforts through free media—news coverage—and paid media—political advertising. The first selection presents the news strategies that political campaigns use to acquire favorable coverage. The second selection explores the interaction between the campaign organization and the public in the campaign's efforts to tailor a paid media message to its intended audience.

21. CAMPAIGN NEWS STRATEGIES

F. Christopher Arterton

Presidential campaigns and the press do not operate in two separate spheres—campaign organizations devising and implementing strategies for achieving electoral victory and reporters observing and reporting their activity. Rather, their behavior is intertwined in a symbiotic relationship.

Candidates rely on the press to aid in the implementation of the strategy of reaching voters. They know that, to voters, the campaign is a reality governed by perceptions—media-directed perceptions. The image of the candidate portrayed in the news media presentation will shape powerfully voters' perceptions of the candidate and affect the candidate's eventual victory or defeat.

F. Christopher Arterton describes the strategies that political campaigns use to employ press coverage in their behalf. He lists four goals that campaigns have in their interaction with news media, and he explains how campaigners attempt to manipulate the relationship with the press to achieve these goals.*

F. Christopher Arterton is dean of the Graduate School of Political Management in Washington, D.C. In addition to *Media Politics* (1984), from which the following is excerpted, he is author of *Teledemocracy* (1987) and co-author of *The Electronic Commonwealth* (1988).

THE CAMPAIGN NEWS STRATEGY

Campaigners use whatever means lie at their disposal to achieve beneficial news coverage. Their strategy is based on their desire to pass some major communication costs over to the media corporations, an understanding that news has more credibility than advertising, and a firm belief that reported news does shape their political support.

*From *Media Politics* (Lexington, Mass.: Lexington Books, 1984), pp. 30–35. Reprinted with permission.

By making desired stories easy to report while attempting to obscure or detract news value from stories deemed harmful to the candidate, campaigners maneuver to limit the agenda of the daily news. Yet, even when they are successful in influencing the content of news reporting, politicians are never able to dictate a journalist's report. Reporters and correspondents retain final control over what they print and broadcast. Yet because politicians normally hold the initiative in generating events that can be reported, they can control—at least to some extent—the range of stories that are available. The predictability in the news process does permit campaigners to plan their political efforts with the headlines in mind.

To what ends do politicians pursue media politics? Campaigners report that several distinct goals shape the development of the campaign news strategy.

NAME RECOGNITION

The first concern of campaign operatives is to achieve access to voters through the news media. They are interested in sheer exposure. Whether accurately or not, politicians assume that name recognition is fundamental to the process of securing votes. If candidates are not covered, they will not become known. The era in which voters pull the lever for their party's candidate—whether or not they have ever heard of him—is over, if it ever existed. Name recognition has become a critical ingredient in the calculus of electability, particularly in primary elections where party identification has less influence and differences in recognition levels can be substantial.[1] But even in general elections, campaigners believe that voters will not support a candidate whose name they do not recognize.[2]

Promoting name recognition by maximizing news coverage is, therefore, the initial step of the campaign's news strategy. For example, during the 1976 presidential campaign, Senator [Frank] Church and his advisers decided to start late in the primary season when, presumably, the other candidates would be nearing exhaustion. However, by mid-May, when Church began to recruit voters in the Nebraska primary, most reporters had already been assigned to other candidates. His political strategy, thus, ran counter to the practical need to provide visibility. Despite their best efforts, Church received very little coverage both before and after his win in Nebraska:

> In April, the networks waited until just before the Nebraska primary to assign crews to Church. They were traveling permanently from that point on. . . . They gave us a few bad shots, but they're not as damaging as just nonexposure. You can't overcome other candidates who are on the screen two or three nights per week.[3]

The goal of expanding name recognition is not, however, as straightforward as it first appears. We cannot predict that campaigners will seek to maximize their news coverage indiscriminantly under all circumstances. Some campaigners may target segments of the electorate and, consequently, focus on gaining exposure through specific news outlets. These segments can be based on policy interests, the probability of campaign involvement (for example, party activists versus mere voters), or geographic concerns. As the general election campaign nears a conclusion, for example, local media in pivotal states may become more important to the candidates than those which deliver a nationwide audience. On the other hand, little-known candidates may count upon the news exposure accompanying early primary victories to boost their national ratings:

> In the primaries, your basic thing is to get known, at least in the states where you're running early, and if you're successful then that takes care of your national recognition problem overnight.[4]
>
> The places that our name recognition had better be high are New Hampshire and Florida. We don't have to worry about the rest of the country. But if we do well in those states, particularly if we win New Hampshire where we're not expected to do well at all—a Southerner in a New England state, you know—we could get on the cover of *Time* and *Newsweek* and all of a sudden this guy nobody ever heard of before is, maybe, the probable nominee. . . .[5]

Finally, during the year preceding the primaries, most campaigners recognize the impossibility of attracting television coverage. Accordingly they devote their efforts to reaping newspaper coverage, knowing that clippings, particularly those from prestigious national papers, can be photocopied for mass mailings to party activists and local journalists. During these initial stages, campaigners seek to communicate with attentive publics through media like newspapers or magazines which may have lower salience to the mass electorate.[6]

In practice, the pursuit of name recognition can include efforts to associate a candidate's name with a particular office. Even well-known politicians will seek news coverage to link their candidacy to a position. The [Ronald] Reagan campaign in 1976 and the [Edward] Kennedy campaign in 1980 experienced great difficulties in generating a continuous flow of news coverage between the end of the primary campaign and the opening of the August conventions.[7] Each sought to maintain public awareness that its man was a credible candidate for the nomination; both faced the obvious disadvantage of an incumbent candidate who could command legitimate news coverage.

Campaigners' attention to the quantity of news coverage, therefore, does not cease with the attainment of a given level of recognition. Campaign personnel attempt to pace the news flow so that the candidate's activities will be continually reported. These considerations can affect such critical decisions as which primaries to enter. Quite apart from the value of votes and delegates, a continuing calendar of state primaries could ensure that a candidate will not drop out of the national headlines.[8]

Patterson has provided empirical support for the relationship between news coverage and name recognition.[9] The number of respondents who felt they "knew something" about Jimmy Carter rose from only 20 percent in February before the New Hampshire primary to 77 percent just after the Pennsylvania primary in late April. Patterson found that, after his New Hampshire victory, Carter received fully half of the news space devoted to the Democratic race, more than three times the volume allotted to any other candidate.

Occasionally, campaigners may seek to limit the quantity of news reported about their candidate. For example, in the latter stages of the 1976 primary campaign, Carter's strategists became convinced that voters were becoming annoyed at seeing Carter on the network news every night.[10] They limited press access to the candidate and his family and decreased the scheduling of reportable political events in the months before the convention.

FAVORABLE IMAGES

The quest for volume in news coverage is based on the campaigners' acceptance of the hypothesis asserting the media's agenda-setting capacities. Journalists are perceived as able to establish the range of candidates from which voters will choose. Campaigners also desire to use the media to project persuasive information about their candidates.

Substantively, the campaign news strategy consists of persuasive messages about the candidate's personal characteristics, policy stands, or prospects for achieving victory. From the politicians' viewpoint, much of the effort of their campaign consists of repeated attempts to cast essentially the same, simple message into seemingly new forms, such that it will continue to be newsworthy. Each campaign organization seeks to communicate a unique theme or message to the electorate. This message is simultaneously intended to attract political support and differentiate the candidate from his opposition. The appeal may emphasize either images or issues. By informal convention, the discussions between politicians and journalists over campaign themes are usually phrased in terms of their attractiveness to the electorate, rather than as a straightforward debate over the virtues of the candidate or his policy positions. In the process, politicians and journalists cooperate in emphasizing the manipulative aspects of the electoral system, rather than leadership. The ethos of the democratic system in their dialogue becomes primarily the mechanics of how a politician achieves electoral victory rather than a presentation by political elites of the policies they believe correct for the country.

THE PROSPECTS OF VICTORY

Political reporters frequently comment upon the progress of the race itself, combining reports of the election strategies of the contenders with forecasts of probable outcomes. These stories are called "horserace reporting," referring to the interpretations and projections of the likely result of the nomination or election, the "thrill of victory and the agony of defeat" of those who would be president. Politicians perceive such stories as a critical element of their news strategies. Few voters, they assume, will support a politician who has no chance for victory. John Anderson's independent campaign in 1980 and numerous nomination candidacies have been caught in this bind. Many campaigners believe that these horserace stories provide voters with a chief source of information about which candidates have serious prospects.

Accordingly, campaigners make a considerable effort to mold the perceptions of journalists about their candidate's electoral prospects—the likelihood of his

eventual success, the standards according to which his progress should be measured, the levels at which his achievements ought to be labeled "expected" or
"surprisingly strong" or "disappointing," and the implausibility of his opponents'
strategies.

As perceived by these politicians, the media's role in establishing and applying
these standards to each campaign is most significant during the preprimary period,
when there is an absence of concrete events, and a multitude of possible predictors.
Later, success is more and more measured by primary delegate counts, so that room
for plausible criteria is narrowed sharply. Nevertheless, in framing political strategies for gaining the nomination, most campaigners assume that interpretations by
journalists continue to be important throughout the election. As one press secretary
remarked:

> the interpretation of the media will be that much more important . . . because, I think,
> that coming into the convention, if you're short of delegates, the real determining fac-
> tor's going to be the psychological momentum the press creates. Is he the winner? Can
> he get the nomination? Is he acceptable? Given that it's not going to be a clear and
> away winner . . . that interpretation, that psychological momentum, is very important.[11]

INSULATION

A fourth goal of the campaign news strategy is to handle the organizational problems that journalists create for politicians. Once journalists decide that a campaign
is newsworthy, they can become quite intrusive into the campaign's activities. The
press office not only secures news coverage, but fends off reporters to enable other
campaign officials to do their jobs.

Most presidential campaigns adopt specific procedures for responding
to reporters' inquiries. All contact with reporters, for example, is usually coordinated through the press office, both to achieve coordination in the flow of information from the campaign and to insulate campaigners from journalists. Of
course, there are numerous instances in which these rules were violated by individual campaigners.

INTRACAMPAIGN COMMUNICATION

Campaigners might circumvent the centralized press office approach to advance
their individual goals through news coverage. For example, campaigners often use
the news media to communicate to other campaigners or the candidate himself,
particularly when internal channels have proved fruitless. Such attempts need not
be entirely self-serving, as, for example, when state-level coordinators are quoted by
the press saying that the state will be lost unless the candidate appears there.[12]

The use of journalists for internal communication is not limited to attempts by
subordinates to signal their superiors. In July 1975, [Democratic presidential candi-
date] Terry Sanford used a press conference to commit his campaign organization
to qualifying for federal matching funds within one month. Internal memoranda
would not have had the same compelling effect, since in his press conference

Sanford invited journalists to enforce this policy upon his own campaign organization. Once the campaign was committed publicly to that goal—particularly one so easy to measure—subordinates knew that newsmen would continually measure their progress.

Technically, this use of the news reporting process falls outside our definition of a campaign news strategy. Rather than securing the goals of individual campaigners, a news strategy refers to the objectives of the organization. Nevertheless, these examples provide a reminder that campaigns are composed of individuals with diverse goals.

To what degree can campaigners rationally plan and implement their strategies? These organizations are composed of individuals operating to fulfill their own agendas.[13] They may produce either strategy by committee or an amalgam of the disjunctive action of campaigners striving to reach individual goals.[14] Yet upper-level campaign personnel do carefully plan the organization's political efforts.[15] Furthermore, at least some evidence indicates that campaigns behave rationally. . . .[16]

NOTES

1. See, for example, the role assigned to name recognition in a study of congressional races by Thomas E. Mann, *Unsafe at Any Margin* (Washington, D.C.: American Enterprise Institute, 1978).

2. For example, Gerald Rafshoon, Carter's advertising manager, worried as late as mid-October that substantial segments of the electorate still knew very little about Carter (speech before the American Association of Advertising Agencies, New York, October 14, 1976).

3. Personal interview with Deborah Herbst, press aide to Senator Frank Church, October 7, 1976.

4. Personal interview with Richard Stout, press secretary to Morris Udall, January 12, 1976.

5. Personal interview with Hamilton Jordan, campaign manager for Jimmy Carter, July 22, 1975.

6. On the notion of "attentive publics," see Donald J. Devine, *The Attentive Public* (Chicago: Rand McNally, 1970); James N. Rosenau, *Citizenship Between Elections* (New York: The Free Press, 1974); Gabriel A. Almond, *The American People and Foreign Policy* (New York: Praeger, 1960), pp. 137ff; or V.O. Key, Jr., *Public Opinion and American Democracy* (New York: Knopf, 1961).

7. Personal interview with Lyn Nofziger, convention coordinator for Ronald Reagan, August 16, 1976.

8. Personal interviews with John Gabusi, campaign manager for Udall, December 10, 1976, and Bob Neumann, press secretary to Udall, July 6, 1976.

9. Thomas Patterson, *Mass Media Election* (New York: Praeger, 1980), p. 109, and "Press Coverage and Candidate Success at Presidential Primaries: The 1976 Democratic Race." Paper presented at the 1977 meeting of the APSA, Washington, D.C., September 1–4, 1977.

10. Personal interview with Hamilton Jordan, campaign manager for Carter, December 3, 1976.

11. Personal interview with Frank Greer, press secretary to Fred Harris, July 7,1975.

12. See, for examples, the remarks by the Carter coordinators in California and New Jersey, the *New York Times*, October 29, 1976.

13. This is explicitly argued by Kayden, *Campaign Organization*, and implicitly by Hershey, *The Making of Campaign Strategy*.

14. For a discussion of how organizational outputs may be other than rationally calculated, see Graham T. Allison, *The Essence of Decision* (Boston: Little, Brown, 1971) or John Steinbruner, *The Cybernetic Theory of Decision* (Princeton, N.J.: Princeton University Press, 1974).

15. Rational theory's strongest advocate for campaign organizations can be found in Arnold Steinberg, *Political Campaign Management* (Lexington, Mass.: D.C. Heath, 1976).

16. See Aldrich, *Before the Convention*, and Hershey, "Social Learning Theory."

22. 30-SECOND POLITICS

Montague Kern

Image making through paid media—campaign advertising—is a crucial element of any modern presidential campaign. But such image making is not conducted in a vacuum. The construction of an image and the advertising that will serve as the medium are developed in conjunction with survey research. Campaign organizations conduct experiments of voter reaction to ads before airing them publicly.

Candidate image making has its limitations as well. The public's preconceptions about candidates are not easily altered. Image making is more successful when it conforms to and reinforces public perceptions rather than attempts a conversion process.

One such candidate with image problems was Walter Mondale. Mondale lost badly in the 1984 presidential election, winning only his home state—Minnesota. His inability to articulate a consistent message that resonated with voters contributed to his defeat.

The following segment reveals the interaction between public opinion and image construction through paid media in the image-making efforts of the Mondale campaign. Montague Kern details the efforts of the Mondale campaign to shape an image congenial with public expectations and concerns in the face of strong preconceptions about Walter Mondale's candidacy.*

Montague Kern teaches communications at Rutgers University. She is the author of *The Kennedy Crises: The Press, the Presidency, and Foreign Policy* (1983) and *30-Second Politics: Political Advertising in the Eighties* (1989), from which this selection is excerpted.

Walter Mondale's 1984 presidential campaign illustrated how even the most philosophically informational media campaign could turn to an emotional style. The campaign set out, as Mondale expressed it, to "grind away," educating people to such complex issues as the deficit and the consequent need to raise taxes. A part of this effort was to prove that his opponent, incumbent president Ronald Reagan, was "blow-dried," a seeming success simply because he was a good video communicator. Ironically, when pressed both during the primary and general election campaigns, the Mondale campaign itself turned to a highly emotional style.[1]

A "mixed," or new informational, Democratic media campaign failed resound-

*Montague Kern, *30-Second Politics: Political Advertising in the Eighties* (New York: Praeger, 1989), pp. 113–30.

ingly, and Walter Mondale lost every state except his native Minnesota and found to his dismay that the public overwhelmingly accepted his opponent's version of both the character and issues of the two candidates. . . .[2]

Because the race was such a significant one in terms of the evolution of political advertising, it will be examined in some detail, but from the perspective of the 1984 ad sample. The lessons learned from this race, as will be seen, were implemented by the 1988 Democratic candidates.

The 1984 Democratic advertising challenge was indeed a difficult one. Mondale was 20 points behind President Reagan on Labor Day, having emerged wounded from a series of bitterly fought primaries and a divided convention and having further selected a running-mate without regard for the regional requirements of victory. Walter Mondale needed all the help he could get in the South and the West but hurt himself both by his selection of a vice-presidential candidate from New York [Geraldine Ferraro] and then by his reversal of a decision to appoint Georgia's Bert Lance to a high campaign position. The Bert Lance affair and Mondale's failure to screen the finances of the vice-presidential candidate, followed by his failure to insist that the national campaign manage press coverage of [Ferraro's husband] John Zaccaro's financial irregularities, were major blows not only of substance but also of communications strategy. They foretold a campaign in which Mondale appeared to be helping Reagan achieve his landslide, a landslide that had an important communications dimension.

THE 1984 SAMPLE

The Mondale ads . . . point to acceptance of the premises of an emotional approach to political advertising. In his last-ditch effort during the final days of the campaign, Mondale drew on an emotional advertising strategy as old as the "Daisy" commercial that had linked Barry Goldwater with nuclear irresponsibility. This time, voters were asked not only to "teach your children well" but also to protect them from the consequences of Reagan's military policies.

As the strains of "Teach Your Children Well" die down, and an old woman and a blue-collar worker ("you can decide on how she lives and whether he works") pass by, we are left with two young children. They look up, concerned, their play interrupted. The narrator renews his appeal to the viewer's sense of responsibility, perhaps even to feelings of guilt. "*You* can speak for those who cannot speak for themselves," he says. A missile is launched, and we see the world from outer space.

In "Elderly" the camera focused on a series of defenseless, lonely elderly women whose faces are pinched. Their voices express deep uncertainty as they speak of their desperate plight and inquire what they will do now that Reagan has cut the food-stamp program. As the camera pans away, one concludes that these women just want to "get by."

In a third advertisement, a series of characters representing traditional Democratic constituencies bemoan hard times, and a laborer concludes that Reagan doesn't understand how poor people live. "He's just an upper-class man."

These and other Mondale spots in the 1984 sample were coded for a negative rhetorical style. Four out of nine Mondale 30-second spots which ran 25 times in the 1984 ad sample were coded for anger, centered around themes of economic injustice and uncertainty, a coding which includes the view that the ad appeals to feelings of uncertainty, insecurity, or suspicion. One was coded for guilt, or the view that the intended recipient of the message (who was ignoring the plight of the poor) was not acting responsibly. Although there were few codings on the positive side, there was one coding for compassion, or an appeal to the viewer's desire to help others. This was quite unusual among the 1984 positive presidential codings, which were dominated by the Reagan advertising focus on trust, hope, reassurance, and national and local pride.[3]

Mondale's negative emotional appeals differed from Reagan's positive ones in that they were those of a challenger trying to stop the music, to interrupt the sound of the incumbent's violins.

Mondale officials interviewed during the final days of the campaign said that the final 1984 ad sequence was intended to identify the candidate with doubts about Reagan's sense of fairness and commitment to arms control. But according to one, it was also an effort to give the viewers an emotional jolt. "We've put our argument in emotional terms, in gut-wrenching ways," said one advisor. "If there's going to be a major shift in voter's preferences, it's got to be from the gut level." According to another, it was an advertising campaign designed to tap liberals' sense of "guilt," bestirring the party's traditional supporters on Mondale's behalf in this period when the campaign knew it would lose but hoped to narrow the gap.[4]

The issues that Mondale had originally intended to stress, and that reporters from the campaign trail described Mondale as being happiest discussing, finally emerged in these closing ads, which were flown to him from the offices of Texas consultant Roy Spence for his review on the campaign trail. The Mondale of these ads in late October and early November was a traditional "compassionate" Democrat who favored strong government intervention on behalf of the poor and was profoundly concerned about arms control. This was the Mondale of the campaign's original plan. But it was a Mondale who had never fully emerged earlier because the decision had been made after the Democratic convention to focus in the fall campaign on articulating issues that would build a strong leadership image for a candidate who, as the polling and focus-group research indicated, was perceived to be "weak," or indeed "just a politician." The issues that would strengthen the candidate with the crucial 25–40-year-old voters were favored in the process of issue selection. It was ironic that Mondale's return during the final days of the campaign to the issues he cared most about was perceived as yet another retreat from a previous advertising plan, yet another sign that his advertising was not helping him control the total televised-message agenda.[5]

For both an anonymous "former Mondale media consultant" and Republican consultant Roger Ailes, quoted in the *Wall Street Journal*, the final ads were a sign of desperation. The fact that former Mondale media consultants were divulging their views on the pages of the *Journal* and agreeing with Roger Ailes was a sign of major difficulties in yet another area: lack of unity in the campaign in general.[6]

According to Richard Leone, who held responsibility for Mondale's paid and unpaid media message at the beginning of September, the problem was that by the fall there was so little else that seemed to hold promise that the advertising effort became crucial, but decisions were made by a committee of whoever happened to be around. Leone, a protege of Jim Johnson, who had devised Walter Mondale's original campaign strategy, was, during these final days, engaged in a spirited disagreement with the "people who run the campaign" who had moved the advertising in what he considered a futile negative direction. Indeed, there were many other signs of disunity in the campaign. One was the fact that such media consultants as Leone and Roy Spence had limited access to the upper echelons of campaign decision making. From this, Spence later concluded that he would never be in a campaign again "where I'm not in control."[7]

The Mondale effort was also heavily outgunned in terms of spot airtime during the final ten days of the election. Mondale's 30-second and 1-minute ads were overshadowed 3 to 1 with 27.5 to Reagan's 79 minutes of airtime. If Reagan's 30-minute ad, broadcast the night before the election, is included, his lead in the 1984 sample airtime rises from 3 to 1 to 4 to 1. The Mondale campaign's modest efforts to focus the debate on questions of food stamps, education, agriculture, and economic opportunity were also overwhelmed in terms of issue advertising airtime by the Reagan themes of government size, inflation, interest rates, and taxes. Part of the difference between the two campaigns during this period, of course, may be due to the fact that Mondale pulled ads from a number of states during the final blitz (including North Carolina and Georgia, the two states included in this sample) in his last-ditch attempt to prevent the loss of Minnesota.[8]

Human symbols and music both confirmed the throwback during this period to the traditional group-oriented Democratic focus of the ads in the 1984 sample. Unlike the Reagan advertising, and much of the other advertising in the sample, the characters represent traditional constituencies. The appeals offered more of an interest-group than an individual orientation, confirming an approach that was more political than commercial. The music was not the broad, swelling sound that would appeal to everyone; it was a Crosby, Stills, and Nash tune designed to rally the aging 1960s liberals who had to turn out if the whole effort was not to become a 50-state rout.

THE IMPORTANCE OF EARLY IMAGES

For months the Mondale presidential primary media campaign had been guided by the need to develop themes that the strategists, pollsters, and focus groups determined would move large numbers of people for immediate ends. Thus, with the whole Democratic primary field committed to arms control, the candidates did not develop an advertising focus on this issue, which the polls indicated was an area of vulnerability for Ronald Reagan. As a result, no groundwork was laid for a race against Reagan in the fall general election. Reagan, whose polls indicated that he was also vulnerable on the age issue (he was a septuagenarian) and on the possibility of "Democratic return to the fold" in the fall, was thus given plenty of time in the spring and summer to develop a carefully coordinated advertising and news media effort to "inoculate" himself on such issues.[9]

At one point in the hard-fought primary season running ahead of Gary Hart in Ohio, the Mondale campaign launched a first salvo against Reagan by running a "Star Wars" ad. But Mondale lost Ohio to Hart, who focused on "hard times" in the traditional industrial states and launched a hard-sell negative integrity attack on Mondale as a "changeling" politician who was not "like us" but at the beck and call of the "special interests."

Mondale returned with a similar attack—in what was clearly becoming the negative coin of the presidential primary race. The commercial was called "Red Phone," and it was of the hard-sell negative genre in its appeal to feelings of public uncertainty, relating fear of nuclear war to the opponent's qualities, in this case not having held public office. Would one want to elect an "inexperienced" president who might not know what to do when that "Red Phone" rang?

This particular ad achieved its objective. According to Texas media consultant Roy Spence, it was inspired by the urgently blinking lights and ringing phones encountered on a hospital visit to his wife, who was imminently expecting the birth of their child while he was under his own deadline to come up with an ad to use in the bitterly contested Hart-Mondale race.[10]

Joe Trippi, who ran the Mondale primary effort in Pennsylvania, said that

> "Red Phone" was used to respond to everything they threw at us. In this case, fear of nuclear war worked for us. The other guy would be arguing, "No guts, no belly, owned by labor." We didn't address that. We spent millions of dollars on that ad.[11]

Not surprisingly, the negative campaigning—in which the "no-guts" and the "dangerously inexperienced" candidates faced off—left a bitter legacy not only in the public opinion polls, in which Mondale started the general election campaign with "high negatives," but also with disaffected supporters who had favored his opponent in a number of states. One of these was California, the largest general election battleground, where many Democrats who gave Hart the nod during the primary remained unrequited into the fall general election.

Campaign manager Robert Beckel later commented that Mondale was damaged by the primary season, in what he described as a "lack of set-up" going into the fall campaign. "We were in the fourteenth round to start the fight. When you can't see light until Labor Day, what are you going to do?" Further, according to Beckel, "we ran an issueless primary campaign as the 'pick of the lot.'" The problem was, thus, that the negative referential primary advertising laid the foundation for Republican attacks on Mondale's character, making them credible. Hart's "no-guts, no-belly" attacks hit home, dovetailing with publicized speeches the candidate had given in seeking interest-group support over three years of campaigning for the nomination. The public suspected he was the "interest-group candidate," and this was confirmed for many by the fact that Mondale had not actually established what he stood for. Reagan could beat him using Mondale's own thesis, as developed in "Red Phone," that the candidate with less experience might endanger the nation. If Mondale had spent four years a heartbeat away from the "Red Phone," Reagan had spent four years even closer to it, and the United States was still at peace.[12]

The hope, according to Mondale media coordinator Richard Leone, was that in the general election campaign, it would be possible to achieve an objective similar to that envisioned by the Reagan campaign: *to make the Mondale-Ferraro candidacy "America."* As Leone expressed it, the idea was to make the campaign the vehicle *for Americans to achieve their own "hopes, dreams and symbols"* (italics mine). The advertising effort should

> build a new vision of America, of this new party featuring Mondale and Ferraro. A good many of the visual symbols and the whole initial media campaign planned by Roy Spence was around that set of themes—family, and patriotism and progress, equality and women.[13]

Although the first three of these were similar to those articulated in the Reagan media, the latter—equality and women—was different, as was the consistent set of issues ("part of Jim Johnson's initial plan") that would also be presented. These were

> fairness, which people felt Reagan might be vulnerable on, war and peace, and the looming problem of dealing with the deficit. At least that was Mondale's conception of what he should make his campaign about, and that's what he wanted his media to be about.[14]

The first task of the campaign, however, was to rehabilitate Mondale, moving him forward from the "Carter–Mondale" image. His "negatives were bad before the convention, and the Lance thing was really bad. Then he came back remarkably quickly." This whole approach "had to be scrapped, however, when the initial scandal broke around [vice-presidential candidate Geraldine] Ferraro, the candidate who by the end of the campaign was the least popular in the race."[15]

FOCUS-GROUP FEEDBACK

Thus, in late August and early September, with the story of John Zaccaro's finances dominating the news, the wounded Democratic campaign tested image and issues ads to use in the race against Reagan. The findings of focus groups conducted by Edward J. Reilly of Boston say a great deal about the problems Mondale faced and offer feedback concerning how a presidential campaign can evaluate its advertising effort. The lessons might equally apply to any candidate attempting to develop a coherent message after his or her credibility has been severely damaged.

In a series of "Mondale to Camera" ads tested on September 4, the Reilly

group concluded that respondents were "distracted by the visuals and by his presence" and "had difficulty understanding the message" concerning education, taxes,
and the deficit. Several remarked that Mondale may be right on the issues, but they
didn't "see how he's going to do it." One undecided farmer reached the conclusion
most feared by the Mondale campaign: "He reminds me of Carter in those ads." Of
one, in which the candidate appeared in a football jersey in an effort to strengthen
his image, an undecided heavy-equipment operator remarked, "Mondale is not a
football player, and I think it looks stupid to have him walking around in a sweat-
shirt."[16]

The view that emerged from such focus groups was that the public believed
Mondale was weak. This perception contributed to the development of the campaign's foreign policy message. The Reilly group tested a number of foreign policy
ads. In one, Mondale outlined a position favoring arms control negotiations. The
report concluded that there was a problem with them. People did not believe
Mondale would be a tough negotiator. The focus group leader concluded, "This
type of thing would work much better with a third party of stature describing his
strengths in foreign affairs." Another 60-second spot, "Arms Unlimited," argued
that every president except Ronald Reagan had achieved an arms control treaty.
Reagan, instead, "has embarked on a massive arms race and . . . refuses to discuss
banning weapons from outer space." The text referred to arms control agreements
concluded from Eisenhower through Carter, over visuals depicting treaty-signing
ceremonies. It ended with a quote from Kennedy's 1961 inaugural speech: "Let us
never negotiate out of fear, but let us never fear to negotiate."[17]

The focus group revealed a public confused by efforts to use spots to articulate
an arms control position based on its historic context. Participants related better to
specific presidents and the "process" in its most general sense, rather than to any
results. For example, Reilly noted that they were "confused by all of the different
information [presented in "Arms Unlimited"] but responded positively to the
Kennedy quote." Further, participants favored "talking" over "treaties" as a solution
to problems caused by nuclear weapons. Treaties were perceived as legal documents
"that got us into the trouble we're in."[18]

Ads were tested that scored Reagan for a joke in which over an open mike he
inadvertently suggested imminent bombing of the Soviet Union. It turned out that
viewers did not perceive this as a serious mistake. The only ads that worked were
"Reagan–Chernenko," which noted the advancing years of *both* leaders and scored
them for holding "the same stalemated ideas for so long, that they cannot find anything new to think," and "Conference Table," which connected this idea with an
empty table. Use of the latter was recommended because voters "want dialogue, and
the conference table is a neat, clear, and dramatic example of Reagan's record."[19]

Polling data confirmed the focus groups' conclusions that Mondale was perceived to be weak. The campaign accordingly avoided the arms control issue, which
was in any event, as the testing indicated, difficult to express visually. This decision
represented the triumph of visual as the fact of talking itself—which is what people
perceive in television coverage of summit meetings between the heads of states,

rather than the results of those talks—*became the Mondale issue.* Thus, failure to talk as symbolized by an empty table was the campaign's main arms control issue. According to Beckel, the feelings of the 25–40 age group were decisive in campaign decision making in this vital area in which the campaign had long realized it must differentiate Mondale from Reagan. The group, quite simply, did not care for the complexities of the arms control process. Concern for the views of this elusive age group also contributed to the decision not to open with "fairness," which implied "big government."[20]

This was a generation raised on television, with its individualism and heroes, and visual memories of a series of ambitious but failed presidents culminating with Jimmy Carter, with whom Walter Mondale was repeatedly linked by fellow Democrats during the primary and by Republicans during the general election campaign. "Our way of dealing with the *wimp* factor," according to Trippi, a youthful addition to the Mondale campaign,

> was the "Nimitz" ad—Mondale on deck, on an inspection tour with jets flying overhead. But after two years of not doing anything to make the average guy think he's a hero, this may have brought attention to whatever may have been causing the problem.[21]

The Reilly group concluded in late August that

> nothing about Mondale stuck, relating either to his family, or his career, or whatever, because there was no sense of an ideological core, something he stood for. Because voters believe that Reagan's ideology is strong, they view his pragmatism in positive terms . . . while Mondale holds up his finger to see which way the wind is blowing. . . . This is particularly disturbing because it leads respondents to a position where they are willing to believe that Reagan is more of a family man, more religious, and more of a decent person. Without a sense of Mondale's soul, respondents were quite willing to take the symbols of Mondale's life and synthesize them into a Mondale that is developed more by the image of Jimmy Carter than Walter Mondale. . . . The sense of "not knowing" Mondale really is a desire to know if there is anything Mondale is willing to fight for regardless of political risk. The tax-truthfulness issue [developed at the Democratic convention] was beginning to do exactly that but has been obscured by recent events [surrounding the Ferraro disclosures].[22]

DOVETAILING: STRESS ON AN ISSUE TO BUILD CHARACTER

Further development of an issue—the deficit—was therefore recommended in September to give Mondale definition as a person of firm beliefs. The deficit issue would work for Mondale because it

> is becoming a term that is representative of personal fears about the individual's economic viability . . . [and] there is frustration with the enormity of the problem, a feeling of helplessness. Respondents, however, demonstrated a clear desire to begin to "clean up the mess" provided they were shown a plan that would work, and that was fair to them personally.[23]

The conclusion was that the campaign should attack on the issue in a way that would "shake up the framework" of economic satisfaction but, equally important, present a plan for what should be done.

Testing of components of a proposed plan, however, produced mixed results. Respondents questioned Mondale's commitment to spending cuts and his ability to be more effective in this area than Reagan, and they were confused by efforts to explain his "15 percent minimum corporate tax." As the respondents' reactions in the arms control area also indicated, it is difficult to explain a complex issue in a spot. The campaign was aware of this but decided to go heavily with the deficit. Beckel said it was necessary to "create issues because people aren't going to go for slogans. 'This guy's better.' Would people believe that? No. So we tried to make the deficit an issue, contrary to people's thinking, first at the convention, and then in September when we had to explain Mondale's position. And Reagan did a very good job of keeping out of that issue."[24]

If the idea was to make Walter Mondale the issues candidate, in part as a way to build his character, to make "being a politician work for him," it was also an attempt to provide some "symbolic negatives" to carry a negative message about the character of Ronald Reagan. The idea was to enhance, by means of a very real issue, the idea that Reagan was a demagogue or "salesman." Despite its general conclusion that attacks on Reagan didn't work, the report recommended that the campaign go with a type of negative ad, "Taxes," which quoted Reagan and Bush inconsistencies on taxes, based on news coverage, and concluded with a Mondale statement: "Mr. Reagan will raise taxes, and so will I. He won't tell you. I just did." The recommendation was based on the view that after seeing the ad, respondents' description of Reagan changed from "leader" to "politician."[25]

Reilly said the campaign should "use actual footage of Reagan 'dancing' on various issues, i.e., new taxes, to politicize him, and move him from the image of an ideological purist to that of a demagogue." At the same time, it should use two negative ads by New York media consultant David Sawyer, "Deficit (Father)" and "Roller Coaster" to bring the deficit issue home in a way people can understand.

HARD-SELL NEGATIVE ADS

Both "Deficit (Father)" and "Roller Coaster" were hard-sell negative ads featuring mixed generations. . . . They were the mirror opposite of the positive Reagan ads that mixed generations. "Roller Coaster" opens with visuals of the hands of a man and boy holding the bar of an ascending car to the sound of the roller coaster's mechanism, "click, click, click." The announcer describes how the deficit could drive interest rates through the roof, cause unemployment, and send "us into a recession again. But . . . most people don't seem to be worried . . . not yet." The car reaches the summit and then begins a precipitous fall down the tracks. The voices become anxious, "Uh-oh! Here we go!" and the last sound is that of the boy taking a deep breath. There is a freeze frame and a super: "If you're thinking of voting Republican in 1984, think about what will happen in 1985."[26]

The report indicated that the spot "worked well. . . . Viewers laughed and nodded as the car went up, and they all knew the fear of the impending decline. The spot induced fear and apprehensiveness . . . [but] when probed for further response, they rejected the impending decline as the fault of Reagan or the Republicans."[27]

"Deficit (Father)" also opens with a close-up of hands, this time the father's, which were wringing in dismay at the burden of his debt. Finally, he asks, "Could I ask you to pay it back?" A child's hand reaches into the frame, takes the man's hand, and comforts him as a small voice says, "Sure . . . Daddy. I'll try." The announcer chides the Republicans for their lack of a plan to deal with the huge national debt and for their willingness to "pass it on to our children and grandchildren."

According to the focus-group report, viewers did not respond very well to this. They were "defensive" about the deficit being "their fault." Like "Roller Coaster," the format was the opposite of the Reagan hope ads, using an inter-generational family mix to raise the level of voter uncertainty about the future. Both conclude, "If you're thinking of voting Republican in 1984 . . . just think of what could happen in 1985." They were ads that, according to the commercial language of the 1980s, tried to create an "experience" or take the viewers across a wheel of emotions. But there was no alternative, no resolution, at the end: There was no "fast, fast relief" in the form of a credible candidate.[28]

Reilly's recommendations on the deficit advertising were followed, despite the argument of some in the campaign that negative advertising against Reagan would not work. The Reilly report also warned, however, that such ads would not work unless they were accompanied by positive ads that would outline Mondale's approach to the subject. And so an effort was put into developing a plan that would be used for this purpose to influence both the paid and unpaid media. The plan came out on the very day that Geraldine Ferraro stole the headlines with details of her husband's finances.

This represented a failure in what is emerging as a key measure of media campaign effectiveness: timing in relation to network news. Both messages were under the control of the Mondale campaign. That it could not control the messages of the two prongs of its campaign, so that one would not interfere with the other, was a sign of problems.

Ultimately, the campaign ran one ad after another on the deficit and other issues, but none ran long enough to dominate the television agenda. For Beckel, this was in part because the campaign had no message that "people wanted to hear." But there was also a problem of simply running any one ad long enough for it to take hold. Not just a theme, an ad. Mondale's media buyer, Judy Press Brenner, was credited by Leone with spending in a fashion that maximized impact and saved money for the campaign. But her superior, campaign co-chair Bob Beckel, believed there was a problem of penetration:

> We had this smorgasbord of stuff that we were trying out. And the problem is that in a lot of major markets we were only running 150–200 points on some of those spots,

which I found out after the fact. . . . You had to infiltrate Reagan. You had to get in and undermine him from underneath. That takes time and an awful lot of exposure. . . .

We were running at a pretty high level [on the deficit issue]. But on particular ads, we were running at low levels. That's one of the things that I complained about. The message may be that we've got a deficit [but] you've got to see the same thing over and over again.[29]

Republican consultant Roger Ailes agreed, but he believed the problem was that Mondale was indecisive, unable to launch one theme and stick with it. Ailes . . . also believed the Mondale campaign would have done better to adopt what became known as the "David Sawyer approach" and stick with it. Sawyer's approach was instead a source of internal campaign disagreement.[30]

BEYOND THE DEFICIT: NEGATIVE ADS ON A SOCIAL ISSUE?

Sawyer believed that by September the Republicans had recovered from their initial waffling on the deficit issue. The Democratic presidential campaign might use deficit ads briefly, but it should move on to tough attack spots on social and religious-freedom topics. . . . Sawyer developed one tough social issues ad, "Abortion."[31]

"Abortion"

VIDEO	AUDIO
A black card with white type: "1985."	
"1985" fades into darkness. Bedside lamp turned on. Viewer sees bedside table with lamp turned on. Viewer sees bedside table with lamp, clock radio, and phone. Man's hand reaches for phone.	Phone begins ringing.
	Man: "Hello?"
	Young woman: "Daddy? It's Mary Ellen. Daddy . . . something terrible . . , Daddy."
	Another man's voice on the line: "Mr. Sawyer? This is Lieutenant Kennan at police headquarters. Your daughter has been raped. . . . Now, she's not been harmed, but if you and Mrs Sawyer . . ." (voice fades)
Camera moves in on phone, perhaps toward picture of kids on the table.	*Announcer:* "The Republican Party platform says that it will be a law . . . if a woman is raped . . . she must carry the child of the rapist. That abortion will be illegal, even in cases of rape or incest. Think about that. If you vote Republican in 1984 . . . think about what they will do . . . in 1985.
Superimposed on the image: If you vote Republican in 1984, think about what they will do in 1985.	*Young woman:* "Daddy? Tell me everything's going to be okay."

The Reilly group tested the ad and recommended further testing before using it.

This spot created a powerful reaction. Respondents put their heads down, they avoid-ed eye contact with the moderators, they tried not to speak to the issue. . . . Without any questions, this spot generated more emotion than anything else tested. What remains unclear is to what end and does this acute discomfort serve Mondale–Ferraro. With respect to drawing a sharp issue distinction with Reagan–Bush, it worked. As far as agreement with our position, it was unanimous. I would like to see further testing of this before airing.[32]

Leone, to whom the Reilly group reported, said he opposed all negative adver-tising. Beckel said he opposed the Sawyer approach because the ads concluded with the slogan, "If you think you've got problems in '84, wait till '85."

My problem with those ads, although I thought they were done very well, was that peo-ple didn't think there was a problem in '84. Thus there was no reason for them to think there was going to be a problem in '85. I'm not sure if in the choice of who would be their leader, Mondale or Reagan, Mondale would have won that debate."[33]

Thus, "the fear of the future under Reagan was a theme that was debated, and we didn't take." Mondale was not inclined to do it, but Pat Caddell's polling showed that any attack on Reagan along the lines of the Sawyer ads would "backfire [on the sponsors]," unless the attack was preceded either by "prior education of voters" on the issue, or "some positive reinforcement of Mondale."[34]

There was, as Leone noted, little consensus within the campaign during "the weeks that followed the Ferraro thing." Decisions were made by a committee, whose membership seemed to change depending on who was in town and who wasn't. It was a product of a frustration, of everybody recognizing that the numbers weren't very promising. And thus opening the campaign to anybody who might seem to have an idea."[35]

According to Leone, Sawyer would have probably had more influence had he been in town—he was spending most of his time working on the Hunt campaign in North Carolina, where he recommended use of the same abortion spot. Pat Caddell, who had worked for Gary Hart in the primaries, gained influence, with his mid-September polling showing the campaign 20 points behind, the first challeng-ing presidential campaign to fail to pick up votes in September.[36]

For Beckel, a "winning strategy required a yuppie emphasis." Ultimately, while they couldn't be reached on economic issues, the right-wing agenda on social issues was the one thing that moved them. It was thus decided to introduce attack adver-tising linking the administration with Rev. Jerry Falwell and a checklist for judges. Further, there was a switch to a heavy emphasis on anti-Star Wars advertising in late September, early October. "As we continued to probe and probe," Beckel reported of this period after Caddell joined the campaign:

The other weakness we found in Reagan was that there was still a little bit of the war-monger problem. That's when we went heavily into weapons in space, trying to attract women who were weak Reagan supporters, and also in our unending quest for the baby-boomers.[37]

The California Mondale campaign did not believe the resulting "Star Wars" ad was effective. California's young males, surveyed in a focus group that the local campaign found credible, "loved the lasers." According to Joe Trippi, who moved to work with the California campaign during the general election, the ad confirmed their belief that Mondale was weak and "did not want to be strong." California consultant Jules Radcliffe, who worked with the Mondale campaign in the general election, said Californians believed the "shield was dandy." They didn't care one whit about complexity. People "like a good, simple, clean fight. The Republicans tapped into that."[38]

Radcliffe, who said he favors "redneck advertising," argued that the "blip" in Mondale's favor in late September, early October, had nothing to do with arms control. It was a decline in Reagan's "comfort level" as people, who were not sure about Mondale, recognized that Reagan "has connections with unsavory people, and a [rich] lifestyle, with riding boots, that's hard to relate to." The difference with Mondale, the son of Presbyterian minister, who was in actuality much more a man of the people, "should have been pointed out."[39]

Instead, the campaign was unwilling to take advantage of the "rich boy" attack theme, which would have given a character side to the Mondale deficit message. Instead, the campaign decided to explain the issue in the abstract. Radcliffe viewed this as an impossible task in a media campaign. "Mondale is gifted, bright, and has his heart in the right place. From an intellectual standpoint, he's right. Life is more complex." But "people won't buy any message from a cerebral liberal. We're suspicious of it." Part of the national campaign was not impressed with the California critique. According to Leone, "Why should the views of a group of Democrats which had *never* been able to win a race against Ronald Reagan be given any credence?"[40]

"Star Wars" ran in California in a 3–2 rotation with ads tailored to the local market. These included "Toxic Wastes," a Gary Hart endorsement spot, and a Geraldine Ferraro ad. This latter was a novelty. Ferraro did not appear alone in any national ad because of her growing unpopularity. But the California campaign fought for, and ran, this one. Tensions within the campaign erupted at one point as the California consultants believed that headquarters had leaked a memo in order to undermine the efforts of one of them, Mickey Kantor. California was, however, a must-win state for Mondale. Locally, likely voters' response would be examined through tracking polls after an ad had run for a few days; if it was determined that the ad wasn't "working," it would be "yanked." In California, the Reagan advertising effort outgunned that of Mondale during the final days of the election.[41]

Like the majority of previous challenging presidential campaigns, it moved heavily into attack advertising. According to Leone:

> Mondale became increasingly convinced that he had to attack Reagan. . . . It was not a very effective strategy. But from a great many strategies that didn't seem to offer much promise, that was the one he selected.[42]

There was controversy not only over the selection of advertising themes but in the crucial area of news strategies as well. Leone attempted to prevent attacks on President Reagan from dominating the news. But in September . . . the television coverage he was making, and she, Gerry, was making was largely attacking Ronald Reagan. . . . The campaign had very little success, particularly with Gerry, in getting the candidate to move from that approach. Gerry was on the news every night, attacking, getting cheers, and thinking that she was being effective."[43]

THE IMPACT OF AN INDIVIDUALISTIC VIDEOSTYLE

Walter Mondale later believed that his lack of television savvy contributed to his loss. There were significant structural problems:

> We were running at a very inopportune time against a very popular incumbent when the nation was starved for continuity with the economy performing well and international problems more or less off the stage at the moment."[44]

But his own inability to communicate through television was important. "I'm not trying to excuse what happened in 1984 on the basis of television technique even though I think [Reagan's] a genius at it and I'm not very good at it." And as for wrapping its message in the flag, Mondale later commented, "I just wasn't in that ballgame."[45]

Mondale's discomfort with television is hardly surprising in view of a further finding: the focus group's conclusion that the campaign's message was "negatively impacted by his presence." The heavy news coverage of John Zaccaro's finances was also reported to have upset him, so that he decided to avoid the press by traveling in an airplane compartment off-limits to reporters. He did not take advantage of opportunities to appear on talk shows and avoided camera sessions with his media consultants. They said he was willing to sit down with them only twice, leaving them with the task of sorting through tons of camera footage to find visuals from campaign speeches—hopefully from an early period of the campaign when he didn't have bags under his eyes. Further, there were complaints that at a rally he would launch a theme that was not a part of their media strategy, thus accentuating discontinuity between the paid and unpaid media.[46] Yet the advisors who traveled with him, according to Leone, "talked about [what was going to be on the news] but in fact the day wasn't structured around it, and that was all that Reagan's day was structured around." The campaign was "old-fashioned." And whether because, as Leone thought, Mondale and Ferraro succumbed to "the most frequent mistake candidates make in a campaign, which is to confuse the experience they're having with the experience the voters are having," or for other reasons, there was no unified effort to pitch the campaign to the home video audience rather than to the crowds. As a result, in Leone's view, the voters "were having the experience of seeing Walter Mondale and Geraldine Ferraro yelling at Ronald Reagan."[47]

Declamations that work well with crowds, the candidate's audience in an earlier, people-centered era, do not go over well on national television in an era of "intimate" communication on television. "I" statements, which work with an audience, appear egoistic in the living room. Nor was the recurring "I" persona who appeared on the screen in the news coverage dovetailing with Mondale's attempted issue positioning during the final days of the campaign: that of a "caring" government that should serve the needy. The candidate made a rare appearance in the blitz ads, which were taken from rally tapes. In one, "Cincinnati," which L. Patrick Devlin described as Mondale at his "communicative best," animated and sincere, with tears welling up into his eyes, Mondale appeared as a man of service to others. This ad was part of the final 1984 ad series examined here. Its creator Roy Spence described it as emotional."[48]

Still, in contrast with the Reagan ads, in which the candidate always used the pronoun *we* and focused on the fact that his life was only a reflection of the American spirit, of *American* greatness, in "Cincinnati" Mondale testified to his own life as an example for others, and he used the first person ten times. "If it hadn't been for the GI bill, *I* couldn't have afforded law school, *I* don't think," he said." *I* paid the government back several times, *I* don't mind it" (and neither should the young girl, young man in uniform, black man, and older woman whose images appear on the screen presumably representing this targeted audience). "And *I* want your generation, of all generations in American history, to get the best. *I* want you to learn, *I* want you to challenge yourself. . . . *I* want you to stretch [hands to temples] that mind, think of new things and dream new dreams. *I* want your life to be thrilling and *I* wanna help ya."

"Who won the debate and projected an image of the future?" he also declaimed at a rally in New York the day after his successful first debate, the first real break in his campaign. "*I* did," he concluded. This was the 20-second snippet concerning the debate that appeared on the news that evening, amid speculation about the as yet perhaps incompletely formed public reaction to the debate. It was an especially significant news segment because, as Patrick Devlin pointed out, the campaign cut no ads to prolong the video life of two of its major communicative successes: the convention and the first debate, relying instead on the news coverage to carry the message. Thus to have what appeared to be bragging appear on this crucial segment was a blow. Whether for this or for other reasons, the campaign was disappointed in the amount of life Mondale's actual debate performance afforded the campaign. Mondale used *rally style*, not videostyle, which did not project well on an intimate medium.[49]

Some claimed that it was the pitch of his voice, which was high. When Mondale was forced to shout over the din of boos and chants by hecklers, it was reported that his voice became "whiny." Thus, at a University of Southern California rally, an effort at self-deprecating humor backfired: "I got these bags the hard way. I earned them" came out "strident and challenging." A critique he similarly launched on Reagan's arms control policies was reported to be "shrill, harsh, sometimes menacing." By contrast, Reagan's whole career, like those of such Hollywood figures as Jack Benny and George Burns, has been built on self-deprecating humor, which has long been key to successful communication on the entertainment-dominated commercial electronic media. . . .[50]

LESSONS

The Mondale advertising in the 1984 sample was highly emotional, part of a last-minute effort to hold the fort against a Reagan landslide. It illustrated how even a philosophically informationally-oriented campaign used emotional appeals. The emotions appealed to, while confirming the campaign's acceptance of the premises of an affect-laden rhetorical philosophy, were almost the reverse of those in the Reagan advertising. In terms of our categories, whereas the latter's ads appealed to hope, reassurance, and pride, Mondale's appealed to insecurity, uncertainty, and even more complex negative emotions. Compassion was also a part of the mix. During the general election, as during the primary, the Mondale campaign turned to referential and wheel-of-emotions negative advertising.

One original purpose in the general election campaign advertising was to associate the candidate—wounded in a divisive primary that had featured hard-sell negative spots—with an idea, a courageous stand on the deficit, and the associated need to raise taxes. This was a way of building character, of making "being a politician work for him." The challenge examined in this chapter was that of Walter Mondale's attempt to build a positive image after lengthy receipt of body blows ("no guts, no belly") during the primary, and a campaign in which he had consequently run as the "pick of the lot."

NOTES

1. Mondale quoted in the *Washington Post*, May 8, 1985, p. 2.

2. ABC post-1984 exit polls.

3. See also Chapter 4. Doug Watts was media coordinator for Reagan–Bush relations with their New York commercial advertising team. Watts confirmed the fact that the Reagan ads were appealing to these coded feelings. Interview with Doug Watts, Washington, D.C., December 13, 1987.

4. Mondale campaign officials quoted in an article by Robert W. Merry and David Shribman, *Wall Street Journal*, November 5, 1984.

5. Interview with Robert Beckel, Mondale campaign manager, Washington, D.C., October 23, 1985.

6. Merry and Shribman.

7. Interview with Richard Leone, director of communications, Mondale campaign, New York, February 1986; Spence is quoted in L. Patrick Devlin, "Contrasts in Presidential Campaign Commercials in 1984," *Political Communication Review* 12 (1987): 37.

8. Data from logs of Atlanta, Georgia, television stations obtained on the author's visit to the stations, March 1985. The logs indicated that Mondale pulled ads from the air during the last few weeks. The reason for this was confirmed by Leone.

9. Interview with Lou Kitchen, Southern regional director, Reagan–Bush campaign, Atlanta, Georgia, March 20, 1985.

10. Interview with Joe Trippi, Washington, D.C., June 20, 1985.

11. Ibid.

12. Beckel interview.

13. Leone interview.

14. Ibid.

15. Ibid.

16. Edward J. Reilly, MRK Research Confidential Focus-Group Report, *Mondale/Ferraro Campaign, Boston* 1 (unpublished document), p. 17.

17. Ibid., p. 58.

18. Ibid., p. 52.

19. Ibid., p. 58.

20. Beckel interview.

21. Trippi interview.

22. Reilly, Focus-Group Report, pp. 6–7.

23. Ibid., p. 7.

24. Ibid., p. 12; Beckel interview.

25. Reilly, Focus-Group Report, p. 43.

26. Ibid., p. 41.

27. Ibid.

28. Ibid., p. 40.

29. Beckel interview.

30. Interview with Roger Ailes, New York, January 16, 1986.

31. Beckel interview.

32. Reilly, Focus-Group Report, p. 47.

33. Beckel interview.

34. Ibid.

35. Leone interview.

36. Ibid.; for Caddell see Jack W. Germond and Jules Witcover, *Wake Us When It's Over: Presidential Politics of 1984* (New York: Macmillan, 1985).

37. Beckel interview.

38. Trippi interview; interview with Jules Radcliffe, Los Angeles, California, July 25, 1985.

39. Radcliffe interview.

40. Radcliffe and Leone interviews.

41. Trippi and Radcliffe interviews.

42. Leone interview.

43. Ibid.

44. *Washington Post*, May 8, 1985, p. 2.

45. Ibid.

46. Leone interview.

47. Ibid.

48. Devlin, *Contrasts*, p. 40.

49. Ibid., p. 42, on the campaign's failure to follow up on its most significant moments by means of ads.

50. William Dickenson, "Mondale's Image Is the Victim of the Public Eye," *Washington Post*, October 5, 1984, p. 4. See also Paul F. Boller, *Presidential Anecdotes* (New York: Oxford University Press, 1981).

C. EFFECTS ON THE ELECTORAL PROCESS

In addition to media effects discussed in section 5, the presence of the press as a player in the electoral process has produced effects on other aspects of that process. Public campaigning for president is a media-oriented activity. Candidates organize their schedules around photo-opportunities, press conferences, and interviews. The campaign stops for speeches and rallies are designed primarily for the benefit of the travelling reporters who will carry the candidate's words far beyond the relatively small audience at any one location.

Also, presidential conventions are media extravaganzas. Since the nominee is known prior to the convention's balloting, and the other issues of the convention— vice-presidential selection and platform construction—are usually settled in advance, the convention is a national campaign rally for the party. Convention officials confer with network officials to schedule the events of the convention for prime-time coverage.

Since 1976, nationally televised debates have become staples of a presidential campaign. Candidates are expected to participate, and they spend many precious hours preparing their presentations because they know their messages will reach far more voters in a two-hour debate than in most of the rest of the campaign.

The means of candidate travel has been affected by press coverage. In 1992, the Clinton/Gore bus tour was an attempt to court favorable media coverage as a novel and populist form of interacting with voters. Through press coverage, the Democratic candidates were able to communicate a message of proximity with everyday Americans.

In the following selections, we address two aspects of media effects on the electoral process: news media coverage of public opinion polls and press scrutiny of the candidate's personal lives. Both issues have engendered debate among scholars, pundits, and journalists.

News media polls have proliferated in recent years and, increasingly, media-sponsored polls have become features of news stories of the campaign. Critics of the extensive use of poll stories argue they affect voters' attitudes about voting and their vote choice. The first selection below addresses those questions.

Another recurring issue in media coverage of campaigns is the acceptable level of press scrutiny of candidates' private lives. The private lives and past personal activity of several presidential and vice-presidential candidates during 1988 and 1992 became the object of intense media scrutiny. In 1988, reporters interviewed vice-presidential candidate Dan Quayle's college professors about his academic performance and National Guard officials about his military service. Senator Joseph Biden, a 1988 presidential candidate, had his Syracuse University Law School academic record dug up by the press.

In 1992, the intensive scrutiny continued with Bill Clinton's alleged extramarital affairs, draft record, and associations with exclusive country clubs. Paul Tsongas's health was the subject of investigative reporting. A new twist in 1992 was examination of a spouse's background. Hillary Clinton's legal activities in Arkansas became the object of press scrutiny as well.

The second and third selections debate the value of this press scrutiny as well as its causes. The first of the two, written by a former presidential candidate, critiques press scrutiny. The second, authored by a political commentator, offers a defense for the practice.

23. THE EFFECTS OF POLLING IN ELECTIONS

Diana Owen

Does the reporting of polls during a political campaign affect voters? Are voters swayed by poll results? Are they less likely to turn out to vote if their candidate is comfortably ahead or apparently doomed to defeat? Or are they likely to change their vote choice based on poll results? Are they more likely to vote for the candidate ahead in the polls? On the other hand, do they switch to give the underdog a boost?

The effects of polls on voters are addressed in the research presented below. Diana Owen surveyed voters in Virginia and Wisconsin in 1984 and in Iowa, New Jersey, and Virginia in 1988 to determine the effects of poll-related news stories on voters.

In the excerpt below, she addresses voters' attention to and trust in public opinion polls. Does a voter's candidate preference affect one's trust in polls? In other words, are people more likely to believe polls are accurate when they confirm their candidate is leading?

Owen's findings suggest voters are not so easily susceptible to poll results as might be expected. This research reaffirms the power of the voter's screening process in interpreting media messages.*

Diana Owen is an assistant professor of political science at Georgetown University. This excerpt is taken from her book, *Media Messages in American Presidential Elections* (1991).

POLLS AS NEWS IN THE 1984 AND 1988 PRESIDENTIAL ELECTIONS

In keeping with established trends, polling stories in 1984 and 1988 were of several types. On television news, poll results were often reported in conjunction with the daily coverage of the candidates on the campaign trail. Frequently, vivid graphics accompanied the poll story and depicted trends in voters' candidate preference throughout the nation. At times, poll data were translated into electoral votes, which were then displayed on color-coded maps of the United States. This type of striking graphic accompaniment to poll stories heightened their impact.

Newspaper coverage incorporating poll results was more extensive and somewhat more varied than on television. In the *Washington Post*, for example, stories were generated either from the results of the polls of media organizations, includ-

*Diana Owen, *Media Messages in American Presidential Elections* (Westport, CT: Greenwood Press, 1991), pp. 96–104.

ing the *Post*'s own, or from those of the candidates. Headlines frequently stressed the fact that one candidate was either gaining or losing in strength (Taylor and Coleman, 1984; Broder and Sussman, 1984). In addition to stating the results, poll stories tracked the candidates' progress throughout the campaign, compared the results of different pollsters, and reported predictions for specialized groups of voters, such as the residents of particular states and the members of various demographic groups.

As in the past, polling information became even more important to the reporting of the campaign around the time of key events. Poll stories were particularly prominent at the time of the debates. Polls were taken after each debate to determine who had won the debate and how this may have influenced voter preference. The candidates responded to these projections by plotting their strategies for the remainder of the campaign. Poll reporting also became more intensive during the final two weeks of the election period.

Poll stories in 1984 proliferated in the news media, but with slightly fewer stories on network news than in 1980. The frequency of newspaper poll reports remained as high as in prior years, however. Polls were often either the lead or the second story in the newscast. Significantly more poll stories were reported during the weekend broadcasts than during weeknight news, apparently because poll stories are thought to fit in better with the "softer" weekend news formats (Keenan, 1986).

Polls generally demonstrated that Ronald Reagan held the lead throughout the campaign, but pollsters disagreed greatly about the exact margin of his lead. Poll stories became more prominent and prevalent after Mondale made a strong showing in the first debate. This marked the only time during the election campaign that polls seemed to move in his direction, only to swing back shortly thereafter (Dickenson and Broder, 1984).

Pollsters had a sense that the mood of the country was relatively buoyant in 1984. They therefore formulated questions about people's trust in government and their self-satisfaction to gauge whether people were voting in favor of Reagan or against Mondale. Polls seemed to demonstrate that the vote in this election was more a positive one for Reagan than a negative one against Mondale (Wattenberg and Ladd, 1985).

Estimates of the number of national polls conducted and released through the mass media during the 1988 general election campaign range from 124 (Germond and Witcover, 1989) to 144 (Ratzan, 1989). More than in any previous election, journalists turned to the pollsters for news. The stories that the polls provided were often devoid of both issue and image information about the candidates —further removing the ability of polls to help the public make informed choices.

In the early days of the campaign, during the convention period, Dukakis was running ahead of Bush in the polls. Dukakis experienced a surge in popularity immediately after the Democratic National Convention that was sparked by his strong showing at that event. Between the two conventions, Dukakis did not campaign much. Instead he retreated to the governor's office. This coincided with the decision by the Bush campaign to emphasize Dukakis' "negatives" by playing up his softness on crime. After the Republican Convention, Dukakis' lead in the polls began to slide, as Bush's negative campaign pressed on and gained force. Once Dukakis lost his lead in the polls, his downward slide continued almost unabated. Although we lack empirical evidence, speculation that a bandwagon effect was at work is not unfounded.

One incident in the 1988 election was a landmark in election coverage and conjured up a vast array of ethical questions about poll reporting. On the night before the second presidential debate, Peter Jennings of ABC News spent approximately thirteen minutes summarizing where the candidates stood in the election campaign to that point. Calling it the "most comprehensive poll of the entire campaign," Jennings proceeded to present presidential preference data on all fifty states, complete with eye-catching visuals. With perhaps the most damaging (for Dukakis) presentation of the entire campaign, a colorful map illustrated Jennings' declaration that Bush had a "lock on the electoral college." Jennings stated that the poll found Bush to be an "overwhelming favorite" for the White House. In reality, the poll was riddled with methodological problems and was proved to be inaccurate in several major respects (see Germond and Witcover, 1989: 417–419; Ratzan, 1989). ABC's polling partner, the *Washington Post*, handled the material with greater caution, pointing out more specifics about the sampling procedures and the timing of what were in actuality numerous polls. The conclusion presented by both television and newspaper coverage was that Dukakis did not have a chance of winning. The graphic presentation, especially coupled with the timing of the poll (just three weeks before the election), made it appear that the election was over.

POLLING EFFECTS IN THE 1984 AND 1988 PRESIDENTIAL ELECTIONS

Given this background of the role of polls in elections and of the specific, pervasive part they played in the 1984 and especially the 1988 general elections, we sought to investigate the audience's relationship to presidential preference polls. We examined respondents' levels of exposure and attention to poll results in our election surveys. We also investigated individuals' faith in the accuracy of polls. Finally, we attempted to assess whether knowing where candidates stood in election polls influenced voters' presidential choice or willingness to turn out to vote.

Awareness of candidate preference polls was high for our respondents in both election years. This is not surprising since the surveys were fielded late in the election cycle. Approximately 95 percent of the respondents in all of the counties under study have been exposed to poll results over the course of the campaign. The vast majority of them had obtained their polling information from more than one source. Most frequently, respondents in all counties acquired their poll data from television, followed closely by newspapers. Far fewer people were exposed to polling information through magazines, while a small number obtained the results of polls from radio and other sources.

In spite of this wide-ranging exposure to polling information, few respondents reported having paid a great deal of attention to polls during the campaign. In 1984, there were some differences between Fairfax and Dane Counties in the proportion of respondents who paid very little or no attention to polls. Approximately half of those interviewed in Dane County reported paying little attention to poll results released either on television or in newspapers. Less than 30 percent in Fairfax County indicated that they had very low levels of attention while about 60 percent said that they paid some attention. For both samples, only 14 percent stated that they were very attentive to poll results.

The findings for the 1988 presidential contest are very similar, including the evidence of greater attentiveness to poll results in Fairfax County when compared to the other samples. Approximately 12 percent in each county reported paying a great deal of attention to media-released poll results. In Carroll and Middlesex Counties, about 37 percent stated that they paid almost no attention to polls, while 50 percent were somewhat attentive. In Fairfax County, 25 percent fell into the low attention category, while 65 percent paid a moderate amount of attention.

Attention to poll results was related to party identification across samples in both campaign years. Republicans paid a lot of attention to poll results, while Democrats were less inclined to do so. Compared to partisans, Independents were least likely to pay attention to poll results. Given these findings, we might speculate that Republican respondents were using polls to reinforce and solidify their vote choice, while Democrats were avoiding polls because they contained dissonant information.

The findings for candidate preference do not strongly support such a hypothesis, however. In 1984, Mondale supporters resembled Reagan voters in that they paid only moderate attention to polls. In fact, in Dane County, a greater proportion of Reagan supporters, than Mondale backers paid very little or no attention to poll results, even though their candidate was well ahead. The results appear in Figure 1.

The findings for the relationship between candidate preference and attention to poll results are similar in 1988, with a few exceptions. In Middlesex and Fairfax Counties, Bush and Dukakis supporters were equally unlikely to pay much attention to polls, but the data for Carroll County provide evidence of some level of selective attention. There, 34 percent of Bush voters reported paying a lot of attention to poll results, compared to only 11 percent of Dukakis supporters. In addition, 16 percent of Bush followers paid very little or no attention to polls, while almost 30 percent of Dukakis supporters were nonattentive. This greater propensity of Dukakis supporters to pay very little attention to poll results was also found, to a far lesser extent, in Middlesex County. See Figure 2 for results. . . .

Our next goal was to examine the respondents' trust in the accuracy of poll results reported through the mass media. A vast majority of people in all five samples believed that poll results were accurate some of the time. When we looked at those who did not take this middling position, the findings indicated that people had little faith in polls. In 1984, substantially more respondents believed that polls were often not accurate than trusted their results. The finding was particularly strong in Fairfax County, where nearly one-quarter of the respondents stated that

FIGURE 1

Attention to Polls and Candidate Preference—1984 Election

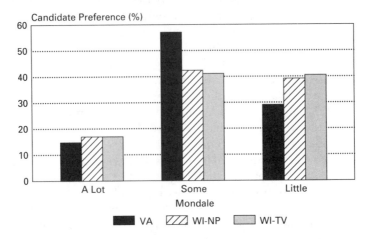

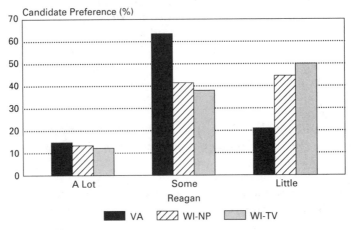

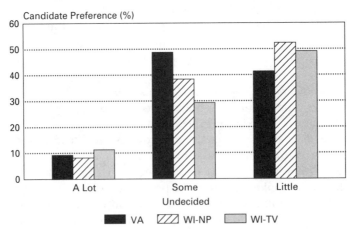

FIGURE 2

Attention to Polls and Candidate Preference—1988 Election

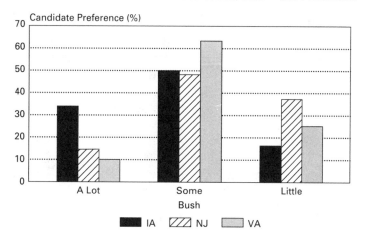

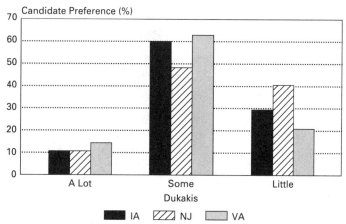

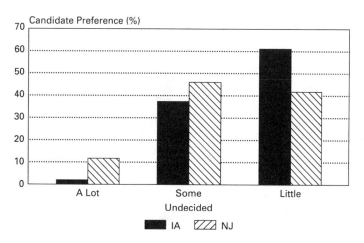

FIGURE 3

Trust in Polls and Candidate Preference—1984 Election

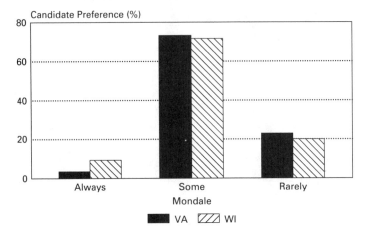

Mondale

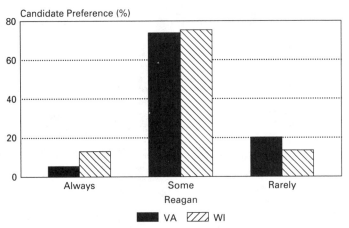

Reagan

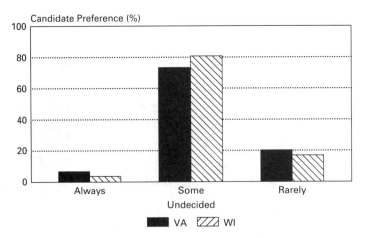

Undecided

FIGURE 4

Trust in Polls and Candidate Preference—1988 Election

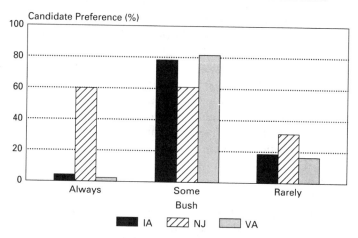

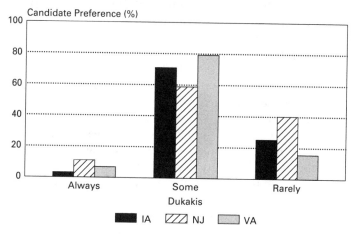

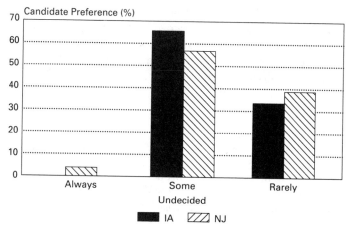

they trusted poll results rarely or never. Comparable findings emerged in 1988 for all three counties. While approximately 3 percent in each county trusted poll results a great deal, 28 percent in Carroll County, 35 percent in Middlesex County, and 17 percent in Fairfax County had almost no faith at all in their accuracy.

Differences in perceptions of polling accuracy were related to candidate preference and particularly to party identification for our 1984 data. Republicans were more likely to say that they always trusted the results of polls than were Democrats or Independents. Independents, particularly in Fairfax County, were less likely to trust the accuracy of polls than were party identifiers.

Reagan supporters were more apt to believe strongly in the accuracy of poll results than were Mondale voters. A larger proportion of Mondale backers stated that they rarely or never trusted polls than either Reagan supporters or undecides. See Figure 3. . . .

The findings for 1988 support the notion that voters are somewhat more likely to trust polls reported through the mass media if their candidate is leading, but the results are less noticeable than for 1984. Only a very weak trend in the data suggests that Republicans trusted polls more than did Democrats in each county; the overall lower level of trust for Independents was substantiated. Bush supporters in Carroll and Middlesex Counties were only slightly more likely to say that they trusted polls a great deal than were Dukakis supporters. More striking was the proportion of Dukakis voters in these counties who felt that polls were rarely or never accurate—28 percent in Carroll County and 40 percent in Middlesex County—as compared to Bush partisans—18 percent and 31 percent, respectively. The findings here are strongest in Middlesex County, while these relationships did not hold true for Fairfax County. One finding, however, was highly consistent in both campaign years. Generally speaking, undecided voters had the least amount of trust in polls when compared to those who stated a candidate preference. The results appear in Figure 4. . . .

From these data we might conclude, with some reservations based on the 1988 data, that voters who found that poll results reinforced their decisions were more likely to trust the polls' accuracy than voters who preferred candidates trailing in the polls. Survey respondents who discovered that the polls disagreed with their choice of candidate were not as interested in polls as those who could use them to justify their decision. The evidence presented demonstrates that selectivity bias exists for poll results, as polls are more relevant to supporters of the winning candidate. . . .

REFERENCES

Broder, David S., and Barry Sussman. "Reagan's Lead in Poll Cut to 12 Points: Mondale Trails 54 to 42 Percent in Latest Post–ABC Survey." *The Washington Post*, 18 October 1984: A1, A6.

Dickenson, James R., and David S. Broder. "Poll Results Indicate Democrat Did Best: Republicans Say 'Knockout' Bid Failed." *The Washington Post*, 9 October 1984: A12.

Germond, Jack, and Jules Witcover. *Whose Broad Stripes and Bright Stars: The Trivial Pursuit of the Presidency 1988.* New York: Warner Books, 1989.

Keenan, Kevin. "Polls in Network Newscasts in 1984 Presidential Race." *Journalism Quarterly* (1986): 616–618.

Ratzan, Scott C. "The Real Agenda Setters." *American Behavioral Scientist* (1989): 451–463.

Taylor, Paul, and Milton Coleman. "Mondale's Polls Show Reagan's Lead Widening." *The Washington Post*, 2 October 1984: A3.

Wattenberg, Ben J., and Everett Ladd. "Moving Right Along? Campaign '84's Lessons for 1988: An Interview with Peter Hart and Richard Wirthlin." *Public Opinion* (1985): 8–11, 59–63.

24. WHY OUR MEDIA MISS THE MESSAGE

Gary Hart

No recent politician has been more wounded by press scrutiny of his private life than Gary Hart. Hart, who ran for the Democratic presidential nomination in 1984 and 1988, was the frontrunner in the primary race when a series of press reports highlighted his extramarital activities. He withdrew from the race in May 1987, and, although he briefly re-entered for two months later in the season, his political career was ruined.

In a speech delivered just before re-entering the race in December 1987, Hart took the media to task for devoting too much attention to a candidate's personal life. He chastised news organizations for spying on politicians to obtain titillating information for their audience. He argued that the trend of character scrutiny by the press was dangerous not only for future political candidates but would eventually result in a loss of privacy for everyone.

But Hart suggests the problem is the making not just of the press but also of the populace who consume a diet of media sensationalism. The American electorate is more interested in news of sex than public policy, and the media are satisfying that urge.*

Gary Hart served as a U.S. senator from Colorado from 1975 to 1987 and as campaign manager to Senator George McGovern when he ran for president in 1972. Hart is currently an attorney in Denver.

Is it any wonder that in an age of television "sound bites" produce bite-sized politics? Or that a culture that treats politics like a sport—and lumps political figures with soap-opera characters—is producing more celebrities than statesmen?

We are, in a word, trivializing our own leadership—together with the offices to which they aspire, including the presidency.

I'll put my argument directly, because it's a central dilemma of our age. Solutions to our problems cannot pass through a media filter which demands simplicity, rewards tactics and is transfixed by personality—particularly when solutions are complex and require serious debate by an informed public.

What forces have contributed to the creation of this media filter? Competition is clearly a factor. News producers seek to be faster, and often more sensational, at lower cost. Local news programs in Denver offer cash give-aways to attract viewers. Two full minutes of news time have been re-allocated to advertisers by CBS Evening News. So-called innovations such as CNN and *USA Today* represent sophisticat-

*From a speech delivered at Yale University, November 11, 1987.

ed news packaging, not news collection. More diversity has not increased competition in serious news gathering. As in other industries, competition in news media has occurred in the style and form of presentation, not in improved substantive quality.

Finally, journalistic standards are eroding as they did earlier in Great Britain, because of a blurring of the distinction between the serious and the sensationalist press. To keep or capture a worried or confused reader or viewer, sex is more expedient than seriousness.

I know this moment a headline is being composed by someone whose attention span has just been exhausted which reads: "Hart Bashes Press." Wrong. First, we are all the press. The distinction between producer and consumer, where news is concerned, is practically non-existent. Second, we all want our news simple and our politics spicy. How else to account for *USA Today* and the ABC NewsBreak? And someone out there is buying the *National Enquirer.*

As a candidate, I have been driven nearly mad by questions from concerned citizens that began, "Why isn't anyone saying . . . ?" Because more often than not some of us were saying close to what the questioner was listening for but hadn't heard. Why the confusion? Because the questioner assumed practically anything a presidential candidate said was newsworthy and would be printed or screened. Therefore, if it wasn't seen in the papers or on television, quite obviously it wasn't being said. And, for all practical purposes, the questioner was right.

Recently, I proposed a national course of strategic investments of public and private resources to ensure opportunity and a stable living standard for our children. But few have heard of these ideas because of greater fascination with stories that dominated the evening news—such things as, for example, the ephemeral charisma of Col. North.

Who wants, after all, to hear about tedious subjects like investments in our future when all television eyes focus on a fascinating or sensational personality. "Television," recently said the eminent historian Barbara Tuchman, "has become our monarch. It has been a great boon to the ill and lonely, but the degree to which it has impaired the brain cells of the general population has not been measured."

While we sat transfixed by such personalities as the charismatic Col. North, the termites of debt continued to undermine the long-neglected foundations of our national economy. In a single day $500 billion worth of corporate America evaporated on the floor of the New York Stock Exchange like raindrops in the sub-Sahara.

And, as Kurt Vonnegut says, so it goes.

We have created—all of us—a media filter that gives us reality short and sweet—as sweet as possible. The filter lets through simplicity, tactics and personality. It resists complexity, strategic thought and genuine character.

Ideas, new policies, are electronically squeezed like lemons. A recent survey measured the average "sound bite" on CBS News at 12 seconds. Military reform, a proposal for a new foreign policy framework, a plan for strategic investment for national restructuring—such new departures must find a home on the too-frequently-unread "op-ed" page, where they can be explicated at the great length of 800 words.

Campaigns, the vehicles by which we select our magistrates, are interpreted as if they were sports events. Political endorsements, fundraising techniques, clever staffs, media strategies, manipulative consultants, sly tactical ploys, all dwarf in media attention the lowly "issues" effort, traditionally relegated to the mustiest, smelliest cranny in the national headquarters.

At the first Democratic candidate debate in 1983, a well-respected, senior political journalist fled the hall within minutes of the opening statements—complaining vigorously that "issues" bored him. And so it goes.

"Personality" has ever been with us in American politics. And, in proper perspective, that's as it should be. But this year's buzz word is "character," and character is defined in a totally negative sense as everything a candidate lacks or every mistake a candidate has made. Now clearly, one must be of sound character to seek to guide our nation. Soundness being judged by a lifetime of performance, the caliber and quality of public service, the demonstration of independence, courage, and conviction in voting, imagination and initiative in governance, utmost respect for the public trust, scrupulous integrity and honesty in campaign finance and handling the public's tax dollars. And cause should not be given to doubt the candidate's ability to conduct the people's business.

But are we seeing a new departure—a departure disturbing, if not dangerous? How far are we prepared to go as a society to peek into areas hitherto precluded? Should candidates be surreptitiously surveilled by reporters or private individuals? Should hidden cameras be used? How far should anonymous tips be pursued? Should rumors and gossip be widely printed? Should reporters tell untruths to obtain sensational responses? What are the limits?

In the occasionally exciting prying into a candidate's minutes and hours, are we not obscuring the years of a lifetime and undramatic acts of courage, fortitude, and determination that reveal true character?

That we are even asking such questions seems a far cry from the America of Jefferson and Madison, from John Winthrop's City on a Hill. More like what might occur in police-state capitals such as Managua, Sofia or Santiago. Little wonder we are the objects of wonder or ridicule around the world from people who simply cannot understand how a news organization can afford to fly six reporters a thousand miles to hide in a candidate's bushes and peek in his windows and cannot send one reporter to the White House to ask the president why he let 250 young marines lose their lives in a barracks in Beirut.

Who's questioning the character of a State Department official who lies to Congress? Or a White House staffer who shreds papers while Justice Department officials wait next door? What about the character of an administration riddled with people who blithely abuse the public trust and get away with it?

Could the very simple human response be that we all find sex more interesting than sound government? Could it be we have confused what's interesting and pruriently exciting with what's important? Could it be we've come to the new point in our history where we entrance ourselves with our leaders' personal lives because we either cannot or will not explore their ideas, their policies, or their vision?

I quote again Ms. Tuchman:

"The passionate interest the Gary Hart episode aroused in the public, contrasted with the flaccid reaction to lost lives and broken laws, illustrates the shallowness and frivolity of public opinion. If the American people do not grow angry when their sons' lives are sacrificed to official neglience, or when statutes are casually violated by the caretakers of the nation's security, one cannot expect any change to a steadier government that commands more respect. Anger when anger is due is necessary for self-respect and for the respect of our nation by others."

Serious people now believe we have put image over substance in our choice of government officers. By our demand for simple answers, we have trivialized ideas, policies and serious debate. By our elevation of political techniques, we have trivialized the process for selecting our leaders. By our acceptance of a cult of personality, we have trivialized the true meaning of character.

A process may be judged by its system of rewards. Our process today rewards simple solutions, media manipulators, political consultants, malleable personalities, and candidates who are neither controversial nor complex. You must decide for yourself whether such a process and system of rewards is designed to produce superior leaders—the Roosevelts, Churchills and DeGaulles of the future.

My fear is that things are going to get worse, not better. There is no privacy—for anyone. And the new rule is that all information—however obtained—is relevant. And, given modern technology, all can be learned.

But, you will naturally ask, if someone has nothing to hide, why should they mind? Part of the answer is self-evident. No one enjoys being spied upon, particularly as a condition for holding public office. But consider the rest of the answer. Rumor and gossip have become the coins of the political realm. When rumor is treated as legitimate news, it not only leads to suspicion but also can be rationalized as authority for surveillance—or spying. Spying, done well or poorly, can produce bits of information, innocent or otherwise. Information thus produced can lead to the threat of publication—an unsubtle form of blackmail—or actual publication and the destruction of a candidacy.

The issue isn't whether a candidate has something to hide. The issue is one of self-respect and the self-evident value of privacy. Take that away and we'll have not only bite-sized policies, we'll have pint-sized leaders.

25. PRIVATE LIVES: HOW RELEVANT?

Michael Kinsley

Michael Kinsley provides a journalistic defense for press scrutiny of a candidate's private life. He argues that the press carries an obligation to reveal such information if large numbers of Americans want to use it to make decisions between candidates. Kinsley explains that, although he personally considers a candidate's sexual activities as irrelevant, as a journalist he must consider what a significant number of voters think is or is not irrelevant.

Kinsley's views are not shared by all journalists. Some believe a candidate's extramarital activities should not be examined by the press. Others suggest some statute of limitations.

Still others believe all such scrutiny is fair game. This diversity of positions suggests the issue of character scrutiny will hardly pass from the American scene any time soon.

Michael Kinsley is an essayist for *Time*, a regular on CNN's "Crossfire," and a frequent print and television commentator on American politics. This is an essay written for the January 27, 1992, issue of *Time.**

Here we go again. Last week two New York City tabloids, the *Post* and the *Daily News*, suddenly front-paged some old allegations about past extramarital activities by Arkansas Governor Bill Clinton, the media-crowned Democratic front runner. And thus, with a heartfelt squeamishness that outsiders will find hard to credit, the American press takes up some unfinished business from four years ago: deciding what to publish about presidential candidates' private lives.

The Gary Hart follies of the 1987–88 campaign left the issue unresolved. But the particulars of that episode established a standard few future candidate sex scandals could hope to match: the misbehavior was current. The perpetrator was virtually caught with his pants down. He had specifically invited scrutiny of his private life: "Follow me around, I don't care." And the behavior was deemed to be specifically relevant to pre-existing questions about the candidate's "character." Since Hart was widely suspected of philandering, evidence that he actually did philander was admissible to the public debate. Evidence of philandering by a candidate not previously suspected of it presumably would fail this odd test.

Many journalists hoped the Gary Hart standard would stick and thereby excuse them from further contemplation of this distressing subject. They hoped especially for an unwritten rule that only ongoing goings-on count. But it's probably not going to be that easy. Nor should it be.

Musings on this ripe topic often muddle three distinct questions: First, what level of proof is required of stories about marital infidelity? Second, should such stories be suppressed, even if probably true, out of respect for the candidate's privacy? And third, are past extramarital affairs (to take the meat-and-potatoes issue here) relevant to a candidate's qualifications for office?

Question One is simple, in theory. Sexual allegations should meet the same standard of proof as allegations on any other subject. By their nature, sexual allegations are often furtive and hard to prove. That is a perfectly good reason not to publish them.

But there is a genuine dilemma. Rumors can become so thick and widespread that not to report their existence—even if they cannot be proved—becomes a kind of dishonesty. The Washington *Post* once got in trouble for publishing a rumor without proof it was true, and defended itself editorially on grounds that, well, it's true there was a rumor. Much chortling and indignation at that. But it's not a worthless point. Past profiles of Clinton, in TIME and elsewhere, have reported vague rumors about marital infidelity as exactly that, and rightly so.

The specific accusations published last week have been peddled for more than a year by a disgruntled former state employee Clinton had fired. The purveyor has

*Reprinted with permission.

zero evidence, and Clinton and the women allegedly involved all deny it. But the stories were published in the *Star*, a supermarket tabloid, picked up by the two New York papers, and thus became fair game for everyone else.

It is easy to sneer at this process whereby the daintier elements of the press can enjoy sex while still claiming to have preserved their virginity: they simply wait for their less fastidious brethren to report something, then report—with distaste—that it has been reported. But it's harder to know how to avoid the problem. The fact that a story claiming that Bill Clinton has had six mistresses appeared on the front page of the New York *Post* is of legitimate news value to the readers of the New York *Times*. At some point the *Times* must have faith that its readers, if offered the same evidence, are as capable as its editors of dismissing such stories as unreliable.

But why should such stories be published even if they are true? The question here is not whether past sexual adventures are relevant to a candidate's fitness for office. That's Question Three. Question Two is who gets to decide Question Three. And the answer is: the voters, not journalists, should decide. I may think that a candidate's past or even present sexual activities are completely irrelevant compared with his views on the federal deficit (which the *Star* has chosen to ignore). In fact, that's pretty close to what I do think. But what right do I have, as a journalist in a democracy, to decide that for others?

Obviously, if there was general agreement among the voters that a candidate's sexual history is politically irrelevant, it would not matter much to candidates what the New York *Post* chose to publish about their sexual histories, or even whether or not what the *Post* published was true. What makes this subject so thorny for politicians and journalists alike is precisely that they fear it is political dynamite and will indeed affect how people vote. And if people wish to vote against a candidate because he has cheated on his wife (even if his wife doesn't care and is, in fact, part of the conspiracy of silence), the press should not be in the business of playing censor and denying them information for fear they'll misuse it.

So the proper test for the journalist is not whether he thinks the information is politically relevant, but whether he thinks it would be politically relevant to a significant number of voters. Obviously this isn't an exact science. My own sense is that the current line is somewhere between a dalliance or two many years ago and more energetic misbehavior recently. More forthright testing of that line might produce *some* pleasant surprises for those journalists who fear that their fellow citizens are too prudish for the country's good. At the least, it would force the citizenry to decide how much they really care about a candidate's sexual history, and might thereby hasten the day when journalists could, with a clean conscience, stop reporting such matters.

SUGGESTED READINGS

Jamieson, Kathleen. *Dirty Politics: Deception, Distraction, and Democracy.* New York: Oxford University Press, 1992.
A prolific observer of political communication in campaigns, Jamieson has provided a highly

readable discussion in this volume and a rare scholarly analysis of the tactics that candidates use to create images through paid advertising.

Jamieson, Kathleen. *Packaging the Presidency*, 2nd ed. New York: Oxford University Press, 1992. A classic in the political advertising literature, this is a history of the rise of political advertising with emphasis on television advertising in presidential campaigns during the 1970s and 1980s.

Lichter, S. Robert, Daniel Amundson, and Richard E. Noyes. *The Video Campaign: Network Coverage of the 1988 Primaries*. Washington, D.C.: AEI, 1989.
Lichter and colleagues at the Media Research Center offer a unique book-length treatment of television coverage of the 1988 primaries.

McCubbins, Mathew D., ed. *Under the Watchful Eye Managing Presidential Campaigns in the Television Era*. Washington, D.C.: CQ Press, 1992.
An edited volume of original works, *Under the Watchful Eye* details changes in campaigns caused by television, but the respective authors differ regarding the effects on American democracy. This book is useful in raising the issues of television effects and presenting some-times conflicting conclusions.

Nelson, Michael, ed. *The Elections of 1992*, Washington, D.C.: CQ Press, 1993.
Nelson and other scholars analyze facets of the 1992 presidential election, including the role of the media in the conduct of the campaign.

Orren, Gary, and Nelson Polsby, eds. *Media and Momentum: The New Hampshire Primary and Nomination Politics*. Chatham, N.J.: Chatham House, 1987.
Orren and Polsby's collection of original works offers readers a view of the role of the media in the public's attention to this first primary of the presidential campaign. Chapters include a discussion of the *Manchester Union Leader*, the differences between national and local news-paper coverage, and the horse-race emphasis of news stories about the primary.

Patterson, Thomas E., and Robert D. McClure. *The Unseeing Eye: The Myth of Television Power in National Elections*. New York: Putnam's, 1976.
A ground-breaking study in the field, *The Unseeing Eye*, with its analysis of the effects of free and paid media on voters' understanding of the campaign, contributed significantly to expanded scholarly interest in the field of political communication.

Patterson, Thomas E. *The Mass Media Election: How Americans Choose Their President*. New York: Praeger, 1980.
Patterson's comprehensive analysis of the news media's role in the 1976 election, using a panel study and content analysis, is a classic work in the field.

Robinson, Michael J., and Margaret Sheehan. *Over the Wire and On TV*. New York: Russell Sage, 1983.
This year-long treatment of coverage by two news media of the 1980 presidential campaign addresses the extent and type of press coverage that presidential contenders received from the beginning of the primary process to the general election.

Sabato, Larry J. *Feeding Frenzy: How Attack Journalism Has Transformed American Politics*. New York: Free Press, 1991.
Sabato explains why the feeding frenzies, especially during presidential campaigns, have become standard journalistic practice. Sabato also provides remedies for this behavior.

chapter **7**

POLITICAL INSTITUTIONS AND ORGANIZATIONS

INTRODUCTION

Although much of the focus of political communication research has been on media effect on political attitudes and behavior, the interaction between press and national political institutions and organizations has attracted increasing interest from scholars. This has been especially true in the wake of media-related developments affecting political institutions.

Increasing presidential use of television as a communication tool (particularly commencing with John F. Kennedy's reliance on live televised news conferences), the role of the press in covering the Watergate scandal, and White House attempts (especially during the Reagan administration) to use TV news to create favorable images have altered presidential–press relations and affected the president's power to shape public policy.

Congressional television has become a staple of cable offerings with the House of Representatives' 1978 decision to permit live broadcasts of floor proceedings. The Senate followed in 1986 when the House's news coverage began to overshadow that of the Senate.

The Supreme Court has been least affected and, not coincidentally, its relationship with the press has not been of great interest to scholars. But the Court has been drawn into the spotlight through the publicity of several highly politicized nominations to the Court during the 1980s. The Supreme Court also has seen the lower levels of the federal court system accept cameras in the courtroom.

Although studies of media effects on mass attitudes and behavior have a clear independent variable (i.e. the media messages), the study of institutions and the press is more murky. A common thread of the readings in this section is the existence of an interrelationship sometimes characterized as symbiotic. Although there is press effect on institutional performance and relationships with other institutions (president with Congress, bureaucracy with president, etc.), institutions also shape the press. By their association with institutions, the press come to reflect the norms and values of the institution covered. Institutions can impact not only the stories reporters write, but also their very definition of what constitutes news.

For example, presidents have succeeded in obtaining press agreement that what the president says and does is news. Efforts by the White House press office help determine the news presented each night on television and the next morning's edition of the daily newspaper. Similarly, congressional use of satellite technology to hold interviews with local TV stations in their states and districts has an effect on the news presented on a local level. Even the Supreme Court has affected the press by focusing press coverage on its product—opinions—while restricting press ability to examine the process of decision making. Moreover, the Court's offering of its highly technical product has led major news organizations with full-time reporters at the Court to encourage a legal background or training for its correspondents.

This section is divided into five subsections according to the four institutions of government, and the role of interest groups as political actors. First, we examine the presidency—the institution where the press relationship has been most visible and the subject of much debate among scholars, politicians, and journalists.

Next, we turn to the Congress. The institutional press coverage and individual members' relationships with journalists are analyzed with special emphasis on the extent to which media coverage has changed Congress.

The most elusive institution from the press's perspective, the Supreme Court, is the focus of the third part. One selection critiques press coverage of the Clarence Thomas nomination and attributes that coverage partly to some of the justices' greater accessibility to the press.

Bureaucracy–press relations are the subject of the fourth section. Stephen Hess describes the interaction between agencies and the press and attempts to dispel the myth that bureaucrats effectively manipulate the news media.

Finally, we look at the efforts of interest groups to influence institutions' actions through the press.

A. THE PRESIDENCY

No other person in the United States receives as much press coverage as the president. News coverage of American government usually focuses on the president—what he does and says, where he goes, whom he meets with.

The intensive press interest in the president has prompted much debate among scholars, politicians, pundits, and journalists concerning the president's relationship with the press. Presidents have been accused by journalists of manipulating press interest to their own advantage. Photo opportunities, press briefings, formal press conferences, and news releases are designed to serve the president's public communication needs, not the press's desire to gather and report news.

Successive administrations have accused the press of concentrating on minor conflict and filtering the president's communication to the public. Presidents have turned to a variety of bypass mechanisms—televised addresses, town meetings, and photo opportunities—to circumvent the press's gatekeeping function.

Despite the flurry of accusations, the constant relationship between the White House and the press corps is highly symbiotic and cooperative. Presidents need the press because of its reach, and the press needs the president as a continual source of news.

The following selections offer a look at the historical development of this relationship and its present state. The relationship between the White House and the press did not spring up with the rise of television in the 1950s and 1960s. In fact, we will begin by tracing the historical development of modern presidential–press relations with emphasis on the contributions of two presidents—Franklin Roosevelt and John F. Kennedy.

Next, we examine the current relationship. The myth of an adversarial press is replaced by one of two images—a press coexisting with the presidency in a cooperative relationship benefiting both sides; or a press manipulated by the White House into a position of witting tool for administration public relations objectives.

The second selection, then, argues that both the White House and the press corps possess certain imperatives that require the development of a cooperative relationship. The stakes of the relationship deter both the White House and the press corps from choosing an adversarial relationship.

The third selection is an excerpt from Bill Clinton's first press conference. This is a sample of the president's more formal interaction with the press corps as a whole.

26. EARLY PRESIDENTIAL–PRESS RELATIONS

Samuel Kernell

From George Washington to George Bush, presidents have interacted with members of the press. However, the strategies for presidential usage of the press and the structure of the press corps has undergone dramatic change over the past 200 years of American history.

The growth of the modern presidency during the twentieth century has altered the relationship as successive presidents have sought press support to shape public and congressional opinion on public policy. Diminishing reliance on the political party as a support base and communication link and increased usage of direct communication tools with the mass public have contributed to presidential interest and cultivation of the press.

Concurrently, the press's imperatives were altered. Commercial and journalistic imperatives predominate; in the past, political imperatives, particularly partisan ones, animated press behavior. Moreover, the devolution of power within news organizations from the publisher to the editor and reporter has affected the nature of the press's relationship with the White House by reducing the length of the conduit between the president and the final news product.

In the following article, Samuel Kernell describes the development of relations between the president and the press during the twentieth century. Kernell traces the growth in professionalization of the White House press corps, the institutionalization of the presidential press conference, and the emergence of methods of direct presidential communication.*

Samuel Kernell is professor of political science at the University of California–San Diego. In addition to *Going Public: New Strategies of Presidential Leadership*, third ed. (1993), he is the co-author (with Gary C. Jacobson) of *Strategy and Choice in Congressional Elections*, 2nd ed. (1983).

When [President Franklin] Roosevelt began his first news conference in 1933, he, like Wilson 20 years earlier, was met by a throng of more than 200 reporters anxiously awaiting word as to how he planned to conduct business. Roosevelt began by announcing that he was dispensing with written questions. He then identified four classes of information that would be presented in these "delightful family conferences": (1) occasional direct quotations permitted only through written authorization from the White House; (2) press conference comments attributed to the president "without direct quotations"; (3) background information to be used in stories without a reference to the White House; and (4) "off the record" remarks not to be repeated to absent reporters. To administer the policy of authorized direct quotations and other relations with the press, Roosevelt appointed the White House office's first press secretary, Stephen Early.

When the conference ended, the correspondents applauded, the first time ever according to some veterans.[1] One seasoned reporter called it "the most amazing performance the White House has ever seen. The press barely restrained its whoopees . . . the reportorial affection for the president is unprecedented. He had definitely captivated an unusually cynical battalion of correspondents."[2] *Editor and Publisher*, the semiofficial scribe and gossip of the profession was unrestrained:

> Mr. Roosevelt is a great hit among newspapermen at Washington. I rubbed my ears and opened my eyes when I heard hard-boiled veterans, men who had lived through so many administrations and been so disillusioned that there are calluses in their brain, talk glibly about the merits of the White House incumbent. If Mr. Roosevelt fails the craft, by any false word or deed, he will break a hundred hearts that have not actually palpitated for any political figure for many a year.[3]

*From *Going Public: New Strategies of Presidential Leadership*, 2nd ed. (Washington, D.C.: CQ Press, 1993, pp. 66–80. Reprinted with permission. Some tables have been omitted and some footnotes have been omitted or edited.

That first day Roosevelt gave them what they had sought for more than a decade: assurance of hard news, openly conveyed. The president had made this pact with the Washington press corps.

Roosevelt strengthened the press conference in other ways. He met with the press frequently and routinely; only rarely did he depart from his biweekly, Tuesday-Friday schedule. By the time of his death in April 1945, Roosevelt had invited correspondents into the Oval Office on 998 occasions. Equally important to White House reporters, he used these conferences as occasions to make significant announcements. Reporters came expecting hard news. "He never sent reporters away empty-handed. . . . [They] are all for a man who can give them several laughs and a couple of top-head dispatches in a twenty-minute visit."[4] The White House correspondents not only appreciated the choice stories he saved for these gatherings, they also praised his "timing" and packaging in ways that enhanced an item's newsworthiness.[5] Frequently over the years, Roosevelt would go so far as to suggest how a story should be written, and rarely did the press find this spoon-feeding unpalatable.

For a talented pluralist president like Roosevelt, these delightful family conferences offered ample opportunity to employ his considerable interpersonal skills. The president was usually a model of cordiality. Even his harshest critics in the press corps freely conceded that they were treated fairly at these conferences.[6] Whenever Roosevelt complained about a particular article, he would frequently blame the paper's editor, who he tactfully asserted must have put the correspondent up to it.[7] This technique reduced tension and gave the reporter a convenient way of dissociating himself from his paper's editorial stance.

Roosevelt also strengthened the press conference by relying upon it almost exclusively. With but one exception, he did not give private interviews. That exception is significant, however, because it reveals the entrenched character of the normative system prevailing in the palmy days of institutionalized pluralism. On February 27, 1937, the *New York Times* published a private interview with Roosevelt by Arthur Krock, perhaps Washington's most carefully read columnist. According to Krock's account of the incident, the next press conference was an angry one. The reporters accused Roosevelt of favoritism, which he had made all the more unacceptable by extending to a bureau chief rather than to a member of the working press. J. Frederick Essary, by then a senior Washington correspondent, asked the president whether he planned to repeat such favoritism. Roosevelt promptly confessed his blame. "My head is on the block. Steve's [press secretary Early] head is on the block. I promise never to do it again."[8] During the next eight years he kept his word.

That the profession got its hard news, openly conveyed, is apparent. To appreciate what Roosevelt gained in return one must largely trust the compliments of correspondents and the testimonials of disgruntled conservative editors. What they indicate is that Roosevelt succeeded in splitting off Washington correspondents from the editorial stance of their papers.

Evidence of this phenomenon is available in the election preferences of these two groups in 1936. In the spring of that year, Leo Rosten conducted an informal survey of Washington correspondents to determine their preferences. Of the 84 he questioned, 54 named Roosevelt as their first choice. Tying for second with 8 votes each were Republican preconvention front-runners Arthur Vandenberg and Alfred Landon. Altogether the Republican candidates had the support of 31 percent of the correspondents against Roosevelt's 65 percent.[9] By contrast, during the fall campaign 61 percent of the nation's major newspapers endorsed Republican opponent [Kansas Governor Alf] Landon.[10] Throughout his twelve years in office, Franklin Roosevelt lived with a hostile newspaper industry and a friendly press corps.

PRESS RELATIONS UNDER TRUMAN
AND EISENHOWER

For Harry S. Truman (1945–1953) and Dwight D. Eisenhower (1953–1961), their styles and the needs of the press continued to shape presidential–press relations. Despite the manifold personal differences between Truman and Eisenhower, relations with the press retained a measure of continuity during the 16 years after Roosevelt, largely because of the professional correspondents' attachment to the FDR system.

When Truman came into office he promptly announced that he would continue FDR's ground rules. Although Eisenhower during the transition period considered dropping scheduled press conferences altogether, he, too, ultimately made few changes in the Roosevelt format. Truman's directness and occasional irascibility at times reduced the news conference to verbal sparring matches; Eisenhower's famous syntactical convolutions left reporters scratching their heads and conferring among themselves after a conference to determine what the president had said. Under both presidents, news conferences displayed the structure if not the substance of the Roosevelt press conference. . . .

THE KENNEDY SYSTEM: PRESS RELATIONS
IN AN ERA OF DIRECT COMMUNICATION

The real break with the Roosevelt system came with John Kennedy. Everyone in Washington recognized the new president's rhetorical talents and expected him to use them. . . . Everyone, including the television networks, was primed for a publicly active president. They were not disappointed. Kennedy's innovations in presidential–press relations departed radically from the past and formed what may be called the Kennedy system. It remains in place today.

THE KENNEDY PRESS CONFERENCE

In early December 1960, at the behest of president-elect Kennedy, press secretary Pierre Salinger privately solicited reporters' views on the possibility of having live, nationwide television of press conferences. We do not know their initial responses, but later in the month when Salinger announced the new policy to the regular White House correspondents, the reaction was clear. Salinger described the scene:

> I shall never forget this press conference. I went right into the live TV decision. . . . As I explained the ground rules, a storm of protest came from the assembled reporters. . . . I heard the gravely voice of Bill Lawrence, then the White House correspondent of the *New York Times.* I do not remember his questions but the introductory phrase is sufficient: "Mr. Salinger, as you plunge deeper and deeper into matters about which you know absolutely nothing. . . ." That did it. I didn't wait for the rest of the sentence. Now I was shouting back. It was the President's press conference—not theirs—and he would run it his own way. The decision was final. They could take or leave it.[11]

. . . The first live telecast of a presidential press conference, in late January 1961, drew 418 correspondents to the new State Department auditorium and an estimated prime time audience of 65 million viewers. Virtually everyone who expressed an opinion agreed that the new president had done well. There was little doubt that live television would be a fixture in Kennedy's press conferences. The networks' news offices were happy. Even some of the newspaper correspondents extolled this innovation. Lester Markel in a *New York Times Magazine* article advocated more public activities by the president and the creation of a Department of Public Opinion within the White House.[12]

By summer, however, many newspaper reporters began to complain on grounds readily understandable to those who appreciate the virtues of the "private" press conference of an earlier era. . . . Clark Mollenhoff of the *Des Moines Register* complained about the declining quality of the questions: "Too many of the questions are lobbed setups, and blooper balls, and there is too little effort to obtain any more than generalized information. I don't blame the President for knocking them out of the lot." . . . According to print journalists, television reporters "hammed it up" with long-winded questions, "thus cheapening the conference."[13]

Almost a decade later newspaper reporters would still be voicing many of the same complaints. A survey of prominent Washington journalists found most of them dissatisfied with the modern press conference, and television received much of the blame.[14] The complaints were chronic because the problem is structural. As background briefings and sustained questioning on issues gave way to presidential position-taking and evasion, the print journalists lost their hard news. With television providing instantaneous transmission to the country, whatever fresh news came out of a press conference was stale by the time their stories were printed.

The press conference consequently matured into something quite different from the biweekly gatherings of Roosevelt. Robert Pierpoint's description of his preparation for the modern, televised conference makes this clear:

> The presence of a vast audience magnifies the significance of any possible errors in questioning or in commentary afterward, and I always feel a slight sickness in the stomach and a sweatiness of the palms and forehead. After more than twenty years, I still go through a "psyching up" period, similar to that of a professional athlete before the big game. I read the morning newspapers and follow the news on radio and television, concentrating on the questions I will ask and the issues that could emerge at that day's conference. That means writing down a half dozen questions which the President should

answer that day. I try to anticipate how each might be answered, phrasing the question carefully so the President cannot evade it. At the same time, questions must be designed to elicit genuine information or reactions of national importance. And finally, the questions cannot be so obscure or so simple as to risk making me look foolish or to waste my colleagues' and the public's limited press-conference time.[15]

Expanded television coverage of the presidency has made celebrities of those who cover the White House for the networks. Many of these men and women come to Washington after being newscasters for local television. On arrival they commonly draw six-figure salaries. To them "professionalism" is as likely to mean free agency as any collective interests of correspondents. The advent of live television brought into the press conference new participants who promptly became stars. They assumed front-rank positions at the conference and vied aggressively with one another as well as with the newspaper correspondents for recognition from the president. And since they were the conduit through which he gained a spot on the evening news, they generally got it.

Another change, which makes the modern press conference more eventful, is its relative infrequency. Since Roosevelt, presidents have wondered how often they could go before the public and retain its attention. . . . Since Kennedy, the average number of conferences per month has further declined. . . .

Once the news conference failed to provide a steady diet of hard news, it quickly lost standing among print correspondents. Over the years journalists have offered numerous proposals to resurrect aspects of the FDR system. For their daily stories, however, they began to look elsewhere in the White House and in the agencies for presidential stories. Consequently, when the press conference became moribund for long stretches under Nixon and Reagan, who preferred political travel and nationally televised addresses, the complaining came most heavily from among network correspondents rather than print journalists.

THE LOCAL PRESS AND THE PRIVATE INTERVIEW

As the press conference became yet more formal under the glare of studio lights, Kennedy introduced other avenues of access to the press. For the most part, these innovations gave the president greater control over the content of information the press received. One such innovation was special, informal news conferences with publishers and reporters of papers from a particular state or region. With Kennedy these generally took the form of White House luncheons. Every subsequent president has adopted some variant of Kennedy's innovation.

Another innovation, if it may be called that, was the frequent use of the private interview. . . . As president, [Kennedy] continued his close personal associations with Charles Bartlett of the *Chattanooga Times* and Ben Bradlee, then with *Newsweek*. He also conducted private interviews with such notables as James Reston of the *New York Times* and columnist Joseph Alsop. A perquisite of friendship with Kennedy was special access to stories. . . . Network correspondents were not to be excluded. Before long, Kennedy opened the Oval Office to television crews for taped interviews.

Initially, this practice—a single instance of which had put FDR's "head on the

block"—raised the ire of many members of the writing press more than did the televised press conference. Reston had personally warned the president-elect that private interviews might generate too much ill will. (Later, after becoming a favored
insider, he recanted)[16]. . . .

Routine use of the exclusive interview, cultivation of the press outside Washington, and live telecasts of news conferences constitute the Kennedy system. . . .
With television, the Kennedy system corrupted this centerpiece of the FDR system.
And by introducing new—and from the perspective of the White House, more
manageable—avenues of contact with the press, the Kennedy system depreciated
the status of the news conference.

THE KENNEDY SYSTEM AS A MODEL
FOR PRESIDENTS WHO GO PUBLIC

During the past quarter century, encompassing five presidents, the Kennedy system
has remained the working model of presidential–press relations. To the degree it
has changed at all, the system reflects more the forces it set in motion than any new
ideas of Kennedy's successors. As the press conference has withered, Kennedy's
alternative forms of press relations have thrived. Precise numbers for each administration are difficult to come by, but Ronald Reagan's 194 press interviews and 150
special White House briefings of the press from outside Washington during his first
three years indicate sharply increased growth in the use of this news outlet since the
Johnson administration.[17]

The development of satellite communications permitting instantaneous transmissions from the White House to local news stations around the country has created a booming market for White House communications beyond Washington. From
1981 to 1984, the number of local news stations with Washington bureaus grew from
15 to more than 50.[18] The business between local Washington television producers
and stations throughout the country has been burgeoning as well. Local television
news coverage offers several advantages over presidents' traditional news outlets.
First, it allows the White House to segment the market—"to narrowcast its message
to a very specific audience," in the words of one Reagan staffer.[19] Second, these
newscasters are interested in presidential activities that the networks and even local
press pay little attention to. The presidency is a ceremonial office. From it flows an
endless stream of medals, commendations, and sometimes just salutations. Private
citizens from all over the country come to the White House daily to receive the president's congratulations. For local television bureaus, these happy, often sentimen-
tal, ceremonies offer wonderful local color. Of importance to the White House, the
president is invariably cast as a sympathetic figure. The third advantage of local television coverage over traditional news outlets is that journalists for these bureaus, as
recent arrivals with few prerogatives and an uncertain mandate, abide by White
House instructions. . . .

Many of the local bureaus began setting up shop during Jimmy Carter's
administration. Given their special attraction, Carter was understandably quick to

invite them to the White House. It was left to the Reagan administration, however, to incorporate local television reporters fully into the ongoing routines of White House media relations. This innovation, wholly consistent with the premises of the Kennedy system, will probably be a normal, and growing, aspect of presidential–press relations in the future.

Presidents have adapted the Kennedy system to their personal styles in other ways as well, but none has altered the system's basic structure. . . . Lyndon Johnson constructed a television studio in the White House and obliged the networks to outfit it with cameras ready to broadcast on a moment's notice. Richard Nixon dismantled the studio, but to offset his numerous, rough dealings with the television networks and particularly the *Washington Post*, he dramatically expanded press relations outside Washington. Jimmy Carter went to the public in his own way, with informal, but well-orchestrated town meetings. Ronald Reagan has shown a special fondness for the radio. His Saturday afternoon broadcasts from the Oval Office have frequently been compared with Roosevelt's famous fireside chats. As important as these and other practices have been to a given president's overall public relations program, they amount to little more than personal and ultimately transient enhancements of the Kennedy system.

What was lost to the press when the news conference became a forum for the president's direct communications to the country was not fully realized as gains to the White House. With the adoption of the Kennedy system, presidents took more away from the traditional relationship than they contributed. It was up to the correspondents to establish a new equilibrium by withdrawing deference to the president's representation of events and policies. While the emergence of an adversarial press can be attributed in part to President Johnson's Vietnam "credibility gap" and Nixon's Watergate cover-up, it is important to understand that it inheres in presidents' strategic reformulation of press relations, and thus will not disappear as memories of these events fade into history. As late as the Eisenhower era, the president and the White House press corps generally followed the rule of institutionalized pluralism; each party sought reciprocity with the other to reduce uncertainty and to advance its own goals. Under the Kennedy system, however, this relationship broke down. Peter Lisagor hit upon this fundamental shift when he complained that the press was merely "one of the props" of the Kennedy press conference.[20]

Live television requires the president to be ever mindful of the public audience, and this setting necessarily gives rise to posturing. The correspondent's job has consequently become one of "isolating fact from propaganda when a president seeks to use the press as a springboard to public opinion, as he does in a televised press conference."[21] Journalists no longer pay homage to unobtrusive, objective journalism. Instead, they speak of getting at the facts behind the president's statement or press release. Senior Washington correspondent James Deakin remarked: "The White House reporter has one accepted role—to report the news—and several self-appointed roles. . . . I feel I'm there, in part, to compel the government to explain and justify what it's doing. A lot of people don't like that, but I feel we're the permanent in-house critics of government."[22]

The adversarial aspect of presidential–press relations is an elusive quality, difficult to quantify, and the systematic evidence on the subject is inconclusive. From the testimonials of the sparring partners, however, the adversarial relationship appears to be a well-established fact of life. The arrival of less deferential correspondents, some of whom were media stars in their own right, frequently has turned the conference into an occasion of irritation and embarrassment for the White House. Although no president has yet been willing to excuse himself altogether from these encounters, none has been reluctant to tamper with its format and schedule in an effort to produce more favorable results. Johnson, Nixon, and Reagan provide examples. As the Vietnam War heated up at home, Johnson sensed that reporters were lying in wait for him at press conferences with loaded questions. To throw them off balance, he switched to impromptu and short-notice press conferences that gave reporters little time to arm themselves. To stave off embarrassing issues, Nixon occasionally limited questions to specified policy areas. (This change, however, was generally well received by many newspaper correspondents because it gave them the opportunity to pursue newsworthy issues in depth.) In early 1982 some of Reagan's aides believed that their president was suffering from unflattering network "take-outs" of his noontime press conferences. They therefore rescheduled these conferences to later in the day, nearly doubling the television audience and reducing the time available to networks to edit the president's remarks. However, the president's aides tweaked the arrangement. He conducted three such sessions in 1987 and four in 1988. By the end of his second term, the formal news conference had become an endangered species.

GEORGE BUSH'S ADAPTATION OF THE KENNEDY SYSTEM

Threatened with extinction, preservation of the press conference became a *cause celebre* during Bush's first campaign for the presidency, if not with voters, certainly with the reporters and a number of organizations that study these matters. In response, Bush announced soon after his election that he would sharply increase the number of news conferences.

Frequency may "depressurize" the relationship, as one White House aide put it, but for Bush it introduced another problem. The president [Bush] and those who work with him agree that he does not perform well on television. (Reflecting our media age, the disjointed phrases that constitute his rhetoric are commonly referred to as "sentence segments.") The White House solved the dilemma by giving the press conference its greatest overhauling since Kennedy's innovations. Instead of prearranged, frequently prime-time sessions, Bush called brief, impromptu morning sessions in which the networks were allowed a few minutes to assemble the cameras if they were interested in covering the conference. Frequently they were not; Cable News Network was the only network to broadcast many of these sessions. As no advance notice was given for these conferences, many correspondents were absent, but this in itself did not prove controversial, probably because the president rarely used the occasion to make newsworthy remarks. By the end of his first year in office, President Bush had conducted 38 such mini-conferences compared with only one that followed the formal, prime-time format. The consensus among Bush's aides that the latter was a "disaster" reinforced the administration's enthusiasm for this new approach to the press. So, up until the reelection campaign, he held only one more formal news conference.

The revamped format should be viewed not so much as a restoration of the press conference but rather as simply a strategy for pacifying the press. The conferences were scheduled at the president's convenience; correspondents had little time to prepare difficult questions, yet they could not complain that the president was inaccessible.[23] While these sessions may have satisfied White House correspondents accustomed to Reagan's sparse offerings, they provided little opportunity for the president [Bush] to advance his policies. In assessing Bush's damage-control approach to the press conference, Reagan's media adviser, Michael Deaver, cautioned that the downside of this strategy would come when the president "will have to go over the heads of this town and go directly to the American people."

NOTES

1. Chalmers Roberts, "Franklin Delano Roosevelt," in *Ten Presidents and the Press*, ed. Kenneth W. Thompson (Washington, D.C.: University Press of America, 1983), 24.

2. Cited in Leo Rosten, *The Washington Correspondents* (New York: Harcourt Brace, 1937), 50.

3. Marlin E. Pew, "Shop Talk at Thirty," *Editor and Publisher*, April 8, 1933, 36.

4. James E. Pollard, *Presidents and the Press* (New York: Macmillan, 1947), 775.

5. Rosten, *The Washington Correspondents*, 50.

6. Raymond Clapper is cited in Pollard, *Presidents and the Press*, p. 780 stating "the president and his most indefatigble critic, Mark Sullivan, still exchanged pleasantries at press conferences."

7. Ibid, 776.

8. Arthur Krock, *The Consent of the Governed* (Boston: Little, Brown, 1971) p. 242.

9. Rosten, *The Washington Correspondents*, 58–61.

10. Walter Davenport reported in *Editor and Publisher* that 45 percent of the nation's major newspapers supported Roosevelt in 1932, 34 percent in 1940, and 60 percent in 1944. "The President and the Press," *Colliers*, February 3, 1945, p. 16. White's *FDR and the Press* takes a revisionist stance arguing that Roosevelt was far more hostile to the nation's publishers than they to him. See especially chapters 3, 4, and 5.

11. Pierre Salinger, *With Kennedy* (New York: Doubleday, 1966), 57.

12. Lester Markel, "What We Don't Know *Will* Hurt Us," *New York Times Magazine*, April 9, 1961, 116–117.

13. James E. Pollard, "The Kennedy Administration and the Press," *Journalism Quarterly* 41 (Winter 1964): 7. See also Alan L. Otten, "Whose Conference?" *Wall Street Journal*, August 5, 1970, 44.

14. Jules Witcover, "Salvaging the Presidential Press Conference," *Columbia Journalism Review* 9 (Fall 1970): 33.

15. Robert Pierpoint, *At the White House* (New York: G.P. Putnam's Sons, 1981), 70–71.

16. Worth Bingham and Ward S. Just, "The President and the Press," *Reporter* 26 (April 1962), 18.

17. The figures for personal interviews come from Lou Cannon, "Phantom of the White House," *Washington Post*, December 24, 1984, 25.

18. Thomas B. Rosenstiel, " 'Local' News Bureaus Polish Reagan's Image," *Los Angeles Times*, July 14, 1984, 1.

19. Ibid, 18.

20. Pollard, "The Kennedy Administration", p. 7.

21. Jules Witcover, "Salvaging the Presidential Press Conference," *Columbia Journalism Review* 9 (Fall 1970): 28.

22. Cited in J. Anthony Lukas, "The White House Press 'Club,' " *New York Times Magazine*, May 15, 1977, 67.

23. "The Presidency, the Press, and the People," University of California, San Diego, January 5 and 6, 1990. Transcript reprinted in *APIP Report* (Jan. 1991): 4–5 . . .

27. CONFLICT AND COOPERATION

Michael B. Grossman and Martha Joynt Kumar

Although the post-Watergate image of an adversarial press challenging the president is a popular one, especially among journalists, the reality is quite different. The relationship, although prickly at times, is highly symbiotic.

In the following selection, Michael B. Grossman and Martha Joynt Kumar describe a relationship marked more by cooperation and accepted routine than by conflict and instability.*

Michael B. Grossman and Martha Joynt Kumar are members of the Department of Political Science at Towson State University. They are co-authors of *Portraying the President* (1981), from which this selection was excerpted. This work was one of the first comprehensive studies of presidential press relations.

THE STAKES OF THE RELATIONSHIP

The president of the United States ordinarily is brought to you by the news media. Images of the White House produced by strategists who advise the president reach their audience after they are processed in the great news factories and fine craft shops of print, broadcast, and television journalism. Reporters, editors, and producers regularly communicate messages from and about the President to workers, businessmen, farmers, ethnic groups, religious groups, and similar segments of the population—all of whom once received them primarily from their own leaders.

The President, the news media, and the people have an enormous stake in the critical relationship between the White House and news organizations. Both White

*From Michael B. Grossman and Martha Joynt Kumar, *Portraying the President* (Baltimore: The Johns Hopkins University Press, 1981), pp. 3–7, 13–16. Reprinted with permission.

House officials and reporters work to capture a national audience that demands information about the presidency. Since each uses the other's prestige to add to its own, the relationship between the two sides is often cooperative. Tensions occur because partisans of the president and partisans of the news media compete to gain the most benefits from the relationship. Both argue that their side speaks for the people.

THE STAKES FOR THE PRESIDENT

Newly elected presidents and their advisers know that their ability to acquire political influence often depends on their ability to use the tools of image-building. White House officials learn quickly that using these tools to bolster their reputation in the Washington community, as well as with the larger public, contributes to the success of their administration. "Presidential leadership is as much a matter of intangibles as of tangibles, as much shadow as substance," wrote Patrick Anderson, [a former] of speechwriter for Jimmy Carter's 1976 presidential campaign, a national political reporter, and a White House aide during the Johnson administration. "What a President does may matter less than what the people think he is doing.[1]

A president requires popular support to obtain political influence because his office's constitutional and institutional prerogatives are insufficient for him to achieve many important objectives. Although his powers to command are considerable, effective leadership requires his ability to use a variety of political skills. A president must be able to persuade Congress, the bureaucracy, his political party, lobbyists for interest groups, state and local officials, and an army of influentials in the private sector that it is in their interest to support his programs.[2] In order to influence and persuade these groups, presidents have found it increasingly necessary to demonstrate their effectiveness as leaders of public opinion.[3]

A president needs news organizations because, as communicator of most of his political messages, they determine his credibility with major public officials and the leaders of the most powerful interest groups. His 600 White House subordinates organize his relations with a long list of crucial individuals including most congressmen, important officials of state and local governments, key figures among the diffuse layers in the domestic and foreign policy bureaucracies, the officers and lobbyists for interest groups, and the leading figures of party organizations. In meetings with them, the president or his aides impart vital specialized information and shape the personal elements in the relationship. Since these contacts take place in a society in which, like the public at large, influential leaders get most of their messages about the White House from the news media, organizing the president's relations with news organizations is an important element of all the relationships. "There is no way to do this job as president if you are not willing to think about the media as part of the process in the same way that Congress is part of the process," Richard Cheney, White House chief of staff for Gerald Ford reflected shortly before that administration left office. "Consciously or unconsciously, the press often becomes an actor in the scenario."[4]

THE STAKES FOR THE MEDIA

News organizations need to cover the president because he represents the focal point in the American political system for their staffs and audience. For many reporters, a White House assignment represents the high point of a career. They know that the stories they prepare are virtually guaranteed a leading position in the daily or weekly editions of their publications or programs. The White House assignment also gives reporters high visibility with the public, which sees their faces, hears their voices, or reads their bylines. For print media editors and broadcast media producers, maintaining a regular correspondent at the White House is an important aspect of the prestige of their publication or programs. They want their organizations to reflect the aura of the presidency.

Because the Chief Executive is an individual, presidential activities can be portrayed more dramatically by the media than can those of Congress or the bureaucracy. The news media presents the president in its columns, telecasts, and broadcasts as an embodiment of national authority. John Herbers, deputy chief of the *News York Times*'s Washington bureau and a former White House correspondent, gave the following explanation for the predictable manner in which the media lavishes time and space to present the president to the public: "It's the way the whole process operates. If you have an institution [the presidency] in which an enormous amount of power is invested, an enormous amount of prestige, an enormous amount of publicity in the past has been centered on, then you get into a situation which is difficult to break out of. . . . It's a matter of habits in people's minds all the way from the reporting staff through the editors. I think it's true of most news organizations. They're conditioned to think in these terms."[5]

News organizations regard themselves as surrogates for the public; this is another reason why they place so much importance on their relationship with the President. . . .

THE STAKES FOR THE PUBLIC

The ultimate significance of the relationship between the White House and news organizations is that most segments of American society depend on what appears in the media for their information about the president. . . . The highest stakes involve two major aspects of the political system: first, that the president be able to communicate with the public; second, that the people get an accurate assessment of his conduct and activities. Because the media is the main intermediary between president and public, conflicts occur between White House officials and news organizations over which messages will appear, what information will be available, and which activities reporters will be permitted to cover. The outcome affects whether the public response will be to provide support for the president or to demand that his policies change.

Other important consequences occur when the relationship becomes too cooperative or too competitive. One probable outcome of a cozy relationship is that reporters, editors, or producers will gloss over official mistakes and thus fail to inform the public who was responsible for a bad decision. For example, because many columnists and reporters had close relations with Henry Kissinger, they minimized his role in the protraction of the Vietnam conflict, his ignorance of international economic policy, and his possible involvement in the Nixon administration's use of methods of dubious legality to track down unauthorized leaks of information. They became collaborators with Kissinger in his largely successful efforts to portray himself as a White House official whose involvement in maintaining America's world position was too important to subject him to close scrutiny on these types of questions. As a result, public demands for closer supervision of some of his policies never became widespread. . . .

There are a number of important consequences for the public when the relationship becomes highly competitive. During the [1970s], the media made it difficult for the president to transmit important messages to the public; at the same time, the White House used manipulative methods to prevent unfavorable stories from appearing. . . .

Ten years during which respected journalists saw deceit in the White House while partisans of the government believed that the media played a major role in the departure of two presidents from office have left visible effects on the contemporary relationship between the White House and news organizations. Perhaps the most enduring effect has been a reinforcement of the already heavy emphasis that the news media give to the presidency. In other ways, as well, the ten-year war accelerated rather than ended existing trends. Thus, although newly arrived White House officials and reporters alike in the post-Watergate era may think of themselves as free agents, they invariably follow the routines dictated by the enduring needs of the organizations they work for. What they attempt to do usually is programmed by their organization's expectations, and what they don't or can't do is the result of organizational constraints. New White House officials find that organizational imperatives dictate the way they can use the media. Newly assigned reporters find that achieving their organization's goals leads them to follow the same routines as the reporters who preceded them to the White House.

So, in contrast to the view that they are adversaries whose relations recently have undergone dramatic change, the argument here is that the White House and the news media are involved in a continuing relationship rooted in permanent factors that affect both sides no matter who is president or who is doing the reporting. Continuing forces shape both sides more than specific incidents, however traumatic, or the impact of particular personalities, however unusual. What's more, the cooperative elements in this relationship are at least as strong as those that are antagonistic, for a fundamental reason: presidents and news people depend on each other in their efforts to do the job for which they are responsible.

Only through news organizations can a president get and keep the attention of the public. Tradition and constitutional proscriptions prohibit him from commandeering the press, except infrequently and with its consent. With the exception of those Pearl Harbor-like crises when the public automatically turns to the White House for explanation and reassurance, the president needs regular assistance from the press to get his message across. Although the White House and news organizations disagree over what and when the public should learn about the character, activities, policies, and decisions of the president, most of what appears about the president in the media is a result of efforts that are at least partly cooperative.

Presidents want the news media to transmit messages to their many constituencies. News organizations must cover the president because his activities represent the single biggest continuing news story that their audience demands they present. The evolution of the present relationship based on the common need to attain these complementary goals began in the late nineteenth and early twentieth centuries, when mass circulation newspapers and magazines were creating a national audience. At that time some presidents and their aides recognized the advantages of establishing a system for the release of news that gave them control over the rules by which reporters gained access to information and individuals at the White House; this enhanced the president's ability to get his unfiltered message across to the public. During the same period Washington became an important center for the press. Reporters assigned to cover national news began to focus on the activities and personalities of presidents, who replaced the Congress as the central interest of their editors and readers.

The current availability of staff and other resources, more than any desire of presidents to make war against the media, accounts for the systematic efforts by recent administrations to coordinate political communications, public information, and publicity policies, although antagonism certainly was an element during the Nixon administration. The larger and wealthier news organizations in turn have developed strategies for covering the president that have made it possible for them to deal on a nearly equal level with White House officials. This rough parity has made some journalists more willing to present critical accounts of White House activity and has led a few, since they are less frightened by the prospect of White House reprisals, to take a stance of almost permanent antagonism. Parity also contributes to the stability of their relationship. Since each side can inflict considerable damage on the other, cooperation suits the needs of both better than an adversary relationship.

Because both the White House and news organizations gain from prominent and even favorable coverage of the activities of the president, senior White House officials and the managers of publishing and broadcasting enterprises try to avoid major conflicts. The public displays of anger and sarcasm at the press secretary's daily briefing are misleading if they are regarded as symptoms of fundamental hostility rather than as an outpouring of personal frustrations and antagonisms reinforced by a physical set-up and organizational structure that provides many opportunities for outbursts. Many observers whose only view of the relationship is at the briefing or at similar events mistakenly label the two sides as adversaries. They are not. They do not always share the same interests, but that is another matter. The evidence, as indicated in the files of the presidential libraries and as substantiated in numerous interviews, indicates that those who lead the major news organizations as well as most of those who serve as senior advisers to the president will go to considerable lengths to attain and maintain cordial relations with each other.

The high intensity with which different versions of reality were presented to the public during Vietnam and Watergate and the attacks by supporters of the president and the press on the credibility of each other have led some observers to believe that the relationship has changed drastically and permanently. . . . The media as a whole have been portrayed as independent actors plotting to undermine the political authority of the administration or even destroy public confidence in the presidency.

There is not much evidence that the media have either the organizational unity or the ideological affinity to mount a sustained attack on the president. Nonetheless, the evidence justifies one White House allegation about the role of news organizations. They have become one of the principal forces on the national political scene, influencing the other major forces—the President, Congress, the bureaucracy, the parties, and the pressure groups—and in turn being influenced by them.

NOTES

1. Patrick Anderson, *The President's Men* (Garden City, N.Y.: Doubleday & Co., 1968), p. 187.

2. See Richard E. Neustadt, *Presidential Power: The Politics of Leadership from F.D.R. to Carter* (New York: John Wiley & Sons, 1980), for the classic study of the theory that presidential power rests on the President's ability to persuade.

3. See Elmer E. Cornwell, *Presidential Leadership of Public Opinion* (Bloomington: Indiana University Press, 1965), for an excellent study that puts forth the theory that the President's most important relationship is the one he has with the public.

4. Interview with Richard Cheney, Nixon administration White House assistant and Ford administration chief of staff (White House: MJK & MBG, December 8, 1976).

5. Interview with John Herbers, *New York Times* White House correspondent and deputy chief of its Washington bureau (Washington, D.C.: MBG, January 11, 1977)

28. *A PRESIDENTIAL PRESS CONFERENCE*

The presidential press conference has been much maligned in recent years. Both White House officials and journalists have questioned its utility for communication between the president and the press. White House staff argue that journalists are more interested in boosting their own reputations by playing "gotcha." Journalists have concluded the event has become too staged.

Presidents have used press conferences as opportunities to focus press attention on the president's desired agenda. Sometimes the press conference is used to announce good news and attract press notice to a favored issue of the administration. In other cases, the press conference is called with the hope of defusing an issue clouding the administration's press coverage, thereby satisfying press interest in the subject so the president can go on to other items.

President Bill Clinton's first press conference below is an example of the latter. As a result of the president's announcement that he would sign an executive order on homosexuals in the military, the first major crisis for the new administration was congressional and public reaction, much of it vocally hostile, to the intended change. Clinton attempted to defuse the issue by announcing a compromise.

PRESS CONFERENCE BY THE PRESIDENT,
January 29, 1993, The Briefing Room

1:44 P.M. EST

THE PRESIDENT: Good afternoon, ladies and gentlemen. I'm sorry, we had a last-minute delay occasioned by another issue, not this one.

The debate over whether to lift the ban on homosexuals in the military has, to put it mildly, sparked a great deal of interest over the last few days.

Today, as you know, I have reached an agreement, at least with Senator Nunn and Senator Mitchell, about how we will proceed in the next few days. But first I would like to explain what I believe about this issue and why, and what I have decided to do after a long conversation, and a very good one, with the Joint Chiefs of Staff and discussions with several members of Congress.

The issue is not whether there should be homosexuals in the military. Everyone concedes that there are. The issue is whether men and women, who can and have served with real distinction, should be excluded from military service solely on the basis of their status. And I believe they should not.

The principle on which I base this position is this: I believe that American citizens who want to serve their country should be able to do so unless their conduct disqualifies them from doing so. Military life is fundamentally different from civilian society, yet necessarily has a different and stricter code of conduct, even a different code of justice. Nonetheless, individuals who are prepared to accept all necessary restrictions on their behavior, many of which would be intolerable in civilian society, should be able to serve their country honorably and well.

I have asked the Secretary of Defense to submit by July the 15th a draft executive order after full consultation with military and congressional leaders and concerned individuals outside of the government, which would end the present policy solely on the basis of—excuse me—of the exclusion from military service solely on the basis of sexual orientation, and at the same time, establish rigorous standards regarding sexual conduct to be applied to all military personnel.

This draft order will be accompanied by a study conducted during the next six months on the real, practical problems that would be involved in this revision of policy, so that we will have a practical, realistic approach consistent with the high standards of combat effectiveness and unit cohesion that our Armed Services must maintain.

I agree with the Joint Chiefs that the highest standards of conduct must be required. The change cannot and should not be accomplished overnight. It does require extensive consultation with the Joint Chiefs, experts in the Congress and in the legal community, joined by my administration and others.

We've consulted closely to date, and will do so in the future. During that process interim measures will be placed into effect which, I hope, again, sharpen the focus of this debate. The Joint Chiefs of Staff have agreed to remove the question regarding one's sexual orientation from future versions of the enlistment application, and it will not be asked in the interim.

We also all agree that a very high standard of conduct can and must be applied. So the single area of disagreement is this: Should someone be able to serve their country in uniform if they say they are homosexuals, but they do nothing which violates the code of conduct or undermines unit cohesion or morale, apart from that statement?

That is what all the furor of the last few days has been about. And the practical and not insignificant issues raised by that issue are what will be studied in the next six months.

Through this period ending July 15th, the Department of Justice will seek continuances in pending court cases involving reinstatement. And administrative separation under current Department of Defense policies based on status alone will be stayed pending completion of this review. The final discharge in cases based only on status will be suspended until the President has an opportunity to review and act upon the final recommendations of the Secretary of Defense with respect to the current policy.

In the meantime, a member whose discharge has been suspended by the Attorney General will be separated from active duty and placed in standby reserve until the final report of the Secretary of Defense and the final action of the President.

This is the agreement that I have reached with Senator Nunn and Senator Mitchell.

During this review process, I will work with the Congress. And I believe the compromise announced today by the senators and by me shows that we can work together to end the gridlock that has plagued our city for too long.

This compromise is not everything I would have hoped for or everything that I have stood for, but it is plainly a substantial step in the right direction. And it will allow us to move forward on other terribly important issues affecting far more Americans.

My administration came to this city with a mission to bring critical issues of reform and renewal and economic revitalization to the public debate—issues that are central to the lives of all Americans. We are working on an economic reform agenda that will begin with an address to the joint session of Congress on February 17th. In the coming months the White House Task Force on Health Care, chaired by the First Lady, will complete work on a comprehensive health care reform proposal to be submitted to Congress within 100 days of the commencement of this administration.

We will be designing a system of national service to begin a season of service in which our nation's unmet needs are addressed, and we provide more young people the opportunity to go to college. We will be proposing comprehensive welfare reform legislation and other important initiatives.

I applaud the work that has been done in the last two or three days by Senator Nunn, Senator Mitchell and others to enable us to move forward on a principle that is important to me without shutting the government down and running the risk of not even addressing the family and medical leave issue, which is so important to America's families, before Congress goes into its recess.

I am looking forward to getting on with this issue over the next six months and with these other issues which were so central to the campaign, and far more importantly, are so important to the lives of all the American people.

Q: Mr. President, yesterday a federal court in California said that the military ban on homosexuals was unconstitutional. Will you direct the Navy and the Justice Department not to appeal that decision? And how does that ruling strengthen your hand in this case?

THE PRESIDENT: Well, it makes one point. I think it strengthens my hand, if you will, in two ways. One, I agree with the principle embodied in the case. As I understand it—I have not read the opinion—but as I understand it, the opinion draws the distinction that I seek to draw between conduct and status. And, secondly, it makes the practical point I have been making all along, which is that there is a not insignificant chance that this matter would ultimately be resolved in the courts in a way that would open admission into the military without the opportunity to deal with this whole range of practical issues, which everyone who has ever thought about it or talked it through concedes are there.

So I think it can—it strengthens my hand on the principle as well as on the process.

Q: Mr. President, there's a glass of water there, by the way, while I ask the question. Do you think, since you promised during the campaign—your literature put out a very clear statement: lift the ban on homosexuals in the military immediately—do you think you didn't think through these practical problems? What have you learned from this experience in dealing with powerful members of the Senate and the Joint Chiefs? And how much of a problem is this for you, to accept a compromise which doesn't meet your real goals?

THE PRESIDENT: Well, I haven't given up on my real goals. I think this is a dramatic step forward. Normally, in the history of civil rights and advancements, presidents have not necessarily been in the forefront in the beginning. So I think the fact that we actually have the Joint Chiefs of Staff agreeing that it's time to take this question off the enlistment form, that there ought to be a serious examination of how this would be done, even though they haven't agreed that it should be done; that the Senate, if they vote for the motion advocated by Senators Nunn and Mitchell, will agree; senators who don't agree that the policy should be changed are agreeing that we ought to have a chance to work through this for six months, and persuade them of that, I think, is very, very significant.

Now, I would remind you that any President's executive order can be overturned by an act of Congress. The President can then veto the act of Congress and try to have his veto sustained if the act stands on its own as a simple issue that could always be vetoed. But I always knew that there was a chance that Congress would disagree with my position. I can only tell you that I still think I'm right; I feel comfortable about the way we have done this; and I'm going to maintain the commitment that I have.

Q: But do you think that you hadn't examined the practical problems—

Q: Sir, I just wonder, do you think in retrospect that—obviously, you didn't intend the first week—I'm sorry, you want to—

THE PRESIDENT: No, I had always planned—I had always planned to allow some period of time during which policies would be developed to deal with what I think are the significant practical problems. This, in effect, may reverse the process over what I intended to do, but there has to be a time in which these issues, these practical issues are developed and policies are developed to deal with them.

Q: Obviously, you didn't intend the first week of your administration, given your promise to have the laser focus on the economy, to be seen around the country as military gay rights week. I wonder if in retrospect you think you could have done things differently to have avoided that happening?

THE PRESIDENT: I don't know how I could have done that. The Joint Chiefs asked for a meeting about a number of issues, in which this was only one. We spent a lot of time talking about other things. This issue was not put forward in this context by me, it was put forward by those in the United States Senate who sought to make it an issue early on. And I don't know how I could have stopped them from doing that.

Q: You don't think that in making the promise and then in promising to follow through on it early that you might have given rise to this, do you sir?

THE PRESIDENT: Well, I think it was pretty clear to me that we were talking about some sort of six-month process, days and days ago, and the people who wanted it debated now were not deterred by that and probably won't—a lot of them won't be deterred by the agreement announced today. I think that we must—they have the perfect right to do this. But the timing of this whole issue was clearly forced by the people in the Senate who were opposed to any change of the policy no matter what the facts are. And I think that was their right to do, but they control the timing of this, not me.

Q: Two questions. First of all, just to make sure that we're clear on this: July 15th this happens, period, regardless of what comes out at these hearings, is that correct? The ban will be issued—or will be lifted, rather.

THE PRESIDENT: That is my position. My position is that I still embrace the principle and I think it should be done. The position of those who are opposed to me is that they think that the problems will be so overwhelming everybody with good sense will change their position. I don't expect to do that.

Q: So you definitely expect to do it. And secondly—

THE PRESIDENT: I don't expect to change my position, no.

Q: What do you think is going to happen in the military? There have been all sorts of dire predictions of violence, of mass comings out, whatever. What do you think the impact of this is going to be, practically?

THE PRESIDENT: For one thing, I think if the—if you look at the last 10 years of experience here, according to the reports we have, this country spent $500 million in tax dollars to separate something under 16,500 homosexuals from the service in the face of—and has dealt with complaints, at least, of sexual abuse—heterosexual abuse—largely against women—far greater volumes. But during this period, we have plainly had the best educated, best trained, most cohesive military force in the history of the United States. And everybody—ask anybody—and the Joint Chiefs will tell you that.

They agreed that we should stop asking the question. This single thing that is dividing people on this debate—I want to make it very clear what this—this is a very narrow issue. It is whether a person, in the absence of any other disqualifying conduct, can simply say that he or she is homosexual and stay in the service. I do not expect that to spark this kind of problem. And I certainly think in the next six months, as people start to work it through and talk it through, a lot of legitimate, practical issues will be raised and dealt with in a more rational environment that is less charged. That is certainly what I hope will happen. Thank you.

Q: Want to tell us what the other problem was you were working on, Mr. President—on the Middle East, sir?

THE PRESIDENT: No, tomorrow or the next day.

END, 1:58 P.M. EST

B. CONGRESS

A debate has raged over the effects on the legislative process of news media coverage of Congress. During the 1970s and 1980s, several scholars decried the emergence of a "show horse" member who thrived on personal publicity in contrast to the "work horse" member who concentrated on the mundane task of passing legislation. This dichotomy has also been characterized as an "outside" versus an "inside" strategy of passing legislation. Members who utilize an "outside" strategy employ press releases, op-ed pieces, news conferences, one-on-one press interviews, and photo opportunities to recruit support for legislative goals. Those choosing the "inside" strategy rely on the traditional tools of persuasion, bargaining, and compromise to enact legislation.

According to conventional wisdom, not only did the emergence of this type of individual affect members' behavior but it also altered power relationships within Congress. Members who used an "outside" strategy gained power over established leaders who excelled in backrooms, not TV studios.

The next three selections address this conventional wisdom view of a dramatic change in members and the legislative process caused by news media coverage. The first reading reflects the notion that the news media generally, and television in particular, have altered the legislative behavior of members, reshaped the power structure within Congress, and consequently changed the legislative process.

The conventional wisdom view is disputed in the second reading. The legislative process has remained largely unchanged. Members of Congress respond to the news media because of their perception of its importance, not because it actually possesses the ability to determine the outcome of the legislative process.

In the third selection, the conventional wisdom and its critique both are labelled as right and wrong. The changes wrought by the role of the news media have altered Congress, but not to the exclusion of other, more traditional factors affecting the legislative process.

29. *BOSS TUBE REPLACES BOSS TWEED*

Hedrick Smith

In this first selection, Hedrick Smith explains and defends the conventional wisdom.* Using words like "revolutionary" and "profound effects," Smith contends that television in particular has reshaped legislative politics. By creating a new breed of politicians who pursue outside strategies to achieve legislative goals, television has shaken the power structure in Congress and shifted power from traditional insiders who serve in leadership roles to younger, mediagenic members who are eager to shape policy and willing to utilize news media coverage to do so.

Hedrick Smith, a former reporter and columnist with the *New York Times*, is author of *The Power Game: How Washington Works*, from which this selection is taken. He has authored *The New Russians* and *The Russians*, and also co-authored several other books on American politics.

Television is the other major revolutionary ingredient in the new power mix. By now, it is a familiar cliche that television has largely replaced the political parties as the middleman between candidates and voters. In effect, Boss Tube has succeeded Boss Tweed of Tammany Hall, Boss Crump of Memphis, and the Daley machine in Chicago. Television brings politicians right into the living room and lets voters form their own impressions, rather than voters having to depend on what local party bosses, union leaders, church spokesmen, or business chiefs say. The campaign impact of television is undeniable. For many candidates it has replaced going door to door.

And it has also profoundly affected the Washington power game. It has eroded still further the cohesive force of the two parties in Congress, feeding centrifugal forces. Television fuels the independence of individual politicians, and that compounds the problems of congressional leaders in rounding up majorities. The trend in television politics is for candidates to build their personal mass appeal and political organizations, bypassing the regular party apparatus. Once they arrive in Congress, candidates who get elected as political Lone Rangers are less responsible to party leaders.

---

*From Hedrick Smith, *The Power Game: How Washington Works* (New York: Ballantine Books, 1988), pp. 35–39. Reprinted with permission.

Television has altered other power relationships, too. In the old days, Arthur Krock, chief correspondent of the *New York Times* in Washington and a premier columnist from Franklin Roosevelt's era to Dwight Eisenhower's presidency, used to host an informal weekly luncheon table at the Metropolitan Club, one of those elite male establishments. When George Tames, the veteran *Times* photographer, retired in 1985, he told me that up to twenty top government officials would show up at Krock's regular lunch table and swap gossip, news, and off-color stories. No senior columnist today commands a similar table. But, illustrating the change, 134 senators and members of Congress showed up one night in October 1985 for Ted Koppel's ABC *Nightline*. Invited in advance, they were vying for a chance, first served, to appear on camera for a minute each—just for the privilege of asking questions of Soviet and American policy experts on the outcome of the Reagan-Gorbachev summit in Geneva.

Television has become the new reality in American politics—in 1960 for the president, in the mid-seventies for other politicians. It has drastically expanded the arena of action. In the past few years, the commercial outlets for political news have mushroomed. On top of established network coverage, change came rapid-fire: *The MacNeil-Lehrer Report* opened on public television in 1975, ABC's *Good Morning America* started in 1975, ABC's *Nightline* went four nights a week in 1980, and that same year the Cable News Network was born. A year later, the Sunday morning news shows got a shot in the arm with ABC's *This Week with David Brinkley*.

In 1979, the House began live telecasts of its floor debates. Howard Baker, before retiring as Senate majority leader, kept urging the Senate to follow suit, as a way of getting cameras to focus on the main action rather than on the publicity antics of individual members. "If you don't let them [the senators] do anything on the floor," Baker commented, "they do it on the Capitol steps and somehow there's always a TV camera out there."[1] The Senate followed Baker's advice eighteen months later.

Quite clearly, television has offered a fast track to those with political sex appeal and a knack for personality politics. It has opened the door to celebrities from other walks of life: Jack Kemp, the former star quarterback for the Buffalo Bills football team; Bill Bradley, the New York Knicks basketball Hall of Famer; astronaut John Glenn; and regional media personalities such as Jesse Helms, not to mention a Hollywood actor such as Ronald Reagan.

Stephen Hess, a political scientist at the Brookings Institution, contends in his book *The Ultimate Insiders* that network news coverage actually reinforces the established leadership. In 1983, for example, he found that some, though not all, of the Senate leaders and potential presidential contenders got the heaviest coverage on the network evening news and Sunday shows and in five major newspapers.[2] Indeed, the sharpest, most telegenic leaders can use TV to enhance their power; Senate Republican leader Bob Dole is a prime example. But Hess's survey showed that, in 1983, some major committee chairmen got less media play than senators with less formal power who were public celebrities, among them John Glenn and Gary Hart.

Both were presidential contenders, but their news–celebrity status came not from the slow patient route of seniority and old-fashioned inside politics, but from their skill at the media game or their notoriety.

Moreover, another study in Hess's book made clear that publicity-sharp middle-rank or junior senators (Christopher Dodd of Connecticut, Paul Tsongas of Massachusetts, Arlen Specter of Pennsylvania, Larry Pressler of South Dakota, and Howard Metzenbaum of Ohio) were doing extremely well on the newer television shows.[3] On the House side, some backbenchers have clearly used video politics to magnify their influence.

"The changes in the media," observed political scientist Michael Robinson, "have given younger members and maverick members more political visibility—and hence greater power—than ever before."[4]

The most talented of the new breed have charm and wit on television; some have become substantive legislators, too. This group combines inside savvy with flair for the media game. What put them on the fast track was the happy combination of being telegenic and pithy—the ability to simplify issues and fashion thematic messages. John F. Kennedy, a lackluster senator impatient with inside politics, was the first to market glamour politicking on TV. This is not to say that Kennedy and his political imitators have lacked substantive achievements, merely that video appeal was central to their rise to prominence. To keep up in the power game, even old-timers such as House Speaker Tip O'Neill have had to learn how to play the game of video politics.

In Congress, the first wave of new-breed politicians who had grown up with television and found it their natural medium was the Democratic class of 1974—bright, articulate, energetic politicians such as Timothy Wirth of Colorado, Thomas Downey and Stephen Solarz of New York, Tom Harkin of Iowa, Robert Edgar of Pennsylvania, Chris Dodd and Toby Moffett of Connecticut. The class of 1974 changed the temper of the Congress, for they were upstart, independent voices, irreverent toward the congressional Establishment. Television helped them get ahead and put their mark on issues. Then in 1978, a big class of new-breed Republicans arrived to be sworn in on the new regular live coverage of the House. Some, such as Newt Gingrich, an outspoken go-getter from Georgia, used media skills to build influence.

Rarely has a new-breed Republican garnered the limelight more dramatically than Phil Gramm, a supremely self-confident Reaganite economist from Texas. Gramm is no stereotyped, blow-dried, airhead TV politician; he is not a glamour boy, but a bespectacled ex-professor with thinning locks. Gramm shot to prominence by combining a shrewd sense of timing, brilliant legislative packaging, and a knack for self-promotion and selling his ideas on television. He came to the House of Representatives as a Democrat in 1978. Just three years later he played a central role in the Reagan budget package by leading the defection of southern conservative Democrats to support Reagan's budget. In 1983, he switched parties and got elected to the Senate as a Republican in 1984. A year later, as a freshman senator—

indeed as a ninety-seventh-ranking senator—he emerged as a prime architect (with another freshman Republican, Warren Rudman of New Hampshire) of the highly controversial plan to balance the budget by 1991 through mandatory annual reductions in the deficit. Gramm's media skills got him wide political notice and legislative results.

Rather caustically, some old hands branded the flashy new-breed legislators as "show horses" who chase publicity while the grubby details of legislation are hammered out in private by the "workhorses." But in fairness, the most effective newcomers offer more than the blow-dried look. They have developed substantive expertise. What has aroused the jealousy of their elders is the refusal of newcomers to sit back and behave like novitiates.

Television helped break up the policy monopolies of established committees and throw open the power game. Overshadowing the grinding "inside" spadework of bill drafting in committee, television offered shortcuts and a showcase. Kemp and Gramm are prime examples of those who learned how to influence Congress and market their ideas with their colleagues through the media. Over television, they sent messages to the voters and generated grass-roots interest that ricocheted back to Congress. Thus, television offered a marketplace for all 435 members of the House and one hundred senators to become policy entrepreneurs. That is one major reason why Congress seems so unruly today. . . .

NOTES

1. Howard H. Baker, Jr., interview with Steve Roberts, Martin Tolchin, and the author, January 15, 1985.

2. Stephen Hess, *The Ultimate Insiders* (Washington, D.C.: Brookings Institution, 1986), pp. 9–19 and table pp. 140–142.

3. Ibid, table on pp. 138–139.

4. Michael J. Robinson, "Three Faces of Congressional Media," in Thomas E. Mann and Norman Ornstein, eds., *The New Congress* (Washington, D.C.: American Enterprise Institute for Public Policy Research, 1981), p. 98.

30. WHY IS TELEVISION SO IMPORTANT IN CONGRESS?

Stephen Hess

In this next reading, Stephen Hess argues that the impact of the news media, particularly television, on the legislative process is vastly overrated. Hess argues that members of Congress solicit media notice not in conjunction with legislative activities but primarily because of celebrity status that results from such exposure.*

*Stephen Hess, *Live from Capitol Hill: Studies of Congress and the Media* (Washington, D.C.: Brookings Institution, 1991), pp. 105–109. Reprinted with permission. Some footnotes have been edited or omitted.

Stephen Hess, a senior fellow in the Governmental Studies program at the Brookings Institution, is the author of several works on politics and the media including *The Ultimate Insiders: U.S. Senators in the National Media* (1986), *The Government/Press Connection* (1984), and *The Washington Reporters* (1981).

The conundrum, then, is why television appears to be so important to the life of Congress. As researchers are finally figuring out how to measure the place of television in the political process, television's importance for Congress is best measured by the degree to which House and Senate are not covered. But members of Congress and congressional reporters do not seem to have noticed. Quite the contrary, in fact; they tend to overestimate the extent of television coverage and hence its importance in the legislative and electoral processes.[1] Partly this stems from the journalist's habit of ignoring the average, the typical, and the routine. When Hedrick Smith in *The Power Game: How Washington Works* made the case for media politics as a staple of the House of Representatives by citing the activities of Stephen Solarz, Les Aspin, Richard Gephardt, and Newt Gingrich, it was as if he had chosen Larry Bird, Patrick Ewing, Michael Jordan, and Magic Johnson as representative players in the National Basketball Association. But a more important explanation is the solipsistic view of the world that permeates Capitol Hill. Reality to reporters is what they can see, to politicians what they can touch. And Capitol Hill is always crammed with cameras, lights, sound equipment, tape recorders, news conferences, handouts, stakeouts. This is their reality. This also contributes to the myth of television's power as they react to its presence rather than to its output.

The output . . . is small. Timothy Cook has told the affecting story of Don J. Pease; a staid and hardworking backbench congressman, who wanted to extend a program of unemployment benefits that was about to expire in 1985. His staff convinced him that a visual aid was just what he needed to get himself on television:

> When his turn came up [at a rally], Pease vigorously deplored official Washington's callousness toward unemployed workers: "If you want to know the truth, the Reagan administration acts as if you don't exist." Then raising the spatula in his right hand, he shouted, "Do you know what this is? This is a burger flipper. This is the Reagan administration's answer to unemployment. And you can flip burgers all day, and your spouse can flip burgers all day, and you still won't get above the poverty line!"

The results of this exercise, according to Cook, were that the "network evening news programs ignored the story . . . and the next morning neither the *New York Times* nor the *Washington Post* mentioned it. The staff's one consolation was a color photograph in the *Baltimore Sun*, although the caption neglected to explain why Pease was waving the spatula." The legislation did not get out of committee.[2]

Nevertheless, Congress and its members are spending more each year trying to influence news media coverage.[3] But the interest is not as pervasive as I had expected after reading some accounts of Capitol Hill activities. . . . Electronic news releases, for instance, are far more rare than is suggested by the newspaper and magazine stories that focus on legislators who produce the tapes and ignore those who do not. Press secretaries by my calculations rank a lowly fifth in the pecking order of both House and Senate offices; in the House they also spend a fair amount of time on activities that have nothing to do with the media. Jamie Whitten, chairman of the House Appropriations Committee, is said never to have held a press conference: "You do your job best when you do it quietly," he summarized.[4]

Indeed, legislators should know that sound bites on the evening news will not get them reelected. Other avenues of publicity in which they can target the audience and control the message are infinitely more effective and involve less risk of losing votes. The odds of being able to move a policy debate by using television news are very long for the average member of Congress. Why then do they devote such energy to this pursuit?

One answer could be that legislators do not know of television's limited impact because it does not appear limited from their vantage point. It is limited only if the question is framed: How many impressions of me, for how long, how positively, is a voter likely to get from my effort? Rather, staff and friends collect and comment upon their appearances, thus magnifying them. (It is similar to what I witnessed a few years ago when I watched a cabinet officer reading his daily press clippings. His senses told him that an awful lot was being written about him. It was harder for him to recall that he was the only one reading all of it). Under this closed system, even an obscure cable program at an obscene hour can produce a reenforcing feedback.

Another answer could be that legislators are cockeyed optimists. Is there not some of this quality in everyone who seeks elective office? Senator William S. Cohen believed that the politicians' common denominator is ambition. "Whether it is noble or ignoble," he wrote, "it is an all-consuming passion which refuses to acknowledge the folly of its relentless pursuit."[5] In pursuit of the elusive sound bite, surely each member of Congress thinks he is as energetic, articulate, and intelligent as Phil Gramm and Newt Gingrich. Moreover, sound-bite journalism protects legislators from themselves. Although television and newspapers work off the same definition, their needs differ—TV needs nine seconds, and thus must edit out redundancy and even the awkward pauses of conversational speech. This will not necessarily make legislators look good, but it keeps them from looking bad.

Add to Senator Cohen's definition of political ambition Joseph A. Schlesinger's theory of progressive ambition: "The politician aspires to attain an office more important than the one he now seeks or is holding." More than a third of the Senate once served in the House. . . . For some legislators, perhaps, being on television has less to do with the next election than with some future election that may only be a dream.

So, as the members of Congress supposedly rush to recording studios to tape instant reactions to the president's State of the Union message, the political pluses outweigh the minuses. Getting on the air is an advantage, even if an exaggerated one. The costs are small, both in time and money, and the money is provided by taxpayers or campaign contributors anyway. Also, because most legislators sincerely wish to be noticed, there is no longer a stigma—the "show horse" label—attached to those who are exceedingly good at getting themselves on television. . . .

For the legislators of Capitol Hill, television is not primarily about politics at all, I realize. Or rather, without elections to be won and legislation to be passed, there would still be the rush to television. For television is about being a celebrity. Television appearances are analogues of the decor of their offices, which are filled with cartoonists' impressions of them and photographs of them taken with famous people at important events. "The celebrity is a person who is known for his well-knowness," said Daniel J. Boorstin. In his brilliant essay, *The Image*, he concluded, "The hero created himself; the celebrity is created by the media."[6] I am on TV; therefore I am.

NOTES

1. See, for example, Michael D. Wormser, ed., *Guide to Congress*, 3d ed. (Washington, D.C.: CQ Press, 1982), p. 744. Scholars, however, have been less likely to fall into the journalists' trap. A number of studies have noted the modest television coverage of congressional campaigns. See, for example, Mark C. Westlye, *Senate Elections and Campaign Intensity* (Baltimore: Johns Hopkins University Press, 1991), pp. 39, 41. John W. Kingdon, *Agendas, Alternatives, and Public Policies* (Boston: Little, Brown, 1984), pp. 61–64, also describes a more limited role for the media in setting congressional agendas.

2. See Timothy E. Cook, *Making Laws and Making News: Media Strategies in the U.S. House of Representatives* (Washington, D.C.: Brookings, 1990), pp. 132–146.

3. See Walter Pincus, "TV Staff for House May Grow," *Washington Post*, April 25, 1990, p. A26; and "House TV Expansion Deferred," *Washington Post*, April 26, 1990, p. A21.

4. Quoted in Peter Osterlund, "Media-Savvy Congress Turns to TV," *Christian Science Monitor*, June 3, 1988, p. 3.

5. William S. Cohen, *Roll Call: One Year in the United States Senate* (New York: Simon & Schuster, 1981), p. 165.

6. Daniel J. Boorstin, *The Image or What Happened to the American Dream* (New York: Atheneum, 1962), pp. 57, 61.

31. OUTSIDER AND INSIDER STRATEGIES: CAN COMPLEMENTARITY WORK?

Timothy E. Cook

The process of legislation has been affected by the intensified relationship between members of Congress and the press. While in the past the most successful legislative efforts relied on an "inside strategy" of direct interaction with other members of Congress, members today have discovered the utility of pursuing an "outside strategy" in attempting to enact legislation. Are these mutually exclusive, as the foregoing debate has assumed? Timothy E. Cook suggests the two strategies actually enjoy a complementary relationship for members of

Congress. The complementarity of these strategies becomes imperative given the inherent deficiencies of either strategy alone.*

Timothy E. Cook is associate professor and chairman of the department of political science at Williams College in Williamstown, Mass. A former Congressional Fellow, he has published widely on the relationship between Congress and the news media. He is the author of *Making Laws and Making News: Media Strategies of the U.S. House of Representatives*, from which this section has been excerpted.

... [I]s [the outside strategy] now *the* way of getting something done in Congress and in Washington? Nonmembers seeking to influence Congress seem to think so. As power became dispersed on Capitol Hill in the 1970s, would-be leaders outside Congress had more to keep track of, more people to deal with, and more potential obstacles. Decision-making inside Congress became more collegial after earlier systems of czar rule by the Speaker and an emphasis on working through committees.[1] It is no longer easy to shape events on the Hill or move a bill along simply by contacting a few strategically placed people. Instead, persuading constituents to lobby their representatives or to write Congress en masse has become the accepted way to get things done. As James Baker, White House chief of staff under Ronald Reagan, said, "A, you've got to have a message, and B, you've got to be able to sell that message.... You've got to be able to sell it not just to the public but also on the Hill. But the key to selling it on the Hill is to sell it publicly.[2]

Presidents have increasingly appealed to the public for support. Even before Ronald Reagan, going public had largely supplanted the bargaining that was once the key to executive power.[3] Rather than turn to an outside strategy only if other efforts have failed, contemporary presidents have begun with public appeals, resorting to backroom bargaining only to win swing votes. Interest groups and lobbies also deal with the media much more often than in the past, whether they proceed like citizens' groups, wooing reporters, or like corporate groups that simply buy advertisements. Either way they avoid the herculean task of lobbying all 535 members of Congress separately.[4]

The adequacy of using only an outside strategy depends on its goals. It may be enough merely to call attention to a problem that someone else has to take care of. The legislative process involves not only enactment of bills, but implementation of their provisions by the executive branch and oversight of the results by Congress. Through the media, which are often ready for stories of government mismanagement, Congress can call attention to practices within the executive branch that ignore public opinion or interpret congressional intent too freely.

Likewise, representatives may not always be interested in passing legislation. Some Republicans, most notably the outspoken members of the Conservative Opportunity Society (COS), have recently argued that setting forth a coherent agenda should be the goal. "This is very much a long-term strategy," said a press assistant to

*Selection from Timothy E. Cook, *Making Laws and Making News: Media Strategies in the U.S. House of Representatives* (Washington, D.C.: Brookings Institution, 1990), pp. 150–66. Reprinted with permission. Some footnotes have been edited or omitted.

a freshman Republican active in COS. "We've been so long with the Republicans in the minority [that] it's easier to be in the minority [than govern] unless we can demonstrate that we could govern, come up with plans and alternatives rather than saying no." Others disagree; the press aide to a conservative Republican on the Appropriations Committee complained, "Some members are advocating philosophical goals through the national media, getting their message across. But they won't get a bill passed all session." But in an era in which parties are becoming polarized, Democrats and Republicans alike set forth issues with partisan truculence, largely for short-term political gain: either they will get the policy they want or they will have ready on hand an issue to run on in the next campaign. Tony Coehlo, when chair of the House Democratic Congressional Campaign Committee, commented, "Politics should not control legislation, but we need to know the politics of the legislation. . . . Republicans are doing this marketing. We need to concentrate more on who delivers the message and how."[5]

Inside strategies have not been entirely displaced, however. Even in the 1981 debate over Reagan's severe budget cuts—the clearest case we have of a campaign to influence Congress by mobilizing public opinion—key votes were won by trading favors. For a president to advocate a policy agenda and then invoke the specter of public disapproval if Congress fails to act has often been enough for some form of legislation to be drafted and passed; but resentment among legislators accustomed to bargaining and to being consulted may build and threaten the president's success. A classic case was the revolt of the House Republicans in 1986 when they were faced with the tax reform package that emerged from Ways and Means. When the adoption of rules necessary to consider the package was defeated because it received almost no Republican support, Reagan had to consult with members of his party in person to win them over. Presidents may also have to turn to bargaining to find agreement on the fine points of an agenda. Likewise, while interest groups report a sharp rise in their use of television and newspaper ads, they are also more active in almost all methods of influence, including direct contact and consultation.[6]

For those who want to be key legislators, the outside strategy can only go so far. The media may help set an agenda and increase the prominence of an issue, but the outside strategy is a blunt instrument. Enacting legislation still requires deliberation on the particulars of a bill and consultation and compromise to build a coalition. Contrary to speculation, however, being a show horse is not incompatible with being a work horse; no empirical investigation has been able to prove that seeking or receiving publicity precludes legislative labor.[7] Work horses can find publicity useful to advance their goals when inside strategies are impractical. Even after the agenda has been set, they can use the media to narrow the debate to consideration of a few alternatives and specification of their main components. One press secretary to a Republican on the House Judiciary Committee pointed out the benefits:

> One is packaging, communicating your idea. Any package has to have proper substance *and* attention getters *and* articulation of what you're doing. . . . If legislation is to go anywhere, it has to be understood. With immigration, we could see the education in

the media; members knew pretty well what was going on. They were asking less often, "What are employer sanctions?" than "Why is [X] pushing this approach to employer sanctions?" It's a big oversight to neglect packaging.

Both leaders and backbenchers are increasingly called on to pursue inside and outside strategies simultaneously. Time routinely elevates members to power committees—Appropriations, Budget, Rules, or Ways and Means—or to leadership of a subcommittee.[8] Yet attaining a position of some influence does not make an outside strategy superfluous; and such a post may make it easier to attract attention. Members seek a good reputation among journalists, which can be translated into influence in Congress, which then leads to increased favorable coverage, and so forth. To be a major player in Washington, a person must now achieve two reputations, one among colleagues and the other among reporters, government officials, lobbyists, and the public. Little wonder that Christopher Matthews, Tip O'Neill's administrative assistant, could list the keys to success on Capitol Hill in clear order: "the right style so that a member can get attention when it matters, the right issues and the ability to get things done internally."[9]

There is, however, a tension between outside strategies and inside strategies that must be managed if legislation is to be enacted. An inside strategy demands pliability to allow bargaining and compromise, and as a result the legendary tacticians of Congress rarely took a clear position on an issue they were considering. This was one of the keys to Wilbur Mills's success as chair of the House Ways and Means Committee: "On many issues, Mills is inscrutable to the members: they don't know if he has a position or, if he does, what it is. . . . To [committee members] he is an extremely skillful leader who responds to them in such a way that his conclusions, drawn from their discussions, become their conclusions."[10] Mills may have been unusually crafty, but party leaders, for whom keeping peace in the family is more important than enacting a given program, and committee leaders, who must be perceived as fair by committee members to stay in their positions, may prefer to avoid the close identification with a particular stand that could impair effectiveness as an inside player.[11]

An outside strategy, because it must rely on the media, needs a clear-cut, possibly definitive position that severely limits flexibility. Backbenchers can win attention by being linked to a particular view on a particular issue. Leaders of parties and committees must often respond in kind to avoid losing the spotlight. If journalists see mostly disingenuous tentativeness, they will turn elsewhere. And members who defer to a colleague on a matter of mutual concern may alert reporters that there is another expert voice on the issue and may lose influence. Far from the fluidity and mutual deference that characterizes the inside strategy, an outside strategy favors members who stake out turf for themselves alone and defend it in no uncertain terms.

Moreover, calling attention to an issue is not the same as responding to it, particularly if the subject occasions divisiveness. When asked about the role of the media in legislative strategies, the press assistant to a three-term moderate Southern Democrat replied,

It depends on the issue being considered. Like the idea for a network for missing children—get it associated with the person and it gets its own constituency right off the bat. If members are not aware whether it's a good thing to support, they can then see that it is. But with highly debated issues, like covert aid to Nicaragua, it doesn't help. There's a confusing debate on the floor and a confusing debate in the papers.

The problem becomes how to exploit media attention while avoiding the disadvantages. The press secretary to a Republican leader provided one option: "Before legislative action, you want exposure, you want to generate public attention and public interest. Then you get to actually legislating and putting the pieces of the puzzle together, and you *don't* want it; you've got everything cranked up and then a story in the *Post* can kill you. . . . Sometimes it becomes a matter of shutting off initiatives: don't go to the press and don't generate an initiative and they won't be there." Turning off the spigot is not always so easy, however; once journalists discover an issue, the trajectory of coverage often has a logic of its own that defies being turned away, let alone turned off.

Balance and adroitness in changing from one strategy to another and back must be the goal, especially for House leaders. . . .

In the 1960s House, inside strategists were usually thought to hold the best cards. Such is no longer the case. Now when members want to shape policy and build their influence, the outside strategy is at least as attractive. Legislating through the media is a reasonable option to a House member who otherwise faces obstacles or inertia. For those looking for new ways to address the public interest and advance their careers, linking media strategies and legislative strategies can call attention to the larger issues and overcome seemingly entrenched interests. . . .

But an outside strategy cannot stand alone. Television and newspapers may help set the agenda, but they do not clearly discriminate among the various potential solutions or reforms. When filtered through reporters' preferences for clear-cut issues, an outside strategy may pressure members to choose sides. How the policy is to be carried out can easily become less important than whether it is enacted in some form. Yes-or-no, either-or appeals are custom-made for achieving publicity. Details of execution are not. So using the media to legislate may require impressive skill at the acrobatics of balancing strategies—even though the training, the tactics, and the expectations for the two diverge more often than they converge.

There is much to be said for making news in order to make laws. The strategy can establish that the general aims of the legislation are worth pursuing. It implicitly encourages members to clarify their positions and may well also push them to look beyond servicing the organized interest groups and toward extrinsic standards of public policy in the public interest. But an outside strategy is no panacea; it can too readily slip into position taking that accomplishes only symbolic or even other ends.

Moreover, the extent to which a media strategy actually involves the public in the legislative process is open to question. Many examples of successfully going public have occurred when the public has been divided or uncertain. The prominence of matters before Congress is a product more of what sells to the media than of what sells to public opinion. Journalists have little knowledge about their audiences, and their priorities often differ from popular concerns.[12] And so long as this is the case, the media will be imperfect guardians of representative democracy.

NOTES

1. Steven S. Smith, "New Patterns of Decisionmaking in Congress," in John E. Chubb and Paul E. Peterson, eds., *The New Direction in American Politics* (Washington: Brookings, 1985).

2. Quoted in Mark Hertsgaard, *On Bended Knee: The Press and the Reagan Presidency* (New York: Farrar Straus Giroux, 1988), p. 23.

3. Samuel Kernell, *Going Public: New Strategies of Presidential Leadership* (Washington: CQ Press, 1986).

4. Kay Lehman Schlozman and John T. Tierney, *Organized Interests and American Democracy* (New York: Harper and Row, 1986), pp. 170–182.

5. Quoted in Richard E. Cohen, "Taking the Very Long View, the Parties Begin Planning for 1992 House Elections," *National Journal*, April 13, 1985, p. 795.

6. Schlozman and Tierney, *Organized Interests*, p. 157.

7. See my "Show Horses in House Elections: The Advantages and Disadvantages of National Media Visibility," in Jan Pons Vermeer, ed., *Campaigns in the News: Mass Media and Congressional Elections* (Westport, Conn.: Greenwood Press, 1987), note 1. See also Laura I. Langbein and Lee Sigelman, "Show Horses, Work Horses, and Dead Horses," *American Politics Quarterly*, vol. 17, no. 1 (1989), pp. 80–95.

8. For example, by 1982 all but one of the members first elected in 1974 sat on power committees or were subcommittee leaders (chairs or ranking minority members). Burdett A. Loomis, "Congressional Careers and Party Leadership in the Contemporary House of Representatives," *American Journal of Political Science*, vol. 28 (February 1984), table 1.

9. Quoted in Richard E. Cohen and Burt Solomon, "Congress's Rising Stars," *National Journal*, January 24, 1987, p. 176.

10. John F. Manley, *The Politics of Finance: The House Committee on Ways and Means* (Little, Brown, 1970), pp. 108–109.

11. Barbara Sinclair, *Majority Leadership in the U.S. House* (Johns Hopkins University Press, 1983); and Glenn R. Parker, "The Selection of Committee Leaders in the House of Representatives," *American Politics Quarterly*, vol. 7 (January 1979), pp. 71–93.

12. Herbert J. Gans, *Deciding What's News: A Study of CBS Evening News, NBC Nightly News, Newsweek, and Time* (Pantheon, 1979), chap. 7; and Robert Darnton, "Writing News and Telling Stories," *Daedalus*, vol. 104 (Spring 1975), pp. 175–94.

C. THE SUPREME COURT

While the president, executive department heads, and members of Congress are active pleaders at the media's gates, the justices of the U.S. Supreme Court maintain a more complex relationship with the press. Justices rarely engage in the tactics of press relations endemic to national policymakers—press releases, news conferences, briefings, press relations staffs. The Court apparently does little to entice the attention of the press.

Neither does the Court avoid press coverage. The opinions of the Supreme Court, many of which are voluminous, are delivered to the press at the moment they are announced. A room is provided specifically for the use of reporters who cover the Court and even desks are available for those who do so on a regular basis. Documents the Court receives on each case, including briefs from interested parties not directly involved in the case (*amicus curiae*), are made available to the press corps. Finally, the Court's Public Information Office serves the function of assisting reporters in a multitude of procedural ways, although rarely with the substance of Court decisions.

It is not that the justices do not care what the press says about them.* However, the justices take care not to respond overtly to the press or even create impressions with the press or the public that there is more than passing interest in or acquaintance with press coverage of the Court. The result would be the emergence of an image of the Court as attentive to the winds of public opinion rather than the law and the Constitution.

The problem for the justices is how to channel attention to reinforce a public image of the institution as primarily a legal body constrained by the U.S. Constitution and the law. The alternative image—nine justices driven by politics and personal policy preferences—would undermine the Court's ability to function as a policymaker by weakening public confidence.

The following selections illuminate aspects of the current relationship between the Court and the press. The first selection analyzes the composition of the press corps covering the Supreme Court and the characteristics of this unique beat. The second selection, by a present member of the Court, examines coverage provided by that press corps. Justice Scalia sets forth his own perspective on the role of the press and offers recommendations to the press on how to cover the Court's decisions.

32. *THE SUPREME COURT PRESS CORPS*

Elliot Slotnick

The journalists who cover the U.S. Supreme Court are known as "The Supreme Court Press Corps." Although they are the gatekeepers for the Court's relationship with the public, they are little known outside the narrow confines of the Court itself. In the following excerpt, Elliot Slotnick describes the journalists who cover the Court and the nature of their work: preparing for stories, analyzing decisions quickly, and writing concisely and simply about complex legal issues.[†]

Elliot E. Slotnick is an associate professor of political science at Ohio State University.

*See, for example, Fred Graham, *Happy Talk: Confessions of a TV Newsman* (New York: W.W. Norton & Co., Inc., 1990).

[†]Selection from Elliot E. Slotnick, "Television News and the Supreme Court: The Case of Allan Bakke." Paper presented at the annual meeting of the American Political Science Association, August 30, 1990. Reprinted with permission.

His work on judicial politics has been published widely in journals such as *The American Journal of Political Science, The Journal of Politics,* and *Judicature.*

The Supreme Court beat is a relatively uncluttered one when compared with the number of reporters who routinely cover the White House or the halls of Congress. Except, perhaps, for landmark decision days and crowded oral arguments in prominent dramatic and, often, emotionally laden cases, approximately fifty reporters cover the Court on a routine basis. Varying numbers are often cited for the number of journalists whose responsibilities exclusively focus on Supreme Court coverage. . . . Among the "regulars" at the Court are wire service reporters for UPI, AP, and Dow Jones, reporters for major "national" newspapers such as the *New York Times, Washington Post,* and *Wall Street Journal,* and broadcast journalists from the three major networks, CNN, and NPR.

In the eyes of many analysts, the Supreme Court beat is not a prized one for journalists since reporting on the Court "has all the features that most journalists try to avoid."

> Reporters sit in a basement room waiting to be presented a complicated legal document that they quickly have to puzzle out for themselves. They cannot interview the major sources of the story to ask them what they meant. . . . Meanwhile they know that . . . editors do not regard most judicial decisions as very important or very newsworthy. . . . An ambitious reporter, already making a name in bylines, is likely to consider assignment to the Court a dead end. (Press and VerBurg, 1988: 253)

Clearly, Supreme Court reporters are less "participatory" in the processes that they cover than are their colleagues in other governmental settings, and it would be difficult to sustain the argument that journalists have any impact on what the Court actually decides. It is in this sense that the Court's press corps "probably has less power and influence than any other major news group in Washington" (Grey 1968:55). Nevertheless . . . the media have a potentially great role in developing public perceptions of the Court and in providing a baseline of information about what the Court has done.

Because of the unique institutional setting in which the Court's reporters find themselves, the skills that are required of them may be very different from those that would best lead to success among their colleagues. Indeed, the prototypical model of the aggressive investigative reporter with all of its connotations gives way in this domain to the primacy of one's analytical skills. Supreme Court reporters spend more time reading than they do on their feet or on the telephone. . . . The posture the Court reporter takes toward the institution tends to be more laden with respect and deference than one finds on other governmental beats. Coupled with the vestiges of intimidation . . . and problems of adequate preparation there is a tendency for the Court to get off relatively "easy." While some facets of Supreme Court activity are critiqued by journalists, "Judicial reasoning and the wisdom of decisions are seldom attacked." There is a "generally accepting philosophy of the press," which "is in marked contrast to relationships existing between the news corps and many other news sources in Washington. Policy decisions are constantly under scrutiny in most areas of government, but Court newsmen give little evidence that they see themselves in such a 'watchdog' role" (Grey 1968:53–54).

One of the major problems confronting the Supreme Court reporter is the great tension that often exists between making a story both understandable to a lay audience as well as accurate. There is an ever-present risk of oversimplifying things to the point where important nuances of a critical ruling are lost in translation. . . .

The unique demands of the Supreme Court journalist's job may be one of the reasons why Court reporters have relatively short tenure. One now outdated analysis found that, as a group, Court reporters were relatively young and well educated. They were highly experienced (averaging over eleven years of professional work), yet they only served, on the average, approximately two and a half years on the Supreme Court beat (Dennis, 1975: 790–792). Young, ambitious journalists may simply not be satisfied "languishing in the basement pressroom of the Supreme Court . . . far from the excitement of the more glamorous political beats. . . . They do not often get to use the tools of the trade, they are locked out of the inner sanctums, and they have few sources and very little power in relation to their colleagues" (Berkman and Kitch 1986:258).

One issue on which most analysts of media coverage of the Court agree is the need for reporters with adequate preparation for the task at hand. . . . In a recent survey focusing on twenty-four Supreme Court "regulars," Sherman found that nine were lawyers including Stephen Adler (*Wall Street Journal*), Richard Carelli (AP), Tim O'Brien (ABC News), Carl Stern (NBC News), Stuart Taylor (*New York Times*), and Stephen Wermiel (*Wall Street Journal*). Among the prominent and well-respected lay reporters, however, were Rita Braver (CBS News), Al Kamen (*Washington Post*), Nina Totenberg (NPR), and Lyle Denniston (*Baltimore Sun*). (Sherman, 1988) Clearly, one needn't possess a law degree to have the kind of background conducive to covering the Court, but as Fred Graham explains, formal legal training may result in the Supreme Court journalist attaining a special status.

> It always amused me to have Burger complain to me about journalists as if I were something else. He did it partly, I felt, because I was a lawyer. I learned, over the years, that the true importance of my law degree was not that it helped me write knowledgeably about the cases but that it removed the stigma of being a "non-lawyer." The fact that nobody has ever been called a "non-dentist" or a non-plumber" suggests that lawyers and judges tend to view the uninitiated with more skepticism than other professions do, and the shingle on my wall made them more likely to talk freely with me. (1990:135)

Whether one is a lawyer or not, advance preparation is generally acknowledged as the key to successful coverage of the Court. According to Clayton, "If a reporter has studied the briefs, listened to the arguments, and thought about the case, he ought to be in pretty good shape to handle the Court's decision when it comes" (Hiebert 1966:191). Anthony Lewis claimed that while he covered the Court he read or looked over every *certiorari* petition that was filed and made a note on each. He tried to discuss cases with "informed lawyers," particularly the government's own watchdogs in the Solicitor General's office. Lewis also attended oral argument which he found instructive "because it discloses better than anything else what the real issues are in a case and what troubles the members of the Court." In addition, "there are moments of tension and drama and humor. The personalities on the bench are unveiled just a bit." For similar reasons Lewis generally attended the announcement of decisions claiming to "absorb more by ear than by eye" (Lewis 1959:368–371).

Few Court reporters are likely to be as thorough in their preparation (and successful in their Court reporting) as was Anthony Lewis. To a certain degree, the nature of this unique journalistic beat renders it less constrained than others with respect to the media's presentation of the news story and "the reporters are free to frame the decision as they wish" (Davis 1987:55). In the best of circumstances, reporters may understand a decision "perfectly" and still be unable to portray it effectively for a mass audience. It is in this sense that Supreme Court reporting remains in a state of continued development, presenting a great challenge to its practitioners. . . .

REFERENCES

Berkman, Ronald, and Laura W. Kitch. 1986. *Politics in the Media Age.* New York: McGraw-Hill Book Company.

Davis, Richard. 1987. "Lifting the Shroud: News Media Portrayal of the U.S. Supreme Court." *Communications and the Law* 9:43–59.

Dennis, Everette E. 1975. "Another Look at Press Coverage of the Supreme Court." *Villanova Law Review* 20:765–799.

Graham, Fred. 1990. *Happy Talk: Confessions of a TV Newsman.* New York: W.W. Norton and Company.

Grey, David L. 1968. *The Supreme Court and the News Media.* Evanston, Illinois: Northwestern University Press.

Hiebert, Ray Eldon, editor. 1966. *The Press in Washington.* New York: Dodd, Mead and Company.

Lewis, Anthony. 1959. "Problems of a Washington Correspondent." *Connecticut Bar Journal* 33:363–371.

Press, Charles, and Kenneth VerBurg. 1988. *American Politicians and Journalists.* Glenview, Illinois: Scott Foresman and Company.

Sherman, Rorie. 1988. "Media and the Law." *National Law Journal.* June 6, 1988:32–36.

33. A JUSTICE CRITIQUES THE PRESS

Antonin Scalia

Justices of the Supreme Court rarely speak publicly beyond their pronouncements from the bench. Even more rare are any statements about the press. These would become a public acknowledgment that the justices do think about the press, which they would prefer not to admit. However, Associate Justice Antonin Scalia has spoken in public about media coverage of the Court. The following excerpts are from a speech Scalia delivered on several occasions. In it, Scalia suggests that law is "a specialized field, fully comprehensible only to the expert." He advises reporters who analyze opinions not to critique them on the basis of the results, but on the opinion's fidelity to the judicial process. Scalia states that he wants to alert the news consumer to the dangers of accepting the press's practice of labelling a decision good or bad on the basis of the result rather than the reasoning.

Justice Scalia has served as an Associate Justice of the United States Supreme Court since 1986. Prior to his appointment to the Court, he was an appellate judge on the District of Columbia Circuit Court of Appeals and a law professor at the University of Chicago.

It is a long and venerable tradition of common law that judges do not respond to public criticism. If a newspaper should carry an article commenting adversely upon the administration of a particular federal program, it would not be unusual to find in the op-ed pages a few days later a response from the responsible Agency head, sometimes even a Cabinet officer.

Likewise with respect to public criticism of legislation or proposed legislation. The sponsoring members of the legislative branch will often come to their own defense. Judges, however, are traditionally confined to the manner of defense that finds its equivalent in the world of boxing, in what Mohammed Ali, after one of his less brilliant fights, a fight that he won but barely, called his rope-a-dope trick. I don't know if you remember that but he described it as a tactic of lying back against the ropes and letting your opponent beat the bejabbers out of you until he gets tired.

There have been some notable exceptions to this judicial practice of defending oneself through the rope-a-dope trick, the most famous of which was perhaps John Marshall's publication of a five-installment response to Spencer Roan's attack in the Richmond press on Marshall's opinion in *McCulloch v. Maryland*.

That example alone is enough to suggest the rope-a-dope technique works better. Like most judges, Marshall was apparently better at writing opinions than editorials. Worse still, the editor of the paper apparently got the installments mixed up and published them in the wrong order.

But I am digressing from my subject before I have even begun. My point is that there is this tradition of judges taking their lumps in silence. I have no intention of abandoning that tradition, since—for reasons I shall allude to later—it is a good one. I think it not within the traditional prohibitions, however, to discuss at a high level of generality some of the characteristics of the judicial process that make it particularly difficult for the reader of criticism of the judicial opinion or, for that matter, the writer of criticism to know whether it is well-founded. I am not referring to criticism in law reviews or in journals of legal scholarship whose readers and writers presumably appreciate the distinctive characteristics of the judicial process.

I am referring to reporting in commentary concerning judicial opinions addressed not to the bar but to the general public. My intent, I should make clear at the outset, is not to disparage that reporting and commentary. It is what it is for a very understandable reason and cannot be expected to be otherwise. I do hope to induce some of you to read that reporting and commentary with an appreciation that things are not always as they seem. It should be apparent from even these opening remarks that I am about to appeal to the principle that the law is a specialized field, fully comprehensible only to the expert. That is not, I must confess, an attractive proposition. The "this-is-too-complicated-for-you-to-understand" argument is trotted out in many fields. Let me try to explain, however, why it has unique validity in the field of judging.

In most areas of human endeavor, no matter how technical or abstruse the process may be, the product at least can be fairly evaluated by the layman. The bridge does or does not sustain the load for which it was designed. The weather forecast is or is not usually accurate. The medical treatment does or does not improve the patient. I maintain that judging or at least judging in a democratic system is different. There is frequently the case that the operation is a success even though the patient dies.

For in judging, process is a value unto itself, and not, except in a very remote sense, merely a means to achieving a desirable end. The result is validated by the process, not the process by the result. To give the simplest example of what I mean, consider the unrepentant and still dangerous serial murderer who has been tried and acquitted, but whose guilt has later been made absolutely clear by newly discovered evidence. The prosecutor seeks to retry him for the same crimes and the trial judge of course dismisses the indictment. The result in the particular case is a terrible one. A serial murderer continues to stalk the streets. But there is no doubt that the decision of the judge was a good one since if the double jeopardy clause of the Constitution means anything at all, it means that the prosecution cannot retry an acquitted defendant simply because he discovers new evidence. The result was bad, but the decision was good because the proper process was followed. The judge applied the law.

Now it is easy to acknowledge that this bad result was the work of a good judge because of two elements that alas do not always come to the rescue of the good judge. First, the legal rule itself was clear. It is easy to understand and to explain that the double jeopardy clause of the Constitution prevents retrial. Second, it is easy to understand and to explain that in the long run, though not in this particular case, that rule produces desirable results. It led to injustice here only because the prosecutors left it too soon and went forward with the case inadequately supported by the evidence. Abandoning the rule would likely produce even greater injustice since prosecutors could repeatedly subject innocent people to the repeated expense and agony of criminal prosecution each time a new piece of evidence was discovered. Such readily apparent vindication of the good judge is, as I say, not always available for the good judge who has to produce a bad result. Often, perhaps most often, only the legal rule is not 100 percent clear. There are those who say the rule is otherwise and the judge is right only because he is a better lawyer than they are, reads the precedents more closely, distinguishes related cases more intelligently, pieces together the statutory or Constitutional text more skillfully. These arcane skills are not easy to understand and, even more difficult, not to mention tedious, to explain. Often, perhaps most often, the long-term beneficial consequences of the decision are difficult to comprehend without detailed knowledge of the law or are emotionally uninspiring or are problematic or even nonexistent.

. . . [A] judicial decision with good results is not necessarily sound, and a judicial decision with bad results is not necessarily faulty. As an example of what goes into a judicial decision, and of the arguments pro and con that must be considered and evaluated before one can intelligently say that is a good one, let me read you a brief excerpt from the decision a few terms ago in the case called *United States v. Hohri*, a case involving an important and highly emotional issue that ended rather inconclusively. Hohri was a suit against the United States for damages arising from the internment of Japanese Americans during World War II. The trial court had held that all the claims were barred by sovereign immunity or by the statute of limitations. An appeal was taken from that trial court to the Court of Appeals for the District of Columbia Circuit, which reversed the decision and sent the suit back to the district court for trial. That decision of the Court of Appeals was appealed to us. After hearing argument (and I, by the way, did not sit in this case so I can describe it dispassionately), we did not even decide the main issue but held that the decision of the Court of Appeals had to be reversed because it had no jurisdiction over the case since the appeal from the district court should have been taken not to the Court of Appeals for the District of Columbia Circuit but to the Court of Appeals for the Federal Circuit. Surely not a very pleasing result.

But to judge whether that was a good decision or rather whether as a newspaper account quoted one of the plaintiffs as saying, the court had, quote, "ducked the issue," this is a portion of what you would have had to plough through:

"This case has claims both under the Middle Tucker Act and the FPCA, a situation not specifically addressed by section 1295-A2. Resolution of this problem turns on interpretation of the second clause of this subsection, the so-called 'except clause.' The solicitor general contended that the except clause merely describes claims which do not suffice to create jurisdiction in the public circuit. Thus, he argues, appeals of FPCA claims must be heard in the federal circuit if, as in this case, they are joined with claims that fall within jurisdiction. By contrast, respondents contend that the except clause indicates that not only FPCA cases fail to create."

One would not expect the public to be interested in it. Indeed, one would feel for the republic if the public were interested in it. Since the public is not interested in it, one would hardly expect the press to report it. That is why the *University of Chicago Law Review* is not sold at Seven-Eleven.

The general-circulation press will ordinarily report the outcome of the case and its practical consequences. That is fair enough. But the public should understand, and this is the burden of my remarks this evening, that those limited data, outcome, and consequences are not sufficient, not necessarily even relevant data for deciding whether the opinion was a good one. . . .

There is one final reason why judicial decisions cannot be properly evaluated by the desirability of their results. Like moral rectitude, judicial rectitude is ultimately determined, not by results, but by reason. Judges must, of course, give reasons unlike umpires who can simply call the runner safe without specifying whether the throw arrived too late, or because the first baseman's foot was off the bag. For judges, decisions without reasons are not good decisions. It is the long tradition of common law systems that reasons must appear, and it is also the long tradition that the reason given in one case will ordinarily be followed in the next, so that they establish a kind of judge-made law filling in the gaps and ambiguities in the statutory and Constitutional texts.

That being so, to get the result right, even textually right, but the reason wrong is a disaster. The litigants immediately before the court will receive justice; but untold numbers of future litigants will be condemned to the opposite, because future cases will be decided on the basis of the wrong reason. Thus the focus on the result but not the reason is to miss the principal point of a judicial decision. Yet how easy it is for the inexpert observer to note that mistake.

Consider the most famous and the most universally acclaimed judicial decision in English literature, the judgment of the young Roman jurist, Dr. Balthasar. . . . This Dr. Balthasar, better known as Portia, pronounced:

> This bond doth give thee here no jot of blood;
> The words expressly are, a pound of flesh:
> Take then thy bond, take thou thy pound of flesh;
> But, in the cutting it, if thou dost shed
> One drop of Christian blood, thy lands and goods
> Are, by the laws of Venice, confiscate
> Unto the State of Venice

Gratiano, Antonio's friend, exclaims "O upright Judge! . . . O Learned Judge!" And poor Shylock says, "Is that the Law?"

The world by and large has agreed with Gratiano, but Shylock, of course, was right. It is absurd to think that was the law. If there were any good lawyers onstage, they would have said, "O idiotic judge! O dull-witted jurist!" Suppose the next case before Judge Portia involved a bond which entitled one farmer to harvest a wheat crop off another farmer's land. Would Portia say, "You may harvest the wheat, but you may not walk across the farmer's land necessary to reach the wheat field." . . . Let's hope not. Surely the right afforded by a contract implicitly includes agreement to all actions and all results that inevitably attend the exercise of that right. With apologies to Shakespeare, or the Earl of Oxford, or whoever you are, it is ridiculous to say that Shylock was given the right to take a pound of flesh without also having been given the necessary implication, the right to spill whatever blood went along with it. Portia's result was right, of course, but for the quite different reason that a contract entitling one person to commit mayhem upon another is contrary to public policy and therefore void.

Ah, but who cares about that detail? Antonio's friends did not. Shylock did not. Three and a half centuries' worth of Shakespeare's readers did not. And if the trial were replayed today, in real life, in modern dress, I would hardly expect the *New York Times* to call the decision a bad one. Yet it would be. Appallingly bad. Because the reason was wrong.

So, whatever your philosophy of judging, but especially if you believe that judges are supposed to discern the meaning of text, but even if you believe that judges are supposed to produce desirable results, it is almost impossible to tell whether a decision is a good or a bad one simply by knowing the facts of the dispute and learning the results. You have to know in addition at least the reasons given and must understand enough about the area of law in question that you can appreciate how those reasons will affect future cases. You must also know whether those reasons are so irreconcilable with reasons given in earlier cases that the law has been thrown into a turmoil. In addition, if you are a textualist, as I am, you must know whether those reasons are really true, that is, whether they reflect the real meaning of the statutory or Constitutional provision involved. You cannot reasonably expect to get all of that information out of a newspaper account. At least not a newspaper account in a newspaper that wants to remain in business.

I emphasize, because although I do not believe in responding to the press, neither do I believe in antagonizing it, that the object of these remarks is not to criticize press coverage of the courts, which gives the public precisely, I think, what the public wants to know. I hope to have explained, however, the wisdom of the judge's ancient reluctance to engage in public debate over the rightness or wrongness of their decisions and their ancient belief that by and large no news is good news.

D. THE BUREAUCRACY

In terms of media coverage, the most ignored branch of American government is the bureaucracy. With the exception of a select group of agencies, primarily the departments of state, defense, and justice, the bureaucracy rarely makes news. One explanation is the "beat" system. Reporters are often assigned to several bureaucratic agencies, which diminishes their coverage of any one. Another is journalistic resistance to the bureaucratic assignment. Effective reporting usually requires a technical knowledge (that is, a specialization) that many reporters shun as detrimental to their career and as inimical to their identification with the nonprofessional who reads their news copy.

In the following selection, Stephen Hess counters the argument that the bureaucracy manipulates the news. Hess spent one year observing the operations of the press-relations offices in five federal agencies. He concludes that press-relations officials are incapable of controlling news coverage of their agency.

Hess found a more symbiotic relationship where agency officials and journalists depend on one another. Journalists, of course, need stories. Agencies, by providing a steady stream of news releases and advisories, allow the journalist to receive a consistent source of information widely regarded as news. In turn, agency officials solicit a channel of communication with their various constituencies—interest groups, Congress, the White House, and the general public. The press offers that channel.

34. THE GOVERNMENT/PRESS CONNECTION

Stephen Hess

One of the most prolific writers on the subject of media role in American politics, Stephen Hess is a senior fellow in the Governmental Studies Program at the Brookings Institution. His "Newswork" series has illuminated press coverage of the bureaucracy, the Congress, and Washington in general. He is the author of several books on political communications including *Live from Capitol Hill! Studies of Congress and the Media* (1991); *The Ultimate Insiders: U.S. Senators in the National Media* (1986); and *The Government/Press Connection* (1984), from which the following selection is excerpted.*

Press offices are like certain animals with undeservedly bad reputations. Reporters seem to feel it necessary to denigrate the services they provide, almost as if their own standing rests on the need to prove that they "skin their own skunks" (a journalist's explanation for not using research assistants).[1] Government workers are less likely to feel strongly about their agencies' press offices, but when they do, they are apt to cast them as an insubstantial lesser order of the bureaucracy. And government political executives, in most cases, use press office personnel as technicians rather than as policy counselors.

The denigration has predictable results. As Carlton E. Spitzer, director of public information at HEW under John Gardner in the mid-1960s, observed, "Every five or six years, some editor taps a young reporter to 'do a story on government information.' The standard result is a piece that dwells on costs and ineptness and concludes that taxpayers are somehow being ripped off."[2] One reporter recently given the assignment begins his survey, "The government spends millions of dollars a year and employs thousands of public relations experts who can supply almost any kind of information, except how much it costs to supply that information."[3] Exactly. The government has been so lax in defining its public affairs functions,[4] often to disguise the costs, that press offices, which constitute only a small part of government public relations, have been lumped together with many questionable activities.[5]

As providers of information for journalists, how competent were the press offices and officers I observed? Were they efficient or wasteful? Industrious or lazy? And of even more importance in a democratic society, how honest or slanted was the information they dispensed?

If press officers are guilty of wastefulness in the conventional sense that they spend government money frivolously or that they do not put in a full day's work, then perhaps I was not a careful enough observer to see it. Most press offices have shabby, government-issued furniture and aging equipment. The Pentagon's press office, perhaps because it is the richest, seemed to take special pleasure in its

*From *The Government/Press Connection* (Washington, D.C.: Brookings Institution, 1991), pp. 107–15. Reprinted with permission.

unkempt appearance. As for working, more than most government offices, press offices look and sound busy; employees cradle telephones, switching from one caller to the next; photocopiers duplicate transcripts or texts of speeches; wire service tickers clatter and occasionally a television news broadcast or press conference intrudes. When the rest of a building is silent and the bureaucrats have gone home, someone is usually still in the press office. Evidence of waste may exist in places I did not look, but in a year of wandering I generally saw press officers who worked hard and produced a useful product.[6] I gained a respect that I had not expected for the humble press release; indeed, sometimes the press releases were more precise than the hurried accounts written by general assignments reporters. I saw a few press officers who were only serving time, but I do not think they were deliberately lazy. They were incompetent, not venal.

The most frequent and serious charge against press offices—that they manage, manipulate, or control the news—I found inaccurate for an almost perverse reason: they are simply not skillful enough or large enough to manipulate news. One writer's notion that press offices should be feared because they are "conduits of a carefully prepared position" and that they are tools of "a tightly knit bureaucracy" is nonsense.[7] That personnel in a government agency march in lockstep is a view that could only be held by an outsider. The view from inside a press office is that most energy seems to be devoted to trying to find out what the rest of the agency is doing (often unsuccessfully), gathering material that has been requested by reporters rather than promoting carefully prepared positions, and distributing information that is neither controversial nor especially self-serving.

Part of the notion that government overwhelms the press with its view of events comes from dividing the number of Washington reporters into the number of federal public affairs officers. Such arithmetic produces a ratio of one to two, calculated one senator.[8] The conclusion, then, is that government has the personnel with which to control or manipulate information. Yet these figures are misleading; Washington press offices also respond to reporters from across the country and overseas. Even a ratio of press officers to all reporters would be meaningless, however; reporters contact many sources on each story. The government/press connection cannot be compared to a game of one-on-one.

A better case could be made that politically appointed officials—generally without consulting their press offices—attempt to manipulate the news; but as I tried to illustrate in examining leaks and other informal communications, the results smack more of confusion than conspiracy and often are merely the product of what Meg Greenfield has called "the sloppy, ebullient, gabby, exasperating nature of the society, especially of the political society."[9] It is this lack of discretion, of course, that eventually buries all presidents to their keisters. Still, there is nothing constructive they can do about it except to take more care to appoint people who are unlikely to give reporters information that works against the president's interests. Although leak-producing confrontations among the secretaries of state and defense and the national security advisers are almost part of each job description, presidents might modulate the shock waves if they paid more attention to potential personality conflicts when setting these keystone relationships of their administrations. . . .

When the purpose of leaks is to communicate between Washington players—officials, politicians, interest group representatives—Washington stories may be of limited value to the public. In these cases the consumers have a right to feel used by both government and press insiders, especially when reporters seem unwilling to pass along their sources' motives for revealing information.[10]

Arguments are also made that the press manages the news, usually through the choices reporters and editors make from the mound of information available to them. Thus according to the learned literature, some journalists become "gate-keepers" of information and "agenda-setters."[11] But I found that both reporters and officials tended to describe themselves as reacting to the other rather than as being initiators. The views largely depended on where they entered the loop: State Department press officers preparing guidances for the noon briefings based on stories they had just read in the morning's *Times* and *Post* saw the government as mainly reactive; reporters at the briefings asking for the department's guidances on the day's crises saw the press as mainly reactive. Both, I think, rather resent what they perceive of as the influence of the other over them.[12]

Without prompting from me, White House Press Secretary Larry Speakes and White House correspondent Andrea Mitchell on the same day complained in the same words: "They [reporters/officials] push the stories they want." Speakes gave an example of a worthy issue that the reporters had ignored; Mitchell gave an example of an event that the press office had manufactured. In these instances both were right. In other cases, although not often, a question asked at a briefing or news conference will have been suggested to the reporter by a government official: *If you ask about X, you will get an interesting answer.* For example, Bruce Drake of the New York *Daily News*, who was to interview President Reagan in December 1983, says "a presidential adviser" told him he "hoped the question [about hunger in Africa] would come up."

Who is reacting to whom—that is, who is initiating or trying to manage the news—partly depends on supply and demand. How valuable is the information? How badly does a press officer want something to appear in the news media? How badly does a reporter want a story? For instance, a press officer at the FDA tries to convince a *Washington Post* reporter that the commissioner's upcoming speech is important and therefore worthy of attention; the reporter does not buy his argument. The commissioner has made essentially the same statement earlier, the reporter later tells me; the reporter is right, the press officer later tells me.

More convoluted is the purpose of a DOT press officer's conversation with White House reporter Judy Woodruff. The president is coming to the department to give a pep talk and receive a briefing, but he will not be making hard news. The press officer wants to make sure that the reporter's expectations of the crosstown trip are in line with the modesty of the event.

At the State Department, reporters are waiting for the British ambassador during the Falklands crisis. They are behind a roped barricade outside the building. This is a conventional stakeout. Suddenly Sir Nicholas emerges. The reporters rip the restraining rope from the wall and rush toward him shouting questions. A young press office secretary, trapped between them, gasps, "My God, I may be killed." The ambassador makes a few comments about the United States as "the leader of the Western world and a very close ally of my country," smiles, and steps into his Silver Wraith 11 Rolls Royce. The reporters return to the newsroom to wait some more. A story of this magnitude is almost wall-to-wall waiting. After six hours of phoning, network correspondent Marvin Kalb reaches a source who says he will take one question. Kalb: "How much time until the U.S. expects the British to invade?" Source: "Seven days." The reporter gets a ninety-second story on the evening news; in the next booth, his competitor also phones and waits, but he is not as fortunate.

White House correspondent Sam Donaldson is asked, "How often do you get used by the White House?" "I get used by the White House every time they trot out a story and I put it on the air in somewhat of the form that they want it on the air. But it's a two-way street. The President makes a speech and enunciates policy. He uses us, because he's communicating with the American people, but why not? We're here to cover his activities, and to cover his speeches, and if he enunciated a new policy, to put it on the air. So I don't feel that I'm being used in some . . . some grimy sense."[13]

Some spokesmen enjoy talking about their management of news as if they were latter-day Machiavellis, but most of their activities behind closed doors as well as in briefing rooms are merely variations of shouting good news and whispering bad news. Some, of course, are more skillful than others. They have a better feel for how to extend the life of a positive story. They have a surer touch at releasing unfavorable information in a manner that the fewest people will notice. They know when and where to shop around for a sympathetic reporter—just as a reporter with a story that he wants to do will shop around for a sympathetic editor to make the assignment. They adjust events to reporters' deadlines for maximum advantage. Reporters will even admire these skills, which fall inside a zone of acceptable conduct. But if, even accidentally, a spokesman steps beyond this zone, as was the case when Jody Powell leaked an untrue story to Love Miller of the *Chicago Sun-Times*, the behavior becomes unacceptable—and as *Washington Post* reporter Douglas Feaver says, "We have long memories."

Organizations, including government agencies, would be sorely tempted to manage the news if they had a monopoly over the sources of information. Organizations always wish to justify their actions. They also think that their actions are correct, which in the case of government agencies means in the best interests of the people. What keeps news management in check—more than lack of manipulative skills and resources—is pluralism: "Under the American system of separation of powers," Francis Rourke reminds us, "it is even possible to find the opposition entrenched within the structure of government itself."[14] And since Rourke's treatise, published in 1961, there has been a quantum jump in the number of sources of information: nongovernmental organizations, think tanks, and public-interest advocates. Walter Friedenberg of the Scripps-Howard newspapers says that he once worried about the absence of "independent verification" when he reported on government, but now he feels surrounded by groups that are anxious to present him with competing data.

Still, most news comes from government, and if it is skillfully presented, it has a significant advantage over the competition. Moreover, as previously noted, most press officers and Washington reporters agree that some lies "for the public good" are justifiable in a democracy.[15] I did not see outright lying. Press officers hedge, they insinuate, but I always felt they thought they were playing by rules that reporters understood. Press officers and reporters were honorable with each other. This may seem faint praise, however, to news readers and listeners. These consumers are not always aware of the rules and are growing less willing to trust officials' and reporters' assurances that their agreements are in the public interest.[16] Does an honest lie protect national security or merely shelter officials from embarrassment? Do conventions of attribution—background or deep background or off the record—help provide more information to the public, or do they simply make official accountability harder to pinpoint?

Most of the charges about government misinformation in recent years have stemmed from the U.S. involvement in Vietnam. One military press officer commented, "There was so much bad blood—on both sides. We briefed every day and it was hot. *It was hot.* They didn't believe anything we said." Perhaps things have changed. An experienced reporter, but not someone who had been at the Pentagon during the war, said, "Vietnam taught them that they can't have second-rate people in public affairs. These are [now] all people who could do well in other places; they're not rejects." There have also been reorganizations. Yet I doubt that changes in personnel and an improved configuration of boxes on a chart explain much. Wars are special situations. The military services close ranks; secrets become synonymous with national security. In World War I and World War II the people rallied round, led by journalists.[17] But Vietnam, the unpopular war, is more likely a harbinger of future encounters that are not on U.S. soil or in Europe. Philip Knightley, in a brilliant account of war correspondents from the Crimea to Vietnam, resurrects a line from Senator Hiram Johnson: "The first casualty when war comes is truth." I happened to observe the government/press connection in peacetime.[18]

Assuming, then, that agency press operations are rarely centers of peacetime misinformation and are even competently staffed, there still remains a question of their value in a society in which there is no shortage of reporters who can search for their own stories inside governmental Washington. But it is, in fact, this very growth in the number of reporters that creates the rationale for press offices. As James Reston told Dom Bonafede of the *National Journal* in 1982, "Once you pass a certain number of people in the press corps, all the ground rules are different and the relationships are all different."[19] There are too many reporters for each of them to be able to interview the top officials of government. One solution is to consolidate interviews into briefings or press conferences and to distribute more routine material. Such functions require a logistical infrastructure, otherwise known as the press office. The other rationale is that the growth in government has outstripped the resources that a for-profit news system can dedicate to Washington coverage, and only the assistance of government, in the shape of the press office, can ensure that reporters get the basic information they need in the time allotted to them by their organizations.

I.F. Stone once wrote that there is "no other city, and no other world capital, in which life is made so easy for the newspaperman." He was referring specifically to "the advance release," "the prepared text," and "the small army of public information officers waiting in every agency to answer his queries."[20] What are the responsibilities of government to provide reporters with data? Not "Mr. Secretary, what is your position on . . . ?" but "How many children did Sadat have?" A State Department press officer says about the Sadat question: "I resent getting information for reporters that my son could have looked up in an encyclopedia." More significantly, the FDA press chief wonders, "Should I let Faye spend hours researching a query on an obscure drug for an obscure publication?" A very good question. Faye's time costs money. To what extent should taxpayers subsidize what Arthur Okun would have called "an extra helping of information"?[21] Besides, the news industry is profitable; there are also information services for hire. Why should government aid the obviously healthy or compete with an efficient part of the private sector?

In none of the agencies I visited did I find guidelines that defined for press officer and reporter the limits of government's intended helpfulness, and this sometimes led to ill feelings. The Pentagon was an exception. Other than during the invasion of Grenada, when the government changed the rule that reporters had come to expect and banned them from the battle scene, I found fewer misunderstandings between the regulars and the press officers at the Defense Department than at other agencies. This, I think, is because Pentagon reporters and military personnel have a much clearer sense of what is off limits.[22] Reporters, for example, know that they will not get answers to questions about the presence or absence of nuclear weapons locations; operational deployments of ships, troops, and aircraft, except during exercises; or contingency operations plans.

Only the press offices must try to abide by the fictions that all news organizations are equal and all reporters are equally talented. Politicians can be expected to favor the reporters and the media most important to their mission, whether it is getting elected or getting a budget authorization bill through a congressional committee. A Washington reporter for a small newspaper complains, "They [the president's assistants] provide access for important reporters *at the top* of the chain of command."[23] Presumably his access is at the bottom. In other words the desirable interviews at the White House, the quintessentially political office, go to the correspondents from CBS and Time, and not to his paper, the *Arkansas Gazette*. But the press offices, as relatively evenhanded dispensers of information, serve as a leveling force in what is otherwise a steeply hierarchical environment. Viewed as a government subsidy program, press operations thus tend to provide benefits that are more valuable to the smallest or the poorest or the most extreme news outlets. That these offices are more often assailed by reporters from other than elite publications may reflect reporters' frustrations over their condition rather than the quality of the services press offices provide them.

In return for having turned itself into a labyrinth that is nearly impossible for the nonspecialist reporter to traverse in the time limits imposed by daily journalism, government agrees to provide the press with a one-stop service center at each agency. The contrast between the needs of the regular reporter on a beat and those of the reporter who comes around for an occasional story can be seen most starkly at the Defense Department. For those reporters who learn to navigate the Pentagon's corridors, the very vastness of the place works to their advantage. "If someone is promoting the M-1 tank, there are plenty of people around who will tell you what's wrong with the M-1. No trouble finding them," says Richard Halloran of the *New York Times*. At an elemental level, explains another regular, David Bond of *Aerospace Daily*, reporters practice a form of triangulation, learning when "to go across the hall [career press officers] or down the hall [political executives] or to the services [army, navy, air force]." But for the outsider lost in the maze, the press office stands out like the golden arch of a fast-food restaurant—no gourmet meal, but easy to locate, affordable, and, if you know what to buy, it may even meet minimum nutritional needs.

From the government's vantage point, the press office system can also represent a significant savings. In 1978 a treasury official told me that most of his unit's time was being consumed by congressional requests for information. He said he was thinking about establishing a separate operation to handle these inquiries so that his staff could get on with the business of implementing policy. Similarly, press office staff can be justified on the grounds of internal efficiency—fewer interruptions for the rest of the staff in an agency.

Press offices also help present information in an orderly manner. While orderly may be a euphemism for *controlled* in some cases, most of the time the orderly release of information serves the public's purpose as well. News outlets have finite dimensions—all information cannot be printed or broadcast each day; press offices help adjust the velocity of the flow. Obviously there is so much competition among government agencies and among news organizations that this is a crude mechanism. But, in the lingo, they try not to top their own stories.

Finally, press offices could be considered not only as a government subsidy or a government efficiency, but as an entitlement that flows from the nature of a free society and the relationship of the state to the citizen. What more natural function of government is there in a democracy than for it to make available information about how it is governing? Standing in the State Department newsroom, waiting for a daily briefing to begin, Barbara Crossette of the *New York Times* said to me, "The United States is the only country where government views dealing with the press as a duty."

NOTES

1. "Self-respecting reporters rarely consult the PR men," claims Stewart Alsop in *The Center* (Popular Library, 1968), p. 102.

2. Carlton E. Spitzer, "Informing the People," *The Bureaucrat* (Winter 1981–82), p. 62.

3. Harry F. Rosenthal, "U.S. Devotes Millions to PR, Experts," *Washington Post*, May 30, 1983. Rosenthal concludes that 120 government agencies collectively budgeted $165 million on public information for the fiscal year, but that "the real cost is far greater."

4. For a compilation of the many ways that government public relations have been defined, I am indebted to Mordecai Kamesar Lee, "Congressional Oversight of Federal Public Relations" (Ph.D. dissertation, Syracuse University, 1975).

5. The considerable controversy in 1971 over a CBS documentary, "The Selling of the Pentagon," was not about press offices but about "staging elaborate war games, circulating propaganda films and sending out officers in uniform to warn about the menace of communism," according to Lester A. Sobel, ed., *Media Controversies* (Facts on File, 1981), p. 31.

6. As I stated at the outset, I did not set out to go to places that are supposed to be models of inefficiency. See "Author's Note."

7. See Charles S. Steinberg, *The Information Establishment* (Hastings House, 1980), pp. 151, 163.

8. Ibid., p. 54.

9. Meg Greenfield, "The Gabby American Way," *Washington Post*, February 17, 1982.

10. The following sentence from a newspaper story is as useful as it is unusual: "Information that withdrawal was under serious consideration was first made available by opponents of an American pullout who are hoping to stop it by bringing the matter into public discussion." See E.J. Dionne Jr., "U.S. Weighs Unesco Pullout Over Budget and Policy Fight," *New York Times*, December 15, 1983.

11. See David Manning White, "The 'Gatekeeper': A Case Study in the Selection of News," *Journalism Quarterly*, vol. 27 (Fall 1950), pp. 383–90; and Maxwell McCombs and Donald Shaw, "The Agenda-Setting Function of Mass Media," *Public Opinion Quarterly*, vol. 36 (Summer 1972), pp. 176–87.

12. Speaking at the same conference, for example, presidential counselor Edwin Meese said that the press plays a large part in shaping American foreign policy because of its influence on public opinion, while Jeff Greenfield [now of ABC News] said that reporters do not have any real influence on forming public opinion or policy. See "Influence of Media Over American Foreign Policy Discussed," *More Facts* (published by the Foundation for American Communications) (April/May 1982), p. 1.

13. The questioner is Hodding Carter on a segment of the PBS television series "Inside Story" called "Mr. President . . . Mr. President . . . ?" Transcript (The Press and the Public Project, Inc., 1981), p. 2.

14. Francis E. Rourke, *Secrecy and Publicity: Dilemmas of Democracy* (Johns Hopkins University Press, 1961), p. 203.

15. For another view, see Sissela Bok, *Lying: Moral Choice in Public and Private Life* (Vintage, 1979), p. 191. Bok would countenance lying for the public good by officials if what constituted that category of lies could be "openly debated and consented to in advance."

16. A National Opinion Research Center poll shows that 13.7 percent of respondents have a great deal of confidence in the press, 13.4 percent in federal government executives, 12.7 percent in television, and 10.2 percent in Congress. See "Journalism Under Fire," *Time* (December 12, 1983), p. 79.

17. See David L. Altheide and John M. Johnson, *Bureaucratic Propaganda* (Allyn & Bacon, 1980), p. 10.

18. See Philip Knightley, *The First Casualty* (Andre Deutsch, 1975). Also, for an account of how the authorities "frequently used the media as an instrument with which to confuse the enemy" during Britain's war with Argentina in 1982, see Robert Harris, *Gotcha! The Media, the Government and the Falklands Crisis* (Faber and Faber, 1983).

19. Dom Bonafede, "The Washington Press Competing for Power with the Federal Government," *National Journal* (April 17, 1982), p. 666.

20. I.F. Stone, "Many Thank-yous, Mr. President," *Washington Post Book World*, February 13, 1966.

21. Arthur M. Okun, *Equality and Efficiency: The Big Tradeoff* (Brookings Institution, 1975), chap. 1, "Rights and Dollars," is especially pertinent if the discussion were to be applied to the rationales for government press offices. Of similar value is Robert A. Dahl and Edward R. Tufte, *Size and Democracy* (Stanford University Press, 1973). Dahl and Tufte warn against romanticizing "the idea that democracy is somehow linked with smallness" (p. 12) by concluding that "no single type or size of unit is optimal for achieving the twin goals of citizen effectiveness and system capacity" (p. 138).

22. Mark Watson, a legendary Pentagon reporter for the *Baltimore Sun*, once "politely interrupted a Defense Secretary who was talking about tank production rates and suggested that the subject was a military secret, not to be discussed in public." See Robert B. Sims, *The Pentagon Reporters* (National Defense University Press, 1983), pp. 24–25.

23. Tom Hamburger, "How the White House Cons the Press," *Washington Monthly* (January 1982), p. 24.

E. INTEREST GROUPS

Government is not the only special pleader at the gates of the news media. Interest groups are even more prevalent and more intertwined with the news media. City-desk editors at major newspapers and assignment editors at broadcast stations daily toss away hundreds of press releases from various interest groups. Nevertheless, much of the news produced is created or shaped to some extent by interest groups.

The relationship between interest groups and the news media is a little explored field of political communication. Yet, as you will see indicated below, interest groups have discovered the media as a weighty tool in acquiring visibility and legitimacy. The media help the interest group further its policy and public education objectives. By acquiring media notice, various groups hope to shape the public's agenda and, therefore, alter policy choices.

The relationship is symbiotic, not parasitical. The press has found some interest groups willing to function as quasi-governmental bodies—feeding regular doses of news, meeting press deadlines, and putting forth group experts as sources. These groups likely gain the most attention because they meet the imperatives of the press.

Many interest groups solicit press attention and crave quasi-authority status, which will allow their views to be heard in the public debate over issues. In turn, the press requires news sources who will offer stories meeting news values and press deadlines.

However, the interaction is not necessarily equal. More interest groups chase the news media than the other way around. Interest groups compete for media attention and status. However, once established as legitimate sources, some interest groups acquire leverage in handling media requests. For example, reporters who cover Supreme Court decisions involving civil liberties come to believe the American Civil Liberties Union's perspective must be included in their story. The tables then are turned in the interest group's favor.

The following selections dramatically demonstrate this supply and demand phenomenon in media coverage of interest groups. They also illustrate how even groups who often lose in the competition can win at times.

35. WHAT'S GOOD FOR MOBIL OIL

Jarol B. Manheim

Most of the interest-group–related news or advertising we see is the product of the public relations efforts by large, well-established entities. Corporations such as Mobil Oil, General Motors, and IBM employ large public relations staffs to influence their news coverage. Interest groups ranging from the National Organization for Women and the National Education Association to the Chamber of Commerce and the AFL-CIO also pursue major public relations strategies.

Although much of this effort is directed primarily at consumers, these groups also target the participants in the public policy-making process. Groups attempting to affect legislation have moved beyond the corridors of Capitol Hill to the grassroots of America. Through the mass media, they seek to shape public opinion and elite opinion on government policy impacting their group or organization.

In the selection below, Jarol Manheim examines advocacy advertising by large, wealthy corporations and trade associations.* These groups use advertising not to sell products but to influence political decisions.

Advertising is not the only means used. Groups now distribute video press releases, which appear much like news stories and, if used by local TV stations, may blend unobtrusively into the news format. Hence, the group's message acquires legitimacy as straight news.

The news media become like coaxial cable for interest groups who design their messages in visually attractive packages meeting the criteria for newsworthiness. This raises questions about the credibility of a news presentation penetrated by interest-group advocates.

Jarol B. Manheim is professor of political communication at George Washington University. In addition to *All of the People All the Time: Strategic Communication and American Politics* (1991), from which this reading is excerpted, he is the author of articles on political communication that have appeared in the *American Political Science Review*, the *Journal of Communication*, and the *British Journal of Political Science*.

Politicians, government leaders, and governments themselves are not the only ones with political interests in our society, and they are not the only practitioners of strategic political communication. Other players—special and public interest

All of the People All the Time: Strategic Communication and American Politics (Armonk, N.Y.: M.E. Sharpe, Inc., 1991), pp. 106–16. Reprinted with permission.

groups, trade associations, and corporations—get into the game as well. And some, like Herb Schmertz, are important and accomplished communicators.

It was the late political scientist V.O. Key, Jr., who pointed out in his classic book, *Politics, Parties, and Pressure Groups*, the vulnerability of business as a favored interest in American politics and the importance of using communication to sustain its position of privilege. In effect, said Key, business must create and continually press forward a myth of its own social value. Business people, he observed, are few in number and lack the inherent moral authority of "the sturdy agrarian yeomanry or the horny-handed toiler of the factory and foundry." But what they lack in votes, he went on, business people make up in money and intelligence, resources they must use to advantage. The politics of business, said Key, must include aggressive attempts to mold the attitudes of both the general and special publics. To gain public favor business associations and corporations employ in large numbers public-relations experts, those masters of the verbal magic that transmutes private advantage into the public good. . . . [Of] fundamental significance is the continuing propaganda calculated to shape public attitudes favorably toward the business system as a whole or toward particular types of business.[1] It was a concern that Herb Schmertz and a host of other business communicators have shared, and advice that they have heeded well.

And there has been good reason for their concern. A 1975 national survey of public opinion, for example, found that 67 percent of the public expressed a "low approval" of big companies, up from 47 percent ten years earlier. Fifty-seven percent thought that the government should limit corporate profits. One American in three thought the oil companies were the worst of the lot when it came to ethics, and three in four thought that they, in particular, made too much profit.[2] By the mid-1980s, only 19 percent of Americans said they had a great deal of confidence in the leaders of business,[3] and a mere 18 percent said that they thought business executives were highly honest and ethical.[4] And no wonder! A 1981 report by the Media Institute, a Washington-based research group, compiled after monitoring portrayals of business on two hundred prime-time television episodes, found that two-thirds of business people were shown in a negative light, that roughly half of the work shown as being done by business people involved illegalities, that the major characters who ran big businesses were presented as criminals, and that few of the portrayals showed business to be either socially useful or economically productive.[5]

The response to this perceived problem from the business community—as the breadth of the Mobil Oil effort suggests—takes many forms. Perhaps the most prominent among these is the placement of so-called "advocacy advertising," advertising that is intended to promote ideas or policies rather than products. Consistent with the idea of selling the myth of American business suggested by Key, some advocacy advertising is intended to promote business in a generic sense. In the mid-1970s, for example, the Advertising Council, a nonprofit organization that produces many of the nation's best-known public service spots, undertook a multi-year educational campaign to overcome what it termed "economic illiteracy," having discovered through research that only 1 percent of the American population could correctly identify all five of the functions in our economy of business, labor, the consumer, the investor, and advertising. With a budget of $150 million and support from the Department of Commerce and several major corporations, the effort was designed "to make the workings of the free enterprise system as familiar to Americans as the batting average of baseball players." The level of "literacy" the council sought may have been in question—the educational booklet around which the advertising campaign was centered was written at a ninth-grade level and featured original "Peanuts" cartoons—but the concept was pure V.O. Key.[6]

Other advocacy advertising is intended to improve the fortunes of individual companies. In 1987, for example, American television viewers were presented with the image of a space station drifting slowly upward across their screens. Another American space triumph? No. As the station drifted further, its outer markings passed slowly through the field of view—a red star and the letters "CCCP." Lest anyone miss the message, a NASA-like exchange of voices in the background carried a conversation in Russian. "Shouldn't we be there, too?" asked the message at the end. The advertisement—produced by McDonnell Douglas, a major contractor in the American space program—was deemed too controversial by all three networks, who declined to run it, but it appeared on local stations across the country. In 1989, the company followed with a more subtle spot, one picturing a little girl putting on a space suit and helmet and gazing upward as a space station floats by to the strains of "Twinkle Twinkle Little Star." "There's a big world waiting out there, little one. . . ," says a female narrator. "For an educated America, even the sky's not the limit," intones a man's voice.

For all of their "morning in America" feel—and in the first instance the *"wake up* America" message—these spots are not exercises in altruism. The United States program to build a space station—worth an estimated $1 billion to McDonnell Douglas—has been in trouble. Stretch-outs and budget cutbacks have delayed its development, and the will to proceed is very much in doubt. Perhaps that is why, in addition to airing on CNN and the three major networks' public affairs programs— they accepted this one—the advertisement was also set to run repeatedly in selected local markets: Baltimore, Maryland, home of Senator Barbara A. Mikulski, chair of the appropriations subcommittee that oversees the NASA budget; Flint, Michigan, where it might be seen by Representative Bob Traxler, who chairs the House committee that controls the NASA budget; and such other major media capitals as Baton Rouge, Louisiana, Jackson, Mississippi, and Springfield, Massachusetts. "These are all areas," said company spokesman Tom Williams, "where we wouldn't be disappointed if people contacted their congressmen."[7]

Even smaller fish can jump into the advocacy pond. In January 1989, for instance, a small Louisiana company, Marine Shale Processors, bought local time in Washington, D.C., during the network evening news programs for a $250,000 campaign to promote its toxic-waste disposal systems. Basically, the company claimed to turn toxic sludge into harmless gravel. Most Washington viewers were not likely to

buy a toxic-waste disposal system that January, but among the audience were legislators and government environmental regulators who very well might. Targeting.

Advocacy advertising does not come cheap. A one-time, full-page advertisement in the *Washington Post*, for example, cost approximately $37,000 ($45,000 on
Sundays) in 1989, while a similar placement in the national edition of the *New York
Times* cost about $46,000 ($55,000 on Sundays). In that year, Northrup Corporation
spent more than $60,000 for local time in Washington to run a television advertise-
ment touting the company's B-2 bomber in advance of a congressional decision on
extending funding for the plane. Since at the time the B-2 had never flown,
Northrup promoted it as "America's most thoroughly *tested* new bomber" [emphasis
added].[8]

Overall, estimates are that some $50 million to $75 million are spent each year
on advocacy advertising, and the pace of such efforts has been increasing. *Advocacy
Reports*, a newsletter that monitors such ads in four outlets—the *New York Times, New
Republic, National Review,* and *Columbia Journalism Review*—reported that the volume
of placements grew from 118 pages in 1984 to 204 in 1988, or some 73 percent in
four years. In addition to government officials, this advertising can be aimed at journalists—some 14,000 of whom work in the Washington area alone. Or, in the case
of advertising designed to stimulate contributions, organizational membership, or
political action—as in the 1981 effort to mobilize support for the Reagan tax reform
package or the 1988 effort to defeat the nomination of Robert Bork to the Supreme
Court, in which the *Washington Post* alone ran $220,000 worth of messages for both
sides—it can be aimed at the public in general.[9]

Labor has joined the image making as well. Who could have escaped the
catchy strains of "Look for the Union Label," the television anthem of the
International Ladies' Garment Workers Union, which first aired in 1975 and which,
by 1980, elicited recognition and a positive response from four out of five
Americans. And the more recent and more pervasive "Made in the USA" campaign
still fills the airwaves. In 1984 the Labor Institute of Public Affairs, an AFL-CLO affil-
iate, began a television series called *America Works*, which aired in a number of cities.
Along with it came pro-union messages such as one that featured then-Washington
Redskins running back John Riggins in a locker room holding up his NFL Players
Association card. "Here's my union card," said Riggins as if it were American
Express gold. "I wouldn't go to work without it."[10] And during the presidential pri-
mary season in 1987 and 1988, the American Federation of State, County, and
Municipal Employees launched a $1.2 million campaign in Iowa, New Hampshire,
and other key states designed to influence the campaign agenda. "It's time for new
priorities," said the union.[11]

Sometimes advocacy advertising strains the limits of truthfulness. The
Tobacco Institute, principal trade association of the cigarette industry, for example,
ran a series of advertisements in nineteen newspapers around the country which
said that a majority of Americans do not support a ban on cigarette advertising, do
not support an increase in cigarette taxes, and do not support smoking bans in

restaurants. Based on a nationwide survey conducted by Hamilton, Frederick & Schneiders, a respected Washington polling firm that has since been reorganized, the industry campaign was designed to dispel the notion that smokers' rights was an unpopular, minority issue. "Enough Is Enough!" proclaimed the advertisements. Strictly speaking—very strictly—each of the three claims just noted was true. A majority did not support a total ban on cigarette advertising—only 41 percent did. But another 34 percent supported continuation of the present prohibition on advertising these products on radio or television. This the Tobacco Institute neglected to mention. Similarly, a majority did not support an increase in cigarette taxes—only 44 percent did. But another 38 percent thought they should remain at the already high level about which the advertisement went on to complain. This the Tobacco Institute neglected to mention. And a majority did not support a total ban on smoking in restaurants—only 24 percent did. But another 74 percent favored continuation of the segregation of smokers into special smoking sections. This left a mere 2 percent of the public supporting the prosmoking position implied by the advertisement. This, too, the Tobacco Institute neglected to mention. How do we know all this? Because the *Washington Post* got hold of the original data and shared them with the world, much to the embarrassment of the institute.[12]

In addition to being more forthright than that of the cigarette industry, much of the promotional effort undertaken by business is more subtle as well. Mobil's use of public television is not only a case in point—it represented the point of a wedge that is now well embedded in the financing of PBS and its member stations. Big Oil followed the Mobil lead in a big way. By 1981, fully 72 percent of all of the programming broadcast by PBS during its thirty-two-hour weekly core schedule, roughly the equivalent of prime time, was funded in whole or in significant measure by four oil companies: Exxon, Mobil, Arco, and Gulf. Indeed, the same four companies had been among the largest PBS underwriters every year since 1976.[13] Nor is this corporate largesse proffered only by companies from the oil patch. For example, shortly after a division of Allied Chemical was found to have dumped tons of the pesticide Kepone into the James River at Hopewell, Virginia, threatening the public health of those in the area and downriver, and bringing an immediate end to the region's lucrative fishing industry, Allied appeared as one of the principal underwriters of PBS's "MacNeil-Lehrer News Hour," with its elite audience. And in the wake of its own problems with chemical discharges at Bhopal, India, and Institute, West Virginia, Union Carbide, too, became a PBS underwriter.

Commercial television can also provide a vehicle for corporate image polishing. A campaign begun in 1989 by Philip Morris, for example, put the company's name back into television commercials for the first time since the 1950s, but not to sell cigarettes—at least not directly. Rather, the campaign, reinforced by full-page newspaper advertisements, was a 200th anniversary devotional to the Bill of Rights, a potent symbol of American values with which it could hardly hurt to be associated. Estimated cost of the campaign: $30 million per year for two years.[14] Similarly, Dow Chemical set out to rehabilitate its corporate image, damaged for a generation by the company's association in the public mind with the napalm it manufactured for the American war effort in Vietnam. After nearly twenty years, the company has begun a major television advertising campaign. The message to the children of the 1960s antiwar protestors: By caring about people, "Dow lets you do great things."

In 1981, the Federal Communications Commission took steps to make corporate underwriting of public television even more attractive for would-be sponsors by removing certain restrictions on the nature of their messages. Prior to that time, underwriters could only be identified by name. Under the revised rules, still in effect, the identification could include a summary of the company's line of business as well as its corporate logo or symbol.[15] After this decision, some companies, such as Norfolk Southern, even went so far as to develop film or animated logos that closely resemble commercials.

The importance of enhancing a corporation's image should not be underestimated. Joseph Downer, at the time a vice chairman of Arco, told a *TV Guide* interviewer in 1981 that, as a direct result of the $15 million his company had contributed to public broadcasting over a five-year period, "We gain an image of quality. Our sponsorship of the Wolf Trap concerts resulted in a tremendous response from people in government. And, my God, you walk into the departments, or the Congress, and you're identified as Arco, and there's a feeling of warmth. There's no question but that it's helpful to our lobbying effort." But some, like Fred Friendly, who himself gave more than $200 million to public television as head of the Ford Foundation, suggested an even more subtle motive: "By deciding which shows they will underwrite," Friendly pointed out, "they have also decided what will not be on the air. By funding those programs . . . that are harmless, so far as controversy goes, they are structuring the program schedule of public television."[16] It's enough to make Nixon and Company very proud.

Public interest advertising as well as public television can also serve the needs of corporate political communication. Under pressure in recent years on the issues of alcohol abuse and, especially, drunk driving, the beer industry has undertaken an extensive campaign promoting "responsible" drinking. Anheuser-Busch, which has for several years now conducted a "Know When to Say When" campaign, quadrupled the campaign's budget in 1989 to $30 million, or roughly 5 percent of the company's annual advertising expenditures, and in that same year Adolph Coors began a "Now/Not Now" effort, showing scenes at a friendly tavern ("Now") and at work and behind the wheel ("Not Now"). The impetus for all of this seemingly counterproductive advertising? A report on drunk driving was issued by the surgeon general of the United States criticizing alcohol ads and recommending, among other things, a voluntary ban on advertising of alcohol on college campuses by September 1990 and elimination of all tax deductions for all but the simplest of advertisements listing brand names and prices. That, you can be assured, sent ripples through the beer vats of St. Louis, Missouri, and Golden, Colorado. To make sure the word got around, the Beer Institute, the industry's lobby, followed up on the individual corporate promotions with a $2.5 million campaign of its own, this one pointing with pride to the efforts of brewers to combat excessive drinking.[17]

Another strategy pursued by business . . . is the "massaging" of the news by creating and distributing video news clips. This strategy, too, was anticipated by Mobil, and has now become commonplace. Sometimes a report produced by a company, or by its public relations firm, will air in its entirety on a local news program, but without any mention of its source. Audio is provided—indeed, one way to recognize these pieces is by the absence of a statement of affiliation at the end of the "report"—"Jane Doe reporting from San Diego" rather than "Jane Doe, Channel 7 News, reporting"—but it is recorded separately from the video track so that it can be stripped off and replaced with an audio track featuring a reporter from the station that runs the tape, thereby giving that station the appearance of vast news-gathering resources, and the company that created the message the added credibility afforded by the local journalists. It is essentially the same game played by the practitioners of negative political advertising, except that these spots are usually served sunny-side up. To further the deception, the names of persons interviewed are not superimposed on the original tape, so that each local station can use its own graphic style. Some stations run these tapes unedited, while others weave pieces of them into locally produced stories. The commercial touches here are often subtle—a feature on schoolchildren learning to take photographs (using Kodak cameras), a reminder to adjust your (large Timex) clock for daylight savings time—but when they are used, they are news.[18]

Finally, corporations and others sometimes use strategic communication techniques for damage control when something goes wrong. In late 1985, for example, when the Environmental Protection Agency (EPA) began to suspect that dioxin—a potent carcinogen—was contaminating discharges from the nation's paper mills, the paper industry saw a crisis on its horizon. By February of 1986, when it became clear to the paper companies that the contamination affected not only their discharges but their products as well, the time for action had arrived. The cap was still securely in place, but word of the problem was sure to leak soon. Would there be enough time to avoid a public relations catastrophe? Under the leadership of the American Paper Institute (API) in Washington, the industry developed a "Dioxin Public Affairs Plan" and budgeted $300,000 to manage official and public perceptions of paper products. The plan included "Intelligence gathering" at the EPA, tempering news media interest—"Really, folks, there's no story here!"—minimizing public health concerns, and hiring outside experts to counter expected EPA comments on the risks associated with dioxin. API hired a Washington public relations firm, trained representatives of the individual corporations involved on how to deal with the issue, and conducted a consumer survey. The association conducted its own independent tests of paper products and, in September 1987, when the story could be held no longer, announced the results while playing down any threats to health. The outcome? A panic over paper as might have been expected, but a short-lived one, as the industry had hoped.[19]

The value of strategic communication in controlling political damage has not been lost on the nation's religious establishment either. In April of 1990, for example, the National Conference of Catholic Bishops, frustrated by the church's performance in framing the debate on the abortion issue, contracted with the Washington office of the public relations firm of Hill & Knowlton and with the Wirthlin Group, home of former Reagan polling guru Richard Wirthlin, to turn things around. The objective of the three- to five-year campaign is to change the terms of debate from a focus on privacy and women's rights to one on the "humanity of the unborn." The price tag: an estimated three to five million dollars, with the majority to be paid by the Knights of Columbus, a Catholic fraternal organization. The initial publicity generated by the contract, however, may not have been what the bishops had in mind. Both clients and some employees reportedly severed their ties with Hill & Knowlton's Washington office, and more than a third of the roughly four hundred New York employees of the firm signed a petition protesting the decision to represent the church, which stated, in part, "We should not be representing any group in its advocacy of a position which would restrict the fundamental rights of all of us as Americans."[20]

... We can see, then, that corporations, industry associations, labor unions, and other groups are just as sophisticated as politicians—often more so—in the use of strategic communication, and that their efforts are very much a part of the information environment in which we live. . . .

NOTES

1. V.O. Key, Jr., *Politics, Parties, and Pressure Groups*, 5th ed. (New York: Thomas Y. Crowell, 1964), pp. 91–92.

2. Connor, "Mobil's Advocacy," *Wall Street Journal.*

3. Elizabeth Harm Hastings and Philip K. Hastings, eds., *Index to International Public Opinion 1984–85* (Westport, Conn.: Greenwood Press, 1984), p. 360.

4. Edmund F. McGarrell and Timothy J. Flanagan, eds., *Sourcebook of Criminal Justice Statistics—1984* (Washington, D.C.: U.S. Government Printing Office, 1985), p. 213.

5. Reported in "TV's Businessman Is Getting Bum Rap as Tube's Big Boob," *Wall Street Journal*, 20 April 1981, p. 10.

6. Michael J. Connor, "Ad Campaign That Seeks to Explain Workings of Free Enterprise System Stirs Controversy," *Wall Street Journal*, 4 August 1976, p. 32.

7. David Olmos, "Lost in Space? Contractor Supports Space Station with TV Ads," *Philadelphia Inquirer*, 11 May 1989.

8. Paul Farhi, "Weapons Firms Carry Out Ad Blitzes," *Washington Post*, 20 July 1989, pp. F1, F5.

9. Paul Farhi, "Advertising That Aims to Sell Ideas," *Washington Post*, 31 January 1989, pp. C1, C6.

10. Stephen Banker, "Look for the Union Label . . . and Much, Much More," *TV Guide*, 31 March 1984, pp. 30–33.

11. Lloyd Grove, "Groups' Ads Seek to Shape '88 Agenda," *Washington Post*, 14 December 1987, p. A24.

12. Richard Morin, "Tobacco Institute Ads Shaded Truth," *Washington Post*, 26 January 1989, p. A 16.

13. John Weisman, "Why Big Oil Loves Public TV," *TV Guide*, 20 June 1981, pp. 4–10.

14. "Philip Morris Returns to TV with Patriotic Ad Campaign," *Washington Post*, 2 November 1989, p. E3.

15. Margaret Garrard Warner, "FCC to Let Public Broadcasting Stations Broaden Identification of Business Donors," *Wall Street Journal*, 24 April 1981, p. 7.

16. Weisman, "Why Big Oil Loves Public TV," *TV Guide*.

17. Paul Farhi, "Brewers' New Ad Pitch: Moderation and Caution," *Washington Post*, 4 July 1989, pp. C1, C3.

18. Jeanne Sadler, "Public Relations Firms Offer 'News' to TV," *Wall Street Journal*, 2 April 1985, p. 6; Michael M. Klepper, "Airing Your Corporate Message on the Evening News," *Wall Street Journal*, 23 February 1987, p. 26; and Herman M. Rosenthal, "Beware of News Clips Massaging Your Opinions," *TV Guide*, 21 April 1984, p. 5.

19. Michael Weisskopf, "They Couldn't Control the Dioxin but the Damage, Maybe," *Washington Post National Weekly Edition*, 9 November 1987, p. 28.

20. Tamar Lewin, "Abortion Divides Firm Hired to Help Fight It," *New York Times*, 18 April 1990, p. A14; Peter Steinfels, "O'Connor Defends Anti-Abortion Aid," *New York Times*, 22 April 1990, p. 30; Peter Steinfels, "Knights Aiding Anti-Abortion Effort," *New York Times*, 13 May 1990, p. 18.

36. RESOURCE-POOR GROUPS

Edie Goldenberg

Not all interest groups possess the financial resources for large-scale public relations campaigns. These poorer, but still quite effective, groups are the subject of the next selection.

Edie Goldenberg offers an entirely different perspective—interest groups attempting to pursue media strategies, but lacking the resources of large, well-established organizations. For these groups, media attention becomes even more critical because the groups often lack the political resources to accomplish their objectives. However, their poverty usually means they are overlooked, especially when more wealthy groups are competing for attention.

These groups must establish credibility as news sources. They must gain acceptance as legitimate representatives of one side of a controversy. In fact, often they must acquire press recognition that their cause—be it homelessness, the elderly poor, or infant mortality—is newsworthy.

Goldenberg describes the tactics these entities use to overcome the enormous advantage of resource-rich groups. She draws on her research with urban interest groups in Boston.*

Edie Goldenberg is professor of political science at the University of Michigan. She is the author of *Campaigning for Congress* (1984) and *Making the Papers* (1975), from which this excerpt has been taken.

This [study] deals with a distinct subsystem in which the media serve as an intermediary mechanism between the governors and the governed. Actors in this subsystem

*From *Making the Papers* (Lexington, Mass.: Lexington Books, 1975), pp. 1–5, 125–34. Reprinted with permission. Some footnotes and tables have been omitted.

include leaders and members of interest groups, reporters and editors who handle news of these groups, and governmental decision makers whom groups seek to influence. The major focus of this study is on a special subset of interest groups—those which are resource-poor and acting in the urban area—and their interactions with the metropolitan press. The intent is to examine the conditions under which resource-poor groups seek access to the metropolitan press and the conditions under which they are successful in gaining it.

Unless a group has direct access to the government officials dealing with its interest, group members interested in influencing those officials must attempt to influence them indirectly. The media are often involved in indirect attempts to influence policy. They are key access points to public officials for all groups. Through the media, issues are frequently brought to the attention of the public and of government officials. News coverage is used by groups in gaining status and visibility, in expanding the scope of conflict, in reinforcing attitudes, in activating third parties on their behalf, and in gaining a hearing in the political process.

News coverage is particularly important to resource-poor groups because they lack most of the other political resources that might enable them to be heard and to affect policy directly. The ability to receive the proper kinds of publicity at the right time enables resource-poor groups to make more effective use of the limited resources available to them and to generate additional resources for the group. In effect, media attention is itself a political resource. For the group that is unable to exert much influence due to its lack of resources, the media can be intervening mechanisms in the political system. They can intervene by serving as an intermediary in carrying the group's message to policymakers or to third parties who, in turn, take it to policymakers. Or they can intervene by helping groups achieve certain media goals intended to maintain and enhance the group itself so that it may be strong enough to exert influence some time in the future.

The mass media do not provide the only channels of access to public decision makers. Direct confrontation, for one, may not require media treatment to gain a hearing, to activate third parties, or to influence targets. News coverage—even sympathetic news coverage—will not necessarily ensure a group influence in the policy-making arena. However, the media can provide important channels of access for resource-poor groups. If these channels are obstructed, the task of bringing issues into the policy-making arena, and of influencing them once they are there, is very difficult.

Neither do the media provide the only mechanism—or even the major mechanism—for building organizational resources. There is clearly a lot of support among organizers for door-knocking and mass mailings as organizational techniques. However, organizers also stress the importance and usefulness of the press for mobilizing potential group members, for providing incentives for active group participation, for bringing in cash donations, and for alerting allies and third parties to developments and planned actions. . . .

THE ACTORS

The four interest groups of primary interest in this study were all located in the Boston area. They were (1) the Legislative Council for Older Americans (LCOA), a mass-based organization of older people that lobbied on behalf of the elderly and tried to meet more immediate needs where possible; (2) The People First (TPF), a neighborhood organization working to improve the Dorchester community of Boston and immediately to oust a district court judge; (3) the Cape Cod and Islands Tenants' Council (CCITC), a group of poor people on Cape Cod who had to move out of their homes every summer at the start of the tourist season and who tried to alleviate the situation by bringing more housing into the pool of available low-cost housing on the Cape; (4) the Massachusetts Welfare Rights Organization (MWRO), a mass-based recipient organization that tried to improve the living conditions mainly for mothers receiving Aid to Families with Dependent Children (AFDC). All four of these groups shared a relative poverty in terms of group resources available for political action. They also shared a willingness to engage in protest activities from time to time as part of their efforts to influence their targets. They represented only four of the resource-poor groups active in the Boston metropolitan area during the late 1960s and early 1970s when this study was undertaken. However, they did provide a variety of types of resource-poor groups interested in a variety of issues. It is hoped that they spanned a fairly wide range of the types of resource-poor groups active in the Boston area.

The governmental decision makers who were targets for these four groups were primarily administrators and elected officials at the state level. They included the governor, the welfare commissioner, and the Massachusetts legislature, particularly the Joint Social Welfare Committee, the Joint Urban Affairs Committee, and the Joint Welfare Investigative Committee. They also included local housing authorities on Cape Cod, the State Department of Community Affairs (DCA), and the court system—in particular, the head of the Boston District courts and the State Supreme Court.

The news organizations that served as intervening mechanisms between interest groups and governmental targets in Boston were three independent daily and Sunday newspapers: the *Boston Globe* (and the *Evening Globe*), the *Herald Traveler*, and the *Record American*. They varied in terms of size, news organization, type of ownership, editorial policy, and profits, providing three cases that included much of the diversity to be found in metropolitan newspapers today. The *Globe*, particularly the morning paper, was universally acknowledged as the metropolitan powerhouse in terms of revenues, circulation, size, and political clout. . . . In 1968 the *Globe* endorsed Humphrey over Nixon. . . . And in 1972 there was no doubt that the *Globe* favored McGovern's candidacy over Nixon's.

In sharp contrast, the *Herald Traveler* was a staunch Republican newspaper, highly conservative in its editorial stance. . . . The newspaper was operating with a reduced staff of reporters who were constantly worried about losing their jobs should the license be lost.

The third metropolitan newspaper in operation in Boston during the 1967–72 period was the *Record American/Sunday Advertiser*. It was part of the Hearst newspaper chain. . . . During the interview period, the *Record American* was a sensational tabloid publication that emphasized soft news in picture format. It was still operating out of its plant at Five Winthrop Square, a five-story building that it had occupied since 1924 and that was recently slated for demolition. The reporting staff was smaller and older than the staffs at the other two newspapers; the rewrite staff was larger and much more important at the *Record* than at the *Herald* or *Globe*. Nearly all stories were rewritten by rewritemen, most of whom had been with the paper for more than twenty-five years. With respect to social welfare stories, the *Record*'s stance was admittedly quite far to the right and written for an uneducated or poorly educated audience.

THE SETTING

Compared with other local settings, the Boston newspaper scene was highly competitive. The number of newspapers operating in one geographical region has relevance for the access problem, both in terms of whether a group seeks and whether it gains access. The more reporters and newspaper institutions, the more potential receivers and transmitters of news. Therefore, in a competitive environment, a group has more potential points of access to the press than in a noncompetitive one.

In addition, in a competitive environment the potential points of access are more likely to be accessible. If one hostile newspaper dominates a market, there seems to be little that a group or individual can do to induce that newspaper or its employees to provide desirable coverage. In a competitive situation, there are strategies that may give the neglected or mistreated source leverage with respect to even the most hostile newspaper organization. When newspapers fold, turning a competitive scene into a noncompetitive one, it can result in a loss of access. Unless the most accessible newspaper is the one to survive, and unless it remains at least as accessible without competition as it was with it, then groups fare better with access to the press in a competitive environment than in a noncompetitive one.

In choosing Boston as a site for this study, the competitiveness of the media situation was judged as a distinct plus. It was assumed that in a competitive situation, any source—and particularly one lacking political resources—would have an easier time gaining news coverage than in a noncompetitive situation. The multinewspaper situation in Boston was also desirable because it provided for the possibility of making comparisons within one context across a number of significantly different types of newspaper organizations. The potential news was roughly the same for all organizations; the potential news sources were the same for all news organizations.

The results reported . . . are based on fieldwork completed during 1971 and

1972. This field experience included working as a reporter intern for the *Boston Globe* during the summer of 1971, observing as a participant and nonparticipant in the *Globe* and *Herald* newsrooms as well as at City Hall and the State House, and completing a total of 142 interviews with newspeople,[a] media executives, spokesmen for local resource-poor groups, policymakers, and social welfare professionals in Boston. . . .

DISCRETE INTERACTIONS

INTRODUCTION

Access is a hearing in which the group presents its point of view to some target in an effort to affect some outcome and the target seriously listens. For the resource-poor group, access usually necessitates direct contact between group member and newspaper personnel. It is rare that newspeople learn of group points of view through intermediaries such as group newsletters or alternative publications. Direct contacts are described as group-newspaper interactions in this section as a number of questions are addressed. How do groups and newspapers interact? What are the particular problems facing the resource-poor group in its efforts to interact with metropolitan newspapers? How did four resource-poor groups come to interact with the three metropolitan newspaper organizations in Boston? Are there recognizable patterns? Do these interactions become regularized? Why or why not? How much access results?

An initial interaction between a group and a metropolitan newspaper occurs the first time that a member of the group interacts with a newsperson working for the newspaper, whether or not news coverage results. Subsequent contacts between a group and a newspaper may become regularized or remain discrete. They tend to remain discrete if either the group person or the newsperson changes or if the contacts occur infrequently. They become regularized if they occur frequently over time with some consistency in pattern. . . .

Discrete interactions are important for a number of reasons. First, understanding the circumstances under which they occur clarifies the limits of group access to the press. At a minimum, access requires an initial interaction. Three of the four groups existed and engaged in potentially newsworthy activities before they ever interacted with the press. Yet, during that period, neither the group nor the newspaper took the initiative to contact the other. What are the circumstances that initially lead resource-poor groups to contact the newspapers? What are the circumstances that lead metropolitan newspapers to contact resource-poor groups? Understanding these circumstances can add to our understanding of the conditions under which access is sought and gained.

Second, the character of the initial interaction can affect subsequent interac-

[a]These interviews included people not only from the three metropolitan newspapers already alluded to but also 13 newspeople associated with various alternative media in Boston and with the *Christian Science Monitor*.

tions between group and newspaper by setting the tone as friendly or hostile, productive or nonproductive. Furthermore, coverage resulting from the initial interaction can establish the newsworthiness of the group and its activities and lead to further contacts in the future. Today's news reports are often stimulated by yesterday's news reports.[1] Once a group receives coverage, it is more likely to be attended to in the future. But the first coverage of resource-poor groups requires some initial interaction between group and newspaper, and the character of that interaction affects the likelihood that coverage will result.

There are two broad ways in which groups and newspapers first interact. One is the result of the group's explicit efforts to contact newspapers and to generate news. The other requires less group initiative. It results more from the workings of the newspaper's news net and from newspaper initiative than from any press-directed group effort.

GROUP INITIATIVE

Sometimes resource-poor groups take the initiative in reaching the press. They contact them directly by calling or by sending a written announcement. If these contacts are focused, group spokesmen contact specific individuals on the newspapers—usually reporters—who they expect will help their group achieve its press goals. For example, a Legislative Council for Older Americans (LCOA) informant took the initiative in contacting a *Boston Globe* reporter by sending him LCOA press releases. The informant described how he and the reporter first got together:

> I read [the reporter's] column and decided it would be nice to have coffee with him and get to know him. I kept sending [the reporter] press releases even though [he] was pretty much ignoring them for quite a while. Then he finally came around. We talked and became friends and have been ever since.

The reporter's description of how he and the LCOA informant first came to meet was essentially the same:

> In the beginning, I paid little attention to them [LCOA]. I received some of their literature and decided it made sense. So I talked with them and I have become their advocate.

Another example of a focused effort of a resource-poor group to contact some individual on a metropolitan newspaper was the Massachusetts Welfare Rights Organization's (MWRO) effort to contact someone on the *Globe*. MWRO's organizer did not know anyone in Boston's metropolitan press prior to his arrival in the summer of 1968. His brother, who worked for the St. Louis Symphony, had given him the name of a contact in the Boston Symphony. When the organizer got to Boston, he called his contact and told him that he was there "to make things happen" and asked whom he could be in touch with in the press. A reporter with the *Boston Globe* who had made a name for himself locally reporting education and civil rights earlier in the 1960s was suggested as a good press contact. MWRO's organizer contacted this reporter, who was then writing a series of profiles of interesting people for the *Globe*'s Sunday magazine. The reporter did a story on the organizer. He also suggested to MWRO's organizer another *Globe* reporter who did most of the *Globe*'s welfare reporting from 1968 through 1970. This welfare reporter eventually became an advocate for MWRO. However, when MWRO first started its actions, he was out of town. Rather than contact anyone else or the newspaper in general, MWRO's organizer contacted no one in the press before the welfare reporter got back.

A third example of focused group initiative in contacting a newspaper was Cape Cod and Islands Tenants' Council's (CCITC) initial interaction with the *Globe*. The newspaper coverage of CCITC was carefully orchestrated by two organizers who were formerly with MWRO. They had established media contacts during their involvement in MWRO. An ex-reporter and member of CCITC was formally in charge of group publicity, but in fact he dealt mainly with the newspapers in Providence, Rhode Island, where he had friends. Contacts with Boston's metropolitan press came through the two organizers and were directed primarily at the *Boston Globe*. By 1971 a new reporter had joined the *Globe*'s staff and was reporting on welfare and poor people's movements. Another member of the *Globe*'s Urban Team had been with the paper for several years, having played a large part in reporting the Roxbury riots of 1967. Afterward, he concentrated as a specialist on reporting poverty, welfare, and housing. CCITC's organizer mentioned both of these reporters in the following comments about his press contacts for CCITC:

> I tried to get [the veteran reporter] to kick off a story on the Cape, but he kept referring me to [the new reporter]. He could have done a great job. . . . With the Cape, before I did anything else, I went to [the new reporter] and told him what we were going to do. I told him what kind of coverage would help—how to start and how to proceed. I wanted him to get the problem out first, then the threat and the action. I saw him in April. I wanted him to write first about people being evicted, then about ethnics and working people, then the threat of the bridge, then the action. I pushed the working poor and ethnics. If ever I could find one in the group, I brought them forward and told [him] about them and suggested a story. . . . [he] would save a story for morning rather than turn it in to the P.M. since he said the editors were bad on the P.M. He was very important to the . . . movement.

Group efforts to contact newspapers can also be unfocused. In those cases, group spokesmen contact the city desk or send press releases to the newspaper without specifying any specific reporter. This allows the newspaper editors to take complete initiative in assigning (or not assigning) the story to any particular reporter. For example, The People First (TPF) called the newspapers' city desks to alert them to the TPF planned rally in July of 1971. Aside from one brief mention in a *Record* article, which was part of a lengthy series on the Massachusetts district courts,[2] TPF's coverage in the metropolitan press did not begin until that rally, a full eight months after the group was formed. Then general assignment reporters were sent to cover the story. Except for court stories handled by courthouse reporters, most TPF stories were written by general assignment reporters assigned by the city desk in response to some TPF unfocused contact.

If a specific reporter on a newspaper can be identified who is judged likely to be sympathetic to the resource-poor group's goals, then from the group's perspective there are advantages to using a focused rather than an unfocused approach to a newspaper. Because of the quantity of material that moves across the city editor's desk, he or she rarely reads all of it. If, in the first few paragraphs, there is not an obvious news story, the release is likely to be discarded and the telephone call forgotten. This is particularly true for a newspaper that is short-staffed. Yet, if the release or call is directed to a specific reporter, that reporter may read it or listen to it in order to stay informed whether or not there is an immediate news story in it. Keeping a reporter informed on group activities can help in establishing a relationship between group and reporter, a relationship that may help the group achieve its press goals in the future. Therefore, with a focused approach, a resource-poor group is more likely to achieve success—to gain a hearing—than with an unfocused approach. A *Record* reporter commented on focused and unfocused group contacts:

> . . . these groups should be here at the *Record American* talking with a reporter once a week. They used to do that with me and would send me notes on what was happening and they would get coverage sometimes. That was when the groups first got started. Now maybe they put out slick press releases and send them to the editor but I think they'd do better on a more personal basis with the individual reporters.

NEWSPAPER INITIATIVE

Interactions between resource-poor groups and newspapers sometimes result from newspaper initiative. Groups can become newsworthy and be contacted by a reporter in a number of ways. Three of these are discussed below, followed by a general discussion of the metropolitan newspaper's news net and how it can be extended into the community where resource-poor groups initially act.

BECOMING NEWSWORTHY AND ATTRACTING NEWSPAPER ATTENTION

There are several ways a resource-poor group can become newsworthy and attract the attention of the metropolitan newspapers. First, a group may become newsworthy by virtue of its association with other newsworthy institutions, events, or people. Groups may emerge at institutions that are regularly covered by newspaper beat reporters and interact with reporters there. That was how LCOA was first covered in the Boston press. The first story concerned the appearance of approximately 100 elderly at a Boston City Council public hearing on rent control where LCOA's leader addressed the City Council.[3] That story was written by the City Hall beat reporters for the various Boston newspapers. That was also the way LCOA first interacted with a *Record* reporter widely recognized as a welfare expert. She was covering an emergency meeting of state health and welfare officials called by a state government official after the federal government had refused to continue Medicaid for elderly patients in certain Massachusetts nursing homes. LCOA's organizer appeared and spoke at that meeting as LCOA president.[4]

Or groups may associate with people of high status who are judged newsworthy but who are not regularly covered by beat reporters. CCITC's initial interactions with *Record* and *Herald* reporters occurred by the middle of May 1971 when various officials of state government were active and involved in the impending Cape housing crisis. Governor Sargent met with CCITC members and appointed a committee, headed by the commissioner of the Department of Community Affairs, which was to seek housing solutions.[5] In addition to the Department of Community Affairs (DCA) personnel on the committee were representatives of CCITC, local housing authorities, and the Department of Housing and Urban Development (HUD), the welfare commissioner, and the governor's urban affairs advisor. With governmental involvement and the committee structure set up, newspaper coverage—particularly in the *Herald* and *Record*—focused on the developments in negotiations. In interacting with the committee, reporters also interacted with CCITC. In all three of the above examples, the groups took no explicit press-directed initiative, but they interacted as a result of newspaper initiative in covering events judged newsworthy by news personnel.

Second, groups may become newsworthy because of some action they engage in, which in and of itself is judged newsworthy. These actions can be dramatic protests or rallies—where there are many people in attendance or where some disruption or threat of disruption occurs—or they may be less dramatic news events. For example, all four of the groups studied here engaged in early protest activities— rallies, marches, and sit-ins. In most cases, the groups initiated the press contact by calling reporters or newsrooms to alert them to the planned activity. Thus, in most cases, dramatic and newsworthy group actions required either a focused or unfocused group-initiated contact. In at least one instance, however, no group-initiated contact was made. The interaction between group and newspaper resulted from a newspaper-initiated effort to cover a dramatic news event. The first MWRO news coverage was a nonbylined article in the *Record* reporting on demands presented by "some 200 mothers" to the welfare office.[6] Neither of the other two newspapers carried a story on this event. It is not clear how the *Record* learned of this presentation of demands, but it could have been from a tipster or from a newspaper employee's good fortune at being in Roxbury at just the right time.

A third way in which groups can become newsworthy is by gaining credibility as legitimate spokesmen for a particular clientele or as a potential threat to established interests. Resource-poor groups can establish their credibility without already having previously interacted with the metropolitan press either through stories in alternative media or through the credibility that specific group leaders or members bring with them from their earlier activities. For example, the credibility of TPF's claims and threats was partially established by one of its organizers, Michael Ansara. Ansara's earlier actions in leading Students for a Democratic Society (SDS) demonstrations at Harvard University had already resulted in news articles and considerable notoriety.[7] His involvement in TPF probably alerted at least one *Globe* reporter to the likely newsworthiness of TPF activities. . . .

THE METROPOLITAN NEWSPAPER'S NEWS NET

Initial interactions are not solely dependent on group action. They also depend on newspaper actions, in particular on those newspaper efforts to broaden the news net.

The metropolitan newspaper's news net is structured in such a way as to maximize the likelihood of gathering in newsworthy events and issues as soon as they surface at particular government institutions. The beat structure at all three newspapers ensured that beat reporters would have an opportunity to cover stories emerging at City Hall, the State House, the courts, and the police stations. Fire bells, indicating how many alarms and the fire's location, rang in the *Globe* newsroom for every fire in Boston. If groups emerge at different government institutions or do not emerge at all, it is problematic whether the newspaper's news net will extend far enough to become aware of the group's existence and activities. Because there are newsworthy developments in the community that are not necessarily visible to beat reporters located at institutions, there are several ways in which newspapers can spread their news net wide enough to become aware of them.

First, they establish issue specialties that cross-cut the institutional beats. As already indicated, of the three metropolitan dailies the *Globe* went furthest in this direction. Furthermore, the urban affairs specialists were expected by editors to pay particular attention to community happenings—to find out what was going on "out there." The *Herald* and the *Record* did much less to expand news nets with specialists. The few specialists who did work for the *Herald* tended to focus on institutions rather than on the community. Management at the *Record* did not value specialists at all.

A second way in which newspapers spread their news net is by doing a series on some topic and investigating it in depth. All of the newspapers did this from time to time. It was through such a series on the Massachusetts District Court system that the *Record American* first mentioned TPF. Doing such a series usually requires that at least one reporter be freed from daily reporting duties for several days, and editors are not willing to do so very often. At the *Globe*, the issue specialists usually also did the series. The Urban Team, organized in 1967, did many series on urban problems of poverty, welfare, housing, and so forth. In the fall of 1970, the *Globe*'s Spotlight Team began conducting investigations, primarily of corruption in local government. At the *Herald*, a series was done every once in a while. One veteran newsman reportedly did a number of influential series, one on welfare. The award-winning education writers also did a number of series. Informants at the *Herald* said that certain members of the *Herald*'s management did not like series and that their dislike made it difficult to do them there. The *Herald*'s publisher, Harold Clancy, had done a number of "blockbusting" series when he was an investigative reporter for the *Traveler*. In 1967, however, after a new editor-in-chief was brought in and the Channel 5-WHDH controversy became even more threatening to the newspaper's future, all controversial reporting was allegedly discouraged. . . .

Series writing at the *Record American* was also an occasional activity. Before 1970, series were encouraged, but since then the *Record* has moved back toward sensationalism, baby pictures, and police reports, according to *Record* informants. What series writing was encouraged at the *Record* was restricted to veteran reporters who tended to have unsympathetic views of the goals and tactics of protest groups. In addition, the *Record* staff was always so much smaller than either of the other dailies that it was relatively difficult to spare reporters for long periods to work up their series.

A third mechanism that newspapers use which spreads the news net is the regular column focusing either on some issue area or on some population segment or on current "goings on." By making some space regularly available that must be filled by someone writing on a specific topic, the newspaper encourages that columnist to initiate contacts with potential sources and ferret out the news stories rather than merely wait for the stories to come to him or to her. It also provides a visible newspaper contact for sources who want to generate stories on that topic. The clearest examples at the *Globe* were the "Senior Set" column, which required material on the elderly three times per week, and regular space on the opposite editorial page made available usually to a community person presenting some minority viewpoint. Examples at the *Herald* were the "Medicare Mailbox" column, which required material on the elderly six times per week, and the Sunday real estate column through which reporters twice wrote about CCITC and Cape Cod housing. In the *Record*, there was a "3 dot" column of tidbits of news and gossip, frequently picking up some local development that otherwise might not have received metropolitan press attention. Of course, it was more common at metropolitan newspapers to have columns written by beat reporters or columnists assigned to some institution, like the State House, than to have columns that intentionally reached into the community, particularly into low-income communities. Much less space was devoted to community views and more spaced to institutional views in the *Herald*'s "Medicare Mailbox" than in the *Globe*'s "Senior Set." Reporting on CCITC was not a necessary result of the *Herald*'s column on Cape Cod real estate. However, when the space was regularly allotted and restricted to a particular topic area, it was much easier for resource-poor groups to gain the attention of the columnist who was constantly pressed to initiate column ideas.

A fourth way that the newspaper spreads its news collection net wide is by encouraging its staff to read publications that report on developments not readily visible to them. At the *Globe* there was a growing emphasis on national and international news. One veteran reporter complained that he no longer had time to read the *Record American* because he had been assigned responsibility for daily perusing a newspaper from another large city. Yet the *Record*, more than the other dailies, printed certain types of local and suburban news. A *Globe* editor said he thought it was "scandalous" that the *Globe* did not even clip copies of the *Herald* for its library. However, *Globe* reporters and editors regularly read the *Phoenix, Boston After Dark*, and the *Harvard Crimson*, three likely places to find news of emerging resource-poor groups. At the other extreme, *Record* reporters and editors read their own newspaper and the *Globe* and little else. Reporters complained that frequently there were not enough copies of even the *Record* and *Globe* to go around. One rewriteman brought in a *New York Times* for a while, but otherwise there were few papers or periodicals available in the *Record* newsroom. Since they could not initiate story ideas anyway, their reading matter was not so important to their newspaper's news net. *Record* editors and senior reporters who could and did initiate stories did not regularly read either the *Phoenix* or *Boston After Dark*. The *Herald* staff was even more well-read on local matters than the *Globe* staff. Reading matter was regularly available, and at least some reporters and editors read the *Phoenix* and *Boston After Dark*. The *Herald* clipped all three metropolitan newspapers for its library, and reporters were assigned to suburban areas that required their familiarity with certain suburban publications as well.

Of the three newspapers, the *Globe* made the most extensive efforts to extend its news net into the poverty community with issue specialists, series, columns, and reading matter. The *Record* and the *Herald* were mixed. While the *Herald* did have several specialists, none focused on the problems of the poor. *Herald* staffers did read widely, but there was little encouragement for reporters to take an in-depth look at a group or issue and little editorial tolerance of series. There was no column space set aside for a community perspective. What columns were printed in the *Herald* usually focused on institutions. The *Record* editors and staffers did not read widely and had no specialists. There were occasional series, however, and at least those done by the welfare expert took cognizance of resource-poor groups.

SUMMARY

In summary, the initial interactions between resource-poor groups and metropolitan newspapers occur as a result of group initiative or newspaper initiative or both. The group initiative is aimed at gaining a hearing for the group's point of view in order to achieve certain press goals. It can be focused on one particular reporter or unfocused. The newspaper initiative is aimed at spreading its news net wide enough to gather in as many important and interesting news developments as possible so that editors can choose among them for press treatment. Newspapers widen their news nets to include resource-poor groups' developments with issue specialists, series, columns, and reading matter. Groups fall within newspaper news nets and become newsworthy by associating with other newsworthy people, offices or events, by engaging in significant group action, or by establishing group credibility.

Access and news coverage do not usually occur without some personal inter-action between resource-poor source and newspaper reporter. Continuing access requires continuing interaction. If the interactions become regularized, then access is usually facilitated. With regularized interactions, sources and reporters enter a bargaining relationship in which each actor exerts efforts to interact with the other. A skillful source can build a relationship similar to that which often exists between resource-rich source and beat reporter, in which the reporter depends on the source for news and, as a result, the reporter is willing to listen to and act on behalf of the source's interests. Without regularized interactions, the main burden of inter-acting with newspaper reporters falls on the source. Newsworthiness must be shown over and over again. The reporter does not become dependent on the source for news. Instead, the source may become dependent on the reporter for attention—so dependent that news management is impossible.

NOTES

1. Bernard C. Cohen, *The Press and Foreign Policy* (Princeton: Princeton University Press, 1963), p. 58.

2. Ed Corsetti, Jack Wharton, and Jim Morse, "Judges Troy, MacLeod Agree—Justice Is Served," *Sunday Advertiser*, 28 March 1971 p. 38.

3. David R. Ellis, "Elderly Near Hub Colleges Demand Rent Control," *Boston Globe*, 12 June 1968, p. 1.

4. Jean Cole, "Medicaid Crisis Mounts," *Boston Record American*, 29 January 1969, p. 2.

5. David Taylor, "Cape Renters Facing Eviction Refuse Otis," *Boston Globe*, 19 May 1971, p. 5.

6. "Aides Refuse Reinstatement," *Boston Record American*, 23 July 1968, p. 2.

7. Richard Connolly, "SDS Organizer Defends Leftists Against Conspiracy Charges," *Boston Globe*, 17 April 1969, p. 16; Frank Mahoney, "Ansara at Harvard," *Boston Evening Globe*, 17 April 1969, p. 2.

SUGGESTED READINGS

Blanchard, Robert. (Ed.). *Congress and the News Media.* New York: Hastings House, 1974.
Although dated now, this is a useful collection of articles and speeches on press relations with the Congress during the 1960s and early 1970s.

Clarke, Peter, and Susan H. Evans. *Covering Campaigns.* Palo Alto, Calif.: Stanford University Press, 1983.
The work done by these two authors was the first exhaustive analysis of congressional candi-dates' use of the press for campaigning and the nature of campaign press coverage.

Cook, Timothy E. *Making Laws and Making News: Media Strategies in the U.S. House of Repre-sentatives.* Washington, D.C: Brookings Institution, 1989.
A seminal work on the ways that members of Congress employ media strategies to accomplish legislative purposes. Cook rejects the thesis that media relations are unrelated to the work of Congress.

Davis, Richard. *Decisions and Images: The Supreme Court and the Press.* Englewood Cliffs, N.J.: Prentice-Hall, 1994.
An examination of the current Supreme Court's interaction with the press—the process of covering the Court, the Court's public relations effort, the justices' relationship with reporters, and the future of Court–press relations in a media age.

Garay, Ronald. *Congressional Television: A Legislative History.* Westport, Conn.: Greenwood Press, 1984.
A history of the acceptance by Congress of the televising of its proceedings, with special emphasis on the introduction of C-SPAN.

Grey, David. *The Supreme Court and the News Media.* Evanston, Ill.: Northwestern University Press, 1968.
Although now dated, this book does provide a glimpse at press relationship with the Supreme Court during the 1960s.

Grossman, Michael B., and Martha Joynt Kumar. *Portraying the President.* Baltimore: The Johns Hopkins University Press, 1981.
The best monograph on the interaction between the White House press corps and the White House Communications Office.

Hertsgaard, Mark. *On Bended Knee: The Press and the Reagan Presidency.* New York: Farrar, Straus & Giroux, 1988.
A journalist's perspective on the presidential–press relationship that emphasizes White House manipulation of the press.

Hess, Stephen. *The Ultimate Insiders: U.S. Senators in the National Media.* Washington, D.C.: Brookings Institution, 1986.
Hess concludes that the news media concentrate not on junior members, but the leaders in the Senate.

Marshall, Thomas R. *Public Opinion and the Supreme Court.* Boston: Unwin Hyman, 1988.
The most exhaustive presentation of research on the Court's response to public opinion.

Miller, Susan H. *Reporters and Congressmen: Living in Symbiosis.* Lexington, Ky: Association for Education in Journalism, 1978.
Miller's work was the first comprehensive analysis of the interaction between members of Congress and reporters in the making of news and legislation.

Powell, Jody. *The Other Side of the Story.* New York: William Morrow, 1984.
This cogent analysis of the role of a presidential press secretary is the best memoir by a former press secretary. Powell addresses some of the issues of presidential–press relations.

Speakes, Larry. *Speaking Out.* New York: Charles Scribner's Sons, 1988.
A controversial memoir by Ronald Reagan's press secretary, including the revelation by Speakes that he manufactured a famous Reagan quote.

Tebbel, John, and Sarah Miles Watts. *The Press and the Presidency: From George Washington to Ronald Reagan.* New York: Oxford University Press, 1985.
A history of presidential–press relations organized chronologically by president and filled with anecdotes of presidential interactions with journalists.

Woodward, Bob, and Scott Armstrong. *The Brethren.* New York: Simon & Schuster, 1979.
A journalistic account of the Burger years that relies heavily on the accounts of clerks, *The Brethren* provides an insider's glimpse into the personal dynamics governing the work of the Supreme Court during the late 1960s and early 1970s.

chapter **8**

PUBLIC POLICY-MAKING

INTRODUCTION

Increasingly, the specter of public opinion has become a powerful determinant in the formulation of public policy. Public opinion is usually referred to in the public-policy process.

The press has acquired the task of informing the public about policy, organizing public opinion, and articulating that opinion to policymakers. The press has become a common carrier of information—serving as a bulletin board for political actors seeking to communicate with one another. Policymakers send messages to each other, as well as to the general public, through the press.

But the press has gone beyond that role. Members have acquired other roles—trustee of the people and government critic. From the forum provided by these roles, they can become a catalyst and a participant in the policy-making process.

Some journalists have articulated a press role as trustee of the people. Speaking of press role, Arthur Ochs Sulzburger, publisher of the *New York Times*, once remarked that "our function is to serve as the eyes and ears of the public."* In this role, the press serves as representative of the people to the powers that be in American government. Drawing on the implications in the First Amendment, some journalists have argued that they are surrogates for the American public in their encounters with public officials.

*Quoted in Tom Goldstein, *News at Any Cost* (New York: Simon & Schuster, 1985), p. 101.

In such a role, they raise issues they believe Americans wish public officials would address. They ask the questions the American public would like to ask, if they could.

But the issues they raise, whether actually issues of concern to the American public, affect policymakers by focusing their attention. Policymakers respond to these issues because these are the issues they are confronted with in their encounters with the press.

Moreover, policymakers respond because they do not know the extent to which the public will respond. They do not wish to be seen as merely reactive or, worse, unresponsive, to public concerns.

As governmental critics, members of the press act as evaluators of governmental actions. As critics, the press notes the failings of public policy—fraud, abuse, waste, mismanagement, as well as ineffectiveness. It then becomes a catalyst for reform.

This chapter addresses the extent to which the news media impact on public policy. The readings that follow discuss media impact on three aspects of public policy. The first is media impact on the domestic policy process. The second aspect is foreign policy. National defense policy is the subject of the third, with special emphasis on media coverage of the nation at war.

A. DOMESTIC POLICY

The domestic policy-making process at the federal level usually includes not only members of Congress, the bureaucracy, and the White House, but also various interest groups related to the policy area. Still another player is the press.

The press performs its most important role in the setting of the policy agenda by identifying problems, which are then dropped on policymakers' doorsteps. Even this role it rarely carries out alone. Rather, various players in the policy-making process (or would-be players) offer events for news coverage designed to focus attention on the favored issue.

Competition for media attention produces a constant pleading from groups seeking public recognition of their policy area. The decision about which group to cover usually hinges on news values.

Simultaneously, press assignment to beats discussed in section three of this chapter centralizes media coverage on a few newsmakers—such as the White House, congressional leaders, and leading cabinet officials. In those settings, domestic policymakers are better able to influence coverage and set the agenda since a large contingent of reporters is competing for exclusive information. But, as discussed in the Introduction to this chapter, the ability of any one player regularly to set the policy agenda through the press is nonexistent.

Three aspects of media role in policy-making are explored in the following selections. The first is the press's capability as a mechanism for enhancing public role in policy-making. Although public opinion in a democracy is expected to dictate public policy, and the press ideally serves as the public's information source, the press is incapable of performing such a role.

The second aspect is the role of the press in setting policy agendas through investigative reporting. Do journalists' stories shape policymakers' reactions and lead to policy change?

Finally, the methods policymakers use to pass information to the press are explored. The leaks are presented not as unethical acts by disgruntled middle-level bureaucrats, but as part and parcel of the relationship between top policymakers and the press.

37. THE SEARCHLIGHT

Walter Lippmann

Some news professionals have encouraged public expectations that the press can perform this function by calling themselves "trustees of the people," which suggests a representative function in a democratic society.

Walter Lippmann, writing over seventy years ago, warned Americans of the danger of placing the press in such a role. He argued the press is incapable of serving in that capacity.

Lippmann opposed the pre-eminence of public opinion as a determinant of public policy. The notion that public opinion could rule public policy and the press could serve as an organizer and articulator of public opinion was a false ideal.

According to Lippmann, the business of the news is not the business of governance. News is the record of events. In a democratic society where public opinion affects public policy and public knowledge determines public opinion, emphasis must be given to the search for truth, not just a record of events.

Only institutions—such as political parties, legislative bodies, bureaucracies—can represent the mass citizenry. These institutions cannot be supplanted by the press since the two serve different functions—one as a signalizer of events, the other as representative of public interests.

Lippmann's views were prescient. The rise of television and the expansion of media pervasiveness through broadcasting have both heightened media role as well as expectations of the media's performance as participant in public policy-making.

Walter Lippmann was a newspaper columnist and prolific author whose opinions dominated American intellectual life for half a century. He died in 1974. This excerpt is from his classic work, *Public Opinion.**

If the newspapers, then, are to be charged with the duty of translating the whole public life of mankind, so that every adult can arrive at an opinion on every moot topic, they fail, they are bound to fail, in any future one can conceive they will con-

---

*From *Public Opinion* (New York: Macmillan, 1961), pp. 358–64. (Original work published 1922.) Reprinted with permission.

tinue to fail. It is not possible to assume that a world, carried on by division of labor and distribution of authority, can be governed by universal opinions in the whole population. Unconsciously the theory . . . puts upon the press the burden of accomplishing whatever representative government, industrial organization, and diplomacy have failed to accomplish. Acting upon everybody for thirty minutes in twenty-four hours, the press is asked to create a mystical force called Public Opinion that will take up the slack in public institutions. The press has often mistakenly pretended that it could do just that. It has at great moral cost to itself encouraged a democracy, still bound to its original premises, to expect newspapers to supply spontaneously for every organ of government, for every social problem, the machinery of information which these do not normally supply themselves. Institutions, having failed to furnish themselves with instruments of knowledge, have become a bundle of "problems," which the population as a whole, reading the press as a whole, is supposed to solve.

The press, in other words, has come to be regarded as an organ of direct democracy, charged on a much wider scale, and from day to day, with the function often attributed to the initiative, referendum, and recall. The Court of Public Opinion, open day and night, is to lay down the law for everything all the time. It is not workable. And when you consider the nature of news, it is not even thinkable. For the news . . . is precise in proportion to the precision with which the event is recorded. Unless the event is capable of being named, measured, given shape, made specific, it either fails to take on the character of news, or it is subject to the accidents and prejudices of observation.

Therefore, on the whole, the quality of the news about modern society is an index of its social organization. The better the institutions, the more all interests concerned are formally represented, the more issues are disentangled, the more objective criteria are introduced, the more perfectly an affair can be presented as news. At its best the press is a servant and guardian of institutions; at its worst it is a means by which a few exploit social disorganization to their own ends. In the degree to which institutions fail to function, the unscrupulous journalist can fish in troubled waters, and the conscientious one must gamble with uncertainties.

The press is no substitute for institutions. It is like the beam of a searchlight that moves restlessly about, bringing one episode and then another out of darkness into vision. Men cannot do the work of the world by this light alone. They cannot govern society by episodes, incidents, and eruptions. It is only when they work by a steady light of their own, that the press, when it is turned upon them, reveals a situation intelligible enough for a popular decision. The trouble lies deeper than the press, and so does the remedy. It lies in social organization based on a system of analysis and record, and in all the corollaries of that principle; in the abandonment of the theory of the omnicompetent citizen, in the decentralization of decision, in the coordination of decision by comparable record and analysis. If at the centers of management there is a running audit, which makes work intelligible to those who do it, and those who superintend it, issues when they arise are not the mere collisions of the blind. Then, too, the news is uncovered for the press by a system of intelligence that is also a check upon the press.

That is the radical way. For the troubles of the press, like the troubles of representative government, be it territorial or functional, like the troubles of industry, be it capitalist, cooperative, or communist, go back to a common source: to the failure of self-governing people to transcend their casual experience and their prejudice, by inventing, creating, and organizing a machinery of knowledge. It is because they are compelled to act without a reliable picture of the world, that governments, schools, newspapers and churches make such small headway against the more obvious failings of democracy, against violent prejudice, apathy, preference for the curious trivial as against the dull important, and the hunger for sideshows and three-legged calves. This is the primary defect of popular government, a defect inherent in its traditions, and all its other defects can, I believe, be traced to this one.

38. BUILDING POLICY AGENDAS

David L. Protess, Fay Lomax Cook, Jack C. Doppelt, James S. Ettema, Margaret T. Gordon, Donna R. Leff, and Peter Miller

The interaction between reporters and policymakers in the policy-reform process is the subject of the next selection. To what extent do news reports cause the public to rise up and demand reform, thus providing a role for the press as catalyst for policy change?

David Protess and his co-authors analyzed six case studies of a press report affecting public policy decisions.* These include broadcast or print media reports on fraud and abuse in federally funded home health care; problems with the prosecution of rape cases; police brutality; toxic waste disposal practices; child abductions; and kidney dialysis clinics making large profits off patients. They examined the impact these news reports had on the general public and on policymakers.

After concluding their study, the authors found these news reports did affect policymaking. Policymakers did respond to varying degrees. They conclude that successful policy agenda setting by the press is due to the presence of certain necessary factors.

One of those factors, however, is not public outrage. They rejected the mobilization model where the general public, upon hearing reports of social problems, insist on governmental reform and get it. According to Protess and associates, the public's role in reform through policy-making is not active, but anticipatory. Policymakers react with the public in mind, not because of public pressure.

Rather, the key players in reform were policymakers and the press. They describe a symbiotic relationship between reporters and policymakers. These alliances they term "coalition journalism," where reporters and policymakers join forces to affect policy reform in a partnership that fulfills the objectives of both.

David L. Protess is associate professor of journalism at Northwestern University. He is

*From *The Journalism of Outrage: Investigative Reporting and Agenda Building in America* (New York: The Guilford Press, 1991), pp. 238–54. Reprinted with permission.

co-author of *Setting the Agenda: Readings in Media, Public Opinion, and Policymaking* (1991). Fay Lomax Cook teaches in the School of Education and Social Policy at Northwestern. She is author of articles in *Public Opinion Quarterly, Legislative Studies Quarterly*, and *Government and Policy*. A former investigative journalist, Jack C. Doppelt is associate professor of journalism at Northwestern. James S. Ettema teaches in the Department of Communication Studies at Northwestern. Margaret T. Gordon, dean of the Graduate School of Public Affairs at the University of Washington, is author of *The Female Fear: The Social Costs of Rape* (1991). Donna R. Leff, a former investigative reporter, teaches journalism at Northwestern. Peter Miller also teaches communication studies and journalism at Northwestern.

It is no easy matter for social problems to get on policymakers' agendas and produce corrective actions. The number of problems that policymakers might address is virtually infinite. The number that actually come to their attention is circumscribed, but each of those must still vie for policymakers' interest. Policymakers must decide which problems will receive priority attention, just as journalists did in building their investigative and media agendas.

Policy agenda building is the process by which some problems "come to command the active and serious attention of government as prospective matters of public policy," Elder and Cobb state.[1] Once a problem becomes salient, some sort of ameliorative outcome often follows. Solutions, however, are not guaranteed. Some problems may languish when they get to the top of the policy agenda and may eventually fall off before corrective actions are taken.[2] Other problems may be addressed incompletely by policymakers or in ways that create new problems.[3]

Despite the hazards, policy agenda building is the ultimate mission of many investigative reporters. Our historical analysis, the evidence from the case studies, and the surveys of journalists all suggest that a primary goal of investigative reporting is fulfilled when media disclosures grab policymakers' attention and produce reforms. This is the final, and perhaps the most vital step, in the Mobilization Model.

In discussing the impact of investigative reporting on policy making, we identify three aspects of agenda building: *priority, pace, and particularity*. When the problem disclosed by an investigative story moves onto the policy-making agenda, we describe it as having attained relative *priority* status. The problem is in a position to compete with others already in the policy-making stream. *Pace* means the relative speed with which policymakers address the problem. Some problems produce faster policy responses than others.

By *particularity*, we mean the effect of investigative reporting on the particular content of the policy initiatives. Some media investigations offer prescriptions for the problems they have revealed. The prescriptions may be presented in editorials, normative story language, and even discussions between reporters and reform-minded policymakers. When these proposals are transformed into specific policy proposals, the agenda-building effect of particularity has occurred.

The selection of policy proposals may heighten or diminish the priority and pace of social problem solving. Indeed, investigative reporting may trigger various policy-making combinations. Significantly, the resulting policy-making processes may affect the eventual policy *outcomes* or "reforms." [This] section examines the policy-making processes and outcomes in our six case studies. We then identify the various motives of policymakers for taking action on the investigative findings and show how the paths to reform depart from the conventional Mobilization Model.

THE REALITIES OF REFORM

Once agenda-building processes have been catalyzed by investigative reporting, several kinds of policy-making results are possible. These may be more or less consistent with the reformist goals of investigative reporters. . . . [T]he revelation of a social problem may affect the priority, pace, and particularity of agenda building without ultimately resulting in meaningful change.

[We] describe . . . three types of possible policymaking outcomes: deliberative, individualistic, and substantive. Deliberative results occur when policymakers hold formal discussions of policy problems and their solutions, such as legislative hearings or executive commissions. Individualistic outcomes occur when policymakers apply sanctions against particular persons or entities, including prosecutions, firings, and demotions. Finally, substantive results include regulatory, legislative, and/or administrative changes.

As Table 1 indicates, each of the media investigations we studied influenced public-policy making in various ways. The rape reports, the police brutality broadcasts, and the dialysis series triggered all three types of agenda building. The rape reports made legislative changes an immediate priority and engendered communi-

TABLE 1

Summary of the Policy-Making Impact of Six Media Investigative Reports

INVESTIGATIVE REPORT	AGENDA-BUILDING IMPACT	POLICY-MAKING OUTCOME
"Home Health Hustle"	Priority, pace	Deliberative (U.S. Senate hearings)
"Rape: Every Woman's Nightmare"	Priority, pace, particularity hearings) Substantive (law signed)	Deliberative (community
"Beating Justice"	Priority, pace, particularity changes)	Substantive (regulatory
"Wasted Time"	Pace enforcement)	Individualistic (local code
"Missing?"	Priority, pace hearings) Substantive (treaty passed/ agency created)	Deliberative (congressional
"Dialysis: The Profit Machine"	Priority, pace, particularity bills/federal audits) Individualistic (state code enforcement) Substantive (additional inspectors hired)	Deliberative (U.S. bills/state

ty hearings that were not previously planned. The police brutality broadcasts mobilized political actors and produced swift and fundamental revisions of regulations regarding police misconduct. The dialysis series fueled a state and federal debate over the regulation of clinics and, in particular, the reuse of dialyzers. In each case, agenda building resulted in substantive reforms.

At the opposite extreme, the toxic waste series affected only the pace of bureaucratic activity at one locale. The problem of toxic waste disposal did not become more salient to policymakers, nor were measures considered to ensure that the problem was not occurring in places other than the University of Chicago. However, the swift actions taken in this case were effective for remedying the problems disclosed.

The other investigative stories involved in-between cases. The home health probe prompted the U.S. Senate to hold immediate hearings that raised significant questions about fraud and abuse in federal social programs, but no bills were introduced to address the problem. In the international child abductions case, treaty legislation that had languished for years moved higher on the State Department and Congressional agendas and passed unanimously after brief legislative hearings.

Clearly, the investigative stories that we studied significantly affected various policy-making arenas. Yet, the effects varied considerably from case to case. To develop a model that explains the impact of investigative reporting, we need to consider the factors that differentially influenced policy-making in the six cases.

In recent years, research on policy agenda building has flourished.[4] These studies have employed different methodologies to try to identify actors who might influence agenda-building processes, including political leaders, bureaucrats, interest groups, citizens, and the media. Some studies have focused on agenda-building influences in specific social problem areas, such as child abuse[5] and criminal victimization of the elderly.[6] Others have examined institutional agenda building.[7]

Regardless of the divergent paths taken by scholars, certain common agenda-building influences have been identified. For example, Cook and Skogan have demonstrated empirically a "convergent voice" model indicating that agenda building "depends upon the same issue being independently articulated by different groups inside and outside government at about the same time, within the context of a ripe issue climate."[8] This model overlaps with Kingdon's theory of agenda building, which holds that issues rise on policy agendas when separate "streams" of policies, problems, and politics join together at an opportune time.[9] Specifically, these theories of agenda-building identify three factors that may be useful for understanding the investigative case study findings: (1) the recognition by policymakers that a legitimate problem exists; (2) the availability of policy alternatives to address the problem; and (3) the presence of a ripe political climate.

The first condition for agenda building, problem recognition, was present in each of our case studies. Interviews with key policymakers indicate that they often learned about the problems in the six cases through different kinds of media disclosures—by reading or viewing the original exposé, by following the proprietary and nonproprietary coverage of the findings, or through interviews with journalists. Further, some policymakers had prepublication knowledge of the problems, either because journalists interviewed them to obtain information or to build reactions into their stories or because they had heard about them earlier from sources other than media.

In each case, policymakers also were readily able to ascertain the legitimacy of the investigative findings. In the reports about home health care, rape, international child abductions, and dialysis, policymakers had independently studied the problems and found them to be credible. In the toxic waste story, policymakers were able to confirm the series findings through a simple inspection at the University of Chicago. In the brutality reports, the police superintendent was unable to deny the problem of repeat offenders. These developments were important, since credible indicators of social problems may enhance the agenda status of those problems,[10] whereas the absence of such indicators may lead a problem to fall off the policy agenda.[11]

In sum, policymakers perceived that legitimate problems were identified in all six of the cases that we studied. Further, the news media, in various ways, played an important agenda-building role by helping draw policymakers' attention to those problems. Specifically, policymakers temporarily set aside other problems they were addressing to react to the media disclosures. Because of this, the *pace* of reform was accelerated in each of the cases, and the underlying problems became *priority* items in five of the six cases. . . .

Problem recognition, though, is not sufficient to explain the content of the various reforms proposed. Here, we need to consider the policy alternatives available to remedy the problems that were disclosed. Once again, problem-solving proposals were under consideration at the time that several of the investigative stories were published.

At the point that the rape series was published, legislation to crack down on gang rape was awaiting the governor's signature, and an Illinois House committee was formulating additional legislation to deal with the problems of sex crimes. In the international child abductions case, a relevant treaty was awaiting action by the State Department. When the *Philadelphia Inquirer* first published a brief story that was a forerunner to its eventual dialysis series, legislation was pending in the U.S. Senate regarding the reuse of dialyzers.

Consequently, policymakers were able to react readily to the investigative revelations and follow-up coverage with reforms that specifically addressed the problems disclosed. This significantly facilitated the agenda-building process in those cases. As Kingdon states:

> Items are sometimes found on a governmental agenda without a solution attached to them. . . . But normally, before a subject can attain a solid position on a decision agenda, a viable alternative is available for decision makers to consider. It is not enough that there is a problem, even quite a pressing problem. There also is generally a solution ready to go, already softened up, already worked out.[12]

This logic also applies to the toxic waste disposal case. Although policy *alternatives* were not at hand when the investigative series was broadcast, and none was proposed, the enforcement of the *existing* fire code was sufficient to ameliorate the problem.

The other two cases did not have alternatives for policymakers to seize, yet they resulted in policy change anyway. In the police brutality case, viable remedies were not available at the time of the series, nor were they in the policy pipeline. Nonetheless, substantive reforms followed the broadcast of the series. In the home health case, policymakers expressed frustration over the lack of apparent remedies. Yet, the media probe set the deliberative agenda of the U.S. Senate.

In sum, our evidence suggests that the availability of the alternatives helps affect the policies that are proposed in the wake of an investigative series. However, this factor is not sufficient to explain the policy outcomes in each of the cases. Moreover, it does not explain policymakers' motivations for offering those alternatives in the first place.

Policymakers' willingness to propose available alternatives or to innovate has been found to depend, to some extent, on the political timing of the appearance of the problem. In particular, the proximity of problem disclosure to an election is conventionally believed to affect this decision.[13] Indeed, the broadcast of the police brutality series in the middle of a hotly contested mayoral campaign may have influenced the priority, pace, and particularity of the reform measures that followed. Similarly, the hearings that followed the "Home Health Hustle" were timed to showcase the new Republican Senate majority's concern for waste in federal social programs.

However, immediate electoral or political interests do not adequately explain the developments in the other case studies. For example, the State Department's willingness finally to submit the child abductions treaty legislation appeared to be timed mainly to get crusading politicians and the media off its bureaucratic back. In the other investigative stories we studied, political events or developments seemed entirely unrelated to the timing of policy reactions to the investigative stories.

Of course, the "ripeness" of a political climate may include more than short-term political stakes. The "national mood" and the actions of organized interests also are political factors that may affect the nature and scope of policy agenda building.[14] Indeed, established theories of American governance place great emphasis on the policy-making influences of the public[15] and of pressure groups.[16] At this juncture, we need to consider the validity of these conventional models for explaining the findings in our investigative case studies.

THE MOBILIZATION MODEL REVISITED

Consistent with recent studies of policy agenda building, we have concluded that the recognition of problems, the availability of alternatives, and the immediate political climate each provide partial explanations for the policy-making processes in our six case studies of investigative reporting. However, none of these factors, nor all of them together, explains the policy-making outcomes that resulted in most of the cases.

The Mobilization Model, on the other hand, proposes a more complete explanation for our findings. The conventional wisdom of journalists and advocates of popular democracy holds that the general public, outraged at the disclosures about fraud and abuse, sex crimes, police brutality, environmental pollution, child abductions, and dialysis rip-offs, responds by demanding reform. The policy results in each of our cases, according to the conventional wisdom, may be explained by the extent of public reaction to the disclosures.

A more contemporary version of this model, offered by pluralist political scientists, suggests that each exposé mobilizes organizations with a stake in the controversy. These groups pressure policymakers to produce changes that serve the interests of its members. Although the general public may not become actively involved in decision making, it is possible for its views to be expressed through group membership or identity. The pluralist model further suggests that where group conflict occurs over policy alternatives, policymakers attempt to facilitate compromises that reflect a broad spectrum of interests.

We find, however, that neither the conventional statement of the Mobilization Model nor its more contemporary version is useful for explaining our particular case study results. The policy developments that we found clearly occurred independently of either manifest changes in public opinion or interest group pressures. This was demonstrated in two ways. First, the policy agenda was set well before there was any overt expression of citizen preferences. Second, the rhetoric and actions of policymakers indicated they were not responding to public pressure but, rather, were seizing the initiative to promote programs in which they had a stake.

In most of the case studies, reform proposals were announced even before the original exposé had been fully published. Viewers of the "Home Health Hustle" were told toward the end of the 18-minute segment that "next week there will be Senate hearings into the home health business." In the rape reports, community hearings were announced the day after the five-part series began, and the gang rape law was signed on the third day of the series.

Between the third and fourth parts of "Beating Justice," [Chicago] mayoral candidate Harold Washington proposed the abolition of the police department's disciplinary review board. The fire department crackdown at the University of Chicago occurred the morning after the first broadcast. The last part of the dialysis series quoted federal officials who promised reforms, several of which were proposed shortly thereafter.

Only in the child abductions story, where the "60 Minutes" producer refused to give credit to policymakers that she believed was undeserved, did policy actions come later. But even there, officials responded only ten days after the broadcast. Clearly, these developments undermine the Mobilization Model's requisite that public outcry in the wake of an investigative story is a necessary precursor to change.

Second, the tone of policymakers appeared inconsistent with the formulation of the Mobilization Model. Officials seemed neither reactive nor defensive about published allegations of wrongdoing, even when the problems were in their bailiwick. Instead, they responded to the investigative disclosures as if they provided policy *opportunities.*

The home health exposé allowed the new Republican Senate majority to showcase its concern for wasteful social welfare programs. The rape series provided a forum for a governor and a state legislative panel to flex their muscle about crime. The toxic waste reports were viewed by a fire department bureaucrat as an opportunity to impress his new reform-minded boss. The child abductions story gave several U.S. senators a chance to obtain widespread recognition for their routine casework. The dialysis series allowed two Congressional committees and other governmental agencies to spotlight their crusade against health care rip-offs.

In each case, policymakers and their spokespersons used the media disclosures to exhibit positive leadership traits. Rather than risk being portrayed as part of the problem, in the conventional terms of adversary journalism, they took steps that allowed them to be described as part of the solution. This occurred even where policymakers actually had contributed to the problems because they had allowed policy reforms to languish (for example, in the child abductions and kidney dialysis cases).

In most of the cases, exposés could be exploited as opportunities because of prepublication transactions between journalists and policymakers. In the home health, toxic waste, and dialysis stories, journalists and policymakers actively collaborated to set policy-making agendas prior to the public dissemination of the investigative findings. Specifically, coalitions were established that ensured both the nature and timing of the post-publication announcements of reforms. We have called these symbiotic alliances between journalists and officials "coalition journalism."[17] The motivations for forming such coalitions are described later.

Prepublication transactions also occurred in the rape series. There, journalists recontacted reform-minded officials to obtain information about the status of legislative initiatives just prior to the publication of the series. Unlike the other cases, however, the nature and timing of the subsequent policy initiatives were decided independently by officials. Nonetheless, the initiatives clearly were prompted by journalists' contacts with those policymakers, and the newspaper covered them as reactions to its series. Contrary to the Mobilization Model, agenda building began in all four of these cases before the public was made aware of the investigative findings.

The policy agendas in the police brutality and child abduction cases were not set by formal journalist–policymaker coalitions. Nonetheless, similar kinds of symbiotic transactions occurred after publication in both cases. In "Beating Justice," the local television station closely covered the reactions of political candidates as part of its proprietary follow-up. Indeed, campaign aides notified investigative reporters as well as nonproprietary media before each round of public announcements. In the follow-up to "Missing?" a senator's staff helped set the nonproprietary media agenda by supplying journalists with fresh information about additional victims and updates on the status of reform proposals that they supported.

As summarized in Table 2, we find that policy-making agendas are catalyzed by the formal transactions between journalists and officials more than by the direct influence of the public or interest groups. Further, those transactional relationships seem more important than the actual publication or broadcast of an investigative series in influencing the agenda-building process. Finally, the character of the policy outcomes—the reforms—may be affected significantly by collaboration among journalists and officials.

This is not to dismiss the role of the public or pressure groups in influencing the possibility of reform. Pressure groups, in particular, played an important agenda-building role later in the policy-making process in three cases. The rape reports, for example, provided a platform for feminist groups to push for sweeping changes in the Illinois criminal code. The Illinois law was fundamentally revised the year after the newspaper series was published. Similarly, American Children Held Hostage, an organization formed one month after the "60 Minutes" report, was instrumental in keeping the problem of international child abductions on the media agenda. The group also broadened the policy-making support for legislative reforms.

Interest group activity also was important in the aftermath of the dialysis series, but with different consequences. There, patients' groups conflicted with providers' organizations over proposed reform legislation, creating at least a temporary policy stalemate. This is consistent with Kingdon's findings: "Much of interest group activity in these processes consists not of positive promotion, but rather of

TABLE 2

The Media–Opinion–Policy-Making Connection

INVESTIGATIVE REPORT	JOURNALIST— POLICYMAKER TRANSACTION	IMPACT ON GENERAL PUBLIC	INTEREST GROUP PRESSURE	TYPE POLICY RESULT
"Home Health Hustle"	Prepublication coalition (formal)	Highly significant	No	Deliberative
"Rape: Every Woman's Nightmare"	Prepublication coalition (informal)	Not significant	Yes— supportive	Deliberative, substantive
"Beating Justice"	Proprietary and non-proprietary follow-up	Moderately significant	No	Substantive
"Wasted Time"	Prepublication coalition (formal)	Not significant	No	Individualistic
"Missing?"	Nonproprietary follow-up	Not significant	Yes— supportive	Deliberative, substantive
"Dialysis: The Profit Machine"	Prepublication coalition (formal)	Moderately significant	Yes— conflictual	Deliberative, individualistic, substantive

negative blocking," he reports.[18] Nonetheless, the dialysis case was the only one in which pressure groups approximated the conventional role assigned by pluralist political scientists. In the other cases, groups played no discernible role in agenda building, or they facilitated reforms already in the works.

The general public also is not to be dismissed entirely as an agenda-building force. To some extent, policymakers have the public in mind when they develop their collaborative media strategies. As Linsky puts it: "Agenda setting (by the media) is accepted by officials because what becomes a high priority issue for the media may be a reflection of what people are thinking about."[19] In an age when the news media have become a vital link between political actors and their constituencies, getting good press on issues of concern to the public may be a prerequisite for career enhancement.[20]

In particular, establishing collaborative relationships with investigative journalists is a double-edged sword. It allows policymakers to send positive messages to the public about their problem-solving abilities, and, with Richard Nixon's mishandling of the media in Watergate fresh in their minds, to avoid negative portrayals of their performance. Indeed, our interviews with policymakers suggest they respond to investigative reporters as if they *were* the public.

Still, this is very different from the role ascribed to the press and the public by the Mobilization Model. As Table 2 indicates, actual public preferences seem unrelated to policymakers' reactions to the investigative findings. In the rape and toxic waste cases, significant policy-making reactions occurred despite the lack of measured changes in public opinion. In the home health and dialysis cases, relevant changes in public opinion were preceded by policy-making initiatives. Following "Missing?" the public became increasingly antagonistic to the government of Norway without becoming more concerned about international child abductions, the larger problem that policymakers actually were addressing.

The conventional role of public opinion in a popular democracy was approximated only in the police brutality case. There, our surveys of the public, journalists, and policymakers suggest public opinion was catalyzed in the immediate aftermath of the investigative reports. But even here, there were significant departures from the linear Mobilization Model. Rather than a media crusade to outrage the general public, it was a mayoral candidate who used the issue of police brutality to mobilize a specific portion of the electorate. Further, the substantive reforms that followed were made without media fanfare by the incumbent administration, and only after it had been defeated at the polls.

Nonetheless, the police brutality case provides evidence that support certain premises of the Mobilization Model. In particular, this case indicates that the public mood may affect the possibility of reform. . . .

In Chicago, in 1983, reform was in the air. The local climate was ripe both for a general change in administrations—the election of the city's first black reform mayor—and a specific change in the regulation of its police force.

Similarly, the political mood in the country in the early 1900s and the mid-

1970s was conducive to building reform agendas. In those periods, an alienated citizenry and organized public interest groups helped facilitate an array of changes in American society by challenging the status quo. The media played a significant role in bringing about those changes by relentlessly unearthing wrongdoings and crusading to right wrongs.

The cases we studied were set in the 1980s, however, where pragmatism and incrementalism dominated our country's social and political milieu. In this context, it is perhaps surprising that we found any evidence of change, much less some of the important corrective actions documented in our case studies. This is testimony to the ongoing spirit of reform, even if it often resulted from surprising coalitions that appear to defy our expectations of adversary journalism. . . .

SUMMING UP AND LOOKING AHEAD

Journalist–policymaker transactions, then, are often symbiotic. Rather than the conventional notion of investigative reporting, which posits adversarial relationships as the norm, the muckraking–policy-making connection may be just the opposite. Mutually self-interested ad hoc alliances appear to be commonplace.

Some investigative reporters we surveyed perceived the coalitional relationship as an easy fix, providing an opportunity for posturing as well as for policy-making. One investigative reporter from Seattle characterized the governmental reaction to investigative stories as "choreographed and shallow." An editor from Milwaukee saw the trend as one in which the results tend to be "bogus, prearranged or negotiated."

Our case study evidence suggests that symbiotic coalitions can also be effective catalysts for setting reform agendas. In some circumstances, such as the toxic waste case study, they provide a sufficient condition for corrective action. In other cases, they are necessary or helpful for triggering the deliberation of reform measures. However, such coalitions may not be enough to carry the day. The availability of policy alternatives, the role of pressure groups, and the existing political climate must converge for investigative influence to be maximized.

. . . [P]olicy reforms result from complex interactive factors rather than from the simple linear progression specified by the Mobilization Model. The journalist–policymaker connection occupies center stage in this alternative Coalition Model of agenda building. However, their dialogue does not play to an empty theater. The actors seek approbation from the public audience, which in turn is affected by what transpires on the stage. Although the audience has no direct influence over the events that unfold before their eyes, they certainly are kept in mind by the scriptwriters.

Further, the stage is set by a host of contextual factors, which the actors also help to rearrange. The timing of the public showing is crucial for determining the effect it has on various audiences. We have found that conditions are more ripe for reform in certain eras, and for certain problems, than for others. In the 1980s, the climate in the country changed. The spirit of reform that so clearly pervaded the Progressive period and the Watergate era began to abate.

At the same time, the willingness of the journalism profession to commit resources necessary for investigative reporting was tempered by corporate owner-ship of the media, by court decisions, and perhaps by a sense of growing public inurement to exposés. The trend instead has been toward less confrontational and more reader-friendly journalism. This trend was bemoaned in a March 1990 speech to the National Press Foundation by Norman Pearlstine, managing editor of the *Wall Street Journal.* Pearlstine expressed "some very real concerns" about the declin-ing willingness of the press to do "the difficult investigative story." Such a story, he said,

> Really tries to take on major institutions, major organizations, important people in our society . . . and to expose them as thieves when it is appropriate. . . . It is very different from the kind of service journalism that all of us are engaging more in. It's not about being reader friendly. It's not about how many items you can get into a paper to appeal to as many people as possible. . . . I do question whether the kinds of large companies that are publicly held will be able to commit themselves (in the 1990s) to the kind of journalism I am talking about.

"But," he concluded, "(investigative reporting) is really fundamental to the republic and really fundamental to journalism."[21]

The *Journal's* managing editor is not the only one in recent times to fret about the future of muckraking journalism. In 1984, *Editor and Publisher* magazine report-ed the "death" of investigative reporting.[22] This prognostication proved to be unnecessarily gloomy. Still, cutbacks in local television "I-teams" and in newspaper investigative units have been widely publicized.[23]

Our surveys of investigative reporters and editors in 1986 and 1989 suggest that investigative reporting retains a core strength, although it may be shifting direc-tions.[24] Both surveys show that most muckrakers continue to spend as much time on investigative reporting as in the past. However, there is a trend toward doing more short-term investigative stories. . . .

Investigative reporters also may be becoming less of an elite breed of journal-ist. The success of Investigative Reporters and Editors' [IRE] workshops for differ-ent kinds of journalists suggests that the techniques of investigative reporting are being adapted by the professional mainstream. Thus, although separate investiga-tive units have been disbanded, investigative practices have become more wide-spread. As we concluded in 1986:

> the IRE survey findings point to the institutionalization of investigative reporting. Rather than bordering on extinction, investigative journalists have merely become less visible as their efforts become more conventional. Today's muckrakers may be more akin to inveterate watchdogs than starving wolves.[25]

These apparent trends in investigative reporting may seem somewhat contra-dictory. However, they have certain common elements that have significant impli-cations for future governing practices. The decline in resources for investigative reporting, especially long-term projects, probably will mean an increase in collaboration among journalists and policymakers. Journalists will more readily seek out policy partners because they will need information more quickly, and because they will not be given the time to follow up their stories to ensure impact. Similarly, the use of investigative techniques by beat reporters, for whom transactions with officials are already routine, will further facilitate Coalition journalism.

For policymakers, these trends will provide additional opportunities for image and agenda building. The institutionalization of investigative reporting creates increased potential to draw the media spotlight to their problem-solving activities. Policymakers will be able to decrease their reliance on a handful of reporters—some of whom see themselves as adversaries of officialdom—and broaden their capacity to achieve results through a diffusion of partnerships.

The implications of these developments for public policy-making are significant. The expansion of the media-policy connection means journalists will play a greater direct role in helping set public policy agendas. The actual content of stories may become even less important for policy-making than the kinds of alliances that form between journalists and officials.

Second, the long-term policy impact of investigative reporting may be circumscribed by the declining commitment to crusade. Media muckrakers may be able to continue to set the deliberative agenda of policymakers. However, as they move fleetingly from one story to another, the action agenda—the substance of reform—will remain under the control of established policy-making interests.

Finally, present trends suggest the general public will play even less of an active policy-making role. American popular democracy has been victimized by twentieth-century developments in media and society. Scholarly analyses have described the American people as the "phantom public," the "captive public," the "semi-sovereign people," and the "bystander public."[26] Our media age has produced, in one scholar's words, a "democracy without citizens."[27] "Manufacturing consent" is what others have called it.[28]

There is every reason to conclude that present trends in investigative reporting will exacerbate this problem in the future. Muckraker–policymaker transactions will continue to bypass the public in the resolution of important public issues. Even where such issues are not resolved, the public will be led to believe they have been resolved by viewing or reading the reaction stories of reporters. Public outrage about important social problems may not have been manifested for some time; in contemporary times, outrage may prove to be irrelevant even where it does surface.

These trends are not immutable. The historical pendulum may swing back to an era of reform at some future juncture. We have concluded that conditions will be ripe for such an era when public alienation toward authority recurs, and at the same time changes in media engender fierce competition for stories about moral disorder. If and when this does happen, conventional notions about popular democracy may once again become relevant. Until that time, investigative reporting will continue to be a catalyst for policy reform without necessarily being a vehicle for mass public mobilization or enlightenment.

NOTES

1. Charles D. Elder and Roger W. Cobb, "Agenda-Building and the Politics of Aging," *Policy Studies Journal*, 13(1984), p. 115. Borrowing from Lang and Lang, ibid., pp. 58–61, we use the term "policy agenda building" to refer to an evolving, interactive process among many actors as opposed to a one-directional influence of media on policy-making. We are primarily concerned here with the effects of those interactions on the "formal" agendas of government policymakers, and secondarily with the influence on the "public" agendas of citizens. This distinction is drawn by Anthony Downs, "Up and Down with Ecology—The 'Issue-Attention Cycle,' " *The Public Interest*, 28(Summer 1972), pp. 38–50.

2. For an example of this phenomenon, see Fay L. Cook and Wesley G. Sloan, "Agenda-Setting: Convergent and Divergent Voice Models and Rise and Fall of Policy Issues," in Maxwell E. McCombs and David L. Protess (eds.), *Agenda-Setting: Readings in Media, Public Opinion and Policymaking* (Hillsdale, NJ: Lawrence Erlbaum, 1991).

3. As we discussed in Chapter 2, the regulatory reforms of the early 1900s provided a partial solution to the problems revealed by muckraking journalists. However, these "reforms" created an array of unanticipated problems. See Richard Hofstadter, *The Age of Reform* (New York: Knopf, 1955). Ironically, as our case studies show, new muckrakers often spotlight failures of the regulatory system that was created partly in response to problems revealed by old muckrakers.

4. See E. Rogers and J. Dearing, "Agenda-Setting Research: Where Has It Been, Where Is It Going?" in J. Anderson (ed.), *Communication Yearbook 11* (Newbury Park, CA: Sage, 1988), pp. 555–594.

5. Barbara J. Nelson, *Making an Issue of Child Abuse* (Chicago: University of Chicago Press, 1984).

6. Cook and Sloan, "Agenda Setting."

7. See Roger W. Cobb and Charles D. Elder, "Communications and Public Policy," in Dan Nimmo and Keith Sanders (eds.), *Handbook of Political Communications* (Beverly Hills: Sage, 1981); and Roger Cobb, Jennie-Keith Ross, and Marc Howard Ross, "Agenda-Building as a Comparative Political Process," *American Political Science Review*, 70 (March 1976), p. 127.

8. Cook and Skogan, "Agenda Setting," p. 2.

9. John W. Kingdon, *Agendas, Alternatives, and Public Policies* (Boston: Little, Brown and Company, 1984). Kingdon's theory in turn draws from Michael Cohen, James March, and Johan Olsen, "A Garbage Can Model of Organizational Choice," *Administrative Science Quarterly*, 17(March 1972), pp. 1–25.

10. For example, social science research about the seriousness of child abuse was found both to facilitate media coverage of that problem and enhance its status on policymakers' agendas. See Nelson, *Making an Issue of Child Abuse.*

11. The lack of credible evidence that the elderly were a high-risk crime population contributed significantly to the decline of that issue on policymakers' agendas. See Cook and Skogan, "Agenda Setting."

12. Kingdon, *Agendas, Alternatives, and Public Policies*, p. 150.

13. For discussions of the role of elections in agenda building and public policy making, see Anthony Downs, *An Economic Theory of Democracy* (New York: Harper & Row, 1957); Benjamin Ginsberg, "Elections and Public Policy," *American Political Science Review*, 70 (March 1976), pp. 41–49; Barbara Deckard Sinclair, "Party Realignment and the Transformation of the Political Agenda," *American Political Science Review*, 71(September 1977), pp. 940–953.

14. Kingdon, *Agendas, Alternatives, and Public Policies*, pp. 153–160.

15. See Harold A. Lasswell, *Democracy Through Public Opinion* (Menassha, WI: Banta, 1941); Robert A. Dahl, *A Preface to Democratic Theory* (Chicago: University of Chicago Press, 1956); Benjamin I. Page and Robert Y. Shapiro, "Effects of Public Opinion on Policy," *American Political Science Review*, 77(1983), p. 175.

16. See Grant McConnell, *Private Power and American Democracy* (New York: Knopf, 1967); E.E. Schattschneider, *The Semi-Sovereign People* (New York: Holt, Rinehart and Winston, 1960); John W. Kingdon, *Congressmen's Voting Decisions* (New York: Harper & Row, 1981).

17. Harvey D. Molotch, David L. Protess, and Margaret T. Gordon, "The Media–Policy Connection: Ecologies of News," in David Paletz (ed.), *Political Communication: Theories, Cases and Assessments* (Norwood, NJ: Ablex, 1987).

18. Kingdon, *Agendas, Alternatives, and Public Policies*, p. 52.

19. Martin Linsky, *Impact: How the Press Affects Federal Policymaking* (New York: W.W. Norton, 1986), p. 90.

20. For discussions of the news media's displacement of political parties as vehicles for linking politicans with constituencies, see Thomas E. Patterson, *The Mass Media Election* (New York: Praeger, 1980); David Broder, *The Party's Over* (New York: Harper & Row, 1972); and Robert M. Entman, *Democracy Without Citizens* (New York: Oxford, 1989).

21. Speech by Norman Pearlstine to the National Press Foundation Annual Awards Dinner, March 2, 1990.

22. *Editor and Publisher*, "Is Investigative Reporting Dead?" August 25, 1984.

23. For example, see William K. Marimow, "Who Silenced the I-Team?" *Philadelphia Inquirer Magazine* (April 14, 1985), pp. 22–30; Jonathan Friendly, "Investigative Journalism Is Changing Some of Its Goals and Softening Tone," *New York Times* (August 23, 1983), p. 8; Michael O'Neill, "The Ebbing of the 'Great Investigative Wave,' " *ASNE Bulletin* (September 1983), p. 26.

24. David L. Protess, "Investigative Reporters: Endangered Species?" *The Investigative Reporters and Editors Journal* (Winter 1976).

25. Ibid.

26. See Walter Lippmann, *The Phantom Public* (New York: Harcourt, Brace, 1925); Benjamin Ginsberg, *The Captive Public* (New York: Basic Books, 1986); and E.E. Schattschneider, *The Semi-Sovereign People* (New York: Holt, Rinehart and Winston, 1960). Lang and Lang, *The Battle for Public Opinion*, refer to the "bystander public," pp. 10–25.

27. This is the title of the book by Robert M. Entman (1989).

28. Edward S. Herman and Noam Chomsky, *Manufacturing Consent: The Political Economy of the Mass Media* (New York: Pantheon, 1988).

39. DISPELLING THE LEAK MYSTIQUE

Martin Linsky

Every president, probably since George Washington, has complained about leaks about policy decisions appearing in the press. Ronald Reagan even attempted to impose criminal penalties on leakers within his administration. Leaks have become a bane for presidents, yet attempts at eradication have never worked. But, owing to their ability to get press attention for their statements, presidents have succeeded in conveying the idea that leaks are an unethical practice carried on by a small group of disgruntled staff.

In the following selection, Martin Linsky attacks that idea as a myth. Leaking is neither conducted by a few disloyal bureaucrats nor is it merely an accidental disclosure of confidential information. Leaking is a widespread practice at various levels of policy-making from middle-level managers to the White House chief of staff. Moreover, according to Linsky, policymakers now live in a climate where leaking is expected, and their activities in the policy-making process—both public and private—are conducted in anticipation of potential leaks.

Linsky describes the various motives for leaks, such as sending messages to others in government and attempting to stop an action the leaker disagrees with, and he offers examples from six case studies he conducted of policy decisions affected by the press. Linsky's study is based on these case studies and interviews with and surveys of a broad range of national policymakers. It is one of the few extant large-scale studies of media effect on policymaking.

Martin Linsky's own career bridges the gap between academia and government. He lectures at the Kennedy School of Government at Harvard University and is the author of *Impact: How the Press Affects Federal Policymaking* (1986), from which this excerpt is taken. He is also a former Massachusetts state representative.*

The American Heritage Dictionary defines a leak as a "secret or accidental disclosure of confidential information."[1] That definition rests heavily on one factor, the confidentiality of the information. The essence of confidentiality is the assumption that the information held would not be revealed. Reporters and officials identify additional elements as important in defining leaks and distinguishing them from other forms of journalist–policymaker communication. Among them are the confidentiality of the source, the nature of the information, and the initiation of the contact. Leaks have a negative connotation and therefore are subject to different definitions depending on where people sit and their own standards of practice. One person's leak is another's profile in courage. That is one reason why talking about them with reporters and journalists is complicated.

On the question of confidentiality of the source, few journalists and reporters would classify as a leak information where the source is revealed, although under the dictionary definition an accidental leak conceivably could be one in which the source is named as part of the story. Anonymity seems an inevitable element of the traditional leak, even though technically it might not be essential.

All leaking by definition is trafficking in confidential information, but there are differences in the nature of the confidentiality. There are at least three types of confidentiality. First is information which is confidential only in the sense that it is not widely known. An example of a leak of such information is the official who gratuitously slips a reporter a copy of an obscure public record that discloses something embarrassing to someone. Most people would call that a leak even though the information itself is theoretically already available to the press. Second, there's information, such as classified documents and grand jury testimony, which is protected by

---

*From *Impact: How the Press Affects Federal Policymaking* (New York: W.W. Norton & Co., Inc., 1986), pp. 169–73, 185–89, 192–97. Reprinted with permission.

laws, regulations, or oaths. Transfer of that information to a reporter would almost always be considered a leak and would be condemned out of hand by most officials in all but extreme circumstances. The third category of confidentiality covers the huge area of typical and more routine leaks, where the information is thought of as confidential by someone and the official knows that life would be difficult if he or she were disclosed as the reporter's source.

There is also confusion about the distinction among a leak, information on background, and a confidential source. The words mean different things to different people, yet the overlap is substantial. What is common to them is the anonymity of the informer. . . . [A]re there anonymous sources who are not leakers? When journalists make the distinction, they often are referring to the process of getting the information: a leaker is more regularly someone who takes the initiative with the journalist; an anonymous source is a person the journalist contacts, often routinely, for information and insight. In the words of Albert Hunt, Washington bureau chief for the *Wall Street Journal*, "Leaks are stories that are instigated, sometimes by the government for a purpose, sometimes for a good purpose, sometimes for a sinister purpose, sometimes for a selfish purpose, whatever." Confidential sources, on the other hand, are often labels for the people reporters go to and rely on.

Yet there is usually something more subtle to the process than that; sometimes it is aggressive reporting more than an aggressive policymaker that results in a leak. Leaks often take months to generate. Leaks also often happen by accident, as when an official lets information slip without thinking about it or incorrectly assumes a reporter already knows a particular piece of information.

When policymakers make this distinction they may be basing it on the nature of the information or its level of specificity. It is a point that officials sometimes make when they try to separate leaking from their own well-honed practice of providing anonymous background and source information to reporters. Officials argue that they don't leak because the only information they provide to journalists is general direction, suggestions as to other sources, and the like. Yet the element of anonymity still exists; the officials want it that way. The line drawing by officials seems as artificial as that based on who initiates the contact which has been suggested by reporters. It may be common usage and common practice to make the distinction among practitioners, but most anonymous source activity seems to fit well within the dictionary definition of a leak. Officials could only explain away such conduct as something other than leaking to an audience of colleagues or reporters. Anyone else would find it a distinction without a difference. Conventional wisdom and usage would argue that there are only two essential elements of a leak, if we want to include all those communications that people might reasonably call leaks: that the information is considered confidential under a broad definition of the term, and the leaker does not want people to know he or she is the source.

Finally, there is the negative connotation of leaking, which makes it difficult to discuss no matter how widespread the practice. Here is a revealing exchange between a group of senior officials in the national security field and a teacher with experience in both government and journalism. The professor started by asking how many in the room had leaked. No hands went up (except his). Then he said, "Okay, forget classified information. How many have leaked nonclassified information?" Still no hands. Then he asked, "How many have ever told a reporter something you wouldn't want your boss to know you had disclosed?" Nearly half of those in the room raised their hands. Cyrus Vance called leaks "childish" and "naive," but that would be too mild for a lot of middle-level managers in the federal government. For many of them, leaking confidential information is unethical, disloyal, and just plain wrong. Yet for many senior federal officials and nearly all journalists, most leaks do not carry that negative moral baggage. They are at worst an annoyance. [Former Secretary of Defense James] Schlesinger called leaks "mainly a source of irritation" and President Ford described them as a "real pain."

While the arguments about leaks continue, so do the leaks. Forty-two percent of the officials who responded to the survey said they leaked, and it is reasonable to assume that the figure is, if anything, understated. Leaks played a significant role in nearly every one of the cases we studied in detail, although we did not choose any of them for that reason. In the neutron bomb story, for example, Richard Burt of the *New York Times* was leaked the information that President Carter had decided to cancel production of the bomb. He went with the story, and the publication may have played a crucial role in softening Carter's final position. In the Love Canal relocation, the leak of the report on chromosomal damage began the process of undoing the carefully worked-out schedule for assessing the validity of the study. It contributed in a major way to the abbreviated process by which the decision to relocate was made. In the Bob Jones University tax exemption decision, a series of leaks occurred following the media criticism of the decision to restore the tax exemptions. First there were leaks from the White House designed to put the responsibility for the policy shift on Edwin Meese. Then, when that created its own brouhaha in the press and in the White House, someone leaked the notation on the president's log, indicating that Reagan had encouraged or endorsed the policy shift before the decision was public. That leak refocused attention on the president and his views on the issue, and eventually resulted in his taking full responsibility for the whole matter. When the Reagan administration was fighting legislation to reform the accelerated Social Security disability eligibility reviews, White House officials used leaks to try to get the message out that bureaucratic changes were underway. Later, when it seemed inevitable that some legislation would be passed, the Department of Health and Human Services (HHS) began drafting its own legislative package, working with both key members of Congress and the White House staff to gain support. After the story broke about Roy Benavidez, the Vietnam war hero who was thrown off the disability rolls, a draft of the HHS legislative package was leaked. The leak made it appear that the department was simply responding to the criticism stemming from the treatment of Benavidez and undermined Secretary Heckler's quiet negotiations with the chief congressional spokesperson on the issue, Congressman Jake Pickle. . . .

****

. . . There is a pattern of leaks affecting the process of policymaking much more than they affected the substance of the policies. In the decision of the Carter administration to relocate over seven hundred families from Love Canal, the leak of the results of the preliminary study of chromosomal damage among residents there in and of itself had no effect on what officials in retrospect believe to have been the inevitable policy choice. But there is no doubt that the leak was one of the key factors in making the policymakers feel that they had to act more quickly than they would have preferred. The leak advanced the story ahead of the policymakers' schedule and put them on the defensive, forcing them to explain themselves and make future commitments to demonstrate that they were on top of the situation. Similarly, in the Bob Jones University tax exemption story, the leaks were used, presumably by White House officials, to try to fix responsibility for the decision on Meese. They did not add very much momentum to what already existed for backtracking and reversing what had taken place. And in the case of the Social Security disability reviews, the leaks were used by government officials as an unsuccessful and last-ditch effort to stave off congressional action by suggesting that the administration was taking sufficient steps on its own.

The only leak that occurred in the cases we studied in depth which seemed to affect policy as much as process was in the neutron bomb case. On March 27, 1978, President Carter had made what appeared to be his definite and final decision to cancel the neutron bomb. Some of his key people, including principally National Security Adviser Zbigniew Brzezinski and Secretary of State Cyrus Vance, continued to urge Carter to reconsider. For several days, the cancellation decision was kept under wraps. Stories appeared, but they were remarkably off base, most of them predicting that Carter would move ahead with the weapon. Both Richard Burt of the *New York Times* and Walter Pincus of the *Washington Post* were tipped off that Carter had decided on cancellation. Pincus discarded the information because, he now says, he "just couldn't believe that after all these months with everybody saying everything was go, Carter was going to cancel." Pincus's information had come from a congressman by way of his editor.

Burt says he was told by a "non-American," who had learned about the cancellation from a senior US official and mentioned it to Burt "in a normal, passing encounter." Burt confirmed the story with three officials and then went to print. On April 4, the *Times* led the paper with Burt's story, under the headline "Aides Report Carter Bans Neutron Bomb; Some Seek Reversal." Burt's scoop was accurate, and some administration officials assumed he got it from a proponent of the bomb, such as Brzezinski, who would have leaked it in a last-ditch effort to generate enough support for production to turn Carter around.

At the State Department and the Pentagon there was general bemusement, and surprise that the story had not leaked earlier. But with the West German foreign minister due in town to talk with Carter about the bomb and other matters that very morning, the White House was extremely upset. The decision was made to deny. Within twenty-four hours, Vance, Hodding Carter, Harold Brown, Jody Powell, and West German chancellor Helmut Schmidt's spokesperson Klaus Boelling all unequivocally denied that a decision had been made and said the story was wrong. Even President Carter, who had been telling his own advisers that he had decided not to go ahead, was now telling leaders in Congress that he had not made up his mind.

News reports covered the Burt article and the denial as a story in itself. Some even speculated that the misleading information was leaked to Burt by an opponent of the bomb in the administration who was trying to put last-minute pressure on the president not to go ahead. The story and the rebuttal unleashed a wave of protest from Congress, from Republican leaders George Bush, Ronald Reagan, and Gerald Ford, and from a large number of the nation's leading newspapers, all outraged at the idea that Carter was even considering cancellation. Even the *Washington Post*, which had started the whole process with Walter Pincus's story almost a year before, urged the president editorially to "make a forthright, no-nonsense decision to proceed,"[2] in light of the strain on relations with the allies and the questions about his leadership.

It is impossible to know for sure what impact the Burt story denial had on Carter, but circumstantial evidence suggests it played an important role. Carter began to reevaluate his position that morning. By his own account, within two or three days, and right in the midst of the protests from the politicians and the press spurred by the story and denial, he had moved from cancellation to deferral. In the *Post*, Walter Pincus gave the Burt article credit for the change, although Powell and NSC Deputy Director David Aaron deny it. During a background session for the press just after the deferral was announced, Brzezinski himself said that the "fourth estate played a significant role." When asked point blank whether the Burt story and the reaction to it made the president shift his stand, Brzezinski said, "I think there may be something to that, but you'd have to ask the president to be sure."

Part of the whole strategy for presenting the new decision to defer had to include the notion that the Burt story was dead wrong, that there never had been a decision to cancel. Otherwise, the president would appear to have changed his mind twice, first going ahead, then cancelling and finally deferral. The administration was fairly successful in making the point. Both *Time* and *Newsweek*[3] characterized Burt's story as false; with the exception of an Evans and Novak column, no one in the press seems to have challenged the administration's denial. One of the consequences of this leak was that the administration felt that it had to resort to a bald-faced lie to counter it.

At a press briefing with Burt in the room, Powell characterized the story as "bad reporting." Burt was incensed, and at the conclusion of the briefing he cornered Powell, whom he had never met before, to express his displeasure. Powell ushered him into the office and, in a disarmingly friendly way, explained how much difficulty the story had caused. Burt says he learned a lesson from the experience: "What Jody was saying was that when you're protecting the president, all is fair in love and war."[4]

. . . When officials are asked about the impact of leaks, they talk about process, rather than substance. The impact of leaks is better understood as having changed the routines of policymaking over time, than in terms of the effect of any single leak in a particular case. Policymakers expect leaks, anticipate their impact, take preventative measures, and use them strategically themselves. . . . Three quarters of those officials who worried about leaks limited the number of people involved in decision making and put less information in writing as a result of their concern. On the other hand, just over 20 percent of our worriers said that leaks caused them to narrow the range of policy options that they considered, and even fewer of them said that their concerns on this score caused them to increase the range of policy options or to reshape their options.

Among the questionnaire respondents, officials who served in the Johnson and Nixon years were just as likely to leak as those who served later, yet the anecdotal evidence we have from the policymakers we interviewed suggests that leaks are much more of a factor now than they used to be. One explanation for this apparent inconsistency is that different information now is leaked, and the leaks themselves are more significant in substance.

Theodore Sorensen believes that leaks are a more serious issue in the 1980s than they were for President Kennedy. Respected policymakers who served in the earlier era, such as Dean Rusk, Elmer Staats, and Wilbur Cohen, said that leaks were not a problem for them, and discounted their significance. Rusk said that the only leak he had any difficulty with in all his years as secretary of state was when someone released his comment made in the midst of the Cuban missile crisis that "they were eyeball to eyeball and the other fella just blinked." "It should not have been leaked," Rusk said, "because it might have had some effect on old man Khrushchev, who was impulsive and unpredictable."

Those who served in recent years were much more likely to worry about leaks than those who served more than a decade ago (75.5 percent to 57 percent). Officials who served in the 1970s and 1980s talked more about the importance of leaks and about what they did to adjust to leaks as a continuing part of policymaking—Elliot Richardson, for example, said that his defense against leaks was to open up the process of decision making. That way there would be enough people involved and aware of what was going on that the number of secrets to be leaked would be kept to a minimum and fewer people would feel that they had to leak to air their point of view. Others used very different tactics. Brzezinski excluded people from meetings in order to prevent leaks. [Former Assistant Attorney General Henry] Peterson said that during his time in the Nixon White House, "they were so upset about the leaks and the effect the leaks were having on policy that they specifically forbade White House people or senior staff members from talking to certain members of certain institutions of the media." Predictably, officials we recontacted who had said they had not leaked were critical of the impact of leaks, suggesting, for example, that less information is now put in files, leaving successors less well equipped to understand what went on before them. . . .

****

. . . [L]eaks are not always, maybe not even usually [be], the product of a rational calculation by the leaker. Leaks may also be elicited by a clever reporter or may come from a person who does not realize the significance of the information imparted. Leaks may occur by accident as well as by design. When by design, they may be just as likely intended for some unrelated purpose—such as ingratiating oneself with the reporter or inflicting harm on an enemy—as to affect the outcome of the issue at hand. . . .

Bernard Gwertzman, veteran diplomatic correspondent for the *New York Times*, believes that officials and the public think leaks are more planned and willful than is usually the case: "There are books that credit me with all kinds of leaks. There's Bill Sullivan, who was our ambassador to Iran . . . saying I got tremendous leaks from the State Department. It's kind of amusing because I think in his vision he had some official reading the cables and then calling me up. . . . Whereas in fact some of the best stories I've got occurred in the following fashion: It was December-January, '78–'79, when the Shah was kind of on the ropes. I remember having lunch with a friend of mine at the State Department in which we weren't really talking about Iran. This was a guy who was senior enough to know what was happening. We got talking about Iran and I said, 'Gee, it must be tough on Sullivan. What does he tell the Shah? Does the Shah ask him for advice?' And the guy agreed. 'Yeah,' he says, 'it is tough. The Shah is a Hamlet-like figure. He doesn't know whether he should use force or not use force, and he asked Sullivan for advice, but we can't decide what to tell Sullivan. And so we tell Sullivan not to tell him anything.'

"I checked this out with a couple of other people, and nobody said, 'That's not right.' So I write a story more or less saying that, that Sullivan's reporting that the Shah is indecisive and he can't get [clear signals]. What I didn't realize when I was writing this was that this was a very top secret. I'm not sure the guy who told me this even knew that Sullivan had been sending these cables. He was just a friend of mine. He had no particular axe to grind with Sullivan. He was sympathetic to Sullivan. I think Sullivan thought somebody in Washington was trying to knife him. It's a funny kind of system."

Gwertzman's story has the ring of truth to it. We tend to assume more rationality, purposefulness, and logic from others than we do for ourselves. The "system," as Gwertzman refers to it, is probably a lot more accidental than orchestrated. Journalists get leaks when they are not expecting them, and what appears in print as a leak from a single source, perhaps confirmed by others, is often the result of a lot of conversations out of which the reporter gets what Gwertzman calls a mosaic of what is happening.

The idea that leaks may be less systematic than they appear does not eliminate intent on the part of the leakers. Almost all the leak suspects in the Agnew story had a reasonable motive at some point for trying to get some of the information out anonymously.

In the leak of the report in the Love Canal case, motivation is more subtle. It seems likely there that the leaker either talked to Jack Watson or was someone who had attended the key Friday meeting that Watson chaired, where the strategy for releasing the report was developed. Since it was going to be released the next day anyway, why would anyone leak it to the *New York Times*? A likely explanation, perhaps the most likely, is that the leaker was someone who had an existing relation-ship with the *Times* reporter, similar to the example offered by Gwertzman. The leak may have come because the reporter pursued his source and because the leaker saw as an opportunity to do a favor for a reporter from a very important news organiza-tion. It does not seem to have been a leak designed to affect policy as much as a leak which was a part of a reporter–source relationship. That type of leak is called either a self-interested leak or an ego leak, and is distinguished particularly from a policy leak.[5] It often occurs when the policymaker is trying to show the reporter that he or she is important by being privy to important information. In a policy leak, the clear purpose is to try to influence the outcome of a particular decision-making process.

There are two variations on the ego leak. In the goodwill leak, the leader has no professional interest in the policy area or in the particular information involved, but is trying to curry favor by providing information that the reporter will find use-ful. In the casual or no-purpose leak, the transfer of information comes as a by-prod-uct of a personal relationship between the reporter and the leaker, which is charac-terized by ongoing conversation and mutual trust. Richard Burt's explanation about the leak in the neutron bomb case may fit into this category.

Another leak is the trial-balloon leak, where the details of an initiative are sur-faced to see what the reaction will be. There is also the whistle-blowing leak, usually when a frustrated official, without routine access to the press, leaks information about some alleged wrongdoing in government. Then there is the grudge leak, when an official releases negative information, often personal and embarrassing, to settle a score or damage someone else. . . .

Finally, and most esoteric, there is the reverse effect or reverse blame leak. For instance, someone may leak material which on the surface appears to be damaging or negative to himself or herself, but serves to get some important information out while minimizing the possibility of being identified as the source. When Alexander Haig was secretary of state, notes from one of his early morning inner staff meetings were leaked to the *Washington Post*. The notes included some personal and uncom-plimentary comments by Haig about world leaders. At first blush, the leak would seem to be intended to undermine Haig; but on further reflection, as pointed out shortly after the incident by William Safire in the *New York Times*, Haig was under criticism at the time for not being tough enough for the job, and the notes present-ed him as a confident and independent official with his own point of view.

These types of leaks represent a range of disinterestedness and different degrees of moral justification. If you ask leaders why they leaked, as we did, you can-not expect them to respond with the more mean-spirited or self-interested reasons which we know do exist. Yet with that limitation, the answers they did give us provide some additional insight into leakers' motivations.

For example, nearly four out of five of the leakers identified countering false or misleading information as the reason they leaked. In their eyes, at least, they were assisting the process of getting at the truth, of helping the reporter do the job, of keeping the public informed. Nearly as many leakers, almost three out of four, said they leaked to put something on the agenda, to gain attention for an issue or policy option. The other two reasons chosen by more than half of the leakers from the list we offered were to consolidate support from the public or a constituency outside of government (64 percent) and to force action on an issue (53 percent). . . .

Developing good relations with the press was indicated as a reason for leaking by just about 40 percent of our leakers. This number is probably underestimated, both because this is a rather candid admission for an official to make, even anonymously, and because experience indicates that it is standard reportorial practice and simple human nature to hold out the hope of good relations as a possible benefit of cooperating on a story.

Six other reasons for leaking were mentioned by about a third of our leakers. Three are clearly policy leaks: to send a message to another branch of government (32 percent), to stop action on an issue (31.5 percent), and to slow action on an issue (29 percent). One is the trial balloon: to inform other officials of a policy consideration or action (30 percent). A fifth may be a combination of policy and ego: to protect one's position (30 percent). The sixth is close to what we earlier called the accidental leak: the result of an enterprising reporter shrewdly eliciting the information (29 percent).

What we can glean from this data is that those who admitted leaking most often leaked for policy-related reasons of putting items on the agenda and sending a message to those outside of government. Leaks are often, if not usually, given more space and time by news organizations because they are exclusive stories. It follows that leaks can be particularly effective in accomplishing those purposes. The other most often-cited reason for leaking, correcting the record, may have a range of goals behind it. It may be a way to further policy interests or a way of trying to earn the gratitude of the reporter. Leaking "the truth" to correct a mistake may help the journalist without embarrassment to anyone. If the reporter's original story was inaccurate, by providing a corrective leak the official can enable the reporter to fix the mistake in such a way as to draw the least possible amount of attention to the original error. On the other hand, if the error was made by one reporter, giving a competitor an exclusive on the right information can help guarantee that it will get the biggest possible play.

However much the cases and the survey results suggest that leaks may be less systematic than officials and the public suspect, there is nothing to suggest that they are less prevalent. On the contrary, everything we have found argues that leaks as broadly defined are a routine and generally accepted part of the policymaking process. There were leaks in five of the six cases we studied, and both journalists and officials with whom we talked confirmed the view that they are a pervasive element of the interaction. There was disagreement over the importance, the propriety, and the value of leaks, but not whether they were a large fact of life in Washington. . . .

NOTES

1. From the *American Heritage Dictionary of the English Language*, paperback edition, based on the hardcover edition (New York: Dell Publishing, 1976).

2. "The Neutron Decision," *Washington Post*, April 6, 1978, editiorial page.

3. "Furor Over the Neutron Bomb," *Newsweek*, April 17, 1978, pages 35 and 38; and "The Neutron Bomb Furor," *Time*, April 17, 1978, page 10.

4. David Whitman, "The Press and the Neutron Bomb," Kennedy School of Government, case C94-84-595, p. 129 (see asterisk at the bottom of the page).

5. This typology of leaks is not original. Many others who have studied the relationship between press and government have examined the various motivations of leakers. One of the best such efforts, and the one on which this section draws most heavily, is from Stephen Hess, *The Government/Press Connection* (Washington, D.C.: The Brookings Institution), Chapter 7, see especially pp. 77–78. Mr. Hess was a member of the study group for this project.

B. FOREIGN POLICY

After having cut diplomatic relations with the government of Iran in the wake of the takeover of the U.S. embassy in Tehran in 1979, the U.S. government had few channels of communication with Iran. American foreign policymakers often had to resort to television coverage of the Iranian militants to glean any messages from the Iranian government.*

News media organizations have become conduits for intergovernmental message transmission. The *New York Times* prides itself on accurately conveying U.S. policy decisions and, not surprisingly, it is perceived by some foreign governments as the mouthpiece of the U.S. government.

But that role has been tainted when the U.S. government engages in a disinformation campaign through the press as it did against Libya in 1986. Or the press poorly performs the conduit role by garbling the message.†

However, the role of the news media in some cases has gone beyond that of "common carrier" of messages between governments. The news media have been accused of actively participating in foreign policy-making. Television news coverage can direct the public debate and shape public opinion about U.S. foreign policy.‡ News media coverage also shapes the perceptions of reality held by foreign policymakers. In a crisis situation, most of Washington, including the White House and the State Department, is tuned to CNN coverage.

The following two selections illustrate how television news has affected foreign policy-making. The first selection claims that TV news has accelerated the process of foreign policy-making forcing policymakers to make hasty decisions. The second selection demonstrates how saturation coverage of a TV news story, complete with

---

*See, for example, David Altheide, "Iran vs. U.S. TV News: The Hostage Story Out of Context," in William Adams, ed., *Television Coverage of the Middle East* (Norwood, N.J.: Ablex, 1981), pp. 138–58; and James F. Larson, "Television and U.S. Foreign Policy: The Case of the Iran Hostage Crisis," *Journal of Communication* 36 (Autumn 1986):108–30.

†Altheide, op cit.

‡See William C. Adams, "Mass Media and Public Opinion about Foreign Affairs: A Typology of News Dynamics," *Political Communication and Persuasion* (1987); and Doris Graber, *Mass Media and American Politics*, 3rd ed. (Washington, D.C.: CQ Press, 1988), p. 353.

dramatic visuals, can set the president's agenda and drive a reversal of a policy decision.

40. FOREIGN POLICY ON DEADLINE

Lloyd N. Cutler

Television news has become the primary medium for conveying images of foreign-policy events. Television news has brought us pictures of world leaders at summits, civilian uprisings in authoritarian regimes, soldiers fighting in foreign lands, anti-American demonstrations in various nations, and children starving in Africa. Television news has become our "window on the world."

However, a former White House official claims that TV news has become a greater force than merely a medium for images. Lloyd Cutler faults television news for producing a climate of pressure on White House policymakers to make instantaneous responses to foreign-policy crises. He also argues that TV news has affected not only the speed but also the substance of foreign-policy decisions. Examples, according to Cutler, are the Vietnam War and the resolution of the Iran hostage crisis.

According to Cutler, television news must police itself more effectively through scrutiny of its own practices. Especially, the tendency of TV journalists to participate in the staging of news should be critiqued.

Lloyd N. Cutler, author of *Regulating Campaign Finance* (1986), is a former White House counsel under President Jimmy Carter.*

When President Jimmy Carter asked me to become White House counsel in the third year of his term, it was because I could bring more Washington experience to his staff. But it came as a distinct surprise to me how much television news had intruded into both the timing and the substance of the policy decisions that an American president is required to make. TV news now has a much greater effect on national policy decisions—especially foreign-policy decisions—than print journalism has ever been able to achieve and more than most experienced observers realize. This impact is not because TV journalism is more policy-oriented than print journalism—far from it—but because, as policymakers are painfully learning, TV news has a wider reach and faster impact that must now be taken into account. If a picture is worth 1,000 words, sounds and pictures together must be worth 10,000.

TV journalists reach much larger audiences than print journalists. The most important newspapers—the *Los Angeles Times*, the *New York Times*, the *Wall Street Journal*, and the *Washington Post*—exert a major influence on what is featured in other dailies and in TV news itself. But none of these newspapers has more than 1 to 3 million readers. Each of the evening TV news has 12 to 15 million viewers. Surveys consistently confirm that two-thirds of the American people regard the

*From "Foreign Policy on Deadline," *Foreign Policy*, Fall 1984, pp. 113–28.

evening TV news as their principal source of information about local, national, and international events.

TV news vastly increases the number of people who get interested in an issue and care about the outcome. Before the dawn of TV news, press reports about peacetime foreign-policy or national security issues probably left the majority of newspaper and magazine readers unmoved. Print readers can select the stories they wish to read. But TV viewers cannot be selective unless they turn off the program altogether. A vivid account on TV news commands the attention and concern of most of the larger TV audience. The impact of TV news thus has major consequences for the foreign-policy agenda of any administration. To sustain its foreign and national security policies, an administration must not merely satisfy the minority of print readers who care about such issues; it must now satisfy the entire national television audience as well. This is especially true of policies that place U.S. forces at risk. Sometimes TV's influence is all to the good, sometimes it's bad. But it is always present, and learning how to adjust to it is central to the art of governing today.

TV's DOOMSDAY CLOCK

Even before the advent of TV news, print articles about troubling events created a political need for prompt presidential responses. Because TV news accelerates public awareness, the time for response is now even briefer. If an ominous foreign event is featured on TV news, the president and his advisers feel bound to make a response in time for the next evening news broadcast. TV news personifies the U.S. government in the image of the president—almost all administration news is announced from the White House lawn—and the country looks to him alone for the nation's reaction to a crisis. If he does not have a response ready by the late afternoon deadline, the evening news may report that the president's advisers are divided, that the president cannot make up his mind, or that while the president hesitates, his political opponents know exactly what to do.

Anyone who has worked recently in the White House has felt this recurring sense of a TV doomsday clock. Many examples can be cited.

• Ratification of the SALT II treaty was the leading political issue in summer 1979. In the last weeks of August, U.S. intelligence agencies collected data they interpreted as showing the presence of a Soviet combat brigade in Cuba. These reports quickly became public, and in the absence of other news they became the leading TV story of the Labor Day weekend. Senators on both sides of the SALT II debate went on camera to demand the removal of the brigade. To save the treaty, Carter also went on camera to announce that the continued presence of the brigade was "not acceptable." Within the next week, closer analysis of the evidence revealed a failure of the intelligence community's institutional memory: The same brigade had been at the same location since the Cuban missile crisis of 1962. While the United States had insisted on its withdrawal at that time along with that of Soviet nuclear missiles and bombers, Washington had dropped the issue after the missiles and bombers were removed. Under the pressure of Vietnam and other subsequent events, the United States has shifted intelligence resources away from Cuba to other areas.

The brigade was not discovered in 1979, it was rediscovered. The administration could not persuade the Soviets to remove a brigade that had been in Cuba for 17 years and had to accept their assurance that its purpose was to train Cubans rather than to become involved in Western Hemisphere conflicts. Since this explanation did not satisfy many senators, SALT II's passage through the Senate Foreign Relations Committee was delayed for 10 crucial weeks.

If the news of the brigade had appeared only in print and not on TV, the Carter administration might have been able to delay its response at least a few days to permit the intelligence agencies to re-examine their findings. With more time to reflect, the administration could have reappraised the faulty initial intelligence report and put the rediscovery in proper perspective.

• The Soviet invasion of Afghanistan began on December 27, 1979. It immediately became the leading TV news story, despite the continuing drama of the U.S. hostages in Iran. It raised public alarm over a Soviet push into the Persian Gulf—the main energy resource of the free world. In order to make a prompt and forceful response, Carter decided on an embargo of grain and other food shipments to the Soviet Union—a decision I still believe was morally and strategically correct, as well as politically courageous. He made the final decision on January 4, 1980. And to achieve maximum impact, he elected to announce it on camera for the evening TV news. While the White House staff managed to get the necessary executive and departmental orders prepared during the day, none of us realized that American grain dealers with large Soviet orders already had contracted with farmers or had negotiated futures contracts for the billions worth of grain exports that would be banned.

But for the good fortune that January 4 was a Friday, the next day's grain markets would have been in ruins. Over a frantic weekend, we persuaded the Commodity Futures Trading Commission to suspend trading on Monday and Tuesday, and the lawyers were able to devise a financial fix before the markets reopened on Wednesday. But the attraction of announcing the decision immediately on the evening TV news led us into making what might have been a critical mistake.

• In August 1982 after the Israeli invasion of Lebanon routed Palestine Liberation Organization (PLO) forces, the American government sent U.S. Marines to Beirut as part of a neutral buffer while the PLO evacuated its forces to other Arab states. With this mission accomplished, the marines withdrew. Soon thereafter came the refugee camp massacres, in which the Christian Phalangist militia allied with the Israelis slaughtered hundreds of Palestinian men, women, and children. TV news cameras graphically recorded the most grisly details of these gruesome events. The world was shocked, most of all America, and U.S. confidence in its Israeli ally was severely shaken. Within 2 days, President Ronald Reagan appeared on camera to announce his response—the return of the marines to Lebanon to redeem the earlier U.S. commitment to protect the Palestinian civilians after PLO chief Yasir Arafat and his fighters departed.

It has since been reported that Reagan made his announcement against the advice of the secretary of defense and the Joint Chiefs of Staff. If TV news had not recorded and instantly reported these massacres, public horror would not have been as instantaneous or acute. The response could have been more deliberately and perhaps more wisely chosen.

• Soviet destruction of a South Korean airliner in September 1983 was a TV news sensation, complete with simulations depicting how the plane veered off course, how the Soviet fighters tracked and shot it down, and also featured recordings of the South Korean pilot's reports to the Japanese air traffic controllers plus translated radio interceptions of the Soviet pilots and their ground command. Based on this and perhaps other evidence, U.S. intelligence agencies jumped to the initial conclusion that the Soviets knew they were tracking a commercial airliner loaded with innocent passengers and deliberately shot it down without prior warning. Within 48 hours, the president appeared on TV news to charge the Soviet Union with murder in cold blood.

During the following week, a closer and more deliberated analysis of the evidence led the U.S. intelligence community to conclude that the Soviets had probably mistaken the South Korean plane for an American electronic reconnaissance plane and had not realized they were attacking a commercial airliner until after its disappearance over the Sea of Japan was announced. Even so, the Soviet action was inexcusable, and the initial Soviet denials of responsibility were outrageous. But the president's premature and probably mistaken on-camera charge—and the equally erroneous Soviet on-camera riposte that the South Korean airliner was being used to collect electronic intelligence for the United States—unnecessarily aggravated the already tense relationship between the superpowers.

• Reagan made his decision to invade Grenada in October 1983 within a day after TV news aired the numbing pictures of the truck bombing of the U.S. Marine barracks in Beirut. For good or ill, the Grenada decision will affect U.S. ties with Latin America and Western Europe for many years. But TV news shortened the time available to weigh these consequences. As an account of White House decision making in the March 10, 1984, issue of the *Economist* suggests, the impact of the pictures from Lebanon on the president and the American people probably hastened his decision to take a bold and prompt action when opportunity knocked in another part of the world.

SUBSTANTIVE IMPACT

TV affects not only the timing of major policy decisions but their substance as well. A TV news lead item hits viewers with the speed and force of a laser beam, and it attracts the interest of a much wider audience that the printed word. It therefore can speed the coalescence of public backing for an initiative the president favors but is reluctant to take before the public is ready to support it. President John Kennedy felt unable to propose civil rights legislation until TV news built the necessary public backing with its dramatic pictures of Sheriff Bull Connor's police force using cattle prods against civil rights demonstrators in Birmingham, Alabama.

The impact of TV news can also dissuade presidents from initiatives they would soon come to reject. Newswatchers who see the miseries of combat and deprivation instantly associate themselves with the victims and their families. TV news can provide a useful early warning that a policy course that costs American lives or jobs will be very difficult to sustain over an extended period. It can force an administration to calculate fully the costs and benefits of such a policy before it casts the die.

The rub is that the national interest sometimes requires launching or sticking with a policy despite the initial cost in lives or jobs. In such cases TV can have a harmful impact on the substance of national policy decisions. TV is quintessentially a medium that transmits simple surface impressions, while national policy issues are infinitely complex and many-sided. The ugliness of military combat or economic deprivation can be graphically conveyed in a few pictures and sounds; the complex policy considerations that usually lie behind a decision to risk these consequences are much more difficult to explain.

TV news does not have the time needed to convey complex ideas. It comes in staccato bursts, resembling a newspaper that consists solely of headlines. Anything that cannot be conveyed in a few brief sentences and dramatic pictures is not carried at all. Even the president is rarely allowed more than a few consecutive sentences. Only 22 minutes of a half-hour network news program are taken up by the news. The aggregate number of words spoken would not fill two-thirds of a single standard newspaper page.

Consider the impact of television on the substance of three recent important policy choices:

¶ Before Vietnam, presidents were able to have their way with Congress and the American people on the conduct of armed conflict once U.S. forces and prestige were committed. Vietnam was the first comprehensively televised war, and many lament the role of television in that war. Its enormous cumulative impact in shaping public opinion helped force three consecutive presidents to modify their war-fighting policies and ultimately to abandon the effort entirely. Clearer to the American people than presidential explanations of the policy reasons for the war was its daily ugliness, reflected on their TV screens. Yet the undeniable impact of television on U.S. war policy was not necessarily harmful. While many still believe the United States should have finished the job, TV helped convince the majority that the war was a policy mistake. The Vietnam intervention would probably not have been sustainable over the long run even in the absence of TV news. The French military effort in Vietnam, after all, failed before the TV era. TV news helped make the war unsustainable much earlier than would otherwise have been the case and thus helped the U.S. government make the policy correction needed to put the original mistake in the past.

¶ The dramatic seizure of the U.S. embassy staff in Iran in November 1979 dominated TV news for more than a year. As the days of captivity ticked by, the daily network news invariably began or ended with the statement, "This is the 121st [or 242nd, or 363rd] day our hostages have been held in Iran." A new, late-night network news program was launched called "America Held Hostage." TV journalists vied with one another to obtain interviews or tapes of the hostages, their captors, and any Iranian official from the Ayatollah Ruhollah Khomeini on down who could be persuaded to go on camera. These daily reports heightened the public sense of anger and frustration, which in turn increased the political value to the Islamic revolutionary movement of continuing to hold the hostages. The American people were outraged to the point where they would undoubtedly have supported a declaration of war; and while such a course would have been politically useful to Carter in an election year, in the longer term it would have been a serious foreign-policy error. The result could have been to ignite the entire Persian Gulf and to bring Soviet forces much closer to its shores. From time to time, the administration tried to play down the hostage crisis so that world attention would abate and quiet diplomacy would have a chance. But the constant drumbeat of TV news removed that public option.

¶ When then presidential candidate Reverend Jesse Jackson decided to visit Syria, Central America, and Cuba, TV news created running-story media events out of each voyage. Sensing the communication opportunities, foreign officials as different as President Hafez al-Assad of Syria and Premier Fidel Castro of Cuba changed policies and released into Jackson's hands Americans held prisoner in their countries. An exchange in Panama exposed the real interests of many of Jackson's hosts. Asked by the press what concrete change Jackson's visit to Central America had brought, the president of Panama thought it was sufficient answer simply to gesture to the rows of TV cameras, photographers, and reporters surrounding Jackson, who had, he said, "succeeded in getting representatives of U.S. mass media to come to Panama and Central America to see firsthand the situation."

What TV coverage of Jackson's trips managed to convey about "the situation" was superficial at best. Yet Jackson's trips not only freed some political prisoners but also undoubtedly affected the political evolution of U.S. diplomacy in these sensitive areas. Even Reagan, who had refused to see him before Jackson went to Syria, was so impressed by the worldwide TV impact of his return with U.S. Navy Lieutenant Robert Goodman that he welcomed both of them at the White House and thus recovered a share of TV's center stage for himself. And he took advantage of the release to open a new negotiating initiative with Assad.

As the above examples show, an appraisal of television's impact on public policy must distinguish between its damaging effect on the time available for crisis decisions and its sometimes harmful effect on the substance of broad policy. The most harmful effect of TV news is its tendency to speed up the decision-making process on issues that TV news is featuring and to slow down and interrupt the process of deciding other important issues that get less TV attention. Whatever urgent but less televised problem may be on the White House agenda on any given morning, it is often put aside to consider and respond to the latest TV news bombshell in time for the next broadcast. In a very real sense, events that become TV lead stories now set the priorities for the policy-making agenda.

Is it possible for an administration to cope with TV's harmful effects? Americans urge their children to be computer literate. Can Americans and their leaders become more TV literate?

To reduce the political risk of leaving a news vacuum for others to fill, administrations can consider creating news about the decision-making process itself. Photo opportunities can be allowed for the arrival and departure of key advisers, for meetings in the cabinet or situation rooms, and for consultation with foreign allies or domestic interest groups. Background interviews can be arranged on the importance of deliberate analysis and measured responses. Image builders can focus on the wise and cautious president, weighing pros and cons, instead of on the superman who comes to the rescue in a flash. And if the administration has the nerve to play down an incipient crisis and delay its reaction long enough, the agenda of TV news may shift to some newer, unrelated development. The pressure for a prompt response to the earlier event may then disappear.

Presidents and their advisers can also be more cautious in responding to an event that is only an intelligence deduction. Intelligence analysts work on the basis of circumstantial data that are rarely conclusive. A single deduction may have a 90 percent chance of being correct, but when five 90 percent deductions are strung together to reach an intelligence judgment, the margin for error rises from 10 to about 50 percent. To protect against misjudgments, several U.S. intelligence services share data and compete in drawing deductive conclusions. But just as journalists are driven to be the first to bring their conclusions to their policymaking customers, intelligence services are driven to be the first to bring their conclusions to their policymaking customers. In the episodes of the Soviet combat brigade and the South Korean airliner, the intelligence analysts made incorrect initial deductions; the policymakers also made decisions without adequately taking into account the possibility that these initial deductions might be wrong.

Administrations can also resort to other TV techniques, such as the live presidential TV press conference and the presidential television address. Both give the president a consecutive half-hour or so of television time—about as much as viewers can absorb. The press conference format creates more suspense and audience interest but sacrifices full presidential control. The address format provides total control but risks viewer loss of interest. Both formats run the risk of overuse; the power that television offers the president is, in British journalist Godfrey Hodgson's apt phrase, a Faustian bargain. Like youth, TV power does not last very long—few TV performers can hold their audience over a 4-year span.

Moreover, television press conferences and addresses are now staged events, as is true of almost every TV program, including the news. Staging is thought to be a necessary technique to permit TV presentations to come across as fresh and natural. News announcers wear make-up to offset the intensity of the lights. Their lines are written in advance and read from hidden teleprompters to simulate impromptu delivery. Pictures are carefully edited. Logos, graphs, and other visual aids are also prepared and displayed to communicate ideas more rapidly than mere speech. For every face on camera, 10 times as many technicians, reporters, and producers are behind the scenes. Presidential press conferences and addresses require the same performing skills and the same careful preparation. That is a great deal to ask of government leaders who also have to manage the national economy, assure social tranquility, and protect the free world.

. . . Mastering the art of TV presentation is now critical to governance. In the television era an administration that cannot present well cannot govern well.

But while better TV skills will help politicians cope with their new environment, they cannot possibly offset the fundamental influence on national policy-making that TV now exerts. . . . Since two-thirds of the people receive most of their information via TV news, one can legitimately infer that on national policy issues— especially issues that require disagreeable choices such as huge continuing budget deficits—TV tends to build negative public reactions to any course of action and that it retards rather than fosters building a political consensus. . . .

No one yet knows how to solve this or many of the other new problems that TV politics presents. As I have argued elsewhere, the U.S. two-party system needs strengthening to offset the decline in party cohesion that television helps create.[1] As America approaches the bicentenary of its Constitution several groups have developed ideas about reforming the basic U.S. political structure that deserve closer attention. But not even structural reform can change the growing impact of TV news on making public policy. The role of TV news can be better managed, but it cannot be undone. What TV news has wrought are the side effects of innovation and a free press, values that are worth pursuing despite such costs.

There is no use deploring the advent of TV news and only limited use criticizing how TV journalists and producers present it. In their competition for ratings, they have probably lost the best of the qualities that made Americans admire Edward R. Murrow and Walter Cronkite. But on the whole, within the time constraints of this medium and the attention span of the viewing public, TV journalists and producers perform their tasks with reasonable objectivity and integrity. According to a 1982 Roper poll, if conflicting versions of the same news event were reported on TV and in newspapers, 53 percent of respondents would regard the TV version as more credible; only 22 percent would pick the newspaper version. According to the same poll, 88 percent of the audience believes TV news does a good to excellent job. Even if it can be charged with many sins, TV can hardly be faulted for conveying information more vividly and to bigger audiences than print. Yet it is most often these qualities of TV news, rather than inadequate journalistic skill or judgment on the part of those who present it, that account for its impact on the making of national policy.

Longer network evening news programs would permit more coverage in depth, but they run counter to the financial interests of local stations and to the habits of television audiences. Most viewers like staccato bursts that shift their attention from one item to another. The "MacNeil-Lehrer News Hour," with about 4 million viewers, may exhaust the audience potential for in-depth network evening news programs.

No doubt TV journalism would profit if it were the target of more and better criticism. Private sources of criticism are likely to be more constructive and less dangerous than official sources. Political scientist Austin Ranney of the American Enterprise Institute for Public Policy Research has suggested that the network news organizations could do more to expose and criticize one another's mistakes. Print journalists have also been slow to recognize the growing importance of TV news and to hold it accountable for what it does. Print journalism is eternally grateful to the late A.J. Liebling's series of *New Yorker* magazine critiques called "The Wayward Press." TV needs a contemporary A.J. Liebling to write or talk about the wayward television press, as well as an annual Edward R. Murrow award for the best in-depth network news service. Some of the many first-generation TV fortunes might be used to endow awards specifically for TV news excellence like the Pulitzer prizes for print journalists as well as scholarships for budding TV journalists. Like some major U.S. newspapers, the TV networks might employ ombudsmen who could offer weekly commentaries on the performance of their colleagues in covering public events. Public television took a small step in this direction with the program "Inside Story."

In particular, print and TV journalists ought to expose the tacit conspiracy of silence about staging, whether practiced by revered network announcers or by politicians in and out of office. Staging is making people or events appear different from what they really are. Staging, of course, has its place in the creative arts, but in the arts its use is not concealed from the audience. The staging of TV news, political press conferences, and public addresses is concealed from the audience. Not to mince words, it is a fraud. When a TV interview is presented as fresh and impromptu even though the journalist and the politician have been through a rehearsal before they appear on the screen, they are jointly deceiving the audience. When news announcers or politicians use hidden teleprompters, they are pretending to express extemporaneously ideas that they are reading from a prepared script, often one prepared by someone else. At the very least, they ought to tell viewers; when they do not, the free press should discharge its duty to inform viewers of the deception.

For news announcers, these frauds may be trivial vanities. But as these deceits become commonplace, they deter TV journalists from exposing the same deceptions when committed by politicians, and that is not a trivial fact. . . . The staging of political interviews, press conferences, and public addresses cheats viewers of television's primary political value—its ability to demonstrate integrity, intelligence, and judgment and to expose incompetence, confusion, and deceit. Unless TV journalists insist on preserving that value, TV technology may succeed in disproving Abraham Lincoln's fundamental political maxim. It may indeed become possible to fool all of the people all of the time. . . .

NOTE

1. See Lloyd N. Cutler, "To Form a Government," *Foreign Affairs* 59, no. 1 (Fall 1980).

41. TEN DAYS THAT SHOOK THE WHITE HOUSE

Daniel Schorr

In the aftermath of the Persian Gulf War, the Bush administration began to withdraw U.S. troops from Kuwait and Saudi Arabia. However, the long-standing hostility between the Iraqi government and the Kurdish people within Iraq broke into open warfare. Taking advantage of the weakness of the Iraqi regime, Kurdish leaders were rebelling against Saddam Hussein's government. But the Iraqi army was conducting a campaign of genocide against the poorly armed rebels and the civilian population. Kurdish families in large numbers were fleeing to escape the fighting.

Daniel Schorr narrates the Bush administration's movement from nonintervention and apathy toward the Kurdish refugee situation to military support.* The news media, especially the television network news programs, Schorr argues, were the impetus for the Bush administration policy reversal. By vividly portraying the Iraqi suffering and placing the responsibility for it on the president's doorstep, the press served as the catalyst for public policy.

Schorr's portrayal of an administration reacting to news coverage is not atypical. However, news organizations must provide the saturation news coverage to capture the attention of both the public and the policymakers. Moreover, the Kurdish refugee problem was another episode in a story the American news audience had already been following attentively, namely the Persian Gulf War.

Daniel Schorr, a former CBS News correspondent, is now a senior news analyst for National Public Radio. He is author of *Clearing the Air* (1977) and co-author of *Within Our Reach: Breaking the Cycle of Disadvantage* (1988).

Score one for the power of the media, especially television, as a policy-making force. Coverage of the massacre and exodus of the Kurds generated public pressures that were instrumental in slowing the hasty American military withdrawal from Iraq and forcing a return to help guard and care for the victims of Saddam Hussein's vengeance.

The Kurdish tragedy was only one in a season of [recent] worldwide disasters—the typhoon in Bangladesh, earthquakes in Soviet Georgia and Costa Rica, famine in Africa.

Scenes of suffering flitted past American television audiences, a succession of miseries almost too rapid and stark to be absorbed. But the suffering of the Kurds stood out from the others. This was not a natural catastrophe, but a man-made disaster, and one that had a special claim on the American conscience. It was America,

*From *Columbia Journalism Review* (July/August 1991): 21–23. Reprinted with permission.

after all, that had invaded Iraq and shaken loose the underpinnings of authority. It was America's president, George Bush, who, on February 15, called on the "Iraqi military and the Iraqi people" to rise up and "force Saddam Hussein . . . to step aside." It was President Bush who, on February 27, had ordered an abrupt cessation of hostilities, leaving the Iraqi dictator with enough armor and aircraft to put down Shiite and Kurdish uprisings. And, finally, it was the Bush administration that, after first warning the Iraqi regime not to use helicopter gunships against its own people, then stood by while they were used to strafe Kurds fleeing to the mountains in the north.

Americans became dimly aware, in the month after the war stopped and the rebellions had started, that their government, having burst the floodgates in Iraq, was trying to run away from the flood. There was even a whisper of tacit collusion with the dictator whom Bush had called "worse than Hitler." The *New York Times* reported on March 27 that the administration had "decided to let President Saddam Hussein put down rebellions in his country without American intervention." This in the name of avoiding being dragged into what the president called "a Vietnam-style quagmire," and in response to Saudi Arabian and Turkish concerns about the possible disintegration of Iraq.

The administration had every reason, at first, to believe that the public supported a policy of getting the troops home quickly and avoiding involvement in ethnic strife. There was some criticism, but it was mainly confined to the editorial pages of newspapers. The Bush administration, like the Reagan administration, seems to work on the premise that print does not move people; only television, with its visceral impact, does.

The Kurds had been let down by America before. As disclosed in the report of the House Intelligence Committee in 1976 (of which I obtained a draft before the House voted to suppress it), President Nixon had the CIA sponsor a Kurdish uprising against Saddam Hussein, starting in 1972, as a favor to the Shah of Iran. When the Shah and Saddam settled their differences, support for the insurrection was withdrawn and the Kurds were abandoned to an Iraqi attack. ("Our movement and people are being destroyed in an unbelievable way, with silence from everyone," Mustafa Barzani, father of the current Kurdish leader, wrote to Secretary of State Henry Kissinger on March 10, 1975. "We feel, Your Excellency, that the United States has a moral and political responsibility towards our people, who have committed themselves to your country's policy.") Thousands were killed and 200,000 fled to Iran, of whom 40,000 were forcibly returned to Iraq.

I reported this on CBS in 1976, but it was a "tell story" without the pictures needed to let the audience experience the dimensions of American betrayal. And it made little impression. So now, in March 1991, the Bush administration was not overly concerned with "tell stories" and commentaries about how America was turning its back on the Kurds.

Jim Hoagland wrote in the *Washington Post* of "an American bug-out from the Persian Gulf," and William Safire wrote in the *New York Times* that the president had experienced "a failure of nerve." But "a senior presidential aide" told *Time* magazine, "The only pressure for the U.S. to intervene is coming from columnists and commentators. And a "top White House aide" (probably Chief of Staff John Sununu in both cases) told *Newsweek*, "A hundred Safire columns will not change the public's mind. There is no political downside to our policy."

Famous last words, politically speaking. What the White House did not seem to realize was that, by the end of March, the issue, as perceived by the public, was changing from military intervention in support of a revolution to compassionate intercession for the victims of Saddam Hussein's genocidal methods. By then, while hundreds of thousands of Kurds and Shiites were being driven into Iran, where they could not be easily seen by the world, hundreds of thousands more Kurds were being driven into the rugged mountains bordering Turkey, where they could be vividly witnessed by television.

The vast panorama of suffering, and perhaps even more the individual portraits of agony, seemed overwhelming. Not easily forgotten were scenes like that of the little girl, her bare feet sinking into the freezing mud, or of the little boy, his face burned, possibly by napalm. The anguished face of a child peered up from the cover of *Newsweek*, with the caption, addressed to Mr. Bush, "Why won't he help us?" In a BBC report on *The MacNeil–Lehrer News Hour*, a woman asked, "Why did George Bush do nothing?"

The quagmire-shunning Bush administration was slow to react, concentrating on a formal cease-fire to speed the return of American troops and continuing to emphasize its refusal to be involved in "an internal conflict."

April 2: On a golf course in Florida, in strange juxtaposition with evening news scenes of shivering and starving refugees, the president brushed off questions about the continued Iraqi use of helicopter gunships against the Kurds, saying, "I feel no reason to answer to anybody. We're relaxing here."

A senior official told the *Washington Post* that the reticence was deliberate: "Engaging on this issue gains us nothing. All you do is risk raising public concerns that are not there now. . . ."

April 3: By now the administration was becoming aware of American and European "concerns," and had begun scrambling for a policy of compassion without intervention. On the Florida golf course, Mr. Bush said, "I feel frustrated anytime innocent civilians are being slaughtered. But the United States and these other countries with us in this coalition did not go there to settle all the internal affairs of Iraq."

Later that day came a written statement in the president's name, departing from the administration's passive role: "I call upon Iraq's leaders to halt these attacks immediately and to allow international organizations to work inside Iraq to alleviate the suffering. . . . The United States is prepared to extend economic help to Turkey through multilateral channels."

April 4: Appearing with Japanese Toshiki Kaifu in Newport Beach, California, Mr. Bush said, "We will do what we can to help the Kurdish refugees." But he also stuck with the position that no American parent "wants to see United States forces pushed into this situation, brutal, tough, and deplorable as it is."

By this time, the Kurdish insurrection all but crushed, television was showing a mass exodus into the mountains. A widely distributed Associated Press photo showed a ten-year-old girl in a hospital in northern Iraq being comforted by her mother. The child had lost a hand and an eye in an Iraqi helicopter attack.

April 5: In Newport Beach, a dogged President Bush declared, "We will do what we can to help there without being bogged down into a ground-force action in Iraq." Again, the press office, hours later, came up with a written new policy—the Air Force would start dropping food, blankets, and clothing to Kurdish refugees in northern Iraq.

As a public-relations answer, the air drops did not go over very well. The supplies landed in random places; television showed where some Kurds had been killed by failing bales.

April 8: Europe was looking at television, too, seeing reporting—particularly in Britain—that was often more vivid and comprehensive than American television was showing. At a European Community meeting in Luxembourg, British Prime Minister John Major proposed the creation of a protected "enclave" for the Kurds in northern Iraq. Secretary of State James Baker, visiting Luxembourg, saw on television what Europeans were seeing. Then, at the bidding of President Bush, worried about an impression of American insensitivity to the refugees' plight, Baker proceeded to the Turkish border. The seven-minute visit turned into a photo opportunity of a special sort. It focused on scenes of desperate Kurds, one saying, in English, "Please, Mr. Baker I want to talk to you. You've got to do something to help us."

April 11: A Reuters dispatch from Washington noted, "Searing pictures of suffering Iraqi refugees have clouded America's gulf war triumph and given President Bush a devilish political problem." Part of his problem was that his vacillation on the Kurdish issue had helped to bring down his approval rating from 92 to 80 percent in a *Newsweek* poll (78 percent in a Gallup poll).

April 12: The administration announced that American troops would be going back into Iraq as part of a relief operation called "Provide Comfort." Military encampments would be set up, guarded by coalition forces, eventually to be turned over to the United Nations. The announcement came so suddenly as to catch off base Defense Secretary Richard Cheney who, an hour before, had told a news conference that there had been no decision to "actually put forces on the ground in Iraq."

Within a two-week period, the president had been forced, under the impact of what Americans and Europeans were seeing on television, to reconsider his hasty withdrawal of troops from Iraq. As though to acknowledge this, Mr. Bush told a news conference on April 16, "No one can see the pictures or hear the accounts of this human suffering—men, women, and, most painfully of all, innocent children—and not be deeply moved."

Military victory over Iraq was threatening to turn into political and moral defeat. The polls that had shown Americans overwhelmingly wanting troops home in a hurry were now showing that Americans did not want to abandon the Kurds, even if that meant using American forces to protect them.

It is rare in American history that television, which is most often manipulated to support a policy, creates an unofficial plebiscite that forces a change in policy.

In a column on May 5, *New York Times* television critic Walter Goodman underscored what the medium had wrought when "it compelled the White House to act despite its initial reluctance." But he also raised the question, "Should American policy be driven by scenes that happen to be accessible to cameras and that make the most impact on the screen?"

The question is a reasonable one. But, in the case of the Kurds, it was not the pictures alone that forced the change. These were not random pictures of random suffering, but pictures that dramatized the suffering of a people for whom Americans felt some responsibility. It was that combination that overwhelmed governmental passivity.

C. NATIONAL SECURITY POLICY

On January 17, 1991, U.S. military planes began bombing Baghdad, Iraq. The world knew of the attack only minutes after the president of the United States—thanks to CNN.

Televised wars—both hot and cold—have become staples of the late twentieth century. Industrialized nations cannot go to war without television cameras in tow.

Some authoritarian governments have restricted Western media access to battlegrounds, but many governments—both democratic and nondemocratic—have attempted to turn press coverage to their advantage. When Iraq's Saddam Hussein staged a televised meeting with foreign hostages his government held or agreed to interviews with Western media organizations, he was using television to attempt to affect national security policy of other nations toward his regime.

But the press's role is not just that of common carrier. The media have been accused of acting as a participant in the making of U.S. national security policy. The entertainment media have been charged with fostering public receptiveness to the Vietnam War and other battles with communism.* News coverage of the Vietnam War, especially TV pictures of lost battles and dead soldiers, was said to contribute to public frustration with the war and eventual decline of support.

The Persian Gulf War resurrected the issues of press role in the conduct of war. For the first time since World War II, the military imposed censorship on news stories. Many reporters were limited to coverage from Saudi Arabia; few actually saw

---

*J. Fred MacDonald, *Television and the Red Menace: The Video Road to Vietnam* (New York: Praeger), 1985.

troops on the move and rarely was combat actually observed by a reporter. Yet, the public seemed to support these restrictions on the press during the engagement.

The first three selections below address the relationship between the press and the military before and during Desert Storm (the Persian Gulf War). These include an analysis of the evolution of the rules governing media coverage of the war, a critique of the military's handling of the press corps attempting to report on the war, and one journalist's experience as a war correspondent in the Persian Gulf.

Finally, an observer who has worked on both sides of the government/press relationship looks at the broader relationship between the press and national security policymakers.

42. *PERSIAN GULF WAR RULES FOR JOURNALISTS*

The Persian Gulf War was the largest U.S. military effort since the Vietnam War and the first opportunity for both media organizations and the military to test Pentagon news coverage policies in an extended conflict. During the fall of 1990, the Pentagon drafted ground rules for press operations and assigned spaces to the Pentagon pool—the group of reporters who would have special access to combat in the earlier stages of a military operation.

The following memoranda demonstrate how these ground rules were modified before their implementation with the inception of Desert Storm on January 17, 1991.

Government press policy was not imposed upon news organizations, but resulted from press input in the policy-making process. The Pentagon sought to satisfy press concerns and impose restrictions that would result from a consensus between the military and the media.

On December 13, 1990, Assistant Secretary of Defense for Public Affairs Pete Williams issued the contingency plan for media coverage of the Persian Gulf conflict including ground rules.

DEPARTMENT OF DEFENSE, CONTINGENCY PLAN FOR MEDIA COVERAGE OF HOSTILITIES, OPERATION DESERT SHIELD, 13 DECEMBER 1990

The objective of this plan is to ensure news media access to combat areas from the onset of hostilities, or as soon thereafter as possible, in Operation DESERT SHIELD. This is a three-phased plan for exercising and deploying rotating correspondent pools, aligned with front line forces to permit combat coverage.

Each pool would consist of eighteen news media personnel: three newspaper correspondents, two wire service correspondents, two three-member television crews, one radio correspondent, one wire service photographer, one newspaper photographer, one news magazine reporter, one news magazine photographer, one Saudi reporter and one third-country reporter. Membership in the pools would be drawn from news media personnel already in Saudi Arabia.

In Phase I of the plan, which would begin immediately, the first two pools would be formed by the Joint Information Bureau in Dhahran and randomly exercised at least once every two weeks to provide training for media participants and U.S. military personnel. These pools will always be exercised simultaneously to ensure that operational security is preserved. During Phase I, the pools would familiarize themselves with troops and equipment, cover activities in the areas to which the pools are sent, and exercise their ability to file news stories from the field.

Phase II would begin by deploying the pools when hostilities are imminent, putting them in place to cover the first stages of combat. If such prepositioning is not possible, the pools would be moved forward from Dhahran as quickly as possible to the immediate area of conflict. As soon as possible, additional pools would be deployed to expand the coverage. The size of these pools will be determined by the availability of transportation and other operational factors. These additional pools could be used to fill the gaps in coverage, if the conflict is spread over a wide area. Air Force, Navy, amphibious, and logistical support units will be covered by additional smaller pools, which will be rotated to ensure continuous coverage.

Security review for all pool material would be performed at the source, where the information was gathered, and transmitted to the Joint Information Bureau at Dhahran, where it would then be available to journalists covering the operation. Ground rules would consist of those currently in effect.

Phase III would begin when open coverage is possible and would provide for unilateral coverage of activities. The pools would be disbanded and all media would operate independently, although under U.S. Central Command escort.

Proposed News Media Listing for DoD [Department of Defense] Contingency Airlift

Media Affiliation	No. of Seats
ABC-TV	10
CBS-TV	10
CNN	10
NBC-TV	10
NBC/ABC/CBS crews for local affiliates	6
AP	5
UPI	5
REUTERS	5
ABC RADIO	2
AP RADIO NETWORK	2
CBS RADIO	2
WESTWOOD RADIO	2
NATIONAL PUBLIC RADIO	2
UPI RADIO	1
UNISTAR RADIO	1
TIME	3
NEWSWEEK	3
U.S. NEWS AND WORLD REPORT	3
WASHINGTON POST	3
NEW YORK TIMES	3
LOS ANGELES TIMES	3

Proposed News Media Listing (Continued)

Media Affiliation	No. of Seats
CHICAGO TRIBUNE	3
WALL STREET JOURNAL	3
KNIGHT-RIDDER	2
BOSTON GLOBE	2
GANNETT NEWS SERVICE	2
COX NEWSPAPERS	2
HEARST NEWSPAPERS	2
SAN FRANCISCO CHRONICLE	1
NEW YORK POST	1
NEWSDAY	1
CHRISTIAN SCIENCE MONITOR	1
BALTIMORE SUN	1
WASHINGTON TIMES	1
DALLAS MORNING NEWS	1
COPLEY NEWS SERVICE	1
NEWHOUSE NEWS SERVICE	1
SCRIPPS-HOWARD	1
MILWAUKEE JOURNAL	1
CAPITAL CITIES COMMUNICATIONS, INC.	1
ARMY-NAVY-AIR FORCE TIMES	1
TOTAL:	120

OPERATION DESERT SHIELD, NEWS MEDIA GROUND RULES, 14 DECEMBER 1990

All interviews with service members will be on the record. Security at the source is the policy. In the event of hostilities, media products will be subject to security review prior to release. Interviews with pilots and aircrew members are authorized upon completion of mission; however, release of information must conform to the ground rules stated below.

All Navy embark stories will state that the report is coming "from the Persian Gulf, Red Sea or North Arabian Sea." Stories written in Saudi Arabia may be datelined Riyadh, Dhahran, or other area by general geographical description, such as "Eastern Saudi Arabia." Stories from other participating countries may be datelined from those countries only after their participation is released by DoD.

You must remain with your military escort at all times, until released, and follow instructions regarding your activities. These instructions are intended only to facilitate troop movement, ensure safety, and maintain operational security.

You must be physically fit. If, in the opinion of the commander, you are unable to withstand the rigorous conditions required to operate with his forward-deployed forces, you will be medically evacuated out of the area.

You are not authorized to carry a personal weapon.

The following categories of information are releasable:

1. Arrival of U.S. military units in the Central Command area of responsibility when officially announced. Mode of travel (sea or air), date of departure, and home station.
2. Approximate friendly force strength figures.
3. Approximate friendly casualty and POW figures by service.
4. Confirmed figures of enemy personnel killed in action (KIA) or detained for each action or operation.
5. Nonsensitive, unclassified information regarding U.S. air, ground, and sea operations, past and present.
6. Size of friendly force participating in an action or operation will be disclosed using general terms such as "multi-battalion," "naval task force," etc. Specific force or unit identification may be released when it no longer warrants security protection.
7. Identification and location of military targets and objectives previously under attack.
8. Generic description of origin of air operations, such as "land" or "carrier-based."
9. Date, time, or location of previous conventional military missions and actions as well as mission results.
10. Types of ordnance expended, in general terms.
11. Number of aerial combat or reconnaissance missions or sorties flown in theater or operational area.
12. Type of forces involved (e.g., infantry, armor, Marines, carrier battle group).
13. Weather and climate conditions.
14. Allied participation by type of operation (ships, aircraft, ground units, etc.) after approval of host nation government.
15. Conventional operation code names.
16. Names and hometowns of U.S. military units or individuals.

The following categories of information are not releasable:

1. Number of troops.
2. Number of aircraft.
3. Numbers regarding other equipment or critical supplies (e.g., artillery, tanks, landing craft, radars, trucks, water, etc.).
4. Names of military installations or specific geographic locations of U.S. military units in the Central Command area of responsibility, unless specifically released by the Department of Defense.
5. Information regarding future operations.
6. Information regarding security precautions at military installations or encampments.
7. Photography that would show level of security at military installations or encampments, especially aerial and satellite photography.
8. Photography that would reveal the name or specific location of military units or installations.
9. Rules of engagement details.
10. Information on intelligence collection activities including targets, methods, and results.
11. Information on operations underway against hostile targets.
12. Information on special operations units, unique operations methodology or tactics, for example, air operations, angles of attack, and speeds; naval tactical or evasive maneuvers, etc.
13. Information identifying postponed or cancelled operations.
14. Information on missing or downed aircraft or missing ships, while search and rescue operations are planned or underway.

15. Information on effectiveness of enemy camouflage, cover, deception, targeting, direct and indirect fire, intelligence collection, or security measures.
16. Additional guidelines may be necessary to protect tactical security.

Casualty information

1. Notification of the next of kin is extremely sensitive. By executive directive, next of kin of all military fatalities must be notified in person by an officer of the appropriate service.
2. There have been instances in which next of kin have first learned of the death or wounding of a loved one through news media reports. If casualty photographs show a recognizable face, name tag, items of jewelry or other identifying feature before the casualty's next of kin have been notified, the anguish that sudden recognition at home can cause is out of proportion to the news value of the photograph or video. Although the casualty reporting and notification system works on a priority basis, correspondents are urged to keep this problem in mind when covering action in the field. Names of casualties whose next of kin have been notified can be verified by the joint information bureaus in Riyadh or Dhahran, the appropriate public affairs office, or the office of the Assistant Secretary of Defense (Public Affairs).

—end—

The ground rules encountered immediate criticism from some press outlets. The following three responses are typical of the reaction to the announcement:

THE WASHINGTON POST

December 18, 1990

The Honorable Pete Williams
Assistant Secretary of Defense (Public Affairs)
Room 2E800
The Pentagon
Washington, D.C. 20301-1400

Dear Pete,

Thanks for the document outlining pool plans and charter status report. I think the pool plans represent some progress but am unclear if you want names submitted now for the charter. If so, please let us know.

I wish I could say thanks for your list of ground rules. I suspect that you may have heard similar assessments from some of my colleagues, to the effect that they are wildly excessive and seemingly a prescription for total control and gridlock. Listing categories of information that are releasable is a new one on me. It should be dropped. You can bet that every story written by a correspondent in-country will have a dozen things that aren't on either of your lists and so we will be subject to essentially unlimited censorship by a battalion of public affairs officers with varying degrees of understanding about the press's role in a democracy who will be acting as editors, reading their list, checking it twice and crossing things out because they don't fit clearly in your list of what is releasable.

The rules about what is not releasable also seems far too broad and are open to all sorts of excessive interpretation, in my view, by large numbers of PAOs caught in what are certain to be hectic conditions. There were very concise rules in Vietnam which, I believe, were well respected by reporters and would be again in the Gulf. Let's get this honed down to legitimate security guidelines.

Finally, the idea that in Phase III one needs a military escort at all times also goes too far. I see no need for that. It seems simply another means of controlling everything.

We should have one more meeting of the group, it seems to me, on these points. If you are open to this, let me know quickly so it can be set up. Time is short.

Thanks,

Michael Getler

HEARST NEWSPAPERS

Dec. 20, 1990

Pete Williams
Assistant Secretary of Defense
The Pentagon
Washington, D.C. 20301-1400

Dear Pete:

This is a response to your Dec. 14 memo and invitation to comment.

First, I offer my applause for your efforts to anticipate and plan for contingencies in the Persian Gulf. Later problems will be minimized by this program. Equally important, a process will have been established so that later unanticipated problems can be overcome by people working together, in good faith and with clear channels of communication.

Many aspects of your plan are excellent and, therefore, I'm going to limit my comments to areas I think should be changed.

1) I'm sorry to see on-site "security review" in your plans. As you know, when the national Pentagon pool was first launched in 1984, no such reviews were contemplated. Correspondents were to comply with the "Vietnam-era rules," which didn't require prior review; if a correspondent violated the rules, the punishment was simple, swift and effective—the loss of accreditation. Those rules won a very high degree of compliance.

Unfortunately, the practice of prior censorship has become embedded in the

Pentagon pool concept in recent years, mainly because all parties quickly recognized that the pool was reliant on military communications.

However, if you're going to have a review, experience with the Pentagon Pool has shown that an on-site commander may not be the best person to perform this duty.

We all recall the episode in the Persian Gulf when the pool was covering the July 1987 reflagging of Kuwaiti tankers; the U.S. Navy commodore in charge of the escort insisted on censoring material that in no way violated news media ground rules but, instead, merely embarrassed him.

Therefore, if the Department of Defense insists on prior review, I urge that it be handled at the Pentagon.

If you stick to on-site review, you should create an appellate process at the Pentagon where disputed material could be examined and the relevant Washington bureau chief consulted. Such a procedure evolved from the 1987 Persian Gulf pools and worked to speed the process.

2) I don't understand the need—or the practical feasibility—for Phase III escorts. If unilateral coverage becomes possible, correspondents will need to move about more freely than pool constraints permitted. In Phase III, escorted unilateral coverage is an oxymoron.

Correspondents covering Desert Shield from August to the present have complained about the DoD requirement for escorts, on the one hand, and about the lack of available escorts, on the other hand. That combination quickly shuts down any coverage other than briefing coverage.

3) The ground rules are needlessly complex and you should go back to the one-page rules previously issued for Desert Shield, which are similar to the Vietnam-era rules referred to above. I'm enclosing a copy of the one-page version.

I recommend you adopt the old axiom that, in the United States, everything is permitted except that which is prohibited. With that as a guiding light, the rules then should become a short list of "don'ts," similar to the one-page version. The forbidden information outlined in #1-16 in the non-releasable section is similar to the Vietnam-era rules.

The danger of trying to spell out in detail what can be released is that there will be instances where a particular fact isn't prohibited from being released but it also isn't covered by one of the can-be-released rules. The result: gridlocked copy that doesn't move. Don't tell us what we can do; tell us what we can't do.

Again, thanks for responding to our needs. I look forward to working with you on further refinements.

Sincerely,

Charles J. Lewis
Bureau Chief

Newsday's *bureau chief responded not to differ with the nature of the rules, but to take issue with the allocation of space in the press pool. He argued* Newsday *deserved two slots because it has made a "major commitment" to coverage of the conflict. Other organizations made similar requests, although most were unsuccessful.*

December 18, 1990

Mr. Pete Williams
Assistant Secretary of Defense
The Pentagon
Washington, D.C. 20301-1400

Dear Pete:

I have received and reviewed your December 14, 1990, memorandum concerning Persian Gulf pools and the C-141 flight in the event of hostilities. While I salute you and your staff for the time and effort you have devoted to this project, I feel compelled to appeal for reconsideration of the decision to allocate only one seat on the C-141 to Newsday.

Newsday has made a major commitment to coverage of the Persian Gulf crisis, with at least one reporter present in Saudi Arabia since soon after the deployment of U.S. forces there. I believe our commitment has equalled or exceeded some newspapers on the list that were granted two or three seats on the flight. In addition, Newsday's circulation far exceeds that of several newspapers ahead of us on the list. With the newspaper shake-out in New York, our daily circulation now approaches one million—and on Sundays exceeds that level.

For these reasons, I request that Newsday be allocated at least two seats on the C-141. If you have questions or need more information please call me or our deputy bureau chief, Mary Leonard, or contact us by fax on (202) 393-7043.

We look forward to hearing from you soon.

Sincerely,
Gaylord Shaw

On December 24, Williams called a meeting of the Washington bureau chiefs of Pentagon correspondents for January 4, 1991, to air their complaints about the DoD ground rules for news coverage of the war. Three days after the meeting, Williams sent a memo to the press corps announcing the changes in the ground rules. In the memo, Williams notes the changes in the ground rules reflecting the criticisms received by press representatives, such as those from the Washington Post *and Hearst Newspapers. Also, the allocation of press pool seats was altered to give* Newsday *two slots.*

ASSISTANT SECRETARY OF DEFENSE

January 7, 1991

MEMORANDUM

To: Washington Bureau Chiefs of the Pentagon Press Corps
From: Pete Williams
Re: Ground rules and flight for auxiliary staff in the event of hostilities in the Persian Gulf

Thank you for attending our meeting last Friday. As in the past, your comments were valuable and appreciated. I believe we share the common goal of working out a system under which information will be disseminated to the American people without jeopardizing operations or endangering the lives of U.S. service members.

The overwhelming view expressed during the meeting was that the ground rules should be brief and clear in order to be effective. We agree and have boiled them down to one page (copy attached). We adopted the suggestions many of you made and now list only that information which should not be revealed. The second page of the attachment contains guidelines to follow, which are intended to meet the specific operational environment of the Persian Gulf.

You will note that we eliminated many of the earlier proposed ground rules, especially those which would have failed the critical test for combat ground rules: whether that information would jeopardize the operation, endanger friendly forces, or be of use to the enemy. As many of you noted, while every military operation has unique characteristics, past experience shows that reporters understand their heavy responsibility in covering combat. In the end, it is that professionalism upon which we will depend.

I am still working with the Saudi embassy to obtain visas for your people who may go over on the Air Force plane. As soon as I have the details worked out, I will pass them to you. In the meantime, we need the information listed below as soon as possible for the staff members you wish to send on the C-141.

    a. Name of news organization
    b. Full billing address of news organization
    c. Fax number of news organization
    d. Full name(s) of representative(s)
    e. Social security number(s)
    f. Passport number(s)
    g. Names and home, business, cellular (if applicable) and beeper phone numbers of two people (primary and backup) who will serve as your points of contact for activation of the flight. . . .

Thank you for your continuing suggestions and comments.

OPERATION DESERT SHIELD, GROUND RULES,
7 JAN 91

The following information should not be reported because its publication or broadcast could jeopardize operations and endanger lives:

(1) For U.S. or coalition units, specific numerical information on troop strength, aircraft, weapons systems, on-hand equipment, or supplies (e.g., artillery, tanks, radars, missiles, trucks, water), including amounts of ammunition or fuel moved by support units or on hand in combat units. Unit size may be described in general terms such as "company-size," "multi-battalion," "multi-division," "naval task force," and "carrier battle group." Number or amount of equipment and supplies may be described in general terms such as "large," "small," or "many."

(2) Any information that reveals details of future plans, operations, or strikes, including postponed or cancelled operations.

(3) Information or photography, including serial and satellite pictures, that would reveal the specific location of military forces or show the level of security at military installations or encampments. Locations may be described as follows: all Navy embark stories can identify the ship upon which embarked as a dateline and will state that the report is coming "from the Persian Gulf," "Red Sea," or "North Arabian Sea." Stories written in Saudi Arabia may be datelined, "Eastern Saudi Arabia," "Near the Kuwaiti border," etc. For specific countries outside Saudi Arabia, stories will state that the report is coming from the Persian Gulf region unless DoD has publicly acknowledged participation by that country.

(4) Rules of engagement details.

(5) Information on intelligence collection activities, including targets, methods, and results.

(6) During an operation, specific information on friendly force troop movements, tactical deployments, and dispositions that would jeopardize operational security and lives. This would include unit designations, names of operations, and size of friendly forces involved, until released by CENTCOM.

(7) Identification of mission aircraft points of origin, other than as land or carrier based.

(8) Information on the effectiveness or ineffectiveness of enemy camouflage, cover, deception, targeting, direct and indirect fire, intelligence collection, or security measures.

(9) Specific identifying information on missing or downed aircraft or ships while search and rescue operations are planned or underway.

(10) Special operations forces' methods, unique equipment or tactics.

(11) Specific operating methods and tactics, (e.g., air ops angles of attack or speeds, or naval tactics and evasive maneuvers). General terms such as "low" or "fast" may be used.

(12) Information on operational or support vulnerabilities that could be used

against U.S. forces, such as details of major battle damage or major personnel losses of specific U.S. or coalition units, until that information no longer provides tactical advantage to the enemy and is, therefore, released by CENTCOM. Damage and casualties may be described as "light," "moderate," or "heavy."

GUIDELINES FOR NEWS MEDIA

News media personnel must carry and support any personal and professional gear they take with them, including protective cases for professional equipment, batteries, cables, converters, etc.

Night Operations—Light discipline restrictions will be followed. The only approved light source is a flashlight with a red lens. No visible light source, including flash or television lights, will be used when operating with forces at night unless specifically approved by the on-scene commander.

You must remain with your military escort at all times, until released, and follow their instructions regarding your activities. These instructions are not intended to hinder your reporting. They are intended to facilitate movement, ensure safety, and protect operational security.

For news media personnel participating in designated CENTCOM Media Pools:

(1) Upon registering with the JIB [Joint Information Bureau], news media should contact their respective pool coordinator for explanation of pool operations.

(2) If you are unable to withstand the rigorous conditions required to operate with the forward-deployed forces, you will be medically evacuated out of the area.

(3) Security at the source will be the policy. In the event of hostilities, pool products will be subject to security review prior to release to determine if they contain information that would jeopardize an operation or the security of U.S. or coalition forces. Material will not be withheld just because it is embarrassing or contains criticism. The public affairs officer on the scene will conduct the security review. However, if a conflict arises, the product will be expeditiously sent to JIB Dhahran for review by the JIB Director. If no agreement can be reached, the product will be expeditiously forwarded to OASD(PA) for review with the appropriate bureau chief.

Casualty information, because of concern of the notification of the next of kin, is extremely sensitive. By executive directive, next of kin of all military fatalities must be notified in person by a uniformed member of the appropriate service. There have been instances in which the next of kin have first learned of the death or wounding of a loved one through the news media. The problem is particularly difficult for visual media. Casualty photographs showing a recognizable face, name tag, or other identifying feature or item should not be used before the next of kin have been notified. The anguish that sudden recognition at home can cause far outweighs the news value of the photograph, film or videotape. Names of casualties whose next of kin have been notified can be verified through the JIB Dhahran.

Proposed News Media Listing for DoD Contingency Airlift

MEDIA AFFILIATION	NO. OF SEATS
ABC-TV	10
CBS-TV	10
CNN	10
NBC-TV	10
NBC/ABC/CBS crews for local affiliates	6
AP	5
UPI	5
REUTERS	5
ABC RADIO	2
AP RADIO NETWORK	2
CBS RADIO	2
WESTWOOD RADIO	2
NATIONAL PUBLIC RADIO	2
UPI RADIO	1
UNISTAR RADIO	1
VOICE OF AMERICA	1
TIME	3
NEWSWEEK	3
U.S. NEWS AND WORLD REPORT	3
BUSINESS WEEK	1
WASHINGTON POST	3
NEW YORK TIMES	3
LOS ANGELES TIMES	3
CHICAGO TRIBUNE	3
WALL STREET JOURNAL	3
KNIGHT-RIDDER	3
BOSTON GLOBE	2
GANNETT NEWS SERVICE	2
USA TODAY	2
COX NEWSPAPERS	2
HEARST NEWSPAPERS	2
SAN FRANCISCO CHRONICLE	1
NEW YORK POST	1
NEWSDAY	2
CHRISTIAN SCIENCE MONITOR	1
BALTIMORE SUN	1
WASHINGTON TIMES	1
DALLAS MORNING NEWS	1
COPLEY NEWS SERVICE	1
NEWHOUSE NEWS SERVICE	1
SCRIPPS-HOWARD	1
MILWAUKEE JOURNAL	1
CAPITAL CITIES COMMUNICATIONS, INC.	1
ARMY-NAVY-AIR FORCE TIMES	1
TOTAL:	126

The ground rules were changed slightly following the 7 January draft, but the changes urged by the press were not affected. The final rules constituted a compromise between Pentagon officials and journalists.

43. THE CENSORED WAR

Ad Hoc Media Group

Many news organizations were still unhappy with the security restrictions and their implementation at the height of the Gulf War. Several major news media organizations, including the major TV networks, the *Washington Post*, the *New York Times*, the *Wall Street Journal*, and the Associated Press sponsored a joint review of the Pentagon's handling of the press during the war. The following selection includes a statement they issued listing their principles for military–press relations during wartime and a report describing their differences with the Pentagon over specific Pentagon practices toward the press during the engagement. The statement and report were sent to Secretary of Defense Dick Cheney.

The following excerpt is this group's perspective on the Pentagon's press policies at the height of the Persian Gulf War and will likely become the news media's starting point in negotiations with the Pentagon over coverage of the next U.S. military intervention.

STATEMENT OF PRINCIPLES

We believe these are the principles that should govern future arrangements for news coverage of the United States military in combat:

1. Independent reporting will be the principal means of coverage of U.S. military operations.

2. The use of pools should be limited to the kind envisioned by the Sidle Commission. Pools are meant to bring a representative group of journalists along with the first elements of any major U.S. military operation. These pools should last no longer than the very first stages of a deployment—the initial 24 hours, to 36 hours—and should be disbanded rapidly in favor of independent coverage. Pools are not to serve as the standard means of covering U.S. forces.

3. Some pools may be appropriate for events or in places where open coverage is physically impossible. But the existence of such special-purpose pools will not cancel the principle of independent coverage. If news organizations are able to cover pooled events independently, they may do so.

4. Journalists in a combat zone will be credentialed by the U.S. military and will be required to abide by a clear set of military security guidelines that protect U.S. forces and their operations. Violation of the guidelines can result in suspension of credentials or revocation of credentials and expulsion from the combat zone.

5. Journalists will be provided access to all major units.

6. Military public affairs officers should act as liaisons but should not interfere with the reporting process.

7. News material—words and pictures—will not be subject to prior military security review.

8. The military will be responsible for the transportation of pools. Field commanders should be instructed to permit journalists to ride on military vehicles and aircraft whenever feasible.

9. The military will supply PAOs with timely, secure, compatible transmission facilities for pool material and will make these facilities available whenever possible for filing independent coverage. In cases when government facilities are unavailable, journalists will, as always, file by any other means available and will not be prevented from doing so. The military will not ban communications systems operated by news organizations.

10. These principles will apply as well to the operations of the standing DoD National Media Pool system.

(Adopted by Ad Hoc Media Group, June 1991)

PROBLEMS OF NEWS COVERAGE IN THE PERSIAN GULF WAR

INDEPENDENT REPORTING: PREVENTION OF

For those American reporters who sought to operate 'unilaterally' during the Gulf war, meaning outside the restricted pool system, their experiences seemed to mirror both the gratification that comes from independent reporting and the worst fears of a reporter in a democracy.

These often gave their readers or viewers the first and best accounts of important milestones in a war, including the battle at Khafji and the entry of allied ground forces into Kuwait City. In doing so, they experienced harassment, interference and sometimes detention from American officers under orders from the high command.

During the battle at Khafji, pool reporters were not sent to the scene for at least 18 hours and even then were kept in rear areas. Associated Press reporter John King, who slipped into the town earlier operating independently, provided eyewitness reports about what was happening. Afterward, King says, several things happened: "Col. William Mulvey (chief of the JIB at Dhahran) gave the Saudis a memo listing eight people (including myself and two AP colleagues) who had been in Khafji or other 'restricted areas.' The Saudis said they were encouraged to pull a few visas to make a point. The memo was withdrawn after protest."

Then, King says, "CentCom strengthened its orders to roadblock guards . . . to turn back anyone carrying press credentials." Later, "I was forcibly detained on the north-south highway by Saudi troops at the direction of a Marine lieutenant." King was detained again, briefly, by the 7th Engineers after stopping to ask questions near the Saudi–Kuwait border.

"There were so many verbal warnings from Mulvey to the unilaterals," says

King, "that another violation could land you on a plane home. He suggested at one point that if I was detained by the US military, I could be held through the war and released afterwards."

AP reporter Fred Bayles was also detained by another US unit in the Hafr al Batin area and AP's Mort Rosenblum and agency photographer Tannen Maury were "busted" by the Army, as Rosenblum describes it, while seeking out the 24th Division "after the JIB said it would not object if field commanders invited reporters to join them."

After the AP pair spotted a colonel from the road and asked him to signal ahead to the division PAO, they were ordered instead into an MP guard house and told to wait for corps PAOs to arrive. When the AP journalists said they wanted to leave to go back to Dhahran, they were told they could not and were "detained." When they said they were leaving, the MP lieutenant "said he'd send vehicles in pursuit."

Washington Post reporter Guy Gugliotta and five colleagues, frustrated by "the virtual non-existence of usable pool reports from the town of Khafji," set out as unilaterals, made contact with US Marines three kilometers outside of town and were conducting interviews with the commander, until a public affairs officer with a pool arrived in the scene. The PAO "told the colonel he wasn't allowed to talk to us" and another PAO "began copying our names—notifying us to leave and threatening to turn us over to Saudi soldiers if we didn't get out of the area," Gugliotta reports.

Newsweek contributing writer, retired Army Col. David Hackworth, reported returning from a unilateral trip to a Special Forces unit with photographer Mark Peters, who took a picture through a car window, "and US troops fixed bayonets and charged us. I had more guns pointed at me by Americans or Saudis who were into controlling the press than in all my years of actual combat," he wrote.

Chris Hedges of the *New York Times*, who operated for two months as a unilateral, writes in the current issue of the *Columbia Journalism Review* of an incident in which he stopped to talk to some officers who ran a field hospital. They then "assigned an armed escort to me and I was driven to the headquarters of the Seventh Corps, some ten miles away . . . and turned over to a Captain Miller. The captain said I was under detention," Hedges reports.

There were scores of other incidents, many of them not involving detention but still, in their seeming triviality, reflecting the dedication to total control of the press by those giving orders and the mindset of many PAOs in carrying them out.

Ed Offley is a military writer for the *Seattle Post-Intelligencer*, a paper that covers Ft. Lewis, Wash., whose commander, Lt. Gen. Calvin A.H. Waller, was sent to Saudi Arabia as Deputy Commander of all U.S. forces there. Offley reports that Waller promised an interview. But when Offley arrived in Saudi, "I attempted for four days to send the message. Several months later, back in Washington State, Waller asked: 'Where were you? Why didn't you get in touch?'"

Stephanie Glass of the *San Antonio Light* reports that after leaving Saudi, she stopped at Little Rissington, England, to see what thousands of San Antonio active duty and reserve Air Force members were doing at a stand-by hospital there. Days of calling in advance yielded what she thought was decent access to the hospital and a choice of whom she wanted to interview.

"When I arrived, the public affairs officer took me to a ward with no patients and brought in five people for me to speak with. He never left the room and abruptly ended the interviews 45 minutes later," Glass writes. "I was not allowed to see any of the 20 other buildings, the hospital, the living quarters, not even the mess hall. I was told that I could speak with the commander, a privilege in their eyes."

Joan Lowy of Scripps Howard News Service, who operated most of the time outside the pool system, reports that the JIB at Dhahran "refused on several occasions to give me a Geneva convention card," which identifies a journalist as a noncombatant to unfriendly forces. The JIB officers argued that no coverage was allowed except pool coverage. Therefore, these cards were withheld precisely from the people who probably needed them the most, even though the JIB officers were well aware that much independent reporting was going on.

Some of the reporters who bucked the system often found allied forces more cooperative than the Americans. ABC News correspondent Forrest Sawyer, for example, was probably the only U.S. journalist to report and record pictures during a bombing raid—with the Royal Saudi Air Force on a Tornado bombing mission.

Sawyer and CBS News correspondent Bob McKeown also provided the first news and pictures during the liberation of Kuwait by operating outside the pool system and by having their own transmission equipment with them, which reporters operating within the pool system were not allowed to carry.

For field reporters in the Gulf, and especially those who sought to operate independently (outside of the restricted pool system), there were two general experiences: (1) Soldiers and many company and field grade officers welcomed press coverage, were not afraid of it, and tried to help reporters. (2) But these officers were often ordered not to be cooperative, indeed to detain and expel independent reporters, by the military high command and public affairs apparatus.

"Unilateral coverage on the battlefield should not be prohibited," writes Molly Moore of the *Washington Post*. "Many commanders were willing to allow reporters to tag along with their outfits, but were ordered not to do so by higher command."

"The level of cooperation from military personnel generally was instinctively high, from enlisted men to generals," adds Edward Cody, also of *The Post*. "The problem was they had been told by their commander (Gen. Schwarzkopf) that cooperation was to be limited, so they obeyed him and not their instincts."

MILITARY ESCORTS: THE BIG CHILL

At 3 p.m. on January 16, the crew of the USS John F. Kennedy was told over the ship's loudspeakers that the war would begin shortly after midnight. Carol Morello of the *Philadelphia Inquirer*, a pool reporter on the JFK, said, "There was euphoria about the ship. I began to cover it."

Crew members jabbed fists into the air and shouted fighting words. The scene was apparently too bloodthirsty for the PAO accompanying Morello and her pool mates; he quickly directed them below decks, where they were confined in a compartment for more than an hour. The PAO explained that he wanted to organize an "orderly" tour of the ship.

"I complained loudly and repeatedly that history was being made and we were there to record it," Morello said. "To no avail. By the time he let us out and led us as a group on a tour of the ship, the euphoria had been replaced by a determined preparation for war."

From the very start of pool operations in Saudi Arabia to the day the war ended, journalists were under the around-the-clock escort of public affairs officers whose mission, the Pentagon said, was to facilitate news coverage.

A handful of the PAOs went to extraordinary lengths to help reporters get the story—and to get the story transmitted rapidly back from the field. But many others saw their duty not as facilitating but controlling. They denied access, tried to prevent servicemen and women from speaking candidly and pressured reporters to avoid the negative and emphasize the positive.

Newspeople appreciated the dedication of PAOs like Capt. Kim Wortham of the Idaho National Guard, who risked his life by driving through dust storms and a mine-strewn battlefield to help the Associated Press and *The Wall Street Journal* file for the next day's papers. They appreciated PAOs at a field hospital who worked rapidly to inform the next of kin of wounded Marines so that stories could be dispatched quickly.

But newspeople also found themselves contending repeatedly with escorts who stepped in front of a camera to stop an interview, stared menacingly at GIs making unfavorable comments, locked up reporters to prevent them from witnessing spontaneous excitement at the start of the war and jawboned about the content of stories.

The interference had nothing to do with operational security. It had everything to do with sanitizing the nature of war and polishing the image of the military.

These experiences—shared by every type of news medium, with every service and in every part of the war theater—make it clear that we cannot again be subjected to a system that requires all newsgathering to be performed under the control of military monitors.

After the pool system was established but before the war began, public affairs escorts seemed especially aggressive about asserting authority over reporters and their work.

As Frank Bruni of the *Detroit Free Press* put it, "The instructions from the top were to watch us carefully, not help us."

Two reporters—Susan Sachs of *Newsday* and Carol Rosenberg of the *Miami Herald*—were barred from a Marine unit after their escorts complained that they asked questions forbidden by military guidelines, rolled their eyes and sighed at answers and were rude to their hosts.

Albert Hunt of *The Wall Street Journal* said that PAOs with his reporters several times stepped into the middle of interviews to stare down military people saying things the PAOs didn't like. "It was as if the escorts were following a policy for which they had been trained," Hunt says. "We and other reporters expressed outrage at this, and after a while the more obvious attempts at intimidation seemed to stop."

But the efforts to control interchanges between reporters and GIs never stopped.

Edie Lederer of the Associated Press said that Capt. Gary Caruthers, deputy PAO at the Al Kharg air base in Saudi Arabia, sat in on every interview, "facing the person being interviewed and shaking his head yes or no as to whether a question should be answered."

Other PAOs carried written advisories they would read to troops before letting reporters ask questions. AP's Fred Bayles said these advisories came to be known among newspeople as the "Miranda warning."

When reporters were able to speak unmonitored with military personnel, the service people understood the difference between legitimate security concerns and image issues. Some said they had been instructed not to talk to reporters, period.

Glass encountered one serviceman who told her, "his officer said that if he did not have anything nice to say, he shouldn't say anything at all."

Just as PAO escorts tried to control interviews, they tried to restrict what reporters could witness, even when operational security was in no way involved.

After the cease-fire, when security was obviously not a concern, [Frank] Bruni attempted to write a story about the only fatality suffered by the Third Armored Cavalry Regiment. With the war over, a young soldier had picked up an unexploded American cluster bomblet, which blew up and decapitated him. Bruni's escort said a story about the incident would be inappropriate. The unit refused to allow him to go to the scene.

Attempts by PAOs to control the content of stories were common.

Morello said her Navy PAO once tried to get her to delete from a story quotes from an on-the-record briefing. She declined but paid the price of a long delay while the story was cleared by the admiral.

Time magazine's Dick Thompson said he interviewed a Marine pilot who had bombed a column of Iraqi vehicles parked at the roadside during prayer time. Thompson said his escort, Maj. John McLean, tried to talk the pool reporters out of including the incident in their report for fear of offending Muslim members of the coalition.

"McLean never threatened to censor the pool report," Thompson said. "But for about 20 minutes he did try to convince us that it was in the best interest of (the) war effort that we drop the prayer bombing reference. This seemed to be a more insidious kind of censorship, trying to get us to self-censor. In the end, we agreed that the information should be in the report and it appeared that way."

That kind of pressure, applied repeatedly by many PAOs, amounted to the real censorship of war coverage. Reporters sometimes felt trapped in circumstances that required them to go along, at least to some degree, in order to keep whatever limited access they had.

In some cases, reporters were hampered by turf disputes between PAOs.

Edward Cody of the *Washington Post* said, "Most escorts were convinced that the pool in their custody was to cover only, repeat only, the unit to which they were assigned. Some escorts were ordering other escorts to leave areas with their charges because they were not assigned to the right unit for the area in question."

As Cody noted, "Military custody means being subjected to military attitudes, in this case unit integrity. . . . Soldiers did not understand what was needed (by reporters) or how to get it done."

Instead of facilitating the flow of news stories, many PAOs prevented it. They refused to allow reporters to use readily available telephones. They refused to press for rapid transportation of copy. They subjected stories to multiple levels of clearance in violation of the military's own guidelines for security review.

Molly Moore of the *Washington Post* noted that, no surprise to newspeople, "Some of the most successful pools in this operation had no PAOs with them for various logistical reasons and had excellent relationships directly with commanders.

"Reporters assigned to the Army Tiger Brigade, for example, were PAO-less for logistical reasons and ended up with some of the best access of anyone."

That access, it must be added, produced news stories without endangering operational security.

ACCESS: LIMITED, RESTRICTED, DELAYED

By controlling what journalists saw, and when they saw it, the military exercised great power to shape and manage the news. Again and again, this power was used to prevent coverage of newsworthy events on a timely basis.

A glaring example occurred on February 26, when a SCUD missile killed 28 U.S. soldiers bivouacked in Dhahran. Although the JIB and media were headquartered only several miles away—and a "quick reaction pool" was standing by—coverage was restricted and impeded. The pool was never deployed. No military officer in Dhahran was authorized to comment. Official information came from Riyadh, 150 miles away.

Denying access was standard procedure when casualties were involved. On January 29, when seven U.S. Marines were killed by "friendly fire" on a light armored vehicle, no coverage was permitted. Requests for a pool to be taken to the scene were refused.

On one occasion when a pool with the Army happened into the vicinity where a soldier had been killed, coverage was prevented. The media were also barred from the battlefield memorial service, even though soldiers welcomed reporters to be present.

Anything resembling a religious observance was usually vetoed for news coverage. "The first Sunday after the war broke out, I saw a bunch of Marines listening to 'Onward Christian Soldiers' on a boombox," said ABC News correspondent Linda Patillo. "It was a story they wouldn't let me do because of Saudi sensitivities." On frequent occasion, "Saudi sensitivities" superseded First Amendment freedoms of speech and religion.

Other "sensitivities" blocked other legitimate stories. No coverage was ever permitted of B-52 bombing missions despite repeated requests. In fact, the request was approved by Assistant Secretary Williams, but the Air Force command refused. On frequent occasions, access granted by one layer of authority was denied by another.

Pools operating in the field were restricted to specific units and not allowed to travel to nearby units even for breaking news. The battle of Khafji was belatedly covered from afar by one pool assigned to the Marines, although a second Marine pool nearby was kept away from the action.

During the air war and westward shift of ground forces, there was only a handful of ground pools deployed, and most of them were too small to adequately cover their units.

There were no pools with the 3rd Armored, 24th Infantry, 101st Airborne, 1st Infantry Division and several other major ground units until just before the ground war. As we argued for more spots, Army Lt. Col. Larry Icenogle said it best: "I've got 26 people trying to cover 250,000 ground troops. You don't have to tell me it's ridiculous."

Even when there was pool "access," there were limitations. The typical ground-pool for a division was eight people. The pools often were kept in the rear with commanders, limiting access to troops.

Logistics played a role in blocking access. Because the military did not dedicate any transportation to the pools it organized, delays were commonplace. It took the military two days to transport a pool to the scene of the Persian Gulf oil spill, a 200-mile drive on paved roads from Dhahran.

Transportation and coordination limited timely reporting on land and sea. No reporters witnessed the firing of 16-inch guns on the battleship Missouri. It took two days to get Navy pictures back to Dhahran.

In virtually none of the incidents where access was denied or delayed were requirements of national security at issue. Instead, the military made decisions based on its notion of what it wanted covered and what it did not. On a scale unprecedented in our history, politics and propaganda became criteria in news coverage of the U.S. at war. "Sensitivities" governed access decisions, with the military acting as news assignment editors for the nation.

SECURITY REVIEW: ONE WEAPON THE PENTAGON DIDN'T NEED

There were fewer complaints from journalists about the "security review" process in the Gulf War than about other methods of control employed by the Pentagon. For one thing, reporters in this war, like their counterparts in other wars, took seriously the Pentagon's legitimate operational security guidelines and did not violate them. Out of 1,351 pool reports filed, only four went to the Pentagon for security review; and of those only one was changed.

Still, despite the pool system's extraordinary control of what reporters did and filed, many reports from front-line units were delayed and/or recommended for censorship by on-scene PAOs. That JIB officers refused in most cases to go along with those recommendations was small consolation, given the transmission delays that resulted. These delays for security review often took days instead of minutes or hours.

Moreover, the PAOs all too often sought to edit not so much security review as the "prior restraint" imposed by the entire pool system, beginning with the DoD National Media Pool and continuing with the local pools that actually covered the war. Indeed, the pool system employed in this war was itself a form of censorship.

Following are some examples of security-review problems:

• Ed Offley of the *Seattle Post-Intelligencer,* a reporter who has specialized in military and defense issues since 1981, learned during an interview with an electronics warfare officer that the EF-111 aircraft carries 10 "exciters" with which the pilot may jam enemy radars and radios. Told by a PAO that this information was classified, Offley deleted it. The next day, he happened to read an Air Force press release mentioning that the EF-111 carries "exciters."

• Chuck Lewis of Hearst Newspapers and others encountered what Lewis calls a "layering effect" imposed by the Army in VII Corps. Copy would be reviewed by the PAO of the 2nd Armored Division, then by the 1st Infantry Division, then by VII Corps' "notorious" Major Cook and finally by the Dhahran JIB. The process added days to an already unacceptably slow process.

• Nicholas Horrock of the *Chicago Tribune* encountered a lack of uniform standards in the security-review process. Unit identifications would be allowed in one pool report and deleted from another without explanation or apparent reason.

• Sometimes violations of the guidelines were encouraged by the military for what turned out later to have been attempts to use the press to disseminate disinformation. For example, one pool report, filed on Feb. 17, described in some detail how the Marines would conduct amphibious warfare against the Iraqis. On its face, this kind of information violated the ground rules, yet it had been provided by officers with the troops and was cleared by the censors. Only after the war was effectively over did Gen. Schwarzkopf explain that the press had been deliberately used to mislead the Iraqis.

• One story submitted by the *Wall Street Journal*'s John Fialka was so heavily marked up by the time it reached the JIB that Lt. Col. Larry Icenogle believed VII Corps wanted the entire report deleted. On more sober analysis, however, the problem was solved at the JIB with the insertion of a single word—"perhaps." But Fialka's story had been delayed for three days.

• Even when there was no actual censorship there were other forms of suppression. John Balzar of the L.A. *Times* wrote a vivid description of how a helicopter attack on Iraqi ground troops looked through night-vision glasses. Among other things, Balzar reported how "one (Iraqi) dropped, writhed on the ground, and struggled to his feet" only to be hit with another burst from the chopper that "tore him apart." None of this was deleted. Balzar, however, was not allowed to see much action again.

In the end, the combination of security review and the use of the pool system as a form of censorship made the Gulf War the most undercovered major conflict in modern American history. In a free society, there is simply no place for such overwhelming control by the government.

44. THE POOL

William Boot

William Boot provides a firsthand account of a journalist's experience with the Pentagon news pool during the Persian Gulf War. Boot's story recounts how military public relations officers tried to shape his story by suggestion. In other cases, stories were inexplicably lost by the military during transmittal to the states or while undergoing security review.

William Boot is the pen name of Christopher Hanson, a contributing editor of the *Columbia Journalism Review* and the Washington correspondent for the *Seattle Post-Inquirer.*

I was a combat pool correspondent, one of the happy few who helped provide America with what Pentagon spokesman Pete Williams called "the best war coverage we've ever had." True, most of us never saw a battle and few of us even saw a dead Iraqi soldier, but at least we got to be part of the big adventure. True, many of our dispatches never made it back to our news organizations, but at least we got to write them. True, military officers controlled our every movement, but that, after all, may be why Williams bestowed his glowing praise, and pool veterans should not take compliments lightly. To help put Williams's tribute in perspective, here is a day-by-day account of what it was like to cover a ground war under the pool system.

February 19—Dhahran International Hotel. Correspondents line up at a U.S. military supply room, hoping to draw the helmets, flak vests, chemical suits, and other gear required to protect them in the field.

"If you can get the gear yourself [that is, from an independent source] you're good to go," says a supply sergeant.

"So it's available independently?" asks a reporter.

"No, only from us." Catch-22.

At the last minute, an army officer announces that the rules have been relaxed: full protective trappings are not required now. Any gear unavailable today will be issued in the field.

February 20—I board a transport plane for the army's Seventh Corps headquarters minus rubber anti-chemical boots—an essential item in the Desert Storm wardrobe. Upon arrival, we are told by a spokesman, Major David Cook, that Seventh Corps is, in fact, *not* prepared to supply missing gear. Anti-chemical boots are in especially short supply.

February 21—With a reporter from the *New York Times* and an AP correspondent, I embark in a Humvee truck on a lurching two-hour journey across the desert.

We are headed for the Iraqi border to visit the Second Armored Calvary Regiment, which we are told will spearhead the most significant American ground assault of the war. The reporters ride in back. In front are two military escorts Captain John Koko, thirty-three, and Sergeant Roy Botkins, twenty-nine, both reservists from Kentucky. Each carries a loaded M-16 rifle and a box of Cracker Jacks. Koko, a fount of wisecracks, is gung-ho about the profession of arms, but contemptuous of his current assignment as a "P.A.O. [public affairs officer] puke." He sings snatches of the Army recruiting jingle, "Be all that you can be."

Under canvas later on, Koko discusses his unique approach to public affairs at the front. "My job is rumor control," he says, and then gives his interpretation of that duty: he controls rumors by spreading them himself. It's all part of the continuing effort to relieve boredom. Koko seems especially proud of his part in spreading one rumor: a soldier uses a gas mask pouch as a pillow, but as he shifts position during the night the pressure of his head accidentally triggers an antidote syringe needle in the pouch. It punctures the soldier's neck, killing him instantly.

Koko—who stands about six foot four and once served as an Army Ranger—is now in high gear, regaling us with tales of how he has been patrolling Seventh Corps territory, apprehending reporters who had made their way to the front without permission. He dutifully, if reluctantly, stops Americans, but truly gets a charge out of busting French and especially Italian reporters, because, in his view, neither country is contributing enough to the war effort.

Ironically, news organizations themselves may have done even more than enforcers like Koko to thwart reporters trying to cover the war. The Pentagon, shrewdly enough, had delegated to U.S. news media in Dhahran many decisions on who got pool slots. In early January, the "sacred sixteen"—the *New York Times*, the *Washington Post*, Cox, Gannett, the *Wall Street Journal*, and other papers that had kept reporters in Saudi Arabia continuously since late 1990 voted to keep pool slots for themselves. Bitter fights with newcomers resulted. (Eventually, the Defense Department created new pool slots to accommodate some of the newcomers.) All told, reporters seemed to spend more energy fighting each other than fighting pool restrictions.

February 22—At breakfast I seek soldiers' reactions to the latest reports that Iraq has offered to withdraw from Kuwait, raising last-minute talk of a peace settlement. One soldier tells me he would just as soon go ahead with the ground offensive because he has just had his head shaved and doesn't want to be seen back home until it grows out. At that point, Koko comes up and gently rebukes me for talking to troops without a military escort.

Next, we get a lesson in just how well the military's communication system for field reporters actually works. With Koko supervising, we three reporters interview the only woman in camp, a sergeant whose classified intelligence duties make her the female closest to Iraqi lines. She is tough and articulate and it all makes for a nice story. The only problem is that, after I write my piece and send it back to headquarters in a Humvee, it disappears. It never reaches Dhahran, never is issued as a pool report, never gets to my editors. (The *Wall Street Journal*'s John Fialka tells me later that my experience is typical—"Seventh Corps was simply a black hole.")

February 23—Word is that the Second Armored Cavalry does not want reporters along on the ground offensive. But the regimental spokesman, Captain Bob Dobson, says this restriction applies only to TV crews. "He can take one pencil" and agrees to take me, but only if I agree to his terms—I can go only where Dobson goes and must never venture out by myself. No other escorts are available. Koko and Botkins will be returning to headquarters. Reluctantly, I agree to the terms. The alternative is sitting out the war in the rear. Captain Dobson is now my assignment editor.

February 24—At dawn, the Second Armored Cavalry convoys form up and move out across the misty desert into Iraq. I ride with Dobson, twenty-nine, a bright, portly West Pointer with a passion for junk food, who gives me a running commentary on the regiment and its role in the war.

Later, we are ordered to don our chemical-weapons protective suits (I have by now managed to scrounge a pair of the special boots). I then write a story in which soldiers react to the prospect of gas warfare and—almost to a man—urge nuclear retaliation if Iraq uses chemicals. No couriers are available. We have outstripped our lines of communication. The only option for filing stories is the regiment's "E-munication" computer system, which in theory can send articles to headquarters via satellite. But the system is on the blink, and remains so for days. My newspaper does not get this dispatch until February 28, when it is far too stale to use.

February 25—A day of massive prisoner-taking and sporadic fighting, including a small engagement just a few hundred yards off to the right of the regimental headquarters column. Dramatic stuff for a newcomer to war, and I write a colorful piece on taking prisoners. Of course, it cannot be filed due to technical difficulties.

At one point, Dobson's public affairs vehicle is bouncing along a rutted track, past a cluster of Iraqis who have just surrendered. They wave and smile. We wave and smile. Then the Humvee hits a huge bump, spilling a good part of its load in front of the Iraqis. It is hard not to feel embarrassed.

The convoy lurches on. I ask Dobson if we can break away from the headquarters detachment and join one of the regiment's squadrons of M-1 tanks and Bradley Fighting Vehicles, which are seeing the real action up ahead. He says he'll try to accommodate me eventually, but can't promise anything. We drive on into the night. At last the convoy halts and circles up. The soldiers dig in as American tank cannons and artillery thunder away nearby. I spend the night sitting up in the Humvee, horrified that the war might be over before I can transmit even one good story.

February 26—A day of excitement, confusion, and frustration. Reports reach headquarters by radio that the regiment's armored squadrons up ahead are engaging Republican Guard tank units. The regiment's assignment, says Dobson, is to locate the main elements of the guard and engage them in battle until heavier U.S. units can move up to finish them off. After pausing during a sandstorm, with seventy-m.p.h. winds, the headquarters column moves off, only to reverse direction and hastily retreat because Iraqi tanks have supposedly been spotted up ahead. Night finds us dug in, watching a light show of explosions and flames along the horizon. The regiment's heavy armor is battling the Republican Guards along a twenty-mile front, but from this distance I can make no sense of the action. What could have been my biggest story ever is playing itself out, and I'm missing it.

February 27—Dobson gets an update on the battle from the regiment's operations center and gives me a briefing—it seems an entire Republican Guard division has been annihilated. I write a story on the battle. This time, with Dobson's help, I actually manage to file it over the computer hookup, along with all the other hoary dispatches that have stacked up.

Later, with the column having paused to rest up, Dobson and I and a couple of Air Force liaison officers drive off to inspect the hulk of an Iraqi armored personnel carrier, which has been knocked out by a U.S. aircraft missile. The Iraqi inside the vehicle has been burned beyond recognition. A gunner who sat atop the carrier has been thrown clear but torn nearly in half and horribly mutilated in other ways. I take detailed notes.

"What angle are you planning to use?" asks Dobson. When I make a noncommittal reply, he says, "Here's the angle I would use: There is no glory in war. . . . No one will ever know what happened to these two. Their families will never know. The sand is already covering that [gunner's] body." He shakes his head.

My assignment editor seems to have good news judgment. I take his advice. The problem is that the piece I write is quite graphic, just the sort of story that the Defense Department—with its smart-bomb videos that make combat seem bloodless—has been trying to avoid. Will this dispatch survive the censor's blue pencil?

As things turn out, the dispatch gets through unaltered and no high-ranking meddler comes after me. But this may be because the war is all but over.

A more telling case is probably that of *Los Angeles Times* reporter John Balzar, who was assigned to cover a helicopter aviation brigade in the Eighteenth Army Corps. Before the ground offensive started, his unit was conducting night attacks into Iraq. Apache helicopter pilots allowed Balzar to view infra-red gun-camera footage of one of these raids.

Here is a sample of what he reported shortly before the ground war was launched:

> Through the powerful night-vision gunsights they looked like ghostly sheep, flushed from a pen—Iraqi infantry soldiers bewildered and terrified, jarred from sleep and fleeing their bunkers under a hellstorm of fire. One by one they were cut down by attackers they couldn't see or understand. Some were literally blown to bits by bursts of 30mm exploding cannon shells. One man dropped, writhed on the ground, and struggled to his feet. Another burst tore him apart. A compatriot twice emerged standing from bursts. As if in pity, the American Army attackers turned and let him live. . . .

This pool report was not censored by the Defense Department, but after it was filed Balzar and the other members of his pool were, in effect, grounded. They were taken to see no combat and spent much of the ground offensive sitting around in a tent.

February 28—My priority today is to interview the soldiers who had fought in Tuesday night's fierce tank battle and to file an after-action report. But Dobson's priority is to collect Iraqi weapons from the battlefield for the regimental museum. So that, needless to say, is what we do. I take notes as Dobson and three Air Force liaison officers, with .45s at the ready, clear Iraqi bunkers (no Iraqis are to be seen) and haul off booty. From one bunker the Air Force men liberate a twenty-six-inch Sanyo color TV set with stereophonic sound.

For much of the day I ride with a young Air Force captain. He, and not Dobson, now sets my news agenda. At one point, he asks, "Would you like a Pop-Tart?" But he can't find the box. It has fallen off the back of the truck and is lost. The captain is crestfallen. As he drives along, he speaks with a consuming intensity of his fondness of Pop-Tarts, a snack with the flavor of home. Suddenly his eyes bulge. He realizes that he has blundered into a dense field of unexploded cluster bomblets dropped by U.S. planes. Slowly, with great care, he eases the truck through the field. When it's finally evident that he has pulled us through intact, he pauses and says softly, as if to himself, "That really bums me out about the Pop-Tarts."

It's unclear what my lead for today should be—the Sanyo TV or the Pop-Tarts. I lean toward the latter.

March 4—After a journey by helicopter and transport plane, I arrive back at the Dhahran International Hotel. The American Military Police at the front door search my bags far more carefully than they had when I arrived two weeks before. The reason for this thoroughness, explains one M.P., is that journalists back from battlefields have been showing up with some interesting souvenirs. He says one member of a CBS crew came in with three Iraqi hand grenades. They turned out to be the trip-wire type, which go off the instant you pull the pin. Other journalists, whom he declined to identify, came in with pistols and anti-tank weapons, and one had four volatile blasting caps in her pocket. The M.P. says he has come to question whether the American press corps has very good judgment.

Back in the hotel, I discuss my pool experience with colleagues and conclude that, astonishingly enough, I have had relatively *good* luck with the system. Some reporters covering Seventh Corps got no dispatches back at all. A great many—and this applied to the entire theater of operations—were far from any combat whatsoever; they will be traumatized for years to come not by what they saw of this war, but by what they didn't see.

In the final reckoning, I'm left with this question: Was joining a pool really worth the aggravation? It's a close call, but probably it was in those cases where you actually got to cover some fighting. On the other hand, those passed over for pool slots were not necessarily the losers. Consider the *New Republic*'s Michael Kelly, who was told he would not get a ground combat pool assignment and opted to go on his own. He and a *Baltimore Sun* reporter drove across the desert toward Kuwait City, ahead of the allied forces. Kelly's poignant March 18 account of desperate, surrendering Iraqis, begging reporters to take them into custody, made far better reading than any pool report I saw during the entire war.

45. THE NEWS MEDIA AND NATIONAL SECURITY

Richard R. Burt

We now turn to a broader discussion of media coverage of national security policy. Richard R. Burt offers a critique of media role in the national debate over national security. He contends that the press has contributed to a trivialization of the issue by failing to provide in-depth analysis of national security policy issues. Burt blames this development on the lack of expertise by reporters and the trends of "herd journalism," excessive competition for scoops, and an emphasis on personalities over substance.

In conclusion, Burt tentatively offers some solutions for reform designed to encourage more comprehensive reporting.* But analyze the effects of these reforms. Who will benefit from them—the media, interest groups, government? Can the trends of journalism toward soft, human-interest news be overcome by these reforms?

Richard R. Burt has been on both sides of the government–media relationship. He is a former assistant U.S. secretary of state and has worked as national security correspondent for the *New York Times*.

The public debate over national security has become more complicated and more important. Yet the media have failed to keep pace in explaining defense and arms control issues to a confused American public. Indeed, the performance of the press and broadcast journalism in reporting and analyzing these issues is one reason why the national security debate in the United States (and the West more broadly) has become increasingly chaotic, simplistic and ill-informed.

This is a provocative thesis and some qualifications are in order. The media, like other major institutions in American society, not only effect change but also reflect broader cultural and political trends. Thus the decline in the quality and coherence of the media's treatment of national security must first of all be seen against the backdrop of more general developments within the American political system, U.S. foreign policy and the media themselves.

One important change, which has been noted by political analysts ranging from Pat Cadell to Lee Atwater, is the growth of populism in American politics over the last two decades. This has not only meant that the "smoke-filled room" has been overtaken by primary elections and techniques of mass advertising, but that political issues themselves have been popularized with the paradoxical and pernicious result that the influence of small, but motivated interest groups has grown.

The popularization of politics has had an important impact on the national security debate. Traditionally, core U.S. national security questions—nuclear doctrine and deployments, arms control goals and objectives—were addressed among a limited community of government officials, interested politicians and academic think-tankers. This community has grown larger, with the profusion of new think tanks and the acquisition by many congressmen of their own national security advis-

ers. And, just as national political parties have steadily lost power in a populist period of American polities, so has the traditional American national security community. The result has been a decline in understanding and support among Western
publics for concepts like extended deterrence and their replacement with more
popular, anti-nuclear solutions ranging from the freeze on the left to a "Space
Shield" on the right.

The debate in recent years over "strategic defense" illustrates the point. Since
the 1960s, the national security community has addressed the pros and cons of bal-
listic missile defense, including its technical feasibility, its impact on deterrence and
the deeper problems of what constitutes adequate deterrence. The 1969–70 Senate
debate over ABM deployment, with its extensive and thoughtful testimony from
analysts on both sides of the issue, remains to this day the classic exposition of the
issue. The debate over the Strategic Defense Initiative [SDI] has had none of the
rigor, coherence or clarity of these deliberations. Instead, it has largely degenerat-
ed into a popularized contest between interest groups and passionate minorities
who have depicted SDI, on the one hand, as the nation's only chance to escape the
threat of nuclear devastation or, on the other, a sure way to make such devastation
possible. Political action committees espousing one or another of these points of
view have been formed, films have been produced and pedalled to local TV stations,
and ardent speakers have crisscrossed the country with their emotional and simplistic messages. . . .

Broader changes within the "media culture" of the United States have also had
an adverse impact on the serious coverage of national security. Television has contributed to a decline in the attention span of viewers, especially young people.
Despite the profusion of news programming on television, the quality and comprehensiveness of national security coverage has declined. The in-depth documentary,
pioneered by CBS during the Murrow-Friendly era, has all but disappeared,
replaced by short, snappy reports on breakfast television. The traditional Sunday
interview programs, which gave officials and reporters time to explore issues, have
evolved into "mediagenic" confrontations in which the views and antics of news
entertainers, like Sam Donaldson, are thought to be more interesting than the officials and experts they interview. The competition created by syndicated and cable
news programming has probably accelerated the merger of news and entertainment
on television. "The McLaughlin Group" and "Crossfire," with their "inside baseball"
gossip, are enjoyable programs, but they contribute little to a real understanding of
SDI, U.S. policy in Central America, or the future of the strategic triad.

As TV has emerged as the main source of news for most people, newspapers
have had to hustle to redefine their role. Some changes have been positive—for
example, the growth of commentary and analysis in newspapers as exemplified by
the op-ed page. Generally, however, the trend has been toward "McNews" coverage
epitomized by *USA Today*: a heavy emphasis on leisure, sports, and entertainment
with hard news boiled down to capsule coverage. Worse, the "McNews" phenomenon has affected all newspapers and magazines, including the most serious. During
my tenure at the *New York Times,* for example, the space allocated for so-called hard

news reporting and analysis shrunk substantially with the decision to move the paper's layout from eight columns per page to six (to make the paper more "readable") and, more importantly, to free up space for special sections covering lifestyle, sports, food and recreation.[1]

These broad trends in American politics and the media help explain why coverage of national security issues has become more superficial, trivial, and sensational. But they don't tell the whole story. Individual news organizations and the reporters, editors, and managers that comprise these organizations are also responsible. Reporters and editors, individually and as a group, need to address what might be termed shortcomings of "tradecraft" in covering national security.

LACK OF SUBSTANTIVE EXPERTISE

Although it is true that there are examples in which individuals with some expertise in security and arms control issues have been recruited to cover these topics, the fact remains that the large majority of reporters who report on these issues do not possess the background to write or speak coherently and authoritatively. Too often, reporters lack the necessary conceptual and historical framework to fully understand events and place them in the proper context.

Examples of this are almost too numerous to cite. There is, for instance, a journalistic "crisis industry" in covering developments within the Atlantic Alliance. Almost any time that differences emerge within NATO, journalists on both sides of the Atlantic seem impelled to suggest that a crisis is at hand and it could threaten the very underpinnings of the European–American relationship. Thus, when many Europeans expressed misgivings over the 1986 American raid on Libya, it was reported several times in both the U.S. and the European press that this was "the worst crisis in the history of the Alliance." Not only is this short-lived dispute hardly remembered today, but its coverage at the time seemed oblivious to the long history of European–American differences over the use of force in the Third World (Suez, Vietnam, Iran, and Afghanistan). There appeared, moreover, to be little understanding that as important as these differences over "out-of-area" contingencies are, they must be seen in the context of a long-standing consensus within NATO over its core strategy of deterring aggression in Europe.

The media's treatment of the infamous "neutron bomb" is another example. The issue was made to hinge not on whether the deployment of a more discriminate nuclear weapon would or would not have enhanced NATO's strategy of flexible response (although I think it would have). The media never discussed the issue in these terms. Instead, the press focused on the incorrect claim that the weapon destroyed people, not things, and thus was the ultimate "capitalist" weapon. Perhaps the height of alarmist, superficial coverage was achieved by the *Washington Post*, which, in an editorial, called the weapon the "killer warhead," as though the tens of thousands of other nuclear and conventional munitions then in the U.S. inventory lacked this attribute.

Coverage of the MX and the 600-ship navy debates has also had a ludicrous quality. The MX issue was mainly presented in terms of whether a new, more capable missile should be procured. The desirability of maintaining the strategic triad and enhancing U.S. countermilitary strategic capability and the MX's relation to these issues were not explored. In the 600-ship navy debate, coverage focused mainly on the cost involved and not on the question of naval roles and missions, including the doctrinal issue of "horizontal escalation."

Although it is probably true that there has been a gradual increase in overall expertise on national security within the media as a whole, the people who have studied and followed security issues most closely are often not those who get to report on important developments. By this I mean that the small cadre of specialists who are able to prepare analytical "think" pieces are very rarely the journalists who are actually assigned to cover newsmaking events. It is the White House correspondent who covers the most important stories, the Reykjavik summit, for example, or President Reagan's March 1983 SDI speech.[2]

The effort to achieve greater expertise must contend with a countervailing tendency in journalism—the declining, but still entrenched, view that the best reporters are "jacks of all trades." There is still a strong belief on the part of editors that the "tradecraft" skills of reporting take precedence over subject-specific expertise or, as one editor told me years ago, "If you know how to cover a major fire, you can cover anything." In fact, there is a tendency for editors as well as fellow journalists to be skeptical of a colleague with special expertise on the grounds that he or she has somehow been co-opted by the people or institutions they are assigned to cover. Thus, sheer ignorance often masquerades as "professional distance."

HERD JOURNALISM AND COMPETITION

It is difficult for non-journalists to understand the terrific competitive pressures of journalism, especially in Washington. The competition, in my view, is responsible for the now-familiar phenomenon of herd journalism: the tendency of the media to cover the same events in much the same way, ignoring other developments and other issues. At the White House, the State Department, and other departments, the press corps often attempts to decide in collective fashion what the "story" of the day will be. The reason, of course, is that reporters do not want to be caught off guard (and thus have an angry editor on the phone) when a colleague suddenly develops a story that they missed. It is safer to agree in advance what the story is and run with the herd.

Ironically, herd journalism offers government spokesmen enhanced opportunities to define the news by steering them toward the story of the day. More important, it means that many important stories never get covered. It also leads to a "sequential" approach to the news—a stream of different stories from day to day and week to week, reported without context and perspective. The consequence is that some stories, such as the "nuclear winter" debate, are reported only briefly and dropped. Other stories, like deployment of INF and arms control, are reported only in pieces, so that it is difficult for the public to establish a connection between

NATO's 1979 double-track decision, the actual deployment of missiles in 1983, and the achievement of an agreement four years later.

SCOOP JOURNALISM

The competitive pressure of Washington journalism means that "scoops" take precedence over policy analysis. This leads to several problems. First, the competitive environment promotes leaks that can damage sensitive operations and negotiations with friends and adversaries. Simply put, there is information that U.S. officials should not divulge to the press and if it is divulged, should not be published. Revelations about U.S. clandestine operations are an example. But it is extremely difficult to dissuade a news organization from running with a juicy news leak.

Second, many scoops are not entirely accurate, but because they pertain to sensitive policy or intelligence issues, it is difficult, if not impossible, to set the record straight. As a State Department official in the early 1980s, I read many accounts in the press of National Security Council meetings which bore little or no relation to what had actually transpired.[3] But for obvious reasons, there was little the administration could do to set the record straight. Third, the "scoop mentality" of many reporters and editors can distort the very definition of news. The fact that some piece of information is "exclusive" sometimes seems of greater importance than the content of the information itself. During the Nixon–Ford and Carter eras, for example, the press placed a great premium on finding out the details of U.S. negotiating positions at SALT and the developments within the negotiations themselves, which were closely held. The Reagan administration, on the other hand, has tended to take a more public position on arms control developments, to the point of unveiling U.S. positions in presidential speeches and briefing reporters in detail afterward. Not surprisingly there was far greater press interest in the nuances of U.S. positions when that information was more difficult to obtain than at present.

Finally, scoops have a perverse impact on how the government itself handles information and makes sensitive information available. As was the case in earlier administrations, scoop journalism and the threat of leaks led the Reagan administration to progressively narrow the circle of people engaged in decision making and analysis. Thus issues that were thrashed out by the full National Security Council in 1981 were later decided in much smaller National Security Planning Groups. This reduced the potential for leaks, but it also reduced the diversity of opinion and the amount of special expertise that could be brought to bear on a problem. This certainly is one of the roots of the Iran-*contra* affair.

THE "PEOPLE MAGAZINE" APPROACH TO NATIONAL SECURITY

Perhaps with the "lessons" of Watergate beginning to fade, there has been a decline in scoop journalism. But there is a danger that it will be replaced by a *People*

Magazine approach focusing on personalities and bureaucratic in-fighting while ignoring the substance of policy issues. There has always been a fascination with going behind-the-scenes in covering Washington, and such reporting is often helpful in understanding how and why decisions are made. Many of the "tick-tock" pieces describing the formulation of President Reagan's March 1983 SDI address were useful in portraying decision making within the administration. But the growing emphasis on highlighting personal and institutional conflict in Washington reporting often means that real issues are forgotten. . . .

BEING THERE

Both "scoop" and "People Magazine" coverage of national security are merely reflections of the growing role of the media and their ability to achieve greater access. The news media today are larger; they can communicate more information more quickly; and people and institutions, here and abroad, are ready and able to provide them with more information. These trends have generally positive implications for individual Americans and the United States as a whole, but they do raise difficult questions in the area of national security.

One of these issues has already been alluded to: Where should the line be drawn between press freedom and the protection of sensitive national security material? Since the publication of the *Pentagon Papers*, most news organizations have felt free, on most occasions, to report whatever information they were able to obtain. Moreover, they have criticized government efforts, such as giving lie-detector tests to suspended leakers, to stem the flow of classified information. Is this a tenable position over the long-term? Should *The Nation* be permitted to publish technical aspects pertaining to the assembly of weapons? Should Bob Woodward, as he did in *Veil*, report that former Egyptian President Anwar Sadat, former El Salvadoran President José Napoleon Duarte, and the current Prime Minister of Dominica, Eugenia Charles, served as CIA "assets"? Should newspaper reporters provide their readers detailed information on U.S. intelligence capabilities used for arms control verification? Equally difficult questions are raised by press coverage of the use of U.S. military force. There is now a voluminous library on the role of the news media in the Vietnam conflict in shaping (or misshaping) U.S. perceptions of the war. One question, posed by Peter Braestrup in *Big Story*, is whether the news media, particularly television, are capable in complex and confused combat situations of providing the real story. Braestrup details how the Tet offensive was universally depicted as a major American military debacle when, in reality, it resulted in a U.S. victory. There is a saying in U.S. government circles that when an international crisis breaks out, "the first reports are always wrong." But these are often the only reports many people read.

Another question is whether the news media should always and in all circumstances be permitted to cover, firsthand, the use of U.S. military force. Obviously, there are circumstances in which even the media respects the right of U.S. military secrecy. No one (to my knowledge) has argued that reporters should have been invited along to cover the ill-fated U.S. hostage rescue mission in Iran. But when the Reagan administration, following Mrs. Thatcher's lead in the Falklands, shut reporters out of the early phases of the Grenada action, there was a terrific hue and cry.

The British, of course, have a very different tradition in handling (and muzzling) the press, but British military history does raise intriguing questions. British World War II archives released in recent years reveal that the evacuation from Dunkirk in 1940 was in many respects a sorry operation. Not only did British troops on the beach fire on their French allies to prevent them from joining in the evacuation, but Churchill, to the last minute, denied to the French that an evacuation was even contemplated. With the help of the BBC, the government was successful in depicting the evacuation as a magnificent rescue operation undertaken by a flotilla of private boats, manned by eager sailors. In fact, many British boat owners refused to make the voyage and had their ships commandeered. It is understandable that Churchill and his colleagues, in this moment of crisis, needed to construct the Dunkirk "myth." The interesting question, however, is what would have been the impact on British morale and the course of World War II had there been TV crews on the beach? Might Dunkirk have had the same effect as the Tet offensive?

GOVERNMENT BY PRESS RELEASE

Perhaps one of the most interesting issues flowing from the news media's greater role and access is the impact this has on national security decision making itself. One thing is clear: U.S. officials spend far more time worrying about what the news media is saying about them and their decisions than is commonly understood by either the public or the media themselves. Early morning staff meetings in government departments focus as much on press problems as "real" problems; as much on how to depict a policy to the press as on what policy should be in the first place. And the higher one goes within the bureaucracy, the more time is devoted to press "spin control" and damage-limitation.

The result is that public affairs staffs have grown and spokesmen wield greater influence. "Good" news is released to coincide with the evening news shows, while the "bad" news dribbles out late Friday night or over a holiday weekend. Abroad, U.S. efforts to influence foreign press have been stepped up, and at home a large "public diplomacy" bureaucracy has come into being, which not only draws on the United States Information Agency, but also the State Department, the Pentagon, the intelligence agencies, and the NSC staff. In the media age, these steps are not only inevitable, they are useful. But there is a danger of making policy exclusively through press release, of basing decisions on the arguments of media specialists rather than those of policy analysts. Thus, the next step from a news media that simplifies complex issues like SDI or MX deployment could be a government (the executive branch and the Congress alike) that does the same.

THE IMPACT OF TELEVISION

I have already referred to the possible role of television in reshaping the national security debate—how the TV generation's shortened attention span and the visual requirements of the medium can contribute to the trivialization of news. But the news media, especially television, creates news itself. Edward R. Murrow's famous "See It Now" broadcast in which he excoriated Joseph McCarthy is considered to have constituted the turning-point in the controversial senator's career. But in more recent years, television's ability to generate news events has depended less on its persuasive powers and more on its entertainment value.

In 1983, as the nuclear freeze movement approached its height in the United States and protesters marched against INF deployment in Europe, the movie *The Day After* was aired. This was truly a modern-day media event, with news organizations covering the controversy created by a second-rate, made-for-TV movie. No doubt the producers believed they were making an important statement about the dangers associated with the arms race. This is certainly how the news media described the program. But the ultimate impact of the program was probably different.

In the United States, after receiving considerable hype, *The Day After* was quickly forgotten within policy circles in Washington. In Europe and particularly West Germany, where it was shown many times, it probably bolstered the determination of the peace movement. Among the American public, the program, in providing a highly emotional and inaccurate picture of how nuclear conflict could start and what its consequences would be, contributed to a growing anti-nuclear bias which complicates the task of maintaining support for deterrence.

SOME PROPOSALS

Because many of the problems I have outlined here reflect deeper trends within the news media, government and U.S. society, it is difficult to suggest any comprehensive solutions. . . .

Nevertheless, the news media, whether they like it or not, have become a participant in national security decision making, and we therefore have the right to demand improved performance on their part. The following suggestions are offered with this in mind.

First, news organizations and individual journalists should work to improve their understanding of national security problems. There are a number of obvious ways this can be done, ranging from making an effort to recruit reporters with specialized knowledge in this area, as the *New York Times* has done, to making it possible for nonspecialists to acquire greater expertise. The John F. Kennedy School of Government at Harvard has an international security program for mid-career government officials. Why not expand this program and others like it to accommodate several reporters? Government can also play a helpful role. In the Reagan administration, the Arms Control and Disarmament Agency (ACDA) sponsored a weekend seminar away from Washington which permitted senior officials to talk and mingle with reporters who regularly cover arms control. These seminars should be institutionalized and other agencies should follow ACDA's lead. The State Department could convene conferences on the [former] Soviet Union or Central America, for example, while the Pentagon could hold retreats with reporters on the defense budget and the military balance.

But the government should also examine its own methods of talking to the press. In my view, the era of the spokesman is waning. While public affairs officials will still be necessary, the best spokesmen on national security are the policy-making officials themselves, from the President and the secretaries of state and defense on down. This does not mean that TV anchormen should be chosen to fill these jobs (although it does not hurt to have a former actor as President). It means that senior- and middle-level officials must become more conversant with the media and how to use them. This must go beyond knowing what "deep background" means to actually understanding how to present complicated problems coherently and intelligibly, thus avoiding distortions and simplifications. In the media age, nearly every national security official is likely, at one time or another, to appear on television. It is surprising how many are totally unprepared to do so. While Strobe Talbott in *Deadly Gambits* was most impressed with Richard Perle's bureaucratic skills, I am more dazzled by his mastery of television. In other words, my advice to national security officials about television is "if you can't beat 'em (and we can't), join 'em."

I have the same advice for think tanks, universities and foundations. The United States is almost unique in having a large "private sector" in the national security field. Since the foundation of the RAND Corporation in the 1950s, most of the original contributions to thinking about defense and arms control have come from this sector. But it, too, must adjust to the media age. It is ironic that lobbying groups, like the Arms Control Association or the Heritage Foundation, that do the least in-depth work on national security issues are the most successful in getting their views across to the press. While more research-oriented institutions may think it unseemly to work closely with the press, this is a mistake. I am glad to see that at least some institutions recognize this. Under the leadership of Peter Tarnoff, for example, the Council on Foreign Relations has begun a series of projects designed to increase the Council's activities in television.

Finally, there is the troubling question of leaks and the news media's competitive incentives to run with them. The government can help with this problem by punishing those leakers it manages to catch, but this is hardly the answer. The news media must recognize their responsibility in this area. An Israeli-style censorship system is out of the question, but a measure of self-policing might be possible. I doubt that major news outlets would participate in some form of press council arrangement which would comment on whether previously published reports had damaged national security, but the idea could at least be discussed. Another idea would be for news organizations to hire former senior officials as consultants for their expert advice on whether and how to report potentially sensitive stories. Networks and newspapers now retain legal consultants to advise them on potentially libelous reports. And while the national security area is much less clear-cut, the potential damage is greater. As a former reporter, even these modest steps make me uncomfortable. But as somebody once said, the First Amendment is not a suicide pact.

NOTES

1. My predecessor at the *Times*, Les Gelb, tells me that his reports averaged roughly 1,200 words. When I came to the *Times*, I was told to keep an average story to about 900 words. By the time I left, reporters were urged to keep their pieces below 750 words.

2. My own experience is instructive here. Although I covered, almost continuously, the negotiations leading to the SALT II treaty for the *Times*, I was not permitted to cover or even attend the 1979 Carter–Brezhnev summit in Vienna. The reason was that the other correspondents, especially at the State Department and the White House, had stronger "turf" claims to cover the event.

3. Earlier, as a journalist, I found that much of the "leaked" information I received was essentially disinformation: inaccurate information provided by axe-grinding and disgruntled officials designed to distort, undermine, and change a real decision that had been taken.

SUGGESTED READINGS

Berry, Nicholas O. *Foreign Policy and the Press.* Westport, CT: Greenwood Press, 1990.
Berry's study of the paramount mass-circulation daily international news source rejects the conventional wisdom that the press is a major player in foreign policy or that it is effectively manipulated by foreign policymakers.

Braestrup, Peter. *Big Story: How the American Press and Television Reported and Interpreted the Crisis of Tet 1968 in Vietnam and Washington.* Boulder, Colo.: Westview Press, 1977.
A classic in this literature because Braestrup demonstrated how the events during Tet were distorted in news coverage by reporters' perspectives and approaches to news reporting.

Cohen, Bernard. *The Press and Foreign Policy.* Princeton: Princeton University Press, 1963.
The classic work on this topic, this monograph was the first to examine the interdependence of the press and foreign policymakers.

Dorman, William A., and Mansour Farhang. *The U.S. Press and Iran: Foreign Policy and the Journalism of Deference.* Berkeley: University of California Press, 1987.
A case study of American media coverage of U.S. foreign policy toward a single country, this monograph concludes that journalists are inclined to follow foreign policymakers' leads in news coverage, rather than perform an aggressive watchdog role.

Hallin, Daniel C. *The "Uncensored War": The Media and Vietnam.* Berkeley: University of California Press, 1986.
Hallin disputes the contention that media coverage of the Vietnam War was critical of U.S. policy and propelled public opinion against the war. He argues that press coverage that was initially supportive and later critical was a reflection of public opinion.

Kaniss, Phyllis. *Making Local News.* Chicago: University of Chicago Press, 1991.
A rare monograph-length treatment of the effect of local news coverage on local public policy decisions.

Linsky, Martin. *How the Press Affects Federal Policymaking.* New York: W.W. Norton & Co., Inc., 1986.
Includes six case studies of policy choices affected by news coverage during the 1970s and early 1980s.

Matthews, Lloyd J. *Newsmen and National Defense.* Washington, D.C.: Brassey's, 1991.
A collection of articles that originally appeared in *Parameters,* this monograph is especially valuable in its discussion of the history of media–military relations and offering government officials' perspectives.

Morgan, David. *The Flacks of Washington.* Westport, CT: Greenwood Press, 1986.
A study of the role of government public relations officers in government relations with the press.

Sefaty, Simon, ed. *The Media and Foreign Policy.* New York: St. Martin's Press, 1990.
A collection of articles by scholars and foreign policymakers dealing with the media effect on a host of foreign policy crises and issues, including U.S. relations with Libya, the salience of news leaks, and the dilemma of media coverage of intelligence agencies.

Smith, Perry M. *How CNN Fought the War: A View from the Inside.* New York: Birch Lane Press, 1991.
CNN became the primary source of television news about the Gulf War not only within the United States, but also internationally. This book provides a glimpse at how CNN covered the war.

Soley, Lawrence C. *The News Shapers: The Sources Who Explain the News.* New York: Praeger, 1992.
Soley analyzes how reporters choose expert public policy sources and how that choice affects policy coverage.

chapter 9

THE FUTURE: TECHNOLOGY AND DEMOCRACY

INTRODUCTION

Up till the end of the twentieth century, the printing press, telegraph, telephone, radio, and television have been the technological innovations revolutionizing the communications industry and thereby reshaping media role in American politics. But the future holds promise for even greater change attributable to technology. Interactive cable, satellite communications, faxes, and personal computers have just begun to influence political communications in the United States.

However, new technology will not resolve tensions between the news media and political institutions and organizations. This is true because the technology of the future will not likely upset the current balance of power in American politics. The news media will not become omniscient or omnipotent. Nor will new technology allow political leaders to exercise enhanced power owing to the technology, and voters will not become more easily duped or suddenly acquire greater wisdom because of new breakthroughs in communication.

Centralization of information will become less likely through the availability of a vast array of news sources, especially through electronic means. Those with near monopolies on some forms of information, such as the intelligence community, will be less successful in controlling access.

But the costs of acquiring the technological capability to gather such information will still place limits on possession. For example, the voters with the least information will remain so since the costs for gaining such information will remain prohibitive.

Methods of communicating within the political system will be altered. Organizing and presenting messages to other actors will require technological knowledge and assistance.

But one unintended by-product of a wave of reliance on sophisticated technology in political decision making may be a backlash against technicians and technocrats who have become wedded to technology. For example, in the popular *Star Wars* film, Han Solo retains his buccaneer mentality in a world driven by sophisticated technology. Beyond the world of science fiction fantasy, there still exists the strong appeal of individuals who retain their humanness rather than conform to the demands of technology. While on the one hand, 1988 Democratic presidential candidate Michael Dukakis, labeled a technocrat, is criticized as devoid of personality, on the other, colorful, earthy, and independent presidential candidate Ross Perot is acclaimed by many Americans as a breath of fresh air.

Whither the effects of technology on American politics?

The first section in this chapter examines some of the new media-related technology and potential political effects. The second section addresses the question of the effects of these technological innovations and innovative uses on American democracy.

A. COMMUNICATIONS REVOLUTION

The technological revolution of the past twenty years has meant dramatic changes in the communications industry. Satellite, cable, video recorders, computer networks, and other marvels have become staples of American life. However, most of the effects of communications technological innovations on American politics in the twentieth century will occur during its last decade.

The breadth of technological development and the impact on political communication cannot be fully addressed in a section of this length. Only a small sample of the issues raised by new technological uses can be examined. The two selections below constitute that small sample by concentrating on the role of two types of satellites on the changing landscape of political use of technology. The first excerpt explains how satellite communications affect presidential campaigning. The second offers a glimpse into the future when news media organizations, using remote sensing satellites, will be capable of reporting on military and foreign policy actions without reliance on government permission.

46. THE USE OF SATELLITES IN POLITICS

Richard Armstrong

When Home Box Office became the first satellite programming service in 1975, the door opened for rapid expansion in the field of commercial TV broadcast satellite programming. With declining costs for both sending and receiving broadcast transmissions, the technology has moved from a corporate luxury to an everyday occurrence for many Americans with earth stations planted in their backyard.

The poltical uses of the technology soon followed—closed circuit fund-raising pitches, intraparty electronic rallies, satellite press conferences, video press releases via satellite, and so forth. More applications and more widespread use are certain through the 1990s and into the next century.

In the following reading, Richard Armstrong describes how satellites operate and tells of their usage in presidential campaigns, congressional press relations, fund-raising, and political organization.*

Richard Armstrong is a political consultant and is the author of *The Next Hurrah: The Communications Revolution in American Politics,* from which the selection is taken.

Before the off-year elections of 1986, few people had ever heard of a political media consultant by the name of Frank Greer. On November 5, 1986, the morning after election day, his name was on everyone's lips.

A Teddy-bearish man with a friendly, open face, Greer doesn't look like anyone's idea of a political mastermind. But in 1986 he scored the media consultant's equivalent of a grand slam, winning all but two of the thirteen campaigns he took on. The national media hailed Greer as the newest political genius. But few reporters noticed what really distinguished Greer from all the geniuses who preceded him. Although it would be hard to say it was the sole reason for his success in 1986, it's not entirely coincidental that Frank Greer is the first major political consultant in America to specialize in the use of satellites.

"We try to keep it simple and not mysterious," Greer says about using satellites in politics. "A lot of people in this business make it sound incredibly complicated and avant-garde. But it's not. It's just a tool, just another way of communicating your message."

"There are really only four ways to use satellites in politics," says Greer. "You can use them for remote press conferences. You can use them to feed new stories [to local media around the country]. You can use them for fund-raising. And you can use them for organizing."

It's that simple. But more than enough to have an impact on the outcome of a political campaign.

REMOTE PRESS CONFERENCES

John Glenn, of all people, should have known better. How ironic that the first American to go into orbit would be outsmarted by a mere earthling like Walter Mondale! But that's what happened when the former vice president hired Frank Greer to consult on his 1984 presidential campaign.

In the presidential primaries, each week brings a new election and a new battleground. Occasionally there are as many as seven different elections in seven different states on a single day. During the heat of a primary campaign it's not unusu-

*From *The Next Hurrah: The Communications Revolution in American Politics* (New York: Beechtree Books, 1988), pp. 196–205, 210–12. Reprinted with permission.

al for the candidate or his aides to lament, "If only there were a way for us to be in two places at once."

It sounds impossible. But if you know how to use satellites, you can do it.

During one such impossible week in 1984, when both Florida and Georgia were preparing for their primaries, Walter Mondale took an hour out of his campaign schedule in Georgia to go to an Atlanta television studio. Greer had arranged for an "uplink" to a satellite and had made appointments with the news anchormen of Miami's three biggest television stations. As Mondale stared into the camera, each Florida newsman took turns asking him questions over long-distance phone lines. Mondale's replies were shot in Atlanta, relayed by microwave to an uplink dish outside the city, beamed 22,300 miles in space to a satellite over the equator, reflected back to the downlink dishes in three Miami television stations, and recorded for use on the evening news later that day.

Meanwhile, John Glenn was doing it the old-fashioned way. He took a precious day out of his own campaign schedule in Georgia (a state of crucial importance to him) and traveled to Miami, where he held a rally. As it happened, Glenn's rally and Mondale's satellite news conference took place on the very same day.

When the six-o'clock news came on in Miami that evening, the interview with Walter Mondale was the lead story on all three network-affiliated television stations. In each case Mondale appeared on the "chroma-key" blackboard behind the news desk as the anchorman swung around in his chair and repeated the questions he had asked on the phone earlier. To the viewers it appeared to be a live interview in the studio, a real coup for the local news team. But as virtually everyone in southern Florida watched Mondale "live" on local TV, Mondale himself was busy meeting his commitments in Georgia.

John Glenn's rally was covered by only one TV station in Miami. "It was the fifth or sixth story," says Frank Greer with a smile.

THE SATELLITE NEWS FEED, OR VIDEO PRESS RELEASE

What we're running here, says Robert Vastine of the Senate Republican Conference, "is a miniature news bureau for the Republican Senate."

Like any newsroom, Vastine's is a beehive of activity. Telephones ring. Typewriters clatter. Technicians and cameramen swarm around a small TV studio. Two mobile crews await word from a harried assignment editor, who sends them scurrying out the door to cover this event or that.

But Vastine's newsroom is very different from all the others in Washington, D.C. For one thing, it's on the grounds of the U.S. Capitol. For another, it's completely financed by the federal government. And for a third, it has only one "beat": the U.S. Senate. In fact, Vastine's newsroom is even more narrowly focused than that: It covers the statements and activities of only *Republican* senators.

Whenever a Republican senator as much as burps on Capitol Hill these days, the Senate Republican Conference is on hand with its cameras to record the event and prepare it for transmission to a satellite later that afternoon. When the Senate is in session, the Conference has a thirty-minute block of time reserved on either *Westar IV* or *Galaxy I* every day at 3:45 P.M. They don't have to worry about renting an uplink dish, though. They have their own. It's on the roof of the Hart Senate Office Building.

Although the Conference has a state-of-the-art television studio, with a set large enough for one moderator and two guests, most of the videotape is shot by two mobile crews, who roam the Hill looking for Republican senators in the act of making news.

"We might shoot them making comments as they leave a committee room, holding a press conference, emerging from the Senate chamber . . . anything a senator does that's newsworthy," says Vastine.

These two crews and the TV studio are tightly scheduled by two assignment editors, who use a variety of sources to find out what's happening on any given day. Once they assign a crew to cover an event, they check with each senator's press secretary to make sure it's okay.

The raw videotape is brought back and prepared by two editing crews for the afternoon feed to the satellite. According to Vastine, the type of material being fed varies widely. But most of it consists of what people in the electronic news-gathering business refer to as "actualities": video newsclips of Republican senators presenting bills, interrogating witnesses, answering questions from reporters, or giving speeches.

Although the programming never smacks of campaign politics—the Republican Senate Conference and its Democratic counterpart, after all, receive six hundred thousand dollars of annual funding from the federal government—it obviously has some cumulative political effect. To put it bluntly, more and more Republican faces are appearing on more and more television screens more and more often. What isn't appearing there as often as it used to is the filtering—some might say, the cynical—effect of the national political reporter. "The boys on the bus" and "the boys in the press gallery" are standing alone in center court while Republican senators send a bounce pass sailing over their heads to local TV reporters back home.

Are local reporters less skeptical? Less sophisticated? Easier to manipulate? More likely to accept things at face value? More respectful?

Who knows?

But whether they are or not, Republican senators have clearly made the judgment that—just like the "telephone game" they played as children—the message is more likely to come out intact when you eliminate the middlemen.

Former National Cable Television Association spokesman Ed Dooley is very impressed with what the Senate Republican Conference has accomplished. In fact, said Dooley in a letter dated October 1986, "[The Conference has] done a really first-rate job. Their equipment—from uplink to studios—is one of the Hill's better kept secrets. The odds a year ago seemed against the Republicans retaining control [of the Senate]. But if they do, I'd be brash enough to give substantial credit to satel-casting."[1]

As it turned out, of course, the Republicans *didn't* retain control. But that doesn't mean Dooley was wrong in his assessment, because if the activity of the Senate Republican Conference is one of Washington's better-kept secrets, then Washington's best-kept secret is this:

The Democrats are doing it, too!

The Democrats call their committee the Senate Democratic Policy Committee, and its communications director is a woman, Linda Peek. But aside from those superficial differences, and aside from the fact that the Republicans have enjoyed a substantial head start, Democrats are busy promoting their own senators in much the same way the Republicans are.

Since the Senate Democratic Policy Committee continues to use its six-hundred-thousand-dollar annual budget to provide a variety of services other than electronic publicity, Ms. Peek does not have the wide range of equipment and resources enjoyed by Mr. Vastine. Her biggest problem, however, is not getting more hardware; it's getting more support from her senators. Although some are better at it than others, Republican senators have, for the most part, taken to the cameras like fish to water. The Democrats, on the other hand, have been camera-shy. Perennial underdogs when it comes to using new technology, some Democratic senators may not even realize that the cameras they see could be their own.

"They've seen us developing [this technology] so fast," says Vastine, "some of them don't realize their own party is doing it, too."

In fact, when I spoke with Mr. Vastine shortly after the November elections of 1986, he expressed some concern about how the new Democratic majority in the Senate would respond to his cameras now that they would be in power.

"I think January will be a miserable month for me," he said ruefully.

And indeed it was.

January was scarcely more than a week old when Senator Wendell H. Ford, Democrat of Kentucky, sent a stern letter to the architect of the Capitol. Under the new Democratic regime, Ford would become head of the Senate Rules Committee. In that capacity, he told the architect to remove all microwave antennas—except those of the national television networks—from the roof of the Hart Senate Office Building. Aside from the network antennas, however, there happens to be only one other dish up there, the one belonging to the Senate Republican Conference.

How odd that one of the first things Senator Ford would want to do after becoming Chairman of the Rules Committee would be to sweep off the roof of the Hart Building. What a tidy man! In politics, this is what's known as "cleaning house" . . . or, er, Senate.

The Republicans were, of course, incensed. And they threatened to fight back. But it didn't really matter. If the Democrats wanted a clean roof, Vastine could always get his uplink from another source. And in time the Democrats would want their own dish on the roof, anyway. After all, you can't stand in the way of progress.

One group that would very much like to stand in the way of this kind of progress, however—that would, in fact, like to throw their limp bodies in front of it—is the national press. If Democratic senators are uncomfortable with the new technology, members of the Washington press corps are downright appalled by it. And although it is the electronic media who presumably are being "controlled" and "manipulated" by the use of video actualities, ironically it's the print reporters who seem to get the most exercised about it.

"The print media find these [satellite] feeds extremely offensive," says Vastine. "They get on their high horse and inveigh against the scandalous practice of [a] television station's using someone else's footage. But ask them how many press releases their reporters just rewrite . . . or how many they don't even bother to rewrite.

"The analogy to a press release is exact," says Vastine. "What we're doing is helping nonnetwork affiliate and nonmetropolitan television, radio, and cable stations build their own programming base. They don't have to scrape to hire their own Washington bureau."

As with any public-relations tool, however, the point of a satellite is not just to help the press tell your story but also to help the press tell your story in the way you want it told. And while the material is not packaged or slanted in any way, it also is not what one would characterize as a warts-and-all view of the Republican Senate.

"You're certainly not going to feed them both sides of the story," says Greer bluntly.

More worrisome from the press's point of view is that the "beat reporter"—the guy who sits in the press gallery every day and who is in a position to know when Senator Jones is telling the truth and when he's not—is being bypassed. In the past he could report the senator's comments and add his own analysis. But now he watches helplessly as the senator's remarks fly over his outstretched arms to a local television reporter, who—as one wag once characterized all local TV anchormen—is scarcely more than a thirty-dollar haircut on a three-dollar head.

Vastine is right when he says that the video actuality and the paper press release are exactly analogous. But in the world of public relations, getting your press release published intact without comment or analysis is the publicist's equivalent of hitting a grand-slam home run. In the world of video actualities, it seems to happen all the time. While network-affiliated and large independent stations look disdainfully at actualities, small broadcast and cable stations gobble them up.

If anything, admits Vastine, "[these stations] would really like for us to do more of the story for them. If [there's a committee hearing] on hazardous dump sites, they'd really like us to put in a picture of a hazardous dump site.

"But that does get to where you're canning the feed," Vastine adds primly.

THE SATELLITE AS A FUNDRAISING TOOL

Why go a few miles to attend a fund-raising dinner when you can go forty-four thousand miles?

That must have been what some Democratic fat cats asked themselves when

Walter Mondale held a fund-raising dinner in Washington that was beamed by satellite to thirty other locations around the country.

One of those locations was in Alexandria, Virginia—only a few miles from where the event was actually taking place. Although the price of a ticket was the same in both locations, approximately three hundred Democrats decided they'd rather watch Mondale on the satellite than cross the bridge to see him in person.

"It was the craziest thing," says Greer, who organized the technical aspects of the event, "but some people are just fascinated by the technology."

Evidently a lot of people were fascinated by it, because the dinner raised more than a million dollars. And the money came at a time when Mondale desperately needed it. You could say Mondale owed his nomination to *Satcom III-R*. But when he finally made it into the general election, Mondale had to face a man who had been raising money by satellite for some time.

Ronald Reagan's experience with satellite fund-raising dated all the way back to 1982, when the president conducted what must have been the shortest, least expensive, and most lucrative whistlestop fund-raising tour in history.

On October 14, 1982, Reagan left the Oval Office and drove two blocks to the U.S. Chamber of Commerce building just across Lafayette Park from the White House. He stepped into a two million-dollar television studio the Chamber had built to broadcast their own satellite-delivered cable program service, BIZNET. When the cameras came on, Reagan's face and voice could be seen at fund-raising events in dozens of different locations around the country. He "visited" ten states, spoke on behalf of fourteen GOP congressional candidates, answered questions from dozens of local GOP donors, raised untold thousands of dollars, and did it all without spending more than an hour away from the Oval Office. The satellite campaign swing was so successful that four days later he did it again.

But you don't have to be a president of the United States with commitments all over the country to take advantage of the satellite's unique ability to put you in two places at one time. In 1986, Representative Bill Richardson, Democrat of New Mexico demonstrated that even a congressional candidate can use the satellite as a fund-raising tool. Richardson held a fund-raiser in Santa Fe that was televised live and beamed up to *Westar IV*. At various locations throughout his district, campaign volunteers invited their friends and neighbors to watch the show on cable or on their own private satellite dishes. When everyone was gathered around the set, the hosts passed peanuts, passed the hors d'oeuvres, and passed the hat.

THE SATELLITE AS AN ORGANIZATIONAL TOOL

In one sense, the use of satellites as a tool for political organization is still in its infancy. In another, it is more highly developed and more pervasive than many people realize.

As an instrument for the nuts-and-bolts work of campaign organization, some labor unions have enjoyed success using satellites. The American Federation of State, County, and Municipal Employees (AFSCME), in particular, has made a substantial investment in satellite technology. So has the AFL–CIO. Both organizations used their facilities to help organize the involvement of their rank-and-file members in the 1984 Mondale campaign. By using satellite teleconferences, the unions could afford to have top-notch political consultants conduct private seminars for their field operatives all over the country. As the technology becomes cheaper and more available, it's likely that more and more political organizations will be using satellites for internal communications. . . . [S]atellites are also being used by media consultants to transmit television commercials from the studio to the field instantaneously, thus contributing to the punch/counterpunch style of today's media campaigns.

But the satellites' greatest impact on politics so far has been as a tool for *external* communications, as a way of reaching out to the uninitiated and bringing them into the fold. No communications medium casts a wider net than a satellite. It literally drops its message like a blanket over an entire continent. It can bring together millions of like-minded individuals, no matter how far apart they may live or how different their lives may be on a superficial level. When it comes to reaching out to a broad constituency, inculcating them with a system of values and beliefs, encouraging them to give their time and money, building a corps of activists and volunteers, creating a sense of shared interests and culture, satellite technology is without peer. . . .

****

. . . Larry Kirkman of the AFL–CIO was trying to create a satellite-delivered program service that would do for the labor movement what CBN [Christian Broadcasting Network] did for fundamentalism. After a successful three-market test of labor-oriented programming on cable TV in 1983, Kirkman began finalizing plans for a satellite-delivered program service that would include comedy and variety shows in addition to public-affairs programming. Among other things, the channel would feature a syndicated program called *American Works*, which had been well received in the initial test. The goal, said Kirkman to *CableVision*, is to provide labor-oriented programming that "viewers want, but cannot find on the dial,"[2] and to "make the public interest interesting."[3]

The U.S. Chamber of Commerce also is trying to make the public interest more interesting with their satellite-delivered program service BIZNET. When it isn't being rented by Ronald Reagan, the two-million-dollar television studio at the U.S. Chamber of Commerce is used to broadcast a complete menu of legislative and economic programs to business subscribers around the country. They include local chambers of commerce, trade associations, and large corporations. The programs themselves go by such names as *Washington Watch, Economic Update,* and *Small Business Report.*

"[BIZNET is] a very powerful force," says a former communications staffer from the Democratic National Committee, "because it's keeping constituents around the country informed. A grass-roots lobbying effort could be put together in a matter of seconds."

All of this raises the possibility that the national political parties themselves will eventually want to create their own satellite-delivered program services. The Senate

Republican Conference's now-defunct *Conference Roundtable* program certainly was a stab in that direction.

Conference Roundtable was produced every two weeks at the Senate Recording Studio, beamed up to a satellite, and offered free of charge to some three hundred cable systems and sixty PBS affiliates around the country. What was remarkable about the *Conference Roundtable*, while it lasted, was how much it resembled the usual fare of Sunday-morning public-affairs shows and how little it looked like partisan propaganda. The show always began with a pop version of one of the Brandenburg concertos, while the camera panned portraits of great Republicans from the Past. "*This* is the *Conference Roundtable*," said the voice of a professional announcer in a grave and momentous tone. From there the show proceeded very much like *The McLaughlin Group*, with two senators, two national political reports, and one moderator sitting in a semicircle and informally discussing the week's hottest issues. The viewer would have to be fairly well acquainted with the names and faces in the U.S. Senate to notice that no one but Republicans were ever invited to appear on the show. When the credits rolled at the end of each episode, the program was identified as a production of the "Senate Conference of the Majority." It did not use the word "Republican." . . . [T]he *Conference Roundtable* clearly wanted to attract new people into the fold without running the risk of dredging up old prejudices about the GOP.

"I don't think it's unrealistic at all to think that the major parties will have their own network," said one former director of campaign planning with the Republican National Committee [RNC].

"When I buy cable today, I get ESPN. Someday I might get RNC."

NOTES

1. Ed Dooley, personal letter to the author.

2. As quoted in Victor Livingston, "Cableline to Launch New Service," *CableVision* (February 20, 1984), p. 22.

3. As quoted in "AFL–CIO Outlines TV Promotion Plans," *Multi Channel News* (October 18, 1982), p. 29.

47. SPYING ON THE GOVERNMENT: THE MEDIA, REMOTE-SENSING SATELLITES, AND U.S. NATIONAL SECURITY POLICY

Richard Davis

In April 1986, a major environmental disaster occurred—the meltdown of a nuclear reactor at the Chernobyl nuclear power plant in the Ukraine. The disaster was exacerbated by its occurrence in the closed society of the Soviet Union, whose government promptly denied outsiders access to information. But American news organizations obtained satellite images of Chernobyl from a commercial remote-sensing corporation in France and broadcast them in the United States. The images provoked a global condemnation of the Soviet government and contributed to the furtherence of *glasnost* (openness) as official Soviet policy. Through media use of remote sensing, the Soviet government's attempts to retain a monopoly on information were unsuccessful.

Although remote sensing has been a surveillance tool of the superpowers ever since the late 1950s, its commercial application is more recent, and its effects on the media's role in politics are in the embryonic stage. The following selection describes the effects on news media coverage of issues of national security of remote-sensing technology. Although the U.S. government has attempted to restrict the news media's access to remote sensing data involving U.S. military intervention, such efforts will become increasingly futile with widespread dissemination and commercial use of the technology.*

Richard Davis is associate professor of political science at Brigham Young University. He is the author of *The Press and American Politics: The New Mediator* (1992) and *Decisions and Images: The Supreme Court and the Press* (1994).

The United States government's national security imperatives and the American news media's news-gathering responsibilities are reaching a point of new conflict with the advent of remote-sensing satellite technology. Technological developments enabling the press to view national security policy implementation, such as military conflicts and covert actions, have taken one step closer to reality since the mid-1980s.

The Persian Gulf War of 1990–1991 was a precursor to the larger conflagration over access to national security-related information that soon will erupt as the news media increase usage of remote-sensing technology for news gathering, and related executive agencies, in an endeavor to restrict access to such sensitive information, attempt to impose restrictions on that usage.

After a brief description of the technology and its prior uses, this article explains the current and potential utility of civilian remote-sensing satellite technology by news media organizations, particularly on national security and American foreign policy issues. It also addresses the problems of implementation of the technology the news media face, including the limitations of the technology itself as a news-gathering tool and US government efforts to restrict media access.

Finally, it is demonstrated that due to the proliferation of national remote-sensing systems, US government efforts to restrict news media use of national security-related information obtained through commercial remote-sensing will become increasingly futile. Hence, this new technology will enhance the news media's capability to retrieve militarily and politically sensitive information previously controlled by government.

*From "Spying on the Government: The Media, Remote Sensing Satellites, and U.S. National Security Policy," *Political Communication*, 9 (Fall 1992): 191–205.

DESCRIPTION OF THE TECHNOLOGY
AND NON-MEDIA USAGE

Remote-sensing has been defined by the UN Committee on the Peaceful Uses of Outer Space (COPUOS) as "a system of methods for identifying the nature and/or determining the conditions of objects on the earth's surface and of phenomena on, below, or above it, by means of observations from airborne or spaceborne platforms."[1]

A remote-sensing satellite system entails one or more orbiting spacecraft with a stable platform for sensors, optics, and receiving and transmitting antennas in contact with one or more receiving stations on the ground.

The resolution of the imagery is determined by the resolving power of the sensor and the distance from the object. The closer the satellite to the earth's surface, the better the resolution even with low resolving power.

Remote-sensing satellites have the capability of viewing vast areas of the earth's surface with low resolution or, with high resolution, observing objects as small as two to four inches across. US military satellites are powerful enough to read numbers on a license plate or view a soccer game in progress.[2] However, since high-resolution sensors image a smaller geographical area, the amount of information received can be overwhelming. Moreover, as the satellite orbits the earth, the higher the resolution, the narrower the band of the earth's surface imaged.

Another problem is the infrequency of coverage of any particular area of the earth's surface. Due to the satellite's orbit and the earth's rotation, it does not remain stationary over the earth's surface.

Two types of resolution exist—spatial resolution and spectral resolution. The former refers to the ability of a sensor to separate objects of a given size. For example, with a spatial resolution of 10 meters, or 33 feet, buildings can be distinguished. Spectral resolution is the ability to distinguish an object due to its color or contrast with the background environment. The American and the French commercial satellites carry both types of imaging systems because their combination enhances the resolution of an image by including objects that can be seen on one but not the other.[3]

MILITARY USES

Since remote-sensing has the advantage of viewing a geographical area without intruding on the political boundaries of the nation or nations within that area, this technology has become the most successful military reconnaissance method.

Post–World War II military reconnaissance initially relied on cameras fitted onto RB-36 and RB-47E aircraft. After experimenting unsuccessfully with weather balloons, and for several years successfully with the U-2, the US launched the first reconnaissance satellite in 1960 following the shoot-down of a U-2 earlier that year.[4] By the early 1960s, remote-sensing satellites moved from film to electro-optical scanning and microwave technology.[5] In the mid-1960s a new camera allowed for resolution of objects as small as two feet from an altitude of 100 miles, and multispectral photography and infrared scanning were first utilized to detect camouflage and nighttime activity.[6]

Military remote-sensing satellites have demonstrated their utility in several national security crises. They were used to locate the American hostages held in the US Embassy in Tehran in 1980 and for planning the US air raid on Libya in April 1986.[7]

During the Persian Gulf War in 1990–1991, six Air Force and CIA spacecraft were operating in orbit over the Middle East. With a resolution of up to six inches, the satellites were used for bomb damage assessment and planning attacks. One satellite, the Lacrosse radar imager, had the capability to image through clouds and was useful during bad weather or at night. The satellites were able to perform tasks such as locate Iraqi armor in the desert and track the movement of mobile Scud launchers.[8]

COMMERCIAL USES

These cameras in the sky became commercial in 1972 with the launching of the Landsat satellite. Since then the commercial remote-sensing industry has grown. Over a five-year period in the early 1980s, remote-sensing data sales equalled slightly more than $30 million.[9] By 1988, sales in that year alone were estimated at more than $30 million, with the US Commerce Department predicting sales in the 1990s reaching over $9 billion.[10]

The resolution for US commercial satellite imagery has lagged far behind that of the military. In 1972, Landsat imagery was capable of a resolution of 80 meters. By 1990, the resolution was down to 30 meters.[11]

The Land Remote-Sensing Commercialization Act of 1984, known as the Landsat Act, turned control of Landsat over to the Earth Observation Satellite Company (EOSAT), a private company free to image and sell their photographs to other commercial interests. Today, the Landsat imagery is used for a variety of purposes including forestry, cartography, mineral and petroleum exploration, oceanography, and land management.[12] The Landsat images were used in 1988 to help firefighters battle forest fires in Yellowstone National Park.[13]

Landsat served as the sole commercial remote-sensing system in the world until 1986. Since 1986, two other commercial systems, one built by the French and the other by the Russians, have begun to compete with, and have now surpassed, EOSAT in the commercial imagery market. The French system, known as SPOT, launched a commercial satellite in 1986 with a resolution of 10 and 20 meters. The Russian satellite system, however, has a five-meter resolution capability.

Administered by a foreign trade organization called Sojuzkarta, the Russian system was established in 1987 to raise hard currency for the space budget. Like SPOT and EOSAT, Sojuzkarta is open to all potential customers, although it has excluded the sale of imagery from any socialist bloc nation.[14] Sojuzkarta has signed contracts with Western companies as exclusive marketers of the Russian imagery within their own countries.[15]

REMOTE SENSING AND NEWS GATHERING

Prior to the mid-1980s, although the technology existed, remote sensing was not employed by news organizations for news-gathering purposes.[16] The barriers to its use were technical and financial.

The technical problems included the low resolution of existing sensors, the infrequency of images from a particular area, the difficulty of redirecting a satellite's orbit, and the lengthy processing time for the imagery. However, more recently each of these impediments has been reduced by technological improvements in remote sensing.

Up until 1986, the only available resolution on commercial satellites was 30 meters, which lacked sufficient detail for news usage, especially in a visual display by broadcast media. Moreover, the difficulty of re-directing the satellite over a certain geographical area and the lengthy waiting period, sometimes months, for processing and enhancement ill-fit the news media's needs.[17]

Also, there was little demand for higher resolution since the majority of customers for Landsat imagery were interested in lower resolutions covering broader areas for geological, oceanographic, or meteorological purposes, rather than highly specific, high-resolution imagery useful primarily for military or political reasons.

However, the launching of more satellites allowing for wider and more frequent coverage and the reduction of processing time from months to days attracted media interest.[18] Moreover, the resolution offered by newer satellites was more compatible with television's high-definition visual needs. Television demands a resolution of three to five meters. The satellites launched in the late 1980s and early 1990s by SPOT and Sojuzkarta possessed sensors with five- to ten-meter resolutions. That resolution can be enhanced by value-added vendors that digitalize the photographs to provide greater clarity.

The commercial remote-sensing companies also have actively solicited the needs of media organizations. For example, in 1988 EOSAT surveyed media representatives to determine press needs in a remote-sensing system.[19]

The financial barrier also has been reduced. Costs for imagery have dropped. In the early 1990s, Sojuzkarta was selling photographs for $1500 a piece, while EOSAT sold its lower resolution imagery for $500 to $3000.[20]

Since 1986, US news organizations have purchased imagery from the three commercial companies for news-gathering purposes. The first major use of this capability by news organizations was coverage of the Chernobyl nuclear power plant accident in late April 1986. Using the imagery as evidence, news organizations were able to challenge the Soviet government's claims about the extent of the damage caused by the meltdown.

Subsequently, American news media, particularly the national television networks, have bought imagery used for dozens of stories, both foreign and domestic. These have included the Persian Gulf War, fire damage at Yellowstone National

Park, a fire at a Libyan chemical weapons plant, deforestation of the Amazon rain forests, and construction of SA-5 sites in Cuba.[21]

But since news organizations constitute only one of a number of clients of remote-sensing satellite companies, the news media are not in a position to dictate the orbital pattern of the satellite or the direction of the sensors. Remote-sensing satellite companies are reluctant to abandon prior missions requested by other clients to meet press needs for imagery of a breaking story. EOSAT was willing to suspend other assignments to image the Chernobyl disaster in April 1986 primarily because it already had a satellite in the area, but such a rapid response in the future would be rare.[22]

The result of these barriers in the past has been use limited primarily to stories where the imagery itself is the primary source and object of the story rather than as a supplemental tool for coverage of breaking stories. The technology is still novel enough to news organizations and the news audience that the existence of the imagery itself becomes sufficient justification for a story.

One proposal to employ the technology specifically to meet media imperatives is development of a jointly owned media remote-sensing system. Dubbed "mediasat," such a system could service a consortium of news organizations—both print and broadcast, general consumer and specialized—with interests in imagery.[23]

Costs for a satellite for news gathering currently would be prohibitive for a single news organization and perhaps even for a consortium. One estimate puts costs of development and launching at $215 to $410 million, and annual operating costs at $10–15 million. However, news organizations could defray some of the costs by tapping the burgeoning commercial remote-sensing market by expanding the sensor's capabilities to uses other than news gathering.[24]

Although no single news organization or group of organizations has committed itself in theory to a mediasat, efforts to promote one have been underway since 1985. The Radio and Television News Directors Association has lobbied and testified before Congress and submitted formal comments to the Department of Commerce to clarify existing rules and propound statutes and regulation favorable to future development of such a media capability. ABC News Producer Mark Brender predicted that through technological advances, and absent governmental intrusion, "commercial remote sensing satellites may become as indispensable as the printing press and the hand-held camera to a free society."[25]

Even without a media satellite, the existing commercial satellite corporations have made their products readily available to news organizations for prices starting at several hundred dollars. One news organization, calling itself the Space Media Network, was formed to buy imagery from commercial satellites, analyze it, and disseminate it. Formed by a Swedish journalist, the organization has broken stories based on imagery documenting Soviet laser weapons sites, the previously secret Saudi Arabia basing of intermediate range missiles purchased from the Chinese government and the location of a 1957 nuclear disaster in the Soviet Union never admitted by the Soviet government.[26]

MEDIA USE AND NATIONAL SECURITY POLICY

Although US networks had used imagery several times during the Iran-Iraq war, the Persian Gulf War of 1990–91 presented the first test of media access to and use of remote-sensing imagery during a large-scale US military conflict.[27]

Media imagery would be particularly significant if news organizations were barred from the combat zone, such as in the 1983 Grenada invasion, or even if their access was severely limited as in Panama in 1989 and during the Gulf War in 1991. With remote-sensing systems, the media could effectively bypass Pentagon restrictions on press access. Independently acquired information such as US troop locations and movements, the success of bombing missions, and estimates of enemy troop strength could challenge US military claims.

However, the Persian Gulf War began badly for news organizations expectant of extensive imagery use. Immediately after the Iraqi invasion of Kuwait, SPOT altered its "open skies" policy by restricting access to its imagery of the Middle East. The new policy, designed to prevent Iraqi use, limited access to individuals with US security clearances. The effect of the policy change was to make the Defense Department the only viable customer.[28]

However, news organizations used imagery of the Gulf from other sources. *ABC World News Tonight* used imagery with a 30-meter resolution from the Landsat satellite. ABC also obtained imagery from NOAA's [National Oceanic and Atmospheric Administration] weather satellite.[29] But neither of these sources offered the high resolution possible with SPOT.

In October 1990, ABC News bought imagery taken in early September from a Soviet satellite company, but was reluctant to air it because of what it showed, or rather did not show. The imagery clearly revealed the huge allied troop deployment in northern Saudi Arabia. But, significantly, there was no evidence of any large-scale buildup of Iraqi forces in Kuwait, which was a direct contradiction to White House and Pentagon assertions.

Rather than display these photographs on network television and risk incurring the wrath of the Bush administration and damaging the network's own credibility if they were wrong, their dilemma was leaked to *Newsweek*. In early December, *Newsweek* ran a short story about it, making public the dilemma over the imagery.[30]

One problem with the imagery bought by ABC News was the absence of a photograph of a section of southern Kuwait where the missing troops could have been located. After the *Newsweek* story, the *St. Petersburg Times* bought the missing photograph and another one showing portions of Saudi Arabia. After showing the imagery to the same experts ABC News used, again they found no evidence of Iraqi buildup.[31]

Several factors could have caused the discrepancy—the placement of Iraqi forces in concealed bunkers, glare from the sun, or the switching by the Soviets of photographs taken in different years. According to the experts who saw the photographs, the last possibility is unlikely because US troop sites in Northern Saudi Arabia were plainly seen in the photographs, and the credibility of the Russian commercial agency, Sojuzkarta, would be ruined if such a deception became public knowledge.

But another more serious problem was the low resolution of the photographs. While the Soviet commercial satellite could see objects as small as 5 meters wide, such as individual houses, US military remote-sensing satellites have much better resolution. However, the experts commissioned by ABC News concluded they should have seen some evidence of military activity at the level of resolution. Peter Zimmerman, a former official in the US Arms Control and Disarmamant Agency during the Reagan administration and one of the experts who saw the photographs, explained:

> We don't see any tent cities, we don't see congregations of tanks, we don't see troop concentrations, and the main Kuwaiti air base appears deserted. . . . There is no infra-strcture to support large numbers of [military] people. They have to use toilets or the functional equivalent. They have to have food. They have to have water at the rate of several gallons per man per day. They have to have shelter. But where is it?[32]

Moreover, the photographs ABC and the *St. Petersburg Times* obtained with five-meter resolution clearly showed details of the US military buildup. According to Mark Brender, "ABC could not only count the transport planes parked on the runway in Dhahran, we could tell you what kind of planes they were."[33]

The whole issue raised enough doubts among Pentagon reporters to lead the Pentagon's spokesman, Pete Williams, to review the US military reconnaissance imagery himself. Subsequently, he reiterated that the evidence confirming the US estimates did exist.[34]

However, after the war concluded, the Pentagon revised its estimates of enemy strength to approximately half of what had originally been estimated. Moreover, the military command admitted they knew of the discrepancy even before the ground war began, but declined to disclose it. Marine Corps General Walter Boomer confessed that "as we began to accumulate evidence during those later weeks, we all began to sense . . . that they were not up to strength. But we weren't going to say anything about it."[35]

IMPLEMENTATION PROBLEMS

Although the technology is available and will increasingly become so, two major problems will halt the expanded usage by the press. One concerns the limitations of remote sensing as a news-gathering tool. The other, and more serious difficulty, is governmental efforts to limit press access to remote sensing.

TECHNOLOGICAL LIMITATIONS

Although the capability will exist to observe large group human activity at any point on the globe, remote sensing is not the penultimate tool for news-gathering. It carries its own limitations.

One such limitation is the sheer volume of possible raw data. One estimate is a five-meter resolution can provide 100 to 150 million bits of data per second.[36] Sorting and analyzing the enormous amount of data produced by a high-resolution satellite would be a daunting task for a news organization, especially given daily or hourly media deadlines.

Unless the news organization received information from an alternative source, such as an unofficial leak, or was covering an already existent news story, it would be difficult to locate and identify a major news story through remote sensing alone. In other words, a news organization first would need to know where to look.

Given the avoidance of investigative reporting on most beats, it is unlikely remote-sensing imagery, with its requirement of some level of technical expertise and the size of the task of sorting data, independent of other sources would produce dramatic news stories.

The visual presentation of the imagery is problematic. The resolution of the imagery will affect the amount of analysis needed to accompany visual display of the imagery. A low resolution image will require substantial analysis. Viewers must be guided to significant points on the image. Even then, the viewer must accept on faith the analyst's conclusions.

However, a higher resolution will allow the viewer to see the objects and identify them as such—airplanes, trucks, ships, etc. The viewer will be less dependent on the analyst and will be enabled to provide their own visual confirmation of the analyst's conclusions.

But even a high-resolution photograph will not explain the meaning of the contents. A high-resolution image of an airport, for example, normally becomes significant only if it is accompanied by analysis explaining, for example, its role as a clandestine, private operation, such as a drug lord's airstrip.

News organizations also must determine the source of analysis—internal or external—to the news organization. Since the news-reporting process is driven by the need for official or quasi-official confirmation of the media-generated data, internal expertise is insufficient as a basis for a story. Thus, conclusions based on the imagery must be confirmed by governmental actors or at least others who carry an authoritative status, such as related interest groups and scholars. The dilemma becomes more acute when a choice must be made between expert analysis and governmental denials, as in the above case.

Remote sensing does not have the capability of revolutionizing the news-gathering business. However, it does hold the greatest promise in enhancing the ability of the press to observe events in conjunction with already established stories where access has been denied by government.

GOVERNMENTAL RESTRICTIONS: THE RATIONALE

Although the US government has fostered the growth of the commercial remote-sensing industry, it has simultaneously remained cautious about potential news-gathering applications. This caution has evolved from the real fear that decisions about disclosure of national security policy will rest in the hands of the American news media, not the US government.

The example above from the Persian Gulf War illustrates some of the national security and foreign policy-related objections critics have propounded to unrestricted media access to remote-sensing imagery. These include disclosure of secret US military information, disclosure of information sensitive to other governments provoking retaliation against the US, possible media misinterpration of data, and loss of control in crisis decision making.[37]

DISCLOSURE OF SECRET INFORMATION

One potential danger to US security interests is media dissemination of secret military information.[38] News gathering by remote sensing allows news organizations to collect and disclose information about secret military activity. Troop or fleet locations or headings or shipments of materiel could be observed by media personnel who would then hold the responsibility of holding or releasing such information. Even smaller military operations such as hostage rescue missions could be detected.

As discussed earlier, however, observation must be underway in order for attention to be focused on a specific geographical area. A military operation which is already secret is not likely to be "given away" by remote sensing. A large-scale military operation would be an exception, but unless the battle zone is a sparsely populated area such as the Iraqi desert or an area where access is in some other way controllable, such as in Grenada, an exercise could not be conducted without disclosure through other methods on the ground.

FOREIGN RETALIATION DUE TO MEDIA DISCLOSURES

Another objection notes the possibility of foreign governments' retaliating for the disclosure by US news media of sensitive information. Although this possibility now exists, remote-sensing technology enhances the media's opportunity to retrieve and publicize such information.

Although no retaliatory act occurred, such an incident could have occurred in 1975 when the Soviet Union complained through diplomatic channels about an *Aviation Week & Space Technology* article including imagery of Soviet launch facilities.[39]

However, one factor minimizing the significance of this objection is the general awareness of the American news media's high level of autonomy from formal governmental control.

MISINTERPRETATION OF DATA

Another objection is the possibility of media misinterpretation of data. In the above example, ABC News relied on the analysis of non-media experts, who, given subsequent alterations in Pentagon estimates, may not have misinterpreted what they saw. However, other news organizations, in haste to report a story, may not be so cautious.

This problem may be ameliorated over time. The possibility of misinterpretation of imagery by the news media will always be a factor in usage of remote sensing. However, it is likely that as use of the imagery becomes more common (particularly if a media satellite is developed), news organizations will hire or train their own in-house imagery reporting and analysis specialists as they have done with other fields such as law, medicine, and science. Moreover, as sensor resolution pushes past the five-meter level, analysis will become less a technical exercise as visual description and precise identification are easier. However, the meaning of the objects could still be misconstrued.

LOSS OF CONTROL IN CRISIS DECISION MAKING

Information and decision-making power in a crisis involving the US and other governments historically has been the monopoly of a small group of players in the White House and two or three executive agencies who work against the clock to find resolutions.

The "grace period" for resolution of the crisis has been reduced since the six days President Kennedy had to respond to Soviet missile buildup in Cuba. Media remote-sensing news-gathering capability will further reduce, if not eliminate, such a grace period. With real-time capability, news organizations will be able to broadcast and the public will be able to follow events simultaneous to their occurrence.

GOVERNMENT RESTRICTIONS: POLICY

In response to these objections, the Congress and related executive agencies have constructed legal barriers to minimize the potential of media possession and dissemination of information potentially damaging to national security interests. These barriers have taken the form of sensor resolution limits, license review, and penalties for disclosure of national security-related information.

Reportedly, a classified executive order was signed by President Jimmy Carter in 1978 limiting commercial satellite resolution to 10 meters.[40] In the wake of media complaints of undue restrictiveness, especially with the advent of the 10-meter SPOT satellite, and concern about effects on the growth of the US civilian remote-sensing system, the Reagan administration later rescinded such a restriction and settled on one to two meters as the limit for national security concerns.[41]

Through the Landsat Act, relevant executive agencies can grant or deny licenses or impose fines on commercial remote-sensing systems.[42] Under the act, the Secretary of Commerce determines whether to grant a license for a remote-sensing system. The Defense and State Departments can intervene in the license review process for national security and US foreign policy issues respectively.

The licensee must agree in writing to comply with US international obligations and national security concerns. Punishment for violation can include revocation of an existing license, retention of license but limitations on the future use of the system, or civil penalties of up to $10,000 per day for each violation. Under NOAA regulations, the administration can seize any "object, record, or report" which is likely to be used in violation of the Landsat Act.[43]

Given the high costs of constructing and maintaining a remote-sensing system, a news media organization may be inclined to avoid application or be overly cautious about the material it uses.

News organizations are unlikely to take the risk of constructing and launching a satellite since the license could be revoked at any time leaving the news organizations with an unusable satellite for covering what would probably be the major news story of the day. As Mark E. Brender suggests, the news organizations are not likely to purchase a sensor if they are not assured that "the First Amendment will accompany that sensor into space."[44]

Under the Landsat Act, only domestic remote-sensing firms were affected. This legal omission, and the subsequent availability of SPOT and Sojuzkarta as sources of imagery, provided a loophole for US media organizations. But the Reagan administration quickly closed the loophole by requiring private foreign firms, such as SPOT and Sojuzkarta, to apply for licenses to do business in the US.[45] The result was equal application of the vague "national security" and "international obligations" clauses to both foreign and domestic firms selling imagery in the US.

These restrictions do inhibit development of an independent media-owned satellite, but also deter a non-media licensed commercial satellite system from providing imagery to a media organization, the publication of which may result in a government-imposed penalty on the non-media licensee. SPOT's unwillingness to sell imagery during the Persian Gulf War may serve as an example.

News media representatives and legal experts have criticized the Landsat provisions as undefined and thus unconstitutional.[46] One legal expert has charged the vagueness of these terms could have a "chilling effect on the news media as potential remote-sensing licensees."[47] They argue the restrictions are constitutionally vague, fail to treat remote sensing as a First Amendment-protected news-gathering tool, and constitute a prior restraint on the press.

General terms such as "national security" and "international obligations" of the United States provide little guidance for news organizations. The likely intended, as well as the actual, result would be media caution leading to self-censorship. Moreover, the Defense Department on national security matters and the Secretary of State on foreign policy would possess broad discretion in defining the circumstances to which the terms apply.

Opponents of the restrictions also argue that remote sensing should be accorded the same rights as other news-gathering tools.[48] The US Supreme Court has granted news-gathering some level of protection under the First Amendment, although not at the same level as news reporting.[49] The Court ruled that the press can be denied access for news-gathering purposes when a compelling national interest is demonstrated, although the government's restrictions must be narrowly drawn to serve that interest.[50]

Thus NOAA may be able to deny the press access to remote-sensing imagery on the basis of compelling governmental interest.[51] However, it would seem to necessitate placing equal restrictions on non-media licensees, which could have economic consequences for commercial remote-sensing systems.

Any attempt to ban media licensing of a remote-sensing system due to its potential national security damage would probably meet with the disapproval of the Supreme Court since it would constitute a broadly, rather than narrowly constructed, governmental interest. Moreover, as two scholars have concluded, the Court has "never declared a novel news-gathering technology off-limits solely because of the information it might reveal. Indeed, such a declaration would appear patently inconsistent with the function of the First Amendment and its place in our system of government."[52]

Another argument is the prior restraint nature of these provisions. By determining licensing or continuation of a license based on content of the photographs and by reserving the right to seize items likely to be used in violation of the Landsat Act, the government may be construed as exercising prior restraint.[53]

For example, had ABC News planned to broadcast the location of US troops in northern Saudi Arabia with the aid of imagery, the Justice Department could have attempted to seize the imagery and impose prior restraint to halt the broadcast. Such a case probably would have met the conditions set by the Supreme Court in the case of *Near v. Minnesota* when Chief Justice Hughes explicitly mentioned troop locations as a justified item for prior restraint.[54] It also may conform to the Court's later test of justification if the government demonstrates the information would cause "direct, immediate, and irreparable damage to our Nation or its people."[55] However, as will be demonstrated below, the practical application of such a doctrine will become increasingly complicated, if not impossible to administer in the future.

THE FUTILITY OF GOVERNMENTAL BARRIERS

The problem of constitutionality is overshadowed by another, even more salient, question: Can the US government maintain these restrictions given the practical difficulties of enforcement?

The US government no longer possesses the legal means to prevent military-related classified information obtained through remote-sensing systems from reaching American citizens. Under current federal espionage laws, the executive branch can impose sanctions for disclosing national security information. But the ability to enforce such laws is arguable.

The erosion of legal control is attributable to the emergence of non-US commercial remote sensing systems willing to sell their products to all comers. In fact, under the "Open Skies" policy and nondiscrimination among users, the commercial systems were encouraged to provide open access.

The US can respond to this burgeoning threat by applying political pressure on other governments to withhold commercial satellite imagery from the news organizations. Such a request may have been made to the French government in August 1990 when SPOT decided to sell photographs of the Middle East only to the US Defense Department.[56] Since goverments own a controlling interest in many, if not all of these enterprises within their own countries, internal pressure could be applied. Failing that, legal means could be employed as in the US to prevent the dissemination of such information.

However, the US cannot rely on such international cooperation to be sustained in future US military actions. Such pressure would be especially difficult to maintain when other nations with remote-sensing capability remain neutral and sell imagery to all comers, as the Soviet Union did during the Gulf crisis.

Moreover, the proliferation of use of remote sensing is expanding rapidly, both for commercial and military uses. The two superpowers have long since lost their monopoly on remote-sensing satellite systems. The Chinese were the first to develop and launch their own spy satellite in the early 1970s.[57] The French announced plans to launch their own military satellite in the early 1990s. Italy and Spain are paying part of the costs and will have some access to the information received. Also, Israel may already have such a system in place. Construction is underway in India, Japan, Canada, and Brazil. Other nations still in the planning stages appear to be Britain, South Africa, and India.[58] The capability to possess militarily-sensitive information will be widespread.

Even those nations uninterested or incapable of building their own systems have been able to obtain imagery from the existing commercial satellite systems. With the expansion of the market and reduction in costs, such purchases will become more common.

Moreover, future technological developments militate against efforts to restrict media observation of US military sites and activities. The sensor resolution gap between military and commercial satellites will be erased as the technological capability spreads. Today, with a resolution of five meters, the imagery provided to media organizations can detect bridges, airfields, surface ships, and large buildings such as warehouses.

By the year 2000, with resolutions of one to three meters, media organizations will be able to identify missile sites, aircraft, nuclear weapons components, radar communications, troop units, and command and control centers. With a resolution of 0.5 meters, other objects such as artillery positions and supply dumps will become visible for identification.[59]

One of the technical drawbacks to media observance of US military activities underway is the real-time capability, i.e., ability to see events on the ground as they occur. Currently, the news media are hampered in fast-breaking coverage by a delay of several days in the receipt of imagery.

The US military now possesses real-time or nearly real-time capability. During the Gulf War, intelligence officers with transportable image transmission facilities in Riyadh received hundreds of images of the Iraqi theater every two to four hours when clouds did not obstruct.[60]

But such capability is not a distant prospect for civilian satellite systems. During the Gulf War, EOSAT offered photographs to media customers in 48 hours after satellite transmission to the ground, which are the current limits of the technology.[61] By the mid-1990s, however, EOSAT plans to provide imagery for use by news organizations in a matter of a few hours or near real-time capability.[62]

Complicating the problem of restricting media use of satellite imagery is international dependence on satellite technology. For example, during the Persian Gulf War, US weather satellites operated by the National Oceanic and Atmospheric Administration (NOAA) transmitted weather imagery to Middle Eastern nations. The imagery was received by nations such as Israel, Turkey, India, and Egypt for weather forecasting.

But the imagery also was received by Iraq, which could have used the data for attack planning. Although the resolution of the satellite was low in contrast to Landsat or SPOT imagery, the Iraqis could have used the imagery to detect the sites of successful Scud attacks or bombing raids on allied positions.[63]

Occluding the satellite's transmissions would have eliminated the Iraqis' potential use. But it also would have crippled the ability of other nations in the Middle East, some neutral in the conflict, to anticipate weather changes. The result could be severe loss of life and property in those nations.

The availability of remote-sensing imagery from a variety of sources will enable American news media to purchase imagery from other sources not subject to US government-imposed restrictions. Even if the American news media are banned from such dissemination, a prospect unlikely to meet the approval of the US Supreme Court, other news media will be exempt from such a ban.

Non-US media such as the Canadian Broadcasting Corporation, the British Broadcasting Corporation, and Reuters may form a consortium to launch and maintain a remote-sensing system. Their potential for global transmission of information would prevent only the US mass public from receiving news banned by the US government. The value of withholding from the American public information about US military activities that is widely disseminated throughout the world would be highly questionable.

Moreover, access to Canadian broadcast news for Americans living along the Canadian border and the commercial development of home satellite receivers with the capability to receive foreign news currently hinders the ability of the US government to prevent foreign-based news from reaching an American television audience. The growth of the home receiver industry in the near future only enhances that difficulty.

CONCLUSION

The news media have now discovered the utility of remote-sensing imagery in news gathering. Despite the limitations of the technology and in its application, it holds great promise for news media usage, especially as a tool to observe areas such as restricted combat zones.

As remote-sensing usage by the news media expands, the US government will be faced with the dilemma of continuing a futile effort to block press coverage in national security-related matters or discovering some other alternative, such as camouflaging operations whose secrecy is deemed imperative to national security. Remote sensing is an issue that will not disappear, but will only offer more complex difficulties for US policymakers in the future.

NOTES

1. UN Doc. A/AC 105/98, January 20, 1972. Quoted in Paul H. Uhlir, "The Public International Law of Civilian Remote Sensing: An Overview," in Robert J. Aamoth, et al., *American Enterprise, the Law, and the Commercial Use of Space. Vol. 11: Remote Sensing and Telecommunications: How Free, How Regulated?* Washington: National Legal Center for the Public Interest, 1986, p. 27.

2. William E. Burrows, *Deep Black: Space Espionage and National Security.* New York: Random House, 1986, pp. 247–250.

3. Curtis Peebles, *Guardians: Strategic Reconnaissance Satellites.* Novato, CA: Presidio, 1987, p. 175.

4. Peebles, *Guardians: Strategic Reconnaissance Satellites*, pp. 7–58.

5. Frederick B. Henderson III, "Private Sector Satellite Remote Sensing: Barriers to Commercialization," in Aamoth, et al., pp. 83–85.

6. Curtis Peebles, pp. 82–84.

7. Burrows, p. 249.

8. Craig Covault, "Recon Satellites Lead Allied Intelligence Effort," *Aviation Week & Space Technology*, February 4, 1991, p. 25.

9. U.S. Congress, Office of Technological Assessment, *Commercial News Gathering From Space—A Technical Memorandum*, OTA-TM-ISC-40 (Washington, D.C.: Government Printing Office, May 1987), p. 26.

10. James W. Rawles, "Commercial Imaging Comes Down to Earth," *Defense Electronics*, April 1989, p. 57.

11. Mark Brender and Peter Zimmerman, "The Day the Open Skies Closed," *Space News*, August 13–19, 1990, p. 15.

12. See, for example, Frederick J. Heimes, *Preliminary Applications of Landsat Images and Aerial Photography for Determining Land-use, Geologic, and Hydrologic Characteristics: Yampa River Basin, Colorado, and Wyoming.* Reston, Va.: Department of the Interior, 1978; D.L. Williams, *Monitoring Forest Canopy Alteration Around the World with Digital Analysis of Landsat Imagery.* Greenbelt, Md.: NASA, 1979; and David A. Greenburg, "Third Party Access to Data Obtained via Remote Sensing: International Legal Theory versus Economic and Political Reality," *Case Western Reserve Journal of International Law*, 15 (Spring 1983):361–391.

13. Gary M. Kramer, "The First Amendment Viewed from Space: National Security Versus Freedom of the Press," *Annals of Air and Space Law*, vol XIV (1989):342.

14. Mark E. Brender, "High-Resolution Remote Sensing by the News Media," *Technology in Society*, vol. 11 (1989): 90–91; and Barry Brown, "Canadians Get Look at Secret NATO Base From Unlikely Source," *The Washington Times*, August 29, 1989, p. A7.

15. See Ian Birrell, "Soviet Satellites Focus on Profits," (London) *Sunday Times*, January 7, 1990; and Brown, "Canadians Get Look," op cit.

16. The sole exception was the specialized publication *Aviation Week & Space Technology.*

17. Robert J. Aamoth "American Enterprise, the Law, and the Commercial Use of Space," in Aamoth, et al., p. 3.

18. Aamoth, "American Enterprise," p. 4.

19. "Survey Results Favor High Resolution Images for Media," Earth Observation Satellite Company press release, February 12, 1988.

20. Melinda Gipson, "Tracing the Line in the Sand," *Electronic Media,* January 22, 1991; and Joan Mower, "Commercial Satellite Companies Selling Photos of Persian Gulf," AP wire story, November 9, 1990.

21. Mark E. Brender, "Remote-Sensing and the First Amendment," *Space Policy,* November 1987, p. 295; and Mark E. Brender, "High-Resolution Remote Sensing by the News Media," *Technology in Society,* 11 (1989):94–95.

22. U.S. Congress, *Commercial News Gathering From Space,* pp. 19–20.

23. For a discussion of the feasibility of "mediasats," see, for example, *Commercial News Gathering From Space,* op cit; Peter E. Glaser and Mark E. Brender, "The First Amendment in Space: News Gathering from Satellites," *Issues in Science and Technology,* Fall 1986, pp. 60–67.

24. David T. Lindgren, "Commercial Satellites Open Skies," *Bulletin of Atomic Scientists,* April 1988, p. 37.

25. Quoted in James W. Rawles, "Commercial Imaging Comes Down to Earth," *Defense Electronics,* April 1989, p. 49.

26. "Space Photos Show Soviet Laser Weapons," *The Washington Times,* October 23, 1987, p. 2; "Saudis Secretly Deploying Missiles," *Washington Times,* September 20, 1988, p. 8; and "Photos Prove '57 Nuclear Disaster," *Chicago Tribune,* December 1, 1988, p. 18.

27. Mark E. Brender, "High-Resolution Remote Sensing by the News Media," pp. 94–96.

28. Peter B. deSelding and Andrew Lawler, "SPOT Halts Sales of Gulf Area Imagery," *Space News,* August 13–19, 1990, p. 3.

29. "Media Taps NOAA Birds for Gulf Views," *Navy News & Undersea Technology,* January 28, 1991, p. 3.

30. "Where Are the Troops?" *Newsweek,* December 3, 1990, p. 6.

31. Peter Blumberg, "Satellite Picture Puzzle: No Iraqis," *Washington Journalism Review,* May 1991, p. 14.

32. Jean Heller, "Public Doesn't Get Picture with Gulf Satellite Photos," *St. Petersburg Times,* January 6, 1991, p. 1.

33. Quoted in Melinda Gipson, "Tracing the Line in the Sand," *Electronic Media,* January 22, 1991.

34. Blumberg, op cit.

35. Colin MacKenzie, "Desertions, Understaffed Units Eroded the Threat of Iraqi Army," *Toronto Globe & Mail,* May 19, 1991, p. 1.

36. *Commercial News Gathering From Space,* p. 23 fn.

37. For a brief presentation of these objections, see *Commercial News Gathering From Space,* pp. 30–33.

38. *Commercial News Gathering From Space,* pp. 30–31.

39. *Commercial News Gathering From Space,* p. 31.

40. Aamoth, "American Enterprise," p. 8.

41. See Lindgren, pp. 34–37.

42. 15 U.S.C. 4201–4292.

43. For a discussion of this provision, see Gary M. Kramer, "The First Amendment Viewed From Space: National Security Versus Freedom of the Press," *Annals of Air and Space Law*, 14 (1989):339–367.

44. Testimony of Mark E. Brender, Chairman, Media in Space Committee, Radio-Television News Directors Association, before the Subcommittee on Natural Resources, Agriculture Research, and Environment, and the Subcommittee on International Scientific Cooperation of the House Committee on Science, Space, and Technology, April 2, 1987, p. 3.

45. Lindgren, p. 37.

46. For samples, see Brender, "High-Resolution Remote Sensing by the News Media," pp. 91–95; and Glaser and Brender, pp. 60–67. For the perspective of legal scholars, see Aamoth, "American Enterprise," pp. 6–8; and J. Laurent Scharff, "News Dissemination of Images from Remote-Sensing Satellites: First Amendment Questions," *Communicator*, June 1989, p. 15.

47. Aamoth, "American Enterprise," p. 8.

48. See Luc Frieden, "Newsgathering by Satellites: A New Challenge to International and National Law at the Dawn of the Twenty-First Century," *Stanford Journal of International Law* (Fall 1988):103–193; and Rita Reimer, "News Gathering From Space: Land Remote-Sensing and the First Amendment," *Federal Communications Law Journal*, 40 (May 1988): 321–349.

49. The most relevant case is Branzburg v. Hayes 408 U.S. 665 (1972) where the Court asserted the First Amendment does grant protection to newsgathering. The Court subsequently defined circumstances where that protection is and is not extended. See Pell v. Procunier, 417 U.S. 817 (1974); Saxbe v. Washington Post Co., 417 U.S. 843 (1974); and Houchins v. KQED, 438 U.S. 1 (1978).

50. Globe Newspaper Co. v. Superior Court, 457 U.S. 596 (1982).

51. Gary M. Kramer, "The First Amendment Viewed From Space: National Security Versus Freedom of the Press," *Annals of Air and Space Law*, 14 (1989):350.

52. Robert P. Merges and Glenn H. Reynolds, "News Media Satellites and the First Amendment: A Case Study in the Treatment of New Technologies," *High Technology Law Journal* 3 (1989):10.

53. See Merges and Reynolds, pp. 14–15; Kramer, op cit; and Reimer, pp. 332–338.

54. 283 U.S. 697, 716 (1931).

55. *New York Times* v. *United States*, 403 U.S. 713 (1971).

56. Peter B. deSelding and Andrew Lawler, "SPOT Halts Sales of Gulf Area Imagery," *Space News*, August 13–19, 1990, p. 3.

57. Peebles, *Guardians*, pp. 172–174.

58. See David T. Lindgren, "Commercial Satellites Open Skies," *Bulletin of Atomic Scientists*, April 1988, pp. 34–37; and William J. Broad, "Non-Superpowers Are Developing Their Own Spy Satellite Systems," *New York Times*, September 3, 1989, p. 1.

59. Ann M. Florini, "The Opening Skies: Third-Party Imaging Satellites and US Security," *International Security*, 13 (Fall 1988):98.

60. Covault, op cit.

61. Mark Brender and Peter Zimmerman, "The Day the Open Skies Closed," *Space News*, August 13–19, 1990, p. 15.

62. Lindgren, p. 35.

63. "Iraqis Still Receive Weather Data From US Satellites," *Aviation Week & Space Technology*, January 21, 1991, p. 26.

B. DEMOCRATIC FUNCTIONS IN A MEDIA AGE

Any discussion of the future of communications technology and politics should raise the question of the impact of the future of democracy. The rise of new communications technology has sparked a debate over the systemic effects. Will technology improve or impair our democratic system of government? Will we become more democratic or less so? If more so, is that really good?

One of the questions is the desirability of direct democracy—one where the public literally makes policy decisions and bypasses elected officials. This system may be viewed by some populists as a solution to elite control of the levers of power in American politics. Those who seek to redistribute power may find these technological innovations encouraging.

However, more traditional commentators argue the potential for danger is more real. A system where the public can respond instantaneously from the comfort of an armchair and with the touch of a button is a highly undesirable one. The public's whim would quickly become public policy with deleterious effects on the stability and cohesiveness of the policy process.

Without the brake of elected representatives and the various layers and cells of American government, democracy would be supplanted by either anarchy, tyranny, or some combination of both.

Another objection is the continued intrusion of a foreign element into the political process. Can a democracy function in an age when an institution, the press, governed by other imperatives—journalistic professional standards and commercialism—performs such vital roles in the system and carries the potential, under certain circumstances, of producing changes in mass attitudes and behavior, public policy-making, and the process of choosing elected officials?

One solution is to reform the press into an institution more responsive to the imperatives of the political system. Calls for media reform usually suggest greater coverage of issues, less attention to sensationalism.

But these efforts have not been successful. In fact, one could argue that those forces within journalism tending toward sensationalism have become more dominant during the 1990s with the rise of drama and scandal news programs and the influence of tabloid journalism on more mainstream news outlets.

Moreover, they carry the seeds of the destruction of the freedom of the press. A press operating under societal expectations of performance in the functioning of the democratic system will eventually have those expectations codified and enforced by government. Such steps will reduce, not enhance, the press's freedom.

Another proposal, then, is to reform the political process to reduce the role of the news media. The latent assumption here is that the news media, however well intentioned, will not, and even cannot, perform functions in American politics formerly conducted by other institutions such as political parties.

The goal is to minimize news media influence by filling vacuums the media have come to fill. An axiom of media role in politics could be stated thusly: The more porous the process, the more significant will the media become.

The process of electing a president, particularly that of nominating candidates, has become a classic example. As political party leadership stepped out of the nominating process and turned it into a mass versus elite-dominated process, the news media filled the vacuum. The U.S. Supreme Court, at the other end, has retained much of its impenetrability and accordingly is little affected by the press in its day-to-day operation. The comparison may not be fair because the electoral process is expected to be inclusive and responsive; the judicial process is expected to be the opposite. But the point lies not with the correctness of porosity. Rather, it is the fact that this state results in enhanced media power.

The proferred solution, then, is to restore the political processes most affected by the press to their prior state by reinvigorating the political parties. The result will not harm the press (nor the First Amendment) since there would be no change imposed on it.

The following two selections address both of these issues. The first analyzes the effects of technology on politics, but adopts a moderate approach to the magnitude of future effects.

The second selection closes the book by proposing an innovation in American politics that would partially remove the press from its public service obligation and reduce the tension between news media and the political system.

48. TOWARD AN ELECTRONIC COMMONWEALTH

Jeffrey B. Abramson, F. Christopher Arterton, and Gary R. Orren

The potential of technological revolution in American politics has sparked both hope and fear in politicians and analysts. Those who view these technologies positively prefer greater democracy in the system. Citizens can possess greater power to check institutions.

The greatest fear is the acceleration of the policy-making process to a dangerous rate. Rapid transmission of public opinion invites hasty, ill-considered judgments by the public, which then become translated into poor public policy. For this school of thought, the process already moves too quickly. Political institutions designed to mediate between public opinion and public policy protect American democracy by slowing down the process of decision making.

The following selection attempts to glean the benefits from both of the above contrasting positions.* Authors Abramson, Arterton, and Orren suggest more limited political

*From *The Electronic Commonwealth: The Impact of New Media Technologies on Democratic Politics* (New York: Basic Books, 1988), pp. 274–80, 295. Reprinted with permission.

effects of the new media; massive restructuring of politics is not on the horizon. They support the importance of not accelerating the political process, but they also agree with the argument for greater citizen involvement. They recommend avenues for harnessing communications technology to improve political communication. According to the authors, the electronic commonwealth empowers citizens by enhancing information sources and including individuals who cannot be present in public debate.

Abramson, Arterton, and Orren argue that the problems of our democracy are not resolved by new technology, but through political choices. Their approach signals a fresh direction—neither euphoria nor hand-wringing—to the role that the media will play in American politics in the future.

Jeffrey B. Abramson is professor of political science at Brandeis University. F. Christopher Arterton is dean of the Graduate School of Political Management in Washington, D.C. and author of *Media Politics* (1984) and *Teledemocracy* (1987). Gary R. Orren is professor of political science at the Kennedy School of Government, Harvard University. He is co-author of *Media and Momentum: The New Hampshire Primary and Nomination Politics* (1987).

The new media are here to stay. Video, satellite, and computer technologies have become so basic to modern communications that the new media can no longer be dismissed as a passing fad. For better or worse, we live and will continue to live in a society where information exchange has become torrential. The traditional obstacles to communications of volume, distance, and time have been eliminated for all practical purposes. Ours is now a world accustomed to global telephone and television service via satellite, accustomed to the computer's ability to process data instantly, accustomed to the storage of 100,000 pages of print on a single five-inch disk. Whole sectors of the economy are by now so dependent on communications volume and speed that there is no turning back. . . .

How will politics fare in this new video age? How do we make the best democratic response to the new media environment? With the 1988 presidential campaign, new media politics have come into their own. Pat Robertson, the former president of the Christian Broadcasting Network, has shown that the electronic church can be sufficiently mobilized to mount a plausible presidential campaign. All candidates have learned to make imaginative use of computerized, direct-mail campaigns to target particular audiences for particular messages. Media wizards have also shown how the new satellite technologies permit politicians to bypass reporters and feed their own video productions to local stations. Local cable stations have proved a boon to candidates who do not have the resources to buy conventional television time or who wish to reach the particular audience in their district. Perhaps most visibly, the new technologies have enhanced the already considerable hold that polls have over the electoral process by quickening the results of polling, fine-tuning their accuracy, and providing detailed information about the demographics of those polled. The information candidates now have about the views of their constituents—with all the possibilities for better representation or more deft manipulation that such information creates—has never been greater.

Although in their infancy, these political uses of the new media suggest that we face a basic value choice between two competing visions of democracy's future. . . .

THE VALUE CHOICES AHEAD

One vision of democracy's future centers on using electronics to keep more constant and instant track of public opinion. [W]e have called this vision *plebiscitary democracy*. According to the plebiscitarian, technology happily renders obsolete the cumbersome procedures of representative democracy; at long last the people can be empowered to vote on issues directly, using the wizardry of electronic voting from the home. Advocates of such electronic plebiscites speak optimistically about the coming revival of citizen participation and direct democracy.

The vision of citizens voting directly on issues and not just for representatives is certainly alluring. Is it not obvious that we become a more democratic nation if, thanks to electronics, individuals can speak for themselves rather than deputizing representatives to speak for them? . . . [We have] argued against the allure of the obvious. Participation in a poll or plebiscite gives only the thinnest experience in self-government. That experience becomes even thinner if electronic communications frees people even from the "inconvenience" of leaving their homes to vote. In the classical conception, participatory democracy required assembly, deliberation, and debate. The value of participation was the education people received in the democratic art of persuading or being persuaded in turn. To persuade others required a person to justify individual opinions in terms of the common good and not merely to vote private interests. At its best, therefore, participation required people to risk their opinions; meetings were hardly idle forums for registering preconceptions on cue. In England and the United States, the jury has long represented this more robust vision of participatory democracy—participation in a process where power goes to the persuasive and not just to the side with the most votes.

In the immediate political present, the electronic voting model has the upper hand in democratic thought. A widespread feeling of powerlessness attracts lay attention to the quick fix of polls and plebiscites. But in our judgment, there is a better and more democratic remedy for lost citizen power—a remedy the new media can help deliver. We have called this alternative vision of democracy's future the *electronic commonwealth*. The electronic commonwealth takes its political cue from the town meeting. It seeks to use the new age of two-way television to restore practicality and substance to participation in local government. At the same time, the ideal of an electronic commonwealth seeks to expand and enrich the traditional town-meeting format in two ways. First, it looks forward to making civic use of computer power, ending the isolation of communities so far as obtaining information is concerned. Second, the electronic commonwealth guards against the parochialism of local politics by using the scale-conquering properties of video, telephones, and computers to bring communities together for regional discussion of regional issues and national discussion of national issues.

Consider an easy if trivial example of an old electronic technology that overcomes physical obstacles to speaking and being spoken to in turn: the microphone. Only a Luddite would refuse in principle to tamper with traditional ways of conducting a meeting by providing speakers with microphones. Of course, in a democracy providing microphones is not risk-free; words of tyrants can be amplified also. But this merely indicates the obvious point that microphones have no politics. Where the politics of the meeting are already democratic, the microphone will not be monopolized but will be equally distributed to speakers. Used in this way, the microphone enriches democracy by expanding the size of the audience that can hear and be heard in turn. Where the politics of the meeting are authoritarian, the microphone reinforces the tyranny by amplifying the speeches of the leader and leaving others more voiceless than ever.

In essence, the democratic promise in the new media is the democratic promise in the microphone writ large. We now have ways to expand the visual as well as the audio part of the meeting; we now have ways to allow persons attending a meeting via television to speak as well as listen. The approximation of electronic communications to face-to-face meetings is thus qualitatively greater than it has ever been before. Greater also is the size of the audience that can now gather electronically at a school board meeting or even at a party nominating convention. The microphone enlarged participation in meetings but did not explode the constraints of numbers and distance. The new electronic age does just that, with all the threats and promises for democracy implicit in mass participation.

Without electronics, the town-meeting model is suitable only for local government. With electronics, there comes to be the new politics of regional electronic meetings. Consider, for example, local government bodies in New England towns separately wrestling with energy or environmental problems. After a certain point, dealing with those problems requires regional solutions. But it is difficult to find time and place for face-to-face regional meetings. Currently such meetings tend to be held infrequently at best. The new media could do much to put regional politics back on the American political landscape.

A mix of local, regional, and national discussion is the aim of the ideal electronic commonwealth. If all the new media promised was a shift from more national to more local television, then we might be trading one set of democratic vices for another. The democratic vice of broadcasting is the blandness and homogeneity of mass-audience programming. The need for ratings success robs television of the programming diversity appropriate to a pluralist society. But in liberating television from the mass audience, the new narrowcast media could conceivably sponsor the ills of fragmentation and faction: members of closed and insular communities talking among themselves but not to outsiders.

. . . [T]he dangers of faction in our culture are real. Among other special-interest networks, cable television now supports the Christian Broadcasting Network, Music Television, the Nashville Network, the Black Entertainment Network, the Spanish International Network, and the National Jewish Network. However much we welcome the arrival of diversity to television, we must guard against the antidemocratic spectacle of separate but equal television. Democratic conversation is conversation among citizens who see themselves as responsible in common for governing a community. Because they share this responsibility and power, citizens have a stake in communicating across ethnic, religious, racial, income, and cultural lines. For all its blandness, mass-entertainment broadcasting has provided Americans with common channels and common entertainments. It is imperative that these common channels not be lost.

The ideal of an electronic commonwealth guards against the ills of faction and closed communities. Consider the case of school committee meetings televised on the local cable access channels. Suppose at one meeting the discussion centers on the adoption of a new math curriculum for the elementary schools. Those present at such a meeting might want more information about the proposed curriculum—information not locally available. Perhaps the curriculum has been tried in a neighboring district or a district across the country. Perhaps a graduate student is completing a dissertation on the effects of the new curriculum at a distant university. Empowering local citizens to make decisions on local education means getting them in touch with these distant sources of information. And the new media can facilitate the exchange of information across the nation every bit as much as it can facilitate televising local politics to local audiences in the first place. Doing both together—empowering citizens to participate in local government and bringing them the sometimes distant information to participate intelligently—is the goal of the electronic commonwealth.

The marketplace itself is not likely to support electronic information services devoted to exchanges of civic information. Currently, the most successful videotex services are those such as Dow Jones News/Retrieval that concentrate narrowly on commercial information. The technology is the same, whether remote advice is sought on the stock market or the math curriculum; the politics is radically different. If the new media are to be harnessed to civic uses, then intervention in the selections of the market in favor of subsidized civic uses of computers, data bases, videotex, and two-way television must become a political priority.[1]

We have stressed that subsidies for civic communications are in the American tradition and not a violation of it. The free library system is testimony to the importance we attach to subsidizing civic education. We do not yet think of computers and information services as the equivalent of printing presses and libraries. But it is crucial that we make this imaginative leap and provide substantial public financing for civic uses of computerized information. Otherwise, we may soon be talking about a communications counterrevolution. Instead of spreading information, the computer's impact could well be to hoard it on data bases purchased only by well-heeled professional audiences. Dow Jones Information Services advertises itself as accomplishing "the democratization of information." This is true, insofar as it uses computer technology to sell more information to more people at less cost than ever before. But the electronic commonwealth demands democratization of information of another sort. The information a democracy needs is about public as well as private matters. And it is information that is publicly held, not privately held for profit. Only politics, and not technology alone, can deliver this sort of democratized information.

****

. . . Now is the time to raise fundamental value questions about how a democracy may best profit from the marvels of electronic communications. As we see it, the basic choice comes down to this. One choice is to use the new technology to quicken democracy and tighten the hold of public opinion over public policy. This is the politics of polls and plebiscites, electronic voting, and instant feedback schemes. The speed and reach of the new media can put such a politics into practice if we want it. Another choice is to use the new technology to slow down democracy, to involve more citizens than ever in meetings and debates, discussion, and dialogue. This is the politics of the electronic commonwealth and the televised town meeting. The congregating or conferencing capacity of the new media can put such a politics into practice if we want it. The choice between racing democracy and slowing democracy is ours. Only politics, not machines, can make that choice.

NOTES

1. For concrete suggestions for subsidizing a civic communications system in the electronic age, see Benjamin Barber, *Strong Democracy: Participatory Politics for a New Age* (Berkeley: University of California Press, 1984), pp. 278–79.

49. IMPROVING JOURNALISM BY ENHANCING CITIZENSHIP

Robert M. Entman

Robert Entman follows a long line of political scientists, journalists, and media critics who have suggested reform of journalism. Most recommendations have focused on the news business.

Entman's goal, however, is twofold: to improve the quality of public information transmitted through the media as well as to invigorate the electoral and policy roles of the political parties, which have become moribund in the areas of organizing campaigns and communicating with their affiliates. Entman suggests the press has failed to provide enough "accountability news"—news that allows the public to assess the performance of government. In that sense, he offers an idea that targets not just the press, but also more traditional mediating mechanisms in American politics freed from the economic marketplace.* Entman's proposal would result in a partial return to the era of the partisan press, but with a twist, since a nonpartisan press would also exist. Is Entman's idea viable—would it accomplish the desired objective and would policymakers, parties, and the public approve of it? You decide.

Robert M. Entman is associate professor of communication studies, journalism, and political science at Northwestern University. He is co-author (with David L. Paletz) of *Media Power Politics* (1981) and author of *Democracy Without Citizens: Media and the Decay of American Politics* (1989).

*From *Democracy Without Citizens: Media and the Decay of American Politics* (New York: Oxford University Press), 1989, pp. 134–40. Reprinted with permission.

... [T]he first step to lasting improvements in journalism is isolating some outlets from the economic market altogether; the boost to their autonomy would allow them in turn gradually to raise the supply and augment the mass public's taste for accountability news. The goal is genuine diversity and richness in ideas, a scenario in which media, audiences, and governing elites participate more often in mutually beneficial democratic debate. The colloquy might actually focus on the merits of ideas and candidates. If this seems too idealistic, we can at least hope for a reduction in the perversities now imposed by media coverage, and an increase in the availability of accountability news.

There are two major options for expanding journalism that operates more independently of economic pressure. One is augmenting public broadcasting, the other creating publicly subsidized private media. The Public Broadcasting Service and National Public Radio both offer arguably the highest quality daily public affairs programming in the form of PBS's "MacNeil/Lehrer NewsHour" and NPR's "All Things Considered" and "Morning Edition." This is no accident; these programs do not seek to maximize the size of their audiences. But their biggest problem is precisely the small audience and meager impact on perceived and actual public opinion. Their very weakness protects the budgets of PBS and NPR from political attack by the commercial networks. In addition, the public broadcasters must maintain cordial relations with the politicians, foundations, and corporations that fund most programming. Only imperfectly insulated from political and economic pressures, sometimes too scrupulously balanced to provide their audiences with clues to truth, they are far from autonomous.

This suggests the option of combining guaranteed, irrevocable, and large tax subsidies for expanded news with a structure that would better protect the autonomy of public broadcasting. If these organizations could mount a news effort funded at the level of the commercial networks (say $250 million a year), it might well alter the course of electronic journalism. With this money they could offer frequent documentaries, investigative projects, and essayists like Bill Moyers doing more topical commentary. ... While audience size might never reach that of the big three networks, if PBS and NPR could generate enough creatively packaged new information, it would significantly supplement and prod the three commercial networks, and even the print media.[1]

Some propose that subsidies for public broadcasting come from a tax on commercial station revenues. The tax would be a fair trade for the de facto perpetual monopoly on their frequencies that stations now enjoy.[2] But such a tax guarantees opposition from an intense organized interest, the broadcast industry. Reformers would do better to obtain the money from general revenue.[3]

The political fate of this proposal would be uncertain. A rich and autonomous public news service could inflict pain on all established institutions. Members of Congress might see a powerful new voice conveying accountability news as a threat to their political interests and oppose any significant change. The commercial networks might not look kindly on a proposal to strengthen PBS and NPR news operations. ... [T]he news divisions of the big three experienced hard times in the

1980s and would not appreciate subsidized competition. Others would raise First Amendment fears. Assuaging those doubts would require ingenious mechanisms for insulating PBS from political manipulation.

Beyond the politically difficult option of strengthening public broadcasting lies the possibility that political parties—and the public's interest in politics—could be invigorated through public subsidies for partisan media. Serious constitutional difficulties and political opposition would confront any move in this direction. If a new policy passed those hurdles, the most likely outcome would be failure to transcend the dilemma of journalism. I offer the following ideas in a spirit of cautious though realistic hope.

I propose to create national news organizations run by the major parties and subsidized by the government. Financial security would increase the autonomy of the organizations. The long-term goal is more analytical information, more diversity, more readily accessible ideas. The targeted audience would be not just the public but other news organizations. The new media might at least stimulate the old to deeper insight.

To be sure, blind party loyalty is no necessary improvement over what we have now. If parties merely reinforced partisanship through manipulative propaganda, citizenship might even deteriorate. But parties appear to be the best vehicle for enhancing the public's inclination and ability to seek and process political information in a more sophisticated way.[4] Party newspapers or television channels might encourage a move toward a system of mass membership and loyalty more akin to the European democracies. Parties might sell newspaper subscriptions as part of membership, providing a selective incentive to join.[5] Partisan papers and TV shows might well contain entertainment features, reviews, and other cultural content along with news and commentary. Their existence might bolster party identification in the public, which in turn seems likely to boost participation.[6] The decline of participation in the U.S. has historically paralleled the dwindling of the partisan press and the rise of objectivity; perhaps an injection of party media would reverse the trend.

If successful, these new media would provide a competitive challenge to the rest of the press by publicizing hearings and other congressional work and exposing bureaucratic activities occurring beyond the normal news net. C-SPAN does this to some extent, but in a haphazard way limited by tiny budgets and a desire for objectivity. The journalists working for the party organs would be free to analyze and evaluate substantively, constructing arguments about truth woven into news narratives.

To free their staffs from the drudgery of covering the standard beats, party newspapers might employ wire services for routine news. They could devote their major resources to building specialists in editorial, policy analytical, and investigative journalism. Ideally, the staffs of the party outlets would constantly uncover new facts, hidden implications, and problems with current policy. They would publicize the findings of congressional investigations, they would mine the hearing records the way I.F. Stone once did to highlight information usually known only by self-interested experts in the policy arena. These revelations might in turn inspire the commercial media to cover the same things or strike out into related territory.

The party newspapers might employ the new technologies of distribution, like *USA Today* transmitting copy by satellite to printing plants around the country. The party television outlets would probably use cable; parties might also put together syndicated shows that commercial stations could broadcast.

These novel news organizations would have partisan and ideological biases; they would also develop considerable dependence upon their own party elites. But the party would have to promote the paper or TV programming to the public and to the rest of journalism. Blatant distortion and predictable diatribes would render the medium virtually useless for the party. So the hope would be that the new media could serve citizenship, not serve up party propaganda.

Still, potential drawbacks abound. One party might develop a much more effective operation than the other. That would be not only a problem for the weaker party but a dilemma for democracy. Severe imbalance in the effectiveness of the two parties' operations would not energize knowledgeable participation. Another danger is that party leaders might engage in struggles over the content of the party organs. Determining who runs the show could turn into a divisive internal issue. One would hope party media could develop a life of semi-independence from party organizations, as appears true in some European democracies. But one can envision a scenario in which both parties produce either bland material carefully balanced to avoid offense to constituencies or constantly changing biases to placate shifting dominant factions. If this occurs, the new party media would become largely irrelevant. Only if they offer a different and respectable product would they receive attention from wide audiences and other journalists.

Another major but surmountable obstacle is funding. Precedent suggests several mechanisms for establishing a subsidy. The government could offer a tax credit for contributions designated to party media funds. A tax check-off might provide support, as it already does for the presidential campaign. The government would prohibit the print or TV outlets from accepting advertising, in order to limit the intrusion of economic market pressures and to prevent vast inequality of resources among the party organs.

An unresolved problem is how to deal with minor parties. On the one hand, the danger of limiting the subsidy to the two big parties would be narrowing the flow of ideas even more by tightening the hold of Democrats and Republicans on the political dialogue. On the other, it is impractical to fund any other party as generously as the big two. A compromise might be to channel publication subsidies to all other parties in proportion to the number of votes they receive in presidential and congressional elections and to allow minor parties to accept advertising in their media. This practice might give more people who sympathize with third parties an incentive to vote for them in order to bolster their media budgets, even if they are sure to lose an election. With richer media, more parties might become viable forces.[7]

Beyond subsidized party media, other forms of government intervention in the news industry are common in Europe, including grants, loans, aid by parties, price regulation, and funding for news agencies.[8] All would be controversial here.

Americans would probably look on such proposals skeptically because of the First Amendment and the deep-seated fear of media-government collusion. In addition, owners of private news organizations dread subsidized competitors. They would mount considerable political opposition to my proposal, based on their economic interests; they and others would also cite the danger to ideals of the free press. So the political process would present serious barriers to the party media proposal. . . .

ACKNOWLEDGING INTRACTABILITY

Despite years of pleas by journalism critics and scholars, and despite occasional attempts at reform, news practices resist change. News coverage cannot transcend the limitations and interests of media audiences. Nor can journalists entirely escape their links to political elites. Any solutions to the dilemma of American journalism remain problematic. We can make progress at least by admitting the real state of citizenship, acknowledging the limits on journalism, and understanding the implications of both for the health of American democracy. The dilemma only deepens when we assume and invoke a mythical marketplace of ideas.

Beyond this, the notion that good journalism can yield government accountability may be exaggerated. Merely presenting enough information might not make government responsive and responsible to the public. Mechanisms that relate public opinion to the behavior of policymakers, such as elections and interest groups, might fail in enforcing government responsiveness even to an enlightened public. In other words, even if we enjoyed a more autonomous press and a more interested, perceptive public, democratic accountability might not closely resemble the ideal portrait. But improving journalism would at least give democracy a better chance.

NOTES

1. The figure I suggest, $250 million, is $1 per capita. John Weisman, "Public TV in Crisis: Can it Survive?," *TV Guide* (August 1, 1987, p. 6), writes that per capita government spending on all public broadcasting (not just news) in the U.S. is 57 cents. In the UK, it is $18; Canada, $22; and Japan, $10. Part of the disparity is that these other countries have much smaller populations while confronting large fixed costs of producing programs that are the same whatever the population. But even adjusting for population differences, these other countries spend several times more than the U.S.

2. Cf. Geller, 1985.

3. Great Britain has funded an alternative channel at $150 million annually. According to one report, it "has emerged as perhaps the most exciting and varied TV channel anywhere, broadcasting much of what is at the cutting edge in the arts . . . as well as current affairs." "Channel of choice, Britain's alternative station: Low budget, high praise," *Washington Post*, November 30, 1986, p. G1. The station has an hour newscast each evening, and also welcomes "passionate partisanship within individual programs (but insists on year-round 'balance')" (p. G2).

4. Cf. Burnham, 1981a, 1981b.

5. Olson, 1965.

6. Abramson and Aldrich, 1982.

7. Of course many politicians favor the two-party system, and the U.S. erects structural obstacles to the emergence of any significant third party. But others think a dose of competition for the big two might be helpful.

8. Pickard, 1985: Chap. 5.

SUGGESTED READINGS

Arterton, F. Christopher. *Teledemocracy: Can Technology Protect Democracy?* Beverly Hills, Calif.: Sage Publications, Inc., 1987.
The most exhaustive analysis of the potential effects of technology on democracy in the United States, this monograph offers a cautious optimism about the utility of technological innovations but notes such change will not guarantee increased citizen interest in and involvement with public affairs.

de Sola Pool, Ithiel. *Talking Back.* Cambridge, Mass.: MIT Press, 1973.
A distinguished political scientist, de Sola Pool wrote this monograph when cable was spreading across the country and offered a prediction of the political effects of interactive cable television.

Hollander, Richard S. *Videodemocracy.* Mt. Airy, Md.: Lomond Publications, 1985.
A call for a more direct democracy through interactive cable technology, this book offers an optimistic perspective on the likely effects of technology on the democratic system.

Katsh, Ethan. *The Electronic Media and the Transformation of Law.* New York: Oxford University Press, 1989.
The legal community attempts to manipulate information, argues Katsh. This is an excellent treatise on the relationship between law and information and the effects of new technology on the judicial system.

Krepon, Michael, et al., eds. *Commercial Observation Satellites and International Security.* New York: St. Martin's Press, 1990.
This collection of articles includes a discussion of how news media organizations' remote-sensing capabilities will affect international relations.

Neuman, W. Russell. *The Future of the Mass Audience.* New York: Cambridge University Press, 1991.
Neuman argues that new communications technology will not revolutionize American politics. More particularly, the mass audience will not become fragmented into disparate parts with deleterious effects on the American political system.

Remote Sensing and Telecommunications: How Free, How Regulated? Washington, D.C.: National Legal Center for the Public Interest, 1986.
A multivolume forum for a debate by scholars, lawyers, and practitioners on U.S. telecommunications policy toward remote sensing.

CREDITS